Brief Contents

Contents

PART III	PROBLEMS OF INEQUALITY
Chapter 6	Poverty 160

Preface

The topics covered in *Social Problems,* Sixth Edition—including racism, sexism, urban poverty, corporate crime, drugs, and mental disorders—are inherently interesting. The typical book on social problems describes these phenomena separately, using a variety of explanations. Students exposed to such a melange of approaches might retain their interest in these problems, but they probably would complete the book with little grasp of how social problems are interrelated and of society's role in their creation and perpetuation. This book is different. The approach is sociological. There is a coherent framework from which to analyze and understand society and the problems found therein.

Our overarching goal in *Social Problems,* Sixth Edition, is to capture the imagination of the readers. We want them not only to be interested in the topics but also to become enthusiastic about exploring the intricacies and mysteries of social life. We want them, moreover, to incorporate the sociological perspective into their explanatory repertoire. The sociological perspective requires, at a minimum, accepting two fundamental assumptions. The first is that individuals are products of their social environments. Who they are, what they believe, what they strive for, and how they feel about themselves are all dependent on other people and on the society in which they live. The incorporation of the sociological perspective requires that we examine the structure of society in order to understand such social problems as racism, poverty, and crime. This method, however, runs counter to the typical explanations people use for social ills. The choice is seen in an example supplied by Thomas Szasz:

> Suppose that a person wishes to study slavery. How would he go about doing so? First, he might study slaves. He would then find that such persons are generally brutish, poor, and uneducated, and he might conclude that slavery is their "natural" or appropriate social status. . . . Another student "biased" by contempt for the institution of slavery, might proceed differently. He would maintain that there can be no slave without a master holding him in bondage; and he would accordingly consider slavery a type of human *relationship* and more generally, a *social institution,* supported by custom, law, religion, and force. From this point of view, the study of masters is at least as relevant to the study of slavery as is the study of slaves. (Szasz, 1970: 123–124)

Most of us, intuitively, would make the first type of study and reach a conclusion. This book, however, emphasizes the second kind of study: looking at masters as well as slaves. An observer cannot gain an adequate understanding of racism, crime, mental illness, or other problems by studying only bigots, criminals, and the mentally disturbed. Therefore, we focus on the social structure to determine the underlying features of the social world in an effort to understand social problems.

Because our emphasis is on social structure, the reader is required to accept another fundamental assumption of the sociological perspective (see Eitzen and Baca Zinn, 1993). We are referring to adopting a critical stance toward all social forms. Sociologists must ask these questions: How does the social system really work? Who has the power? Who benefits under the existing social arrangements and who does not? We should also ask such questions as: Is the law neutral? Why are some drugs illegal and others, which are known to be harmful, considered legal? Why are so few organizations in the United States—which is characterized as a democracy—democratic? Is our society a meritocratic one in which talent and effort combine to stratify people fairly? Questions such as these call into question existing myths, stereotypes, and official dogma. The critical examination of society can demystify and demythologize. It sensitizes the individual to the inconsistencies present in society. But most important, a critical stance toward social arrangements allows us to see their role in perpetuating social problems.

In conclusion, the reader should be aware that we are not dispassionate observers of social problems. Unlike the chemist, who can observe the reaction of chemical compounds in a test tube objectively, we are participants in the social life we seek to study and understand. As we study riots in South Los Angeles, child abuse, poverty, urban blight, or the behavior of the CIA, we cannot escape our feelings and values. The choice of topics, the order in which they are presented, and even the tone of the discourse in the book, reveal our values. We cannot, however, let our values and our feelings render the analyses invalid. All pertinent findings must be reported, not just those that support our point of view. In other words, we must be as scientific as possible, which requires a recognition of our biases so that the findings will not be invalidated.

Let us, then, briefly make our values more explicit. We oppose social arrangements that prevent people from developing their full potential. That is, we reject political and social repression, educational elitism, institutional barriers to racial and sexual equality, economic exploitation, and official indifference to human suffering. Stating these feelings positively, we favor equality of opportunity, the right to dissent, social justice, an economic system that minimizes inequality, and a political system that maximizes citizen input in decisions and provides for an adequate care system and acceptable living conditions for *all* persons. Obviously, we believe that U.S. society as it is presently organized falls short of what we consider to be a good society. The problem areas of U.S. society are the subjects of *Social Problems,* Sixth Edition. So, too, are structural arrangements around the globe that harm people.

Ordinarily, when revising a book for the fifth time, the task is rather routine—updating and other cosmetic changes with, perhaps, a new chapter. Not so, this time. Since the fifth edition was published in 1992 (and actually written a year earlier), several important trends have intensified, requiring a significant revision. For example:

- The chance for nuclear war among the superpowers is remote, while the chances for localized wars and terrorism have increased.
- The magnitude of domestic and global environmental problems has accelerated.
- Racial and ethnic tensions throughout the world and within the United States have escalated.
- The world has added 200,000,000 people, most of whom are poor.
- The Savings and Loan scandal (the largest scandal in United States history) has revealed, once again, the cozy relationship between money and politics.
- The large cities of the U.S. are more troubled with growing dependent populations, shrinking job markets, increased racial tensions, and declining economic resources to meet their problems. For the most part, the cities have been abandoned by federal and state governments, as well as by the political parties.
- The economy continues its massive transformation, adding workers in some areas and displacing workers in others. Among other consequences, the middle class continues its decline in numbers.

This sixth edition of *Social Problems* considers each of these important trends and events and others as well. Specifically, the chapter on war and militarism has been dropped. Replacing it is a chapter on domestic urban problems. The chapters on global inequality and environmental problems have been changed considerably to reflect the ever-greater magnitude of these social problems. Other chapters have been reorganized to include new data, current research, and new interpretations. Observations have been added on such subjects as multinational corporations, labor unions, the politics of drugs, tracking in schools, financial inequality among school districts, urban enterprise zones, Amerasians, political lobbying, and corporate polluters.

A feature retained in this edition is the inclusion of cross-national panels entitled "Another Society, Another Way" to illustrate how other societies deal with a particular social problem. Societies included in these panels are those in Sweden, Canada, the Netherlands, Japan, and France. This global emphasis is also found in panels and tables that compare the U.S. with other nations on such topics as crime/incarceration, medical care, and education. A popular feature from the previous editions—Forums presenting contrasting views or a provocative single essay on a significant question—are included again.

At the end of each chapter there are a glossary, chapter review, and selected bibliography.

To summarize, this sixth edition of *Social Problems* improves on the earlier editions by focusing more deliberately on four themes: (1) the structural sources of social problems; (2) the role of the United States in global social problems; (3) the centrality of class, race, and gender as sources of division, inequality, and injustice; and (4) the critical examination of society.

A Note on Language Usage

In writing this book we have been especially sensitive to our use of language. Language is used to reflect and maintain the secondary status of social groups by defining them, diminishing them, trivializing them, or excluding them. For example, traditional English uses masculine words (*man, mankind, he*) when referring to people in general. Even the ordering of masculine and feminine, or of Whites and Blacks, within the discussion or the reference to one category consistently preceding its counterpart, subtly conveys the message that the one listed first is superior to the other. In short, our goal is to use language so that it does *not* create the impression that one social class, race, or gender is superior to any other.

The terms of reference for racial and ethnic categories are changing. Blacks increasingly use the term *African American,* and Hispanics often refer to themselves as *Latinos.* In *Social Problems,* Sixth Edition, we use each of these terms for each social category because they often are used interchangeably in popular and scholarly discourse (see the first Observation in Chapter 7 for an elaboration on this issue of "What shall we call each other?").

Also, we do *not* use the terms *America* or *American society* when referring to the United States. *America* should be used only in reference to the entire Western hemisphere—North, Central, and South America (and then in the plural, *Americas.* Its use as a reference only to the United States implies that the other nations of the Western hemisphere have no place in our frame of reference.

Acknowledgments

We wish to thank several graduate students for their assistance: Karen L. Lambourne, Jenna Cook, and Dan Dahlstrom. We are especially indebted to Doug A. Trimmer for writing the chapter on urban problems.

Our thanks also go to:

Verghese Chirayath, John Carroll University
Keith Crew, University of Northern Iowa
Kurt Finsterbush, University of Maryland
David Greenwald, Bloomsburg University
Phillip Grimaldi, Westchester Community College
Donald Hayes, Sam Houston University
Patrick Horan, University of Georgia
Larry Horn, LA Pierce College
Drew Hurley, Santa Fe Community College
Dennis Kalob, Loyola University
Charles Norman, Indiana State University
Michael Nusbaumer, Purdue University at Fort Wayne
Peter Remender, University of Wisconsin-Oshkosh
Jerrold Starr, Pittsburg, PA

Focusing on the poor and ignoring the system of power, privilege, and profit which makes them poor, is a little like blaming the corpse for murder.

Michael Parenti

uman beings are plagued by problems that result from the social arrangements within society. U.S. newspapers, magazines, and television continually remind us of these problems. Consider some representative newspaper headlines:

- "As Many as 3 Million Americans Are Homeless"
- "10 percent of Americans are on Food Stamps."
- "Women in the Work Force Make Less Than 70 Cents for Every Dollar Paid to Men"
- "One in Four High School Students, Mostly Minorities, Never Graduate"
- "Acid Rain Threatens Lakes and Streams in the Region"
- "GM Closes Local Plant and Moves Operation to Mexico"
- "The Savings and Loan Scandal Will Cost Taxpayers over $500 Billion"

These headlines highlight social problems such as poverty, sexism, racism, environmental degradation, economic dislocations, and corporate and political crimes. These problems and others, which are examined in detail in this book, are inherently interesting. The description and analysis provided here can enhance the reader's understanding and appreciation of the complexity of social life.

Sociologists have always been intrigued with the causes, consequences, solutions, and changing definitions of social problems. The following historical sketch of how sociologists have approached social problems provides a useful background to the focus of this book.

History of Social Problems Theory

Typically, social problems have been thought of as social situations that a large number of observers felt were inappropriate and needed remedying. Early U.S.

"Where did we go wrong?"

Drawing by Richter; © 1992 The New Yorker Magazine, Inc.

sociologists applied a medical model to the analysis of society in order to assess whether some pathology was present. Using what were presumed to be universal criteria of normality, sociologists commonly assumed that social problems resulted from "bad" people—maladjusted people who were abnormal because of mental deficiency, mental disorder, lack of education, or incomplete socialization. These social pathologists, because they assumed that the basic norms of society are universally held, viewed social problems as behaviors or social arrangements that disturb the moral order. For them, the moral order of U.S. society obviously defined such behaviors as homosexuality, alcoholism, suicide, theft, and murder as social problems. But this approach did not take into account the complexity inherent in a diverse society.

In a variation of the absolutist approach sociologists in the 1920s and 1930s focused on the conditions of society that fostered problems. Societies undergoing rapid change from the processes of migration, urbanization, and industrialization were thought to have pockets of social disorganization. Certain areas of the cities undergoing the most rapid change, for example, were found to have disproportionately high rates of vice, crime, family breakdowns, and mental disorders.

In the past few decades many sociologists have returned to a study of problem individuals—deviants who violate the expectations of society. The modern study of deviance has developed in two directions. The first sought the sources of deviation within the social structure. Sociologists saw deviance as the result of conflict between the culturally prescribed goals of society (such as material success) and the obstacles to obtaining them that some groups of people face. The other, of relatively recent origin, has focused on the role of society in creating and sustaining deviance through labeling those people viewed as abnormal. Societal reactions are viewed as the key in determining what a social problem is and who is deviant.

Most recently, some sociologists have tried to alert others to the problematic nature of social problems themselves (see Spector and Kitsuse, 1987). These theorists emphasize the **subjective nature of social problems.** They say that what is defined as a social problem differs by audience and by time; pollution, for example, has not always been considered a social problem. This perspective also examines how particular phenomena come to be defined as social problems, focusing on how groups of people actively influence those definitions.

This brief description reveals several issues that must be addressed in looking at social problems. First, sociologists have difficulty agreeing on an adequate definition of social problems. Second, there is continuing debate over the unit of analysis: Is the focus of inquiry individuals or social systems? Related to the latter is the issue of numbers: How many people have to be affected before something is a social problem?*

---

*C. Wright Mills made an appropriate distinction. If a situation such as unemployment is a problem for an individual or for scattered individuals, it is a "private trouble." But if unemployment is widespread, affecting large numbers of people in a region or the society, it is a "public issue" (social problem) (Mills, 1962).

Toward a Definition of Social Problems

There is an **objective reality to social problems:** There *are* conditions in society (such as poverty and institutional racism) that induce material or psychic suffering for certain segments of the population; there *are* sociocultural phenomena that prevent a significant number of societal participants from developing and using their full potential; there *are* discrepancies between what the United States is supposed to stand for (equality of opportunity, justice, democracy) and the actual conditions in which many of its people live; people *are* fouling their own nest through pollution and the indiscriminate use of natural resources (Eitzen, 1984). This normative approach assumes that some kinds of actions are likely to be judged deleterious in any context. Therefore, one goal of this book is to identify, describe, and explain situations that are objective social problems.

There are several dangers, however, in defining social problems objectively. The most obvious is that subjectivity is always present. To identify a phenomenon as a problem implies that it falls short of some standard. But what standards are to be used? Will the standards of society suffice? In a pluralistic society like ours there is no uniform set of guidelines. People from different social strata and other social locations (such as region, occupation, race, and age) differ in their perceptions of what a social problem is and, once defined, how it should be solved. Is marijuana use a social problem? Is pornography? Is the relatively high rate of military spending a social problem? Is abortion a social problem? There is little consensus in U.S. society on these and other issues. All social observers, then, must be aware of differing viewpoints and respect the perspectives of the social actors involved.

Even sociologists and other social scientists do not agree among themselves on the definition of social problems and on what types of phenomena should be included under that rubric. Nor can they escape making value judgments as they pursue their work. It is impossible to do research that is uncontaminated by personal and political sympathies (Becker, 1967). The values of the scholar-researcher affect both the choice of questions and the answers. In the study of poverty, for example, should the social scientist examine the poor people or the system that tends to perpetuate poverty among a certain segment of society? In the study of the problems of youth, should the major question be why some youth are troublesome for adults, or why adults make so much trouble for youth? These quite different questions will yield very different results.

We should recognize, then, that the study of social problems cannot be value-free and that the type of problems researched and the strategies used tend either to support or to undermine existing societal arrangements. Seen in this way, both types of social research are political. Yet there is a tendency to label as political only the research that challenges the system. Research that finds fault with the social system in behalf of the powerless implies that the system is being questioned, and the charge typically arises that such research is biased. Becker has described the logic of this situation:

> When do we accuse ourselves and our fellow sociologists of bias? I think an inspection of representative instances would show that the accusation arises, in

one important class of cases, when the research gives credence, in any serious way, to the perspective of the subordinate group in some hierarchical relationship. In the case of deviance, the hierarchical relationship is a moral one. The superordinate parties in the relationship are those who represent the forces of approved and official morality; the subordinate parties are those who, it is alleged, have violated that morality. . . .

It is odd that, when we perceive bias, we usually see it in these circumstances. It is odd because it is easily ascertained that a great many more studies are biased in the direction of the interests of responsible officials than the other way around. (Becker, 1967: 240, 242)

In looking for objective social problems, we must also guard against the tendency to accept the definitions of social problems provided by those in power. Because the powerful—the agencies of government and business—provide the statistical data (such as crime rates), they may define social reality in a way that manipulates public opinion, thereby controlling behaviors that threaten the status quo (and their power). The congruence of official biases and public opinion can be seen in several historical examples. Slavery, for instance, was not a social problem in the South, but slave revolts were. In colonial New England the persecution of witches was not a social problem, but the witches were (Szasz, 1970). Likewise,

According to public opinion of the time, dispossessing Native Americans of their land was not a social problem, the Native Americans who resisted were.

Are families to blame for their poverty or is society responsible for their plight by not providing jobs, adequate wages, and health care?

racism was not a social problem of the Jim Crow South, but "pushy" Blacks were. From the standpoint of U.S. public opinion, dispossessing Native Americans of their lands was not a social problem, but the Native Americans were.

Thus, to consider as social problems only those occurrences so defined by the public is fraught with several related dangers. First, to do so may mean over-looking conditions that are detrimental to a relatively powerless segment of the society. In other words, deplorable conditions heaped on minority groups will tend to be ignored as social problems by the people at large. If sociologists accept this definition of social problems as their sole criterion for what is a social prob-lem, they have clearly taken a position that supports existing inequities for minor-ity groups.

Second, defining social problems exclusively through public opinion diverts attention from what may constitute the most important social problem: the exist-ing social order (Liazos, 1972). If defined only through public opinion, social prob-lems will be limited to behaviors and actions that disrupt the existing social order. From this perspective, social problems are manifestations of the behaviors of abnormal people, not of society; the inadequacies and inequalities perpetuated by the existing system are not questioned. The distribution of power, the system of justice, how children are educated—to name but a few aspects of the existing social order—are assumed to be proper by most of the public, when they may be social problems themselves. As Skolnick and Currie have noted, "conventional social-problems writing invariably returns to the symptoms of social ills, rather than the source; to criminals, rather than the law; to the mentally ill, rather than the quality of life; to the culture of the poor, rather than the predations of the rich; to the 'pathology' of students, rather than the crisis of education" (Skolnick and Currie, 1973:13).

By overlooking institutions as a source of social problems (and as problems themselves), observers disregard the role of the powerful in society. To focus exclusively on those who deviate—the prostitute, the delinquent, the drug addict, the homosexual—is to exclude the unethical, illegal, and destructive actions of powerful individuals, groups, and institutions in U.S. society and to ignore the covert institutional violence brought about by racist and sexist policies, unjust tax laws, inequitable systems of health care and justice, and exploitation by the corporate world (Liazos, 1972).

Types of Social Problems

This book examines two main types of social problems: (1) acts and conditions that violate the norms and values present in society, and (2) societally induced conditions that cause psychic and material suffering for any segment of the population.

Norm Violations

Sociologists are interested in the discrepancy between social standards and reality for several reasons. First, this traditional approach directs attention to society's failures: the criminal, the mentally ill, the school dropouts, and the poor. Sociologists have many insights that explain the processes by which individuals experience differing pressures to engage in certain forms of deviant behavior because of their location in the social structure (social class, occupation, race, and role) and in space (region, size of community, and type of neighborhood). A guiding assumption of our inquiry here, however, is that norm violators are symptoms of social problems, not the disease itself. In other words, most deviants are victims and should not be blamed entirely by society for their deviance; rather, the system they live in should be blamed. A description of the situations affecting deviants (such as the barriers to success faced by minority group members) helps explain why some categories of persons participate disproportionately in deviant behavior.

Another reason for the traditional focus on norm violation is that deviance is culturally defined and socially labeled. The sociologist is vitally interested in the social and cultural processes that label some acts and persons as deviant and others as normal. Because by definition some social problems are whatever the public determines, social problems are inherently relative. Certain behaviors are labeled as social problems whereas other activities (which by some other criteria would be a social problem) are not. People on welfare, for example, are generally considered to constitute a social problem, but slum lords are not; people who hear God talking to them are considered schizophrenic, but people who talk to God are believed perfectly sane; murder is a social problem, but killing the enemy during wartime is rewarded with medals; a prostitute is punished, but the client is not; aliens entering the country illegally constitute a social problem and are punished, but their U.S. employers are not. The important insight here is that "deviance is not a property *inherent* in certain forms of behavior; it is a property *conferred upon* these forms by the audiences which directly or indirectly witness them" (Schur, 1971:12). The members of society, especially the most powerful members, determine what is a social problem and what is not.

Powerful people play an important role in determining who gets the negative label and who does not. Because there is no absolute standard that informs citizens of what is deviant and what is not, our definition of deviance depends on what behaviors the law singles out for punishment. Because the law is an instrument of those in power, acts that are labeled deviant are so labeled because they conflict with the interests of those in power. Thus, to comprehend the labeling process, we must understand not only the norms and values of the society but also what interest groups hold the power (Quinney, 1970).

Social Conditions

The second type of social problem emphasized in this text involves conditions that cause psychic and material suffering for some category of people in the United States. Here, the focus is on how the society operates and who benefits and who does not under existing arrangements. In other words, what is the bias of the system? How are societal rewards distributed? Do some categories of persons suffer or profit because of how schools are organized or juries selected, because of the seniority system used by industries, or because of how health care is delivered? These questions direct attention away from individuals who violate norms and toward society's institutions as the generators of social problems.

Social problems of this type generate individual psychic and material suffering. Thus, societal arrangements can be organized in such a way as to be unresponsive to many human needs. As a benchmark, let us assume, with Abraham Maslow, that all human beings have a set of basic needs in common: the fundamental needs for shelter and sustenance, security, group support, esteem, respect, and self-actualization (the need for creative and constructive involvement in productive, significant activity) (Maslow, 1954). When these needs are thwarted,

> individuals will be hostile to society and its norms. Their frustration will be expressed in withdrawal, alcohol or other drugs, or in the violence of crime, terrorism, and aggression. People will take up lives outside of the pale of social control and normative structure; in so doing they will destroy themselves and others. They will rightly be condemned as "bad" people, *but this is so because they have lived in bad societies.* [Italics added] (Doyle and Schindler, 1974:6)

When health care is maldistributed, when poverty persists for millions, when tax laws permit a business to write off 80 percent of a $100 luncheon but prohibit a truck driver from writing off a bologna sandwich, when government is run by the few for the benefit of the few, when businesses supposedly in competition fix prices to gouge the consumer, then society is permitting what is called **institutionalized deviance** (Doyle and Schindler, 1974:13). Such a condition exists when the society and its formal organizations are not meeting the needs of individuals. But these conditions often escape criticism and are rarely identified as social problems. Instead, the focus has often been on individuals who vent their frustration in socially unacceptable ways. A major intent of this book is to view individual deviance as a consequence of institutionalized deviance.

In summary, here we consider **social problems** to be (1) societally induced conditions that cause psychic and material suffering for any segment of the population, and (2) acts and conditions that violate the norms and values found in society. The distribution of power in society is the key to understanding these social problems. The powerless, because they are dominated by the powerful, are likely to be thwarted in achieving their basic needs (sustenance, security, self-esteem, and productivity). In contrast, the interests of the powerful are served because they control the mechanisms and institutions by which the perceptions of the public are shaped. By affecting public policy through reaffirming customs and through shaping the law and its enforcement, powerful interest groups are instrumental in designating (labeling) who is a problem (deviant) and who must be controlled. Our focus, then, is on the structure of society—especially on how power is distributed—rather than on "problem" individuals. Individual deviants are a manifestation of society's failure to meet their needs; the sources of crime, poverty, drug addiction, and racism are found in the laws and customs, the quality of life, the distribution of wealth and power, and the accepted practices of schools, governmental units, and corporations. As the primary source of social problems, society, not the individual deviant, must be restructured if social problems are to be solved. (See the Observation comparing the United States with other nations on social problems.)

OBSERVATION

COMPARING THE UNITED STATES WITH OTHER INDUSTRIALIZED NATIONS ON SELECTED SOCIAL PROBLEMS

Andrew L. Shapiro has compiled data on the nineteen major industrial nations—Australia, Austria, Belgium, Canada, Denmark, Finland, France, Germany, Ireland, Italy, Japan, the Netherlands, New Zealand, Norway, Spain, Sweden, Switzerland, the United Kingdom, and the United States. Of these nations, Shapiro finds that the United States ranks Number One on some positive dimensions. For example the United States is Number One in real wealth; number of billionaires; big homes; defense spending and military capability; executive salaries; physicians' salaries; ethnic diversity; percentage of population with access to safe drinking water; and the percentage of inhabitants enrolled in higher education.

At the same time, however, the United States ranks first in a number of social problems indicators: murder rate, reported rapes, robbery rate, incarceration rate, drunken driving fatalities, cocaine use, greenhouse gas emissions, contributing to acid rain, forest depletion, hazardous waste per capita, garbage per capita, children and elderly in poverty, homelessness, inequality of wealth distribution, bank failures, military aid to developing countries, divorce, single-parent families, reported cases of AIDS, infant mortality, the death of children younger than five, and teenage pregnancy.

Also, among these nations, the United States ranks *last* in spending on the poor; preschoolers fully immunized against polio, DTP (dipththeria-tetanus-pertussis), and measles; humanitarian aid to developing countries; percentage of people with health insurance; and providing paid maternity leave; and 17th in public spending on education; 15th in women's wages as a percentage of men's; 15th in life expectancy; and 9th in early childhood education.

The U.S. ranks number 1 in the rates of murder, robbery, reported rapes, and drunken driving fatalities.

Social Structure as the Basic Unit of Analysis

There is a very strong tendency for individuals—lay people, police officers, judges, lawmakers, and social scientists alike—to perceive social problems and prescribe remedies from a psychological perspective. For example, they blame the individual for being poor, with no reference to the maldistribution of wealth and other socially perpetuated disadvantages that blight many families generation after generation; they blame Blacks for their aggressive behavior, with no understanding of the limits placed on social mobility for Blacks by the social system; they blame dropouts for leaving school prematurely, with no understanding that the educational system fails to meet their needs. This type of thinking helps explain the reluctance of people in authority to provide adequate welfare, health care, and compensatory programs to help the disadvantaged.

The fundamental issue is whether social problems emanate from the pathologies of individuals (**person-blame**) or from the situations in which deviants are involved (**system-blame**) that is, whether deviants are the problem itself or only victims of it. The answer no doubt lies somewhere between the two extremes, but since the individual- or victim-blamers have held sway, we should examine their reasoning (Ryan, 1976).

Person-Blame Approach versus System-Blame Approach

Let us begin by considering some victims, such as the children in a slum school who constantly fail. Why do they fail? The victim-blamer points to their "cultural deprivation."* They don't do well in school because their families speak different dialects, because their parents are uneducated, because they have not been exposed to the educational benefits available to middle-class children (such as visits to the zoo, computers in the home, extensive travel, attendance at cultural events, exposure to books). In other words, the defect is in the children and their families. System-blamers look elsewhere for the sources of failure. They ask, What is there about the schools that makes slum children more likely to fail? The answer is found in the irrelevant curriculum, class-biased IQ tests, the tracking system, overcrowded classrooms, differential allocation of resources within the school district, and insensitive teachers whose low expectations for poor children create a self-fulfilling prophecy.

Criminals constitute another set of victims. Why is the recidivism rate (reinvolvement in crime) so high? The victim-blamer points to the faults of individual criminals: their greed, their feelings of aggression, their weak control of impulse, their lack of conscience. The system-blamer directs attention to very different sources: the penal system, the scarcity of employment for ex-criminals, and the schools. For example, 20 to 30 percent of inmates are functionally illiterate; that is, they cannot meet minimum reading and writing demands in U.S. society, such as filling out job applications. Yet these people are expected to leave prison, find a job, and stay out of trouble. Illiterate ex-criminals face unemployment or at best the most menial jobs, with low wages, no job security, and no fringe benefits. System-blamers argue that first the schools and later penal institutions have failed to provide these people with the minimum requirements for full participation in society. Moreover, lack of employment and the unwillingness of potential employers to train functional illiterates force many to return to crime in order to survive.

The inner-city poor are another set of victims. The conditions of the ghetto poor, especially Blacks, have deteriorated since the mid-1960s. Some observers believe that this deterioration is the result of the transplantation of a southern sharecropper culture (Lemann, 1986), welfare programs (Murray, 1984), and laziness. The more compelling system-blame argument, however, is made by William J. Wilson (1987). He claims that the ghetto underclass endures because of the disappearance of hundreds of thousands of low-skill jobs, those mainly involving physical labor, in the past twenty-five years or so. Wilson's contention, supported by research results, is that all of the pathologies of the ghetto (such as teenage pregnancy, illegitimacy, welfare dependency, and crime) are fundamentally the consequence of no available jobs.

The strong tendency to blame social problems on individuals rather than on the social system lies in how people tend to look at social problems. Most people define a social problem as behavior that deviates from the norms and standards

---

*Cultural deprivation** is a loaded ethnocentric term applied by members of the majority to the culture of the minority group. It implies that the culture of the group in question is not only inferior but also deficient. The concept itself is patently false, because no culture can be inferior to another; it can only be different. The concept does remind us, however, that people can and do make invidious distinctions about cultures and subcultures. Furthermore, they act on these distinctions as if they were valid.

According to one system-blame argument, the problems of the ghetto are the result of unavailable job opportunities.

of society. Because people do not ordinarily examine critically the way things are done in society, they tend to question the exceptions. The system not only is taken for granted but also has, for most people, an aura of sacredness because of the traditions and customs they associate it with. Logically, then, those who deviate are the source of trouble. The obvious question observers ask is, Why do these people deviate from norms? Because most people view themselves as law-abiding, they feel that those who deviate do so because of some kind of unusual circumstance, such as accident, illness, personal defect, character flaw, or maladjustment (Ryan, 1976:10–18). The flaw, then, is a function of the deviant, not of societal arrangements.

Interpreting social problems solely within a person-blame framework has serious consequences. (The following material is adapted from Caplan and Nelson, 1973, 1974.) First, it frees the government, the economy, the system of stratification, the system of justice, and the educational system from any blame. This protection of the established order against criticism increases the difficulty of trying to change the dominant economic, social, and political institutions. A good example is the strategy social scientists use in studying the origins of poverty. Because the person-blamer studies the poor rather than the nonpoor, the system of inequality (buttressed by tax laws, welfare rules, and employment practices) goes unchallenged. A related consequence of the person-blame approach, then, is that the relatively well off segments of society retain their advantages.

Not only does the person-blame approach justify the authorities in protecting the established order from criticism, but it also enables them to control dissidents under the guise of being helpful. Caplan and Nelson have provided an excellent illustration:

Normally, one would not expect the Government to cooperate with "problem groups" who oppose the system. But if a person-blame rather than system-blame action program can be negotiated, cooperation becomes possible. In this way, the problem-defining process remains in the control of the would-be bene-factors, who provide "help" so long as their diagnosis goes unchallenged.

In 1970, for example, while a group of American Indians still occupied Alcatraz Island in San Francisco Bay, a group of blacks took over Ellis Island in New York Harbor. Both groups attempted to take back lands no longer used by the Federal Government. The Government solved the Ellis Island problem by getting the blacks to help establish a drug-rehabilitation center on it. They solved the Alcatraz problem by forcibly removing the Indians. Had the Indians been willing to settle for an alcoholism-treatment center on Alcatraz, thereby acknowledging that what they need are remedies for their personal problems, we suspect the Government would have "cooperated" again. (Caplan and Nelson, 1974:104)

Another social control function of the person-blame approach is that trouble-some individuals and groups are controlled in a publicly acceptable manner. Deviants—whether they are criminals, homosexuals, or social protesters—are incarcerated in prisons or mental hospitals and administered drugs or other forms of therapy. This approach not only directs blame at individuals and away from the system, but it also eliminates the problems (individuals).

A related consequence is how the problem is to be treated. A person-blame approach demands a person-change treatment program. If the cause of delin-quency, for example, is defined as the result of personal pathology, then the solu-tion must clearly lie in counseling, behavior modification, psychotherapy, drugs, or some other technique aimed at changing the individual deviant. The person-blame interpretation of social problems provides and legitimates the right to ini-tiate person-change rather than system-change treatment programs. Under such a scheme norms that are racist or sexist, for example, will go unchallenged.

The person-blame ideology invites not only person-change treatment pro-grams but also programs for person-control. The system-blamer would argue that this emphasis, too, treats the symptom rather than the disease.

A final consequence of a person-blame interpretation is that it reinforces social myths about the degree of control individuals have over their fate. It pro-vides justification for a form of **Social Darwinism:** that the placement of people in the stratification system is a function of their ability and effort. By this logic the poor are poor because they *are* the dregs of society. In short, they deserve their fate, as do the successful in society. Thus, in this viewpoint there is little sympa-thy for government programs to increase welfare to the poor. (See the insert on William Graham Sumner for an example of this philosophy.)

Reasons for Focusing on the System-Blame Approach

We emphasize the system-blame approach in this book. We should recognize, however, that the system-blame orientation has dangers. First, it is only part of the truth. Social problems are highly complex phenomena that have both indi-vidual and systemic origins. Individuals, obviously, can be malicious and aggres-sive for purely psychological reasons, and perhaps only a psychologist can explain why a particular person shoots at cars passing on the freeway. Clearly, society

William Graham Sumner and Social Darwinism

William Graham Sumner (1840–1910), the sociologist who originated the concepts of folkways and mores, was a proponent of Social Darwinism. This doctrine, widely accepted among elites during the late nineteenth and early twentieth centuries, was a distorted version of Charles Darwin's theory of natural selection. From this viewpoint, success is the result of being superior. The rich are rich because they deserve to be. By this logic the poor also deserve their fate because they are biological and social failures and therefore unable to succeed in the competitive struggle.

Social Darwinism justified not only ruthless competition but also the perpetuation of the status quo. Superior classes, it was believed, should dominate because their members were unusually intelligent and moral. The lower classes, on the other hand, were considered inferior and defective. Their pathology was manifested in suicide, madness, crime, and various forms of vice.

On the basis of this philosophy, Sumner opposed social reforms such as welfare to the poor because they rewarded the unfit and penalized the competent. Such reforms, he argued, would interfere with the normal workings of society, halting progress and perhaps even contributing to a regression to an earlier evolutionary stage.

needs to be protected from some individuals. Moreover, some people require particular forms of therapy, remedial help, or special programs on an individual basis if they are to function normally. But much behavior that is labeled deviant is the end product of social conditions.

A second danger of a dogmatic system-blame orientation is that it presents a rigidly deterministic explanation of social problems. Taken too far, this position views individuals as robots controlled totally by their social environment. A balanced view acknowledges that human beings may choose between alternative courses of action. This issue raises the related question of the degree to which people are responsible for their behavior. An extreme system-blame approach absolves individuals from responsibility for their actions. To take such a stance would be to argue that society should never restrict deviants; this view invites anarchy (Caplan and Nelson, 1973:209).

Despite these problems with the system-blame approach, it is the guiding perspective of this book, for three reasons. First, because average citizens, police officers, legislators, social scientists, and judges tend to interpret social problems from an individualistic perspective, a balance is needed. Moreover, as noted earlier, a strict person-blame perspective has many negative consequences, and citizens must recognize these negative effects of their ideology.

A second reason for using the society-blaming perspective is that the subject matter of sociology is not the individual—who is the special province of psychology—but society. Because sociologists focus on the social determinants of behavior, they must make a critical analysis of the social structure. An important ingredient of the sociological perspective is the development of a critical stance toward social arrangements. Thus, the sociologist looks behind the facades to determine the positive and negative consequences of social arrangements. The sociologist's persistent questions must be, Who benefits under these arrangements, and who does not? For this reason, there should be such a close fit between the sociological approach and the society-blaming perspective.

A final reason for the use of the system-blame approach is that the institutional framework of society is the source of many social problems (such as racism, pollution, unequal distribution of health care, poverty, war, and economic cycles). An exclusive focus on the individual ignores the strains caused by the inequities of the system and its fundamental intransigence to change. A guiding assumption of this book is that because institutions are made by human beings (and therefore are not sacred), they should be changed whenever they do not meet the needs of the people they were created to serve. As Skolnick and Currie have stated:

> Democratic conceptions of society have always held that institutions exist to serve people, and not vice versa. Institutions therefore are to be accountable to the people whose lives they affect. Where an institution—any institution, even the most "socially valued"—is found to conflict with human needs, democratic thought holds that it ought to be changed or abolished. (Skolnick and Currie, 1973:15)

One goal of this book is to help the reader understand the social nature of social problems. Accepting the system-blame perspective is a necessary first step in efforts to restructure society along more humane lines. The job of social scientists in this endeavor should be to provide alternative social structures (based on theory and research) for those we complain about. To do this job, social scientists must ask very different research questions from those posed in the past, and they must study not only the powerless but also the powerful.

Organization of the Book

The organizing theme of this book is that many aspects of social problems are conditions resulting from cultural and social arrangements. It therefore begins by examining the fundamental organization of U.S. society. The remainder of Part I elaborates on the political economy of social problems, emphasizing the political and economic organization of society and its impact on social problems. The focus is on power because the powerful, by making and enforcing the laws, create and define deviance. They determine which behaviors will be rewarded and which ones punished. The powerful influence public opinion, and they can attempt to solve social problems or ignore them. Through policies for taxation and subsidies, the powerful determine the degree to which wealth is distributed in society. They also determine which group interests will be advanced and at whose expense.

The economy is equally important. The particular form of the economy establishes a distribution process, not only for wealth but also for goods and services. In many important ways Karl Marx was correct: The economy is the force that determines the form and substance of all other institutions—the church, school, family, and polity.

Critical scrutiny of the polity and the economy provides clues for the bias of society. It helps explain the upside-down qualities of society whereby the few benefit at the expense of the majority; how reality gets defined in contested issues; how political and economic processes affect what is currently being done about social problems; and thus, why so many social policies fail.

Part II focuses on problems of people, resources, and location. The topics examined are world population, global inequality, environmental degradation and resource depletion, and U.S. urban problems.

Part III examines a crucial element of U.S. social structure: the various manifestations of social inequality. It describes inequality based on wealth, race/ethnicity, gender, age, and sexual orientation.

Part IV describes problems found within four representative institutions. One chapter looks at the family-related problems of single-parent families, child care, violence, and divorce. The chapter on education illustrates how this institution of society, while necessary as the source for transmitting the proper skills and attitudes to each generation, is also a generator of social problems. Thus, it shows once again how social problems (in this case, inequality) originate in the basic structure of society. The chapter on health care focuses on the reasons for the high cost of health care in the United States and on the unequal delivery of health care. The final chapter in Part IV addresses the allocation and remuneration of jobs. The number and types of jobs are undergoing a major shift as society deindustrializes and moves toward a service economy. While the resulting changes bring many opportunities, they also bring many problems, in particular, the widening gap between the haves and the have-nots and the emergence of a new form of poverty.

Part V examines the impact of social structure on individuals. Deviant behavior is activity that violates the norms of an organization, community, or society. Consequently, deviance is culturally defined and socially labeled. Certain behaviors are also labeled as deviant because they conflict with the interests of the powerful in society. Public policy, then, reflects the values and interests of those in power and is codified into law. Members of society are also taught how to respond to deviants. The law and these structured responses to deviants are societal reactions that establish deviance in social roles; paradoxically, the degraded status that results from societal reactions reinforces the deviance that society seeks to control. Deviance, then, is fundamentally the result of social structure. We examine these processes in relation to several types of deviance: crime, mental disorder, and drug use.

CHAPTER REVIEW

1. Historically, U.S. sociologists have viewed social problems in terms of social pathology: "Bad" people were assumed to be the sources of social problems because they disturbed the prevailing moral order in society.

2. In the 1920s and 1930s sociologists focused on the conditions of society, such as the rapid changes accompanying urbanization and industrialization, as the sources of social problems.

3. More recently, many sociologists have returned to a study of problem individuals—deviants who violate the expectations of society. The modern study of deviance has developed in two directions. The first sought the sources of deviation within the social structure. The other, of relatively recent origin, has focused on the role of society in creating and sustaining deviance through labeling those viewed as abnormal. In this view, societal reactions are assumed to determine what a social problem is and who is deviant.

4. There is an objective reality to social problems; some conditions or situations do induce material and psychic suffering. There are several dangers, however, in defining social problems objectively. Subjectivity cannot be removed from the process. A standard must be selected, but in a pluralistic society there are many standards. Moreover, social scientists not only disagree on what a social problem is but also cannot escape their own values in the study of social problems. Most important, the objective approach to social problems entails acceptance of the definitions provided by the powerful. The acceptance of these definitions diverts attention away from the powerful and toward those the powerful wish to label negatively, thus deflecting observations away from what may constitute the most important social problem—the existing social order.

5. This book examines two types of social problems: (a) acts and conditions that violate the norms and values of society, and (b) societally induced conditions that cause psychic and material suffering for any segment of the population. The key to understanding both types of social problems is the distribution of power.

6. The focus is on the structure of society rather than on "problem" individuals. A guiding assumption of our inquiry is that norm violators are symptoms of social problems. These deviants are for the most part victims and should not be blamed entirely for their deviance; the system in which they live should also be blamed.

7. The person-blame approach, which we do not use, has serious consequences: (a) It frees the institutions of society from any blame and efforts to change them; (b) it controls "problem" people in ways that reinforce negative stereotypes; (c) it legitimates person-control programs; and (d) it justifies the logic of Social Darwinism, which holds that people are rich or poor because of their ability and effort or lack thereof.

8. The system-blame orientation also has dangers. Taken dogmatically, it presents a rigidly deterministic explanation for social problems, suggesting that people are merely robots controlled by their social environment.

KEY TERMS

Subjective nature of social problems. What is and what is not a social problem is a matter of definition. Thus, social problems vary by time and place.

Objective reality of social problems. There are societal conditions that harm certain segments of the population and, therefore, are social problems.

Institutionalized deviance. When a society is organized in such a way as to disadvantage some of its members.

Social problems. Societally induced conditions that harm any segment of the population and acts and conditions that violate the norms and values found in society.

Person-blame. The assumption that social problems result from the pathologies of individuals.

System-blame. The assumption that social problems result from social conditions.

Cultural deprivation. The assumption by the members of a group that the culture of some other group is not only inferior but also deficient. This term is usually applied by members of the majority to the culture of a minority group.

Social Darwinism. The belief that the place of people in the stratification system is a function of their ability and effort.

FOR FURTHER STUDY

Lawrence G. Brewster. *The Public Agenda.* 2d ed. New York: St. Martin's Press, 1987.

Joe R. Feagin and Clairece Booher Feagin. *Social Problems: A Critical Power-Conflict Perspective.* 3d ed. Englewood Cliffs, N.J.: Prentice-Hall, 1990.

R. C. Lewontin, Steven Rose, and Leon J. Kamin. *Not in Our Genes.* New York: Pantheon Books, 1984.

Michael Parenti. *Power and the Powerless.* 2d ed. New York: St. Martin's Press, 1978.

Earl Rubington and Martin S. Weinberg, eds. *The Study of Social Problems: Six Perspectives.* 4th ed. New York: Oxford University Press, 1989.

William Ryan. *Blaming the Victim.* Rev. ed. New York: Random House (Vintage), 1976.

Malcolm Spector and John I. Kitsuse. *Constructing Social Problems.* Hawthorne, N.Y.: Aldine de Gruyter, 1987.

FORUM

WHO OR WHAT IS ULTIMATELY THE SOURCE OF CRIME: THE INDIVIDUAL OR SOCIETY?

Person-blamers believe that the individual offender is the primary source of crime.

Stanton E. Samenow

We have identified a total of fifty-two thinking patterns that are present in all the criminals in our study. At the outset, we surmised that we would discover different profiles for criminals who had committed different kinds of crimes—property, sex, and assault. This turned out not to be the case. Criminals do differ in the types of crimes they commit and in their *modi operandi*. The man who uses stealth and cunning may avoid fights for fear of physical injury, but, more significantly, he looks down on the criminal who uses force, seeing him as crude. The criminal who uses "muscle" regards the conman as "weak" or "sissy." However, if one examines how criminals live their lives, how they regard themselves and the outside world, the similarities far outweigh the differences. Furthermore, we found that the criminal charged with a sexual offense has committed other types of crimes. The same is true of the others, although their police records do not reveal this. Both the white-collar criminal and the street criminal conduct their lives in the same way, even though their styles in crime suggest that they are different types of people. All criminals are habitual liars. They fail to put themselves in the place of others

(unless it is to scheme a crime). They do not know what responsible decision making is, because they have prejudged most situations and find no need to ascertain facts and consider alternative courses of action. They believe that the world is their oyster and that people are pawns, while they have no obligation to anyone. In short, they share all fifty-two thinking patterns that we describe in our writings. Criminality goes far beyond mere arrestability. It pertains to the way in which a person thinks and lives his life. . . .

Changing the environment does not change the inner man. Slums are cleared, job opportunities are offered, schooling is provided, but crime remains. More of our criminals had jobs than were unemployed. But providing a criminal with job skills and then a job results in a criminal with a job rather than a criminal without a job. He remains a criminal. He may utilize his job for his own gain, commit crimes on the job, or use his job as a mantle of respectability, which leaves him free to live a secret life of crime outside his work.

Source: "The Criminal Personality: New Concepts and New Procedures for Change," by Stanton E. Samenow first appeared in the September/October 1978 issue of *The Humanist* and is reprinted with permission.

System-blamers argue that crime is caused by how societies and their institutions are organized and operate.

Jeffrey Reiman

Any criminal justice system like ours conveys a subtle, yet powerful message in support of established institutions. It does this for two interconnected reasons: first, because it concentrates on *individual* wrongdoers. This means that *it diverts our attention away from our institutions, away from consideration of whether our*

institutions themselves are wrong or unjust or indeed "criminal."

Second, the criminal law is put forth as the *minimum neutral ground rules* for any social living. We are taught that no society can exist without rules against theft and violence, and thus the criminal law is put forth as politically neutral, as the minimum requirements for *any* society, as the minimum obligations that any individual owes his fellows to make social life of any decent sort possible. Thus, it not only diverts our attention away from the possible injustice of our social institutions, but *the criminal law bestows upon those institutions the mantle of its own neutrality.* Since the criminal law protects the established institutions (e.g., the prevailing economic arrangements are protected by laws against theft, etc.), attacks on those established institutions become equivalent to violations of the minimum requirements for any social life at all. In effect, the criminal law enshrines the established institutions as equivalent to the minimum requirements for *any* decent social existence—and it brands the individual who attacks those institutions as one who has declared war on *all* organized society and who must therefore be met with the weapons of war.

This is the powerful magic of criminal justice. By virtue of its focus on *individual* criminals, it diverts us from the evils of the *social* order. By virtue of its presumed neutrality, it transforms the established social (and economic) order from being merely *one* form of society open to critical comparison with others into *the* conditions of *any* social order and thus immune from criticism. . . .

Consider, for example, the law against theft. It does indeed seem to be one of the minimum requirements of social living. As long as there is scarcity, any society—capitalist or socialist—will need rules preventing individuals from taking what does not belong to them. But the law against theft is more: It is a law against stealing what individuals *presently* own. *Such a law has the effect of making present property relations a part of the criminal law.*

Since stealing is a violation of law, this means that present property relations become the implicit standard of justice against which criminal deviations are measured. Since criminal law is thought of as the minimum requirements of any social life, this means that present property relations become equivalent to the minimum requirements of *any* social life. And the criminal who would alter the present property relations becomes nothing less than someone who is declaring war on all organized society. The question of whether this "war" is provoked by the injustice or brutality of the society is swept aside. Indeed, this suggests yet another way in which the criminal justice system conveys an ideological message in support of the established society.

Source: Reprinted with permission of Macmillan Publishing Company from *The Rich Get Richer and the Poor Get Prison: Ideology, Class and Criminal Justice,* Third Edition by Jeffrey Reiman. Copyright © 1990 by Jeffrey Reiman.

The thesis of this book is that the problems of U.S. society are the result of the distribution of power and the form of the economy. This chapter begins the analysis of U.S. social problems by looking at the political and economic realities of interest groups, and also at power, powerlessness, and domination. As we discuss, the state is *not* a neutral agent of the people but is biased in favor of those with wealth—the upper social classes and the largest corporations. As we analyze the bias of the system, we begin to see that, contrary to popular belief, the U.S. system does not produce a society that is democratic, just, and equal in opportunity. Rather, we may find that the United States is an upside-down society, with the few benefiting at the expense of the many. Finally, we see how our society itself is the source of social problems.

This chapter is divided into four sections. The first section describes the two polar types of economic systems, capitalism and socialism. The second describes the U.S. economy, with its concentration of corporate and private wealth. The third examines the political system and its linkages to the economic elites. The final section shows how the politicoeconomic system is biased in favor of those who are already advantaged.

Capitalism and Socialism

Industrialized societies organize their economic activities according to one of two fundamental forms: capitalism or socialism. Although no society has a purely capitalist or socialist economy, the ideal types provide opposite extremes on a scale that help us measure the U.S. economy more accurately.

Capitalism

Three conditions must be present for pure **capitalism** to exist—private ownership of property, personal profit, and competition. These necessary conditions constitute the underlying principles of a pure capitalist system. The first is private ownership of property. Individuals are encouraged to own not only private possessions but, most important, also the capital necessary to produce and distribute goods and services. In a purely capitalist society there would be no public ownership of any potentially profitable activity.

The pursuit of maximum profit, the second essential principle, implies that individuals are free to maximize their personal gains. Most important, the proponents of capitalism (see the inserts on Adam Smith and Milton Friedman) argue that profit seeking by individuals has positive consequences for society. Thus, seeking individual gain through personal profit is considered morally acceptable and socially desirable.

Competition, the third ingredient, is the mechanism for determining what is produced and at what price. The market forces of supply and demand will ensure that capitalists will produce the goods and services wanted by the public, that the goods and services will be high in quality, and that they will be sold at the lowest possible price. Moreover, competition is the mechanism that keeps individual profit seeking in check. Potential abuses such as fraud, faulty products, and exorbitant prices are negated by the existence of competitors who will soon take

Adam Smith

Adam Smith (1723–1790), a Scottish economist, is the godfather of laissez-faire capitalism. His *Inquiry into the Nature and Causes of
the Wealth of Nations,* written in 1776, presented a logical vision of how society was bound
inextricably by the private decisions of entrepreneurs and consumers alike.

Of the many issues that Smith addressed, one is paramount for our concerns:
How does society hang together when everyone is pursuing his or her self-interest? For Smith the answer is in the laws of the marketplace; the needs of society
and its citizens are met by each person producing what will bring a profit.
According to Smith, someone will provide whatever is needed, because demand
increases the likelihood of profit. But if all entrepreneurs are profit-hungry, what
will prevent them from taking unfair advantage of their consumers? The answer,
simply, is competition. The existence of competition will keep prices fair and product quality high.

The market also regulates the incomes of those who produce the goods. If
wages are too high in one kind of work, other workers will rush to that type of job,
bringing down the exorbitant wages. Similarly, if wages are too low, then workers
will change to better-paying jobs. The marketplace also reduces the possibility of
surpluses because entrepreneurs, foreseeing the problem, will move to more profitable arenas where the demand and profits are high. Thus, the laws of the marketplace provide an "invisible hand" that regulates the economy without
government intervention. The government is not needed to fix prices, to set minimum wages, or to protect against consumer fraud. All that is needed is a free and
competitive marketplace.

The question, of course, is whether the nature of the marketplace in a world
of huge multinational corporations, multimillion-member labor unions, and con-
glomerates is the same as it was in the eighteenth century.

business away from those who violate good business judgment. So, too, economic inefficiency is minimized as market forces cause the inept to fail and the efficient to succeed.

These three principles—private property, personal profit, and competition—
require a fourth condition if true capitalism is to work: a government policy of laissez-faire, allowing the marketplace to operate unhindered. Any government
intervention in the marketplace will, argue capitalists, distort the economy by neg-

Milton Friedman

Milton Friedman (b. 1912), a Nobel laureate in economics, is the leading contemporary advocate of a free market economy to solve society's ills. He is fundamentally opposed to central planning on the grounds that such a system is coercive. Rather, people should be free to work and produce whatever they feel will bring a fair price. According to Friedman, price is the key. If the price is high for a certain product because of demand, individuals will be attracted to producing it; if the price is low, many producers will turn to other, more profitable activities. The result of such a system, Friedman has argued, is peaceful cooperation among millions of persons in societies and among societies. More important, because such a system is based on freedom of choice, it promotes political, human, and religious freedom as well.

Friedman maintains that government intervention interferes with the natural mechanism of the free market. Thus, for him the basic problem of U.S. society today is too much government, not too little. He is especially fearful of the move toward socialism. Friedman characterizes capitalist societies as voluntarily cooperative, whereas the essential notion of a socialist society is force. Either the individual is master or the government is. In the former case freedom reigns, and the dignity and the individuality of people are respected. In a socialist society, on the other hand, individuals must be coerced to work for what the government considers the common good. Thus, for Friedman capitalism tends to give freer rein to the more humane values by fostering a climate of individual responsibility and achievement:

> I am only saying that a set of social institutions that stresses individual responsibility, that treats the individual—given the kind of person he is, the kind of society in which he operates—as responsible for and to himself, will lead to a
> higher and more desirable moral climate than a set of institutions that stresses
> the lack of responsibility of the individual for what happens to him and relieves
> him of blame or credit for what he does to his fellowmen.*

*Milton Friedman, *The Economics of Freedom* (Cleveland: Standard Oil Company, 1978), p. 11.

atively affecting incentives and freedom of individual choice. If left unhindered by government, the profit motive, private ownership, and competition will achieve the greatest good for the greatest number in the form of individual self-fulfillment and the general material progress of society.

The traders on the New York Stock Exchange are the brokers of capitalism, buying and selling shares of businesses for their clients.

Socialism

The five principles of **socialism** are democratism, egalitarianism, community, public ownership of the means of production, and planning for common purposes. True socialism must be democratic. Representatives of a socialist state must be answerable and responsive to the wishes of the public they serve. Nations that claim to be socialist but are totalitarian violate this fundamental aspect of socialism. The key to differentiating between authentic and spurious socialism is to determine who is making the decisions and whose interests are being served. Thus, it is a fallacy to equate true socialism with the politicoeconomic systems found in the People's Republic of China or Cuba. These societies are socialistic in some respects; that is, their material benefits are more evenly distributed than those in the United States. But their economies and governments are controlled by a single political party in an inflexible and authoritarian manner. Although these countries claim to have democratic elections, in fact the citizens have no electoral choice but to rubber-stamp the candidates of the ruling party. The people are denied civil liberties and freedoms that should be the hallmark of a socialist society. In a pure socialist society democratic relations must operate throughout the social structure: in government, at work, at school, and in the community.

The second principle of socialism is egalitarianism: equality of opportunity for the self-fulfillment of all; equality rather than hierarchy in decision making; and equality in sharing the benefits of society. For some socialists the goal is absolute equality. For most, though, equality means a limit to inequality, with some acceptable disparities in living standards. This more realistic goal of socialism requires a fundamental commitment to achieving a rough parity by leveling out gross inequities in income, property, and opportunities. The key is a leveling of advantages so that all citizens receive the necessities (food, clothing, medical care, living wages, sick pay, retirement benefits, and shelter).

The third feature of socialism is community, which is the "idea that social relations should be characterized by cooperation and a sense of collective belonging rather than by conflict and competition" (Miller, 1991:406).

The fourth characteristic of socialism is the public ownership of the means of production. The people own the basic industries, financial institutions, utilities, transportation, and communication companies. The goal is serving the public, not making profit.

The fifth principle of socialism is planning. The society must direct social activities to meet common goals. This means that socialists oppose the heart of capitalism, which is to let individuals acting in their own interests in the marketplace determine overall outcomes. For socialists, these uncoordinated activities invite chaos and while possibly helping some people in the society will do damage to others. Thus, a purely socialist government requires societal planning to provide, at the least possible individual and collective cost, the best conditions to meet the material needs of its citizens. Planning also aims to achieve societal goals such as protecting the environment, combating pollution, saving natural resources, and developing new technologies. Public policy is decided through the rational assessment of the needs of society and how the economy might best be organized to achieve them. In this situation the economy must be regulated by the government, which acts as the agent of the people. The government sets prices and wages; important industries are run at a loss if necessary. Dislocations such as surpluses or shortages or unemployment are minimized by central planning. The goal is to run the economy for the good of the society.

The U.S. Economy: The Concentration of Corporate Wealth

The U.S. economy has always been based on the principles of capitalism; however, the present economy is far removed from a free enterprise system. The major discrepancy between the ideal system and the real one is that the U.S. economy is no longer based on competition among more or less equal private capitalists. It is now dominated by huge corporations that, contrary to classical economic theory, control demand rather than respond to the demands of the market. However well the economic system might once have worked, the increasing size and power of corporations disrupt it. This development calls into question what the appropriate economic form is for a modern industrialized society.

Monopolistic Capitalism

Karl Marx, more than 100 years ago, when bigness was the exception, predicted that capitalism was doomed by several inherent contradictions that would produce a class of people bent on destroying it (see the inset on Karl Marx and "self-destruct" capitalism). The most significant of these contradictions for our purposes is the inevitability of monopolies. Marx hypothesized that free enterprise would result in some firms becoming bigger and bigger as they eliminate their opposition or absorb smaller competing firms. The ultimate result of this

Karl Marx and "Self-Destruct" Capitalism

Karl Marx (1818–1883) was one of history's greatest social theorists. His ideas have fueled revolutionaries and revolutions. His writings have had an enormous impact on each of the social sciences. His intellectual contributions to sociology include (1) elaboration of the conflict model of society, (2) the theory of social change based on antagonisms between the social classes, (3) the insight that power originates primarily in economic production, and (4) concern with the social origins of alienation.

Marx believed that the basis of social order in every society is the production of economic goods. What is produced, how it is produced, and how it is exchanged determine the differences in people's wealth, power, and social status. Marx argued that because human beings must organize their activities in order to clothe, feed, and house themselves, every society is built on an economic base. The exact form this organization takes varies from society to society and from era to era. The form that people chose to solve their basic economic problems would, according to Marx, eventually determine virtually everything in the social structure, including the polity, family structure, education, and religion. In Marx's view all these social institutions are dependent on the basic economy, and an analysis of society will always reveal its underlying economic arrangements.

Because it owns the means of production, the social class in power uses the noneconomic institutions to uphold its position. Thus, Marx believed that religion, the government, the educational system, and even sport are used by the powerful to maintain the status quo.

Marx argued that every economic system except socialism produces forces that eventually lead to a new economic form. In the feudal system, for example, the market and factory emerged but were incompatible with the feudal way of life. The market created a professional merchant class, and the factory created a proletariat. Thus, new inventions create a tension with the old institutions, and new social classes threaten to displace old ones. Conflict results, and society is rearranged with a new class structure and an alteration in the division of wealth and power based on a new economic form. Feudalism was replaced by capitalism; land ownership was replaced by factories and the ownership of capital.

Capitalism, Marx maintained, also carries the seeds of its own destruction. Capitalism will produce a class of oppressed people (the proletariat) bent on destroying it. The contradictions inherent in capitalism are (1) the inevitability of monopolies, which eliminate competition and gouge consumers and workers; (2) lack of centralized planning, which results in overproduction of some goods and underproduction of others, encouraging economic crises such as inflation, slumps, and depressions; (3) demands for labor-saving machinery, which force unemployment and a more hostile proletariat; and (4) control of the state by the wealthy, the effect of which is passage of laws favoring themselves and thereby incurring more wrath from the proletariat. All these factors increase the probability that the proletariat will build class consciousness, which is the condition necessary to class conflict and the ushering in of a new economic system.*

*See Robert J. Werlin, "Marxist Political Analysis," *Sociological Inquiry* 42 (No. 3–4, 1972), 157–181; *Karl Marx: Selected Writings in Sociology and Social Philosophy,* T. B. Bottomore, trans. (New York: McGraw-Hill, 1956), pp. 127–212. See also Michael Harrington, *The Twilight of Capitalism* (New York: Simon & Schuster, 1976).

---

process is the existence of a monopoly in each of the various sectors of the economy. Monopolies, of course, are antithetical to the free-enterprise system because they, not supply and demand, determine the price and the quality of the product.

For the most part, the evidence in U.S. society upholds Marx's prediction. Most sectors of the U.S. economy are dominated by **shared monopolies.** Instead of a single corporation controlling an industry, the situation is one in which a small number of large firms dominate an industry. When four or fewer firms supply 50 percent or more of a particular market, a shared monopoly results, which performs much as a monopoly or cartel would. Most economists agree that above this level of concentration—a four-firm ratio of 50 percent—the economic costs of shared monopoly are most manifest. Government data show that a number of industries are highly concentrated (e.g., each of the following industries has four or fewer firms controlling at least 60 percent: light bulbs, breakfast cereals, turbines/generators, aluminum, chocolate/cocoa, photography equipment, brewing, guided missiles, and roasted coffee).

This trend toward ever-greater concentration among the largest U.S. business concerns has accelerated because of two activities—mergers and interlocking directorates.

Megamergers. In 1988 there were 5,417 mergers and leveraged buyouts costing $453 billion. Some of the largest recent mergers were Standard Oil of California's purchase of Gulf Oil for $13.3 billion and Texaco's buyout of Getty Oil for $10.1 billion. The largest takeover occurred in 1989, when RJR-Nabisco was purchased for $25 billion. The federal government encouraged these mergers by relaxing the antitrust law enforcement on the grounds that efficient firms should not be hobbled. Critics have argued, however, that such financial excess will have a crippling effect on the economy.

> The speculative frenzy yields . . . dismal figures: $1.3 trillion spent on mergers and buyouts over the 1980s, equal to roughly one-third the amount spent for new productive plant and equipment over the same period; about $13 billion spent just arranging these deals, forty-five times the government's annual outlay for worker health and safety. And because buyouts were financed mostly through debt, corporations now devote more than 60 percent of their pretax

Many foods in a grocery story have high prices because they are in highly concentrated industries (shared monopolies).

profits to interest payments, nearly double the burden carried in the 1970s. (Pollin and Cockburn, 1991:231)

This trend toward megamergers has at least four negative consequences: (1) it increases the centralization of capital, which reduces competition and raises prices for consumers; (2) it increases the power of the huge corporations over workers, unions, and governments; (3) it diminishes the number of jobs; and (4) it is nonproductive. Jim Hightower emphasizes this last point:

> In the last three years [1983–1986], 9,000 companies changed owners at a cost of nearly half a trillion dollars. For what? Not for new plants, products or jobs, but for paper shuffling, for lawyers, accountants, brokers, bankers and big investors—hundreds of millions of dollars paid in nonproductive fees to achieve nonproductive ends. (Hightower, 1987:25)

The amount of money made by the brokers on these deals can be incredible. At the extreme, Michael Milken, as an employee of Drexel Burnham Lambert, Inc., created high-risk junk bonds to finance leveraged buyouts and was paid $550 million in 1987 for his services.*

> More than half a billion dollars a year is $1.5 million a day. We're counting all 365 days because Mr. Milken often works seven days a week, even during vaca-

---

*Some of Milken's work was legitimate; other activities were not. In 1990 Milken pleaded guilty to six felony counts related to securities fraud. He agreed to pay $600 million in fines and restitution. He was later sentenced to ten years in prison.

tion. That's a bit over $107,000 an hour, based on his normal 14-hour day. The 42-year-old financier's 1987 compensation, paid for his 1986 work, was more than the gross national product of the Republic of Guyana, whose 779,000 citizens produced only about $460 million in goods and services in 1985. (Swartz, 1989:1)

Defenders of a free and competitive enterprise system should attack the existence of monopolies and shared monopolies as un-American. There should be strong support of governmental efforts to break up the largest and most powerful corporations. Nearly two decades ago, Mark S. Green offered the following commentary:

> Huey Long once prophesied that fascism would come to the United States first in the form of antifascism. So too with socialism—*corporate* socialism. Under the banner of free enterprise, up to two-thirds of American manufacturing has been metamorphosed into a "closed enterprise system." Although businessmen spoke the language of competitive capitalism, each sought refuge for himself: price-fixing, parallel pricing, mergers, excessive advertising, quotas, subsidies, and tax favoritism. While defenders of the American dream guarded against socialism from the left, it arrived unannounced from the right. (Green, 1972:4)

Interlocking directorates.   Another mechanism for the ever-greater concentration of the size and power of the largest corporations is **interlocking directorates,** the linkage between corporations that results when an individual serves on the board of directors of two companies (a direct interlock) or when two companies each have a director on the board of a third company (an indirect interlock). Such arrangements have great potential to benefit the interlocked companies by reducing competition through the sharing of information and the coordination of policies. As a Senate report has put it:

> Personal interlocks between business leaders may lead to a concentration of economic or fiscal control in a few hands. There is in this the danger of a business elite, an ingrown group impervious to outside forces, intolerant of dissent, and protective of the status quo, charting the direction of production and investment in one of several industries. (U.S. Senate, 1978:6)

In 1914 passage of the Clayton Act made it illegal for a person to serve simultaneously on corporate boards of two companies that were in direct competition with each other. Financial institutions and indirect interlocks, however, were exempt. Moreover, the government has had difficulty in determining what constitutes "direct competition." The result is that, despite the prohibition, interlocking directorates are widespread.

Interlocking directorates proliferate throughout U.S. industry. When directors are linked directly or indirectly there is the potential for cohesiveness, common action, and unified power. Clearly, the principles of capitalism are compromised when this phenomenon occurs.

Instead of functioning as a free enterprise system, then, the U.S. economy is controlled by huge corporations. To illustrate the enormity of the largest corporations, consider the assets of the top three in 1990: General Motors ($180 billion), Ford ($173.6 billion), General Electric ($153.9 billion); and profits: IBM ($6.02 billion); Exxon ($5.01 billion), and General Electric ($4.3 billion) (*Fortune,* 1991:286).

These companies need not be concerned with sound business principles and quality products, because there is no real threat of competition. In other words, the concentration of industrial wealth means that the principles of free enterprise cannot work. Nevertheless, many large corporations devote considerable efforts to convincing the public that the U.S. economy *is* competitive despite the evidence. Many advertisements depict the economy as an Adam Smith-style of free market with competition among innumerable small competitors. This, however, is a dream. Competition does exist among the mom-and-pop stores, but they control only a minute portion of the nation's assets. The largest assets are located among the very large corporations, and competition there is virtually nonexistent.

Multinational Corporations

The thesis of the previous section is that there is a trend for corporations to increase in size, resulting eventually in huge enterprises that join with other large companies to form effective monopolies. This process of economic concentration provides the largest companies with enormous economic and political power. Another trend—the globalization of the largest corporations in the United States— makes their power all the greater. This fact of international economic life has very important implications for social problems, both domestically and abroad.

A number of U.S. corporations have substantial assets overseas. In 1991, for example, the top five U.S. corporations in foreign assets were Citicorp ($95,927 million), Ford Motor ($55,053 million, Exxon ($51,118 million), IBM ($50,210 million), and J. P. Morgan ($48,390) (*Forbes,* 1992:298–299). There has been a tendency of late for U.S. corporations to increase their foreign investments sharply. Why are U.S. corporations shifting more and more of their total assets outside the United States? The obvious answer is that the rate of profit tends to be higher abroad. Resources necessary for manufacture and production tend to be cheaper in many other nations, and labor costs are substantially lower. Wages in general are much lower than in the United States, and unions are nonexistent.

The consequences of this shift in production from the United States to other countries are significant. Most important is the drying up of many semi- and unskilled jobs. The effects of the increased unemployment are twofold: increased welfare costs and increased discontent among people in the working class. We return to this problem of domestic job losses through overseas capital investments in Chapter 14, when deindustrialization is discussed.

The problems of domestic unemployment exacerbated by overseas investment are the problems of lost revenues through taxes and a negative balance of payments. Tax revenues are lost because corporations can escape paying domestic taxes by having goods produced overseas and by undervaluing exports and overvaluing imports. Indirectly, taxes are also lost by increased unemployment. The balance-of-payments problem is aggravated by the flow of investment money overseas and the purchase of goods produced in foreign countries.

Another result of the twin processes of concentration and internationalization of corporations is the enormous power wielded by gigantic multinational corporations. In essence, the largest corporations control the world economy. Their decisions to build or not to build, to relocate a plant, or to start a new product or to scrap an old one have tremendous impacts on the lives of ordinary citizens in the countries they operate from and invest in.

Finally, multinational corporations tend to meddle in the internal affairs of other nations in order to protect their investments and maximize profits. The multinationals have paid millions in bribes and political contributions to reactionary governments and conservative leaders in countries like South Korea, Bolivia, Taiwan, Japan, and Italy (Parenti, 1988:147).

Concentration of Wealth

The other discrepancy between free enterprise in its real and ideal states is the undue concentration of wealth among a few individuals and corporations. This imbalance makes a mockery of claims that capitalism rewards the efforts of *all* enterprising individuals.

The concentration of corporate wealth.   Wealth in the business community is centralized in a relatively few major corporations, and this concentration is increasing. In 1950 the largest 100 manufacturing corporations held 39.7 percent of all manufacturing assets; in 1985 they held almost 50 percent (Marger, 1987:97). The following examples show just how concentrated wealth is among the major U.S. corporations.

- Less than 1 percent of all corporations control two-thirds of the corporate assets of the United States (Parenti, 1988:11). In 1989 the largest 500 companies had a total of $7 trillion in assets, with each of the 500 corporations exceeding $2.644 billion (*Forbes,* 1990a:248–254). The top 10 corporations controlled 20 percent of the assets owned by the top 500 (*Forbes,* 1990a:248–249). The top 200 companies held more than 60 percent of *all* manufacturing assets (Marger, 1987:97).
- Of the 15,000 commercial U.S. banks, the largest 50 hold more than one-third of all assets. The top 10 hold 20 percent of the assets (Marger, 1987:102). Moreover, the 49 biggest banks have a controlling interest in the 500 largest corporations (Report of the Joint Economic Committee, 1986).
- One percent of all food corporations control 80 percent of all the industry's assets and about 90 percent of the profits (Parenti, 1988:12).

The concentration of private wealth and income.   Capitalism generates inequality. Wealth is concentrated not only in the largest corporations but also among individuals and families. For example, there are 12 counties in the United States where the average household wealth exceeds $200,000 (Cooper, 1991). In 1992, according to *Forbes,* there were 101 individuals or families in the United States with an estimated net worth of $1 billion or more (*Forbes,* 1992:161).

The concentration of wealth at the top is growing. Moreover, a recent study by two Federal Reserve System analysts found that

> the top one-half percent of families owned 29 percent of total family net worth—including homes and cars as well as investments such as stocks and bonds, an increase from 24 percent in 1983. Everybody else lost some of their share to the ultra-rich, who controlled 60 percent of bonds and business assets. The bottom 90 percent of families owned only 32 percent of total net worth—about the same share as the top one-half percent, primarily their homes, bank accounts, autos, and life insurance (Moberg, 1992:7).

White households have more than 10 times the wealth of Black households.

Personal wealth is badly skewed by race and gender. According to the Census Bureau, White households in 1988 had a median net worth of $43,279, compared to $5,524 for Latino households and $4,169 for Black households. In other words, White households have more than 10 times the wealth of Black households and 8.5 times the wealth of Latino households (U.S. Census Bureau, 1991d:20–21. In terms of income by gender, in 1990 the median income for families headed by a male was $40,331 compared to $19,528 for those families headed by a female (U.S. Census Bureau, 1991d:3).

The data on wealth always show more concentration than income statistics, but the convergence of money among the few is still very dramatic when considering income. Thus, the share of the national income of the richest 20 percent of households was 46.6 percent while the bottom 20 percent received only 3.9 percent of the nation's income in 1990. The data in Table 2.1 show that income inequality is increasing in U.S. society. Especially noteworthy is the sharp gain in

Table 2.1 Share of aggregate income by each fifth of households in 1970, 1980, and 1990

Year	Percentage Distribution of Aggregate Income					
	Lowest Fifth	Second Fifth	Third Fifth	Fourth Fifth	Highest Fifth	Gini Ratio*
1990	3.9	9.6	15.9	24.0	46.6	.428
1980	4.2	10.2	16.8	24.8	44.1	.403
1970	4.1	10.8	17.4	24.5	43.3	.394

*The income inequality of a population group is commonly measured using the Gini index. The Gini index ranges from 0, indicating perfect equality (i.e., all persons having equal shares of the aggregate income), to 1, indicating perfect inequality (i.e., one person has all the income and the rest have none). The increase in the Gini index for household income between 1970 and 1990, from .394 to .428, indicates a significant increase in income inequality.

Source: Bureau of the Census, "Money Income of Households, Families, and Persons in the United States: 1990," *Current Population Reports,* Series P–60, No. 174 (August 1991), p. 6.

the Gini index, which measures the magnitude of income concentration from 1970 to 1990. The difference in income between the top 20 percent and the bottom 20 percent is the greatest since the Census Bureau began gathering this information.

The Center on Budget and Policy Priorities found that in the 1980s the incomes of the richest 1 percent of Americans grew more than 87 percent, while the incomes of the poorest U.S. households dropped more than 5 percent. This report noted that the gap in income is so wide in U.S. society that the "combined incomes of the richest 2.5 million Americans . . . nearly equal the combined incomes of the 100 million Americans with the lowest incomes" (reported in Meisler, 1990:1C). Shown another way, the top 4 percent of earners in 1989 made the same total amount of wages and salaries as the bottom 51 percent of earners (Barlett and Steele, 1992:ix).

Another measure of this increasing gap is the difference in earnings between the heads of corporations and the workers in those corporations. In the mid-1970s the typical CEO (Chief Executive Officer) of a *Fortune* 500 company made 34 times what the average manufacturing worker earned. By 1989 the CEOs of these companies made $2.8 million in yearly salary—109 times more than the average U.S. worker (*USA Today,* 1991b:12a).

The inequality in wealth and income has risen dramatically for a number of reasons. The gain at the top reflects the increased tax benefits received by the affluent from changing tax laws during the 1980s (a reduction for the wealthy from a top tax rate of 50 percent to 28 percent and a concomitant raise in Social Security taxes, which especially affects people making less than $53,000 a year). Another factor explaining this inequality gap is the changing job structure as the economy shifts from manufacturing to service and as U.S. jobs are exported (Reich, 1989). At the upper end, "corporate chairmen and presidents as a class feasted in the 1980s, but the number of mid-level management jobs lost during those years was estimated to be as high as 1.5 million (Phillips, 1990:21). For a look at a society that is organized to minimize inequality, see "Another Society, Another Way."

The Political System: The Links Between Wealth and Power

In many ways the U.S. government represents the privileged few rather than the majority. Although the government appears democratic, with elections, political parties, and the right to dissent, the influence of corporate wealth prevails. This influence is seen in the disproportionate rewards the few receive from the politico-economic system and in government decisions that consistently benefit them.

Government by Interest Groups

Democracy may be defined as a political system in which the majority will prevail, in which there is equality before the law, and in which decisions are made to maximize the common good. The U.S principle of majority rule is violated by the special interests, which by deals, propaganda, and the financial support of political candidates attempt to deflect the political process for their own benefit. Individuals, families, corporations, unions, and various organizations use a variety of means to obtain tax breaks, favors, subsidies, favorable rulings, and the like from congressional committees, regulatory agencies, and executive bureaucracies (Domhoff, 1978:25–60). To accomplish their goals, along with the slick brochures, expert testimony, and technical reports, corporate lobbyists still have the succulent campaign contributions, the secret slush funds, the "volunteer" campaign workers, the fat lecture fees, the stock awards and insider stock market tips, the easy-term loans, the high-paying corporate directorship upon retirement from office, the lavish parties and prostitutes, the prepaid vacation jaunts, the luxury hotels and private jets, the free housing and meals, and the many other hustling enticements of money.* (Parenti, 1988:201)

The existence of lobbyists does not ensure that the national interest will be served or that the concerns of all groups will be heard. Who, for example, speaks

ANOTHER SOCIETY, ANOTHER WAY

REDUCING INEQUALITY IN SWEDEN

In return for taxes [a progressive tax on income, from 5 to 45 percent for individuals and 52 percent for corporations, and average local income taxes of about 30 percent] and fees people are provided with a broad spectrum of public services and social welfare benefits that guarantee a minimum living standard, provide aid in emergencies, redistribute income more evenly over a person's life cycle and narrow the gaps between different income groups.

All residents in Sweden are covered by national health insurance. If a person is ill, or must stay home to care for sick children, he receives a taxable daily allowance, in most cases 90% of lost income. Except for modest fees the health insurance pays all hospitalization costs, prescribed drugs, lab fees and visits to doctors at public outpatient clinics. A large proportion of private doctors' fees and about 40% of dental care costs are also covered by this insurance.

When a child is born, the parents are legally entitled to a total of twelve months of paid leave from work, which can be shared between them, with the option of saving six of these months for use during the child's first four years. They also receive tax-free child allowances, equal for everyone, until the child's 16th birthday. Children who then continue their education are entitled to study allowances. At university level these consist chiefly of repayable loans. Municipalities provide a growing number of children with day-care and after-school activities at low costs. Low-income families and pensioners are eligible for housing allowances.

National work injuries insurance pays all health insurance costs in case of work-related accidents. The great majority of those working in Sweden have unemployment insurance through their trade unions, while unemployed without such coverage can receive a smaller cash benefit from the government. There are extensive government programs of job retraining and

sheltered employment as well as relocation grants to help the unemployed find new work.

Workplaces are adapted to the needs of the disabled with the help of government subsidies. The disabled who cannot work are provided with early pensions.

A basic old-age pension, financed by tax revenues, is payable to everyone from the age of 65. The State also pays an income-related supplementary pension financed from employer payroll fees. The two types of pension, which both rise automatically with inflation, are designed to provide two-thirds of a pensioner's average real earnings during his 15 best-paid years.

Nine years of schooling are compulsory for all children starting at age 7. Over 90% go on to at least two years of upper secondary school, choosing from among numerous vocational or academic study lines. An extensive system of municipal adult education enables adults to acquire the same primary and secondary education as young persons. Schools are run by municipalities and provide free instruction, books and lunches.

Altogether there are in Sweden more than thirty institutions of higher education, operated by the State and providing free instruction. Slightly more than half of the students in higher education are women, and a large number of students are people over 25 taking advantage of liberalized admission rules for those with work experience.

Private, government-subsidized adult education associations arrange study circles for 2.5 million course participants a year.

Most cultural institutions are subsidized with public funds. A guiding principle for Swedish cultural policy is to spread cultural activities throughout the country, for example through traveling organizations for theater, concerts and exhibitions.

Source: "General Facts on Sweden," *Fact Sheets on Sweden* (Stockholm, Sweden, The Swedish Institute, December 1988), p. 2.

for the interests of minority groups, the poor, the mentally retarded, renters, migrant workers—in short, who speaks for the relatively powerless? And if there is a voice for these people, does it match the clout of lobbyists backed by immense financial resources?

The Financing of Political Campaigns

Perhaps one of the most undemocratic features (at least in its consequences) of the U.S political system is how political campaigns are financed. Campaigns are becoming more and more expensive, with money needed to pay for staff, direct-mail operations, phone banks, computers, consultants, and advertising. The 1988 campaigns for Congress and the presidency cost $1.2 billion, including monies from the federal government (each major presidential candidate received about $70 million in public funds), individuals, political parties, and Political Action Committees (PACs). The average victorious senator spent $3.6 million in 1988, up from $610,000 in 1976. "Since this meant he had to raise $12,000 a week for six years, incumbents and challengers have become increasingly dependent on PAC money" (Rukeyser and Cooney, 1991:145).

These expensive campaigns are funded by the candidates' personal wealth, individual contributions, and (in the case of congressional candidates) money donated from special-interest groups through PACs. In 1974 PACs gave $12.4 million to congressional candidates; in 1980 they gave $45 million; and $181 million in 1992.

The wealthy and politicians are connected through the contributions of the former and the decisions of the latter.

These increasingly higher sums given to congressional candidates have led some cynics to comment that we have "the best Congress money can buy" (Stern, 1988). PACs are formed to represent interests such as labor unions, doctors, realtors, auto dealers, teachers, and corporations. Each PAC may give up to $5000 to any candidate in a primary and another $5000 in a general election. As *U.S. News & World Report* editorialized, "PACs of every ilk have a way of contributing their allowed $5,000 chunks to candidates who either have voted 'right' or had better do so shortly" (Stone, 1978:112).

In addition to PACs, there are two other legal ways for individuals and special interests to funnel money to the candidate or party of their choice. Each individual can give $1000 to a candidate. A common tactic is for the executives of a corporation to "bundle" their $1000 contributions so that a sizable gift is given to a political candidate. The other legal way to contribute is through what is called "soft money." Here any amount can be given by individuals, corporations, unions, and other organizations to political parties at the national, state, and local levels, or to other private organizations that are technically independent of the candidates. These gifts are not covered by the federal election laws and thus the amounts can be unlimited. This loophole was used by wealthy persons to contribute to the Republican and Democratic national parties (and indirectly to the presidential candidates) in 1988 and 1992.

In 1988 Bush received $100,000 contributions from 249 individuals, many of whom had substantial business pending with the U.S. government. There were 66 individuals associated with the investment and banking community (including Charles H. Keating, Jr., later found guilty of fraud and racketeering in a major Savings and Loan scandal), 58 in real estate and construction, 17 in the oil industry, and 15 from food and agriculture. Seven of these contributors later were nominated by Bush for ambassadorships (*Common Cause Magazine,* 1990:iii). *The New York Times* called this major loophole in the financing of presidential campaigns "sewer money" (1992:A16).

What did the 249 people who donated $100,000 or more to the Republican National Committee in 1988 receive for their donation? Obviously, they have access to the president, perhaps even influence. Consider the case of one contributor, Frank Lorenzo, chairman of Eastern and Continental airlines. Lorenzo's two airlines had several important matters pending with federal agencies in 1988. The two most important were the National Mediation Board's attempt to settle a dispute between Eastern and its unions. And, at the behest of the unions, two federal agencies were conducting investigations to determine whether Eastern and Continental should continue to operate. After being in office for two months George Bush sided

> with Lorenzo in the continuing Eastern dispute by rejecting the recommendation of the National Mediation Board, which had urged the president to create a federal emergency strike settlement board providing a 60-day cooling-off period. . . . It's the first time in the board's 56-year history that a president had declined to take its advice in any airline labor dispute. . . .
>
> Months later, Bush vetoes Lorenzo-opposed legislation that would have created a congressional "blue ribbon" commission to investigate the Eastern strike. And [Bush threatened a veto] against a House-passed bill that [included] a "two-time loser" provision targeted at preventing airline owners in bankruptcy—read: Lorenzo—from buying out other airlines. . . .

"Frank Lorenzo knows how to use and abuse the system very well," [says Rep. Doug Bosco, Democrat from California]. "A hundred thousand dollars is a big contribution. You don't give it anonymously and send it to a post office box; you give it to people who guarantee you'll be remembered for it. Anytime you give that kind of contribution you do it to have your name known among the highest echelons of the party" (Cobb et al., 1990:22).

It is difficult to prove conclusively that receiving campaign contributions from a special interest buys a vote, but there is some indirect evidence that such contributors do gain advantage:

- In the 1988 election $8.4 million was given to 53 candidates for the House of Representatives *who were running unopposed.* House Speaker James Wright, for example, ran without an opponent and yet received $566,000 from PACs.
- Some PACs give money to both sides in an election. Other PACs contribute after the election to the candidate they opposed but who won anyway.
- In 1992 some corporations gave "soft money" to both parties. Some examples: Archer Daniels Midland gave $397,000 to the Republican Party and $76,500 to the Democratic Party; Atlantic Richfield gave $226,000 to the Republicans and $120,000 to Democrats; RJR-Nabisco gave $382,500 to the Republicans and $231,500 to the Democrats; and U.S. Tobacco gave $308,000 to the Republicans and $56,200 to the Democrats (Hasson, 1992:11A).
- Some PACs contribute *after* the election to the candidate they opposed but who won anyway.

As the *Dallas Times Herald* editorialized:

> The power of PAC money threatens increasingly to turn Members of Congress into legalized political prostitutes. It drives them to sell to the highest bidders their one most easily and legally salable product—access. But worst of all, it erodes the public's confidence in the integrity of the congressional system. (quoted in Wertheimer, 1986:60)

There are many examples of how PAC money seemed to make a difference in legislation passed or defeated. Two cases make the point. In 1982 the National Automobile Dealers' Association opposed a proposed law suggested by the Federal Trade Commission that would require used-car dealers to disclose known defects to potential buyers. The dealers' association, through various PACs, distributed campaign contributions of more than $840,000 to more than 300 senators and representatives, 85 percent of whom voted against the used-car rule, killing it by a greater than two-to-one margin (*The Nation,* 1982; see also Green, 1984). Another example concerns a congressional vote on whether to fund the Clinch River nuclear breeder reactor in 1981. Ralph Nader's Public Citizen's Congress Watch noted that the five companies involved in designing and building the reactor contributed about $280,000 to members of Congress. Of eleven representatives receiving more than $3000, ten voted to build the reactor (the other was absent at the time of the vote); of those representatives who received $1500 to $3000, 76 percent voted for the project; and of those representatives who did not receive any money, 71 percent voted to kill it (Pike, 1982).

Money presents a fundamental obstacle to democracy because only the interests of the wealthy tend to be served. It takes money and lots of it to be a successful politician. The candidate must either be rich or be willing to accept

Danziger in *The Christian Science* Monitor © 1990 TCSPS.

contributions from others. In either case, the political leaders will be part of or beholden to the wealthy.

The Candidate Selection Process

Closely related to the financing of campaigns is the process by which political candidates are nominated. Being wealthy or having access to wealth is essential for victory because of the enormous cost of the race. Thus, the candidates tend to represent a limited constituency—the wealthy.

The two-party system also works to limit choices among candidates to a rather narrow range. Each party is financed by the special interests—especially business. As William Domhoff puts it:

> When all of these direct and indirect gifts (donations provided directly to candidates or through numerous political action committees of specific corporations and general business organizations) are combined, the power elite can be seen to provide the great bulk of the financial support to both parties at the national level, far outspending the unions and middle status liberals within the Democrats, and the melange of physicians, dentists, engineers, real-estate operators and other white-collar conservatives within the right wing of the Republican Party. (Domhoff, 1978:148)

Affluent individuals and the largest corporations influence candidate selection by giving financial aid to those candidates sympathetic with their views and withholding support from those who differ. The parties, then, are constrained to choose candidates with views congruent with the monied interests.

The Bias of the Political System

Most people think of the machinery of government as a beneficial force promoting the common good. But although the government can be organized for the benefit of the majority, it is not always neutral (Parenti, 1978). The state regulates; it stifles opposition; it makes and enforces the law; it funnels information; it makes war on so-called "enemies" (foreign and domestic); and its policies determine how resources are apportioned. In all of these areas the government is generally biased toward policies that benefit the wealthy, especially the business community. In short, power in the United States is concentrated in a **power elite,** and this elite uses its power for its own advantage.

Power in the United States is concentrated among people who control the government and the largest corporations. This assertion is based on the assumption that power is not an attribute of individuals but rather of social organization. The elite in U.S. society are those people who occupy the power roles in society. The great political decisions are made by the president, the president's advisers, cabinet members, members of regulatory agencies, the Federal Reserve Board, key members of Congress, and the Supreme Court. Individuals in these government command posts have the authority to make war, raise or lower interest rates, levy taxes, dam rivers, and institute or withhold national health insurance.

Formerly, economic activity was the result of many decisions made by individual entrepreneurs and the heads of small businesses. Now, a handful of companies have virtual control over the marketplace. Decisions made by the boards of directors and the managers of these huge corporations determine employment and production, consumption patterns, wages and prices, the extent of foreign trade, the rate at which natural resources are depleted, and the like.

The few thousand persons who form this power elite tend to come from backgrounds of privilege and wealth. It would be a mistake, however, to equate personal wealth with power. Great power is manifested only through decision making in the very large corporations or in government. We have seen that this elite exercises great power. Decisions are made by the powerful, and these decisions tend to benefit the wealthy disproportionately. But the power elite is not formally organized; there is no conspiracy per se. The interests of the powerful (and the wealthy) are served, nevertheless, through the way in which society is structured. This bias occurs in three ways—by the elite's influence over elected and appointed government officials at all levels, by the structure of the system, and by ideological control of the masses.

As noted earlier, the wealthy are able to receive favorable treatment either by actually occupying positions of power or by exerting direct influence over those who do. Laws, court decisions, and administrative decisions tend to give them the advantage.

More subtly, the power elite can get its way without actually being mobilized at all. The choices of decision makers are often limited by what are called **systemic imperatives;** that is, the institutions of society are patterned to produce prearranged results regardless of the personalities of the decision makers. In other words, there is a bias that pressures the government to do certain things and not to do other things. Inevitably, this bias favors the status quo, allowing people with power to continue to exercise it. No change is easier than change. The current political and economic systems have worked and generally are not subject to questions, let alone change. In this way, the laws, customs, and institutions of society resist change. Thus, the propertied and the wealthy benefit while the propertyless and the poor continue to be disadvantaged. As Parenti has argued:

> The law does not exist as an abstraction. It gathers shape and substance from a context of power, within a real-life social structure. Like other institutions, the legal system is class-bound. The question is not whether the law should or should not be neutral, for as a product of its society, it *cannot* be neutral in purpose or effect. (Parenti, 1978:188)

In addition to the inertia of institutions, there are other systemic imperatives that benefit the power elite and the wealthy. One such imperative is for the government to strive to provide an adequate defense against our enemies, which stifles any external threat to the status quo. Thus, Congress, the president, and the general public tend to support large appropriations for defense, which in turn provide extraordinary profit to many corporations. In addition, the government will protect U.S. multinational companies in their overseas operations, so that they enjoy a healthy and profitable business climate. Domestic government policy also is shaped by the systemic imperative for stability. The government promotes domestic tranquility by squelching dissidents.

Power is the ability to get what one wants from someone else, by force, authority, manipulation, or persuasion. In Parenti's words, "The ability to control the definition of interests is the ability to define the agenda of issues, a capacity tantamount to winning battles without having to fight them" (Parenti, 1978:41). U.S. schools, churches, and families possess this power. The schools, for instance, consciously teach youth that capitalism is the only correct economic system. This indoctrination to conservative values achieves a consensus among the citizenry concerning the status quo. Each of us comes to accept the present arrangements in society because they seem to be the only options that make sense. Thus, there is general agreement on what is right—and wrong. In sum, the dominance of the wealthy is legitimized. Parenti observes, "The interests of an economically dominant class never stand naked. They are enshrouded in the flag, fortified by the law, protected by the police, nurtured by the media, taught by the schools, and blessed by the church" (Parenti, 1978:84).

Finally, popular belief in democracy works to the advantage of the power elite, as Parenti has noted:

> As now constituted, elections serve as a great asset in consolidating the existing social order by propagating the appearances of popular rule. History demonstrates that the people might be moved to overthrow a tyrant who shows himself provocatively indifferent to their woes, but they are far less inclined to make war upon a state, even one dominated by the propertied class, if it pre-

serves what Madison called "the spirit and form of popular government." Elections legitimate the rule of the propertied class by investing it with the moral authority of popular consent. By the magic of the ballot, class dominance becomes "democratic" governance. (Parenti, 1978:201)

The Consequences of Concentrated Power

Who benefits from how power is concentrated in U.S. society? At times, almost everyone does; but for the most part, the decisions made tend to benefit the wealthy. Whenever the interests of the wealthy clash with those of other groups or even of the public at large, the interests of the former are served. Consider how the president and Congress deal with the problems of energy shortages, inflation, or deflation. Who is asked to make the sacrifices? Where is the budget cut—are military expenditures reduced or are funds for food stamps slashed? When Congress considers tax reform, after the clouds of rhetoric recede, which groups benefit from the new legislation or from the laws that are left unchanged? When a corporation is found guilty of fraud, violation of antitrust laws, or bribery, what are the penalties? How do they compare with the penalties for crimes committed by poor individuals such as welfare chiselers and thieves? When there is an oil spill or other ecological disaster caused by huge enterprise, what are the penalties? Who pays for the cleanup and the restoration of nature? The answers to these questions are obvious: The wealthy benefit at the expense of the less well-to-do. In short, the government is an institution made up of people—the rich and powerful or their agents—who seek to maintain their advantageous positions in society.

The bias of the system today is nothing new. Since the nation's founding, the government's policy has primarily favored the needs of the corporate system. The founding fathers were upper-class holders of wealth. The Constitution they wrote gave the power to people like themselves—property owners.

This bias continued throughout the nineteenth century as bankers, railroad entrepreneurs, and manufacturers joined the landed gentry as the power elite. The shift from local business to large-scale manufacturing during the last half of the nineteenth century saw a concomitant increase in governmental activity in the economy. Business was protected from competition by tariffs, public subsidies, price regulation, patents, and trademarks. When there was unrest by troubled miners, farmers, and laborers, the government invariably sided with the strong against the weak. Militia and federal troops were used to crush railroad strikes. Antitrust laws, though not used to stop the monopolistic practices of business, were invoked against labor unions. President Cleveland's attorney general, Richard Olney, a millionaire owner of railroad stocks,

used antitrust laws, court injunctions, mass arrests, labor spies, deputy marshals and federal troops against workers and their unions. From the local sheriff and magistrate to the President and the Supreme Court, the forces of "law and order" were utilized to suppress unions and serve "the defensive needs of large capitalist enterprises.* (Parenti, 1988:71)

*Copyright © 1988 from *Democracy for the Few*, Fifth Edition, by Michael Parenti. Reprinted with permission of St. Martin's Press, Incorporated.

During this time approximately 1 billion acres of land in the public domain (almost half the present size of the United States) were given to private individuals and corporations. The railroads in particular were given huge tracts of land as a subsidy. These lands were and continue to be very rich in timber and natural resources. This active intervention by the government in the nation's economy during the nineteenth century was almost solely on the behalf of business. Parenti notes, "The government did exercise laissez-faire in regard to the needs of the common people, giving little attention to poverty, unemployment, unsafe work conditions, child labor, and the spoilation of natural resources"* (Parenti, 1988:72).

The early twentieth century was a time of great government activity in the economy, which gave the appearance of restraining big business. However, the actual result of federal regulation of business was to increase the power of the largest corporations. The Interstate Commerce Commission, for instance, helped the railroads by establishing common rates instead of ruinous competition (Huntington, 1965:73–86); federal regulations in meat packing, drug manufacturing, banking, and mining weeded out the weaker cost-cutting competitors, leaving a few to control the markets at higher prices and higher profits. Even the actions of that great trustbuster, Teddy Roosevelt, were largely ceremonial. His major legislative proposals reflected the desires of corporation interests. Like other presidents before and since, he enjoyed close relations with big businessmen and invited them into his administration (Parenti, 1988:73–74).

World War II intensified the government bias on behalf of business. Industry was converted to war production. Corporate interests became more actively involved in the councils of government. Government actions clearly favored business in labor disputes. The police and military were used against rebellious workers; strikes were treated as efforts to weaken the war effort and therefore as treasonous.

The New Deal is typically assumed to be a time when the needs of people impoverished by the Great Depression were paramount in government policies. But as Parenti has argued, "the central dedication of the Franklin Roosevelt administration was to *business recovery* rather than *social reform*" (Parenti, 1980:82). Business was subsidized by credits, price supports, bank guarantees, stimulation of the housing industry, and the like. Welfare programs were instituted to prevent widespread starvation, but even these humanitarian programs also worked to the benefit of the big business community. The government's provision of jobs, minimum wages, unemployment compensation, and retirement benefits obviously aided people in dire economic straits. But these programs were actually promoted by the business community because of the benefits to them. The government and business favored social programs not because millions were in misery but because violent political and social unrest posed a real threat.

Two social scientists, Piven and Cloward, in a historical assessment of government welfare programs, have determined that the government institutes massive aid to the poor *only* when the poor constitute a threat (Piven and Cloward, 1971). When large numbers of people are suddenly barred from their traditional occupations, they may begin to question the legitimacy of the system itself. Crime, riots, looting, and social movements aimed at changing existing social, political, and economic arrangements become more widespread. Under this threat the government initiates or expands relief programs in order to diffuse the social unrest. During the Great Depression, Piven and Cloward contend, the government remained aloof from the needs of the unemployed until there was a surge of political disorder. Added proof for Piven and Cloward's thesis is the contraction or even abolition of public assistance programs when stability is restored.

The historical trend for government to favor business over less powerful interests continues in current public policy. This bias is perhaps best seen in the aphorism enunciated by President Calvin Coolidge and repeated by subsequent presidents: "The business of America is business."

Subsidies to Big Business

There is a general principle that applies to the government's relationship to big business: Business can conduct its affairs either undisturbed by or encouraged by government, whichever is of greater benefit to the business community. The following are examples of governmental decisions that were beneficial to business.

- In 1979 the Chrysler Corporation, after sustaining losses of $207 million in the previous year, appealed to the government and received $1.5 billion in loan guarantees. The government's aid to Chrysler is typical—if the company is big enough. Earlier in the 1970s Penn Central received $125 million when it faced bankruptcy, and the government guaranteed Lockheed $250 million in new bank loans. In other celebrated cases the banking industry and certain large banks have received large sums of government aid. In 1983 the International Monetary Fund was bailed out with $8 billion in federal monies to offset the bad debts incurred by U.S. bank loans to Third World nations. Also, in 1984, when Continental Bank of Illinois was on the brink of bankruptcy, the federal government put together a $7.5 billion rescue package (Parenti, 1988:83).
- In 1987 the government bailed out two Texas financial concerns—$970 million to Houston's First City Bancorporation and $1.3 billion to Vernon Savings. This bailout of savings and loan institutions was only the beginning as Congress in 1989 approved an administration package that will cost an estimated $500 billion over ten years for aid to about 500 of these failing enterprises.
- State and local governments provide businesses with a variety of subsidies such as low-interest loans, tax-free financing, subsidized employee training, and tax breaks to entice them to locate in their jurisdictions. In 1991 these handouts by the states to corporations amounted to $16 billion (Grochot, 1992).
- Quotas are placed on imports of beef, wheat, oil, and other products to protect the profits of U.S. industry.
- A number of major U.S. corporations, such as Du Pont, General Motors, Ford, Exxon, and ITT, owned factories in enemy countries during World War II. These factories produced products for the Axis war effort. "After the war, rather than being prosecuted for trading with the enemy, ITT collected $27 million from the U.S. government for war damages inflicted on its German plants by Allied bombings. GM and Ford subsidiaries built the bulk of Nazi Germany's heavy trucks which served as 'the backbone of the German Army transportation system.' GM collected more than $33 million in compensation for damages

to its war plants in enemy territories. Ford and other multinational corporations collected lesser sums." (Snell, 1974:14–16; see also Di Baggio, 1976; Borkin, 1978; Higham, 1983)

- The federal government directly subsidizes the shipping industry, railroads, airlines, and exporters of iron, steel, textiles, paper, and other products.
- From 1965 to 1967 several major petroleum companies leased acreage in Alaska for oil exploration, paying $12 million for leases worth at least $2 billion. In another oil lease auction, the companies paid the government $900 million for lands that were expected to be worth some $50 billion within a decade (Parenti, 1983:93).
- The government develops new technologies at public expense and then turns them over to private corporations for their profit. This transfer occurs routinely with nuclear energy, synthetics, space communications, and mineral exploration. For example, taxpayers spent $20 billion to develop the satellite communications system, which in 1962 was put under the control of AT&T. Similarly, in 1982 two major corporations built a synthetic fuel plant for $4.5 billion, with the government paying 98 percent of the cost (Parenti, 1988:83–84). A variation of this government subsidy to business occurs with universities as the link. Universities are permitted to sell to companies exclusive licenses on discoveries made under a company's sponsorship. "This adds up to a fat public subsidy for private business. In 1988, the federal government allocated approximately $7 billion to universities for research and development. That same year, corporations bought control of many of the fruits of that research for a puny $750 million" (Bourke, 1989:495).

Perhaps the best illustration of how business benefits from government policies is the system of legal loopholes allowed on federal income taxes. Corporations pay a much smaller percentage of their income in taxes than do individuals. They legally escape much of the tax burden through a number of loopholes (e.g., investment tax credit, accelerated depreciation, and capital gains). Some corporations escape taxes altogether even when they are profitable because of these tax subsidies. For example, after the tax cuts of 1981, General Electric, which

> had corporate profits of $6.5 billion during 1981–1983 . . . received a tax rebate of $283 million from the federal government. Its tax burden went from $330 million a year to minus $90 million a year—money the government now owed GE. By rough estimate, the 1981 tax legislation yielded as much as $1.3 billion for General Electric over several years and probably much more in the long run. (Greider, 1992:341–342)

Trickle-Down Solutions

Periodically, the government is faced with finding a way to stimulate the economy during an economic downturn. One solution is to spend federal monies through unemployment insurance, government jobs, and housing subsidies. In this way, the funds go directly to the people most hurt by shortages, unemployment, inadequate housing, and the like. Opponents of such plans contend that the subsidies should go directly to business, which would help the economy by encouraging companies to hire more workers, add to their inventories, and build new plants. Subsidizing business in this way, the advocates argue, benefits everyone. To provide subsidies to businesses rather than directly to needy individuals is based on the assumption that private profit maximizes the public good. In effect, proponents argue, because the government provides direct benefits to businesses and investors, the economic benefits indirectly trickle down to all.

There are two possible reasons government officials tend to opt for these trickle-down solutions. First, because they tend to come from the business class, government officials believe in the conservative ideology that says that what is good for business is good for the United States. The second reason for the probusiness choice is that government officials are more likely to hear arguments from the powerful. Because the weak, by definition, are not organized, their voice is not heard or, if heard, not taken seriously in decision-making circles.

Although the government most often opts for trickle-down solutions, such plans are not very effective in fulfilling the promise that benefits will trickle down to the poor. The higher corporate profits generated by tax credits and other tax incentives do not necessarily mean that companies will increase wages or hire more workers. What is more likely is that corporations will increase dividends to the stockholders, which further exacerbates the existing problem of the maldistribution of resources. Job creation is also not guaranteed because companies may use their newly acquired wealth to purchase labor-saving devices. If so, then the government programs will actually have widened the gulf between the "haves" and the "have-nots."

The Powerless Bear the Burden

Robert Hutchins, in his critique of U.S. governmental policy, characterized the basic principle guiding internal affairs as follows: "Domestic policy is conducted according to one infallible rule: the costs and burdens of whatever is done must

The chances of getting killed while in the service are three times greater for the less educated than for the college edcuated soldier.

be borne by those least able to bear them" (Hutchins, 1976:4). Let us review several examples of this statement.

When threatened by war, the government institutes a military draft. A careful analysis of the draft reveals that it is really a tax on the poor. During the height of the Vietnam War, for instance, only 10 percent of men in college were drafted, although 40 percent of draft-age men were in college. Even for those educated young men who ended up in the armed services, there was a greater likelihood of their serving in noncombat jobs than for the non-college-educated. Thus, the chances for getting killed while in the service were about three times greater for the less educated than for the college-educated (Zeitlin, Lutterman, and Russell, 1977; Baskir and Strauss, 1978). Even more blatant was the practice that occurred legally during the Civil War. The law at that time allowed the affluent who were drafted to hire someone to take their place in the service.

The poor, being powerless, can be made to absorb the costs of societal changes. In the nineteenth century the poor did the backbreaking work that built the railroads and the cities. Today, they are the ones pushed out of their homes by urban renewal and the building of expressways, parks, and stadiums (Gans, 1971).

The government's attempts to solve economic problems generally obey the principle that the poor must bear the burden. A common solution for runaway inflation, for example, is to increase the amount of unemployment. Of course, the poor, especially minorities (whose rate of unemployment is consistently twice the rate for Whites), are the ones who make the sacrifice for the economy. This solution, aside from being socially cruel, is economically ineffective because it ignores the real sources of inflation—excessive military spending, excessive profits by energy companies (foreign and domestic), and administered prices set by shared monopolies, which, contrary to classical economic theory, do not decline during economic downturns (Harrington, 1979).

More fundamentally, a certain level of unemployment is maintained continuously, not just during economic downturns. Genuine full employment for all job seekers is a myth. But why is it a myth, since all political candidates extol the work ethic and it is declared national policy to have full employment? Economist Robert Lekachman (1979) has argued that it is no accident that we tolerate millions of unemployed persons. The reason is that a "moderate" unemployment rate is beneficial to the affluent. These benefits include the following: (1) people are willing to work at humble tasks for low wages; (2) the children of the middle and upper classes avoid the draft as the unemployed join the volunteer army; (3) the unions are less demanding; (4) workers are less likely to demand costly safety equipment; (5) corporations do not have to pay their share of taxes because local and state governments give them concessions to lure them to their area; and (6) the existing wide differentials between White males and the various powerless categories such as females, teenagers, Hispanics, and Blacks are retained.

Foreign Policy for Corporate Benefit

The operant principle here is that "foreign policy seems to be carried on in the light of the needs of the munitions makers, the Pentagon, the CIA, and the multinational corporations" (Hutchins 1976:4). For example, military goods are sold overseas for the profit of the arms merchants. Sometimes, arms are sold to both sides in a potential conflict, the argument being that if we did not sell them the arms, then someone else would, so we might as well make the profits.

The government has supported foreign governments that are supportive of U.S. multinational companies regardless of how tyrannical these governments might be. The Reza Shah's government in Iran, Chiang's regime in China, Chung Hee Park's dictatorship in South Korea, and Ferdinand Marcos's rule in the Philippines are four examples of this tendency.

The U.S. government has directly intervened in the domestic affairs of foreign governments to protect U.S. corporate interests. In Latin America, for example, the United States has intervened militarily since 1950 in Guatemala, the Dominican Republic, Chile, Uruguay, Nicaragua, and Panama. As Parenti has characterized it:

> Sometimes the sword has rushed in to protect the dollar, and sometimes the dollar has rushed in to enjoy the advantages won by the sword. To make the world safe for capitalism, the United States government has embarked on a global counter-revolutionary strategy, suppressing insurgent peasant and worker movements throughout Asia, Africa, and Latin America. But the interests of the corporate elites never stand naked; rather they are wrapped in the flag and coated with patriotic appearances.* (Parenti, 1988:94)

In sum, the current politicoeconomic system is biased. It works for the benefit of the few at the expense of the many. Because the distribution of power and the organization of the economy give shape and impetus to the persistent social problems of U.S. society, the analysis of these problems requires a politicoeconomic approach.

CHAPTER REVIEW

1. The state is not a neutral agent of the people but is biased in favor of the upper social classes and the largest corporations.
2. There are two fundamental ways in which society can organize its economic activities: capitalism and socialism.
3. Capitalism in its pure form involves (a) private ownership of property, (b) the pursuit of personal profit, (c) competition, and (d) a government policy of allowing the marketplace to function unhindered.
4. Socialism in its pure form involves (a) democracy throughout the social structure; (b) equality of opportunity, equality rather than hierarchy in decision making, and equality in sharing the benefits of society; (c) public ownership of the means of production; (d) community; and (e) planning for common purposes.
5. Marx's prediction that capitalism will result in an economy dominated by monopolies has been fulfilled in the United States. But rather than a single corporation dominating a sector of the economy, the United States has *shared*

monopolies, whereby four or fewer corporations supply 50 percent or more of a particular market.

6. Economic power is concentrated in a few major corporations and banks. This concentration has been accomplished through mergers and interlocking directorates.

7. Private wealth is also highly concentrated. Poverty, on the other hand, is dispersed among 34 million officially and many more millions who are not so designated by the government but are poor nonetheless.

8. The government tends to serve the interests of the wealthy because of the influence of interest groups and how political campaigns are financed.

9. An obvious undemocratic feature of the United States is the exclusion of minorities from economic and political power.

10. The powerful in society (those who control the government and the largest corporations) tend to come from backgrounds of privilege and wealth. Their decisions tend to benefit the wealthy disproportionately. The power elite is not organized and conspiratorial, but the interests of the wealthy are served, nevertheless, by the way in which society is organized. This bias occurs through influence over elected and appointed officials, systemic imperatives, and ideological control of the masses.

11. The government supports the bias of the system through its strategies to solve economic problems. The typical two-pronged approach is, on the one hand, to use trickle-down solutions, which give the business community and the wealthy extraordinary advantages; and, on the other hand, to make the powerless bear the burden and consequently become even more disadvantaged.

12. Finally, business benefits from governmental actions through foreign policy decisions, which typically are used to protect and promote U.S. economic interests abroad.

KEY TERMS

Capitalism.   The economic system based on private ownership of property, guided by the seeking of maximum profits.

Socialism.   The economic system in which the means of production are owned by the people for their collective benefit.

Shared monopoly.   When four or fewer companies control 50 percent or more of an industry.

Interlocking directorate.   The linkage between corporations that results when an individual serves on the board of directors of two companies (a direct interlock) or when two companies each have a director on the board of a third company (an indirect interlock).

Power elite.   People who occupy the power roles in society. They either are wealthy or represent the wealthy.

Systemic imperatives.   The economic and social constraints on political decision makers that promote the status quo.

Power.   The ability to get what one wants from someone else.

FOR FURTHER STUDY

Donald L. Barlett and James B. Steele. *America: What Went Wrong?* Kansas City, Mo.: Andrews and McMeel, 1992.

G. William Domhoff. *The Power Elite and the State: How Policy Is Made in America.* Hawthorne, N.Y.: Aldine de Gruyter, 1990.

Milton Friedman and Rose Friedman. *Free to Choose.* New York: Avon Books, 1979.

George Gilder. *Wealth and Poverty.* New York: Basic Books, 1981.

William Greider. *Who Will Tell the People: The Betrayal of American Democracy.* New York: Simon & Schuster, 1992.

Michael Harrington. *The New American Poverty.* New York: Holt, Rinehart and Winston, 1984.

Michael Harrington. *The Next Left: The History of a Future.* New York: Henry Holt, 1986.

Martin N. Marger. *Elites and Masses: An Introduction to Political Sociology.* 2d ed. Belmont, Calif.: Wadsworth, 1987.

Philip Mattera. *Prosperity Lost.* Reading, Mass.: Addison-Wesley, 1990.

Ralph Nader and William Taylor. *The Big Boys: Power and Position in American Business.* New York: Pantheon Books, 1986.

Michael Parenti. *Power and the Powerless.* 2d ed. New York: St. Martin's Press, 1978.

Michael Parenti. *Democracy for the Few.* 5th ed. New York: St. Martin's Press, 1988.

Kevin Phillips. *The Politics of Rich and Poor.* New York: Random House, 1990.

Michael Useem. *The Inner Circle: Large Corporations and the Rise of Business Political Activity in the U.S. and U.K.* New York: Oxford University Press, 1984.

Howard Zinn. *A People's History of the United States.* New York: Harper and Row, 1980.

FORUM

SHOULD LOBBYISTS REPRESENT A FOREIGN NATION ON
CAPITOL HILL? THE CASE OF JAPAN

No, lobbyists for Japan are a threat to American interests.

Pat Choate, economist

Imagine a foreign country spending more than $100
million each year to hire 1,000 Washington, D.C. lobbyists, superlawyers, former high-ranking public officials,
public relations specialists, political advisors—even former presidents. Imagine it spending another $300 mil-
lion a year to build a nationwide grass roots political
network to influence public opinion. Imagine that its
$400 million per year political campaign sought to
advance its economic interests, influence U.S. trade
policy and win market share in the United States for its
target industries.

None of this is imaginary; none of it is illegal. The
country that is actually undertaking this political campaign is Japan. Today Japan controls the most sophisticated and successful political-economic machine in the
United States. . . .

In politics, as in manufactured products, Japanese
strategy follows a simple and predictable pattern: protect your own domestic markets from foreign penetra-
tion, capture as much of your competitor's market
share as possible. . . .

Japan is gaining political market share in the
United States, spending hundreds of millions of dollars
for competitive advantage. To the Japanese, politics is
another legitimate business expense. . . .

Japan's political machine in the United States is
designed to serve six national and corporate goals:

1. To keep the U.S. market open for exports from
   Japan.

2. To smooth the way for additional purchases of key
   assets in the United States.
3. To blunt criticism of Japan's adversarial trade
   practices.
4. To neutralize or, even better, to capture the political
   influence of the U.S. companies that compete with
   Japan.
5. To influence U.S. trade policies toward Japan,
   Europe, and all other markets where Japan has
   significant economic interests.
6. To create an integrated U.S.-Japan economy that
   prevents the United States from confronting Japan
   economically and politically. . . .

In one critical industry after another, U.S. companies, originally challenged by Japanese manufacturing
prowess, now run the added risk of losing out to the
Japanese competition because of Japan's well-managed
political strategy. American companies, pressed in the
market for the consumer's favor, may now face the
defection of their own government as an ally in global
competition. For the American public, the issue is even
more stark. With so much Japanese money influencing
so many officials in government, the question for the
American people is, "Who do you trust?"

Yes, lobbyists for Japan represent legitimate concerns of Japanese corporations and industry organizations. They are not a threat to U.S. interests.

Tomohito Shinoda, Washington representative for Taro Kimura, Inc.

Like many critics of Japan, Pat Choate has a monolithic view of Japanese corporate activities that is inaccurate. When the U.S. media write about Japanese investments in the United States, reporters say, "Japan bought Rockefeller Center," or "Japan bought Columbia Pictures," rather than say Americans sold them to the individual Japanese corporations, Mitsubishi and Sony. Such reports give the impression that the Japanese business community has teamed up to buy America. In the same way, Mr. Choate argues, "Japan's political machine in the United States is designed to serve six national and corporate goals," including "to keep the U.S. market open for Japanese exports." . . .

My research suggests that the only example of concerted multisector effort to influence U.S. government policy by Japanese corporations was against the unitary tax, a state tax that would impose double taxation on foreign corporations in the United States. This lobbying effort was organized only because the participants had the common commercial interests in that specific matter.

Japanese corporations and industry organizations, independent of one another, do spend outstanding amounts of money on their lobbying activities. Each individual corporation, however, like its U.S. counterpart, seeks its own commercial interest, not "national" interests.

Undoubtedly, Japanese corporations do spend large sums on lobbying (which itself seems to me proof of its ineffectiveness), and for this reason, Japan's lobby is probably the largest "foreign" lobby. But this fact is often exaggerated. Choate compares Japan's "1,000-person lobby" with domestic groups—a rather misleading comparison. Large U.S. institutions, including the National Association of Manufacturers, have at least a dozen full-time lobbyists, besides hundreds of consultants and public relations personnel within their own organizations, so they do not have to be as dependent on outside lobbyists as do Japanese interests in Washington. . . .

My research shows that Japanese lobbying is rarely arm-twisting. Japan's presence in Washington is, in effect, a kind of insurance policy, which is usually defensive rather than offensive and usually not as effective as domestic groups. When rational arguments are used and reasonable requests are made, Japanese lobbying can be effective. . . .

The issue involved is not whether or not foreign influence is good but whether or not the consequent policy outcomes are in the best interest of U.S. society.

Source: Tomohito Shinoda, "Letter to the Editor," *Harvard Business Review 68* (November–December 1990), pp. 187, 190 (excerpts).

3 Global Inequality: The Third World and the United States

Today 1.2 billion people live beneath the threshold of basic needs. The gap dividing the rich from the poor has never been wider: the top fifth of the population on the global economic ladder enjoys 60 times the goods and services of the lowest fifth. (Ruth Leger Sivard, 1991:33)

The countries of the world vary widely in levels of material conditions. One way to assess this variation in standard of living is to use the measure of gross national product per capita. The gross national product (GNP), according to Kriesberg, "refers to the monetary value of all goods and services annually produced for sale in a country plus an estimate of the value of such government services as police, education, and national defense. To compute the GNP per capita, the country's GNP is divided by its population" (Kriesberg, 1979:84).

The GNP is admittedly a crude measure of living standards, because it omits, for example, the goods and services consumed by the producers, which is the case in most underdeveloped countries. However, the per capita GNP does provide a reasonable way to determine overall differences in level of development and technology, the accessibility of services such as schools and hospitals, and the material conditions available to the populace. Table 3.1 compares the richest nations in the world with the poorest, using GNP per capita. The wide disparity in wealth by nation is also seen in Table 3.2. Most glaring, more than three-fourths of the world's population live in countries in which the per capita GNP is $710. At the extreme, more than 1 billion people had incomes below the poverty line. "In the 41 least developed countries of the world, per capita income averaged less than $250 a year, and was deteriorating rather than improving" (Sivard, 1991:9).

Table 3.1 Per capita gross national product 1990, for richest and poorest countries (U.S. dollars)

Classification	Country	Per Capita GNP	Percentage of U.S.
Richest	Switzerland	$32,790	151.1%
	Luxembourg	28,770	132.6
	Finland	26,070	120.1
	Japan	25,430	117.2
	Sweden	23,860	110.0
	Norway	23,120	106.5
	Denmark	22,090	101.8
	United States	21,700	100.0
	Iceland	21,150	97.5
	Canada	20,450	94.2
Poorest	Laos	$200	0.92%
	Malawi	200	0.92
	Chad	190	0.88
	Bhutan	190	0.88
	Guinea-Bissau	180	0.83
	Nepal	170	0.78
	Somalia	150	0.69
	Tanzania	120	0.55
	Ethiopia	120	0.55
	Mozambique	80	0.37

Source: Data from Population Reference Bureau, *1992 World Population Data Sheet* (Washington, D.C.: Population Reference Bureau, Inc., 1992). Used by permission.

Table 3.2   World population data for selected countries, about 1990

Country	Mid-1992 Population (millions)	Birth Rate per 1000	Death Rate per 1000	Annual Rate of Natural Increase(%)	Years to Double Population	Population in 2010 (millions	1990 per Capita GNP (US $)
Australia	17.8	15	7	0.8	83	23.9	17,080
Austria	7.9	12	11	0.1	495	8.2	19,240
Bangladesh	111.4	37	13	2.4	29	165.1	200
Brazil	150.8	26	7	1.9	37	200.2	2,680
Canada	27.4	15	7	0.8	89	32.1	20,450
China	1165.8	20	7	1.3	53	1590.8	370
Cuba	10.8	18	6	1.1	62	12.3	–
Egypt	55.7	32	7	2.4	28	81.3	600
Ethiopia	54.3	47	20	2.8	25	94.0	120
Finland	5.0	13	10	0.3	224	5.0	26,070
France	56.0	13	9	0.4	169	58.8	19,480
Germany	80.6	11	11	−0.1	–	78.2	–
India	882.6	30	10	2.0	34	1383.1	350
Iran	59.7	41	8	3.3	21	105.0	2,450
Israel	5.2	21	6	1.5	45	6.9	10,970
Italy	58.0	10	9	0.1	1,386	56.4	16,850
Japan	124.4	10	7	0.3	217	129.4	25,430
Kenya	26.2	45	9	3.7	19	44.8	370
Mexico	87.7	29	6	2.3	30	119.5	2,490
United Kingdom	57.8	14	11	0.3	257	59.9	16,070
United States	255.6	16	9	0.8	89	295.5	21,700
Dev. Countries	1224.0	14	9	0.5	148	1333.0	17,900
Less Developed	4196.0	30	9	2.0	34	5781.0	810
World	5420.0	26	9	1.7	41	7114.0	3,790

Source: Data from Population Reference Bureau, *1992 World Population Data Sheet* (Washington, D.C.: Population Reference Bureau, Inc., 1992). Used by permission.

The reasons for such global inequality include, as one might suspect, the degree of geographic isolation, the climate, and natural resources. A key determinant is the effect of power. The poor are poor, as we discuss, because they have been and continue to be dominated and exploited by powerful nations that have extracted their wealth and labor. This continuing domination by the powerful of the weak has resulted in an ever-widening gap between the rich and poor nations.

This chapter examines the plight of the poorest countries and the role of the richest—especially the United States—in maintaining global inequality. The first section examines the worldwide social problems generated by such massive inequities—overpopulation, poverty, hunger, unhealthy living conditions, and economic/social chaos. The second part explores the relationship of the United States with the poor nations, historically through colonialism, and currently through the impact of multinational corporations and official government policies.

The Third World

The **Third World** refers to the underdeveloped and developing nations in which poverty, hunger, and misery abound. They are also characterized by relative powerlessness because most of them were colonies and remain economically dependent on the developed nations, especially those of North America and Europe. The Third World nations are also characterized by rapid population growth, high infant mortality, unsanitary living conditions, and high illiteracy. This section documents the poverty, hunger, squalor, and marginality of life in these countries. The description begins with the problem of population.

World Population Growth

The number of people on this planet constitutes both a major problem and future calamity. The world population in 1992 was estimated to be 5.4 billion, and at its current rate of growth the net addition annually is about 93 million people (*Population Today,* 1990:6; Haub, 1992:6). By the year 2000 the estimated population will be 6.25 billion, with an average annual increase of 96 million during the decade (Brown, 1990:5). To put this annual increase of 96 million in perspective, the world population is increasing by the combined current populations of Austria, Denmark, Finland, Iceland, Ireland, Norway, Sweden, Switzerland, and the United Kingdom *every year.* Also, the growth during the 1990s of 959 million (almost 1 billion) is the fastest in history. Again, to put the population growth curve in perspective, the world first achieved a population of 1 billion about 1830. The next billion took 100 years (1930); the third billion, 30 years (1960); the fourth billion, 15 years (1975); the fifth billion, 12 years (1987); and apparently the next billion will take about 11 years (see Figure 3.1). If the 1990 growth rate of 1.7 percent is sustained, the world population will double in 41 years. In short, in the year 2031 the world population will be about 10.8 billion.

About 90 percent of the world's population growth is occurring in the undeveloped and developing nations of the Third World. Table 3.2 contrasts the population data for Third World countries with data for much more affluent nations. The data reveal, most obviously, that there is a strong inverse relationship between per capita GNP and population growth rates—the lower the per capita GNP, the higher the population growth. For example, the Third World countries, on average, double in population in 34 years (with Kenya doubling every 19 years), compared with an average doubling time of 148 years in the developed countries (with some nations not growing in population size at all).

The population growth rates in these poor countries make it difficult to provide the bare necessities of housing, fuel, food, and medical attention. Ironically, there is a relationship between poverty and fertility: the greater the proportion of a given population living in poverty, the higher is the fertility of that population. This relationship is not as irrational as it first appears. Poor parents want many children so that the children will help them economically and take care of them in their old age. Because so many children die, the parents must have a large number to ensure several surviving children. Large families make good economic sense to the poor, because children are a major source of labor and income. As Murdoch has put it, "That poor people are breeding themselves into poverty out of ignorance, religious superstition, poor economic judgment or lack of handy contraception is a persistent, but a false notion. Poor parents have large families because they are poor—they are not poor because they have large families" (Murdoch, 1981:3).

Figure 3.1   Earth '88

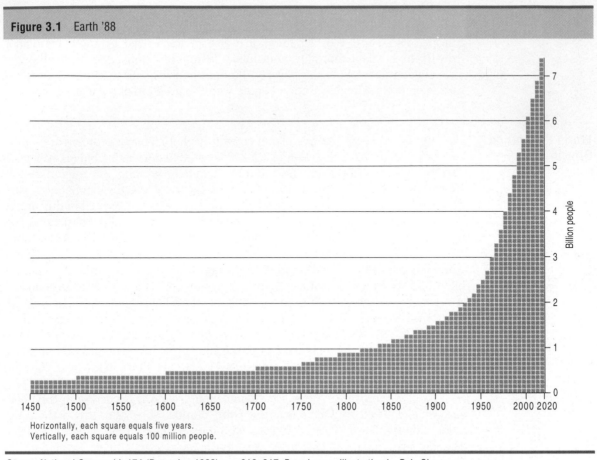

Horizontally, each square equals five years.
Vertically, each square equals 100 million people.

Source: National Geographic 174 (December 1988), pp. 916–917. Based on an illustration by Dale Glasgow.

Poverty

Robert McNamara, while head of the World Bank, defined **absolute poverty** as "a condition of life so degraded by disease, illiteracy, malnutrition and squalor as to deny its victims the basic necessities" (cited in Associated Press, 1981). Paul and Anne Ehrlich define absolute poverty as "being too poor to buy enough food to maintain health or perform a job" (Ehrlich and Ehrlich, 1990:41). About one-fifth of the world's people are trapped in this condition, living typically in the rural areas and urban slums of the Third World.

Poverty translates into inadequate diet, high infant mortality, low life expectancy, and high illiteracy rates. Table 3.3 provides comparative data on these dimensions for Third World countries, the United States, and the more developed nations in general. This table shows a striking maldistribution in life chances—the chances for life, health, and education—between the developed and less developed nations.

The significance of worldwide poverty and its concentration in the Third World nations cannot be overstated. The gap between the rich and poor countries is increasing. The number of people living in absolute poverty grew by 200 million

Table 3.3 How families differ around the world

	Kenya	China	Hungary	India	Brazil	United States
	Population: 6,100,000 in 1950	Population: 550,000,000 in 1950	Population: 9,300,000 in 1950	Population: 369,900,000 in 1950	Population: 53,400,000 in 1950	Population: 152,300,000 in 1950
	23,300,000 in 1988	1,087,300,000 in 1988	10,600,000 in 1988	816,800,000 in 1988	144,400,000 in 1988	246,100,000 in 1988
	79,200,000 projected in 2020	1,404,000,000 projected in 2020	10,500,000 projected in 2020	1,308,800,000 projected in 2020	233,800,000 projected in 2020	296,600,000 projected in 2020

Number of children
The average number of children a woman will bear at current birthrates

Symbol equals one child

Life expectancy
The average life span of a newborn today

Symbol equals ten years

Energy consumption
The average amount of energy consumed per person per year (primary types of energy, excluding fuelwood and crop residues, are converted to oil equivalents)

Symbol equals one U.N. standard barrel of oil

Per capita income
Gross national product (GNP) divided by population

Symbol equals $1,000 (U.S.)

Daily calories
The average caloric intake per person per day

Symbol equals 800 calories

Rooms per dwelling
The average number of rooms in each household

Symbol equals one room

Low birth weight
Babies weighing less than 5.5 pounds, indicating maternal malnutrition and high mortality risk

Symbol equals 5%

Literacy
Males and females over the age of 15 who can read and write (accuracy varies widely by country)

Symbol equals 20%

Male

Female

Doctors and nurses *per 1,000 people*

Symbol equals one doctor or nurse

Source: National Geographic 174 (December 1988), pp. 942–943. Based on an illustration by Allen Carroll.

during the last decade to 1.2 billion (Sivard, 1991:33). These increased numbers of people will suffer from disease, malnutrition, squalor, stigma, illiteracy, unemployment, and hopelessness. Thus, they will be likely candidates for extreme solutions, such as terrorist movements and government policies of military expansion.

Food and Hunger

Through the middle 1980s the growth of food supplies was keeping up with population growth. The annual production of food was adequate for every person on earth, even in the most impoverished Third World nations (Lappe and Collins, 1986). Yet nearly 1.2 billion people are chronically undernourished, and some fifty thousand children die every day from starvation and hunger-related diseases. How can we explain these chilling figures?

An obvious source of the problem is rapid population growth, which distorts the distribution system and strains the productive capacity of the various nations. The annual increase of 96 million people, for example, means that each year an additional increase of 38.4 million tons of grain is needed just to keep up. Between 1950 and 1984 the world's grain output increased 2.6 times, a phenomenal gain. Recent data suggest that the grain harvests are no longer keeping pace with population. The 1989 harvest of 1.67 billion tons, for example, was up only 1 percent from that of 1984, which means that the grain output per person was actually *down* nearly 7 percent (the data in this section are taken from Brown, 1990). A number of factors are shrinking the productive land throughout the world, in rich and poor countries alike. The earth loses 24 billion tons of topsoil each year. Overgrazing of the grassland areas is slowly converting the marginal areas to desert. Irrigation systems that tap underground reserves are dropping water tables to dangerously low levels in many areas, causing the land to revert to dry-land farming. Air pollution and acid rain have damaged some crops and water sources. The rising concentration of greenhouse gases (see Chapter 3) may be changing the climates negatively. And finally, each year millions of acres of productive land are paved over or built on. As Brown has summarized:

> At a time when demand for various biological products is rising rapidly, the earth's biological production is shrinking. The even greater annual additions to world population in prospect for the nineties will further reduce the earth's ability to supply our food and raw materials. (Brown, 1990:7)

Most significant, of course, is that almost all of the population increase is occurring in regions and countries that are already poor. Because of low levels of economic development, the various levels of government, farmers, and others in these countries lack adequate money and credit for the machinery, fertilizer, pesticides, and technology necessary to increase crop production to meet the always-increasing demand. The dramatic price increases for oil since 1990 have had an especially devastating effect on food production in the poor nations. Food production in Third World nations is also more adversely affected by natural disasters (floods and droughts) than it is in more affluent nations because Third World nations are less likely to have adequate flood control, irrigation systems, and storage facilities.

Another way to explain the food problem is to view it as a poverty problem. Food supplies are adequate, but people must have the resources to afford them.

Because the poor cannot afford the available food, they go hungry. This view of poverty is correct. But if it is limited to viewing the poor as the problem, it has the effect of blaming the victims for their plight, ignoring the political and economic conditions that keep prices too high, make jobs difficult to obtain and poorly paid, and force too many people to compete for too few resources.

The major problem with food shortages is not food production, although that is exceedingly important, but the political economy of the world and of the individual nations. Economic and political structures thwart and distort the production and distribution of agricultural resources. (The following discussion is adapted from Lappe and Collins, 1979, 1986, and Murdoch, 1980.) The primary problem is inequality of control over productive resources. In each country in which hunger is a basic problem, most of the land is controlled by a small elite; the rest of the population is squeezed onto small plots or marginal land or is landless. The evidence is that when the few control most of the agriculture, production is less effective than when land is more equally apportioned among farmers. Yields per acre are less, land is underused, wealth produced is not reinvested but drained off for conspicuous consumption by the wealthy, and credit is monopolized. Most important, monopoly control of agricultural land is typically put into cash crops that have value as exports but neglect basic local needs.

Lappe and Collins have supplied two examples. One study found that thirty-six of the forty countries classified by the United Nations as having serious food shortages actually exported agricultural commodities to the United States; another showed that more than half the arable land in the Caribbean is used to produce crops and cattle for export. Over two-thirds of the arable land in Guadeloupe

When land is controlled by a few landowners, agricultural activities tend to be centered on one or two crops for export rather than on a variety of crops for local consumption.

produces sugar cane, cocoa, and bananas; 77 percent of land in Barbados grows just sugar cane (Lappe and Collins, 1979:16, 42).

Agriculture controlled by a few landowners and agribusiness interests results in investment decisions made on the basis of current profitability. If prices are good, producers breed livestock or plant crops to take advantage of the prices. This approach results in cycles of shortages and gluts. Small farmers, on the other hand, plant crops based on local needs, not world prices.

The way food surpluses are handled in a world in which more than 1 billion people are chronically hungry is especially instructive. The grain surplus is handled by feeding more than one-third of the world's production to animals. Crops are allowed to rot to keep prices high. Surplus milk is fed to pigs or even dumped to keep the price high. The notion of food scarcity is an obvious distortion when the major headaches of many agricultural experts around the world are how to reduce mountains of surplus and keep prices high.

From this view, then, the problem of food scarcity lies in the social organization of food production and distribution. (See the observation on Hunger in Africa.) The solution to hunger is to construct new forms of social organization capable of meeting the needs of the masses. The problem, though, goes beyond the boundaries of individual countries. The policies of the rich nations and multinational corporations are also responsible for the conditions that perpetuate poverty in the Third World. The United States, for example, supports the very conditions that promote hunger and poverty. The last section of this chapter documents this role.

Sickness and Disease

Chronic malnutrition, an obvious correlate of greater numbers of people and poverty, results in shorter life expectancies and a stunting of physical and mental capacities. We know, for example, that "one in ten babies born in [poor] countries will not make it to its first birthday" (Ehrlich and Ehrlich, 1990:67). We also know that protein deficiency in infancy results in permanent brain damage. Malnourishment during the years of growth results in an increased probability of dwarfing. Reporting the findings of several studies, the Ehrlichs have stated that

> a child's body grows to 10 percent of its adult size in the first three years, while the brain grows to 80 percent of its adult size. This rapid brain growth is primarily a result of protein synthesis (more than 50 percent of the dry weight of brain tissue is protein). When protein is not available in the diet to supply the amino acids from which brain proteins are synthesized, the brain stops growing. Apparently it can never regain the lost time. Not only is head size reduced in a malnourished youngster, but the brain does not fill the cranium. (Ehrlich and Ehrlich, 1972:92)

Vitamin deficiencies, of course, cause a number of diseases such as rickets, goiter, and anemia. Iron deficiency is a special problem for hungry children.

> The earliest functions to be affected by iron deficiency are those of brain enzymes involved in cognition and behavior. [Through a number of studies] it is now firmly established that iron deficiency can impair cognitive performance at all stages of life, and that, when it occurs in infancy and childhood, its effects may not be reversible. (Scrimshaw, 1991:140)

OBSERVATION

HUNGER IN AFRICA: WHY 30 MILLION PEOPLE ARE STARVING AND HOW TO STOP IT

Key to Africa's condition is "development," a term that means distinctly different things to those being developed and those doing the developing. In the northern sense of the word, Africa's development began some five hundred years ago with the internationalization of trade. As Europeans gained control of the world's waterways, the saw the "dark continent" as a course of raw materials and the gold to underpin their growing money economy. Between 1500 and 1870, Europeans ripped the heart out of the continent, taking some 22.9 million able-bodied farmers out as slaves. By the late 1800s, Africa was divided into spheres of European influence based not on the equitable development of the African economy, but on Europe's interests.

Early in the twentieth century, Africans began to demand control over their own political futures. Country by country, they fought for and won political independence from European colonists—but economic independence proved harder to gain. The structure of African economies, which had been "developed" not to feed Africans, but to meet the needs of Europe, remained intact.

Sudan, Africa's largest country, is a good example of the kind of development that has made Africa the "Third World's Third World," a site of recurring famines and unpayable debt. Although never wealthy, the Sudanese had maintained the ability to feed themselves for centuries. When Britain governed the country, it decided that Sudanese farmers should grow cotton, to supply burgeoning British mills. Using the latest in agricultural technology, the British developed huge cotton-growing schemes on Sudan's most fertile land.

When Sudan became independent in 1956, the new government, encouraged by "development" banks and foreign donors, continued to emphasize cotton production. Two things happened: over time, the world market price of cotton fell, and Sudan's supply of foreign currency plummeted. Since agricultural resources were tied up in cotton, food production kept steadily declining. With no foreign currency, the country had to take out loans to import food. The mills of northern England,

however, still had a constant supply of cheap Sudanese cotton.

Not all of Africa's problems, of course, began or ended with colonialism. Local struggles for power, unjust and corrupt regimes, and inter-African wars have played major roles in the continent's economic decline. But the North has had its own agenda for developing Africa—one that sees the continent as the source of supply for its production and a market for its goods. Ironically, it is the foreign aid ostensibly provided to ease Africa's suffering that is often the instrument for carrying out this agenda.

The aid that goes to Africa from the North—from governments, from nongovernmental organizations (NGOs), and from multilateral lending agencies—includes military, economic, development, and relief aid.

Military aid is the most obvious culprit in the wreck of Africa. The expanding international arms industry has had a field day in Africa, which spends more than fourteen billion dollars a year on weapons and ammunition. . . .

It is no coincidence that over the last decade, some of the largest recipients of U.S. and Soviet military aid in sub-Saharan Africa—Sudan, Ethiopia, Mozambique, and Angola—have been nations where war and famine are the most common.

Economic aid is provided by investors, including USAID and the World Bank, in the form of loans that yield interest to the donor. (Though it presents itself as a development agency, it is important to remember that the World Bank is a bank, and lends money to make a profit.) These northern investors urged African governments to take out huge loans in the seventies—right before two oil-price hikes and a drastic fall in world market prices for Africa's commodities crashed the Third World's economies. OPEC countries invested the profits from these price hikes in northern banks, which then made another round of loans to African governments. Many of the loans went to projects that ten years later loomed as vast monuments to stupidity, and millions in loaned project money were spirited out of Africa into foreign bank accounts by corrupt rulers. The debt still stands—and the interest payments keep growing.

Development aid is usually provided in the form of grants by governments and NGOs. While activists in the South have been somewhat successful in insisting on "appropriate" development—small-scale projects oriented toward local conditions and needs—the "bigger is better" mystique still persists in many cases. The tomato-paste processing plant built in an area of Sudan where no tomatoes were grown and the milk-powder factory in an area where cows could not survive are classic examples.

And development aid includes food aid—which helps the United States deal with its own agricultural surplus, and looks good on television, but has often helped destroy people's ability to feed themselves. . . .

Finally, there's relief aid. If relief aid is what comes in when all other kinds of aid have failed, then there's ample evidence that failure has come to Africa. Since 1980, Africa has received billions in foreign aid, most of it from the United States. During this period, the continent has charted a course of steady decline. Africa today produces less food, has more starving people, and owes more money than it did ten years ago. At best, the aid programs of the past are not very effective; at worse, they have been part of the problem. . . .

Breaking this famine-breeding cycle requires a fundamental shift in how we think about development and how we think about Africa. The first step is to realize that development is something done by people, not to them. As it stands now, development policies are designed by "experts" who sit in capital cities of the North. To change the often destructive impact of these policies, the North has to listen to, and support, Africa's priorities for its own development. High on the list among the community organizers and development workers I talk with is "self-reliance."

Central to self-reliance is food production aimed not at external markets but at local consumption. This seems basic common sense; yet during the 1984–85 famine, Ethiopia was exporting green beans to England. For famines to end, Ethiopia and countries like it will have to shift away from the capital-intensive, import-dependent agribusiness promoted by the North toward producing grains and vegetables for their own people. . . .

Breaking the cycle of famine would also mean abandoning the charity mentality that prevails in the aid industry. Donors should insist that aid go for rehabilitation projects, not just for emergency food. And we need to remember that white northerners do not have the answers for Africa. Our aid organizations and NGOs need to listen more carefully to what their African counterparts are saying.

Vitamin deficiencies make the individual more susceptible to influenza and other infectious diseases. Health in overpopulated areas is also affected by such problems as polluted water and air and by inadequate sewage treatment.

A final health problem brought about by malnourishment is a low level of energy. Not only lack of food but also intestinal disorders commonly associated with poverty cause general lassitude in the afflicted.*

Concentration of Misery in Cities

Although the majority of the poor in the Third World are landless and near-landless rural peasants, the greatest growth in poverty and other problems is occurring in cities. Whereas the population is doubling in many Third World countries

---

*Although low energy levels are a result of poverty, many persons have blamed poverty on a lack of energy, or "drive," in the poor—a classic example of blaming the victim.

Finally, African development needs to be seen in a political context. In the last year, popular protest led to fundamental political changes in some thirty-two African governments. In the last twelve months, more countries have made moves toward democracy than in the last twenty-five years combined. The U.S. government sees "democratization" as scheduled elections and free markets. Those of us who understand the limitations of this—and the high cost that free-market economics has already exacted from Africans—can push for alternative models by supporting small, grass-roots demo-cracy projects, like those backed by many African NGOs. But we cannot support the changing relationship between Africans and their government without democratizing as well, the relationship between Africa and the rest of the world. From the sixteenth century onward, Africa has supported the North—with its labor, its resources, and the money its hungry people send to northern banks. It is time for the North to play fair.

In the short term, however—this month, this year—an immense wave of famine is sweeping the continent, and real people are dying in frightening numbers. Aid must be forthcoming. But I hope that when Americans write their checks this time around, they'll think about why they're keeping Africans alive. I hope they'll write their checks to African organizations and to the few northern organizations that follow the leadership of African development activists,* and that they'll call the networks to complain about the endless images of helpless African children. I hope that relief agencies will match, dollar for dollar, the aid that goes for emergency relief with aid targeted for basic agricultural rehabilitation. And I hope that after this famine recedes, people will remember that the fight for Africa's future is a long one.

*Because most African NGOs are not registered in the United States, think about donating to those Northern groups that support community-level African initiatives, including:

- Oxfam America: Will direct donations to grass-roots relief and development programs designed and implemented by Africans. 115 Broadway, Boston, MA 02116; 1–800–225–5800.
- Development Group for Alternative Policies: Brings activists from grass-roots African NGOs into the policy debates that affect development. 1400 I St. NW, Suite 520, Washington, DC 20005.
- Global Exchange: Publishes *Beyond Safaris: A Guide to Building People-to-People Ties with Africa.* Send $12.95 plus $1.50 for postage to 2141 Mission St. #202, San Francisco, CA 94110.

Source: Gayle Smith, "The Hunger," *Mother Jones* 16 (September/October 1991), pp. 36–37, 41, 61–62, (excerpts.) Reprinted with permission from *Mother Jones* magazine, © 1991, Foundation for National Progress.

about every 33 years, it is doubling in Third World cities every 13.5 years. From 1950 to 1990, for example, the urban population of the Third World increased from 286 million to 1.5 billion. In 1950 only one Third World city, Shanghai, had a population of more than 5 million. According to projections by the United Nations, by the year 2000 "there will be 40 such cities including 19 with more than 10 million inhabitants" (McFalls, 1991:29–30). The Ehrlichs describe the unlikely prospect of these cities meeting the needs of their poor inhabitants:

The prospects for these gigantic agglomerations are not bright. They have grown so fast that they have far outstripped their ability to care for their inhabitants. Lack of sewage systems, inadequate water supplies laced with pathogens, air pollution, and gigantic garbage dumps (often occupied and "mined" by the poorest of the poor) plague these overgrown metropolises. (Ehrlich and Ehrlich, 1990:154)

Urban growth in the Third World is greatest in Latin America, where 8 to 10 million people annually are either migrating to cities or being born there.

Latin America is the most urbanized part of the underdeveloped world. In 1950, only 42 percent of Latin Americans were city dwellers; today almost 73 percent live in cities, according to the United Nations. This compares with 34 percent in Africa and 33 percent in Asia. (Nash, 1992:1, 10)

A major problem of these cities is providing employment for their citizens. The special problem is to find employment for new immigrants to the cities, the farmers pushed off the land because of high rural density and the resulting poverty. The people who are pushed into the cities are, for the most part, unprepared for life and work there. They do not possess mechanical skills; they are illiterate; they are steeped in tradition. The cities, too, are unprepared for them. Aside from the obvious problems of housing and sanitation, the cities of the Third World do not have the industries that employ many workers. Because their citizens are usually poor, these countries are not good markets for products, so there is little internal demand for manufactured goods.

Another massive problem of the Third World cities is the mushrooming of squatter settlements. In the next thirty years some 3 billion persons will be added to the world population. About 60 percent of that number (1.8 billion) will be added to the cities of Asia, Africa, and Latin America that in many cases are

Shantytowns are the fastest-growing sections of Third World cities.

already bursting at the seams. The sources of this growth are urban fertility and the immigration of people from rural areas. Most of these people have merely exchanged the squalor of rural poverty for that of urban poverty. They have neither money nor skills that are useful in an urban setting.

The immediate question for these immigrants is where to live. They have little choice but to create houses out of scraps (tin, plywood, paper) on land that does not belong to them (in streets, alleys, or ravines, or on hillsides). Shantytowns are the fastest-growing sections of the Third World cities. For example, 25 percent of the citizens of Seoul are illegal homesteaders, as are 67 percent of those in Ankara.

The shantytowns of squatters have none of the amenities normally associated with urban life. Palen has described their situation:

> Since shantytowns almost by definition are illegally occupying the land on which they are built, they cannot demand city services. Streets, police and fire protection, and—most important—sanitary services are usually nonexistent. Water almost always has to be carried from the nearest public tap. Schools are rare. Electricity is the most commonly found utility, since wires can easily be strung from shack to shack.
>
> Health problems are exacerbated by the crowding and lack of proper disposal for sewage and refuse, and by the fact that the settlements are frequently built on the least desirable terrain, such as city dumps, marshlands, or hillsides. Attempts by the government to remove squatters are invariably unsuccessful: if one slum is destroyed, another is built overnight with the refuse from the earlier settlement. When no other city housing is available, there is little alternative to the squatter settlements. (Palen, 1975:324–325)

How do squatters react to their deplorable situation? They are unemployed or work at the most menial of tasks. They are hungry. Their children remain illiterate. They suffer the indignities of being social outcasts. Will they revolt? Some observers believe that for those experiencing abject poverty, the struggle is for the next meal, not for a redistribution of power. Others see the growing squatter settlements as breeding grounds for riots and radical political movements.

The prospects for the cities of the developing countries are bleak. Their growth continues unabated. Unbelievable poverty and hunger are common. Jobs are scarce. Resources are limited and becoming more scarce as the number of inhabitants increases. The capital necessary for extensive economic development or for providing needed services is difficult to raise.

In sum, the high growth rates of cities, combined with the high concentration of people who are poor, unemployed, angry, hungry, and miserable, magnifies and intensifies other problems (such as racial and religious animosities, resource shortages, and pollution), "producing enormous strains on existing political, social, and economic structures and on relations between nations" (Green, 1981:5).

Is Overpopulation Inevitable?

How can the nations of the world deal with the problems of expanding population? Basically, there are three ways to reduce fertility—through economic development, family-planning programs, and social change (see Kammeyer, Ritzer, and Yetman, 1990:609–616). We now examine these briefly.

Historically, as nations have become more urban, industrialized, and modernized, their population growth has slowed appreciably. Countries appear to go through three stages in this process, which is known as the **modern demographic transition.** In the agricultural stage both birth and death rates are high, resulting in a low population growth rate. In the transition stage, birth rates remain high but the death rates decrease markedly due to access to better health practices, better sanitation, and better diets. Many nations are presently in this stage, and the result for them is a population explosion. Much later in the process, as societies become more urban and traditional customs have less of a hold, birth rates decline, slowing the population growth and eventually stopping it altogether (as is now occurring in many nations of Europe and Japan). The solution in this stage, then, is economic development. The problem, of course, is that the modern demographic transition experienced in Europe took about 200 years. This length of time is unacceptable because the planet cannot sustain the massive growth that will occur while the demographic transition runs its course.

The second possibility is to control population growth immediately. Some leaders in the developing countries believe that the idea of population control is racist because most of the control would limit the fertility of Blacks and Asians. Nevertheless, nearly all developing countries have instituted family-planning programs. Several countries have reduced fertility dramatically in just a few decades, most notably China, Taiwan, South Korea, Singapore, Thailand, Colombia, Costa Rica, and several Caribbean countries. Other countries have failed to make much progress. The United Nations estimates that half of the married women in developing countries do not want more children but that they do not have access to effective methods of birth control. The World Bank estimates that it would take $8 billion to make birth control readily available on a global basis. Such availability would reduce the projected world population from 10 billion to 8 billion during the next sixty years (Toufexis, 1989:49). A major reason this effort has stalled is that the United States under the Reagan and Bush administrations reduced its assistance because of their opposition to abortion and such procedures as RU 486 (use of the drug that induces a relatively safe miscarriage in the early stages of pregnancy).

The third strategy to reduce population growth involves societal changes. Ingrained cultural values about children as evidence of the father's virility or as a hedge against poverty in old age must be changed. One method is for the government to provide economic incentives for having fewer children. Religious beliefs such as the resistance of the Roman Catholic hierarchy to the use of contraceptives are a great obstacle to population control. "Still, religious objections need not entirely thwart population planning. Where such resistance is encountered, vigorous campaigns should be mounted to promote natural birth-control techniques, including the rhythm method and fertility delay through breast feeding" (Toufexis, 1989:49). Perhaps the most significant social change needed to reduce fertility is to change the role of women. When women are isolated from activities outside the home, their worth depends largely on their ability to bear and rear children (Kammeyer, Ritzer, and Yetman, 1990:615). Women need to be included in the formal education process. Research has shown that educated women are more apt than less educated women to apply their education to

WORLD POPULATION NOW GROWING at the RATE of a LOS ANGELES EVERY MONTH

Danziger in *The Christian Science* Monitor © 1991 TCSPS.

upgrading their families' health and nutrition and to be receptive to family planning (Ehrlich and Ehrlich, 1988:945).

Priorities of Third World Nations: Military Security or Economic Security?

Third World governments, anxious to protect themselves from outside threats (and from internal insurgents), have opted, usually, for spending their meager resources on military strength. The fears leading to these decisions may be realistic given their relative weakness, the imperialistic schemes by other nations, and border disputes. The priorities of the ruling elites in these countries have been for guns rather than education, health care, agricultural development, and other desperately needed social programs that would enhance the social and economic well-being of their citizens and society. The following data are supplied by Sivard, 1989, 1991:

- Since 1960 developing nations have increased their military expenditures more than twice as fast as their living standards, measured by per capita income (1989:5). This means that "while in 1960 the military bill took the equivalent of 76 million man-years of income to pay it, in 1987 it took 197 million man-years" (1989:19). Thus, the military burden on the economy has grown increasingly heavier.

- Developing countries have eight times as many soldiers as physicians (1991:5).
- The developing nations have spent more for armaments from the industrialized nations than they received in development aid from those countries. Between 1960 and 1987 the governments of the poorer countries spent almost $400 billion (much of it increasing their debt) for military imports (1989:21).

There are at least three major consequences of the disparate spending for military goods over social expenditures in the developing countries. First, military expenditures impeded social development by reducing the monies that could have been spent on education and health care. During the 1980s the gap in spending even increased as the poor countries burdened by foreign debt ($1.2 trillion in 1991) reduced social expenditures even further while *increasing* military expenditures. Extravagant military expenditures must be added to the rapidly growing population, inefficient land use, and the like as major reasons for the increased poverty, illiteracy, disease, and high infant mortality in the Third World.

A second result of overexpenditures for the military in the Third World is that the poor countries have become poorer and more dependent on the industrialized nations because of the increased debt to finance the military.

Finally, the overreliance on military expenditures is a major source for the likelihood of military personnel holding major positions of power in the poor countries. According to Sivard (1989:21), sixty-four governments, more than half of the developing countries, were under military control.

> The arms buildup has . . . changed the political landscape, bringing more military personnel into positions of power. Large budgets dedicated to national defense may not help the economy but they do provide a solid economic base for entry into the political arena. In most countries the military are the biggest element of the official bureaucracy and in many the military budget is the major component of the central government's budget. Size alone assures political clout; rich buying power, plus guns, guarantee it. (Sivard, 1989:21)

Most significant, there is a strong tendency of military controlled governments

> to use force against the people, including torture, brutality, disappearances, and political killings. . . . In the ultimate mockery of 'defense,' military power wedded to political control turns inward to terrorize the people it is intended to protect. (Sivard, 1989:21)

U.S. Relations with the Third World

There is a huge gap between the rich and poor nations of the world. About 75 percent of the world's people live in the overpopulated and poverty-afflicted Third World, yet those nations produce only one-tenth of the world's industrial output and one-twelfth of its electric power output.

The nations of the Third World are underdeveloped for a number of reasons, including geography, climate, lack of arable land and minerals, and a history of continuous warfare; but the rich nations are also responsible. The Third World economies are largely the result of a history of colonialism and of economic domination by the developed nations in the postcolonial era.

As recently as 1914, approximately 70 percent of the world's population lived in **colonies** in areas now designated as the Third World. As colonies of superpowers, their resources and labors were exploited. Leadership was imposed from outside. The local people were treated as primitive and backward. Crops were planted for the colonizer's benefit, not for the needs of the indigenous population. Raw materials were extracted for exports. The wealth thus created was concentrated in the hands of local elites and the colonizers. Population growth was encouraged because the colonizer needed a continuous supply of low-cost labor. Colonialism destroyed the cultural patterns of production and exchange by which these societies once met the needs of their peoples. Thriving industries that once served indigenous markets were destroyed. The capital generated by the natural wealth in these countries was not used to develop local factories, schools, sanitation systems, agricultural processing plants, or irrigation systems. Colonialism also promoted a two-class society by increasing landholdings among the few and landlessness among the many.

Although the process began centuries ago, the legacy of colonialism continues to promote poverty today. In short, the heritage of colonialism that systematically promoted the self-interest of the colonizers and robbed and degraded the resources and the lives of the colonized continues to do so today. Vestigial attitudes, both within and outside these countries, and the continued dependency of Third World nations on the industrialized superpowers exacerbate their problems. As a result, the gap between the Third World and the industrial nations continues to widen.

This section explores the relationship of the United States to the Third World, focusing on the economic mechanisms that maintain Third World dependency and the political policies that promote problems within these countries.

Multinational Corporations

Gigantic **multinational corporations,** the majority of which are U.S.–based, control the world economy. Their decisions to build or not to build, to relocate a plant, to begin marketing a new product, or to scrap an old one have a tremendous impact on the lives of ordinary citizens in the countries they operate from and invest in.

In their desire to tap low-wage workers, the multinational corporations have tended to locate in poor countries. (See the Observation on Women on the Global Assembly Line for the devastating results this policy has had on women workers.) Although the poor countries should have benefited from this new industry (by, say, gaining a higher standard of living and access to modern technology), they have not. One reason is that the profits generated in these countries tend to be channeled back to the United States in the form of dividends. Second, global companies do not have a great impact in easing the unemployment of the poor nations because they use advanced technology whenever feasible, which reduces the demand for jobs.

The global corporations have enormous advantages over local competition when they move into an underdeveloped country. Foremost, they have access to the latest technology, whether it be computers, machinery, or genetic engineering. Second, they receive better terms than local businesses when they borrow money. They are preferred customers because their credit is backed by their

Multinational corporations tend to locate in poor countries where low wages and weak environmental laws result in lower operating expenses.

worldwide financial resources. Moreover, global banks and global corporations are, as we discuss in Chapter 2, closely tied through interlocking directorates and shared ownership. Thus, it is in the interest of these banks to give credit under favorable conditions to their corporate friends. Finally, the global corporations have an enormous advantage over local companies through their manipulation of the market, influence over local government officials, and their control of workers.

An important source of the Third World countries' current dependency on the United States and on other industrialized countries is their growing public and private debt. This debt totalled $1.2 trillion in 1991, nearly half the collective gross national product of these countries. This debt is so large for some nations that they cannot spend for needed public works, education, and other social services. Available monies must be spent, rather, on servicing the debt. Thus, the debt treadmill stifles progress. This situation is further exacerbated by the toll on the natural resources of the developing countries. "Forests have been recklessly logged, mineral deposits carelessly mined, and fisheries overexploited, all to pay foreign creditors" (Durning, 1990:144).

The United States is negatively influenced as well by being the lender nation. First, the United States is encouraged to buy imports and reduce exports, which eliminates domestic jobs. Second, to the degree that foreign governments default on their loans, the U.S. banks that made the bad loans are subsidized by the U.S. taxpayers, ensuring the banks' profit.

Two activities by multinationals are highly controversial because they have negative costs worldwide and especially to the inhabitants of Third World nations—arms sales and the sale of products known to be harmful.

Arms sales.   According to a report by the Congressional Research Service, Third World nations in 1990 purchased $43 billion worth of armaments. The United States ranked first in arms sales, selling $18.5 billion (44.8 percent of the total), followed by the Soviet Union, which sold $12.1 billion (reported in Associated Press, 1991). These sales were motivated by what was deemed to be in the national interests of the countries involved and by the profit to the manufacturers (in the United States the multinationals most involved were Boeing, Lockheed, and Northrop). But, at least from the perspective of the United States, these sales can sometimes backfire. For example, from 1980 to 1988 Iran purchased $17.5 billion in armaments from various countries (not the United States) and Iraq bought $47.3 billion. These purchases fueled the war between these two countries. Moreover, these weapons buys added to the arsenals and the power of these two countries, leading in 1990 to Iraq's invasion of Kuwait and the subsequent U.S. blockade of Iraq and the massive military effort by the United States and other countries to reject further expansion by Iraq and ensure the flow of oil from the Middle East around the world.

Corporate sales that endanger life.   **Corporate dumping,** the exporting of goods that have either been banned or not approved for sale in the United States because they are dangerous, is a relatively common practice. Most often the greatest market for such unsafe products is among the poor in the Third World. These countries often do not bar hazardous products, and many of their poor citizens are illiterate and therefore tend to be unaware of the hazards involved with the use of such products.

The United States and other industrialized nations continue to use the Third World as a source of profits as nations purchase these unhealthy products. For example, the Dalkon Shield intrauterine device was sold overseas after the manufacturer withdrew it from the United States market because of its danger to women. Similarly, after the Consumer Product Safety Commission forced children's garments with the fire retardant called tris off the domestic market because it was found to be carcinogenic, the manufacturer shipped several million garments overseas for sale (Simon and Eitzen, 1990:188–192).

Twenty-five percent of the pesticides exported by the United States are restricted or banned by the Environmental Protection Agency for domestic use. One such pesticide, DBCP, was severely restricted domestically because it was proven to cause male sterility. Nevertheless, Castle & Cooke and Standard Fruit, both American banana producers, used DBCP at their Costa Rican and Honduran plantations. As a result, more than 1,000 men on those plantations were permanently sterilized from contact with the poison (*Multinational Monitor,* 1989b). For another example, consider the following:

> No chemical company its size has as dirty a record as the Velsicol Chemical Co. of Tennessee. Velsicol is the world's only producer of the pesticides chlordane and heptachlor, two pesticides banned in the United States because they are considered probable human carcinogens. Yet, according to a report by the environmental group Greenpeace, over the last two years Velsicol has exported approximately 5 million pounds of the chemicals to at least 25 countries. (Mokhiber, 1989:17)

In 1990, the trade association of U.S. pesticide makers, the National Agricultural Chemicals Association, lobbied heavily in Washington as Congress considered a

OBSERVATION

WOMEN ON THE GLOBAL ASSEMBLY LINE

There are over one million people employed in industrial free trade zones in the Third World. Millions more work outside the zones in multinational-controlled plants and domestically owned subcontracting factories. Eighty to 90 percent of the light-assembly workers are women. This is a remarkable switch from earlier patterns of foreign-controlled industrialization. Until recently, economic development involved heavy industries such as mining and construction and usually meant more jobs for men and—compared to traditional agricultural society—a diminished economic status for women. But multinationals consider light-assembly work, whether the product is Barbie dolls or computer components, to be women's work.

Women everywhere are paid lower wages than men. Since multinationals go overseas to reduce labor costs, women are the natural choice for assembly jobs. Wage-earning opportunities for women are limited and women are considered only supplementary income earners for their families. Management uses this secondary status to pay women less than men and justify layoffs during slow periods, claiming that women don't need to work and will probably quit to get married anyway.

Women are the preferred workforce for other reasons. Multinationals want a workforce that is docile, easily manipulated and willing to do boring, repetitive assembly work. Women, they claim, are the perfect employees, with their "natural patience" and "manual dexterity." As the personnel manager of an assembly plant in Taiwan says, "Young male workers are too restless and impatient to be doing monotonous work with no career value. If displeased they sabotage the machines and even threaten the foreman. But girls, at most they cry a little."

Multinationals prefer single women with no children and no plans to have any. Pregnancy tests are routinely given to potential employees to avoid the issue of maternity benefits. In India, a woman textile worker reports that "they do take unmarried women but they prefer women who have had an operation," referring to her government's sterilization program. In the Philippines' Bataan Export Processing Zone the Mattel toy company offers prizes to workers who undergo sterilization.

Third World women haven't always been a ready workforce. Until two decades ago, young women were vital to the rural economy in many countries. They worked in the home, in agriculture, or in local cottage industries. But many Third World governments adopted development plans favoring large-scale industry and agribusiness as advocated by such agencies as the World Bank and the International Monetary Fund. Traditional farming systems and communities are now crumbling as many families lose their land and local enterprises collapse. As a result of the breakdown of the rural economy, many families now send their daughters to the cities or the free trade zones in an attempt to assure some income.

The majority of the new female workforce is young, between 16 and 25 years old. As one management consultant explains, "when seniority rises, wages rise"; so the companies prefer to train a fresh group of teenagers rather than give experienced women higher pay. Different industries have different age and skill standards. The youngest workers, usually under 23 years old, are found in electronics and textile factories where keen eyesight and dexterity are essential. A second, older group of women work in industries like food processing where nimble fingers and perfect vision aren't required. Conditions in these factories are particularly bad. Multinationals can get away with more because the women generally can't find jobs elsewhere.

bill to bar the export of pesticides banned in the United States. The argument presented in opposition to the bill was that such a ban would cost jobs in plants throughout the United States and would impede scientific research (Schneider, 1990).

Not all companies want young women, although this is the exception rather than the rule. In Singapore, some companies had problems with young women workers who went "shopping for jobs from factory to factory." Management consultants suggested "housewives-only" assembly lines. Older and too responsible for "transient glamour jobs," housewives would make better candidates, they reasoned. One consultant recommended that "a brigade of housewives could run the factory from 8 A.M. to 1 P.M. and leave. Then a second brigade could come in and take over till 6 P.M. This way housewives need only work half a day. They will be able to earn and spend time with their families. The factories will get a full and longer day's work. Deadlines will be met."

Corporate apologists are quick to insist that Third World women are absolutely thrilled with their new-found employment opportunities. "You should watch these kids going to work," said Bill Mitchell, an American who solicits U.S. business for the Burmudez Industrial Park in Ciudad Juarez. "You don't have any sullenness here. They smile." A top-level management consultant who advises U.S. companies on where to relocate their factories said, "The girls genuinely enjoy themselves. They're away from their families. They have spending money. They can buy motor bikes, whatever. Of course it is a regulated experience, too—with dormitories to live in—so it's a healthful experience." Richard Meier, a professor of environmental design believes that "earning power should do more for the women of these countries than any amount of organization, demonstration and protest. . . . The benefits and freedom to be gained by these women from their employment in these new industries are almost always preferred to the near slavery still associated with the production of classical goods, such as batik."

Liberation or virtual slavery? What is the real experience of Third World women? A study of Brazilian women working in a textile factory drew positive conclusions: work "represents the widening of horizons, a means of confronting life, a source of individualization. The majority of women . . . drew a significant part of their identity from being wage-workers." By earning money and working outside the home, factory women may find a certain independence from their families. Meeting and working with other women lays the foundation for a collective spirit and, perhaps, collective action.

But at the same time, the factory system relies upon and reinforces the power of men in the traditional patriarchal family to control women. Cynthia Enloe, a sociologist who organized an international conference of women textile workers in 1982, says that in the Third World, "the emphasis on family is absolutely crucial to management strategy. Both old-time firms and multinationals use the family to reproduce and control workers. Even recruitment is a family process. Women don't just go out independently to find jobs: it's a matter of fathers, brothers and husbands making women available after getting reassurances from the companies. Discipline becomes a family matter since, in most cases, women turn their paychecks over to their parents. Factory life is, in general, constrained and defined by the family life cycle."

One thing is certain: when multinational corporate-style development meets traditional patriarchal culture, women's lives are bound to change.

Source: Annette Fuentes and Barbara Ehrenreich, *Women in the Global Factory.* (New York: South End Press, 1983), pp. 11–15. © Institute for New Communications/South End Press, Boston, 1983. Reprinted by permission.

Another form of corporate dumping, in the literal sense of the word, is the practice of shipping toxic wastes produced in the United States to the Third World for disposal. This practice is attractive to U.S. corporations because the Environmental Protection Agency requires expensive disposal facilities, whereas

Sometimes U.S. corporations sell pesticides to foreign buyers for use in their countries even though the products are banned in the U.S. because the are unsafe.

the materials can be dumped in Third World nations for a fraction of the cost. The host nations engage in such potentially dangerous transactions because they need the money (Simon and Eitzen, 1990:190–192).

Some companies dump workplace hazards as well as hazardous products and waste materials in poor nations. Governmental regulations often require U.S. corporations to provide a reasonably safe environment for their workers. These requirements, such as not exposing workers to asbestos, lead, or other toxic substances, are often expensive to meet. Thus, many corporations move their manufacture (and unsafe working conditions) to a country with few or no restrictions. This move saves the companies money and increases their profits, but it disregards the health and safety of workers outside the United States.

Corporate dumping is undesirable for three reasons. First, and most obvious, it poses serious health hazards to the poor and uninformed consumers of the Third World. Second, the disregard of U.S. multinational corporations for their workers and their consumers in foreign lands contributes to anti–United States feelings in the host countries. And, third, many types of corporate dumping have a boomerang effect; that is, some of the hazardous products sold abroad by U.S. companies are often returned to the United States and other developed nations, negatively affecting the health of the people in those countries. The United States imports about one-fourth of its fruits and vegetables, and some of this produce is tainted with toxic chemical residues.

Many of the pesticides that are banned domestically reenter the United States on produce from countries using these products; about 50 percent of imported produce is pesticide contaminated. And, up to 60 percent of the food the FDA [the Food and Drug Administration] has identified as tainted reaches the consumer. (*Multinational Monitor,* 1989b:6)

U.S. Government

The U.S. government spends about $15 billion yearly on foreign aid programs to Third World nations. There are two reasons for this generosity. First, U.S. governments have reacted to the food, medical, and other needs of people in distress. This humanitarian concern has also led to efforts to help the poorer nations begin to help themselves through agricultural and technical assistance. The other reason for U.S. aid is self-serving, that is, the apparent generosity actually masks the intention for the aid to further U.S. interests. This aim is accomplished at two levels. First, the government provides aid to the Third World to help U.S. corporations make profits. The aid is given on condition that it be used to purchase U.S. goods and that these goods be transported on U.S. ships. Money for roads, bridges, dams, and utilities is appropriated to meet the needs of U.S.–based factories, mines, refineries, and plantations.

At a second level of self-interest, aid is given to Third World governments that further U.S. foreign policy aims. Economic and military aid goes to leaders who support U.S. corporations in their country and who suppress peasant and worker movements, which are viewed as anticapitalist and prosocialist. Most recently, U.S. support has been given to right-wing regimes in Argentina, Chile, El Salvador, Pakistan, and South Africa. In effect, U.S. money and military strength are often used to support the rule of dictators and to smother the efforts of social change groups working for agrarian reform within poor countries. Ironically, then, U.S. policies undermine the efforts that would most help to solve the poverty, dependency, and hunger of the Third World.

U.S. foreign policy also involves clandestine interventions in other countries to defend U.S. interests (i.e., to defend democracy or to halt the predatory behavior of a leader such as Saddam Hussein of Iraq and to protect U.S. corporate interests in the region). These efforts have involved helping favored political groups either retain their power or attain it through the provision of monies, weapons, and expertise; economic sabotage; and even assassinations. Evidence from a Senate Investigating Committee has shown, for example, that over a twenty-year period following World War II the Central Intelligence Agency (CIA) was involved in more than 900 foreign interventions, including paramilitary operations, surreptitious manipulation of foreign governments, and assassinations. These and subsequent efforts to intervene in the affairs of other nations for U.S. interests have occurred in dozens of countries.

What is most ironic is that U.S. foreign policy over the past century has betrayed, as Ahmad says, "the principles embodied in the Declaration of Independence, in the Bill of Rights, and in George Washington's First Inaugural Address. [These] policies have been consistently antinationalist, opposed to revolution, supportive of dictatorship and fascist states, and violently interventionist in the American sphere of influence" (Ahmad, 1980: 2). In short, U.S. interventions are proclaimed "in the defense of democracy," but in effect they are done to contain social change and therefore make "the world safe for capitalism." In the words of Parenti:

To justify interventionism in other countries, our policy makers . . . claim they are defending democracy from communism. But closer examination shows they are defending the capitalist world from social change—even if the change be peaceful, orderly, and *democratic.* Guatemala in 1954, the Dominican Republic in 1962, Iran in 1953, Brazil in 1964, and Chile and Uruguay in 1973 are cases in point. In all these countries popularly elected governments began instituting progressive changes for the benefit of the destitute classes and began to nation-alize or threatened to nationalize U.S. corporate holdings. And in each instance, the United States was instrumental in overthrowing these governments and instituting right-wing regimes that accommodated U.S. investors and ruthlessly repressed peasants and workers. Similarly, in Greece, the Philippines, Indonesia, East Timor, and at least ten Latin American nations, popular govern-ments have been overthrown by military oligarchs—largely trained and financed by the Pentagon and the CIA—who prove themselves friendly to capitalism.

For all their talk about "human rights," U.S. government leaders have propped up regimes throughout the world that have used assassination squads, torture, and terror to support the allies of the corporate world order. In many U.S.–supported states, strikes have been outlawed, unions destroyed, wages cut, and dissidents murdered.* (Parenti, 1988:45)

The ultimate interest of the United States is best served if there is peace and stability in the Third World. These goals can be accomplished only if population growth is slowed significantly, hunger and poverty alleviated, the extremes of inequality reduced, and if, to editorialize, the developed nations, including the United States, would not furnish these nations with armaments and not meddle in their internal affairs.

If the United States and other developed nations do not take appropriate steps, then human misery, acts of terrorism against the affluent nations, tensions among neighbors, and the possibility of war—even nuclear war—will increase. The last factor becomes especially relevant given the knowledge that the follow-ing Third World nations have nuclear bomb capabilities: China, India, Pakistan, North Korea, Taiwan, Iran, Iraq, South Africa, Uruguay, Argentina, and Brazil (Sivard, 1991: 16). Moreover, a number of Third World countries have been alleged to have used chemical weapons (Burma, Ethiopia, the Philippines, Sudan, Egypt, South Africa, Thailand, and Vietnam (Sivard, 1991:16). The ultimate ques-tion is whether the way these steps are implemented will help the Third World reduce its dependence on the more developed nations, the hunger and misery within their countries, and, in the process, international tensions.

CHAPTER REVIEW

1. The Third World refers to the underdeveloped and developing nations where poverty, hunger, and misery are found disproportionately. These nations also are characterized by relative powerlessness, rapid population growth, high infant mortality, unsanitary living conditions, and high rates of illiteracy.

*Copyright © 1988 from *Democracy for the Few,* Fifth Edition, by Michael Parenti. Reprinted with per-mission of St. Martin's Press, Incorporated.

2. The world population exceeds 5.4 billion and will increase by 96 million annually during the 1990s. About 90 percent of this growth will occur in the Third World, where food, housing, health care, and employment are inadequate to meet *present* needs.

3. While world population is growing rapidly, the amount of productive land is shrinking in rich and poor countries alike because of the loss of 24 billion tons of topsoil annually; the lowering of water tables from irrigation; overgrazing; and pollution.

4. Within the nations experiencing the most rapid population growth, cities are growing much faster than are rural areas. The problems of survival for individuals and families are increased dramatically in cities: food is too expensive, jobs are scarce and poorly paid, and sanitation problems increase the likelihood of disease. The concentration of the poor in the limited space of cities increases tensions and the probability of hostility.

5. Poverty is a special problem of the underdeveloped nations of the Third World: 1.2 billion people have inadequate diets, high infant mortality, low life expectancy, and high rates of illiteracy. Poverty also contributes to high fertility.

6. Hunger is a worldwide problem, especially in the Third World, but even there food production is adequate to meet the needs of all of the people. The problem of hunger results from high prices, unequal distribution of food, overreliance on cash crops, and concentration of landownership among very few people—all the consequences of the political economy in these nations and the world.

7. There are three ways to reduce high fertility in the Third World: (a) economic development (modern demographic transition); (b) family planning programs; and (c) social change, especially through the changing of traditional women's roles.

8. The ruling elites of the poor countries have typically used their meager resources to arm themselves rather than to upgrade education and agriculture, improve health care, and provide better housing and sanitation. This emphasis on military spending has resulted in (a) the inequality gap in these poor countries increasing, (b) increased overall impoverishment of these countries and their greater dependence on industrialized nations because of higher debts, and (c) a strong tendency for the military to control these countries.

9. The Third World is underdeveloped for a number of reasons, the most important of which is a heritage of colonialism. Colonialism destroyed local industries and self-sufficient crop-growing patterns, drained off resources for the benefit of the colonizers, and promoted local elites through concentration of landownership among the few. In the postcolonial era the dependency of the Third World and its control by outside forces continue.

10. The world economy is controlled by multinational corporations, the majority of which are U.S.–based. Their power in the underdeveloped nations perpetuates the dependency of many Third World nations on the United States.

11. Multinationals add to the tensions in Third World countries through arms sales, corporate dumping of products known to be dangerous, and intervention in the domestic affairs of host countries.

12. The United States provides aid to Third World countries for two reasons: (1) to meet the food, medical, and technical needs of impoverished peoples; and (2) to further U.S. interests.
13. The U.S. government has also intervened in the affairs of Third World nations to promote its interests. The modes of intervention have included assassinations, economic support of authoritarian regimes, and paramilitary operations.

KEY TERMS

Third World.   The underdeveloped and developing nations where poverty, hunger, and misery abound.

Absolute poverty.   A condition of life so degraded by disease, illiteracy, malnutrition, and squalor as to deny its victims the basic necessities.

Modern demographic transition.   A three-stage pattern of population change occurring as societies industrialize and urbanize, resulting ultimately in a low and stable population growth rate.

Colony.   A territory controlled by a powerful country that exploits the land and the people for its own benefit.

Multinational corporation.   A profit-oriented company engaged in business activities in more than one nation.

Corporate dumping.   The exporting of goods by a business that have either been banned or not approved for sale in the United States because they are dangerous.

FOR FURTHER STUDY

Lester R. Brown et al., eds. *State of the World 1992.* New York: W. W. Norton, 1992.

Dissent. "Africa Today: Crisis and Change," *Dissent* 39 (Summer 1992), entire issue.

Paul R. Ehrlich and Anne H. Ehrlich. *The Population Explosion.* New York: Touchstone, 1991.

James P. Grant. *The State of the World's Children 1992.* New York: A UNICEF publication by Oxford University Press, 1992.

Robert L. Heilbroner. *An Inquiry into the Human Prospect: Looked at Again for the 1990s.* New York: W. W. Norton, 1991.

Ellen Jamison. *World Population Profile: 1991.* Washington, D.C.: U.S. Bureau of the Census, 1991.

Frances Moore Lappe and Joseph Collins. *World Hunger: Twelve Myths.* New York: Grove Press, 1986.

Joseph A. McFalls, Jr. "Population: A Lively Introduction." *Population Bulletin* 46 (October 1991), entire issue.

David R. Simon and D. Stanley Eitzen. *Elite Deviance.* 4th ed. Boston: Allyn and Bacon, 1993.

Ruth Leger Sivard. *World Military and Social Expenditures 1991.* Washington, D.C.: World Priorities, 1991.

Kathryn Ward, ed. *Women Workers and Global Restructuring.* Ithaca, N.Y.: Cornell University ILR Press, 1990.

FORUM

IS FOOD PRODUCTION LIKELY TO KEEP UP WITH POPULATION GROWTH?

There is plenty of food, the problem is distribution.

Frances Moore Lappe and Joseph Collins

Myth: With food-producing resources in so much of the world stretched to the limit, there's simply not enough food to go around. Unfortunately, some people have to go hungry.

Our response: The world today produces enough grain alone to provide every human being on the planet with 3,600 calories a day. That's enough to make most people fat! And this estimate does not even count the many other commonly eaten foods—vegetables, beans, nuts, root crops, fruits, grass-fed meats, and fish.

Abundance, not scarcity, best describes the supply of food in the world today. Rarely has the world seen such a glut of food looking for buyers. Increases in food production during the past 25 years have outstripped the world's unprecedented population growth by about 16 percent. Indeed, mountains of unsold grain on world markets have pushed prices downward over the past three decades.

All well and good for the global picture, you might be thinking, but doesn't such a broad stroke tell us little? Aren't people starving because of food shortages where most hungry people live—in Africa, Asia, and Latin America?

Hunger in the face of ample food is all the more shocking in the third world. In every region except Africa, gains in food production since 1950 have kept ahead of population growth. During the 1970s, only 12 percent of the world's population lived in countries where food production per person was falling.

One hypothetical question best highlights how misleading it is to think of food shortages in the third world as the root cause of hunger: how much of the food now available within third world countries would it take to make up for the total food lacking in the diets of each country's chronically hungry people?

According to the World Bank, the answer is but a tiny percentage. In India, home of over a third of the world's hungry people, the reallocation of a mere 5.6 percent of current food production would wipe out hunger, making an active life possible for everyone. For Indonesia, with the second greatest number of undernourished people in the world, only 2 percent of the country's food supply would make the difference. And in Africa, 7.8 percent of the food supply of Tanzania and 2.5 percent of that of both Senegal and Sudan could meet the needs of the hungry.

This is, we underline, a hypothetical exercise. As the World Bank itself cautions, even though enough food exists, the poor are not able to purchase it.

Thus, even most "hungry countries" have enough food for all their people right now. This finding turns out to be true using official statistics even though experts warn us that newly modernizing societies invariably underestimate farm production—just as a century ago at least a third of the U.S. wheat crop went uncounted. Moreover, many nations can't realize their full food production potential because of the gross inefficiencies caused by inequitable ownership of resources.

Finally, many of the countries in which hunger is rampant export much more in agricultural goods than they import. It is the industrial countries, not the third world countries, that import more than two-thirds of all food and farm commodities in world trade. Imports by the 30 lowest-income countries, on the other hand, account for only 6 percent of all international commerce in food and farm commodities.

Looking more closely at some of the world's hunger-ravaged countries and regions confirms that scarcity is clearly not the cause of hunger.

India. India ranks near the top among third world agricultural exporters. While as many as 300 million Indians go hungry, the country exports everything from wheat to beef and government officials agonize over how to get rid of mounting "surpluses" of wheat and rice—24 million tons in 1985, more than double the entire world's annual food aid shipments in a typical year.

Bangladesh. Beginning with its famine of the early 1970s, Bangladesh came to symbolize the frightening consequences of people overrunning food resources. Yet Bangladesh's official yearly rice output alone—which some experts say is seriously underreported—could provide each person with more than a pound of grain per day, or 2,064 calories. Adding to that small amounts of vegetables, fruits, and legumes could prevent hunger for everyone. Yet the poorest third of the people in Bangladesh eat at most only 1,500 calories a day, dangerously below what is needed for a healthy life.

With about 100 million people living in an area the size of Wisconsin, Bangladesh may be judged over-crowded by any number of standards, but its population density is not a viable excuse for its widespread hunger. Bangladesh is blessed with exceptional agricultural endowments, yet its current rice yields fall significantly below the all-Asia average. The extraordinary potential of Bangladesh's rich alluvial soils and plentiful water has hardly been fully used. If the country's irrigation potential were realized, experts predict its rice yields could double or even triple.

Source: Frances Moore Lappe and Joseph Collins, *World Hunger: Twelve Myths* (New York: Grove Press, 1986), excerpt from pp. 9–12. Reprinted with permission.

Food production is not keeping up with population growth

Lester R. Brown and John E. Young

Projecting future food production was once a simple matter of extrapolating historical trends. But as yields in many countries approach the upper bend on the S-shaped growth curve, this approach becomes irrelevant. The grain outputs of several countries, including China, Indonesia, Mexico, and the Soviet Union, have shown little or no growth since 1984. In addition, land degradation and hotter summers—the former difficult to measure and the latter impossible to project with precision—will shape future production trends.

In one respect, projections are simpler now than in the past. Since the cultivated area is not likely to change appreciably during the nineties, assessing the production prospect becomes solely a matter of estimating how fast land productivity will rise. Historically, the largest gain in world cropland productivity, as measured by grain yield per hectare, came during the six-ties, when it climbed 26 percent over the decade. It rose only 21 percent during the seventies, and an estimated 20 percent in the eighties.

Given the adverse effects of environmental degradation . . . it seems likely that the rise in world cropland productivity will slow further during the nineties. Perhaps as a harbinger of the future slowdown, it increased very little between 1984 and 1989. At this point, it is difficult to know whether this recent plateau is merely a short-term interruption in a long-term trend that will soon resume its vigorous climb, or an indication of how difficult it has become to continue raising land productivity rapidly in countries where yields are already high and in a world where environmental degradation is reducing production potential.

For example, since 1950 U.S. corn yields and West European wheat yields have nearly tripled. In the Third World, wheat yields in India have more than doubled since 1965, and rice yields in China have more than

For example, since 1950 U.S. corn yields and West European wheat yields have nearly tripled. In the Third World, wheat yields in India have more than doubled since 1965, and rice yields in China have more than doubled since 1960. Obviously countries cannot continue doubling and tripling grain yield per hectare every few decades. But what kind of further increases can reasonably be expected? And how quickly will they come?

Trends in land productivity in Japan may help answer these questions. Grain yields there started their long upward climb around 1880, several decades before those in other countries. The world grain yield today, taking into account the wide range of growing conditions, appears to be roughly where Japan's yields were in 1970. For instance, the 1989 rice yield in China, the world's largest rice producer, was an estimated 3.8 tons of milled rice per hectare, exactly the same as Japan's rice yield in 1970. Today, yield per hectare of corn in the United States is nearly double that of rice in Japan in 1970. The yield of wheat in Western Europe is currently a fourth again as high. On the other end of the scale, 1989 rice yields in India were less than half those of Japan in 1970.

Since 1970, Japan's rice yield per acre has risen an average of 0.9 percent per year, scarcely half the 1.7 percent projected annual growth in world population during the nineties. If the world can raise yields during the nineties at this rate, then grain output will increase by 158 million tons, an overall gain of 9 percent. But with world population expected to increase by more than 959 million (18 percent), per capita grain production would fall 7 percent during the decade. If the world cannot do any better over the next decade than Japan has over the last two, in other words, a steady

deterioration of diets for much of humanity and increasing hunger for many of us seem inevitable.

The key question for the nineties is whether the world will even be able to match the Japanese record. Despite the powerful incentive of a domestic price support for their rice pegged at four times the world market, Japanese farmers have run out of agronomic options to achieve major additional gains in productivity. Farmers in the rest of the world—who are not as literate or as scientifically oriented as those in Japan—will find it difficult to do any better.

A deterioration in diet and an increase in hunger for part of humanity is no longer a matter of conjecture. In Africa, both the absolute number of people and the share of population that is hungry are increasing. In Latin America, increasing poverty, declining food production per person, and rising food prices indicate a similar trend. Progress in reducing infant mortality, the most sensitive indicator of a society's nutritional state, has been slowed, stopped, or reversed in dozens of countries.

If the world continues with business-as-usual policies in agriculture and family planning, a food emergency within a matter of years may be inevitable. It would extend beyond low-income people in the Third World, with its repercussions affecting the entire world. Soaring grain prices and ensuing food riots could both destabilize national governments and threaten the integrity of the international monetary system.

Barring any dramatic technological breakthroughs on the food front, the widening of the gap between population growth and food production of the last several years will continue.

4 *Threats to the Environment*

n the introductory essay to *State of the World 1992,* Sandra Postel points to several ominous environmental trends:

- The protective ozone shield in heavily populated latitudes of the northern hemisphere is thinning twice as fast as scientists thought just a few years ago.
- A minimum of 1140 plant and animal species are condemned to extinction each day.
- Atmospheric levels of heat-trapping carbon dioxide are now 26 percent higher than the preindustrial concentration, and continue to climb.
- The earth's surface was warmer in 1990 than in any year since recordkeeping began in the mid-nineteenth century; six of the seven warmest years on record have occurred since 1980.
- Forests are vanishing at a rate of some 17 million hectares per year, an area about half the size of Finland.
- World population is growing by 92 million people annual, roughly equal to adding another Mexico each year; of this total 88 million are being added in the developing world. (Postel, 1992:3).

The magnitude of environmental problems has become so great that the ultimate survival of the human species is in question. Because environmental problems are global, this chapter examines them at both the domestic and international levels. The first section describes the nature of these problems and their consequences. The second focuses on the U.S. case. The third section examines the social sources of these problems and alternative solutions. The final section describes the long-range international implications of environmental problems.

Worldwide Environmental Problems

The earth's **biosphere** (the surface layer of the planet and the surrounding atmosphere) provides the land, air, water, and energy necessary to sustain life. This life-support system is a complex, interdependent one in which energy from the sun is converted into food.

> The mechanisms that supply [human beings with the essentials for life] are **ecosystems**—plants, animals, and microorganisms interacting with each other and their physical environments. The energy that flows through these ecosystems and the oxygen, nitrogen, carbon, and other materials they recycle are the essence of the life-support system within which [5.5] billion people are inextricably embedded. Ecosystems supply civilization with public services both free and irreplaceable. They include regulation of climate and the makeup of the atmosphere, generation and maintenance of soils, control of potential crop pests and carriers of human diseases, pollination of many crops, and provision of food from the sea. Ecosystems supply the nutrients without which we could not survive, and in the process they dispose of our wastes. (Ehrlich and Ehrlich, 1988:916)

These ecosystems are being disturbed profoundly by three social forces. First, the tremendous increase in population increases the demand for food, energy, and other products. As the 1992 world population of 5.5 billion increases to 6.3 billion by 2000, the stress on an already overburdened environment will be increased manyfold.

A second source of the problem is the concentration of people in urban areas, where the air, water, and land cannot absorb their waste and often toxic products.

Finally, environmental problems are the consequence of modern technology and its consumptiveness. Some people have argued that the main source of present environmental problems is the tremendous population growth in the underdeveloped countries, but this is a myth. Of course, the addition of every human being impacts ecosystems, but the effect is uneven, depending on the level of technology.

> While developing countries severely tax their environments, clearly the populations of rich countries leave a vastly disproportionate mark on the planet. The birth of a baby in the United States imposes more than a hundred times the stress on the world's resources as a birth in, say, Bangladesh. Babies from Bangladesh do not grow up to own automobiles and air conditioners or to eat grain-fed beef. Their life-styles do not require huge quantities of minerals and energy, nor do their activities seriously undermine the life-support capability of the entire planet. (Ehrlich and Ehrlich, 1988:917)

These statistics make this point forcefully: the United States has 5 percent of the world's population, yet it uses 25 percent of the world's energy, and it emits, disproportionately, 22 percent of all the carbon dioxide produced in the world. India, on the other hand, has 16 percent of the world's population, but it only uses 3 percent of the world's energy, and it emits only 3 percent of the world's production of carbon dioxide (Elmer-Dewitt, 1992:42–43).

Degradation of the Land

A thin layer of topsoil provides food crops for 5.5 billion people and grazing for about 4 billion domesticated animals. That topsoil is being depleted or lost because of careless husbandry and urbanization. Farm land is lost because of the plowing of marginal lands, leading to wind and water erosion. "Each year, the world's farmers lose an estimated 24 billion tons of topsoil; during the past two decades, they have lost an amount of topsoil equal to that on India's cropland" (Durning, 1991:29). The fertility of farm land is lost because it is exhausted by overuse. It is also lost due to irrigation practices that poison the land with salt, a process called salinization. The result of all of these processes is that fertile land becomes infertile; it becomes desertlike.

> Desertification refers broadly to the impoverishment of the land through overgrazing, overcultivation, deforestation, and poor irrigation practices. Under these pressures, land degrades gradually and insidiously toward a desert-like state.
>
> Each year, desertification claims an estimated 15 million acres worldwide— an area the size of West Virginia lost beyond practical hope of reclamation. An additional 50 million acres annually become too debilitated to support profitable farming or grazing. Hundreds of millions of acres lie somewhere on the degradation continuum, between fully productive and hopelessly desertified. Unfortunately, much of this land is sliding down the diminishing productivity side of the scale. (Postel, 1991:25)

In addition to the degradation and loss of topsoil, productive land is lost through the growth of cities, the building of roads, and the damming of rivers. In the United States, for example, "16 million hectares—more area than the entire state of Georgia—is now under pavement" (Durning 1991:29).

Environmental Pollution and Degradation

The following description of the various forms of pollution present in industrial societies, especially the United States, presents a glimpse of how humanity is fouling its nest.

Chemical pollution. More than 7 million chemicals have been discovered or created by humankind, and several thousand new ones are added annually (Gore, 1992:148). At the world level, the annual production of organic chemicals has risen from 1 million tons in 1930 to 63 million in 1970, and half a billion in 1990 (Gore, 1992:147–148). These chemicals are found in food. They are used in detergents, fertilizers, pesticides, plastics, clothing, insulation, and almost everything else. Consumers are exposed to the often-toxic substances in what they buy, but the danger is more acute for the workers involved in the manufacture of these chemicals.

The manufacture of chemicals requires disposing of the waste. Waste disposal, especially the safe disposal of toxic chemicals, is a huge problem. The amount of toxic chemicals released into the air, water, land, underground, and public sewage, as reported by U.S. corporations in 1990, was 4.81 billion pounds. "Of that, 408.3 million pounds were known or suspected carcinogens; 1.2 billion pounds were known or suspected to cause birth defects" (Kanamine, 1992:13A). See Table 4.1. Typically, corporations choose the cheapest means of disposal, which is to release the waste products into the air and waterways and to bury the materials in dump sites. In one infamous instance, the Hooker Chemical and Plastics Corporation over a number of years dumped 43.6 million pounds of 82 different chemical substances into Love Canal, New York, near Niagara Falls. Among the chemicals dumped were 200 tons of trichlorophenol, which contained an estimated 130 pounds of one of the most toxic and carcinogenic substances known—dioxin. Three ounces of this substance can kill more than a million people. As a result of exposure to the various chemicals dumped at Love Canal, nearby residents had an unusual number of serious illnesses, a high incidence of miscarriages, and an unusual number of children born with birth defects.

The Love Canal dump site is only one of many dangerous locations in the United States. Of the nearly 50,000 dump sites nationwide, some 2,000 have been labeled as potentially dangerous by the federal government and 350 have been documented as sure sources of toxic wastes.

U.S. corporations are also involved in global chemical pollution (see the Observation on Du Pont). They not only dump wastes into the oceans and the air, which, of course, can affect the people in other countries, but they also sell to other countries chemicals (such as pesticides) that are illegal to sell here because they are toxic. In addition, U.S. corporations have used other countries as dump sites for their hazardous substances, because the U.S. government outlawed indiscriminate dumping of toxic wastes in this country in 1975.

In 1988 some 3 million tons of hazardous waste from the United States and western Europe were transported to impoverished countries in Africa and eastern Europe that desperately need hard currency. This is a type of "trash imperialism," whereby the richer countries can push off their problems onto the poorer countries. (Feagin and Feagin, 1990:369)

OBSERVATION

DU PONT: THE WORST POLLUTER OF 1991

Earlier this year, E. I. Du Pont de Nemours & Company began running a television advertisement featuring sea lions, otters, dolphins and penguins playing in their natural environments while Beethoven's "Ode to Joy" plays in the background. The 30-second commercial shows a shoreline and pans the horizon, as the narrator remarks, "Recently, Du Pont announced that its energy unit would pioneer the use of new double-hulled oil tankers in order to safeguard the environment."

Friends of the Earth's Jack Doyle points out, however, that Du Pont's oil subsidiary, Conoco, does not have any double-hulled ships in service and that its fleet will not be double-hulled until the year 2000. And the company has no plans to put double hulls in two of its supertankers, according to Doyle.

The advertisement "is doubly effective, because it doesn't just make us feel good about Du Pont—it makes us feel good about Du Pont the environmental company," Doyle says.

In fact, Du Pont is the nation's number one corporate polluter. According to an exhaustive report issued by Friends of the Earth earlier this year, Du Pont has paid out nearly $1 million in fines, penalties or lawsuit settlements for alleged environmental and public health problems between March 1989 and June 1991. Du Pont reported that it emitted 348 million pounds of pollution in 1989—14 times more than Dow Chemical, 20 times more than Chrysler, and 30 times more than Mobil. The Friends of the Earth report, "Hold the Applause," found that, among the largest 10 companies in 1989, Du Pont had the highest ratio of pollution to profit and the lowest value of sales generated per pound of U.S. pollution.

According to the study, Du Pont has dumped pollutants into the world's oceans, invented chemicals which are now destroying the earth's protective ozone layer, injected millions of pounds of hazardous wastes underground with unknown consequences, produced pesticides that have infiltrated the world's foodstuffs and drinking water, sold lead additives for gasoline in developing countries and lobbied Congress, state legislatures and foreign governments to oppose or weaken environmental measures.

An incident reported earlier this year sheds light on the company's callousness and disregard for human life. The News Journal of Wilmington, Delaware reported that, in its quest to develop a method of dry-cleaning women's clothing, Du Pont exposed volunteers to Freon 113 during early experiments, leading to the death of a company secretary. Du Pont continued the experiments even after the death of 44-year-old Beverly B. Manning, according to documents obtained by the Journal.

But if large megacorporations go the way of the dinosaurs, Du Pont will probably be most remembered for producing chlorofluorocarbons (CFCs), the chemicals which destroy the earth's protective ozone layer. The Environmental Protection Agency estimates that increased exposure to ultraviolet rays brought on by ozone destruction will result in 200,000 additional U.S. skin cancer-related deaths over the next 50 years.

"Du Pont is perhaps most culpable for stringing out the CFC era for its own business reasons and for delaying a shift to safe alternatives," asserts Doyle.

Source: Russell Mokhiber, "Corporate Crime & Violence in Review: The 10 Worst Corporations of 1991," *Multinational Monitor* 12 (December 1991), pp. 12–13. Reprinted with permission from *Multinational Monitor*, PO Box 19405, Washington DC 20036. Individual subscription $25/yr.

Table 4.1 Cancer-causing chemical releases 408.3 million pounds of cancer-causing chemicals were released in 1990. Major releases: dichloromethane, styrene, trichloroethylene.

Top Ten States	Releases/lbs.
1. Texas	42,102,856
2. Indiana	30,460,347
3. Louisiana	28,326,133
4. Pennsylvania	21,864,011
5. Ohio	20,981,940
6. Michigan	18,116,842
7. Illinois	17,850,062
8. California	17,366,655
9. North Carolina	16,986,961
10. New York	12,993,453

Top 10 Companies	Releases/lbs.
1. Monsanto Co.	10,726,650
2. General Electric Co.	10,531,270
3. Hoechst Celanese Corp.	8,391,569
4. Du Pont Co.	6,461,424
5. Foamex L.P.	5,704,827
6. Upjohn Co.	5,245,116
7. General Motors Corp.	5,116,191
8. Dow Chemical Co.	4,916,159
9. Industrial Paper	4,316,407
10. Hickory Springs Manufacturing	4,221,720

Top 10 Facilities	Releases/lbs.
GE Plastics, Mount Vernon, Ind.	4,906,341
Upjohn, Portage, Mich.	4,566,117
Monsanto, Alvin, Texas	3,628,200
PPG Industries, Westlake, La.	3,171,049
Rohm & Haas, Philadelphia	2,866,236
Boeing, Wichita, Kan.	2,803,166
Uniroyal Chemical, Geismar, La.	2,753,759
Rubicon, Geismar, La.	2,714,203
Angus Chemical, Sterlington, La.	2,706,780
Celanese, Bishop, Texas	2,580,458

Source: USA Today, "Cancer-Causing Chemical Releases," (October 1, 1992), p. 13A.
Copyright 1992, USA Today. Reprinted with permission.

Toxic wastes are also exported when U.S. multinational corporations move operations to countries with less stringent environmental laws. For example, the 2000 foreign-owned (mostly U.S.) factories along the U.S. Mexico border in Mexico (Maquiladoras) have created environmental hazards on both sides of the border (Elmer-Dewitt 1991a).

Another problem with toxic wastes is accidental spills from trucks and trains as the wastes are transported. These spills number about 400 a year just in the United States. When these incidents occur, the air is polluted, as is the ground water. Fires sometimes occur along with explosions. The result is that people, animals, and plant life are endangered.

In 1989 agents of the FBI and the Environemntal Agency raided the Rocky Flats nuclear weapons plant in Colorado and found that the contractor (Rockwell) and the Department of Energy had illegally stored, treated, and disposed of hazardous and radioactive waste in violation of the Resource Conservation and Recovery Act.

Finally, the proliferation of chemicals in this century is a fundamental cause of the increase in cancer. "The sharp increase in chemical wastes and contamination over the past few decades is unprecedented in human history. Human beings and their genetic systems have never had to adapt so quickly to so much chemical bombardment" (Feagin and Feagin, 1990:371).

Solid waste pollution. Each day in the United States about 200,000 tons of garbage must be disposed of (about 3.5 pounds for each person). Each year Americans throw away 1.6 billion pens, 2 billion razors and blades, 220 million tires, and 16 billion disposable diapers (Langone, 1989:45). The diapers present a special problem of disposal. They account for 2 percent—3.6 million tons—of the solid waste dumped into U.S. landfills. They are not currently biodegradable, which means that they may be preserved in these landfills for hundreds of years. Moreover, their use means that about 3 million tons of untreated feces and urine end up in landfills rather than in sewage systems, where they would be treated (Day, 1990).

The United States is running out of landfill space. Twenty-seven states expect to run out of space in their landfills by 1995. In 1992 there were about 5,000 landfills, 15,000 fewer than in 1979. As an example of the enormity of the landfill problem, the largest, Fresh Kills Landfill on Staten Island, receives 44 million pounds of New York City garbage *every single day* (Gore, 1992:151). See the Observation on "America's Killing Ground."

The problem of what to do with solid waste is compounded by the increased amounts of waste that are contaminated with compounds and chemicals that do not appear in nature. These wastes pose new and unknown threats to human, animal, and plant life. All landfills leak, seeping toxic residues into the groundwater. Many communities have contaminated drinking water and crops as a result. With the problem clearly becoming serious, some experimentation is now being conducted with landfills that have impermeable linings to prevent such pollution.

There are several alternatives to dumping trash in landfills. The environmentally preferred solutions are for the trash to be reprocessed to its original uses (paper, glass containers, metals) or converted into new products such as insulation (see "Another Society, Another Way" on the excellent program in Japan).

The alternative most commonly selected is to incinerate the garbage. The burning of trash has two major benefits. It reduces the volume of garbage by almost 90 percent, and it can generate steam and electricity. The downside of burning trash is significant. The incinerating of plastics and other garbage releases toxic chemicals, including deadly dioxins and heavy-metal emissions, into the air. The residue (ash) is contaminated with lead and cadmium. Thus, says environmentalist Barry Commoner, what these incinerators produce makes this cure for the garbage problem much worse than the disease (cited in Shabecoff, 1987).

Currently, the United States recycles 10 percent of its trash, incinerates 10 percent, and sends 80 percent to landfills.

Water pollution.   The major sources of water pollution are industries, which pour into rivers, lakes, and oceans a vast array of contaminants such as lead, asbestos, detergents, solvents, acid, and ammonia; farmers, whose pesticides, herbicides, fertilizers, and animal wastes drain into streams and lakes; cities, which dispose of their wastes including sewage into rivers to end up downstream in another city's drinking water; and oil spills, caused by tanker accidents and in offshore drilling. These are problems throughout the world.

Water pollution is a most immediate problem in the Third World. Contaminated water in poor countries results in high death rates from cholera, typhoid, dysentery, and diarrhea. According to the latest data, 1.7 billion people do not have enough safe drinking water. Another 3 billion people are at risk of contaminated water because of improper sanitation (Gore, 1992:110).

In the United States, the Mississippi River provides an example of the seriousness of water pollution. Greenpeace USA, the environmental organization, surveyed pollution in the Mississippi River and found that in 1988 industries and municipalities along the river discharged billions of pounds of heavy metals and toxic chemicals into it. This occurs along the 2,300 miles of the river; the worst pollution is concentrated along 150 miles in Louisiana, where 25 percent of the nation's chemical industry is located.

> The Greenpeace report called the area by its local nickname, the "cancer corridor." Compared to the rest of the Mississippi corridor, the 10 Louisiana parishes where the chemical industry is concentrated "consistently suffered some of the highest rates of mortality from all diseases [and of] cancer deaths and infant deaths." (cited in *Newsweek,* 1990b:77)

OBSERVATION

AMERICA'S KILLING GROUND

U.S. waste brokers and the U.S. federal government believe that they have found the solution to the nation's garbage disposal problem: dumping industrial and household waste on Native American land.

In 1989, Colorado-based Waste Tech Incorporated, a subsidiary of Amoco, approached Dilkon, an isolated Arizona Navajo community with a 72 percent unemployment rate. Waste Tech proposed taking over 100 acres of Navajo land to build an incinerator for burning hazardous waste and a landfill for burying its toxic ash. In exchange, the company promised 175 jobs, a new hospital and a $100,000 signing bonus.

In 1991, the O&G Corporation of Torrington, Connecticut approached the Rosebud Lakota in South Dakota with a proposal to build the largest U.S. landfill on their reservation. The 5,000 acre dump would hold solid waste, incinerator ash and sewage sludge ash.

These types of offers are becoming increasingly common. Since 1990, toxic waste disposal companies have approached more than 50 U.S. indigenous groups, offering millions of dollars in exchange for the right to dump U.S. trash on Native American grounds. The waste companies seek to avoid state, county, municipal and many federal waste-facility operating standards, which do not apply to Native American reservations because of their sovereign status. The corporations also prey on the economic vulnerability of indigenous communities, touting their disposal plans as unique opportunities for "economic development" and increased employment on impoverished Native American reservations—but not mentioning the serious health threats posed by the incineration and storage of hazardous and other wastes.

Instead of working to halt the waste industry's exploitation of Native American communities, the federal government, which has "trustee" responsibility to protect Native American lands, has promoted waste disposal on the reservations. In 1990, for example, the U.S. Department of Commerce awarded a $248,000 minority business grant to a promoter who arranged for a company to bring hazardous waste to an Oklahoma Kaw reservation.

Most disturbing is the federal government's efforts to push nuclear waste on to Native American reservations. The Office of the Nuclear Waste Negotiator, established by the Department of Energy (DOE) in 1987, has solicited every Native Nation in the United States to become an "interim" or permanent recipient of highly radioactive used fuel from nuclear power plants. One of the federal government's many proposed nuclear waste pro-

Pollution of the oceans occurs from wastes dumped into rivers. Thus, industrial wastes, fertilizers, and pesticides flow into the oceans. Winds carry pollutants from cities and factories to the oceans. And, oceans have been used as dumping grounds for ages. The result is that coastal regions, home for 85 percent of the world's fish, are especially polluted.

Jacques Cousteau, the famous oceanographer, says that pollution of the oceans has now

> damaged the ultra-thin membrane on the ocean's surface—called the neuston—which plays a crucial role in capturing and stabilizing the food supply for the tiniest sea organism, phytoplankton, which actually constitute the neuston and which begin the food chain. The consequences of this damage are not yet known, but phytoplankton play a significant role in ocean ecology and in coupling the ocean to the atmosphere. (cited in Gore, 1992:108)

Radiation pollution. Human beings cannot escape radiation from natural sources like cosmic rays and radioactive substances in the earth's crust. Technology has

jects for indigenous lands is the Yucca Mountain Nuclear Waste repository, which is being planned for the Western Shoshone reservation in Nevada, located about 85 miles northwest of Las Vegas. The DOE has allotted $32.5 billion for carving Yucca Mountain into a receptacle for 70,000 metric tons of high-level nuclear waste.

Native Americans are not passively accepting the onslaught against their lands and people, however. Indigenous people throughout the United States have rejected offers from waste companies and ignored overtures from the Office of the Nuclear Waste Negotiator. The Paiutes in northern Arizona, the Kaws in Oklahoma, the Choctaws in Mississippi and Los Coyotes in California have invalidated initial agreements made by tribal officials to accept hazardous waste or garbage. Reservation-wide organizing and education among the Rosebud Lakota led to the rejection of the O&G South Dakota landfill proposal.

The Navajo community group Citizens Against Ruining our Environment (CARE) successfully fought back and forced the cancellation of the Waste Tech toxic waste proposal that had been approved by Dilkon officials in Arizona. CARE continues to work with Native American communities throughout the United States to defend reservations against waste companies and to establish recycling centers.

Non-native U.S. citizens can begin to support indigenous people's rights to self-determination and a clean environment by demanding that their tax dollars no longer be used to peddle nuclear and other toxic waste to Native Americans and by supporting Native American calls for grassroots economic and community development plans. More generally, government, industry and citizens must sharply limit the waste they produce in the first place, and recycle a far greater percentage of what they do create.

As the dangers of waste storage, disposal and incineration are further exposed, indigenous resistance to corporate and government waste facility schemes will continue to build. In the meantime, each incinerator, landfill or toxic storage facility that is built on a reservation poisons thousands of Native Americans and their lands.

Source: "America's Killing Ground," *Multinational Monitor* 13 (September 1992), p. 5.

added greatly to these natural sources through the extensive use of X rays for medical and dental uses, fallout from nuclear weapons testing and from nuclear accidents, and the use of nuclear energy as a source of energy.

The dangers of radiation are evidenced in the extreme in the physical effects on the survivors of the atomic bombs at the end of World War II. These victims experienced physical disfigurement, stillbirths, infertility, and extremely high rates of cancer. In 1986 the most serious nuclear accident to date occurred at Chernobyl in the Soviet Union. The full consequences of this accident will not be known for years, but so far there have been numerous deaths in the Soviet Union and widespread contamination of food and livestock as far away as Scandinavia and Western Europe. The major nuclear accident in the United States occurred at Three Mile Island in Pennsylvania in 1979.

Less dramatic than nuclear accidents but lethal just the same have been the exposures to radiation by workers in nuclear plants and those living nearby. The Hanford nuclear weapons plant in Washington state provides an example. For more than 40 years, the U.S. government ran this facility, monitoring nuclear emissions but not notifying the workers or the 270,000 residents in the surrounding area of the dangers.

> From 1944 to 1947 alone, the Hanford plant spewed 400,000 curies of radioactive iodine into the atmosphere. The bodily absorption of 50 millionths of a single curie is sufficient to raise the risk of thyroid cancer. For years thereafter, Hanford poured radioactive water into the Columbia River and leaked millions of gallons of radioactive waste from damaged tanks into the ground water. . . . Some 13,700 persons absorbed an estimated dose of 33 rads to their thyroid glands [equivalent to about 1,650 chest X rays] some time during the last 40 years. . . . There was no diagnostic or therapeutic purpose. No one told them; there was no informed consent. Some have called this situation a "creeping Chernobyl" but there is a difference. Chernobyl was an accident. Hanford was deliberate. Chernobyl was a singular event, the product of faulty reactor design and human error. Hanford was a chronic event, the product of obsessive secrecy and callous indifference to public health. (Geiger, 1990:E19; see also Ackland, 1990)

Similar situations occurred at the weapons factories at Rocky Flats near Denver, Fernald near Cincinnati, the Savannah River in South Carolina, and at the testing sites for weapons in Nevada and other areas in the Southwest.

The most obvious problem with radioactivity involves the safe storage of nuclear waste. The generation of nuclear power creates radioactive by-products such as uranium mill tailings, used reactors, and the atomic waste itself. The safe storage of these materials is an enormous and perhaps impossible task, because some remain radioactive for as long as 250 thousand years. Neither the nuclear industry nor the government has a long-term technology for safe nuclear waste disposal.

High-level nuclear waste—that which is most radioactive—amounts to a thirty-year total of 17,000 tons. Even though this is "a thimbleful compared to the slag that would result from generating equivalent power by burning coal, [it] threat-

ANOTHER SOCIETY, ANOTHER WAY

JAPAN'S EFFORTS TO CONSERVE

Compared to people in the United States, the Japanese are less wasteful (each Japanese produces 1.9 pounds of trash daily, compared to 3.5 pounds for each American) and they are more serious about reusing and recycling the waste they produce. The United States recycles 10 percent of its trash; Japan recycles 40 percent, including half of its paper, more than half of its glass bottles, and two-thirds of its food and beverage cans. The United States incinerates 10 percent of its solid waste; Japan incinerates 72 percent of what is not recycled. In Japan whatever is not recycled or burned is buried in landfills (24 percent compared to the 80 percent that end up in landfills in the United States).

Japanese communities vary in their regulations concerning trash. One community, Zentsuji, insists that the residents separate trash into 32 categories. Others are less stringent in their demands, but some demands are always made. Since the early 1970s, government officials have strictly enforced mandatory separation of burnable from noncombustible trash. Every Japanese community has access to an incinerator that is equipped with electrostatic precipitators to "scrub" waste gases.

Yet for all its efforts Japan has not conquered its garbage problem. There is still too much waste for this tiny country (in land size) to absorb.

Tokyo and three neighboring prefectures will have an excess of 3.43 million tons of garbage by 2005, and might have to ship it elsewhere. Before that happens, the government will probably promote greater recycling and changes in consumption patterns to reduce the amount of trash that its citizens generate. (Begley, 1989:70).

The 150 miles of the Mississippi River in Louisiana is called the "Cancer Corridor" because of the heavy metals and toxic chemicals dumped into it by the many chemical companies located there.

ens to fill all available storage space at generating facilities, and the U.S. has made little headway in developing a safe final resting place for more of it" (Greenwald, 1991:57). If the United States converted to a nuclear power-based energy system, the radioactive waste generated annually would increase sixfold (*Multinational Monitor,* 1989a).

Air pollution.   Air pollution is a major source of health problems such as respiratory ailments (asthma, bronchitis, and emphysema), cancer, impaired central nervous functioning, and cirrhosis of the liver. These problems are especially acute among people who work in or live near industrial plants in which waste chemicals are released into the air and among people who live in metropolitan areas where conditions such as temperature and topography tend to trap the pollutants near the ground (cities such as Mexico City, Los Angeles, and Denver). The poor are especially adversely affected (see the Observation on Los Angeles).

A University of Southern California study found, for example, that 80 percent of youths who had died as a result of violence, accident, or other nonmedical causes had abnormal lung tissue (reported in Mann, 1990). The pollutants emitted into the air also have extremely serious consequences for the environment; the greenhouse effect and the loss of ozone protection are topics discussed later in this chapter.

OBSERVATION

CLASS, RACE, GENDER, AND AIR TOXICITY IN LOS ANGELES

And as with all destructive byproducts of our society, pollution takes its greatest toll on the poor, on workers and on people of color. Most of the youths in that U.S.C. study were from the inner city; more than half of them were Latino or black. The scientists were careful to point out that contributing to lung disease were factors such as "poor hygiene and poor nutrition which predispose the youth to the harmful effects of frequent viral infections, smoking, air pollution, and other noxious agents." From the point of view of a scientific study, it is necessary to factor out socioeconomic conditions so as to develop a "pure conclusion." But from an organizer's point of view, the interaction between the injuries of class, race and toxicity is what makes the issue so explosive. In L.A., working people often live near freeway exits and on crowded streets, where idling cars pump pollution directly into their lungs. The metal plating and furniture industries, both extremely toxic, are located in Latino and black communities in East Los Angeles, Huntington Park and Watts. The people working in the electronics, oil, chemical, auto, furniture, metal plating and military plants are exposed to the most toxic solvents and chemicals. And while women in these workplaces and neighborhoods are warned about drinking, smoking or using drugs during pregnancy, there is no public outcry against corporate officials who knowingly discharge poisons into the air and directly contribute to birth defects and high infant mortality.

Meanwhile, residents of wealthier neighborhoods closer to the ocean boast of the "breathability" of "their" air—protected by location, lower traffic density and strict residential zoning not enforced in minority areas. Air has become a commodity. As one real estate agent told me, "Air quality is one of the most significant factors that determine property values in Los Angeles."

The County of Los Angeles reflects the demographics of polarization: great concentrations of corporate and private wealth, an inordinately large upper middle class, a rapidly shrinking middle class and unionized working class, and a growing corps of the working poor, the unemployed, the homeless and the criminally employed. This class structure is overlaid with the politics of race. Of L.A.'s 8.6 million people, 3 million are Latino, 1 million are black, 1 million are Asian-American and 3.5 million are white. Presiding over this largest industrial center in the United States is a small white corporate elite.

These facts portend a qualitative social deterioration over the next twenty years. Recently, *LA Weekly* published projections for the year 2010: 10 million people in the county, 5 million of whom will be living in poverty; 500,000 homeless; a two-hour average daily commute; an average freeway speed at rush hour of 15 miles per hour; air quality contributing to 100,000 deaths per year. These projections may be exaggerated, but the trends are not. If class and race contradictions are not resolved we could be seeing a Blade Runner L.A. on the horizon.

Source: Eric Mann, "L.A.'s Smogbusters," *The Nation,* magazine © 1990. This article is reprinted from *The Nation* magazine. © The Nation Company, Inc.

The two major sources of air pollution are emissions from automobiles and from industrial plants (lesser but nonetheless serious sources are toxic waste dumps, burning trash, wood burning, and aerosols). Automobiles, for example, emit four gases implicated in global warming: carbon dioxide, nitrous oxide, chlorofluorocarbons, and ozone smog. The amount of carbon dioxide emitted is directly related to a car's gasoline use (during a car's lifetime, if it averages 18 miles per gallon it emits 57.75 tons of carbon dioxide, compared to 25.93 tons for a car averaging 45 miles per gallon) (*Environmental Action,* 1989:18).

Industrial emissions is the second major source of air pollution in the United States. By 1990 industrial plants and factories were releasing 2.8 billion pounds of

Of all the world's cities, Mexico City has the most polluted air.

poisonous chemicals annually. In 1989 the Environmental Protection Agency cited 205 industrial plants as posing the greatest risks to human health.

Global Environmental Crises

Each form of pollution just described threatens human life. This section focuses on environmental threats to the earth itself. The discussion is limited to three interrelated threats: dependence on fossil fuels for energy, destruction of the tropical forests, and global warming.

Fossil fuel dependence, waste, and environmental degradation. The Industrial Revolution involved, most fundamentally, the replacement of human and animal muscle by engines driven by fossil fuels. These fuels (coal, oil, natural gas) are also used for heating, cooking, and lighting. Their use has increased exponentially.

> History itself is defined by rapid technological evolution. Whereas the planet was home to only a few hundred million human beings at the start of the industrial revolution, it now shelters some five billion people, who occupy around a billion dwellings, drive 500 million motor vehicles and expend much effort to produce a variety of industrial products to further their well-being. Total delivered energy (the amount that reaches the end user—the electricity, say, needed to light a lamp or the natural gas needed to heat a home) rose from the equivalent of about eight million barrels of oil a day in 1860 to 123 million barrels a day in 1985. (Davis, 1990:57)

Put another way, carbon dioxide emissions from fossil fuels, the main villain among the greenhouse gases, has "gone from near zero a century ago to more than a ton of carbon per person [annually] on the planet today" (Durning,

1991:28). In addition, each person in the United States produces an average of twenty tons of carbon dioxide each year (Gore, 1992:146–147).

The industrial nations, of course, are the greatest users of fossil fuels. The average person in a developing country uses the equivalent of 1 or 2 barrels of commercial fuel annually, compared to 10 to 30 barrels per capita in Europe and Japan and more than 40 barrels in the United States (Davis, 1990:58). The United States, for example, has only 5 percent of the world's population, yet it has one-third of the world's cars and drives 50 percent of the total world mileage. To provide for this extravagance, the United States in 1990, at the time of the Iraq crisis, imported 8 million barrels of oil a day (nearly 50 percent of its needs).

The worldwide demand for energy will rise sharply as the developing nations, where 90 percent of the world's population growth is taking place, industrialize and urbanize. People in these countries will be replacing traditional fuels such as wood and other organic wastes with electricity, coal, and oil.

If present energy use trends continue, then world energy consumption is expected to increase by 50 or 60 percent by the year 2010. This trend has important consequences for the world and its inhabitants. First, the demand for fossil fuels has given extraordinary wealth to the nations of the Middle East. At the beginning of 1990, for example, the crude oil reserves in Saudi Arabia, Iraq, Kuwait, United Arab Emirates, and Iran amounted to 740.5 billion barrels, compared to 58.4 billion barrels in the countries that formerly made up the Soviet Union, 25.9 billion barrels in the United States, and virtually nothing in Western Europe and Japan (*Oil and Gas Journal,* reported in Passell, 1990). The primary reason the United States, with the backing of the United Nations, sent troops to Saudi Arabia in 1990 to stop Iraq's attempts to control Kuwait and other oil-rich nations was to keep the oil from the Persian Gulf flowing to the industrialized nations. In short, the maldistribution of the world's energy supply heightens world tensions.

Second, because most nations need to import oil, vast amounts are carried across the world's oceans in about 2,600 tankers. Along with off-shore drilling, these voyages increase the probability of accidents that damage aquatic life, birds, and coastal habitats. Four examples of large-scale spills are the wreck of the *Amoco Cadiz* off the coast of France in 1978, spilling 68 million gallons of crude oil; the blowout of the Ixtoc I oil well, which poured 140 million gallons of oil into the Gulf of Mexico in 1979; the grounding of the *Exxon Valdez* in Alaska's Prince William Sound in 1989, which released 10.5 million gallons of crude oil into an ecologically sensitive region; and the grounding of an oil tanker north of Scotland in early 1993, which dumped 26 million gallons of oil into the North Sea.

Finally, and most important, the combustion of fossil fuels results in the emission of carbon dioxide, which appears to be related to climate change. If, as mentioned, the world's energy consumption increases by 50 or 60 percent by 2010, then carbon dioxide emissions will also increase by 50 or 60 percent. The consequences of the present level of carbon dioxide emissions, plus the expected increase in the near future, may have disastrous consequences for the earth in the form of global warming, as discussed below.

The destruction of the tropical rain forests.   Tropical rain forests cover about 7 percent of the earth's land surface. About 1.9 billion acres of these forests remain in equatorial countries in the Caribbean, West Africa, Southeast Asia, and Latin America. These rich forests are being destroyed at the rate of "one and a half acres a second, night and day, every day, all year round" (Gore, 1992:118). This massive destruction continues to occur because of economics, from the greed of developers to the desperation of poor peasants.

Lumber and mining companies build roads into the jungles to extract their products and transport them to markets. Governments encourage the poor people to settle in these regions by building roads and offering land to settlers, who must clear it for farming. Cattle ranchers require vast expanses for their herds (5 acres of pasture for each head). Land speculators clear huge areas for expected profits. The recovered land, however, is fragile, which leads to a cycle of further deforestation.

> The first step is always a road that opens untouched areas to encroachment. Typically, it is bulldozed in by a lumber company, which removes just one or two valuable tree species. Next down the road are land-hungry farmers who slash the forest and torch it. Fire is the most efficient way to clear a field of debris and pests, and the ash enriches the often poor tropical soil. Crops are abundant for a couple of years, but then the soil loses its fertility, and the farmers move on, often collecting a little money for their tree-clearing efforts from cattle ranchers. They, in turn, use the field for another 7 to 10 years until it is infested with weeds, the dirt hard-packed by hoofs. (Carpenter, 1990:64)

The sources of deforestation are not just local. The poverty of these nations (often the result of their colonial heritage), their indebtedness to wealthy nations, and the products needed by the wealthy nations are also responsible for the destruction of the tropical forests.

> Throughout the tropics, developing nations are struggling to feed their peoples and raise cash to make payments on international debts. Many countries are chopping down their forests for the sake of timber exports. In Central America forests are giving way to cattle ranches, which supply beef to American fast-food chains. (Linden, 1989:34)

The two major environmental consequences of this deforestation are climate change and the vanishing of species. The climate is affected in several related ways. As hundreds of thousands of forest acres are destroyed, rain patterns change. Huge areas once covered with plants, which give off moisture, are replaced by exposed, sandy soils. Also, the massive burning required to clear the land creates clouds of smoke that block the sun and lead to weather change. Thus, lush, green areas often become near deserts. The tropical forest in Brazil (the world's largest) has so much rainfall that it provides 20 percent of the earth's fresh water supply. What will be the long-range effects as this water supply dwindles? Just as important, forests absorb huge quantities of carbon dioxide through photosynthesis. Thus, as forests are diminished so, too, is the earth's capacity to absorb the gas most responsible for global warming. This diminished capacity to process carbon dioxide, changing it into oxygen, leads to changes in the climate and to desertification.

The second critical environmental consequence of deforestation is the loss of animal and plant species. Although these tropical forests cover only 7 percent of the earth's land surface, they are earth's richest factory of life, containing more than half of the world's species of plants, insects, birds, and other animals. As the forests are cleared and burned, species become extinct. One estimate is that the destruction of the tropical forests results in the extinction of 17,500 plant and animal species a year (Carpenter, 1990:65).

Humanity benefits from nature's diversity in many ways. One important aspect is that exotic plants and animals are major sources of pharmaceuticals. For example, Squibb used the venom of the Brazilian pit viper to develop Capoten, a drug for high blood pressure. The yew, which grows in the Pacific Northwest, produces a potent chemical, taxol, which shows promise for curing certain forms of lung, breast, and ovarian cancer. Biotechnology provides the potential to improve agricultural crops by transferring genes from wild plants to domestic crops so that they can be drought-resistant, repel insects, or create their own fertilizers naturally (Linden, 1989). By destroying the forests, we may be eliminating future solutions to disease and famine.

Global warming.   As noted, the burning of fossil fuels and the destruction of the tropical forests contribute to the greenhouse effect. The **greenhouse effect** occurs when harmful gases (carbon dioxide, nitrous oxide, chlorofluorocarbons, and methane)—all products of diverse human activities—accumulate in the atmosphere and act like the glass roof of a greenhouse. Sunlight reaches the earth's surface and the gases trap the heat radiating from the ground. The results, according to the theory, are a warming of the earth, the melting of the polar ice cap, and a significant changing of climate.

Before the Industrial Revolution, forest fires, plant decomposition, and ordinary evaporation released carbon dioxide into the atmosphere, but in small enough amounts to be absorbed by growing plants and by the oceans without noticeable environmental effect. But in the past century or so, human activities, especially the reliance on fossil fuels for internal combustion engines and in smokestack industries, and the use of chlorofluorocarbons to make plastic foam and as coolants in refrigerators and air conditioners, coupled with the destruction of the tropical forests, have increased the prevalence of dangerous gases beyond the earth's capacity to absorb them; hence, a gradual warming.

The evidence supports this view. The earth is now the warmest it has been in the past six thousand years or so. Worldwide, the year 1990 was the warmest year since record keeping began in 1951, and the number of heat waves, droughts, floods, and hurricanes was unusually high. The area of ground covered by snow in the spring of 1990 and the area of ocean covered by ice in the summer of that year were the *least* in the Northern Hemisphere since satellite mapping began in 1973 (Kanamine and Kelly, 1991). Scientists do not debate that the earth is warmer or that carbon dioxide is emitted into the air in ever-increasing amounts, but they do differ on the relationship between the two facts. Some scientists are cautious, arguing that recent warming and dramatic climatic events are random events and part of the natural year-to-year variations in weather. Their caution is countered by the majority of scientists, who are convinced that the magnitude of the greenhouse effect is great and accelerating.

"We're talking about rates of climate change perhaps 100 times faster than at any time in human history," said Stephen Schneider of the National Center for Atmospheric Research. Ecosystems will not be able to adjust so quickly, he said, "and the faster things change, the more likely it is that the impact will be negative." Warned Thomas Lovejoy of the Smithsonian Institution: "There will be no winners in this game of ecological musical chairs, for it will be fundamentally disruptive and destabilizing, and we can anticipate hordes of environmental refugees dwarfing the numbers of the Dust Bowl era or the boat people." (cited in Lemonick, 1989:37)

Sources of U.S. Environmental Problems

The United States has been blessed with an abundance of rich and varied resources (land, minerals, and water). Until recently, people in the United States were unconcerned with conservation because there seemed to be so vast a storehouse of resources that waste was not considered a problem. And as a result, Americans have disproportionately consumed the world's resources. For example, although slightly less than 5 percent of the world's population, people in the United States use 25 percent of the world's oil output each year. This is because we own 180 million cars and trucks and drive some 1,250 billion miles annually, almost as much as all the rest of the world.

Although the perception of abundance may explain a tendency to be wasteful, it is only a partial and superficial answer. The underlying sources of our present environmental problems can be located in the culture and structure of U.S. society.

Cultural Sources   **Culture** refers to the knowledge that the members of a social organization—in this case, a society—share. Shared ideas, values, beliefs, and understandings shape the behaviors, perceptions, and interpretations of the members of society. The dominant ideologies of U.S. society have tended to legitimize or at least account for the wastefulness of Americans and their acceptance of pollution.

The cornucopia view of nature.   Most people in the United States conceive of nature as a vast storehouse waiting only to be used by people. They regard the natural world as a bountiful preserve available to serve human needs. In this **cornucopia view of nature,** nature is something to be used; it is free and inexhaustible. This belief is widespread and will likely persist as a justification for continuing abuse of the environment even in an age of ecological consciousness. Jonathan Turner believes that to turn events around,

it will cost the public money to visualize nature as a common good: Industries will have to pay for their pollution, which in turn will mean that they will raise prices; the federal government will have to engage in expensive monitoring and control of pollution emitted by industries, with the result that federal taxes will be raised; and local communities will have to increase taxes to pay for their pollution and to expand their sewage and garbage treatment facilities. Thus, the belief that nature is a free good may persist for some time as an ideology for keeping prices and taxes down. (Turner, 1977:408–409)

Faith in technology.   There are three basic ways in which human beings can relate to nature. They can view it as a controlling force, thereby submitting to the environment in a fatalistic manner. They can strive to attain harmony with it: People need nature and nature needs people. Finally, they can try to attain mastery over nature.

Most people in the United States regard human beings as having mastery over nature. Rather than accepting the environment as given, they have sought to change and conquer it. Damming rivers, cutting down timber, digging tunnels, conquering space, and seeding clouds with silver nitrate are a few examples of this orientation to overcoming nature's obstacles rather than acquiescing to them. Most Americans, then, view nature as something to be subdued and used.

From this logic proceeds a faith in technology; a proper application of scientific knowledge can meet any challenge. If the air and water are polluted and if we are rapidly running out of petroleum, science will save us. We will find a substitute for the internal combustion engine, create plants that will "scrub" the air by using carbon dioxide as food, find new sources of energy, develop new methods of extracting minerals, or create new synthetics. While this faith may yet be vindicated, we are beginning to realize that technology may not be the solution and may even be the source of the problem.

Scientific breakthroughs and new technology have solved some problems and do aid in saving labor. But often, new technology creates unanticipated problems. Automobiles, for example, provide numerous benefits, but they also pollute the air and each year kill about 50 thousand people in the United States. It is difficult to imagine life without electricity, but the generation of electricity pollutes the air or causes the thermal pollution of rivers. Insecticides and chemical fertilizers have performed miracles in agriculture but have polluted food and streams (and even "killed" some lakes). Obviously, the slogan of the Du Pont Corporation—"Better living through chemistry"—is not entirely correct. Jet planes, while helping us in many ways, cause air pollution (one jet taking off emits the same amount of hydrocarbon as the exhausts from 10 thousand automobiles) and noise pollution near busy airports.

The growth ethic.   Americans place a premium on progress; they dislike the status quo. They tend never to be entirely satisfied. Something better is always attainable. This desire (which is encouraged by the advertising industry) causes people to discard items that are still usable and to purchase new things. Thus, industry continues to turn out more products and to use up natural resources.

The presumed value of progress has had a negative effect on contemporary U.S. life. Progress is typically defined to mean either growth or new technology. Community leaders typically want their cities to grow. Chambers of commerce want more industry and more people (and, incidentally, more consumers). The logic of capitalism is that every company needs to increase its profits from year to year. Thus, we all benefit if the gross national product increases each year. For all these things to grow as people wish, there must be a concomitant increase in population, products (and use of natural resources), electricity, highways, and waste. Continued growth will inevitably throw the tight ecological system out of balance, for there are limited supplies of air, water, and places to dump waste materials; and these supplies diminish as the population increases.

Materialism.   The U.S. belief in progress is translated at the individual level into consumption of material things as evidence of one's success. The U.S. economic system is predicated on the growth (progress?) of private enterprises, which depend on increased demand for their products. If the population is more or less stable, then growth can be accomplished only through increased consumption by individuals. The function of the advertising industry is to create a need in individuals to buy a product that they would not buy otherwise. Consumption is also increased if products must be thrown away (such as nonreturnable bottles) or if they do not last very long. The policy of planned obsolescence by many U.S. companies accomplishes this goal of consumption very well, but it overlooks the problems of disposal as well as the unnecessary waste of materials.

The belief in individualism.   Most people in the United States place great stress on personal achievement. They believe that hard work and initiative will bring success. There is a tendency to sacrifice present gains for future rewards ("deferred gratification"). Many people will sacrifice by working days and going to school at night in order to get a better job. Parents may make great sacrifices so that their children will have the opportunity for a college education or other advantages they never received. In this manner, success is accomplished vicariously through the achievements of one's children.

This self-orientation (as opposed to collective orientation) forms the basis for a number of the value configurations of work, activity, and success mentioned above. The individual is successful through his or her own initiative and hard work. The stress on individualism is, of course, related to capitalism. Through personal efforts, business acumen, and luck, the individual can (if successful) own property and see multiplying profits. Most people in the United States share this goal of great monetary success—the so-called American dream—and believe that anyone can make it. Curiously, people who are not successful commonly do not reject capitalism. Instead, they wait in the hope that their lot will improve or that their children will prosper under the system.

The belief that private property and capitalism should not be restricted has led to several social problems: (1) unfair competition (monopolies, interlocking directorates, price fixing); (2) an entrepreneurial philosophy of caveat emptor ("let the buyer beware"), whose aim is profit with total disregard for the welfare of the consumer; and (3) the current ecology crisis, which is due in great measure to the standard policy of many people and most corporations to do whatever is profitable while ignoring conservation of natural resources. Industrial pollution of air and water with refuse and agricultural spraying with pesticides that harm animal and human life are two examples of how individuals and corporations look out for themselves with little or no regard for the short- and long-range effects of their actions on life.

As long as people hold a narrow self-orientation rather than a group orientation, this crisis will not only continue but also steadily worsen. The use people make of their land, the water running through it, and the air above it has traditionally been theirs to decide because of the belief in the sanctity of private property. This belief has meant in effect that individuals have had the right to pave a pasture for a parking lot, to tear up a lemon grove for a housing development, to put down artificial turf for a football field, and to dump waste products into the ground, air, and water. Consequently, individual decisions have had the collective effect of taking millions of acres of arable land out of production permanently, polluting the air and water, and covering land where vegetation once grew with asphalt, concrete buildings, and Astroturf even though green plants are the only source of oxygen.

In summary, traditional values of U.S. citizens lie at the heart of environmental problems. Americans want to conquer nature. They want to use nature for the good life and this endeavor is never satisfied. In the words of Al Gore:

> One is almost awestruck by our relentless and seemingly compulsive drive to dominate every part of the earth. Always, the unmet needs of civilization fuel the engine of aggression; never can these needs be truly satisfied. The invaded area is laid waste, its natural productivity eviscerated, its resources are looted and quickly consumed—and all this destruction merely stokes our appetite for still more. (Gore, 1992:234–235).

Our individualistic and acquisitive values lead us to resist group-centered programs and humanitarian concerns. Will the energy crisis (and other resource shortages) and the recognition of the peril of continued pollution change our values? Or will we continue to rely on the traditional values for guidance?

Structural Sources

The structural arrangements in U.S. society buttress the belief system that reinforces the misuse of resources and abuses the ecosystem. (The following discussion is adapted from Turner, 1977:410–429.)

The capitalist economy. The U.S. economic system of capitalism depends on profits. The quest for profits is never satisfied: companies must grow; more assets and more sales translate into more profits. To maximize profits, owners must minimize costs. Among other things, this search for profits results in abusing the environment (such as strip mining and the disposal of harmful wastes into rivers), resisting government efforts to curb such abuse, and using corporate and advertising skills to increase the consumption of products, including built-in obsolescence.

This last point needs elaboration. Profits require consumers; growing profits require overconsumption. Corporations use several mechanisms to generate the desire to purchase unnecessary products. Advertising generates hyperconsumerism by creating demand for products that potential consumers did not know they needed. Innovative packaging designs also help to sell products with the size, shape, and colors of the package and its display affecting choices. Another common tactic is product differentiation, where existing products (such as an automobile) are given cosmetic changes and presented to consumers as new. This **planned obsolescence** creates consumer demand as purchasers trade or throw away the "old" product for the "new."

The increased production that results from greater levels of consumption has three detrimental consequences for the environment: more pollution of air and water, depletion of resources, and a swelling of waste products (sewage, scrap, and junk).

That the profit motive supersedes the concern for the environment is seen in the unwillingness of corporations to comply with government regulations and to pay damages for ecological disasters such as oil spills. In addition, the possibility of solving environmental problems is further minimized under a capitalist system because jobs depend on profit of businesses. Economic prosperity and growth mean jobs. Thus, most observers see only a narrow alternative between a safe environment or relatively full employment. The fate of many workers depends on whether companies are profitable. Solving environmental problems appears to be incompatible with capitalism unless ecological disasters occur.

The polity.   As we discuss in Chapter 2, political decisions are fundamentally influenced by powerful interest groups. This bias of the political system is readily seen in government's relatively cozy relationship with large polluters: corporations. Consumer advocate Ralph Nader has provided several illustrations of this upside-down effect (i.e., the benefits accrue to the wealthy few). (The following examples are adapted from Nader, 1970, 1977.)

- Those who define violence are those who perpetuate most of it. The government focuses its attention on the violence that occurs from street crimes but tends to ignore the violence that emerges from the chemical assault on the environment. Much more is lost in money and health through pollution, yet only tangible physical assaults are defined officially as violence.
- Before the liberalization of marijuana laws an individual in some states could get a jail sentence exceeding ten years for smoking pot, yet industrialists knowingly causing smog in a city could be fined just a few hundred dollars a day while they continued to endanger public safety.
- A person who throws a banana peel out of a car window in Yosemite will be fined $25; yet the oil companies responsible for the oil spill in Santa Barbara paid nothing for its cleanup or for restoring the beaches.
- It is a crime for individuals to relieve themselves in Puget Sound but legal for a corporation to do it twenty-four hours a day.
- The size of a business enterprise legitimizes its right to pollute the environment. Suppose you own a fifteen-room house and rent out rooms to six tenants. You employ several people, such as a cook, gardener, and janitor; and to keep costs down, you throw all your garbage and trash into the street. The city officials do not permit this wanton disregard for the welfare of the city and its citizens. You argue, however, that you must keep your costs down in order to contribute to the employment of some of the city's inhabitants. If you are forced to pay for garbage collection or recycling of waste materials, your profits will be reduced and you will have to close down, throwing your few employees out of work. Faced with your threat, the city orders you to desist. The problem is that your operation is not big enough. If you employed thousands of employees, the city would allow you to continue polluting the environment lest thousands be added to the city's unemployed—a clear case of industrial extortion.

These examples illustrate the bias of the law. Moreover, the efforts of the administrative agencies operating under the regulatory laws have been superficial at best. Typically, government intervention has had the effect of administering a symbolic slap on the wrist, and pollution of the environment has continued virtually unabated. The government apparently will not or cannot push the largest and most powerful corporations to do something unprofitable. Not only are these corporations the largest polluters, but they also have a vested interest in the status quo. General Motors and Ford, for example, resist congressional attempts to legislate stricter standards for reducing pollution because the necessary devices add to the cost of automobiles and might curb sales. The government has achieved gradual change, but the powerful automobile industry has consistently responded more slowly than the environmental lobby wanted.

The government, then, has enacted laws to curb pollution, but they are largely ineffective. Turner has listed some of their defects (Turner, 1977:419–420):

- The laws are often phrased in ambiguous language, making prosecution difficult.
- The laws typically mandate weak civil penalties and hardly ever carry criminal penalties.
- The vast majority of the laws do not attack the sources of pollutants after they have been created.
- Many state antipollution laws are enacted with "grandfather clauses" that allow established companies to continue their harmful activities.

The mildness of the pollution laws and their enforcement indicates the ability of the powerful to continue their disregard for people and nature in their search for profits.

The government could take a much firmer stance if it chose to do so. Suppose, as Henslin and Reynolds have suggested, that the situation were reversed: "Can you possibly reverse this situation and imagine the poor polluting the streams used by the rich, and then not only getting away with it and avoiding arrest, but also being paid by the rich through the government to clean up their own pollution?" (Henslin and Reynolds, 1976:220–221). In such a case, how would the poor be treated? The answer is obvious. The powerful would punish them severely and would immediately curb their illegal behaviors. The implication is that whoever has the power can use it for his or her own benefit, disregarding both nature and other people.

Demographic patterns.   The population of the United States is generally concentrated in large metropolitan areas. Wherever people are concentrated, the problems of pollution are increased through the concentration of wastes. Where people are centralized, so too will be the emission of automobile exhausts, the effluence of factories, and the dumps for garbage and other human refuse.

The location of cities is another source of environmental problems. Typically, cities have evolved where commerce would benefit the most. Because industry needs plentiful water for production and waste disposal, cities tend to be located along lakes, rivers, and bays. Industry's long-established pattern of using available water to dispose of its waste materials has caused rivers like the Missouri, Mississippi, and Ohio, lakes like Erie and Michigan, and bays like Chesapeake and New York to be badly polluted.

The ready availability of the automobile resulted in the development of suburbs. The growth of suburbs not only strained the already-burdened sewage

107

facilities but also increased air pollution through increased use of the automobile. The greater the urban sprawl, the greater the smog is.

The system of stratification.   One major focus of this book (and of Chapter 6, in particular) is how U.S. society victimizes the poor. Because of where they live and work, poor people are more susceptible than are the well-to-do to the dangers of pollution, whether it takes the form of excessive noise, foul air, or lead poisoning. Another inequity is that the poor will have to pay disproportionately for efforts to eliminate pollution. As Turner has concluded:

> The affluent are in the vanguard of the ecology movement not only because they are sincerely concerned but also because they can afford to be. It is the poor who are likely to have to pay a greater *proportion* of their limited income in the higher prices and taxes that will inevitably result from an attack on America's ecological problems. Furthermore, since it is likely that much of the money to fight pollution will be taken out of the domestic rather than the military budget, the poor will see many of the programs that directly benefit them cut back under future efforts to clean up the environment. As one ghetto resident cynically observed, "friends of the earth are not the friends of the poor." It is therefore not surprising that the poor have been slow to join the ecology bandwagon; they have much to lose. (Turner, 1977:414)

The bitter irony of the poor having to sacrifice the most to abate environmental problems is that they are not the polluters—the affluent are. The affluent drive excessively; travel in jet planes; have air-conditioned, large homes; consume large quantities of resources (conspicuous consumption); and have the most waste to dispose. Their demand increases economic demand and, concomitantly, industrial pollution.

In summary, the United States is a wasteful, inefficient, and vulnerable energy-centered economy. The natural environment is being destroyed by pollution and waste, primarily because the economic system exploits people and resources. The emphasis on profit requires growth and consumption. Thus, meeting short-term goals supersedes planning to prevent detrimental long-term consequences. Second, we depend on a technology that is wasteful. Third, most people believe in capitalism, growth, and consumption. Finally, population growth increases the demand for products, energy, and other resources.

Solutions to the Environmental Crises

The Probusiness Voluntaristic Approach

The solution advocated by conservatives is based on the premise that if left alone, mechanisms in the marketplace will operate to solve environmental problems. When cleaning up pollution becomes profitable enough, entrepreneurs will provide the services to clean the air, treat the water, and recycle waste. There is a contradiction here, though; the free market approach will not eliminate pollution because companies must maximize their profits. A possible compromise is for the government to provide incentives to industries to curb their polluting activities. These incentives could take the form of tax breaks for the purchase and use of pollution controls or outright grants for the use of effective controls.

The Egalitarian/ Authoritarian Plan

According to its opponents, the business-oriented plan just described has a basic flaw: it lacks overall provision for the whole society. To allow individuals and companies free choice in what to consume, how much to consume, what to produce, and in what quantities is a luxury that society cannot afford in a time of scarcity and ecological crises. Let's look at the two main authoritarian alternatives to solving the problem of pollution.

The government must operate on the premise that pollution is a crime against society and will not be tolerated. This approach entails the enactment of comprehensive laws carrying severe criminal and civil penalties for harming the environment. At the corporate level it means rigorous inspections of companies and prosecution of violators. Moreover, if penalized, these companies must not be allowed to pass the fines on to consumers through higher prices. At the individual level it means inspection of vehicles and homes to enforce compliance with accepted standards.

One obstacle to a comprehensive plan to curb pollution is our federal system of government in which states and communities are free to set their own standards. In principle this system makes sense, because the people in an area should be the most knowledgeable about their situation. However, mining operations along Lake Superior cannot be allowed to dump tailings in the lake on the rationale that having to pay for recycling would reduce local employment levels. Similarly, air pollution is never limited to one locality; wind currents carry the pollutants beyond local borders and add to the cumulative effect on an entire region. Therefore, it seems imperative that the federal government establish and enforce minimum standards for the entire country. Localities could make the standards stricter if they wish. For example, because of its high altitude, Denver has special problems with air pollution. Denver is susceptible to temperature inversions that trap pollutants near the land surface, and automobiles at high altitude emit more pollutants than they would at lower elevations. The city of Denver may therefore want to impose very strict automobile emission standards, just as California has to meet the unusual conditions of its geography.

But while it is easy to list what the government should do, it is also obvious that the implementation of a centralized, authoritarian plan will meet many obstacles and much opposition. Industries, corporations, and communities will resist what will be commonly interpreted as arbitrary and heavy-handed tactics by bureaucrats who do not understand the necessity of profits for maintaining employment and a good local tax base. Will Congress, faced with these pressures, institute a national antipollution program with the necessary clout to be effective? Unless people and their representatives take a more realistic view of the ecological dangers that now exist, Congress will not act.

The Control of Resource Use

To start any effective system, the government must begin by gathering correct information about the extent of natural resource reserves. Currently, government data depend largely on information provided by private firms. Data must also be gathered about the use of the various resources. How much actual waste is there? Can the waste be recycled? What is the turnaround time for renewable resources? Are there alternatives to existing resources? Once authoritative answers to these questions are determined, the government can plan rationally to eliminate waste, develop alternatives, and limit use to appropriate levels.

A rational plan to conserve energy, for example, could include government insistence that new-car fuel economy average 40 miles per gallon (this increase from the current 27 miles per gallon would reduce U.S. oil consumption by 2.8 million barrels a day by the year 2005) (Flavin, 1990); the plan also could include universal daylight saving time, strict enforcement of a relatively low speed limit, the use of governors on automobiles and thermostats, the ban of neon signs and other energy used in advertising, minimal use of outdoor lighting, and a reversal of the current policy that reduces rates for electricity and natural gas as the volume increases. These steps are important, but the key ingredient to conservation is mandatory rationing, which would reduce consumption in an equitable fashion.

Regardless of the plan that is eventually chosen, most people would agree that the waste of energy must be curtailed. Conserving energy will require not only individual alterations of life-styles but also changes in the economic system. Under the current private enterprise system based on profits, corporations seek the profitable alternative rather than the conserving one. In the search for greater profits we have shifted from railroads (the most energy-efficient means of moving people and freight on land), to energy-inefficient cars, trucks, and planes. Instead of using energy-sparing and renewable resources such as wood, cotton, wool, and soap, companies have switched to synthetic fibers, plastics, and detergents made

In a private enterprise system, profits are more important to corporations than the conservation of natural resources.

from petroleum. Barry Commoner has summarized why these changes have occurred:

> The basic reason is one that every businessman well understands. It paid. Soap companies significantly increased their profit per pound of cleanser sold when they switched from soap to detergents; truck lines are more profitable than railroads; synthetic plastics and fabrics are more profitable than leather, cotton, wool, or wood; nitrogen fertilizer is the corn farmer's most profit-yielding input; power companies claim that capital-intensive nuclear plants improve their rate of return; and as Henry Ford II has said, "minicars make miniprofits." (Commoner, 1975:28)

Can the United States continue to operate on an economic system that allows decisions about what to produce and how to produce it to be governed by profit rather than by the common good? The heart of the capitalists' argument, going back to Adam Smith more than two hundred years ago, is that decisions made on the basis of the entrepreneur's self-interest will also accomplish the needs of society most efficiently. This fundamental precept of capitalism is now challenged by the environmental crisis, the energy crisis, and the problems related to them. As Commoner has suggested, "the operative fault, and therefore the locus of the remedy, lies in the design of our profit-oriented economic system" (Commoner, 1975:29).

The exact form that the economy should take in an energy-short and polluted world is a source of controversy. At one extreme are people who believe that

*"And may we continue to be worthy of consuming a
disproportionate share of this planet's resources."*

Drawing by Lorenz; © 1992 The New Yorker Magazine, Inc.

capitalism is the solution, not the problem. Others would demand a socialistic system as the only answer. At a minimum, it would seem that (1) there must be central planning; (2) pollution must be controlled and tightly enforced; (3) the monopoly structure of the energy industry must be broken up (currently, the largest oil companies control the production, refining, transportation, and retail distribution of oil and are the largest owners of coal, uranium, and geothermal energy); (4) there must be mandatory conservation measures; and (5) the government must subsidize efforts to obtain alternative, nonpolluting sources of energy, and the resulting structures should be publicly owned so that the public good, not profit, is the primary aim.

A final problem is that an energy-short world will not continue to tolerate the disproportionate use of energy and other resources by the United States. The possibility of war increases with the growing resentment of have-not nations toward the haves. Heilbroner has used a train analogy to make this point, saying that the peoples

> of the underdeveloped world are aware of the ghastly resemblance of the world's present economic condition to an immense train, in which a few passengers, mainly in the advanced capitalist world, ride in first-class coaches, in conditions of comfort unimaginable to the enormously greater numbers crammed into the cattle cars that make up the bulk of the train's carriages. To the governments of revolutionary regimes, however, the passengers in the first-class coaches not only ride at their ease but have decorated their compartments and enriched their lives using the work and appropriating the resources of the masses who ride behind them. Such governments are not likely to view the vast differences between first class and cattle class with the forgiving eyes of the predecessors. (Heilbroner, 1974:39–40)

At the international level, the United States, along with other developed nations, must seek solutions to the environmental crises facing the planet. This means mandating that the developed countries *reduce* the production of materials that pollute the air, water, and land. This was suggested at the 1992 Earth Summit in Rio de Janeiro, but the United States changed the language so that limits would be *voluntary* rather than mandatory. The United States could also help to fund family planning worldwide to reduce population. But this, too, was resisted by the Reagan and Bush administrations because they did not want government funds used to purchase any birth control technology. The United States must also develop for itself and for other countries environmentally appropriate technologies that will sustain economic progress and be substituted for the ecologically destructive technologies currently in use (see Gore, 1992:317–337). As the United States makes trade agreements such as the ones encouraging free trade with Mexico and Canada, agreements must include standard environmental protections. Similarly, loan agreements must contain environmental protections as a condition to receive monies. Finally, the wealthy nations can help themselves and help the debtor nations by engaging in debt-for-nature exchanges. Many poor nations are helplessly in debt to the rich nations. Presently, many pay the interest (rarely the principle) by cutting down their forests or by farming marginal lands. The creditor nations could reduce debt in exchange for enforceable agreements by the debtor nation to protect vulnerable parts of their environment.

International Implications of Environmental Problems

Environmental problems are not confined within political borders. The oceans, rivers, lakes, and the air are shared by all the world's inhabitants. If a corporation or a nation pollutes, the world's citizens are the victims. If the tropical forests are destroyed, we are all affected. If a country wastes finite resources or uses more than its proportionate share, the other nations are shortchanged.

What will the world be like in fifty years or so? In all likelihood, its population will have leveled off at about 10 billion. The planet will be crowded; the production of enough food and its fair distribution will be problematic. Oil will have been replaced by some other energy source. Unless dramatic changes are instituted, the quality of air and water will have deteriorated greatly and the climate will have been altered. Global warming will have altered climates and flooded low-lying regions.

What should the nations of the world do about environmental crises? One school of thought is pessimistic: the cupboard is almost bare and there is no hope; we must therefore prepare for a world of subsistence living and chaos. At the other extreme, optimists assert that science has always found a solution and will save us again. We cannot foresee now the discovery of new sources of energy, new synthetics, and new processes of recycling wastes. Throughout history skeptics have looked at existing technology and foreseen shortages of items currently in demand. But the future for us may be different, in the sense that we and the next few generations face a future in which the limits of space and resources are reached. Will something yet save us?

The safe prediction is that nations that are now affluent will undergo dramatic changes. Expanding technology will have to be limited because of its demands on precious resources, its generation of harmful heat, and other negative ecological effects. People's freedom to order life as they please—to pave a vacant lot, to have children, to acquire things, to consume fuel on a pleasure trip—will be controlled. The needs of the group, community, society, and perhaps even the world will take precedence over those of the individual. Other values people in the United States hold dear—such as growth and progress, capitalism, and the conquest of nature—will no longer be salient in a world of less space, endangered ecology, and hunger. These values will die hard, especially the choice of individual freedom. No doubt there will be a great deal of social upheaval during the period of transition from growth to stability, from affluence to subsistence. But these changes must occur or we will perish.

The dangers posed by the future require solutions at two levels. At the physical level efforts must be directed to finding, for instance, new sources of energy, methods to increase the amount of arable land, new types of food, better contraceptives, and relatively inexpensive ways to desalt seawater. At the social level there must be changes in the structural conditions responsible for poverty, wasted resources, pollution, and the like. One such target would be to determine ways of overcoming the cultural habits (customs, values, beliefs) that reinforce high fertility, people's refusal to eat certain foods or to accept central planning, and the dependence on growth and technology. New forms of social organization, such as regional councils and world bodies, may be required to deal with social upheavals, economic dislocations, resource allocation, and pollution on a global scale. These new organizations will require great innovative thinking, for it is likely that the dominant modes of the present age not only are unworkable for the demands of an overpopulated planet but also are in large measure responsible for many of our present and future difficulties.

One complicating factor is that, currently, nations tend to focus on national problems rather than on cooperative efforts. Moreover, they are directing their efforts to physical rather than social solutions. They are seeking answers in technological and developmental wizardry. These solutions are important and should not be neglected, but massive efforts should also be directed to finding ethical, legal, religious, and social solutions.

CHAPTER REVIEW

1. The earth's biosphere is disturbed profoundly by three social forces: population growth, the concentration of people in urban areas, and modern technology.
2. Even though population growth, which occurs mostly in the developing countries, has adverse effects on the environment, the population of rich countries are much more wasteful of the earth's resources and generate much more pollution.
3. Chemicals, solid waste disposal, and radiation pollute the land, water, and air.
4. The three major interrelated environmental crises that the earth faces are the burning of fossil fuels, the destruction of the tropical forests, and global warming.
5. The five cultural bases of the wasteful and environmentally destructive U.S. society are the dominant ideologies of (a) the cornucopian view of nature, (b) faith in technology, (c) the growth ethic, (d) materialism, and (e) the belief in individualism.
6. The four structural bases for the misuse and abuse of the U.S. environment and resources are (a) urbanization, (b) the system of stratification, (c) capitalism, and (d) the bias of the political system.
7. The probusiness voluntaristic solution to the environmental crises is to rely on the marketplace rather than on the government. If energy sources are in short supply, prices will rise and two beneficial results will occur: (a) consumption will be reduced among those who cannot afford the high prices, and (b) corporations and individuals will be motivated to search for new sources.
8. The egalitarian/authoritarian solution is based on government planning and control to reduce problems and promote conservation. This solution shares the burdens throughout the social strata. Moreover, it controls consumption to meet societal goals.

9. The worldwide problems of pollution and resource depletion will become more acute in the future because of population growth, urbanization, expanding technology, and the lack of planning by nations individually and collectively.
10. The dangers posed by these critical problems require solutions at two levels: (a) needed at the physical level are discoveries and inventions of nonpolluting technologies and renewable resources; and (b) needed at the social level are changes in the structural conditions responsible for these problems and the creation of new forms of transnational social organizations.

KEY TERMS

Biosphere of the earth. The surface layer of the planet and the surrounding atmosphere.

Ecosystems. The mechanisms (plants, animals, and microorganisms) that supply people with the essentials of life.

Greenhouse effect. When gases accumulate in the earth's atmosphere and act like the glass roof of a greenhouse, allowing sunlight in but trapping the heat that is generated.

Culture. The knowledge (ideas, values, beliefs) that the members of a social organization share.

Cornucopia view of nature. The belief that nature is a vast and bountiful storehouse to be used by human beings.

Planned obsolescence. Existing products are given superficial changes and marketed as new, making the previous product out-of-date.

FOR FURTHER STUDY

Lester R. Brown, ed. *The World Watch Reader on Global Environmental Issues.* New York: W. W. Norton, 1991.

Lester R. Brown, Christopher Flavin, and Hal Kane. *Vital Signs 1992: The Trends That Are Shaping Our Future.* Washington, D.C.: Worldwatch Institute, 1992.

Lester R. Brown et al., eds. *State of the World 1992.* New York: W. W. Norton, 1992.

Center for Investigative Reporting and Bill Moyers. *Global Dumping Ground: The International Traffic in Hazardous Waste.* Washington, D.C.: Seven Locks Press, 1990.

Al Gore. *Earth in the Balance: Ecology and the Human Spirit.* New York: Houghton Mifflin, 1992.

Russell Mokhiber. *Corporate Crime and Violence: Big Business Power and the Abuse of the Public Trust.* San Francisco: Sierra Club Books, 1988.

National Geographic. "Can Man Save This Fragile Earth?" *National Geographic* 174 (December 1988), entire issue.

Scientific American. "Energy for Planet Earth," *Scientific American* 263 (September 1990), entire issue.

Time. "Planet of the Year," *Time* 133 (January 2, 1989), entire issue.

FORUM

CAN MARKET FORCES BE USED TO CONTROL POLLUTION?

No, asserts an editorial in the Multinational Monitor.

In early May, accompanied by great media and corporate fanfare about the wonders of using market forces to control pollution, the Wisconsin Power and Light Company sold "pollution credits"—in effect, a license to spew out sulfur dioxide—to the Tennessee Valley Authority (TVA), an electricity utility serving Tennessee, Alabama and Kentucky. For about $3 million, TVA purchased the right to emit an additional 10,000 tons of sulfur dioxide, the chemical which is the primary cause of acid rain, from the Wisconsin utility.

The deal is the first to be implemented under the pollution credit trading system authorized by the 1990 Clean Air Act. The Act granted plants pollution allowances which set ceilings on the amount of sulfur they will be able to emit after 1995. If a plant reduces its emissions more than is required by the law, it can sell its "extra" emissions reductions—or "unused credits"—to another plant that fails to reduce its emissions to the required level.

The concept was most recently proposed by Dan Dudek of the Environmental Defense Fund (EDF), which pushed the concept with the Bush administration. EDF defends the plan, saying that the emissions trading provision in the Clean Air Act paved the way for a reduction requirement that was tougher than what President Bush would otherwise have agreed to accept. But compromise is often the first step to corruption, and the pollution credits deal advocated by EDF has the potential to do more harm than good for the environment.

Pollution credits serve the interests of polluting utilities, at the expense of consumers, the environment and public health, in several ways:

- Pollution credits undermine positive effects of straight regulation. In the past, when governments mandated lower pollution levels, they forced companies to develop and adopt cleaner technologies because that was the only way to meet the government requirements. Under the credit system, instead of buying smoke scrubbers, companies buy the right to pollute.

- Pollution credits work against the future reduction of emissions. Although credits are not legally property rights, they are effectively property rights that will make further sulfur reductions much more difficult. The government should be constantly moving to reduce emissions, not guaranteeing companies the right to pollute for an indefinite period of time.
- Because allowances are based on past fuel use and emissions rates, companies that were wasteful of fuel and, in some cases, companies that polluted excessively, received the biggest allowances. It is then possible for these companies to profit most by selling credits.
- Cleaner air in Wisconsin comes to mean more pollution in Tennessee. Even if the system does reduce overall sulfur emissions, it allows some companies to continue emitting pollution. Companies that are doing well can afford to buy the right to pollute, and people living around their plants continue to breathe in toxic fumes. A system intended to control pollution should not force a trade-off between reducing acid rain and protecting the general public health.
- Credits were granted to companies in existence at the time of the 1990 Clean Air Act. Since the right to emit pollution has in effect been turned into a commodity, this means that the federal government simply handed over assets of considerable value to these utilities.
- The system does not even stop the acid rain as it is intended to. Even if some companies in a region clean up, others in the area may choose to buy credits to allow them to emit pollution that continues to cause acid rain.

This bad idea is spreading: Southern California has implemented a similar program in an effort to reduce smog-causing emissions; Canada is considering pollution trading for air and water emissions; the United Nations has even tossed around the notion of setting up a global market in which greenhouse gas credits would be bought and sold. The TVA/Wisconsin exchange sets a dangerous precedent.

The Clean Air Act pollution credits program is based on the fundamentally flawed premise that a certain level of pollution is acceptable. As Chris Blythe of Wisconsin's Citizens Utility Board says, "Clean air should be protected, not traded and sold like a used car. What's next—the Los Angeles Police Department trying to buy civil rights credits from Wisconsin?"

The value of human health and the environment cannot be determined by market forces. It is no surprise that the idea plays well with the Bush administration and anti-regulation big business, but an environmental organization like EDF is tainted by pushing a plan which accepts the health and environmental costs associated with pollution.

Most environmental organizations oppose this EDF initiative. U.S. citizens should demand strict limits on polluting sources, much stronger emphasis on pollution prevention, moves toward a total elimination of emissions and the abandonment of a system that turns harmful sulfur fumes into valuable assets. Creating a market in pollution will never clean the air.

Source: "Selling Pollution," *Multinational Monitor* 13 (June 1992), p. 5.

The cities of the United States are in trouble. No other industrial nation has allowed the kind of decline and deterioration that face U.S. urban centers. Most of the social and economic problems discussed in this book are primarily concentrated and have their severest consequences in the city, particularly the largest cities. It is this locale, more than any other, that many of these problems are expanding and intensifying. In this sense, place is crucial to understanding U.S. social problems.

Urban poverty, for example, is especially acute and contributes to and is associated with a host of other city problems. Some problems are a decaying infrastructure, a shortage of affordable housing, homelessness, inadequate public transit, pollution, lack of health care, failing public school systems, and drugs, gangs, and crime. These problems are discussed in the four parts of this chapter: the mugging of U.S. cities, the declining quality of urban life, urban unrest, and urban public policy.

The Mugging of U.S. Cities

Many people in the United States fear being mugged in the city. But individuals are not the only ones who have been mugged. The cities also have been victimized and abandoned since World War II by suburbanization, metropolitan deconcentration, job flight, disinvestment, and the federal government. Thus, the mugging of the city is an apt metaphor for cities in the United States.

Suburbanization

For more than forty years there has been a dramatic population shift in the United States—people moving from cities to the suburbs. Although this shift had begun in some metropolitan areas at the turn of the century or even earlier, it accelerated and became the dominant demographic trend in almost every major U.S. metropolitan area after World War II. Table 5.1 documents the growing suburban percentage of the total metropolitan population, particularly since 1950, for the fifteen largest metropolitan areas in 1980. By 1980, only one of these cities accounted for a majority of the metropolitan population and some major cities were as little as 20 percent of their metropolitan areas (Choldin, 1985:361). The process did not stop in 1980. Between 1986 and 1987, more than 2 million more people moved to the suburbs. During the 1980s, nineteen major U.S. cities lost population and all but seven of them were in growing metropolitan regions (Kemper, 1991:13).

Since it has been predominately upper-middle-class, middle-class, and to a lesser extent working-class Whites who have fled to the suburbs, the process has increased and continues to increase class and race segregation. As suburbs grew and became essentially middle class and White, shrinking central cities were left with a greater proportion of their remaining population who were poor and minority. The suburbanization of the United States has meant the geographic separation of classes and races, particularly of middle-class Whites from poor Blacks.

*This chapter was written by Doug A. Timmer, Department of Sociology, North Central College.

Table 5.1 Suburban percentage of total SMSA population for the 15 largest 1980 SMSAs, 1900–1980

Metropolis	1900	1910	1920	1930	1940	1950	1960	1970	1980
New York**	32.2*	32.4	33.8	36.2	36.1	38.9	47.3	51.2	n. a
Los Angeles	44.9	37.4*	36.6*	40.7*	42.8	46.5	53.2	54.9	55.5
Chicago	18.5	19.1	20.4	24.1*	25.7	30.1	42.9	51.8	57.7
Philadelphia	31.6	31.7	32.8	37.8	39.6	43.6	53.9	59.6	64.3
Detroit	33.1*	24.1	23.9*	28.0*	31.7	38.7	55.6	64.0	72.4
San Francisco	24.5	26.7	28.4	31.9	35.9	45.7	58.2	65.4	68.7
Washington	26.4	25.7	23.5	27.6	31.5	46.8	63.2	73.6	79.2
Dallas-Fort Worth	79.8*	65.8*	54.7*	43.2*	44.1*	44.4*	39.3*	45.7*	56.7
Houston	30.0*	31.9*	25.9*	18.6*	27.3*	36.3*	33.9*	38.0*	45.1
Boston	57.5	58.1	60.0*	64.0	65.1	66.8	73.1	76.7	79.6
St. Louis	30.4	33.4	33.7	40.7	44.3	51.2	64.4	73.7	80.8
Pittsburgh	58.3*	63.7	66.6*	66.9	67.7	69.4	74.9	78.3	81.3
Baltimore	26.6	27.5	18.7*	22.4*	24.6	34.8	47.9	56.3	63.8
Minneapolis-St. Paul	20.4	16.9	15.5*	16.6	19.4	27.6	46.3	59.0	69.7
Atlanta	54.7	43.3	42.4	41.5	45.9	54.5	52.1	69.0	79.1
Mean for all	37.9	35.4	34.0	35.4	37.3	41.4	48.6	54.2	59.9.

* First census following greater than 10 percent territorial annexation by the central city.
** Standard Consolidated Area data.
Source: Based on Muller, 1981, p. 22, with additional data from U.S. Bureau of the Census, 1963, 1970, 1982a.

Today, very high levels of racial segregation persist in most major U.S. metropolitan areas (O'Hare and Usdansky, 1992). Some areas continue to experience increasing levels of residential segregation (Goldsmith and Blakely, 1992; Massey and Denton, 1989). Even when Blacks leave the city they are often resegregated in Black suburbs or in Black neighborhoods in White suburbs (Shannon, Kleniewski, and Cross, 1991).

Middle-class Whites moved to the suburbs for a better place to raise their children, better schools, and less crime. Race played a part in all of motives. "A better place to raise children" often meant a neighborhood with few or no African Americans or Latinos. "Better schools" often meant virtually all-White schools not under court order to desegregate. And "crime" was synonymous with inner-city Blacks for many suburbanites. Those people moving to the suburbs were also attracted to the open space and the prospect of an unattached, single-family dwelling with a yard. This prospect was made more attainable by generally lower real estate costs and lower property tax rates outside of the city.

The exodus to the suburbs was not limited to people. Property taxes moved with them. That broad segment of the population most likely to own property and most likely to pay taxes left the city for the suburbs. And with it went the city's ability to raise revenue for and provide for schools, infrastructure, and other

The exodus to the suburbs involves the movement of people, their taxes, and jobs.

essential city services. The suburbs now had this revenue for their own schools, streets, sanitation, sewers, police, and fire protection as well as for other municipal services.

The other part of the property tax base the cities lost with suburbanization was business and industry. They, too, along with the jobs they generate, moved to the suburbs. There, they could sidestep inner-city minorities and equal employment opportunity and affirmative action mandates. Land was cheaper, as were property taxes and utility rates. Also, unions were fewer and weaker in the suburbs. The suburbs also provided a work site and environment perceived to be safe by the plentiful, skilled white-collar and high-tech workers living in the nearby so-called pink ghetto suburbs. In the end, as the White middle class, business, industry, and jobs fled, suburbanization left the central cities with a poorer population and a reduced tax base to provide the schools, infrastructure, services, and jobs this population needs.

Under these circumstances, inequality between the cities and their suburbs could only increase. As late as 1960, the per capita income of city dwellers was still higher than that of suburbanites—105 percent of suburban per capita income. But by 1980, residents of the nation's 62 largest cities had per capita incomes averaging only 89 percent of those who lived in the suburbs surrounding their cities. And only seven years later, in 1987, city, per capita income was only 59 percent of suburban. In Newark, N.J., the poorest city in the country, residents have incomes only 32.1 percent of their suburban neighbors. (These data are from U.S. League of Cities study reported in Kemper, 1991:14, and from Dreier, 1992:22.)

Suburbanization and the resulting inequality, segregation, and other problems it caused for the central cities were not naturally occurring phenomena.

They were encouraged, supported, and directly subsidized by the federal government, and they profited large developers and corporations.

As Kenneth Jackson's history of U.S. suburbanization, *Crabgrass Frontier* (1985), makes clear, federal government policies and spending shaped consumer choices that pushed people out of the cities and pulled them into the suburbs. The federal government financed the construction of the interstate highway and expressway system, which opened the suburbs to speculation and development and connected them to the city, where many suburbanites still worked. Housing policies implemented by the FHA (Federal Housing Authority) and VA (Veterans Administration) that offered government-insured mortgages—reserved, for the most part, for Whites and the suburbs—facilitated the population shift. So did the availability of federal urban renewal funds. As government supported bulldozers destroyed working-class and lower-middle-class neighborhoods to make way for downtown business development, thousands more displaced residents scattered to the suburbs.

Metropolitan Deconcentration

The kind of dispersal and sprawl of population, retail business, and jobs that suburbanization brings continues to the present. The population of the Los Angeles metropolitan area increased more than fourfold during the past fifty years, but its geographic size increased twenty times. Metropolitan Chicago's population increased only 4 percent over the past two decades, but its geographic area grew by 46 percent. But now the spreading out and deconcentration of metropolitan areas over more land is becoming more extreme. The deconcentration of U.S. metropolitan areas is proceeding beyond the suburbs to what are being called "urban villages" or "edge cities" even more remote from the central cities (see Garreau, 1991). It is to this urban fringe that jobs, particularly the good jobs, are going.

> the locations of the best-paying new jobs are changing radically. These jobs are now overwhelmingly concentrated in obscure crossroads like King of Prussia (Philadelphia metropolitan area), Newport Beach (Los Angeles area), Tyson's Corner (Washington, D.C. area), and Schaumberg (Chicago area). These new suburbs are fourteen, forty, sixteen, and twenty-five miles, respectfully, from the central business district.* (Leinberger, 1992:10)

About one-third of the jobs in major U.S. metropolitan areas are with corporations that export goods and services outside the metro area. These are the highest paying jobs with the best benefit packages. These jobs are in such industries as aerospace, defense, international trade, oil refining, computer software and hardware development, pharmaceuticals, and entertainment. These export jobs create a second type of employment in metropolitan areas—regional-serving jobs. About a quarter of jobs in most metropolitan areas are regional-serving—in finance, real estate, utilities, media, and other professional services. These jobs generally pay less than export jobs but still represent good employment opportunities. The remainder of jobs in metropolitan areas are local-serving. The best of

*Christopher B. Leinberger, "Where Good Jobs Go: Business Flees to the Urban Fringe," *The Nation* (July 6, 1992): 10. This article is reprinted from The Nation magazine. © The Nation Company, Inc.

these include school teachers, police, fire fighters, other municipal employees, and neighborhood doctors and lawyers. The worst include low-wage insecure, temporary, part-time, dead-end work with few or no benefits in retail, clerical, custodial, food service, and private security work. These first two categories of jobs are the ones leaving, or in the case of business expansion and new jobs, not locating in the central city or in the older near-in suburbs. The good jobs are going farther and farther away from the growing proportion of poor and minority persons in the city (see Leinberger, 1992).

> Nearly all new export and regional-serving jobs moved north of Atlanta during the 1980s; the vast majority of low-income, Black neighborhoods are on the south side of town. In Dallas, nearly all new jobs have been created in the north and northwest quadrants of the metropolitan area; the Black and Hispanic populations are concentrated to the east and south. In the Philadelphia metropolitan area, from 1970 to 1990 the number of export and regional-serving jobs that located in the high-income Main Line to the northwest of the city, as well as in the White middle-income areas of lower Bucks County to the northeast and New Jersey to the east, increased by more than 50 percent. The number of these types of jobs in the increasingly Black and Hispanic city dropped by 15 percent over the same time period. In Los Angeles—an extremely complex metropolitan area because of its immense size (more than 14 million people) and because it has more growth paths than other metropolitan areas—nearly all new export and regional-serving jobs were created to the west, northwest and southeast during the 1980s. The largest Black neighborhood, south of downtown, and the largest Hispanic concentration, to the east, are located very close to the center city and quite far from the emerging new job centers in West Los Angeles, Warner Center (northeast) and Newport Beach (southeast).
>
> . . . J.C. Penney, which left midtown Manhattan in 1988 for several temporary sites in near-in suburban Dallas, is now building a campus-style headquarters in Plano, Texas, at the outermost exurban edge of that metropolitan area, twenty-five miles from downtown and eight miles from its current suburban location. U.S. Borax's headquarters (Los Angeles); I.B.M.'s software development facility (Dallas); the R & D facilities for Rohm and Haas, Sterling Drugs and Smithline Beecham (Philadelphia); and Chrysler's new R & D facility (Detroit) have all been built in equally distant, fringe locations.* (Leinberger, 1992: 11–12)

Symbolizing the relocation of U.S. business and industry, by 1992, of the U.S. Big Three automakers, only General Motors had a Detroit address. Ford Motor Company's headquarters were in suburban Dearborn, and Chrysler was moving to Auburn Hills, some 40 miles north of the Motor City (Associated Press, 1992b).

Race and class, as well as the fear of crime, play into the corporate motivation to move to the fringes of urban areas. The perception of many corporations and their employees is that not just the central city, but near-in suburbs as well, are now unsafe and have a large minority work force. Sears and Roebuck's relocation from the Sears Tower in downtown Chicago to Hoffman Estates, thirty-seven miles to the northwest, even twelve miles beyond far-suburban Schaumburg, is a prime example of this perception. Hoffman Estates cannot be

---

*Christopher B. Leinberger, "Where Good Jobs Go: Business Flees to the Urban Fringe," *The Nation* (July 6, 1992): 10. This article is reprinted from The Nation magazine. © The Nation Company, Inc.

reached by public transit, and a number of prominent local realtors have said privately that Sears wants to get rid of its predominantly Black workforce from Chicago's Southside. The move will allow Sears to hire more highly educated workers, mostly White, who live near the 1.9 million square foot campus-style complex. The state of Illinois used taxpayer dollars to subsidize Sears's relocation with lowered land costs, infrastructure and expressway improvements, and tax abatements.

Unstopped, this kind of metropolitan deconcentration to the extreme urban fringe will continue and accelerate the post–World War II middle-class exodus from the central cities and will encourage the same sort of movement out of the near-in suburbs. The results will be fewer jobs and poorer residents in both the city and the older suburbs.

Other Sources of Urban Job Loss

In addition to the jobs that cities have lost to the suburbs and now to the edge cities, there has been a net loss of good-paying and well-benefitted jobs in the wider U.S. economy. Over the past two decades in particular, deindustrialization, the shift from manufacturing to services, and corporations moving their operations outside the United States, have devastated the domestic economy is general and worsened the decline of the cities. These economic charges and their impact on U.S. society are discussed in detail in Chapter 14.

As the business of cities shifted from manufacturing to legal, financial, real estate, and the other service work discussed above, the worst of the local-serving jobs, the low-skill workers—especially those of color in the inner city—were hit hard.

> Low-skilled White men in their 20s saw their annual income fall by 14 percent, after adjusting for inflation, from 1973 to 1989. The annual earnings of White male dropouts in their 20s fell by 33 percent. But Black men in their 20s, at the core of the inner-city employment problem, suffered the most. Their earnings over the same time period fell by 24 percent and by a stunning 50 percent for high school dropouts. (*Business Week,* 1992:40)

According to the U.S. Census Bureau, 14.4 million people in 1990 who worked full-time, year-round made less than $12,195, the amount needed to lift an urban family of four above the federal government's official poverty line (Wartzman, 1992). This figure represents nearly one-fifth of all full-time jobs in the U.S. economy. Meanwhile, federal monies for job programs dropped from $6 billion in 1980 to $4 billion in 1990. As low-wage employment proliferates throughout the U.S. economy, it is increasingly the only kind of employment available to less skilled central city workers.

Often not even low-wage employment is available. For growing numbers of people in the city, there are no jobs. Microchip technology and the electronics revolution have fueled the development of a global economy in which large corporations have little or no loyalty to any particular local or country; they are footloose multinational corporations. Since the early 1970s, many high-wage industries have fled U.S. cities to locate or relocate in places with a more advantageous business climate—lower wages, weak or nonexistent unions, and lax environment laws. Sometimes these places have been suburbs, the urban fringe, or sprawling new metropolitan areas in the Sunbelt states; and often they have been Third World countries, as when GM moves assembly plants to Mexico and Ford to Brazil. This corporate flight has been promoted in the United States by tax policies that encourage business to relocate to new sites rather than to modernize and expand their old plants in the cities. Since 1980, the Fortune 500 industrial companies have cut 3.9 million employees from their payrolls in the United States (Dreier, 1992).

Disinvestment

Systematic patterns of investment and disinvestment have also mugged U.S. cities. Banks, savings and loans, and insurance companies have redlined cities and metropolitan areas—literally drawing red lines on the map and making loans and providing insurance on one side of the line and not on the other. **Redlining** refers to the practice of not providing loans, or insurance in what are deemed undesirable areas. These areas are almost always made up of high concentrations of poor minorities and in the central cities. They are the communities that suffer the consequences of the disinvestment that denies loans to homebuyers, small business entrepreneurs, and real estate developers.

For the most part, the federal government has allowed redlining, even though in 1977, Congress passed the Community Reinvestment Art requiring local institutions to make a fair proportion of their loans in poor neighborhoods and communities in decline. Another federal law, the Mortgage Disclosure Act, mandated

Banks and other investment entities often refuse (redline) to invest in poor areas of cities.

lending institutions to document and make available to the federal government, as well as to their customers, their record regarding investment in poor and decaying areas. But assisted by little or no enforcement of these laws by federal bank regulators, most banks and savings and loans have not responded to the financial needs of these communities. The Observation on the South Shore Bank provides an example of an exception—a bank that has made community development its primary activity.

OBSERVATION

INVESTING IN INNER-CITY NEIGHBORHOODS: SOUTH SHORE BANK

Twenty years ago, the South Shore neighborhood in Chicago, an inner-city bedroom community of approximately 80,000 working-class Blacks, was headed for economic disaster. A downward spiral of redlining, housing deterioration, and slum lording had devastated the once prosperous community, which in 1960 had been completely White and middle class.

Into this demoralized climate stepped four idealistic bankers—three Whites and one Black—who managed to pull off the seemingly impossible. The neighborhood's downward spiral has been reversed to one of growth, without displacing the African American residents of the community. And perhaps most significantly, the process of urban decay was halted while South Shore Bank simultaneously made a profit.

The founders of South Shore Bank call it a combination of "radical values and conservative principles" (Grzywinski, 1991:87). Their conviction was an old-fashioned one—that banks had geographical market areas to which they owed services. Banks, they believed, had a social responsibility to invest in their local communities, even though that investment might entail a slightly higher risk or lesser profit margin. Following through on this principle, residents in the capital-starved South Shore were given priority access to credit and loans by the local bank, fostering a shared social and economic stake on the community. This infusion of capital was not granted without standards, but through prudent loaning practices that rewarded hard work and careful planning but did not unduly and stereotypically penalize those with no credit history or a lack of business experience.

Most of South Shore Bank's loans were made for multifamily dwelling rehabilitation in the neighborhood, since the primary small business in the community was and continues to be residential housing. The targeting of the South Shore neighborhood resulted in the concentration of housing upgrades, so that improved properties fed upon each other, collectively improving each project's odds for success.

Where did the money for these loans come from? In most poorer communities, there is a net savings outflow. That is, residents deposit their relatively meager savings in the local bank, but the bank makes loans in other, less-risky communities. At South Shore Bank, the opposite is the case. A net savings inflow results from money outside the service area coming into the bank, which is then invested locally. "Development Deposits," as South Shore Bank terms them, are marketed to non-South Shore residents who know how their money is being used and can support the bank's social goals without risk by investing in federally insured deposits paying regular interest rates. At the end of 1991, more than 55 percent of South Shore Bank's deposits were from people living outside the South Shore community (Quint, 1992).

South Shore's revitalization has been so successful that other Chicago banks are now competing to make loans there. South Shore Bank has grown from $40 million to more than $200 million in assets and has been profitable every year since 1975. Its loan default rate remains well below the national average (South Shore Bank, 1992).

Source: This essay was written expressly for *Social Problems,* the Sixth Edition, by Kathryn D. Talley, Department of Sociology, North Central College, Naperville, Ill.

The patterns of disinvestment and investment that have resulted from redlining in U.S. metropolitan areas have discriminated by both race and location.

Race. The most significant factor determining the flow of mortgage credit in U.S. cities is the racial composition of a neighborhood. In fourteen metropolitan areas nationwide, in a one year period, banks and savings and loans made on the average three times more loans in White census tracts than in minority census tracts. In New York City, between 1985 and 1986, home loans were seven times more likely to be given to applicants from White neighborhoods than from predominately minority neighborhoods. In a recent seven-year period in Atlanta, five times as many mortgages in predominantly White areas of the city were approved by local banks and savings and loans as were mortgages in Black neighborhoods with the same income level. Another study found the lending ratio in Detroit was three-to-one in favor of White neighborhoods. One Detroit bank preferred White loan applications forty-four to one, in a city that is three-fourths Black. In Denver, an analysis of seven communities showed "a clear and inverse relationship between the percentage of Blacks within a focus area and the amount of residential lending that area received" (Hanrahan and Rankin, 1990:38). Nationwide, Black home mortgage applicants are rejected at savings and loan institutions twice as often as Whites, even when their income level and other indicators of credit are similar. In fact, a study by *The Atlanta Journal* and *The Atlanta Constitution,* the two major daily newspapers in metropolitan Atlanta, has indicated that the home lending rate disparity between Blacks and Whites was greatest in areas where Blacks had the highest incomes. According to the Atlanta study, "In 35 of the 100 [largest metro areas nationwide], high-income Blacks were rejected more often than low-income Whites in at least three of . . . five years" (Hanrahan and Rankin, 1990:38).

Location. Patterns of lending also discriminate with regard to location. Suburbs receive a much greater and disproportionate share of loans than does the inner city. This discrimination, of course, is clearly related to the patterns of disinvestment and investment based on race described above since suburban areas are predominately White and low-income, inner-city neighborhoods are often Black or Latino.

City dollars, inner-city capital, regularly goes to the suburbs. Bank deposits made by inner-city residents in city banks are more likely to be used for home and business loans in the suburbs than in the cities where the need for capital is so apparent. In Baltimore, banks loaned 39 percent more city deposits to suburbs than they did to communities in Baltimore itself. Chicago banks used the deposits of city residents to make 47 percent more loans to the suburbs than to their own urban neighborhood. In Detroit it was 50 percent more (studies reported in Hanrahan and Rankin, 1990).

This sort of redlining, discrimination, and disinvestment ultimately leads to a self-fulfilling prophecy of decline in inner-city neighborhoods. When banks disinvest in a neighborhood, residents and small businesses cannot maintain their homes and property. Without loans, small businesses often fail and the jobs, goods, and services they provide are lost to the neighborhood. Indeed, often the banks themselves are among the businesses that physically leave the community. Disinvestment by banks, savings and loans, and insurance companies also discourages other private investors and government from investing in poor and minority neighborhoods.

The racist myth in the metropolitan United States is, for example, that Black inner-city neighborhoods are rundown because Blacks lack pride and other middle-class values. In reality, they lack capital, not pride and good values. Thus capital is denied to them and to their communities by primarily White-controlled financial institutions.

The inability of poor and minority residents and communities to acquire loans and capital from the private sector of the economy has become even more critical to the decline and decay in the inner city over the past dozen or so years. This is because, beginning in the late 70s, the federal government, as we discuss, began to curtail drastically its investment in cities in general and in inner-city neighborhoods in particular.

Federal Abandonment

We have seen how federal government policies have supported and encouraged suburbanization, metropolitan deconcentration, corporate and job flight, and disinvestment patterns that have contributed to the decline of U.S. cities. Social historian Jacqueline Jones has pointed out how the federal abandonment of the cities has a long history. It began with the intense industrialization of the northeastern and midwestern United States after the Civil War that was allowed to evict farmers and other agricultural workers from the rural South, continued with the creation of wartime (World War II) job opportunities in northern cities and the subsidization of the flight of the predominantly White middle-class from the city to the suburbs, and over the past decade and a half has included huge cuts in dollars and services for the central cities (Jones, 1992).

Federal aid to cities was cut drastically under the Reagan and Bush administrations. In 1980, federal government dollars made up 14.3 percent of city budgets nationwide. In 1992 federal monies accounted for less than 5 percent (Dreier, 1992:22). By 1992, federal assistance as a percentage of city budgets declined to 64 percent below what it was in 1980. Federal aid to cities was cut from $47.2 billion in 1980 to $21.7 billion in 1992 (*USA Today,* 1992a). In 1981, 16 percent of New York City's revenues came from the federal government. Ten years later it had been reduced to only 9.6 percent. In Philadelphia in 1980 about 10 percent of the budget came from Washington; today it is about 4 percent. With federal cuts, Philadelphia lost more than 80 percent of its housing aid and more than 60 percent of its job training funds in the past decade (Kemper, 1991:13; *The Economist,* 1992a:22). Comparable budget figures can be found throughout urban United States, including for both larger and smaller cities.

The Reagan administration eliminated the existing federal revenue sharing program with the cities. Welfare, medical, and other essential social services have been reduced dramatically. Successful urban programs—for public works, economic development, job training, housing, schools, and health and nutrition—have been slashed by more than 70 percent (Dreier, 1992:22).

Initially, state governments were able to provide some of the dollars to cities that the federal government had taken away. But by the mid- to late 1980s, with the economy mired in a deep recession and federal funds to state government also decreasing, states with big cities were increasingly forcing them to go it alone. Facing their fiscal crisis alone and with a shrinking tax base, cities had to cut services or raise taxes—and most had to do both. Raising taxes while closing schools, hospitals, police and fire stations, laying off municipal employees, neglecting health and housing codes, cutting public transit, and postponing infrastructure maintenance and improvements had the effect of encouraging more business, industry, jobs, and middle-class residents to leave the city. This movement, of course, only deepens the budgetary crisis of the downward spiralling cities. And as urban government downsizes, the poor and working-class residents of the city are left to compete for the dwindling resources and services still available.

In a May 8, 1991, television address, Mayor David Dinkins explained New York City's fiscal crisis this way: " 'Our city, like every urban center, has been abandoned in the past decade by the federal government' " (quoted in Kemper, 1991:13). In spite of wide-ranging urban unrest in the spring of 1992 in South Central Los Angeles (discussed later in this chapter), neither the Bush administration nor Congress made any significant commitments to changes in urban policy or increased financial support for our cities. As Republican U.S. Congressman Christopher Shays of Connecticut said, "There's almost a conspiracy of silence between the Democrats and Republicans in Congress and between the White House and Congress not to talk about urban problems." When asked which members of Congress are "good" on the issue of federal support for cities, Frank Shafroth, chief Washington lobbyist for the National League of Cities, replied, " 'There is nobody' " (both quotes in Kemper, 1991:13, 16).

At the level of state government much the same situation exists. As the central cities lose population, jobs, and businesses, they also lose political clout in state legislatures. As the suburbs and edge cities gain these things, they also gain in power. According to Alan Rosenthal, director of the Eagleton Institute of Politics at Rutgers University, " 'Everybody agrees that it's important to help the cities, but when push comes to shove [state legislations] are out for their districts and their constituents [and] the view of . . . suburban legislators is that it doesn't do any good to dump money into the cities' " (in Kemper, 1991:14)

Not surprisingly, given all of the ways U.S. cities have been and continue to be mugged, U.S. Senator Bill Bradley recently concluded, "America's inner cities are now poorer, sicker, less educated, and more violent than at any time in modern memory" (cited in Kirkland, 1992:40).

The Declining Quality of Urban Life

Urban Poverty

In the past fifty years poverty has shifted from a primarily rural phenomenon to an urban one. In 1959, for example, 56 percent of poor people lived in rural areas and small towns, 27 percent in the cities and, 17 percent in the suburbs. By 1985, the situation was much different: 43 percent of the poor were in the central cities, 28 percent in the suburbs, and 29 percent in rural areas and small towns (Goldsmith and Blakely, 1992:46).

This increasing urban poverty is even more concentrated in the nation's largest cities. Typically, as these cities lose population overall, the proportion of poor people increases (Adams, Duncan, and Rogers, 1988:90–91).

Urban poverty is also becoming more concentrated geographically and by race. Neighborhoods in which at least one in five households live below the official poverty line are designated by the federal government as "poverty areas." In 1975, 10.8 percent of the Whites in these areas were poor, as were 29.1 percent of African Americans. By 1989, 31.7 percent of Whites and 42.8 percent of Blacks living in these poor neighborhoods were living below the poverty line (Goldsmith and Blakely, 1992:47).

Child poverty is also concentrated in U.S. cities. While the overall child poverty rate hovered around 20 percent at the end of the 1980s, the poverty rate for children in cities grew from 24.9 percent in 1979 to 28 percent in 1989. Between 1980 and 1990, in 100 cities with at least 100,000 residents, child poverty rates increased significantly in 84 of them. Almost half of the children in 2 cities, Detroit and Laredo, Texas, lived below the poverty line (Associated Press, 1992c).

Metropolitan areas with the *highest* poverty rates tend to have the largest proportions of poor people crowded into high poverty areas. As we have seen, poverty areas are census tracts in which at least one in five households is poor; in high-poverty areas, however, at least two of every five households are below the official poverty line:

> . . . Cities with the greatest concentration of poor people in such isolated districts include New York, Chicago, and Philadelphia: each had more than 100,000 poor people in high-poverty tracts in 1980. While these three cities, together with Newark and Detroit, had the largest increases in concentrated poverty, the phenomenon was widespread throughout the country's big cities. (Goldsmith and Blakely, 1992:47)

Most important, the growing concentration of poor people in central cities is occurring in the context of two overall trends in U.S. poverty. First, both the poverty rate and the number of poor people are on the rise. According to the U.S. Census Bureau, 14.2 percent of people in the United States were below the poverty line in 1991, which was higher than the rate five years ago, ten years ago, fifteen years ago, twenty years ago, even twenty-five years ago. The actual number of poor people in 1991, 35.7 million, was higher than in any year since 1964, when President Johnson and the federal government declared war on poverty (*Denver Post* Wire Services, 1992).

A second trend is that the poor are getting poorer. According to the Center on Budget and Policy Priorities, in 1979, 32 percent of all poor people lived in families with incomes that were below half of the poverty line. Ten years later, in 1989, more than 38 percent of those living in poverty were in families with incomes this low (in *All Chicago Focus,* 1990:3). These overall trends in poverty in the United States are discussed in greater detail in Chapter 6.

Urban poverty and race.   For many people, cities and urban have become metaphors or euphemisms for race. The media, for example, have increasingly equated cities with poor Blacks and Latinos. This, of course, is not the whole truth.

Not all Blacks and Latinos live in cities. Not all Blacks and Latinos are poor. Neither are all Whites middle class and living in the suburbs. Some are poor and living in the central city. Nevertheless, people of color are more likely to be impacted by poverty in United States cities. For example, about three out of five poor Blacks and poor Latinos live in central cities, whereas only one out of three poor Whites reside there (Eitzen and Baca Zinn, 1993:274).

People of color are also more likely to be concentrated in so-called poverty areas in the city. In 1989, 40 percent of poor Whites who lived in central cities were concentrated in poverty areas, but 71 percent of poor Blacks in central cities lived in this kind of neighborhood. Between 1970 and 1980 the number of poor Blacks in high-poverty areas grew by 58.6 percent while the number of poor Whites living in those sorts of areas increased only 1.6 percent (Goldsmith and Blakely, 1992:48). People of color are also much more likely to be among the poorest of the poor. The increase over the past decade in the proportion of poor people who fell into the poorest of the poor category hit Black children particularly hard. In 1979, 38 percent of all poor Black children lived in families with incomes below half the poverty line, but by 1989, half of all Black children lived in families that poor (*All Chicago Focus,* 1990:3).

Urban poverty, race, and segregation.   Not only are poor Blacks and Latinos highly concentrated in poverty and high-poverty areas, but they also comprise a large proportion of the urban poor. In 1989, for example, Blacks accounted for 42 percent of all the poor people in central cities and 56 percent of all the poor in central city poverty areas. Throughout the 1980s and into the 90s, at least one-third of all Blacks living in central cities were poor (Goldsmith and Blakely, 1992:48, 52).

Matching the high rates of Black central-city poverty are extremely high rates of residential segregation. High proportions of Blacks live in overwhelmingly racially segregated neighborhoods. Analysis of 1990 census data for twenty-five large metropolitan areas has shown little or no change in levels of residential racial segregation when compared to 1980 (O'Hare and Usdansky, 1992). And again, some metropolitan areas actually became more racially segregated during the 1980s. Even when statistics show declining segregation, it is usually more apparent than real. Neighborhood racial change at any given time may produce a better mix of Blacks and Whites in a particular neighborhood. Most times, however, this does not indicate stable, long-term, voluntary integration. It more likely indicates a nearly all-White neighborhood in the process of becoming a virtually all-Black one. Although data may show 50 percent Blacks and 50 percent Whites, the figures usually reflect involuntary integration and the fact that all Whites have not yet been able to flee.

> Not only are Blacks in our largest cities disproportionately likely to share tracts with other Blacks, they are very unlikely to share a tract with any Whites at all. Moreover, if they go to the adjacent neighborhood, or to the neighborhood adjacent to that, they are still unlikely to encounter a White resident. These agglomerations of monoracial tracts are densely settled and geographically restricted, comprising a small portion of the urban environment closely packed around the center city. (Massey and Denton, 1989:389)

Estimates based on preliminary 1990 census data for the nation's ten largest cities confirm extreme or hypersegregation. In Chicago, 71 percent of Blacks live in virtually one-race census tracts where at least 90 percent of their neighbors are also Black. In Detroit, 61 percent of Blacks live in this kind of racially segregated area. In Philadelphia, 53 percent do. New York City, Washington, D.C., Atlanta, Dallas, and Houston also have very high proportions of Black residents similarly isolated and segregated. New York, Philadelphia, and Detroit actually become more racially segregated between 1980 and 1990 (Goldsmith and Blakely, 1992:49–50). Other data indicate that metropolitan areas in which Blacks make up a larger proportion of the population in general, and the minority population in particular, are the most racially segregated. This includes the metro areas of Detroit, Cleveland, St. Louis, and Chicago. The metro areas with the lowest levels of segregation are Los Angeles-Long Beach, San Francisco, Oakland, Denver, San Diego, Phoenix, Anaheim-Santa Ana, Seattle, and Riverside-San Bernardino. These areas tend to have larger percentages of Hispanics and Asians, but smaller Black populations (O'Hare and Usdansky, 1992).

In reality, even the extremely high levels of segregation reflected in census tract data underestimate racial separation and isolation. Racial segregation is even more severe when smaller units, like immediate neighborhoods and blocks, are analyzed. High levels of segregation in residence and housing also lead to segregation in schools, churches, and other neighborhood institutions.

This means that not only are the urban poor a growing proportion of all poor people in the United States, but also that a growing proportion of the urban poor are racially segregated in poverty and high-poverty areas in the central city. Racial segregation contributes to and perpetuates poverty because it isolates poor people from the educational and economic opportunities they need. The schools, as we discuss below, in racially segregated, poor Black communities in the inner city are separate but *not* equal. The poor people living in the poorest, racially segregated central city neighborhoods are disconnected—both socially and physically—from urban labor markets. Most adults in high-poverty areas do not have jobs. In 1980, three-quarters of the adults in these areas were out of the labor force altogether; only 20 percent had jobs. Only 38.1 percent of families in high-poverty areas had earnings; 61.1 percent received public assistance (see Goldsmith and Blakely, 1992: 51–52). Because these areas are disproportionately made up of racially segregated Blacks, it is clear that antipoverty efforts must include the desegregation and racial integration of U.S. metropolitan areas.

The Urban Housing Crisis

Low-income and affordable housing in U.S. cities is dwindling. The sources of this shrinkage are recent trends in the urban housing market that affect both the affordability of existing housing and the supply or number of low-income units.

One trend is the concentrated ownerships of retail housing in U.S. cities. In both New York City and Houston, for example, 5 percent of all landlords control more than half the rental housing stock. In Boston, only twenty individuals own 40 percent of the city's rental units (Gilderbloom, 1991:31). Urban rental housing is increasingly controlled by a decreasing number of large owners who cooperate in and through landlord management firms and formal and informal professional associations and groups. In such groups, they are able to reduce competition and ensure rising and higher rents. In this way urban housing affordability is negatively affected, particularly for the poor and working class (Gilderbloom and Appelbaum, 1988).

Poor people living in the poorest, racially segregated central city neighborhoods are disconnected—both socially and physically—from urban labor markets.

Another factor reducing housing affordability and the supply of low-income housing units in urban areas is that private developers and builders, throughout the 1970s and 1980s, tended to invest only in middle-class and luxury housing, where the market provided the highest margins. In many cities, this exclusively middle-class/luxury focus led to considerable overbuilding of this kind of housing. Relatively high vacancy rates, however, do not solve the housing problems of the people who simply cannot afford middle-class or luxury rents and prices. Nevertheless, developers and owners often profited more, because of higher margins, from less than full upscale middle-class developments than from full low- and moderate-income ventures. This private real estate investment included both condo conversion and gentrification.

Condominium conversion involves taking rental units and turning them into apartments for sale. This process often displaces people who cannot afford a down payment and do not qualify for a home mortgage with more affluent residents who can and do. **Gentrification** typically includes buying up older and sometimes run-down properties in poor and working-class neighborhoods and rehabilitating them into middle-class condominiums, townhouses, single-family dwellings, and upscale lofts and apartments. Often, the original residents are displaced because they are unable to afford the increased rents, purchase prices, and property taxes based on the neighborhoods' rising property values. The National Urban Coalition found displacement of low- and moderate-income families in two-thirds of the gentrified neighborhoods it studied (National Urban Coalition, 1978). Research by Phillip Clay (1979) found displacement in 80 percent of the fifty-seven gentrifying neighborhoods he studied in thirty cities. And, as in so much of the rest of urban life, Clay found that race played a role in this displacement. Before gentrification, about half the neighborhoods had been predominately Black. After gentrification, 80 percent were dominated by Whites; only 2 percent were predominately non-White.

The redevelopment of the downtown areas in many U.S. cities during the past decade and a half has also led to the loss of significant numbers of low-income housing units. As the economy moved from manufacturing to services, many big city downtowns were remade as financial, real estate, legal, and retail centers. Building often boomed on the fringes of the old downtown areas and in the process destroyed most of the SROs (single-room occupancy hotels) in many cities. SROs had historically provided housing for economically marginal single persons in the city. Although apartments were small, and occupants often had to share a bathroom or a kitchen or both, the units were affordable and available for this part of urban population. Now, the SRO is becoming a thing of the past. Since 1973, Chicago has lost 70 percent of its SRO units. The figures are comparable for New York, and the losses have been significant in other large cities (see Hoch and Slayton, 1989).

Slumlords have also contributed to the housing shortage in the inner city. Slumlording occurs when landlords buy properties in poor neighborhoods and have no intention of investing in their upkeep and maintenance. Slumlords often fail to pay utility and property tax bills as well. Over time, serious housing code violations develop, roofs leak, stairways deteriorate, plumbing fails, and electrical wiring becomes dangerous. Often the utilities are turned off and tenants are left without water, gas, electricity, and heat. Finally, the city must condemn the building, evict the residents, and take it over for nonpayment of back taxes. With few city funds available for rehabilitation, the building stands vacant and is boarded up. All along the way, of course, slumlords collect as much rent as they can from their poor tenants.

Another urban housing market phenomenon that adds to the housing crisis in some cities is **warehousing,** when urban real estate speculators withhold apartments from the housing market. Speculators buy up buildings and gradually empty them by not renting the units. They hold the property until approaching developers on the edges of gentrifying areas become interested and purchase them for considerably more than their original cost. Developers, of course, are especially attracted to warehoused apartments, which spare them the trouble of getting rid of poor and working-class tenants who will not be able to afford the newly gentrified property.

Failed housing policies. All of the forces in the urban housing market that have led to the shrinking supply of affordable and low-income housing have been met with, or encouraged by, failing government housing policies.

As early as the 1960s, federally financed urban renewal projects were bull-dozing low-income housing in poor and working-class neighborhoods. In theory, federal urban renewal funds were meant for the rehabilitation and redevelopment of decaying urban neighborhoods. In practice, what usually happened was quite different. Cities applied for the federal funds and when they received them used their legal powers of eminent domain and other powers granted them under both federal and state urban renewal legislation to declare an area to be blighted. Once so designated, all structures were eliminated in the area. Often, this was done to facilitate the development of public projects like airports and colleges or universities, medical centers, or even private commercial projects on the now available land (see Hirsch, 1983). The second phase of federal urban renewal was to include replacement housing for people who lost their home or apartment and neighborhood. For the most part, however, funds were never appropriated for this phase, and urban renewal projects continued to reduce the supply of low-income housing throughout the 1970s. Much of the housing stock lost was in fact blighted, but for many people, it was at least an affordable place to live.

More recently, rollbacks in public housing have further reduced the supply of low-income housing in the cities. During the Reagan and Bush administrations, federal housing funds were cut by 70 percent (Dreier, 1992:21). In the face of the urban housing crisis of the 1980s, the Reagan administration slashed federal housing assistance for low- and moderate-income families by 85 percent (Feagin and Parker, 1990). Federal monies for low- and moderate-income housing dipped from $32.2 billion in 1981 to $6 billion in 1989 (Eitzen and Baca Zinn, 1993:275). Federal dollars to finance construction of new low-income housing units were reduced from $4 billion in 1981 to only $400 million in 1987 (Feagin and Feagin, 1990:395).

New construction of low-income housing by the Department of Housing and Urban Development (HUD) decreased from 183,000 units in 1900 to 28,000 in 1985. Presently, the department plans to sell to private interests—referred to as the privatization of public housing—or to demolish 100,000 low-income public housing units over the next five years. Previous commitments for about 250,000 new federally financed low-income units have been cancelled. Growing waiting lists for public housing have forced two-thirds of cities with public housing authorities to stop taking new applications (Gilderbloom, 1991:30–31). By the late 1980s, 800,000 families who had qualified and applied for low-income housing could not get in. There were only 17,000 vacant public housing units in the entire country. Many of these were boarded up and uninhabitable due to HUD's failure to provide adequate maintenance funds. The average wait for an available public housing unit in U.S. cities is now more than a year (Feagin and Feagin, 1990:395). In some cities the wait can be much longer. In Chicago, for example, some Chicago Housing Authority public housing projects have waiting lists as long as twenty years.

These recent cutbacks in public housing in the United States come on top of an already meager public housing sector. When compared to the industrial democracies of Europe, for example, U.S. public housing makes up a small share of the total housing stock. In England and other European nations, urban public housing often accounts for as much as 40 percent of all housing. In the United States, only 1.3 percent of the housing stock is publicly owned. Throughout Europe there has been a more widespread recognition that the private housing market, housing for profit, will not adequately house all parts of the population. Therefore, a larger share of the housing stock, as compared to the United States, has been provided by the not-for-profit or public sector.

In European industrial democracies public housing has been for middle-class as well as for poor and working-class residents. In U.S. cities, public housing has been the housing of last resort for the poorest of the poor only. In 1988, the average tenant's annual income was only $6,539 (Dreier, 1992:20). Only about 6 percent of U.S. households who qualify for low-income housing assistance get it from the government (Gilderbloom, 1991:31). And only one-fifth of the poor live in government-subsidized housing of any kind, be it public housing run by local government, privately owned projects subsidized by HUD, or private apartments where tenants pay rent with government vouchers (Dreier, 1992:21). Hence, with only the poorest of the poor inhabiting it, public housing has remained low on the U.S. political agenda.

No federal program has ever reached more than a fraction of the urban households in the United States that need housing assistance. Government expenditures have never provided the decent, safe and sanitary housing guaranteed all Americans by the Housing Act of 1949. Instead, government housing policy and funds were designed to make the provision of low- and moderate-income housing profitable for private developers, builders, and landlords. The government could have chosen, as was done in much of Europe, to provide this affordable housing by building, owning, and managing it itself. Rather than do this, U.S. housing policy has relied on subsidizing the private sector to provide low- and moderate-income housing that the market was not otherwise providing. This approach has proven to be inefficient, ineffective, costly, and a contributing factor in the dwindling supply of low-income housing in U.S. cities.

When subsidizing private developers is the mechanism relied on for low-and moderate-income housing, a permanent, public, not-for-profit stock of affordable units is not developed. The running out, buying out, and corruption of federal HUD mortgages to private builders and developers illustrate this. Typically, HUD makes something like a twenty-year low-interest loan available to private interests to build a low-income apartment complex. For the duration of the loan, the owners are required to rent a percentage of their units at below market rates to low- or moderate-income households. The problem with this arrangement became apparent in the 1980s, when a number of these developments built in the 1960s now were able to rent all units to middle-class households at market rates because the mortgages were paid off. In this way, federal dollars spent on the provision of low-income or affordable housing now could claim fewer units. HUD mortgages run-out in this way.

Some developers buy out their loans early with the same effect. Instead of taking twenty years to repay the loan, developers may pay them off in five or ten years, thus freeing their units to be rented at market rates to the middle-class even earlier. In this way, private real estate ventures may use low-interest government loans to develop housing without any real commitment to long-term affordable shelter for poor or working-class households. This situation is made worse by the high potential for corruption whenever public monies are used to subsidize the private housing market. For example, throughout the 1980s, when already meager HUD dollars for low-income housing assistance were often diverted to politically connected real estate firms that were given an exemption from the federal law requiring a percentage of their units be rented to low-income renters or that simply used federal dollars to develop middle-class townhouses and even golf courses and country clubs.

Another problem is that government housing policy in the United States is heavily biased toward the middle-class and above. About 60 percent, or about $50 billion, of all federal housing subsidies currently go to the homeowning middle- and upper-middle class. Most of this subsidy comes in the form of tax shelters: local property tax deductions and home mortgage interest payment deductions. Sixty percent of these tax shelters go to U.S. families in the top 20 percent income bracket. The poor, on the other hand, receive a total of only about $15 billion in government housing subsidies. In 1990, middle-class homeowners received approximately $47 billion in tax subsidies, but HUD spent only $9 billion on low-income housing programs (Gilderbloom, 1991:31; *The Economist,* 1992a:24). Canada does not allow this kind of subsidy for middle- and upper-class homeowners and, not coincidentally, does a much better job of housing low-income residents in its cities.

U.S. housing policies have also contributed to the **jobs/housing mismatch.** What little affordable low-income housing there is in U.S. metropolitan areas is kept out of the suburbs and urban fringe. Suburbs and edge cities have used legal, political, and economic means to prevent this kind of housing from being built in their communities. The problem with this is that job growth, as we have seen, is occurring on the remotest edges of metropolitan areas. Thus, people who need the jobs the most, the poor in the central city, were the farthest from them. The jobs are located where the inner-city poor cannot afford to live. The poor are also the least likely to be able to afford to own a car, and public transit systems rarely extend to the extreme urban fringe. An example of this jobs/housing mismatch is the construction of the new Denver International Airport. At a cost of $3.1 billion, it is currently the largest construction project in the United States. The new airport is twenty-eight miles from downtown Denver. There is no public transportation to it. The New Airport Employment Office has reported that more than 4,000 poor people have applied for the relatively high-paying construction jobs, but only 600 have been hired because getting to the job requires a car (McBean, 1992).

Before job growth became concentrated in the urban fringe it was centered in the closer-in suburbs. Although low-income residents of the central city were unable to afford housing in these communities as well, their proximity allowed more of them to hold jobs in these locations. This has changed dramatically with more and more metropolitan deconcentration, and many exurban areas and edge cities are experiencing a labor shortage while growing numbers of central city residents go without jobs.

Because it better increases the property tax base, and hence, revenues, city and state economic development policies and practices have tended to support and encourage both market trends and public policies that favor middle-class residential and commercial development at the expense of low-income and affordable housing.

Consequences of the urban housing crisis.   Trends in the urban housing market together with failed housing policies have had, and continue to have, predictable consequences for a growing number of urban households.

One consequence is that more and more households are experiencing a rent squeeze. By 1990, the amount of tenants' income going for rent had reached a record level. More than half of all tenants were paying rents that exceeded the federal governments definition of affordable housing—not more than 30 percent of household income (upped from 25 percent during the 1980s). More than one-quarter of all renters now devote more than one-half of their income to rent. Since 1970, rents have tripled, while tenants' income has only doubled (Gilderbloom, 1991:30). When urban residents, particularly poor urban residents, have to pay more for housing, they have less money available for food, transportation, education, and health care.

Fewer and fewer families can afford to buy a home. This makes the rent squeeze even worse by flooding the rental market with more renters, thereby putting another upward pressure on rents. During the 1950s, roughly two-thirds of U.S. families could have afforded the average-price new single-family dwelling without spending more then one-quarter of their income on the house. By 1970, the proportion of all families who could do this had dropped to about one-half. And by the early 80s, fewer than one in ten families could afford the average new house without spending more than one-quarter of their income on it. Throughout the 1980s the foreclosure rate on home loans increased dramatically, and defaults on home mortgages have reached record highs in recent years (Feagin and Feagin, 1990:396, 398).

Many people are squeezed out of the urban housing market altogether. There have been significant increases in urban homelessness each year since the late 1970s. Estimates of the number of homeless persons in the United States now range as high as 4 to 5 million. Here, too, the problem is most concentrated in big cities—there are probably many more than 100,000 homeless persons in New York City, 90,000 in Los Angeles, and as many as 60,000 in Chicago.

The number of urban homeless persons will increase because of the even larger number of near homeless and ill-housed persons and households in U.S. cities. Many urban dwellers are on the edge of homelessness. Many are paying too great a portion of their income in rent and are only one personal tragedy, or financial disaster, or job loss from being without shelter. Many are presently living doubled or tripled up with other people, often in public housing. Across the country it has been estimated that more than 3 million families are now living doubled up, including more than 300,000 in New York City (Kozol, 1988). Millions more are ill-housed—in unsafe, unsanitary housing conditions without heat, electricity, and working plumbing. A recent study in Chicago found one in ten households living with these sorts of major code violations, as well as others like leaking roofs, chipping lead paint, and toxic asbestos insulation (Timmer, Eitzen, and Talley, forthcoming).

The near homeless in U.S. cities, if present trends in both public housing and the urban housing market are allowed to continue, will become tomorrow's homeless. Within fifteen years, according to MIT professor Phillip Clay, "the gap between the total low-rent housing supply (subsidized and unsubsidized) and households needing such housing is expected to grow to 7.8 million units" (quoted in Appelbaum, 1989:7). This would entail the loss of affordable housing for roughly 19 million people (Timmer, Eitzen, and Talley, forthcoming).

Decaying Infrastructure

The fiscal crisis of the cities has also impacted them physically. The urban infrastructure is crumbling. Old water mains regularly erupt in the winter. Streets are marred with potholes. Clogged and overburdened expressways deteriorate. Sewer systems are decaying and overstressed. Public transit stations, subway tunnels, and rail and trolley tracks all make mass transportation less efficient as years go by without needed maintenance. The U.S. Department of Transportation has rated 40 percent of all U.S. bridges, many in the oldest cities, as structurally deficient or functionally obsolete (Dorning, 1992).

The U.S. Department of Transportation has rated 40 percent of all bridges in the U.S. as structurally deficient or functionally obsolete.

The United States has fallen far behind Europe and Japan in maintaining its urban infrastructure. The U.S. Conference of Mayors recently released a report, *Ready to Go,* that identified more than 7,200 public works projects on hold because U.S. cities lack the funds for them (Dreier, 1992:23). The American Society of Civil Engineers has estimated it would take $50 billion spent over the next ten years just to bring New York City's public infrastructure up to a state of good repair (Dorning, 1992). In the past two years, Chicago has witnessed the flooding of its Loop (downtown) from the Chicago River into old and unmaintained leaking underground railway tunnels, causing more than $1 billion in damage and lost business revenue; millions of dollars of damage, injuries, and deaths from the explosion and fire coming from outmoded and unmaintained gas mains in a Northwest Side residential neighborhood; a malfunctioning drawbridge over the Chicago River between the Loop and the exclusive Gold Coast commercial area on North Michigan Avenue, again resulting in huge retail sales losses as many potential customers were blocked in their efforts to shop there.

Many economists now believe that investing public dollars in a job-creation program to rebuild the nation's infrastructure and a much needed and expanded mass transit system are the best ways to revive the sluggish U.S. economy. According to the U.S. Conference of Mayors, these projects could create nearly 420,000 jobs within the next year (Drier, 1992:23).

There is a strong link between declining infrastructure and declining economic growth and productivity in the U.S. economy. Overburdened and deteriorating expressways, closed bridges, moratoriums on new connections to sewer systems straining beyond capacity that stop new construction, congested airports—all have real economic costs. Studies by economist David Aschauer indicate that a pattern of less spending on public works in cities leads to declines in economic growth. Aschauer has found that the current low levels of infrastructure spending first occurred around 1968, just before the persistent pattern of slow economic growth and declines in productivity that prevail now began. Furthermore, Aschauer believes that as much as half of the drop in productivity growth in the U.S. economy in the last two decades can be attributed to deterioration of the infrastructure, much of it in the cities. He also estimates that each dollar invested in public infrastructure today improves national economic productivity about four times as much as a dollar invested in new plant or equipment by private companies (see Dorning, 1992).

Transportation, Pollution, and the Environment

The urban transportation system in the United States, again in contrast to most European cities, is dominated by the private automobile. In 1940, public mass transit accounted for about 30 percent of all passenger miles—a measure of transportation use defined as one person traveling one mile—in urban areas. By 1970, public transit was used for only 6 percent of passenger miles, and by 1983 this figure had fallen to less than 3 percent (Shannon, Kleniewski, and Cross, 1991:154–155). The United States ranks number one in the world in cars per capita and also in using cars rather than public transportation (Shapiro, 1992: 159–161).

This was not always the case. As late as the 1930s, U.S. urban areas had a fairly diverse transit system. But by 1949, General Motors Corporation had replaced more than 100 electric transit systems—trolleys and trains—in 45 cities with gas-driven buses. This occurred in places like New York City, Philadelphia, Baltimore, St. Louis, Oakland, Salt Lake City, and Los Angeles, among many others. In April 1949, a federal jury in Chicago convicted General Motors of conspiring with Standard Oil of California and Firestone Tire to replace electric transportation with gas- and diesel-powered buses and to monopolize the sale of buses and related products (gas, oil, and tires) to local transit authorities. In most instances, these corporations accomplished this by creating a holding company and buying up the electric transportation systems. General Motors was fined $5,000. H. C. Grossman, treasurer of General Motors and chief engineer of the campaign, was fined $1. General Motors continued the practice into the 1950s (Liazos, 1982).

Between 1936 and 1955, the number of operating trolley cars in U.S. cities dropped from 40,000 to 5,000. Between 1945 and 1970, cities and states spent $156 billion constructing hundreds of thousand of miles of roads, but only 16 miles of subway were built in the entire country during the same time period (Liazos, 1982).

To a large extent, the auto-dependency of U.S. cities was created by powerful oil and auto lobbies. These corporate interests sometimes literally tore up city mass transit systems and shaped federal, state, and local legislation to develop the highway system instead of railroads and subways.

Consequences of auto dependency. The development of the auto-dependent urban transportation system was responsible for the suburbanization and deconcentration of metropolitan areas. Highways, interstates, expressways, and cars helped to gut the central cities, taking away middle-class taxpayers, jobs, business, and retail and commercial activity. As auto dependency sprawls and decentralizes urban areas, a vicious cycle of more cars and highways sets in. Mass transit is less expensive, most energy efficient, and most cost-effective under conditions of high density. Urban neighborhoods, where population is high and dense, require fewer stops and stations, less track, and fewer train and subway cars and buses to move large numbers of people efficiently. The auto-reliant transportation system that has aided the deconcentration of U.S. cities has contributed to lower densities in suburban and urban fringe areas. These lower densities remove many of the energy, environmental, and cost advantages of urban mass transit and lead to the construction of more and bigger highways with more cars, further decentralizing metropolitan areas.

The reliance on the private automobile at the expense of mass public transportation also further disadvantages the urban poor. Unable to afford owning and operating a car, they must rely on an underfunded and often undependable public transit system with limited service. We have seen the problems many poor and working-class central-city residents have getting to jobs in the suburbs and edge cities.

The decentralization that comes with auto transportation has destroyed the landscape and encouraged the spread of commercial strips, shopping malls, and multilane roads and streets. It has also led to increasing congestion and perhaps most critical of all has polluted the air that urbanites breathe.

According to the Road Information Program, 40 percent of U.S. major urban roads are congested (*USA Today,* 1992b). The proportion of urban interstate highways that are congested during rush hour rose from 23 percent in 1975 to 45 percent in 1990 (Dorning, 1992). This congestion has significant economic cost. Traffic jams add to the shipping cost of goods with added wages paid to drivers, more fuel used, and larger inventories maintained to meet customer orders (Dorning, 1992).

Cars and trucks stuck in traffic burn more gasoline and thus pollute the air more. The air over urban areas is still dirty and toxic, with particulate, lead, and carbon monoxide, still pouring from gas engines. Automakers still resist higher miles per gallon standards. The federal government is still slow to implement higher air quality standards, and during the Reagan and Bush administrations, even cut mass transit funds to cities. The continued growth in traffic has cancelled out much of the effectiveness of pollution control attempts by states and cities. Perhaps most important, the federal Environmental Protection Agency (EPA) has not enforced the federal Clean Air Act provision, which withholds federal funds for new highway or industrial construction in urban areas that do not comply with the air quality standards required by the Act (Shannon, Kleniewski, and Cross, 1991:163, 208). Recently, however, the EPA has served notice on the metropolitan areas where auto emissions are the highest and air quality the farthest from conforming to federal law. Although there may have been some improvement in air quality and smog levels in medium-sized cities, more than 86 million people still live in areas that do not meet national standards. Most of those people live in the largest cities—Los Angeles, Chicago, Boston, Atlanta, Washington, and New York City (Saker, 1992).

Other environmental threats in the central city.   The air is not the only source of the environmental pollution concentrated in urban areas. Illegal dumping, lead paint poisoning, and abandoned hazardous waste sites also plague the central city. Low-income neighborhoods, especially those with predominately minority populations, are home to a disproportionate share of the nation's polluted sites (Swanson, 1992; Bullard, 1990). This pattern suggests a perception among corporate polluters that poor minority residents will be less likely to have the organized political clout to resist the environmental degradation of their neighborhood; that they either won't, or can't, fight back.

Evidence of **environmental racism** abounds in urban areas. For example, a recent investigation by *The Chicago Reporter* (see the Observation on environmental racism), a publication focusing on the issues of race and poverty, found that:

- One of the five worst concentrations of toxic waste in the United States is on Chicago's South Side. Of the city's 162 toxic hot spots recorded by the EPA in March 1992, 99 are in postal ZIP code areas that are at least 65 percent minority. All but one of these spots are on the predominately African American South Side.
- In 1989, five of the six Chicago ZIP code areas with the highest levels of toxic releases by industry were at least 78 percent minority.
- Of the ten community areas in Chicago with the highest incidence of lead poisoning among children, all were at least 70 percent minority. Of 485 individual cases of lead poisoning studied by the Chicago Department of Health, 94 percent were minorities.

OBSERVATION

ENVIRONMENTAL RACISM: A TOXIC DOUGHNUT

No matter which way the wind is blowing, unpleasant odors waft through Altgeld Gardens, a housing project on Chicago's Southeast Side. To the west, the coke ovens at Acme Steel Co. spew benzene and other poisons into the toxic mix. To the south is suburban Dolton's municipal landfill; to the east, the CID Corp. landfill, owned by Waste Management Inc., processes garbage and hazardous waste. To the north, near 130th Street and Stony Island Avenue, beds of sewage sludge are spread daily at a Chicago Metropolitan Water Reclamation District facility.

"We live in a toxic doughnut," said Hazel M. Johnson, one of about 8,000 residents in the all-black project, ironically nicknamed "The Gardens."

Only four Chicago landfills take hazardous wastes, all on the far Southeast Side: Paxton Land Fill Corp., at 122nd Street and Torrence Avenue; Land & Lakes Co., at 12200 S. Stony Island Ave. and 13416 S. Indiana Ave.; and CID Corp., at 138th Street and the Calumet Expressway.

But landfills are only the beginning of the story. The area has been a regional dumping ground for at least a century. The old company town of Pullman, now a Chicago neighborhood, once dumped its waste on the spot where Altgeld Gardens now stands. Aging industries have long poured pollution into the air, and closed and rusting factories hide hazardous waste piles, drums and tanks, leaking toxic contents into the ground.

The federal EPA monitors sites where hazardous wastes have been dumped or stored through its Comprehensive Environmental Response, Compensation and Liability Act Information System.

In March, Chicago had 162 hot spots on the CERCLIS list—99 are in ZIP codes that are at least 65 percent minority. ZIP code 60608, which includes parts of the West Side, tops the list with 14 sites. The area is 81 percent minority. There are 13 sites in ZIP code 60622, which includes West Town and is 73 percent minority.

The Southeast Side has 42 sites. ZIP codes 60617 and 60628, which include South Deering and Pullman, each have 12 hot spots. 60617 is 82 percent black and Latino; 60628 is 95 percent black.

The EPA can order a cleanup for the worst toxic waste sites, paid for by the Superfund, an environmental endowment financed by industry and government.

Because Chicagoans drink Lake Michigan water instead of ground water that may be contaminated by toxic dumps, the city has been ineligible for Superfund money. EPA officials said they plan to reevaluate the Chicago sites, but have set no specific timetable.

Source: Linc Cohen, "Waste Dumps Toxic Traps for Minorities." *The Chicago Reporter* 21:4 (April 1992):6. Reprinted by permission.

- Illegal dumping disproportionately affects the city's minority neighborhoods. Twenty-four city wards (out of a total of 50) that are 65 percent or more minority account for almost 80 percent of the tonnage of illegally dumped garbage in the city (all findings in Cohen, 1992).

As a result of how race and class determine where urban areas dump their waste, people of color are twice as likely as Whites to live in counties with the highest levels of industrial toxins. People of color are also twice as likely to live in counties with the highest mortality rates from all diseases. They are three times as likely as Whites to live near one of the largest toxic waste dumps in the country, and 50 percent more likely to die from acute exposure to hazardous material outside of their home (Goldman, 1992:349).

Environmental racism extends beyond the pollution of particular urban neighborhoods to the federal government's attempts to control it. Although the EPA found in January 1992 that minority communities face a disproportionate number of environmental problems from *all* types of pollution, they have enforced environmental laws and standards less vigorously there (Associated Press, 1992c). An investigation by *The National Law Journal* has revealed that the EPA consistently levies lower fines on polluters in minority communities (reported in Goldman, 1992). Fines in minority communities have averaged about one-fifth of the fines in White communities for violations of the hazardous waste law. The study also confirms that the EPA is slower to put toxic waste sites in minority communities on the federal government's Superfund clean-up priority list. And more frequently than in White neighborhoods and communities, the EPA chooses to contain waste rather than treating or removing it from minority neighborhoods. This racist response is perhaps best symbolized in the nation's capitol, where the federal government has spent $1 billion to clean up the Potomac River as it rolls through the complex of U.S. government buildings and only 3 percent of that amount on the highly polluted Anacostia River in the impoverished Black neighborhood of Southeast Washington, D.C. (Goldman, 1992).

As poor minority communities are illegally dumped on and find themselves on top of more and more toxic and hazardous wastes, waste management corporations scramble to locate their incinerators and disposal facilities in these neighborhoods. This often places these impoverished communities in the position of choosing between at least some kind of economic development and their collective health. Recently, for example, poor Black suburbs to the south of Chicago, some of the very poorest suburbs in the country, have had to choose between jobs that come with incinerators and/or toxic waste dumps and their own health and well being.

Health and Health Care

Health and health care problems in U.S. society are discussed at length in Chapter 13. But here, these problems in urban locations deserve special attention because some health and health care problems are more concentrated in large cities.

Because poverty is concentrated in the central city, so is the disease that goes with it. Poor people in the city get tuberculosis and other diseases almost unheard of among the middle class. They are much more likely to die of cancer. Low birthweights plague poor children in the inner city and reduce their chances for survival. Chronic conditions, like diabetes, often go untreated. Many of the urban poor, without health insurance of any kind, cannot afford to burden their families with the hugh debt that life-saving technologies would bring.

Infant mortality rates are highest in poor minority neighborhoods in the inner city and are as high or higher than in many Third World countries. Infant mortality among inner-city Blacks is presently on the rise. In Bedford Stuyvesant and Harlem in New York City, 21 out of every 1000 babies die before their first birthday. That rate is more than twice the U.S. average and three times the Canadian rate. It is the same as the infant death rate in Malaysia and Chile (McNish, 1991; Munoz, 1991).

Many poor inner-city children who survive their first year are then threatened by such diseases as measles, tetanus, polio, tuberculosis, diphtheria, and whooping cough. In New York City, in 1990, for example, only 40 percent of children had received the recommended vaccinations against these diseases by age two. According to the World Health Organization and the United Nations Children Fund, 76 percent of the children in El Salvador, 77 percent in Uganda, and 98 percent of the children in North Korea and Cuba had been vaccinated against all of these diseases by age one (Lee, 1991).

Perhaps more than any other disease, tuberculosis is associated with poor living and working conditions and thus is a good indicator of the overall level of urban health. During the 1970s, tuberculosis rates steadily declined, continuing the trend of several decades. But in the 1980s, this trend reversed. Tuberculosis began to resurge, particularly in poor minority neighborhoods in New York City, Los Angeles, and Chicago. By 1990, the tuberculosis rate in these three cities was one-third higher than it had been in 1980 and was three times the national average (Fordham Institute for Innovation in Social Policy, 1991). Making the situation worse was increasing evidence that in these cities strains of tuberculosis were developing that are resistant to the antibiotic drugs historically used to control the disease.

Tuberculosis is a highly contagious disease that requires immediate detection and treatment. This, however, is often not the case in poor inner-city neighborhoods. One study found that 83 percent of 181 tuberculosis patients discharged from Harlem Hospital in New York City in 1988 were lost in follow-up and did not continue in treatment (reported in McCord and Freeman, 1990).

Other research has established that asthma deaths have recently been increasing at an alarming rate in poor Black communities in the central city, and that rates of sexually transmitted diseases are highest in these same places (Jones and Capitanini, 1992; Capitanini, 1991). Many pockets of the highest overall mortality rates in the United States are found in poor minority communities in the inner city (McCord and Freeman, 1990).

Many of the poor in the central city lack access to adequate medical care. Eric Munoz, medical director of a public hospital in Newark, New Jersey, puts it this way:

> Compounding the problem is the lack of access to primary care for many minorities. Those of us in the medical field sense that the ghettos are growing larger and the health problems becoming worse. Data from the Secretary of Health and Human Services concerning minorities support this decline. None of the Great Society programs of the 1960s have succeeded. As Harlem, Watts, and other inner-city areas continue to grow, a new wave of hopelessness, disease, and suffering is striking millions of Americans. (1991:29)

Many poor and working-class central city residents have seen their small neighborhood or community hospitals close under the pressure of rising costs. For many, the number of indigent non-paying patients became too high a proportion of their total number. This has happened in at least six Chicago communities over the past five years, for example. Other city hospitals have begun to turn away patients who are uninsured and/or cannot pay the prevailing charge for medical treatment they require. More than one in ten U.S. hospitals are now routinely refusing to treat those people (Jacobson, S., 1992).

This means that more and more central city residents are unable to find any medical care in private for-profit or private not-for-profit hospitals and clinics. Increasingly they have only one alternative—the large, underfunded, understaffed, underequipped public hospital that cannot legally deny them care. These facilities are being overwhelmed by the number of patients and the cost of treating them. Because they are unable to afford doctor visits or are unable to find doctors who will accept the lower fees of Medicaid (the state and federal government's insurance program for the poor), patients are coming to the emergency room sicker and in need of more costly care. But the urban public hospitals are less and less able to provide adequate care.

Urban public hospitals are forced to practice triage—treating the most urgent emergencies first. Other patients must wait, sometimes for days.

Many private hospitals that have remained open have done so by cutting high-cost services. Many have closed emergency rooms and trauma units. Trauma networks, for example, have collapsed in Chicago, Detroit, Los Angeles, Miami, and San Diego. In Chicago, ten hospitals have left the city's trauma network in the last five years, leaving only two private hospitals with a trauma center in the third largest city in the country. High-risk obstetrical care and drug and alcohol abuse treatment programs also have been shut down. As private hospitals in the city abdicate these high-cost services, more of them must be taken over by public hospitals, increasing their burden with more patients and higher costs. Cook County Hospital in Chicago estimates that it will treat at least 1000 more nonpaying trauma victims this year than last—at a cost of roughly $10 million (Frankel, 1991).

Another urban problem adding to the burden of public hospitals is AIDS. The National Centers for Disease Control in Atlanta has confirmed that the incidence of AIDS, the numbers of AIDS victims, and the costs of caring for AIDS patients are all highest and most concentrated in central cities. Again, a disproportionate share of the cost has been passed on to the urban public hospitals. The annual and lifetime cost of treating an AIDS patient is higher in the United States than anywhere else in the world—$38,000 a year, $102,000 over the life span (Altman, 1992). In addition, there are the treatment costs for HIV-infected persons who have not yet developed AIDS. Many of the AIDS and HIV patients who come to urban public hospitals, of course, are not paying patients.

In short, the increasing number of uninsured and underinsured persons seeking health care in the emergency rooms of public hospitals, the lack of federal government support for these hospitals, and the inability of city governments caught in a budgetary crisis to fund them all ensure that without major reforms urban health and health care can only deteriorate further.

Urban Schools

Public schools in the United States are separate and unequal. Nowhere is this more evident than in the nation's largest metropolitan areas. Education critic and reformer Jonathan Kozol, after spending considerable time in both urban and suburban schools, noted the "remarkable degree of racial segregation that persisted almost everywhere" Kozol, 1991:2), especially outside of the deep South. Most city schools he visited were 95 to 99 percent non-White. In St. Louis, Chicago, New York, New Jersey, Washington, D.C., and San Antonio he found the same pattern. The more affluent middle class has moved to the suburbs, where their children attend virtually all-White schools; or if they have remained in the city and can afford it, they send their children to private schools. The less affluent and racial minorities are left in the city.

Urban schools are also class segregated. More than 80 percent of the students in the Chicago Public Schools are minority, primarily Black and Latino. In addition, more than 70 percent of the system's students live below the poverty line (Heard and Davis, 1992). This is typical of many big-city school districts. The amount of money spent on the education of the children attending city schools pales in comparison to what is spent on each student in the more affluent suburbs. Chapter 12 provides the details of these severe inequities.

The consequences for the separate and unequal schools and their students in the city are devastating. Underfunded urban public schools are plagued with shortages of teachers, textbooks, equipment, and facilities. The school buildings themselves crumble and deteriorate from a lack of long-overdue maintenance. These schools often go without playgrounds, basic gym equipment, up-to-date science labs, and even without enough toilets and toilet paper. Often guidance counselors in city schools are assigned between 500 and 1000 students; in the most affluent suburban schools, counselors may be responsible for no more than two dozen. Many times urban school districts must severely cut funds for extracurricular activities. The Chicago Public Schools, for example, recently cut 43 percent of their annual budget for these activities, which means no high school sports in the city beginning in 1993. This will remove the one remaining route that the city's young skilled athletes have to higher education (Temkin, 1992).

The results of all of this are predictable: lower standardized test scores and high dropout rates in many urban school districts. Already disadvantaged inner-city students are further disadvantaged.

Crime, Drugs, and Gangs

The problems of crime and drugs in the United States are discussed in Chapters 15 and 17. These problems also have a special relation to urban areas. In the United States, crime has become a euphemism for cities. More specifically, there is a media and popular identification of crime, and the drugs and gangs assumed to be related to it, with the inner city. And because crime is also a code word for race, it comes to be associated in both media and popular accounts primarily with young Black males in the inner city.

Admittedly, the FBI's *Uniform Crime Report* and the U.S. Justice Department's *National Crime Survey* have shown for some time that poor minority males in the inner city have the highest arrest rates for serious felony offenses and are, along with other members of poor minority inner-city communities, the most likely to be victims of this sort of crime in U.S. society. Why is this so?

Throughout this chapter, we see how suburbanization and metropolitan deconcentration have gutted the cities, taking away jobs, businesses, and industries. Private lending institutions have disinvested in our cities, and the federal government and its policies have encouraged growth and affluence in the suburbs and the urban fringe while promoting decay and decline in the central cities. Cities have increasing and concentrating poverty, rising unemployment and low-wage employment, a dwindling supply of decent and affordable housing, a crumbling infrastructure, and an inadequate public transportation system unable to connect central city residents with the job growth on the edges of the metropolitan area. More central city residents are becoming sicker, unable to gain access to adequate health care. Underfunded urban school systems are ill-prepared to ready students for the current metropolitan labor market. These socioeconomic conditions lead to crime, drug use, and gangs in the cities.

Official crime statistics have shown for several decades that there is more property or economic crime in the United States than violent crime, often ten times as much. And many violent offenses, such as robberies, have an economic dimension. The transition of many U.S. cities from manufacturing centers to service economies has severely limited the ability of many low- and semi-skilled workers to find jobs with livable wages and benefits. Because migration to the suburbs has been extremely limited for low-income and minority populations, poor Black, Latino, and immigrant neighborhoods in the inner city have become fertile ground for the development of an alternate or **informal economy** to ensure their survival. An important part of this informal economy is criminal.

Over the past two and one-half decades participation of minority teenagers in the legal labor market has declined significantly. Labor force participation rates for eighteen- and nineteen-year-olds dropped from more than 70 percent in 1960 to 55 percent in 1984—nearly a 28 percent decline. These rates also declined for minority young adults. During the same time period, rates decreased for twenty- to twenty-four-year-olds by 17 percent and for twenty-five- to thirty-four-year-olds by 9 percent (Currie, 1985; Wilson, 1987; Staley, 1992).

When work and survival are not forthcoming from the legal or formal economy, young persons in the inner city become more susceptible to and attracted to opportunities in the informal or criminal economy. Street crime becomes their work (Sullivan, 1989). Participation in drug rings can spell money and survival. Illicit drug trafficking now accounts for at least $100 to $150 billion by standard estimates, as much as 40 percent of the income derived from underground or informal economic activity in the United States (Staley, 1992:23). That the socioeconomic conditions in the inner city make it an ideal location for the illegal drug economy has not been lost on the people who control international drug growing, processing, and distribution. The gangs that provide members with meaningful social relationships and status in the barren and isolated inner city and with protection from other sources of violence in their communities also ensure survival with specialized stolen property, drug, and weapons sales (Hagedorn, 1988).

Official U.S. drug policy has deleterious effects on inner-city communities as well. By criminalizing them, the official strategy is to eliminate drugs and their negative consequences by arresting, prosecuting, convicting, and imprisoning all drug users, buyers, and sellers. This war on drugs actually escalates drug selling, use, and addiction and magnifies the negative consequences that go with them (see Chapter 17). Criminalization sends drug prices and profits upward, thus making the drug trade more attractive. Sellers thus can recruit more users and addicts. Because their drugs and behavior are illegal, users and addicts may have to steal or sell drugs themselves to afford their own habits.

Intravenous drug users and addicts are pushed underground to avoid detection and criminal sanction. They share contaminated needles, giving the United States the highest proportion of AIDS victims who have contracted the disease through intravenous drug use anywhere in the world. By contrast, many European countries and cities are decriminalizing drug use and curbing the illegal drug trade by reducing its profitability, thus lowering drug use and addiction rates. They also are controlling the spread of AIDS among IV drug users and addicts with clean-needle exchange programs that are used because they are free of stigma and legal punishment. In Dutch cities, for example, where drugs are treated as a public health problem instead of a criminal one, de facto decriminalization of drugs and harm reduction policies and programs have produced the lowest proportion of IV drug-using AIDS victims in the industrialized world (see Schmoke, 1992).

Besides failing as a drug control strategy, the war on drugs is not being waged justly. Although the official claim is one of zero tolerance, pursuing all users, buyers, and sellers no matter who or where they are, in fact the war is racist and focused on young Black males in poor inner-city neighborhoods. According to federal studies, about 12 percent of drug users in the United States are Black. Yet in 1989, 41 percent of those arrested on drug charges were Black, and the overwhelming majority were young Black men from the inner city. The National Council on Crime and Delinquency attributes this to the war on drugs, which is not a zero tolerance war on drugs, but a war on the poor and Black in U.S. inner cities (see Timmer, 1991). One in four Black males is now under the supervision of the criminal justice system—on probation or parole, in jail or prison (Mauer, 1991). This only serves to marginalize further the already highly marginal poor Black inner-city residents, with ripple effects throughout Black families, schools, and communities in the inner city (Gordon, 1990).

Fear of crime in the city. Fear of crime is often exaggerated in comparison to the reality of, or actual potential for, criminal victimization. Often the fear is not of crime at all. What people identify as a fear of crime is often a fear of persons of cultural and racial groups different than their own (Fischer, 1976). Nonetheless, such misdirected fear of crime often is a significant factor in central city decline. If people, industry, corporations, retailers, and other small businesses will not stay in or move to the city because they believe it is not safe, then the process of urban decline cannot be turned around. A self-fulfilling prophecy of central city decline sets in. Because of the belief that the city is crime-ridden and unsafe, people, businesses, and jobs leave the city, thereby making it more crime-ridden and unsafe and further removing the possibility that the business and jobs that could begin to change the socioeconomic conditions that produce crime will go there in the future.

Urban Unrest and Riot: What Happens in Places Like South Central Los Angeles?

In late April 1992, a virtually all-White jury in a virtually all-White suburb of Los Angeles, Simi Valley, found four White Los Angeles police officers innocent of the brutal beating of a young Black man, Rodney King. The not-guilty verdict came in spite of the fact that the beating had been videotaped by a Los Angeles resident and viewed by the entire nation.

The acquittal was followed by urban unrest in the South Central neighborhood of Los Angeles that left 58 persons dead, more than 4000 injured, and at least $1 billion worth of property damage with 5000 buildings damaged or destroyed (*The Economist,* 1992b). On a smaller scale, the unrest spread to several other inner-city areas, in large and small cities, across the country. It is important to understand that the exoneration of four LAPD officers was only the triggering event for the violence and looting that followed.

Historically, injustice at the hands of the criminal justice system, normally the police but in this case combined with the courts, has tended to be the spark that has ignited urban unrest. The underlying socioeconomic conditions in the inner cities described throughout this chapter set the stage for these episodes of disorder in U.S. cities. This was the case in Los Angeles in the Spring of 1992 as well, where:

- 200,000 jobs had been lost in the year prior to the unrest.
- By 1987, per capita income was only 67 percent of suburban income.
- Countywide, there were 1068 supermarkets in 1970, but only 694 in 1990, with most of the boarded up markets in the city's minority communities.
- In the industrial corridors of South Central Los Angeles, 50,000 jobs have been lost over the past three decades.
- In South Central Los Angeles and neighborhoods adjacent to it, 70,000 high-paying manufacturing jobs were lost between 1978 and 1982. General Motors Corporation, Bethlehem Steel, Goodyear, and Firestone Tire all relocated or closed their plants.
- The only growth in the manufacturing sector is in textile sweatshops that illegally employ undocumented immigrants at less than minimum wage.
- In South Central Los Angeles and other inner-city neighborhoods, unemployment rates are as high as 50 percent, compared to the nation's 7.2 percent rate at the time of the disturbance.
- The riot-torn area, home to more than 500,000 people, had only 19 branch banks (the above data are from *The Economist,* 1992b; Wilkins, 1992; Dreier, 1992).

The results of this job loss and disinvestment are predictable. Residents of places like South Central Los Angeles are cut off from mainstream society. People of color live in neighborhoods without the basic social supports found in middle-class communities. Opportunity structures and resources that provide people with hope are absent. People have been discriminated against by employers, businesses, and lenders. They have been abandoned by the federal government and abused by the police. For them the American Dream is a nightmare. Disconnected from mainstream social and economic institutions, they have no stake in U.S. society. Sociologically, this is how the disorder and unrest must be understood. The violence and damage are the outcome of an economy and a government that have failed urban America; by Spring 1993 not one federal dollar has been spent in South Central Los Angeles to address the underlying causes of the disturbances.

Urban Policy: Rebuilding U.S. Cities

Why Save the Cities?

There are moral and political reasons to rebuild U.S. cities and improve the quality of life for all urban residents. Cities have also been cultural and intellectual centers and should thrive once again on those grounds. Perhaps the most compelling argument for saving U.S. cities is economic. Few people would allow the decay of their cities if they believed it would limit economic growth in general and their own economic opportunity in particular. Two recent studies have shown that the decline of cities does just that.

Research by Larry Ledebur of Wayne State University and William Barnes of the National League of Cities and by Hank Savitch of the University of Louisville indicates that declining cities lead to declining suburbs. Many older near-in suburbs now share many of the same social, economic, and fiscal problems facing the central cities. Not even the bedroom suburbs on the urban fringe can isolate themselves and escape all the economic and social problems created by a troubled economy, widening income inequality, and rising urban poverty. If large sections of big cities are left to rot, entire metropolitan areas and U.S. society as a whole, not just the local residents, will ultimately pay a heavy price (see Dreier, 1992).

Policy Alternatives

Three broad policy alternatives exist for rebuilding urban areas: moral exhortation, the market, and a Marshall Plan.

Moral exhortation. This view blames the problems in our cities on urban residents, particularly poor Blacks in the inner city. The poor themselves, their families, their culture, and their neighborhoods produce values and behavior that are the essential cause of poverty and of all the urban problems connected to it. The values and behavior of the poor and Black in the inner city must be brought up to middle-class standards. The poor must be shown the error of their ways.

This approach assumes that the values and behavior of poor people are different from the values and behavior of the White middle- and upper-middle classes (see Chapters 6 and 7 for an elaboration and critique of this approach). A growing body of evidence suggests that this is not true, that poor Black people in the city and affluent White people outside of it display similar behavior under similar socioeconomic conditions and circumstances (see di Leonardo's review, 1992, for example). By focusing on the behavior of the poor, this approach fails because it ignores the social, economic, and political sources of urban decline. Urban anthropologist Micaela di Leonardo delivers the fatal blow to policy rooted in this perspective:

> I'll say it one last time. Of course we have to love, control and enlighten all our children. Street crime and drug addiction are terrible things. Early childbearing isn't great. People, including poor people, ought to be kindly and sensitive to one another in public and private. But prior to all these considerations are public policies that have created and maintain poverty and racial stratification. (1992:186)

The market. This policy position is shared by most conservatives and liberals, by both major political parties, and by both the Republican and Democratic candidates for president in 1992. It holds that if government provides the proper subsidies and incentives to business, the private sector will redevelop urban areas and the benefits will ultimately trickle-down to all urban residents. To promote economic development, this approach advocates government financial assistance for new businesses in the city and urban enterprise zones.

In the first case, city and federal low-interest loans, loan guarantees, and sometimes outright subsidies have been used to prod private developers and corporations to participate in urban renewal projects. The problems with this approach have been twofold. One, public monies are most often used for upscale development—office towers, middle-class residential complexes, exclusive retail shopping, and luxury hotels. Normally the economic benefits do not trickle-down to poor and working-class city residents. And second, many times the loans sour. The private sector reneges on its financial commitments to government when its projects fail to turn a profit and the businesses involved would just as soon have the property turned over to the city or federal government. The much heralded renovation of Baltimore's Inner Harbor is a prime example of this. The city now stands to lose $60 million in development loans, much of which went to upscale hotels, retail outlets, and apartment houses (Jacobson, S., 1992).

As for urban enterprise zones, the notion is that tax incentives and credits will encourage businesses to locate or relocate in depressed inner-city areas, thereby creating the jobs that will lead to the redevelopment of these neighborhoods. In conjunction with these zones, President Clinton has advocated relatively small amounts of money being spent directly on improving urban infrastructure and transportation.

But evaluation of existent enterprise zones is not encouraging (see the Forum at the end of this chapter). For the most part, businesses relocate jobs to urban enterprise zones for tax advantages, but this does not create significant numbers of new jobs. Moreover, the jobs that do come to the inner city generally do not go to inner-city residents. Studies from around the country find high inner-city unemployment rates even in areas close to jobs. Evidence also suggests that the tax revenues lost in urban enterprise zones could have been used to create education and training programs, employment programs, better police protection, and subsidized housing construction that would create more jobs and thus improve the quality of life in these poor neighborhoods (Williams and Breslow, 1992).

Critics of this urban policy perspective point to the irony in offering the market as the solution to urban problems. For them, the market has caused the problems. What but the market, they ask, has taken decent jobs farther from the central city? What, more than the market, has influenced the decline of our cities?

A Marshall Plan for the cities.   Advocates of this policy reject the other two alternatives. The first blames the victims of bad public policy, and the market clearly has failed the cities and many of those who live there. What is required is massive intervention by both regional and federal governments, a government plan for rebuilding urban areas that rivals the Marshall Plan that rebuilt Europe after World War II. Public investment in U.S. cities needs to proceed on a level never seen before.

Regional government should be encouraged. Here, more affluent suburbs and edge cities share tax revenues and services with less affluent cities, improving the quality of life throughout the metropolitan area. This will, of course, be opposed by many suburbanites who do not see it as serving their interest. There is some precedent for it, however. Louisville, Kentucky, and its suburbs have come to such an agreement. In Minneapolis-St. Paul, any county in the metropolitan area that exceeds the average growth rate by 40 percent or more shares the excess tax revenue with the rest of the area, including the central city (*The Economist,* 1992a).

For its part, the federal government must stop underwriting the deconcentration of metropolitan areas with its policies and subsidies. It must enforce prohibitions against disinvestment in the city. On the positive side, it must fund a public works job creation program modeled after those of the Great Depression and the New Deal era. This public works program could be used to rebuild the decaying urban infrastructure. The federal government's urban policy ought to increase public assistance and welfare payments, build more affordable public housing, develop an adequate public mass transit system, and fund the clean up of toxic and hazardous waste, particularly in poor and minority neighborhoods. The federal government must provide health insurance to all people, including inner-city residents, and increase financial assistance for urban public hospitals. It must also, along with state government, take on a greater share of the funding of public schools. This will help remove the educational inequalities between suburban and urban schools that result from the reliance on local property taxes.

These changes in the federal government's urban policy will not come easy. Presently, urban residents are not viewed as a constituency by either major political party. Compared to the past, fewer members of Congress represent cities. More congressional districts incorporate cities and suburbs. Members of Congress, even those from the cities, are now more loyal to national political action committees (see Chapter 2) than they are to local urban political machines and organizations. And in the post–cold war era with cutbacks in military spending, the democratically controlled U.S. Senate and House passed legislation preventing the transfer of funds from the military budget to the domestic budget. This ensured that no peace dividend would be available to rebuild urban areas. Democrats, long the party of the cities, could have stopped this, but they chose not to (Dreier, 1992).

Meanwhile, city governments, city employees, and poor and working-class residents lose ground as cities cope with the myriad of problems by raising local taxes, cutting services, and, through the process of privatization, turning as many city functions as possible over to the profit-making private sector.

CHAPTER REVIEW

1. Many social problems in the United States, beginning with poverty, are concentrated in large cities.
2. At least since the end of World War II, U.S. cities have been increasingly abandoned by the economy and the federal government and its policies.
3. Through its process of suburbanization and metropolitan deconcentration, the central cities have lost people, jobs industry, business,and their tax base. Central cities have also lost jobs in the transformation from a manufacturing

to a service economy. Central city jobs, particularly in the Midwest and Northeast, have been lost to the Third World, the Sun Belt, and also the suburbs. Federal transportation, housing, economic, and tax policies have encouraged this gutting or mugging of the cities.

4. Race and class have played an important role in suburbanization and metropolitan deconcentration. The middle class and White tend to move to the suburbs and urban fringe, the poor and minorities remain in the city. As a result, over the past forty years, many large cities have lost population, even in growing metropolitan areas. They have also become poorer and seen their proportion of minority residents increase.

5. Beginning in the 1950s, U.S. business and financial and lending institutions have tended to disinvest in cities and invest in suburbs and edge cities, to disinvest in Black and Latino neighborhoods and invest in White communities. This pattern of disinvestment is directly responsible for neighborhood and central city decline.

6. Suburbanization, metropolitan deconcentration, disinvestment, and the federal policies that have encouraged them, along with cuts in federal funds for programs that assist poor and working-class city residents that began in the late 1970s, have led to a declining quality of life in U.S. cities.

7. The declining quality of life in U.S. big cities is reflected in increasing and intensifying poverty, the lack of affordable housing, homelessness, decaying infrastructure, inadequate public transit, pollution, health problems, and the lack of access to adequate health care, underfunded and failing schools, and crime, drugs, and gangs.

8. Urban poverty has been increasing and becoming more concentrated in particular areas in the central city. The poor have also been getting poorer, especially the minority poor. African Americans and Latinos are more likely than Whites in the city to be poor, and Blacks are much more likely to live in highly segregated neighborhoods that are also high-poverty areas.

9. Both the urban housing market and government subsidized and public housing have failed to provide enough decent and affordable shelter in U.S. cities. The results are a dwindling supply of low-income housing and increasing urban homelessness.

10. The lack of public investment in the urban infrastructure has begun to significantly limit growth and productivity in the U.S. economy.

11. An automobile-dependent transportation system has polluted U.S. cities and prevented the development of public mass transit. Inadequate public transit impacts the poor in the central city who cannot afford to own and operate a car and are thus unable to reach jobs in the suburbs and urban fringe.

12. Poor and minority communities in the inner city are the site of a disproportionate amount of illegal dumping and toxic and hazardous waste.

13. Poor and minority inner-city neighborhoods have the highest rates of many health problems—infant mortality, asthma, sexually transmitted diseases, lead poisoning, tuberculosis, and AIDS. Residents of these same places suffer most from lack of access to adequate health care as private hospitals in cities close their doors to under- and uninsured patients. The emergency rooms of underfunded, ill-equipped, and understaffed urban public hospitals become their only alternative.

14. Because U.S. public education is funded primarily with local property taxes, gross inequalities exist between suburban and city schools. Urban schools are increasingly characterized by crumbling facilities, textbook and teacher shortages, outdated equipment and technologies, few extra curricular activities and special programs, low standardized test scores, and high dropout rates.

15. When opportunities in the formal and legal economy are not forthcoming, young minority males turn to the informal economy for survival. Much of the informal economy is illegal, involving property crime, drug trafficking, and certain gang activities.

16. Fear of crime contributes to urban decay as it works against the people, business, and jobs that could increase economic development and reduce crime from remaining in, or relocating to, the city.

17. By criminalizing drugs, drug users, and addicts, the war on drugs makes the drug trade in the cities more attractive and profitable and then further marginalizes already marginal poor Black inner-city neighborhoods.

18. The recent urban unrest in South Central Los Angeles, although triggered by the acquittal of four White police officers in the beating of a Black man, had its source in the underlying socioeconomic conditions in urban areas described in this chapter.

19. One can make a very pragmatic and economic argument for rebuilding U.S. cities; research shows that declining cities lead to declining suburbs and metropolitan areas.

20. There are three broad policy positions on rebuilding U.S. cities. One position essentially blames urban decay on the values and behavior of the minority poor; urban redevelopment will only occur when they change their behavior. A second position relies on the market. Government should provide incentives to businesses to develop and locate in the central city. Urban enterprise zones will begin the rebirth of cities. A third view argues that the first two approaches misdiagnose the source of urban ills and fail to redevelop the central city. What is needed is massive public intervention and investment in our cities on the part of both regional and federal governments.

KEY TERMS

Redlining.   When banks, savings and loans, government agencies, and insurance companies refuse to make home and small business loans and insure property in poor and minority neighborhoods.

Gentrification.   The redevelopment of poor and working-class urban neighborhoods into middle- and upper-middle class enclaves; often involves displacement of original residents.

Warehousing.   The withholding of apartments from the housing market by speculators who hope to sell them at a profit to developers.

Jobs/housing mismatch.   The inability of central city residents most in need of decent jobs to reach them on the urban fringe because they cannot afford to operate a private auto and the public transportation system is inadequate; moving to the urban fringe is not an option because of housing costs and racial segregation.

Environmental racism.   The tendency for poor and minority areas in cities and metropolitan areas to be the targets of a disproportionate share of illegal dumping and the site where most toxic and hazardous waste is disposed; these communities also suffer, as compared to more affluent White communities, from lax enforcement of environmental regulations and laws.

Informal economy.   When opportunities are not present in the regular legal economy, people in poor inner-city neighborhoods often turn to this alternate economic exchange and activity for survival; much of the informal economy is illegal activity involving crime and drug trafficking.

Regional government.   A single metropolitan governmental unit, encompassing the central city and its suburbs.

FOR FURTHER STUDY

Joe T. Darden, Richard Child Hill, June Thomas, and Richard Thomas. *Detroit: Race and Uneven Development.* Philadelphia: Temple University Press, 1987.

Mike Davis. *City of Quartz: Excavating the Future in Los Angeles.* New York: Vintage Books, 1992.

Joe R. Feagin. *Free Enterprise City: Houston in Political and Economic Perspective.* New Brunswick, N.J.: Rutgers University Press, 1988.

Chester Hartman. *The Transformation of San Francisco.* Totowa, N.J.: Rowman and Allanheld, 1984.

Gregory D. Squires, Larry Bennett, Kathleen McCourt, and Philip Nyden. *Chicago: Race, Class, and the Response to Urban Decline.* Philadelphia: Temple University Press, 1987.

Clarence N. Stone. *Regime Politics: Governing Atlanta, 1946–1988.* Lawrence: University of Kansas Press, 1989.

Todd Swanstrom. *The Crisis of Growth Politics: Cleveland, Kucinich, and the Challenge of Urban Populism.* Philadelphia: Temple University Press, 1985.

FORUM

ENTERPRISE ZONES: URBAN HOPE OR TRICKLE-DOWN HOKUM?

Enterprise zones have become the new silver bullet cure-all for the woes of urban America in this presidential season. Several versions of this idea are being pushed by President George Bush, Gov. Bill Clinton and congressional leaders in their stated goal of helping inner cities. (And, in Bush's version, even the countryside.) But making themselves look good to urban dwellers seems to be the real goal of these politicians. And given the record of enterprise zones, an appearance of change is about all we can expect. If Washington really wants to help the inner cities, it needs to put aside this trickle-down, supply-side gimmick and institute a real program of jobs and training for the urban unemployed.

What are enterprise zones. An "enterprise zone" is a geographical area of a city designated to qualify for certain benefits. Zones can be selected on the basis of unemployment levels, housing stock, neighborhood conditions or lack of business activity. The concept was initiated in Great Britain in 1978, and during the '80s hundreds of zones were set up throughout the United States.

Businesses that start up, relocate or expand within the defined area receive tax breaks and other prescribed benefits. Those most frequently given by states include sales-tax credits, wage credits, employer income-tax credits, easing or exemption of regulations, tax credits for hiring disadvantaged residents of the area, capital financing, property-tax credits and investment tax credits.

The enterprise zone notion is based on an assumption that business expansion in run-down areas will create jobs and revitalize the community better than direct government programs that provide social services, jobs and training.

Mixed results. Some zones appear to have attracted new businesses, but others—perhaps most—have seen businesses move in but little or not improvement in the area. In virtually no case have social and economic benefits to the community outweighed their tax cost.

Some of the larger state enterprise zone projects include:

- **Baltimore:** Park Circle is the home of 60 businesses that employ 1,400 people, but the adjacent neighborhood has not improved. Teenage unemployment among blacks in the area still hovers near 40 percent.
- **Connecticut:** Eleven cities and towns in the state have enterprise zones, but the state has no way to assess whether the programs have been cost-effective. In spite of a 50 percent credit on corporate business taxes for the first 10 years, the zones have not helped the state recover from its disastrous economic slump.
- **Kansas:** Several years' experience led to cancellation of the program last year. Cities gerrymandered zone boundaries to include wealthy and prosperous neighborhoods and to take in existing facilities of healthy companies such as Boeing, Beech Aircraft and even a Coors beer distributorship. Some cities established zones entitling businesses to 10-year tax abatements, then moved the zones to take in a new set of businesses without taking back the earlier abatements. They thus created a shell game with enterprise zone boundaries that benefited business but had little effect on jobs and inner-city conditions.
- **Los Angeles:** Since 1988, the Pacoima zone has created only 212 jobs, the Watts zone 159 and the Central City zone 220. Pacoima has seen a spurt of industrial activity, but city planners doubt that it has been a result of enterprise zone tax incentives. Some of the businesses moved from other areas, creating no new jobs.
- **St. Louis:** Since a zone was established in the Manchester Avenue area in1983, only four small businesses have been created. Of the 328 new jobs created by these businesses and others that expanded or relocated into the zone, a paltry 25 have gone to area residents.

In short, state-authorized enterprise zones have worked poorly or not at all. Some jurisdictions have assembled extensive data on tax costs of enterprise zone legislation, but none has developed credible estimates of benefits to depressed areas. State and local economic development officials who we interviewed consistently voiced the view—never on the record—that social benefits were unlikely to equal the tax costs.

Even Richard Cowden, executive director of the American Association of Enterprise Zones, warns that programs consisting only of tax incentives have little chance for success. He argues that the most effective zones provide additional funds for improved law enforcement, social services, job training and infrastructure.

Current proposals. Despite evidence that state-level programs have failed, the Bush administration's four-part plan for enterprise zones calls for federal tax incentives for business owners and investors. Bush proposes:

- Appropriation of $2.5 billion to create 50 new zones, half to be in rural areas.
- A 15 percent tax credit to employers for the first $20,000 of wages paid to each employee who both lives and works in the zone.
- No capital-gains tax on the sale of enterprise zone assets held at least two years.
- Tax deductions for investors of up to $50,000 in a year or $250,000 in a lifetime, for the purchase of stock in small enterprise zone companies.

Democratic leaders in Congress appear to support the concept but with modifications. House Speaker Tom Foley would endorse a capital-gains tax cut for enterprise zones but does not think it is necessary to cut the rate to zero, as in the administration's proposal. House Ways and Means Chairman Dan Rostenkowski would defer capital-gains taxes and would provide a lower tax credit of $3,000 for each zone resident employed. Senate Finance Committee Chairman Lloyd Bentsen supports enterprise zone legislation but wants it focused on creating jobs rather than just attracting investment.

On the surface, the enterprise zone idea can be appealing. It would be good to stimulate business expansion and new enterprise creation that would provide jobs to the unemployed and be a catalyst for neighborhood renewal of depressed areas.

But while an enterprise zone neighborhood might, over the course of a decade, count a small number of new jobs traceable to the proposed legislation, accountants and lawyers would be busily at work determining how to exploit the capital-gains and stock-investment provisions of the act, provisions that would appear to have virtually no potential for producing either new business or new jobs in depressed areas.

The Bush administration's proposals, as well as the congressional alternatives, would subsidize business and investors from the national treasury. They would not provide concomitant benefits to economically depressed areas.

Tax expenditures for these purposes, totaling billions of dollars, must come from the pockets of other taxpayers or from reduced spending on other programs. Given Congress' self-imposed barrier to transferring budget funds from military programs to social programs, any such reduction would almost certainly come out of the hide of already starved social programs and most likely out of existing programs to aid cities and communities.

The policy question is straightforward: Is this the best use of taxpayers' money to help cities? And the answer is no. Enterprise zone legislation currently being considered, whether originating with the Republicans or the Democrats, is an election-year response to a serious crisis in the cities. It is another gimmick of supply-side, trickle-down economics.

Enterprise zones, for all the grandiose claims to the contrary, are not a cost-effective use of taxpayers' dollars. Bribing business to induce it to help the inner cities will always mean that the bulk of the benefits will go to business.

Washington should take the billions of dollars it is talking about putting into enterprise zones and invest it more productively in direct aid to communities. (The

U.S. Conference of Mayors has already identified 7,252 projects that would put people back to work and repair the urban infrastructure.) Invest in public employment programs to hire the inner-city unemployed. Equip them with training, transportation, appropriate health support. Give them jobs repairing streets, sewers and sidewalks, cleaning vacant lots, renovating buildings, planting trees and shrubbery, removing graffiti, building and staffing libraries, parks and recreation centers. Provide a jobs safety net the unemployed can count on to put food on the table and use as a springboard to employment in the private sector.

In other words, invest taxpayers' dollars in people, not in corporations.

Source: Ralph Estes, "Enterprise Zones: Urban Hope or Trickle-Down Hokum?" *In These Times* (September 16–29, 1992): 16. Reprinted from *In These Times,* a Chicago-based bi-weekly.

T he United States is envied by most peoples of the world. It is blessed with great natural resources, the most advanced technology known, and a very high standard of living. Despite these facts, a significant portion of U.S. residents live in a condition of **poverty** (with a standard of living below the minimum needed for the maintenance of adequate diet, health, and shelter). Millions are ill fed, ill clothed, and ill housed. These same millions are discriminated against in the schools, in the courts, in the job market, and in the marketplace; and discrimination has the effect of trapping many of the poor in that condition. The so-called American dream is just that for millions of people—a dream that will not be realized.

This chapter is descriptive, theoretical, and practical. On the descriptive level we examine the facts of poverty—who the poor are, how many there are, where they are located, and what it means to be poor. Theoretically, we look at the various explanations for poverty—individual and structural. On the practical level we explore what needs to be done if extreme poverty is to be eliminated.

There are two underlying themes in this chapter. The first theme is that the victims of poverty are not to be blamed for their condition; rather, the inequities present in U.S. society are responsible. That is, the essence of poverty is inequality—in money and in opportunity. The second theme is important when we take up the possible solutions to this social problem: The United States has the resources to eliminate poverty if it will give that problem a high enough priority.

The Extent of Poverty in the United States

What separates the poor from the nonpoor? In a continuum there is no absolute standard for wealth. The line separating the poor from the nonpoor is necessarily arbitrary. The Social Security Administration (SSA) sets the **official poverty line** based on what it considers the minimal amount of money required for a subsistence level of life. To determine the poverty line, the SSA computes the cost of a basic nutritionally adequate diet and multiplies that figure by three. This multiplier is based on a government research finding that poor people spend one-third of their income on food. If we use this standard, in 1991, 14.2 percent of the population (35.7 million persons) were defined as living in poverty (the 1991 data on poverty are from U.S. Census, reported in Pear, 1992). See Figure 6.1 for the poverty rate data over time.

In this chapter, we consider the poor as people below this arbitrary line. However, the government procedure not only is arbitrary but it also minimizes the extent of poverty in the United States. Some economists have argued that a more realistic figure would be 50 percent of the median income. In 1991, for example, the official poverty line was $13,924 for a nonfarm family of four. If the 50-percent-of-median-income standard were used, the line would have been $15,052, adding many millions of people to the poverty category. Such a procedure might shock the government into more action to alleviate suffering in this country. In effect, though, a poor person is anyone denied adequate health, diet, clothing, and shelter because of lack of resources.

Exact figures on the number of poor are difficult to determine. For one thing, the amount of money needed for subsistence varies drastically by locality. For

Figure 6.1 Number of poor and poverty rate: 1959 to 1991

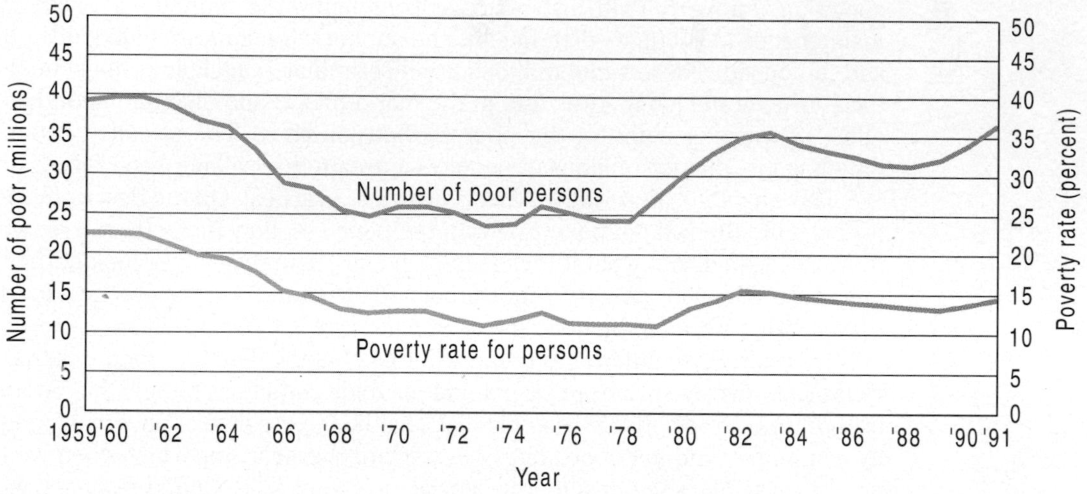

Note: The data points represent the midpoints of the respective years

Sources: U.S. Bureau of the Census, "Poverty in the United States: 1990," *Current Population Reports,* Series P–60, No. 175 (Washington, D.C.: Government Printing Office) 1991, p. 3; and data from Pear, 1992.

example, the money needed for rent in New York City is much greater than the money needed in rural Arkansas. Another difficulty is that the poor are most likely to be missed by the U.S. Census. People most likely to be missed in the census live in ghettos (where several families may be crowded into one apartment) or in rural areas, where some homes are inaccessible and where some workers follow the harvest from place to place and therefore have no permanent home. Transients of any kind may be missed by the census. The conclusion is inescapable that the proportion of the poor in the United States is underestimated, because the poor tend to be invisible, even to the government. This underestimate of the poor has important consequences, because U.S. Census data are the basis for political representation in Congress. These data are also used as the basis for instituting new governmental programs or abandoning old ones. Needless to say, an accurate count of total population is necessary if the census is so used.

Despite these difficulties and the understating of actual poverty by the government's poverty line, we do know some facts about the poor.

Racial Minorities Income in the United States is maldistributed by race. In 1991, the median family income for White households was $31,569 compared to $22,691 for Latino households, and $18,807 for Black households. Not surprisingly, then, 11.3 percent of Whites were officially poor, compared to 28.7 percent of Latinos, and 32.7 percent of African Americans.

Latinos will soon replace Blacks as the racial group with the highest poverty rate. This prediction is based on several facts regarding the Latino population. First, Latinos generally tend to be much younger than Whites or Blacks, making them more likely to be newer to the work force and therefore among the lowest paid. Second, they tend to be concentrated in the lowest segment of the labor market, where pay is at or near the minimum wage regardless of longevity. Third, high unemployment is prominent in geographical areas heavily populated by Latinos. Finally, Latinos tend to have larger families than do Whites or African Americans, and they are more likely than those in the other two racial groups to have only one wage earner.

Native Americans have about the same poverty rate as African Americans (Snipp, 1992). As with other racial categories, though, there is a wide variation among Native Americans, with some in the middle class, some poor, and some extremely poor. In the latter category are the 25 percent of Native Americans who live on reservations. There, poverty rates and unemployment tend to be very high, health problems rampant, and educational attainment comparatively low (Ropers, 1991:49–50). On the Pine Ridge reservation in South Dakota, for example, the poverty rate was 63.1 percent in 1989 (Kilborn, 1992).

Women

Two out of three impoverished adults in the United States are women, a consequence of the prevailing institutional sexism in society. With few exceptions, U.S. society provides poor job and earnings opportunities for women. This fact, combined with the relatively high frequency of divorce and the large number of never-married women with children, has resulted in the high probability of women who head families being poor (in 1991, single-parent families headed by women had a 35.6 percent poverty rate, compared to a poverty rate of only 6 percent for two-parent families).

This trend, termed the **feminization of poverty** (see Pearce, 1978; Ehrenreich and Stallard, 1982; Stallard, Ehrenreich, and Sklar, 1983), implies that the relatively large proportion of poor women is a new phenomenon in U.S. society. Thus, the term obscures the fact that women have always been more economically vulnerable than men, especially older women and women of color. But when women's poverty was mainly limited to these groups, their economic deprivation was mostly invisible. The plight of women's poverty became a visible problem when the numbers of White women in poverty increased rapidly in the past decade or so with rising marital disruption. Even with the growing numbers of poor White women, the term *feminization of poverty* implies that all women are at risk, when actually the probability of economic deprivation is much greater for certain categories of women. The issue, then, is not only gender but class, race, and gender (Burnham, 1986).

Race and gender contribute independently to the poverty equation. "The black woman, with two strikes against her, is almost three times more likely to be

Black women are almost three times more likely to be poor as White women.

poor as is a white woman. And an Hispanic woman is two and a half times more likely to be poor" (Shortridge, 1989:486).

Children

The nation's poverty rate was 14.2 percent in 1991, but the rate was 21.8 percent for children under age eighteen and 25 percent for children under three. Slightly more than one-half of all Black children under age six were poor, compared to 45 percent of Latino children and 17 percent of White children under six. The Children's Defense Fund provides the following facts and projections:

> All groups of children are poorer today than they were at the beginning of the decade—especially white children, whose poverty rates have increased by almost a third. If present trends persist, white children may eventually face the same savage levels of poverty in the future that now afflict black and Hispanic children. Today nearly one in two black and one in three Hispanic children is poor.
>
> If we do not rise off our national rear end and mobilize to prevent and reduce child poverty, between now and the year 2000 *all* of the growth in our

child population will consist of poor children and our children in the next century will be poorer than today.

■ In the year 2000, one in four of all American children, 16 million children, will be poor—3 million more than in 1987.
■ By the year 2030, one in three, or 25 million American children, will be poor—about double the number today. (Children's Defense Fund, 1989b:xvi–xvii)

Elderly

Contrary to popular belief, the elderly as a category have a lower poverty rate (12.4 percent in 1991) than the general population (14.2 percent). In fact, there are four times as many children as elderly people living in poverty in the United States. This seeming anomaly is the result of government programs for the elderly being indexed for inflation whereas many welfare programs targeted for the young were reduced or eliminated, especially since 1980.

Place

Poverty is not randomly distributed geographically but tends to cluster in certain places. Regionally, dividing the nation into fourths, the area with the highest poverty is the South (16 percent), followed by the West, Midwest, and Northeast. The states with the highest poverty rates in 1991 were Mississippi (23.7 percent), New Mexico, Louisiana, Kentucky, and Alabama. Each of these states has a disproportionate number of racial minorities and has a higher rural population than urban population. The states with the lowest poverty rates were New Hampshire (7.3 percent), Delaware, Hawaii, Connecticut, and Maryland.

In metropolitan areas the poverty rate is higher in the central cities than in suburban areas. Nonmetropolitan areas have a higher poverty rate than do metropolitan areas. People living on farms have a higher rate of poverty than does the nonfarm population.

There are important differences between the rural and the urban poor. The rural poor have some advantages (low-cost housing, raising their own food) and many disadvantages (low-paid work, higher prices for most products, fewer social services, fewer welfare benefits) over the urban poor (Maharidge, 1992). As a result, "the rural poor are more likely than the urban poor to be long-term poor" (O'Hare and Curry-White, 1992:6).

Finally, the United States, when compared to other major industrialized democracies, has more poverty, more severe poverty, and supports its poor people least. A study by the Joint Center for Political and Economic Studies found that

the United States stands in ignominious isolation. Among industrialized counties, the United States has the highest incidence of poverty among the non-elderly and the widest distribution of poverty across all age and family groups. It is also the only western democracy that has failed to give a significant portion of its poor a measure of income security. (cited in Albelda, 1991:20)

The Poor-Poor

Before leaving the description of the poor, let's examine the characteristics of the **poor-poor**—those people living at or below half the poverty line (the following is taken from Whitman, 1990). In 1989 there were 12 million people—1 out of every

20 people in the United States—who lived below *half* the poverty line. Some facts about these people who are among the poorest of the poor:

- 4.9 million of these 12 million (41 percent) are children.
- One of 7 African Americans are in the category. "While the number of poor Black children living above 50 percent of the poverty line actually *decreased* 10 percent from 1979 to 1989, the number living below half the poverty line skyrocketed 52 percent" (Whitman, 1990:42).
- Six of ten live in female-headed families.
- Only two of five are on welfare.

This category of the **poor-poor** has increased by nearly 45 percent from 1979, when unemployment was roughly the same as in 1989. This upsurge in the truly destitute also occurred during a decade when at least seven of the ten years saw economic upswings. The explanation for this seeming anomaly appears to be that (1) many of the poor-poor live in rural areas that experienced economic hard times while many other regions of the country were relatively prosperous; (2) a decline in marriage resulted in single mothers and unattached men; and (3) public assistance benefits, especially in the South, were reduced during the 1980s (e.g., Aid to Families with Dependent Children benefits fell 18 percent in real terms during that decade). We return to the explanations for poverty later in this chapter.

Myths About Poverty

What should be the government's role in caring for its less fortunate citizens? Much of the debate on this important issue among politicians and citizens is based on erroneous assumptions and misperceptions. "These myths need to be dispelled in order to direct public policy intelligently" (O'Hare, 1986:22).

Refusal to Work

Several facts belie the faulty assumption that poor people refuse to work. Forty percent of poor people in 1991 age fifteen and older worked; 9 percent had year-round, full-time jobs. The main increase in the number of poor since 1979 has been among the working poor (Whitman, 1988). This increase is the result of declining wages, the increase in working women who head households, and a minimum wage of $3.35, unchanged from 1981 to 1989, when in two steps it finally rose to $4.25 an hour in 1991. The Census Bureau reported that there was a sharp rise between 1979 and 1990 in the proportion of full-time workers with low earnings (defined as less than a poverty-level income for a family of four), with the rate rising from 12.1 percent to 18 percent (reported in *Chicago Tribune,* 1992). In other words, nearly one worker in five was in the low-pay category in 1990. When race is considered, the rate for White workers in 1990 was 17.1 percent, compared to 25.3 percent among Black workers, and 31.4 percent among Latino workers.

**Welfare
Dependency**

We should recognize, first, that most poor people do *not* receive welfare. Only about one-third of poor families receive public assistance payments, and only about 40 percent of the poor receive noncash benefits such as food stamps, free or reduced school lunches, public housing, or Medicaid. Second, the average welfare recipient stays on welfare less than two years (Sklar, 1992:10). Third, welfare is inadequate to meet the needs of the poor, falling far short. In 1990, for example, the average poor family of three had an annual income $3,039 *below* the poverty line.

> Many poor families manage by cutting back on food, jeopardizing their health and the development of their children, or by living in substandard and some-times dangerous housing. Some do without heat, electricity, telephone service, or plumbing for months or years. Many do without health insurance, health care, safe child care, or reliable transportation to take them to or from work. (Children's Defense Fund, cited in Sklar, 1992:10)

There is a fundamental misunderstanding by the U.S. public about where most governmental benefits are directed. We tend to assume that government monies and services go mostly to the poor (**welfare**) when in fact the greatest amount of government aid goes to the nonpoor (**wealthfare**). Most (about three-fourths) of the federal outlays for human resources go to the nonpoor, such as to all children in public education programs and to most of the elderly through Social Security Retirement and Medicare.

The upside-down welfare system, with aid mainly helping the already affluent, is also accomplished by two hidden welfare systems. The first is through tax loop-holes (called **tax expenditures**). Through these legal mechanisms the govern-ment officially permits certain individuals and corporations to pay lower taxes or no taxes at all. The government estimate for tax expenditures—savings for the already fortunate—in 1990 was $294.3 billion (U.S. Bureau of the Census, 1991b:320). In a telling irony, the government tax breaks to homeowners who deducted interest and real estate tax payments amounted to a housing subsidy of $51.03 billion in 1989 (U.S. Bureau of the Census, 1991b:320), whereas the amount the poor received in public and subsidized housing in that year amount-ed to only about $7 billion.

The second hidden welfare system to the nonpoor is in the form of direct sub-sidies and credit to assist corporations, banks, agribusiness, defense industries, and the like. These subsidy programs, which may have noble purposes such as helping an ailing industry (e.g., a $500 billion bailout of savings and loans begun in 1989), do transfer substantial sums primarily from the middle class upward to large corporations and to individuals who own stock in them. Elliott Currie and Jerome Skolnick argue that this is

> "socialism for the rich"—that is, they supply money and support to corporate businesses, not according to the much-applauded principles of the free market, but according to need as determined by the government. [We should recognize that government welfare to a corporation or an industry may be necessary to avert an economic disaster. This is also the principle that] underlies govern-ment spending for *individuals* who have floundered in the "free" market. There, the government seeks to maintain the individual as a productive member of

Government tax breaks to homeowners (the deduction of interest and taxes) amounted to a housing subsidy of $51 billion in 1989, while expenditures for public and subsidized housing for the poor in that year were only about $7 billion.

society. Applauding the government's commitment to corporate welfare while condemning its support for individuals facing economic difficulties seems less than consistent. (Currie and Skolnick, 1984:139–140)

Welfare Is a Black Program

The myth is that most welfare monies go to Blacks. The facts, however, are different (the following is from Ehrenreich 1991). Sixty-one percent of the population receiving welfare (i.e., means-tested cash assistance) is White. Because Blacks are disproportionately poor and they are disproportionately among the poorest of the poor, they, while only 12 percent of the population, are one-third of the welfare population. Blacks are also twice as likely as Whites to be unemployed, and more likely to be disabled. Whites, only 11 percent of whom are below poverty, are disproportionately welfare recipients. Ehrenreich states:

> So our confession stands: white folks have been gobbling up the welfare budget while blaming someone else. But it's worse than that. If we look at Social Security, which is another form of welfare, although it is often mistaken for an individual insurance program, then whites are the ones who are crowding the trough. We receive almost twice as much per capita, for an aggregate advantage to our race of $10 billion a year—much more than the $3.9 billion advantage African Americans gain from their disproportionate share of welfare. One sad reason: whites live an average of six years longer than African Americans,

meaning that young black workers help subsidize a huge and growing "over-class" of white retirees. (Ehrenreich, 1991:84)

The Costs of Poverty

Some 35.7 million people in the United States were officially poor in 1991. These people and those just above the poverty line generally receive inferior educations, live in substandard housing, are exposed to toxic chemicals, are malnourished, and have health problems. Here are a few examples of the conditions of the poor. Some of these items are discussed in more detail at other points in the text.

- In 1991 37 million people had no private or public health insurance. About 1 million families a year are refused medical care for financial reasons.
- The infant mortality rate in some poor urban neighborhoods exceeds the rate in Third World countries. Compared with all countries, the United States ranks 18th in infant mortality, 22nd in under-age-five mortality, and 36th in infants with low birthweight (Sivard, 1991:48).
- 5.5 million children under age twelve suffer from hunger (Sivard, 1991:48). In 1991 an estimated 30 million people were hungry.
- Twenty percent of U.S. adults are functionally illiterate (Kozol, 1985).
- About 25 percent of people live in substandard housing without adequate plumbing, heat, or other facilities (Sivard, 1991:48). About 3 million do not have any permanent shelter at all (Kozol, 1988).
- Economic hardships increase the likelihood of a number of pathologies, such as alcoholism, suicide, and child abuse (Brenner, 1973; Trafford, 1982; Horwitz, 1984).

The psychological consequences of being poor are many. The poor are rejected and despised by others in the society, looked down on as lazy, shiftless, dirty, and immoral. Being poor is therefore degrading. The poor are not wanted by the more well-to-do as neighbors, friends, mates, or colleagues. Thus, many of the poor define themselves as failures. They are the rejects of society, and they feel it.

Being poor also engenders hopelessness and, thus, apathy. The poor have virtually no power. They cannot afford lawyers or lobbyists. They cannot afford to go on strike against low wages or high rent. Consequently, they tend to feel that their fates are in the hands of powerful others.

There is also a great deal of anger among the poor. They pay higher interest rates (because they are poor credit risks—another vicious circle); they are the last to be hired and the first to be fired; they must live in poor housing and often filthy conditions. One of the most important sources of anger is that they see affluence all about them but, no matter how hard they try, are unable to share in it.

Given the propensity for alienation, hostility, and lack of ego strength among the poor, there are three ways in which the individual poor cope with the conditions in which they find themselves: put up with the aversive situation, withdraw from it, or fight it.

What are the consequences for society if a significant proportion of the populace is poor? In economic terms the cost is very high. For example, the poor constitute a relatively unproductive mass of people. In a sense these persons are wasted; their work output is marginal, and they pay few or no taxes (usually only sales tax, since they have little property and low incomes). The cost to other tax-payers is quite large, in the form of welfare programs, urban renewal, and crime prevention. If poverty were eliminated through more better-paying jobs and more adequate monetary assistance to the permanently disabled or elderly, the entire society would prosper from the increased purchasing power and the larger tax base.

But economic considerations, though important, are not as crucial as human-itarian ones. A nation that can afford it must, if it calls itself civilized, eliminate the physical and psychological misery associated with poverty.

The Causes of Poverty

Who or what is to blame for poverty? There are two very different answers to this question. One is that the poor are in that condition because of some deficiency: either they are biologically inferior or their culture fails them by promoting char-acter traits that impede their progress in society. The other response places the blame on the structure of society: some persons are poor because society has failed to provide equality in educational opportunity, because institutions dis-criminate against minorities, because private industry has failed to provide enough jobs, because automation has made some jobs obsolete, and so forth. In this view society has worked in such a way as to trap certain persons and their off-spring in a condition of poverty.

Deficiency Theory 1: Innate Inferiority

In 1882 the British philosopher and sociologist Herbert Spencer came to the United States to promote a theory later known as **Social Darwinism.** He argued that the poor were poor because they were unfit. Poverty was nature's way of "excreting . . . unhealthy, imbecile, slow, vacillating, faithless members" of society in order to make room for the "fit," who were duly entitled to the rewards of wealth. Spencer preached that the poor should not be helped through state or pri-vate charity, because such acts would interfere with nature's way of getting rid of the weak (*The Progressive,* 1980). Social Darwinism has generally lacked support in the scientific community for fifty years, although it has continued to provide a rationale for the thinking of many individuals. Recently, however, the concept has resurfaced in the work of two respected scientists. Both suggest that the poor are in that condition because they do not measure up to the more well-to-do in intel-lectual endowment.

Arthur Jensen, professor of educational psychology at the University of California, has argued that there is a strong possibility that Blacks are less well endowed mentally than Whites. From his review of the research on IQ, he found that approximately 80 percent of IQ is inherited, while the remaining 20 percent is attributable to environment. Because Blacks differ significantly from Whites in achievement on IQ tests and in school, Jensen claimed that it is reasonable to hypothesize that the sources of these differences are genetic as well as environ-mental (Jensen, 1969, 1980).

Richard Herrnstein, a Harvard psychologist, agrees with Jensen that intelli-gence is largely inherited. He goes one step further, positing the formation of hereditary castes based on intelligence (Herrnstein, 1971, 1973). For Herrnstein, social stratification by inborn differences occurs because (1) mental ability is inherited and (2) success (prestige of job and earnings) depends on mental ability. Thus, a meritocracy (social classification by ability) develops through the sorting process. This reasoning assumes that persons close in mental ability are more likely to marry and reproduce, thereby ensuring castes by level of intelligence. According to this thesis, "in times to come, as technology advances, the tendency to be unemployed may run in the genes of a family about as certainly as bad teeth do now" (Herrnstein, 1971:63). This is another way of saying that the bright people are in the upper classes and the dregs are at the bottom. Inequality is justified just as it was years ago by the Social Darwinists.

To buttress their claim for the overwhelming primacy of heredity over environment in intelligence, both Jensen and Herrnstein used data from the classic studies of identical twins by the famous British psychologist Sir Cyril Burt. These studies from the 1940s and 1950s have come under a cloud of suspicion. Burt, who died in 1971, has been accused of fraud, of having faked much of his research, of reporting tests that were never done, and of signing fictitious names as coauthors (Gillie, 1977).

Notwithstanding the flaws in the logic and in the evidence used by Jensen and Herrnstein, one must consider the implications of this thesis for dealing with the problem of poverty.

Jensen and Herrnstein have argued that dispassionate study is required to determine whether intelligence is inherited to the degree that they state. Objectivity is the sine qua non of scientific inquiry, and one cannot argue with its merits. We should recognize, however, the important social consequences implied by the Jensen-Herrnstein argument. First, it is a classic example of blaming the victim. The individual poor person is blamed instead of schools, culturally biased IQ tests, or social barriers of race, religion, or nationality. By blaming the victim, this thesis claims a relationship between lack of success and lack of intelligence. This relationship is spurious because it ignores the advantages and disadvantages of ascribed status. According to William Ryan, "Arthur Jensen and Richard Herrnstein confirm regretfully that black folks and poor folks are born stupid, that little rich kids grow up rich adults, not because they inherited Daddy's stock portfolio, but rather because they inherited his brains" (Ryan, 1972:54).

A second implication is the belief that poverty is inevitable. The survival-of-the-fittest capitalist ideology is reinforced, justifying both discrimination against the poor and privilege for the privileged. Inequality is rationalized so that little will be done to aid its victims. The acceptance of this thesis, then, has obvious consequences for what policy decisions will be made or not made in dealing with poverty.

This thesis divides people in the United States further by appealing to bigots. It provides scientific justification for their beliefs in the racial superiority of some groups and the inferiority of others. By implication, it legitimates segregation and unequal treatment of so-called inferiors. The goal of integration and the fragile principle of egalitarianism are seriously threatened to the degree that members of the scientific community give this thesis credence or prominence.

Another serious implication of the Jensen-Herrnstein argument is the explicit validation of the IQ test as a legitimate measure of intelligence. The IQ test attempts to measure innate potential, but this measurement is impossible, because the testing process must inevitably reflect some of the skills that develop during the individual's lifetime. For the most part, intelligence tests measure educability—that is, the prediction of conventional school achievement. Achievement in school is, of course, also associated with a cluster of other social and motivational factors, as Joanna Ryan observes:

> The test as a whole is usually validated, if at all, against the external criterion of school performance. It therefore comes as no surprise to find that IQ scores do in fact correlate highly with educational success. IQ scores are also found to correlate positively with socio-economic status, those in the upper social classes tending to have the highest IQs. Since social class, and all that this implies, is both an important determinant and also an important consequence of educational performance, this association is to be expected. (Ryan, 1972:54)

The Jensen-Herrnstein thesis, however, overlooks the important contribution of social class to achievement on IQ tests. This oversight is crucial, because most social scientists feel that these tests are biased in favor of those who have had a middle- and upper-class environment and experience. IQ tests discriminate against the poor in many ways. They discriminate obviously in the language that is used, in the instructions that are given, and in the experiences they assume the subjects have had. The discrimination can also be more subtle. For minority group examinees the race of the person administering the test influences the results. Another, less well-known fact about IQ tests is that in many cases they provide a **self-fulfilling prophecy,** as Ryan notes:

> IQ scores obtained at one age often determine how an individual is subsequently treated, and, in particular, what kind of education he receives as a consequence of IQ testing will in turn contribute to his future IQ, and it is notorious that those of low and high IQ do not get equally good education. (Ryan, 1972:44)

The Jensen-Herrnstein thesis also provides justification for unequal schooling. Why should school boards allot comparable sums of money for similar programs in middle-class schools and lower-class schools if the natural endowments of children in each type of school are so radically different? Why should teachers expect the same performance from poor children as from children of the more well-to-do? The result of such beliefs is, of course, a self-fulfilling prophecy. Low expectations beget low achievement.

Finally, the Jensen-Herrnstein thesis encourages policymakers either to ignore poverty or to attack its effects rather than its causes in the structure of society itself.

Deficiency Theory 2: Cultural Inferiority

One prominent explanation of poverty, called the **culture-of-poverty** hypothesis, contends that the poor are qualitatively different in values and life-styles from the rest of society *and that these cultural differences explain continued poverty.* In other words, the poor, in adapting to their deprived condition, are found to be more permissive in raising their children, less verbal, more fatalistic, less apt to defer gratification, and less likely to be interested in formal education than the well-to-do.

Most important is the contention that this deviant cultural pattern is transmitted from generation to generation. Thus, there is a strong implication that poverty is perpetuated by defects in the lifeways of the poor. If poverty itself were to be eliminated, the former poor would probably continue to prefer instant gratification, be immoral by middle-class standards, and so on. This reasoning **blames the victim.** From this view, the poor have a subculture with values that differ radically from values of the other social classes.

Edward Banfield, an eminent political scientist, has argued that the difference between the poor and the nonpoor is cultural—the former have a present-time orientation while the nonpoor have a future-time orientation (Banfield, 1977). He does not see the present-time orientation of the poor as a function of the hopelessness of their situation. Yet it seems highly unlikely that the poor see little reason to complain about their slums: What about the filth, the rats, the overcrowded living conditions, the high infant mortality? What about the lack of jobs and opportunity for upward mobility? This feeling of being trapped seems to be the primary cause of a hedonistic present-time orientation. If the structure were changed so that the poor could see that hard work and deferred gratification really paid off, they could adopt a future-time orientation. Needless to say, there have been many severe criticisms of Banfield's position (see Ryan, 1970).

Critics of the culture-of-poverty hypothesis argue that the poor are an integral part of U.S. society; they do not abandon the dominant values of the society but, rather, retain them while simultaneously holding an alternative set of values. This alternative set is a result of adaptation to the conditions of poverty. Elliot Liebow, in his classic study of lower-class Black men, has taken this view. For him street-corner men strive to live by society's values but are continually frustrated by externally imposed failure:

> From this perspective, the street corner man does not appear as a carrier of an independent cultural tradition. His behavior appears not so much as a way of realizing the distinctive goals and values of his own subculture, or of conforming to its models, but rather as his way of trying to achieve many of the goals and values of the larger society, of failing to do this, and of concealing his failure from others and from himself as best he can. (Liebow, 1967:222)

Most people in the United States, however, believe that the poor are poor because they have a deviant system of values that encourages behaviors leading to poverty. To illustrate, a 1989 Gallup poll asked a national sample: "In your opinion, which is more often to blame if a person is poor—lack of effort on his part, or circumstances beyond his control?" Thirty-eight percent responded "lack of effort," 42 percent answered "circumstances," and 17 percent felt that both lack of effort and circumstances were to blame (*Gallup Report,* 1989a:4). Those most likely to choose "lack of effort" were men, young adults, Whites, people making $30,000 and over, and Republicans.

Structural Theories In contrast to blaming the biological or cultural deficiencies of the poor, the structural theory states that how society is organized creates poverty and makes certain kinds of people especially vulnerable to being poor.

Institutional discrimination.   Michael Harrington, whose book *The Other America* was instrumental in sparking the federal government's war on poverty, has said, "The real explanation of why the poor are where they are is that they made the mistake of being born to the wrong parents, in the wrong section of the country, in the wrong industry, or in the wrong racial or ethnic groups" (Harrington, 1963:21). This is another way of saying that the society is to blame for poverty, not the poor. When the customary ways of doing things, prevailing attitudes and expectations, and accepted structural arrangements work to the disadvantage of the poor, it is called **institutional discrimination.** Let us look at several examples of how the poor are trapped by this type of discrimination.

Most good jobs require a college degree, but the poor cannot afford to send their children to college. Scholarships go to the best-performing students. Children of the poor most often do not perform well in school, largely because of low expectations for them among teachers and administrators. This attitude is reflected in the system of tracking by ability as measured on class-biased examinations. Further evidence is found in the disproportionately low amounts of money given to schools in impoverished neighborhoods. All of these acts result in a self-fulfilling prophecy—the poor are not expected to do well in school and they do not. Because they are failures as measured by objective indicators (such as the disproportionately high number of dropouts and discipline problems and the very small proportion who desire to go to college), the school feels justified in its discrimination toward the children of the poor.

The poor are also trapped because they get sick more often and stay sick longer than the well-to-do. The reasons, of course, are that they cannot afford preventive medicine, proper diets, and proper medical attention when ill. The high incidence of sickness among the poor means either that they will be fired from their jobs or that they will not receive money for the days missed from work (unlike the well-to-do, who usually have jobs with such fringe benefits as sick leave and paid-up medical insurance). Not receiving a paycheck for extended periods means that the poor will have even less money for proper health care—thereby ensuring an even higher incidence of sickness. Thus, there is a vicious cycle of poverty. The poor will tend to remain poor, and their children will tend to perpetuate the cycle.

The traditional organization of schools and jobs in U.S. society has limited the opportunities of racial minorities, women, and the elderly. The next four chapters describe at length how these three groups are systematically disadvantaged by the prevailing laws, customs, and expectations of society. We summarize some of the disadvantages here:

- Racial minorities are deprived of equal opportunities for education, jobs, and income.
- Women typically work at less prestigious jobs than do men and, when working at equal-status jobs, receive less pay and fewer chances for advancement.
- The elderly are the victims of job discrimination, mandatory retirement policies, and, typically, inadequate pensions. Social Security and other pension plans discriminate especially against the female elderly (see Chapter 9).

The political economy of society.   The basic tenet of capitalism—that who gets what is determined by private profit rather than collective need—explains the persistence of poverty. The primacy of maximizing profit works to promote poverty in several ways. First, employers are constrained to pay their workers the least possible in wages and benefits. Only a portion of the wealth created by the laborers is distributed to them; the rest goes to the owners for investment and profit. Therefore, employers must keep wages low. That they are successful is demonstrated by the more than 2 million persons who worked *full-time but were below the poverty line.*

A second way that the primacy of profit promotes poverty is by maintaining a surplus of laborers, because a surplus depresses wages. Especially important for employers is to have a supply of undereducated and desperate people who will work for very low wages. A large supply of these marginal people (such as minorities, women, and undocumented workers) aids the ownership class by depressing the wages for all workers in good times and provides the obvious category of people to be laid off from work in economic downturns.

A third impact of the primacy of profits in capitalism is that employers make investment decisions without regard for their employees (potential or actual). If costs can be reduced, employers will purchase new technologies to replace workers (such as robots to replace assembly line workers and word processors to replace secretaries). Similarly, owners may shut down a plant and shift their operations to a foreign country where wages are significantly lower.

In sum, the fundamental assumption of capitalism is individual gain without regard for what the resulting behaviors may mean for other people. The capitalist system, then, should not be accepted as a neutral framework within which

More than 2 million persons work full-time but remain below the poverty line because of low wages and little or no benefits.

goods are produced and distributed but, rather, as an economic system that perpetuates inequality.

A number of political factors complement the workings of the economy to perpetuate poverty. Political decisions made to fight inflation with high interest rates, for example, hurt several industries, particularly automobiles and home construction, causing high unemployment.

The powerful in society also use their political clout to keep society unequal:

> Poverty exists in America because the society is unequal, and there are overwhelming political pressures to keep it that way. Any attempt to redistribute wealth and income will inevitably be opposed by powerful interests. Some people can be relatively rich only if others are relatively poor, and since power is concentrated in the hands of the rich, public policies will continue to reflect their interests. (*Denver Post,* 1982a:11A)

Clearly, the affluent in a capitalist society will resist efforts to redistribute their wealth to the disadvantaged. Their political efforts are, rather, to increase their benefits at the expense of the poor and the powerless. (See the Observation on who benefits from poverty.)

OBSERVATION

WHO BENEFITS FROM POVERTY?

Herbert Gans, a sociologist, has some interesting insights about the benefits of poverty. He begins with the assumption that if some social arrangement persists, it must be accomplishing something important (at least in the view of the powerful in society). What, then, does the existence of a relatively large number of persons in a condition of poverty accomplish that is beneficial to the powerful?

1. Poverty functions to provide a low-wage labor pool that is willing (or unable to be unwilling) to do society's necessary "dirty work." The middle and upper classes are subsidized by the existence of economic activities that depend on the poor (low wages to many workers in restaurants, hospitals, and in truck farming).
2. The poor also subsidize a variety of economic activities for the affluent by supporting, for example, innovations in medicine (as patients in research hospitals or as guinea pigs in medical experiments) and providing servants, gardeners, and house cleaners who make life easier for the well-to-do.
3. The existence of poverty creates jobs for a number of occupations and professions that serve the poor or protect the rest of society from them (penologists, social workers, police, pawn shop owners, numbers racketeers, and owners of liquor stores). The presence of poor people also provides incomes for doctors, lawyers, teachers, and others who are too old, poorly trained, or incompetent to attract more affluent clients.
4. Poor people subsidize merchants by purchasing products that others do not want (seconds, dilapidated cars, deteriorated housing, and day-old bread, fruit, and vegetables) and that otherwise would have little or no value.
5. The poor serve as a group to be punished in order to uphold the legitimacy of conventional values (hard work, thrift, honesty, and monogamy). *The poor provide living proof that moral deviance does not pay* and, thus, an indirect rationale for blaming the victim.
6. Poverty guarantees the status of those who are not poor. The poor, by occupying a position at the bottom of the status hierarchy, provide a reliable and relatively permanent measuring rod for status comparison, particularly by those just above them (that is, the working class, whose politics, for example, are often influenced by the

The Elimination of Poverty

As we have discussed, about 35.7 million people in the United States are officially poor. Probably another 30 million or so hover just above the poverty line. Must some portion of U.S. society live in poverty? Is there a way to get everyone above the poverty level to a level at which they are not deprived of the basics of adequate nutrition, health care, and housing? The remainder of this chapter enumerates some assumptions that appear basic to achieving such a goal and some general programs that adoption of these assumptions requires.

Assumption 1: Poverty can be eliminated in the United States. Michael Harrington has argued forcefully that poverty must be eliminated because the United States has the resources: "In a nation with a technology that could provide every citizen with a decent life, it is an outrage and a scandal that there should be such social misery" (Harrington, 1963:24).

The Children's Defense Fund has calculated (based on 1987 figures) that poverty can be eliminated for $51.646 billion.

need to maintain social distance between themselves and the poor).

7. The poor aid in the upward mobility of others. Many persons have entered the middle class through the profits earned from providing goods and services in the slums (pawn shops, second-hand clothing and furniture stores, gambling, prostitution, and drugs).

8. The poor, being powerless, can be made to absorb the costs of change in society. In the nineteenth century they did the backbreaking work that built the railroads and the cities. Today, they are the ones pushed out of their homes by urban renewal, the building of expressways, parks, and stadiums. Many economists assume that a degree of unemployment is necessary to fight inflation. The poor, who are "first to be fired and last to be hired," are the ones who make the sacrifice for the economy.

Gans notes:

This analysis is not intended to suggest that because it is often functional, poverty *should* exist, or that it *must* exist. For one thing, poverty has many more dysfunctions than functions; for another, it is possible to suggest functional alternatives. For example, society's dirty work could be done without poverty, either by automation or by paying "dirty workers" decent wages. Nor is it necessary for the poor to subsidize the many activities they support through their low-wage jobs. This would, however, drive up the costs of these activities, which would result in higher prices to their customers and clients. . . . In sum, then, many of the functions served by the poor could be replaced if poverty were eliminated, but almost always at higher costs to others, particularly more affluent others. Consequently a functional analysis must conclude that poverty persists not only because many of the functional alternatives to poverty would be quite dysfunctional for the affluent members of society. . . . Poverty can be eliminated only when they become dysfunctional for the affluent or powerful, or when the powerless can obtain enough power to change society.

Source: Herbert J. Gans, "The Uses of Poverty: The Poor Pay All," *Social Policy* (July/August 1971): excerpts from p. 24. Reprinted by permission. © 1971 by Social Policy Corporation.

These numbers sound like a lot of money. And they are. But this is also a large and wealthy country. The cost of eliminating poverty ($51.646 billion) is equivalent to only 1 percent of our gross national product. . . . We *can* save our children—and our future—but only by making hard national choices and reordering our national investment priorities. The issue is not money but national will and values. (Children's Defense Fund, 1989b:xx)

With the breakup of the Soviet Empire and the lessening of global tensions, the United States could reduce its defense budget ($290 billion for fiscal 1993) by $50 billion without threatening national security. These savings, called the Peace Dividend, could be committed to bringing all people in the United States above the poverty line.

Similarly, we could make a commitment to help children living in poverty, with a commitment like we do to meet a national emergency. In the words of Albert Shanker, president of the American Federation of Teachers:

When a great disaster, like a hurricane or an earthquake, strikes people in our country, the president often declares a state of emergency. This mobilizes resources; it cuts through red tape; and it focuses attention on the people who are in danger so they get the help they need—and get it right away. . . . Victims of floods and earthquakes didn't bring their misfortunes on themselves, and we give them help in rebuilding their lives. How can we deny poor children the chance to *build* theirs? (Shanker, 1992a:E9)

Or sometimes the government makes a huge financial commitment to bolster a sagging part of the economy. If, for example, the government can agree to bail out the deregulated, imprudent, and sometimes fraudulent savings and loan industry for an estimated $500 billion (prorated over a number of years), then surely the government is able to spend one-tenth of that amount to lift 31.5 million people out of poverty.

Assumption 2: Poverty is caused by a lack of resources, not a deviant value system. Basic to a program designed to eliminate poverty is the identification of what keeps some people in a condition of poverty. Is it lack of money and power, or the maintenance of deviant values and life-styles? This question is fundamental because the answer determines the method for eliminating poverty. The culture-of-poverty proponents would address non-middle-class traits. The target would be the poor themselves and making them more socially acceptable. Developing the social competence of the poor—not changing the system—would bring an end to poverty. This approach treats the symptom, not the disease. The disease can only be cured by attacking its sources within the society—the structural arrangements that maintain inequality. Thus, the attack must be directed at the structural changes that will enable lower-class persons to earn a living to support their families adequately.

Assumption 3: Poverty is not simply a matter of deficient income; it results from other inequities in the society as well. Poverty involves a reinforcing pattern of restricted opportunities, deficient community services, powerful predators who profit from the poor, institutional racism and sexism (see Chapters 7 and 8), and unequal distribution of resources. These problems can be eliminated through structural changes, including, first, the enforcement of the laws regarding equal opportunity for jobs, advancement, and schooling; and second, the redistribution of power on the local and national levels. The present system works to keep the poor powerless. What is needed, rather, is the organization of the poor into groups with power to determine, or, at least, to shape, policy in local communities. The poor need to have some power over school policies. They need to have a voice in the decisions about the distribution of resources within the community (such as money for parks and recreation, fire protection, street maintenance, and refuse collection). The U.S. system of representative democracy is one of winner take all and is therefore to blame for the powerlessness of all minorities. A system of proportional representation would guarantee a degree of power. A third structural change involves an increasing reliance on planning and action at the national level to alleviate the causes of poverty.

Assumption 4: Poverty cannot be eliminated by the efforts of the poor themselves. The poor have neither the power nor the resources to bring about the structural changes necessary to eliminate poverty. A few of the individual poor may escape poverty by their own efforts, but the others will remain poor unless the people and groups with the power and the resources change the system. This is not to say that the poor cannot have some effect. They can, but usually only indirectly through influential persons or groups who become concerned about their plight.

Assumption 5: Poverty cannot be eliminated by the private sector of the economy. Assuming that private enterprises will not engage in unprofitable activities, we can assume also that private enterprise efforts will never by themselves eliminate poverty. In other words, private profit will tend to subvert the human needs that are of public concern; businesses will not provide jobs that they consider unnecessary or not immediately profitable, nor will they voluntarily stop activities that are profitable (e.g., renting deteriorated housing because the unimproved land may increase in value, or lobbying to keep certain occupational categories outside minimum-wage restrictions, or moving to another state or nation where wages are lower).

Conventional wisdom, however, suggests that private business is the answer, because it will generate new and better-paying jobs. This solution simply will not work, because the "new poor," as Harrington has referred to them, differ dramatically from the "old poor" (Harrington, 1984). The **old poor**—that is, the poor of other generations—had hopes of breaking out of poverty; if they did not break out themselves, at least they believed their children would. This hope was based on the needs of a rapidly expanding economy. There were jobs for immigrants, farmers, and grade school dropouts because of the needs of mass production. However, the poor of the present generation, the **new poor,** are much more trapped in poverty. There is now a much greater probability that poverty will persist from generation to generation and hence a much greater pessimism among poor persons. Some of the new poor are workers who have been displaced by robots, word processors, and other labor-saving devices. The jobs of others have moved—moved from the urban core to the suburbs; moved to other regions of

The new poor have a much harder time finding employment than did the poor of a generation ago. Today, unskilled jobs are being replaced by technology and growing regional and international competition for job-producing industries.

the country; or moved to other countries. The jobs were lost because of rational business decisions. In short, the private sector, with its emphasis on profit (and therefore efficiency), will not generate the new jobs needed to eliminate poverty.

Assumption 6: Poverty will not be eliminated by a rising economy. A common assumption is that a growing economy will help everyone—"a rising tide lifts all boats." To a degree this premise is true, as more people are hired and more opportunities exist during economic expansion. For the poor, though, the conditions of poverty limit and deny. Cities with low tax bases do not provide the needed social services such as pre- and post-natal health care and good schools. The federal government, with other priorities, does not fund programs such as Head Start adequately. Employers do not have jobs with decent wages and benefits, even in good times, for those with inadequate education and training. In the words of George Will, a conservative who usually argues for market-based solutions; "A rising tide does not raise all boats . . . those stuck in the mud have unique problems and a uniquely powerful claim on our help" (Will, 1991:115).

Assumption 7: Poverty will not be eliminated by volunteer help from well-meaning individuals, groups, and organizations. In 1988 candidate George Bush called for a "thousand points of light" as the solution to social problems such as poverty. By this Bush meant that charities and volunteers are the answers, not big government. At one level, this makes good sense. That is, churches, private organizations, and the like can *and do* provide food for the hungry, shelters for the homeless, emergency care for the victims of natural disasters. In Fort Collins, Colorado, for example, a retired physician began a health clinic for indigent children. With volunteer help and donations this clinic provides free medical care for thousands of youth each year. This wonderful program provides services not provided by the city, county, state, and federal government. The problem, however, is that since it is voluntary the children in many communities will be denied these services. Only a national program will ensure that the needs of all children will be met.

Assumption 8: Poverty will not be eliminated by the efforts of state and local governments. A basic tenet of political conservatism is decentralization of government. Relatively small and locally based governmental units are believed to be best suited for meeting the needs of the people. This theory, though logical, has not always worked in practice. In fact, it has increased the problems of some localities.

A good deal of money is gathered and dispensed at the city, county, and state levels for the purpose of alleviating the misery associated with poverty. Some federal programs function only through local units of government. The basic problem is that these local units differ dramatically in their willingness and resources to attack poverty. For example, there are vast differences among states in levels of welfare assistance. In 1990, for example, Idaho spent 24 cents per child to help low-income parents with either child care or preschool programs. At the other extreme, Massachusetts spent $152.04 per child (Gannett News Service, 1992). A family of three needed $11,568 per year for subsistence in 1991, yet the typical state paid $7,968 a year in Aid to Families with Dependent Children, which is supplemented by the federally funded food stamp program. Combining AFDC payments and food stamps, the most generous of the forty-eight mainland states, California, provided $9,906 per three-person family, while the least generous state, Mississippi, provided $4,764 (Rom, 1992; DeParle, 1992).

Contrary to popular thinking, welfare grants *have been declining.* In constant 1991 dollars, the national average (AFDC and food stamps) was $10,169 in 1972 compared to $7,471 in 1991, a *decrease* of 27 percent (DeParle, 1992).

A common assumption (and a justification for some for miserly welfare) is that the needy will migrate to the more generous states. However, the evidence, according to O'Hare, is that the promise of jobs is a greater lure than generous welfare:

> Between 1980 and 1985, the 28 states with below-average AFDC benefits attracted, on average, 97,000 more migrants than states with high benefits, largely reflecting the greater economic strength of the South relative to the Northeast and Midwest. Clearly, the attraction for those willing to move to another state is the promise of jobs rather than the potential for generous welfare benefits. (O'Hare, 1987:11)

Because many politicians believe that relatively high welfare benefits attract poor people from other states and because many states are in a fiscal crisis, there is a current trend to reduce welfare benefits at the state level. In 1991 and 1992, for example, fourteen states, including Ohio, Michigan, Wisconsin, and California, reduced welfare benefits to the poor.

Assumption 9: Poverty is a national problem and must be attacked with massive, nationwide programs financed largely and organized by the federal government. Poverty can be eliminated through the massive infusion of money and compensatory programs, coupled with centralized planning. This procedure is a form of socialism and therefore is suspect by many. Governmental control and government subsidies are not new phenomena in the United States, yet it is a curious fact that subsidies for the poor are generally decried while other subsidies go unnoticed or even praised. The federal government has subsidized, for example, defense industries (loans), the oil industry (oil depletion allowance), all corporations (tax write-offs), students (government scholarships and interest-free loans), professors (research grants), homeowners (the interest on mortgages is tax-deductible, usually saving homeowners hundreds of dollars a year), newspapers and magazines (through lower-cost postage), churches (no property tax or income tax), and farmers (farm subsidies).

What can the federal government do to achieve the goal of getting all persons permanently above the poverty line? Three quite different programs are needed, because there are three kinds of poor people: (1) those who are unemployed (or employed at jobs that pay the minimum wage or below) because they lack the skills needed in an advanced technological society; (2) those who cannot work because they are too old, are physically or mentally handicapped, or are mothers with dependent children; and (3) the children of the poor.

The able-bodied poor need three things: (1) adequate training; (2) guaranteed employment; and (3) a guaranteed minimum income that provides the necessities of food, clothing, shelter, and medical care. New jobs and even new occupational categories must be created. Michael Harrington has suggested that these new jobs may involve working as "indigenous" neighborhood social workers, teacher's aides, community organizers, or research assistants. These new opportunities would be in the service sector of the economy rather than in the goods-producing sector, where automation occurs (Harrington, 1965:35). Other jobs could be in such public works areas as highway construction, mass transit, recycling waste materials, and park maintenance. An important component of such jobs is social usefulness. Jobs with high social productivity would also have some beneficial by-products (latent consequences) in the form of less estrangement of workers from their jobs and overall improvements for the society itself.

All segments of society benefit under full employment. If the poor are paid adequately and therefore have more money to purchase products, the private sector of the economy will be stimulated by increased demand for goods and services. At the same time, full employment and decent pay will give power to the poor. The greater their resources are, the greater is their likelihood to organize for political and social power, to vote their interests, and to become respected by others.

The disabled and incapacitated who cannot or should not be employed require government subsidies to rise above the poverty line. These subsidies may be in the form of money, food, housing, recreational facilities, or special-care centers for the physically and mentally handicapped. An important need is adequate low-cost housing, since most of the poor currently live in deteriorated housing units. Whatever the cost, there must be a nationwide commitment to provide a decent standard of living for these persons. According to an editorial in *Saturday*

Review, "One hallmark of a civilized society is its willingness to care for its poor, ill, elderly, dependent young, and permanently handicapped" (*Saturday Review,* 1970:19).

About 40 percent of the poor in the United States are children. Their economic disadvantage translates into educational disadvantages. Many drop out of school for dead-end jobs, criminal activities, or just hanging out because they have lost hope. How can this cycle of disadvantage be broken? One clear need is for compensatory programs. In the words of Michael Harrington:

> The poor, so to speak, cannot be given the same voucher as everyone else. Having been systematically deprived for so long, they require the use of federal power to make the schooling market more favorable to them than to the children of the affluent. (Harrington, 1968:34)

Head Start is one federally funded program that has documented positive effects for economically disadvantaged children. Lisbeth Schorr has summarized what is known about this excellent program:

> The basic Head Start model has proved to be sound. When three- to five-year-old children are systematically helped to think, reason, and speak clearly; when they are provided hot meals, social services, health evaluations, and health care; when families become partners in their children's learning experiences, are helped toward self-sufficiency, and gain greater confidence in themselves as parents and as contributing members of the community, the results are measurable and dramatic. (Schorr, 1988:192)

The problem with Head Start is that it is underfunded, with only one in four eligible children able to be included.

Michael Harrington has suggested a more comprehensive program than just Head Start for disadvantaged youth:

> We should have a GI bill in the war against poverty and pay people to go to school, pay for their tuition, their books, and give them an additional living allowance if they have a family. The GI bill was one of the most successful social experiments this society ever had. Why does it require a shooting war for us to be so smart? Why can't we in the war on poverty say that the most productive thing a young person between ages 16 and 21 can do is go to school, and that this is an investment in the Great Society? (Harrington, 1965:xii–xiii)

The positive consequences of this plan would be, first, that a significant segment of potential workers would be kept out of the labor force for a time, thereby reducing the number of jobs needed. Second, individuals would learn the skills needed in an automated society. Third, the educated workers could command greater wages and therefore pay more in taxes. The lifetime earnings for veterans who took advantage of the GI bill were significantly greater than for those who chose to bypass the plan—so much so that they will pay back to the government in taxes approximately six times the amount the government invested in their education. A similar approach could work for the poor.

The problem with this emphasis on education (and with alleviating poverty in general) is the difficulty of creating enough socially useful jobs with a decent U.S. standard of pay. Leon Keyserling, former chairman of the Council of Economic Advisors, had said that "education and training as a conduit to a job is itself a travesty unless the jobs are created first: training for jobs can be meaningful only if the jobs are going to be available, and the training itself does not create jobs" (Keyserling, 1960:93). The creation of jobs, then, is the key to eliminating poverty. Because most of these jobs will no doubt be in the public sector of the economy, the government must divert its best minds to tackling this immense problem.

General programs such as these are necessary if the United States is to get everyone above the absolute minimum level of economic security. This goal is easily attainable because the productive capacity of the United States is great enough to make it possible without too much sacrifice. *These programs, however, will not solve the basic problem of inequality;* there is no insurance that they will eliminate urban riots, demonstrations, or crime; they will not eliminate the anger and bitterness that persons feel as they experience deprivation. They can, however, eliminate the human suffering associated with extreme deprivation.

CHAPTER REVIEW

1. According to the government's arbitrary dividing line, which minimizes the actual extent of poverty, 14.2 percent of the U.S. population (1991) is officially poor. Disproportionately represented in this category are African Americans, Latinos, Native Americans, children, women (especially female heads of families), and people living in central cities and rural areas.

2. The poor are *not* poor because they refuse to work. Most adult poor either work at low wages, cannot find work, work part-time, are homemakers, are ill or disabled, or are in school.

3. Government assistance to the poor is *not* sufficient to eliminate their economic deprivation. Less than half of the poor actually receive any federal assistance. When compared to the nonpoor, the poor have a higher incidence of health problems, malnutrition, social pathologies, and homelessness.

4. Most governmental assistance is targeted to the affluent rather than the poor. The nonpoor receive three-fourths of the federal monies allocated to human services. Tax expenditures and other subsidies provide enormous benefits to the already affluent, which further redistributes the nation's wealth upward.

5. One explanation for poverty is that the poor themselves are to blame. The culture-of-poverty hypothesis, for example, contends that the poor are qualitatively different in values and life-styles from the successful and that these differences explain their poverty and the poverty of their children.

6. Another position that blames the poor for their condition is the innate-inferiority hypothesis. This theory, a variant of Social Darwinism promoted by Arthur Jensen and Richard Herrnstein, holds that certain categories of people are disadvantaged because they are less well endowed mentally.

7. Critics of the culture-of-poverty and the innate-inferiority hypotheses charge that in blaming the victim, both theories ignore how social conditions trap individuals and groups in poverty.

8. The homeless are the poorest of the poor. The proportion of people in the United States who are homeless is the highest since the Great Depression, and the numbers have risen rapidly in the past decade. The structural reasons

for this sudden rise in the homeless population are (a) the sudden dwindling of low-income housing; and (b) the increased economic vulnerability among the poor and the near poor resulting from the transformation of the economy, changes in family structure, and public policies that have substantially reduced programs to help the needy.

9. The elimination of poverty requires (a) a commitment to accomplish that goal; (b) a program based on the assumption that poverty results from a lack of resources rather than from a deviant value system; (c) a program based on the assumption that poverty results from inequities in the society; (d) recognition that poverty cannot be eliminated by the efforts of the poor themselves, by the private sector of the economy, by charitable individuals or groups, or by the efforts of state and local governments alone; and (e) recognition that poverty is a national problem and must be attacked by massive, nationwide programs largely financed and organized by the federal government.

10. Three quite different programs are needed because there are three kinds of poverty. The unemployed or underpaid need adequate training, guaranteed employment, and a guaranteed minimal income that is adequate to provide the necessities. The disabled and incapacitated require government subsidies to meet their needs. Finally, the children of the poor need education and opportunities to break the poverty cycle.

KEY TERMS

Poverty. A standard of living below the minimum needed for the maintenance of adequate diet, health, and shelter.

Official poverty line. An arbitrary line computed by multiplying the cost of a basic nutritionally adequate diet by three.

Feminization of poverty. Viewed erroneously as a trend for contemporary women to be more economically vulnerable than men. This view obscures the fact that women have always been poorer than men, especially older women and women of color.

Poor-poor. People whose cash incomes are at one-half the poverty line or less.

Welfare. Government monies and services provided to the poor.

Wealthfare. Government subsidies to the nonpoor.

Tax expenditures. Legal tax loopholes that allow the affluent to escape paying certain taxes and therefore to receive a subsidy (e.g., the tax deduction to home owners).

Social Darwinism. The belief that the principle of the "survival of the fittest" applies to human societies, explaining why the poor are poor and the rich are rich.

Self-fulfilling prophecy. An event occurs because it is predicted. That is, the prophecy is fulfilled because people alter their behavior to conform to the prediction.

Culture of poverty. The view that the poor are qualitatively different in values and lifestyles from the rest of society and that these cultural differences explain continued poverty.

Blaming the victim. The belief that some individuals are poor, criminals, or school dropouts because they have a flaw within them, thus ignoring the social factors affecting their behaviors.

Institutional discrimination. When the social arrangements and accepted ways of doing things in society disadvantage minority groups.

Old poor. The poor of an earlier generation, who had hopes of breaking out of poverty because unskilled and semiskilled jobs were plentiful.

New poor. The poor who are displaced by new technologies or whose jobs have moved away to the suburbs, to other regions of the country, or out of the country. They have less hope of escaping poverty than do the old poor.

FOR FURTHER STUDY

Joel Blau. *The Visible Poor: Homelessness in the United States.* New York: Oxford University Press, 1992.

Fred Block, Richard A. Cloward, Barbara Ehrenreich, and Frances Fox Piven. *The Mean Season: The Attack on the Welfare State.* New York: Pantheon, 1987.

Children's Defense Fund. *A Vision for America's Future.* Washington, D.C.: Children's Defense Fund, 1989.

David T. Ellwood. *Poor Support: Poverty in the American Family.* New York: Basic Books, 1988.

Michael Harrington. *The New American Poverty.* New York: Holt, Rinehart and Winston, 1984.

Charles Hoch and Robert A. Slayton. *New Homeless and Old.* Philadelphia: Temple University Press, 1989.

Jacqueline Jones. *The Dispossessed: America's Underclasses from the Civil War to the Present.* New York: Basic Books, 1992.

Michael B. Katz. *The Undeserving Poor: From the War on Poverty to the War on Welfare.* New York: Pantheon, 1989.

Mickey Kaus. *The End of Equality.* New York: Basic Books, 1992.

Jonathan Kozol. *Illiterate America.* Garden City, N.Y.: Anchor Press/Doubleday, 1985.

Jonathan Kozol. *Rachel and Her Children: Homeless Families in America.* New York: Crown, 1988.

Nicholas Lemann. *The Promised Land: The Great Black Migration and How It Changed America.* New York: Knopf, 1991.

Richard H. Ropers. *Persistent Poverty: The American Dream Turned Nightmare.* New York: Insight Books, 1991.

Ruth Sidel. *Women and Children Last: The Plight of Poor Women in Affluent America.* New York: Viking Press, 1986.

William J. Wilson. *The Truly Disadvantaged: The Inner City, the Underclass, and Public Policy.* Chicago: University of Chicago Press, 1987.

James D. Wright. *Address Unknown: The Homeless in America.* Hawthorne, N.Y.: Aldine de Gruyter, 1989.

FORUM

WHAT IS THE CAUSE OF THE NEW POVERTY?
IS IT WELFARE OR THE LACK OF JOBS?

*The programs designed to help the poor—welfare—have served to encourage low-income
people to avoid work and marriage.*

Charles Murray

Basic indicators of well-being took a turn for the worse
in the 1960s, most consistently and most drastically for
the poor. In some cases, earlier progress slowed; in
other cases mild deterioration accelerated; in a few
instances advance turned into retreat. The trendlines
on many of the indicators are—literally—unbelievable
to people who do not make a profession of following
them.

The question is why. Why at that moment in history did so many basic trends in the quality of life *for the
poor* go sour? Why did progress slow, stop, reverse?

The easy hypotheses—the economy, changes in
demographics, the effects of Vietnam or Watergate or
racism—fail as explanations. As often as not, taking
them into account only increases the mystery.

Nor does the explanation lie in idiosyncratic failures of craft. It is not just that we sometimes administered good programs improperly, or that sound
concepts sometimes were converted to operations
incorrectly. It is not that a specific program, or a
specific court ruling or act of Congress, was especially
destructive. The error was strategic.

A government's social policy helps set the rules of
the game—the stakes, the risks, the payoffs, the trade-
offs, and the strategies for making a living, raising a
family, having fun, defining what *winning* and *success*
mean. The more vulnerable a population and the fewer
its independent resources, the more decisive the effect
of the rules imposed from above. The most compelling
explanation for the marked shift in the fortunes of the
poor is that they continued to respond, as they always
had, to the world as they found it, but that we—meaning the not-poor and un-disadvantaged—had changed
the rules of their world. Not of our world, just of theirs.
The first effect of the new rules was to make it profitable for the poor to behave in the short term in ways
that were destructive in the long term. Their second
effect was to mask these long-term losses—to subsidize irretrievable mistakes. We tried to provide more
for the poor and produced more poor instead. We tried
to remove the barriers to escape from poverty, and
inadvertently built a trap.

Source: Excerpt from *Losing Ground* by Charles Murray.
Copyright © 1984 by Charles Murray. Reprinted by permission of Basic Books, a division of HarperCollins Publishers.

*The issue is not that welfare entices some able-bodied people away from work but that work
is either unavailable or what is available has very low wages.*

Frances Fox Piven and
Richard A. Cloward

The argument underpinning the attack on the welfare
state and the research questions stimulated by the

attack flow from a model that explains human behavior
as responses to economic incentives. Presumably, the
availability and liberality of the "welfare-package," consisting of the several income, nutritional, health, and
housing programs for which a family may be eligible,

constitute an incentive that draws people away from stable labor-market participation and from marriage.

Although we think an economic-incentive model falls considerably short of explaining human behavior as a whole, we agree that it explains a good deal of what people do. It accounts, after all, for the historic opposition of employers to social provision; a labor force that is guaranteed a measure of income security will be less likely to work at jobs that do not offer something more or something better. But this is to say that it is the *relative* incentives of welfare and work that are at issue. To speak only of the work disincentives generated by welfare benefits implies that recipients simply cease making work efforts. A more reasoned way to state the incentive point is that it takes more favorable job opportunities to draw them into the market. This is surely the main meaning of the work-disincentive effects of the guaranteed-income experiments: the experimental income payments were relatively high, so that people did not have to take any job on any terms, and some reduced their work effort. But because the research agenda has been so closely limited by the charges against the welfare state, attention has been focused almost exclusively on the work-disincentive effects of welfare payments, without comparable attention to the question of whether the incentives associated with work have been weakening.

A consistent use of the incentive model would explore the impact of the availability of welfare benefits on labor-market behavior in the context of changes in real wages, benefits, and working conditions. That requires directing attention both to the decline of the mass-production industries, such as auto, steel, and rubber, with their unionized and relatively well paid jobs even for the unskilled, and to the expansion of the service sector with its low-wage, nonunion jobs. Manufacturing employment declined from 28.2 percent to 22.2 percent of the total labor force between 1960 and 1980. The largest relative decline occurred among production workers, and quickened as the years wore on so that, by 1980, the manufacturing sector was shrinking in absolute terms and the largest losses were in the durable-goods sector where the highest-paying manufacturing jobs are concentrated. The contraction was more than offset by service sector expansion, but these new jobs were concentrated in the lowest-paid categories of the service sector. The Bureau of Labor Statistics reported in May of 1986, for example, that 30.5 percent of the jobs added since January 1980 were in retail trade, and nearly 60 percent were in the category of miscellaneous services, such as hotel and motel jobs, business services (including temporary office jobs), and hospital jobs.

The dramatic shift from industrial to service-sector employment has been accompanied by comparably dramatic changes in the terms of work. Annual wages in retailing average $9,036, or about $2,000 less than the poverty level for a family of four, and only 44.3 percent of average earnings in manufacturing, down from 63.1 percent of manufacturing wages in 1962. Annual wages in miscellaneous services of $13,647 did not much exceed the poverty line. But in fact, almost no attention is paid to the impact on work patterns of declining real wages in sectors of the economy in which potential or actual welfare recipients are likely to be employed. Similarly, little is made of the steady erosion of the real value of the minimum wage at which so many jobs in the expanding service sector are pegged. The National Council on Employment Policy reports that in 1984, about 8 million workers received wages at or below the minimum wage of $3.35 an hour, and according to Sar Levitan, another 6 million received wages just above the minimum. Nor is there attention to the spread of temporary and part-time work, or to the revival of home work, or to the reduction or elimination of work-related benefits which occurs under these arrangements. In April 1986, according to the Bureau of Labor Statistics, nearly 20 percent of the work force was employed part-time. When added to those employed in temporary jobs, the numbers of such "contingent workers" have increased from 23.5 million in 1975 to 29.5 million in 1985. In a nutshell, welfare benefits may have become more attractive simply because work has become less so.

Source: From *The Mean Season,* by Fred Block, Richard Cloward, Barbara Ehrenreich, Frances Fox Piven. Copyright © 1987 by Random House, Inc. Reprinted by permission of Pantheon Books, a division of Random House, Inc.

7 Racial and Ethnic Inequality

Dramatic racial transformations of the past two decades have shattered the hope that civil rights victories would end racial inequality and injustice. Instead, the United States now faces serious new racial problems. These problems include the increasing isolation of minorities in central cities, growing minority unemployment and other forms of economic dislocation, the largest ten-year wave of immigration in U.S. history, growing racial diversity (see Figure 7.1), and growing racial conflicts throughout society. The Los Angeles riots have refocused attention on race relations in the United States. These problems are created in large part by national and global economic changes. They are making race a central social issue of the 1990s.

The United States is a mosaic of different social groups and categories. However, these groups are not equal in power, resources, prestige, or presumed worth. They are differentially ranked on each of these dimensions. But why is one group alleged to be superior to another? The basic reason is differential power—power derived from superior numbers, technology, weapons, property, or economic resources. The people holding superior power in a society establish a system of inequality by dominating less powerful groups, and this system of

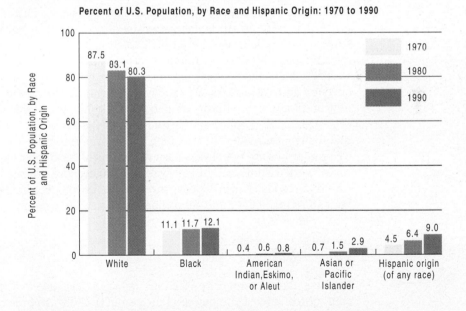

Percent of U.S. Population, by Race and Hispanic Origin: 1970 to 1990

Figure 7.1 Percentage of U.S. population, by race and Hispanic origin: 1970 to 1990

Source: U.S. Bureau of the Census, 1990 Census Profile. "Race and Hispanic Origin," (June 1991): 2.

inequality is then maintained and perpetuated by power. The terms **majority** and **minority** describe the differences in power. The critical feature of the minority's status is its inferior social position in which its interests are not effectively represented in the political, economic, and social institutions of society. The term *dominant* may be used as a synonym for *majority* and *subordinate* as a synonym for *minority* (Yetman, 1991:11).

Like the class and gender hierarchies, racial and ethnic stratification is a basic feature of U.S. society. It is built into society's policies and practices that appear neutral but systematically deny equal access to power, prestige, and privilege. Normal arrangements provide privileges for Whites at the expense of Blacks, Hispanics, and other people of color.

Racial privilege, like class privilege, reaches far back into America's past. The racial hierarchy with White groups of European origin at the top and people of color at the bottom serves important functions for society and for certain categories of people. It ensures that some people are available to do society's dirty work at low wages. Racial hierarchy has positive consequences for the status quo: it enables the powerful to retain their control and their advantages. **Racial stratification** also offers better occupational opportunities, income, and education to White people. These advantages constitute racial privilege.

This chapter examines racial inequality from several different vantage points. First, the characteristics of minority groups and racial and ethnic groups are presented. Then, the historical victimization of Blacks, Chicanos, and Native Americans is discussed. Explanations of racial inequality are followed by a look at its effects on Blacks and Hispanics in terms of income, jobs, education, and health. Finally, the chapter turns to contemporary trends in racial and ethnic relations.

A **minority group** is dominated by a more powerful group and, as a result, singled out for differential and unfair treatment. The theme of this chapter is that the unequal placement of minority groups is the result of structural inequality. Forms of inequality have changed over time, but racial domination remains a persistent feature of U.S. society. Today, old forms of discrimination thrive alongside new and more subtle forms of inequality. Problems of race are created by social organization. The oppressed people are not the problem; the structure of society that distributes resources unequally is the problem. It is important to understand that minorities are not always passive victims of racial oppression. Their histories reveal varied strategies of survival, resistance, and coping in the face of overwhelming odds. Nevertheless, the magnitude of discrimination in the United States has maintained the subordination of people of color.

The Characteristics of Minority Groups

Because majority-minority relations operate basically as a power relationship, conflict (or at least the potential for conflict) is always present. Overt conflict is most likely when the subordinate group attempts to alter the distribution of power. Size is not crucial in determining whether a group is the most powerful. A numerical minority may have more political representation than the majority, as is the case in the Union of South Africa and in most colonial situations. Thus, the most important characteristic of a subordinate minority group is that it is dominated by a more powerful group.

A second characteristic of a **minority group** is that it is composed of people with similar characteristics that differ significantly from those of the dominant group. These characteristics are salient; they are visible, though not necessarily physical, and they make a difference.

The behavior and/or characteristics of minority group members are stereotyped and systematically condemned by the dominant or majority group. Minority groups typically inspire stereotypes in the minds of the dominant group, presumably because these negative generalizations keep them down.

One last characteristic that all minority groups have in common is that they are singled out for differential and unfair treatment. The discrimination may be subtle or blatant, but it is always detrimental. A sizable portion of this chapter focuses on the various manifestations of discrimination toward minority groups in the United States.

These criteria—relative powerlessness, visible differentiation from the majority, negative stereotyping, and unfair discrimination—determine what social categories are minority groups. Typically, eight categories of people are commonly designated as minority groups. Each type is described in the paragraphs that follow.

A **racial group** is a socially defined category that serves as a basis for differential treatment. The term *race* is meaningless in a biological sense because there are no pure races. The crucial aspect of any racial category is that the characteristics that distinguish it are *socially defined* (Yetman, 1991:3). Even though racial groups are set apart and singled out for unequal treatment, race is a social historical group that changes over time. Michael Omi and Howard Winant (1986) call this "racial formation," meaning that society assigns different worth and unequal treatment to groups on the basis of its definition of race. Racial formation touches people throughout society, not just those who are subordinated. Most Whites think that race does not apply to them because they are not people of color. They do not see Whiteness as a racial category (McIntosh, 1992:79). Yet, race shapes the experiences of all people not just those who are most victimized by racial inequality.

A second category, *ethnicity,* is also a traditional basis for inequality. An **ethnic group** has a culture distinctive from the dominant one. An Amish rural community and an Italian neighborhood in Boston are examples of ethnic groups. Of course, racial groups may also differ culturally from the dominant group—say, the Chinese in San Francisco's Chinatown or any tribe of Native Americans.

The third classification, *religion,* also places some categories in inferior positions. Throughout most of their history Jews have been persecuted because of their religion (or assumed religious ties) in one country after another. Much of the unrest in Northern Ireland stems from religious differences. The Protestants in that country are dominant, and the Catholics are the objects of discrimination.

Another category, the *impoverished,* constitutes a minority group in all societies. As we discuss in Chapter 6, the poor in the United States are powerless and are the victims of varied forms of discrimination.

One basis for differentiation, *gender,* has only recently been recognized as a basis for minority status. Women in U.S. society are relatively powerless, perceived in terms of stereotyped qualities (e.g., incapable of leadership because of being highly emotional), and victimized by discrimination, as we discuss in Chapter 8.

Certain *deviant* groups also have the characteristics of minority groups (see Chapter 10). Unmarried mothers (and their offspring), homosexuals, ex-criminals, and ex-mental patients are examples of deviant groups with minority status.

A seventh category, the *aged,* meets the criteria for a minority group in many societies. The elderly in the United States are clearly objects of discrimination, possess negative stereotypes, and are relatively powerless (see Chapter 9).

The *physically different* also have minority group status. People who are deformed, disabled, obese, ugly, and short experience discrimination because they look different.

Racial and Ethnic Groups

Both race and ethnicity are significant in U.S. society. Groups labeled as races by the wider society are bound together by their common conditions. As a result, they develop distinctive cultural or ethnic characteristics. Groups with common national origins or common religious traditions also develop separate cultural or ethnic characteristics. **Ethnicity** is the condition of being culturally distinct on the basis of race, religion, or national origin. Ethnic groups such as Jews, Poles, and Italians have distinguishing cultural characteristics that are rooted in national origin and religion. Racial groups also have distinctive ethnic and cultural characteristics. Therefore, they can be referred to as **racial ethnic groups** (or racially defined ethnic groups) (See and Wilson, 1988:224). The term *racial ethnic* is meant to include both structural discrimination and cultural diversity.

Racial discrimination creates unequal access to society's resources. In order to survive, racial groups must often create distinctive social and cultural arrangements. Cultural diversity is often a way of coping with subordination (Baca Zinn and Eitzen, 1993). African Americans, Chicanos, Chinese Americans, and Native Americans are examples of racial ethnics because each of these groups has a distinctive culture or subculture, shares a common heritage, and has developed a common identity within a larger society that subordinates them. The racial characteristics of these groups have become meaningful within a context that continues to change. Terms of reference are also changing. For example, Blacks increasingly use the term *African Americans* and Hispanics often refer to themselves as *Latinos.* In this chapter we use such interchangeable terms because they are currently used in both popular and scholarly discourse. (See the Observation "What Shall We Call Each Other?")

Differences among Ethnic Groups

Both race and ethnicity are traditional bases for systems of inequality, although there are historical and contemporary differences in society's placement of racial ethnics and White ethnics in this society. Some ethnic groups have moved into the mainstream of society whereas others have remained in a subordinate status. The Germans, Italians, and Irish, for example, experienced discrimination when they migrated here in the late nineteenth century but have been accepted into the dominant majority. Native Americans, Blacks, Chicanos, and other groups, however, have not become assimilated and continue to be objects of discrimination. Two factors combine to explain much of this apparent anomaly.

OBSERVATION

WHAT SHALL WE CALL EACH OTHER?

Working together across the lines of race, gender and national origin teaches us that there can be no easy certainty about what to call each other, only continuing dialogue. The words that name our differences are emotionally charged. If we are members of groups that have suffered discrimination and name calling, we are apt to be sensitive about the choice of these terms. As educators working together toward equity we should help each other learn to use the most acceptable terms. Should we say African-American, Afro-American, or Black? Should we say American Indians or Native Americans? Should we say Hispanics or Latinos? At what age in their lives should females be called women and males be called men?

An important guideline is the principle of self-determination. Each of us has the right to decide what labels are acceptable to us. Our membership in a group may seem obvious to others, but our feelings of affiliation are more complex. The strength of our internal identification with a group and its name can range from denial through mild curiosity to passionate commitment.

If our social setting focuses on our commonality with all human beings (our need for food–shelter–security, our concern for family–children–community, our hope for the future), we may identify less strongly with the subgroups of humanity to which we belong. However, if our differences are at issue (stereotypes about us, prejudices and discrimination against us), we may identify more strongly with our own race, gender, and national origin. Social conditions and interactions can affect our sense of identity and our preference for one name over another.

And preferences do change. For example, Jesse Jackson and other Black leaders said in December 1988 that they preferred to be called African-Americans. "Every ethnic group in this country has some reference to some land, some cultural and historical base. African-Americans have hit that level of maturity," Jackson said.

What should the press do? *Editor and Publisher* ombudsman Henry McNulty said, "I think people should be called whatever they want to be called, within reason, but the question is, Who can tell what 'the people' want?" He added, "I go along with Jackson's reasoning that it is better to refer to someone's ancestral land than to skin color."

The Bill Cosby Show also dealt with this issue when Denise taught her step-daughter Olivia that she should say African-American not Black, Asian not Oriental, and Caucasian not white. This popular show may influence some people to adopt these terms.

Similarly, American Indian and Native American are competing terms. Jim Beck, an Ojibwa administrator at the University of Michigan, prefers the term American Indian (despite its origin in Columbus's "ignorant navigational error"), but he also uses the term Native American. However, he strongly believes Indian should be capitalized when used in words such as paleoIndian.

Hispanic and Latino are also competing terms. In 1968 Sen. Joseph Montoya of New Mexico persuaded President Johnson to declare National Hispanic Heritage Week, and the Census Bureau uses the term Hispanic. However, for some Hispanic evokes only Spaniards or their descendents whereas Latino embraces Portuguese, Spanish, Indian, and African peoples and cultures.

Gender bias is such a part of our language that it resists change. Ms. now seems to be used more often than Miss or Mrs., and "he or she" as often as the generic "he," but inclusive terms like "fire fighter" are still not as common as sexist terms like "fireman."

Source: Adapted from Ted Wilson, "What Shall We Call Each Other?" *Equity Coalition* (Fall 1989):7. Program for Educational Opportunity, University of Michigan.

The most obvious reason is color. Groups easily identified by physical characteristics find it difficult if not impossible to escape the devalued label. Second, the conditions under which the ethnic groups came into contact with the dominant majority appear to be crucial. A key to how ethnic groups were ultimately treated is whether they migrated to the United States voluntarily. (The following discussion is adapted from Luhman and Gilman, 1980:8–27.) Voluntary migrants came to the New World to enhance their inferior status or to market their skills in a land of opportunity. They came with hope and sometimes with resources to provide a foundation for their anticipated upward mobility. Most also had the option of returning if they found the conditions here unsatisfactory.

The voluntary migrants came to the United States in several waves. In colonial times the English, Scotch-Irish, and Germans were the most notable ethnic groups. The Catholic Irish came in great numbers just before the Civil War as a result of the great potato famine in Ireland. They were rural, unskilled, Catholic, and anti-English in sentiment. They settled in urban areas and experienced a good deal of discrimination. During this same period Chinese and later the Japanese migrated to western states. They experienced great discrimination by Whites apprehensive about jobs.

From about 1870 to 1920 a great wave of voluntary immigrants came to the United States mainly from the Catholic areas of Europe—Poland, Italy, and Eastern Europe; Jews from Eastern Europe also came. These new immigrants were different from the dominant English Protestant culture. As a result, they experienced more discrimination than many of the earlier immigrants. The anti-immigrant feeling was exposed in a 1924 federal law, the National Origins Act, which restricted immigration from southern and eastern Europe and stopped it altogether for Asians.

The voluntary immigrants came to the United States and experienced varying forms of labor exploitation and other forms of discrimination. Blacks, Chicanos, and Asians were forced into preindustrial work that was low in pay, status, and chances for upward mobility. To understand the plight of racial ethnic groups, let us look briefly at the historical experiences of four such groups—Blacks, Chicanos, Asians, and Native Americans.

African Americans

In 1991, African Americans (30 million) were 12 percent of the population—the largest and most visible minority group in the United States. The slave trade brought Blacks to America from Africa from 1619 until the Civil War, when they constituted one-eighth of the population. The slaves were defined as property and were denied the rights given to other members of society. Families could be broken up for economic or punitive reasons. The slave owners used their power in several ways to maintain their dominance over their slaves. They demanded absolute obedience; to question the authority of the master meant physical punishment, often severe. Blacks were taught to defer to their masters and to accept their own inferiority. The masters used public displays of power to create in slaves a sense of awe. Slaves were taught to identify with their masters' economic success. Finally, slaves were made to feel dependent on their masters, primarily by restrictions on their education. Typically, it was illegal in the South to teach a slave to read or write.

Following Emancipation the newly freed Blacks, except for the brief period of Reconstruction, remained powerless. They did not have the skills and resources to break away from their dependence on Whites. Because Whites owned the land, Blacks were forced to enter into sharecropping agreements, under which they would farm the land, take all the risks, and return a percentage of the crops harvested to the owner. Typically, the sharecroppers would borrow on the next year's crop to purchase equipment, food, and clothing. Thus, a cycle of indebtedness was set up that bound the sharecroppers as if they were still slaves.

During this same period many states passed Jim Crow laws mandating racial segregation in almost all areas of life (schools, transportation, neighborhoods, drinking fountains, and public eating establishments). These laws, which legalized White domination, remained in effect until about 1965.

The hallmark of representative democracy is that all citizens have the fundamental right to vote for people who will administer and make the laws. Those in power have often defied this principle of democracy by minimizing, neutralizing, or even negating the voting privileges of Blacks (Simon and Eitzen, 1990:231–232). Although the Fourteenth Amendment gave Blacks the right to vote after the Civil War, the White majority in the southern states used a variety of tactics to keep them from voting. Most effective was the strategy of intimidation. Blacks who tried to assert their right to vote were often beaten, sometimes lynched, or their property was destroyed. A more subtle approach, however, was quite effective in eliminating the Black vote in the southern states: through legal means laws were passed to achieve illegal discrimination. One tactic was the White primary, which excluded Blacks from voting in the party primary (Key, 1949:619–643). The Constitution prohibited the states from denying the vote on the basis of race. A political party, however, because it was a private association, *could* discriminate. The Democratic party throughout most of the South chose the option of limiting the primary to Whites. Blacks could legally vote in the general election, but only for the candidates already selected by Whites. And since the Democratic party in the South was supreme, whoever was selected in the primary would be the victor in the general election. This practice was nullified by the Supreme Court in 1944.

Other legal obstacles for Blacks in the South were the literacy test and the poll tax, which were finally prohibited by the Twenty-Fourth Amendment, passed in 1964. Both obstacles were designed as southern suffrage requirements to admit Whites to the electorate and exclude Blacks (without mentioning race). The literacy test and its related requirements were blatantly racist. The object of the test was to allow all adult White males to vote while excluding all Blacks. The problem with this test was that many Whites would also be excluded because they were illiterate. Legislators in various southern states contrived alternatives to the literacy requirements that would allow the illiterate Whites to vote. One loophole was the grandfather clause. This provision, based on Louisiana law, "exempted persons from the literacy test who were registered voters in any state prior to or on January 1, 1867, the sons and grandsons of such persons, and male persons of foreign birth naturalized before January 1, 1898" (Key, 1949:577). Obviously, the use of these dates prevented Blacks from voting and thereby served to maintain White domination.

Beginning with World War I, a time of labor shortage and industrial expansion, Blacks began to move from the rural South to the urban North. After the war, Blacks in the North experienced large-scale discrimination as jobs became scarce. World War II brought another great wave of migrants to the industrial cities of the North, and again after the war Blacks faced unemployment and discrimination from many fronts.

Several conditions following World War II made the Black experience different the second time. Blacks were now concentrated in cities, increasing the likelihood of group actions to alter their oppression. Also, more Blacks were educated and could provide leadership. More important, many Blacks had served the country in the war and now were unwilling to accept continued inferiority at home. The result of these factors and others was the civil rights movement of the 1960s. Although there were significant positive changes for Blacks resulting from this movement, including favorable legislation and court decisions, these gains have faltered due to economic conditions and racial discrimination.

Chicanos

The growing Hispanic presence in the United States has blinded many people to the diversity within this community. In 1991, Hispanics or Latinos numbered 22.4 million—9 percent of the U.S. population. Latinos have diverse origins and diverse histories. In 1991, 64 percent of all Hispanic Americans were Chicanos or Mexican Americans, 10.5 were Puerto Ricans, 4.9 percent were Cubans, 13.7 percent Central and South American, and 6.9 percent were "other Hispanic" (U.S. Bureau of the Census, 1991a:1). Even though all groups have made major numerical impact on the United States since World War II, this section discusses Chicanos, who involuntarily became part of the United States largely because of military conquest (Moore, 1976; Estrada et al., 1981).

Beginning around 1600 the southwestern part of the present United States was controlled by Spain. Mexico gained control over this area when it gained independence from Spain in 1821. Mexico permitted immigrants to settle in this territory (primarily in what is now Texas), and by 1830 there were some 20,000 Anglo* settlers (Barrera, 1979:1, 4).

By 1835 these settlers were hostile toward Mexico and Mexicans. As one historian has described it, "The Texans saw themselves in danger of becoming the alien subjects of a people to whom they deliberately believed themselves morally, intellectually, and politically superior" (Baker, 1965:52). This feeling of superiority, Mexico's abolition of slavery, and other factors led to the Texas revolt of 1835 and an independent Texas republic. When the United States granted statehood to Texas in 1845, despite the fact that Mexico still claimed it, war was inevitable. Many U.S. politicians and business interests supported the war because of the high probability of winning and of subsequent territorial expansion (Acuna, 1972). As a result of the war, which lasted from 1846 to 1848, Mexico lost half its national territory and the United States increased its area by one-third (Arizona, California, Colorado, New Mexico, Texas, Nevada, Utah, and parts of Kansas, Oklahoma, and Wyoming).** Under the Treaty of Guadalupe Hidalgo (1848), Mexicans living on the U.S. side of the new border who decided to remain would have all the rights of U.S. citizens according to the Constitution.

Despite the guarantees to the Mexicans who remained, their status under the new regime was clearly secondary. Their civil and property rights were rou-

---

*Anglos, as used by Chicanos, refers to all Caucasian Americans, not just to those who trace their origins to the British Isles.

**In 1853 the United States purchased from Mexico (the Gadsden Purchase) an additional 45,000 square miles in Arizona and New Mexico.

tinely violated. Most important, the U.S. military, judicial system, and government were used to establish Anglos in positions of power in the economic structures that Mexicans had developed in mining, ranching, and agriculture (McWilliams, 1949). The techniques used to accomplish this control were taxation; a court system unfamiliar with Mexican and Spanish landowning laws, traditions, and customs; and the appropriation of land for the National Forest Service with little if any compensation to the Mexican Americans. In short, Mexican Americans were largely dispossessed of power and property. With the coming of the railroads and the damming of rivers for irrigation, the Southwest became an area of economic growth; but the advantages accrued mainly to Anglos. Mexican Americans no longer owned the land; now they were the source of cheap labor, an exploited group at the bottom of the social and economic ladder. As Barrera has summarized:

> Dispossession from the land . . . depleted the economic base of Chicanos and
> put them in an even less favorable position to exercise influence over the politi-
> cal process. In addition, it had other far-ranging consequences, including facili-
> tating the emergence of a colonial labor system in the Southwest, based in large
> part on Chicano labor. (Barrera, 1979:33)

What emerged in the nineteenth-century Southwest was a segmented labor force, which Barrera refers to as a colonial labor system: "A colonial labor system exists where the labor force is segmented along ethnic and/or racial lines, and one or more of the segments is systematically maintained in a subordinate position" (Barrera, 1979:39).

The twentieth century has been a period of large-scale immigration from Mexico to the Southwest. The number of persons born in Mexico living in the United States was 103,393 in 1900, 221,915 in 1910, and 639,017 in 1930.

The Great Depression was an especially difficult time for Chicanos. Not only were they vulnerable because of their marginal jobs, but they were also the object of hostility from many Anglos, who believed they were flooding an overcrowded labor market, depressing wages, and functioning as a drain on the welfare system. As a result, from 1929 to 1934 more than 400,000 Mexicans, many of them U.S. citizens, were forced to repatriate in Mexico. Those who applied for welfare benefits were the most likely to be victims: "Those who applied for relief were referred to 'Mexican Bureaus,' whose sole purpose was to reduce the welfare rolls by deporting the applicants. Indigence, not citizenship, was the criterion used in identifying Mexicans for repatriation" (Estrada et al., 1981:117).

In contrast, after World War II, when the economy was booming and jobs were plentiful, the U.S. government instituted the bracero program, which permitted Mexicans to migrate to the United States to work in agriculture. Farmers favored such a program because it assured them of a steady supply of cheap labor. This program was terminated in 1964, after nearly 5 million Mexicans had come to the United States, and a total annual immigration quota of 120,000 was imposed on all nations in the Western Hemisphere.

Since World War II there has been another source of migrants (illegals or undocumented workers) who came to the United States in great numbers seeking work. A current estimate is that perhaps more than 1 million people a year cross the border to work in the United States without legal permission. These immigrants are especially vulnerable to low wages and other abuses by employers and landlords.

In addition to the current Hispanic population of more than 22 million, an estimated 4 million undocumented workers live in the United States. Some demographers project that the Hispanics will be one-third of the U.S. population within 100 years (Brimelow, 1992:75).

Currently, Chicanos experience discrimination not only in jobs and wages but also through segregated schools, the use of Anglo-oriented tests for placement in schools, residential segregation, and exclusionary policies by private organizations.

Asian Americans

In 1991, Asian Americans accounted for 3 percent of the U.S. population. With 7 million in number, Asian Americans are more diverse than the other racial ethnics. Their characteristics vary widely according to their national origins and time of entry into the United States.

The history of Asian Americans begins with the arrival after 1848 of Chinese men recruited to work in California, the beginning of a large influx touched off by the gold rush. The numbers grew rapidly, with thousands working on construction of the transcontinental railroads in the 1860s. Agitation against the Chinese during the 1870s included rioting, special taxes, and an anti-Chinese law passed in 1887. In 1882 Congress passed the Chinese Exclusion Act, which essentially banned immigration of Chinese people into the United States. One result of such anti-Chinese sentiment was the substitution of Japanese workers for Chinese (Gardner, Robey, and Smith, 1985:8).

Strict immigration laws of the 1920s (e.g., the National Origins Act of 1924) virtually halted Asian immigration into the United States. Immigration was also low during the depression of the 1930s. After 1952, some easing of Asian immigration restrictions was permitted with the McCarren-Walter Act. Asian immigration then skyrocketed with liberalized immigration policy in 1965 (Gardner, Robey, and Smith, 1985).

In 1970, Asian Americans numbered 4.1 million (1.5 percent of the total U.S. population). Since then, they have migrated in larger numbers to the United States, including more than 700,000 Indochinese refugees after the Vietnam War (See the Observation on Amarasian refugees). Asians are the fastest growing group in the United States, now accounting for 42 percent of the nation's immigrants—as many as from all Latin American countries. It is estimated that the number of Asian Americans will double by the year 2000 to about 10 million (Gardner, Robey, and Smith, 1985).

Asian Americans are often characterized as the "model minority," a label that masks great disparities among them. The population is extremely diverse, giving rise to the term *Pan Asian,* which encompasses immigrants from Asian and Pacific Island countries and native-born citizens descended from those ethnic groups (Lott and Felt, 1991:6). The largest Asian American groups are Chinese (22.6 percent), Filipinos (19.3 percent), Japanese (11.2 percent), Vietnamese (8.4 percent), Korean (11 percent), and Asian Indian (11.2 percent). There are also Laotians, Kampucheans, Thais, Pakistanis, Indonesians, Hmongs, and Samoans.

Asian Americans are the fastest growing ethnic minority in the United States.

Most of the pre–World War II Asian immigrants were peasants, but the recent immigrants vary considerably by education and social class. Many arrived as educated middle-class professionals with highly valued skills and some knowledge of English. Others, such as the Indochinese, arrived as uneducated, impoverished refugees. This is reflected in the differences in income and poverty level by ethnic category. Asian American households are more affluent than are any other racial or ethnic group including Whites. In 1989, well over one-third of all Asian Americans lived in households that had incomes of $50,000 or more. This picture of economic well-being contrasts sharply with the situation of most other minority groups in the United States. The high income level of Asian Americans may be related to their concentration in areas such as Los Angeles, San Francisco, and Honolulu, where salaries are high. To the extent that they are concentrated in high cost-of-living areas, their family income may provide a misleading picture of their economic well-being. There may be another reason the Asian American population is not as well-off as their high family incomes would indicate. Asian-Americans tend to have larger-than-average families with more workers per household (O'Hare and Felt, 1991:7).

While a large segment of this population is financially well-off, many are poor. Given this diversity in social classes among the immigrants, some Asian American leaders say it is misleading to use the term *Asian American* at all (Butterfield, 1991:A11).

Native Americans   In 1990 Native Americans or American Indians numbered 1,878,000, up from 1.4 million in 1980. This 38 percent leap exceeds the growth rate for African Americans (6 percent) but not the growth of Hispanics (53 percent) or Asians (108

OBSERVATION

AMERASIAN REFUGEES: "CHILDREN OF THE DUST"

On December 22, 1987 the United States Congress passed into law the Amerasian Homecoming Act allowing children born in Vietnam, to an American father, between January 1962 and January 1976 to enter the U.S. with their families and with full refugee benefits. As of September 30, 1990 22,392 Amerasian immigrants from Southeast Asia had been admitted to the U.S.; the majority come from Vietnam but Laos and Cambodia are also sources of Amerasian refugees. To give these new arrivals the specialized care and services they need, 26 "cluster sites" deemed to be able to absorb this special population most easily were selected. In 1990 California and New York were the major receiving areas followed by Texas, Florida, Washington State, Illinois, Pennsylvania and Massachusetts.

Several theoretical approaches are used to explain the adaptation, assimilation and general resettlement process undergone by refugees. The *enculturation* model focuses on the resocialization and "Americanization" process which eventually results in the gradual assimilation of the refugees. The *economic adaptation* perspective emphasizes work placement, sustained employment, and language skills as the key measures of assimilation. The *ethnic enclave* viewpoint stresses the fact that Asian refugee and immigrant groups will cluster together in centers of ethnic concentration to bridge the chasm between the old and new cultures and societies. Each of these perspectives assumes that the immigrant or refugee family eventually will adapt or assimilate to American society; however, longstanding psychological, social and cultural barriers can continue to hinder the adjustment process and in no instance are these barriers more applicable than in the case of Amerasian refugee families, particularly among children and young Amerasians.

Life for Amerasians in Vietnam was exceptionally difficult. In their homeland Amerasian youth were known as "children of the dust"; half-breeds from the underside of society who were often stripped of their possessions and experienced much prejudice and discrimination because they were the children of prostitutes and were without a father in a culture where an individual's sense of self stems from identification with a father. In Vietnam many of the Amerasians lead very unstable lives. Many of the children 'dropped-out' of school because of ridicule and discrimination or because of eventual discrimination in the work-place. Health care provision (physical and mental) was inadequate, emotional and behavioral problems were common and tensions within families were great.

The turmoil and tensions experienced by Amerasian families in Vietnam make their resettlement in the U.S. extremely difficult. Most resettled Amerasians are teenagers or young adults admitted to the U.S. together with their accompanying mothers and half siblings or wives and children. One study estimates that only 2% of Amerasian youth eventually meet or live with their American father and that many of the Amerasian adults and late adolescents are very poorly equipped to conform to the norms of contemporary American Society. Furthermore, these refugees identify themselves as Amerasian rather than Asian, American or other races.

Psychological and social difficulties make resettlement an extremely difficult process. Behavioral and attitudinal problems cited as above normal in this population include: mood disturbances, extreme stress, somatization, withdrawal, disillusionment, depression, anxiety and poor self-concept. For the younger Amerasians the recognized pres-

percent) (Fost, 1991:26). Now at 1 percent of the total U.S. population, American Indians have lived continuously in North America for at least 30,000 years. The tribes located in North America were and are extremely heterogeneous, with major differences in physical characteristics, language, and social organization. There were theocracies, democracies, and hereditary chiefdoms; matrilineal and

sures associated with adolescence and also those associated with being an Asian minority member are compounded by the uniqueness of being labelled Amerasian. Furthermore, Amerasians whose fathers' are minority group members may find it very difficult to accept that they are half Black, Hispanic or other Asian and are thus subject to even greater socio-psychological pressures.

Relationships within the Amerasian family unit are often strained because the child may not have lived with his/her mother or may not even have known the mother well in Vietnam. In the U.S. a single Vietnamese mother of an Amerasian child and that child's half siblings may often have difficulty exerting authority and the normal teenager-parent tensions and anxieties are often greatly intensified. A report on Vietnamese Amerasians prepared by the Office of Refugee Resettlement in December 1989 emphasizes that Amerasians have lower educational levels, literacy and language skills and that despite their high expectations and motivational levels, "their measured levels of preparedness suggest the need for the availability of sustained, long term support services."

Data collected as part of a local needs assessment survey of Amerasian refugees conducted by the Refugee Social Services Administrative Unit of the Jewish Federation of Metropolitan Chicago permit limited quantitative sociological analysis of this unique subpopulation. Some of the salient findings include:

- a large percentage of Amerasian youth had one or more recognized 'problems' upon resettlement (counted as 'problems' were difficulties in school, participation in gangs, drug abuse, crime involvement, suicide attempts and problems in family relationships).

- the percentage of youth with problems does not vary substantially with age; approximately 63% of those aged 14 to 17 encountered problems while the corresponding figure for those over age 18 was 58%.

- individual Amerasians experiencing the most difficulties tended to be poorly educated male youths whose fathers were minority members and who were members of multi-sibling family units. An unstable home environment and living outside an established Southeast Asian Community were also important predictors of difficulties.

In short, within this particular sample of Amerasian refugees, Amerasian youth with various difficulties were more likely to be male, to have fathers who were Black, Hispanic or other Asian and to be individuals living within households where, in addition to the absence of a father figure, the mother was intermittently employed and where the environment was described as unstable by assistance workers and Amerasians' mothers.

Amerasian refugee families experience high levels of social and psychological difficulties upon resettlement and these problems persist over a long period of time. Conventional theoretical frameworks are inadequate for understanding this population. It is necessary now to go beyond impressionistic theories and initial analytic work to better understand Amerasian refugees.

Source: Makja Lorraine and Brendan Mullan, *Vietnamese Amerasians in the U.S.: Their Social History and Current Problems.* (1990). Paper presented at the American Sociological Association Meetings, Washington, D.C. 1990. Reprinted by permission.

patrilineal systems; hunters and farmers; nomads and villagers. Some tribes were basically cooperative; others were fiercely competitive.

In 1492, when Columbus landed at Watling's Island in the Bahamas, the North American continent was an area of astonishing ethnic and cultural diversity.

North of the Rio Grande was a population of 12 million people, something like 400 separate and distinct cultures, 500 languages, and a dazzling variety of political and religious institutions and physical and ethnic types. (Cook, 1981:118)

Native Americans, then, lived in a pluralistic world, with tribes of different cultures and social organizations coexisting. In contrast, the Europeans who settled in the New World were quite similar: They spoke some variant of Indo-European language; they had a common religious tradition—Christianity; political and social conventions were similar (patrilineal descent, male dominance, property rights, and political organization as a nation-state). They shared a belief in what they considered the international law of the right of discovery. This belief held that the European nation first landing on and claiming the right to territory not formerly held by other Europeans had the exclusive authority to negotiate with the natives for the absolute ownership of the land. This ethnocentric notion was buttressed further by the Europeans' belief that they represented the highest level of civilization. They were convinced of their superiority to the natives of the New World, whom they considered to be not only infidels but inferior beings.

From the beginning, the Europeans took the land once owned by the natives. One way they took land was through treaties. The English and the French offered inducements to tribes to cede some of their land in exchange for the promise of material goods, health benefits, and the guaranteed security of Indian lands. Often these treaties included a perpetuity clause—that the treaty would remain in effect and the Indians could live in peace, security, and independence in their lands "as long as the waters flow and the grasses grow." The Indians accepted the treaties but were quickly disillusioned; "virtually all were broken by the European signatores" (Dorris, 1981:49).

As new waves of settlers moved westward, the lands the Indians had been promised were forcibly taken. Native Americans protecting their lands fought battles with settlers and with U.S. troops. Always the result was that Native Americans were forced to move farther west to remote areas.

Native Americans were also forced to move to other places against their will. Although the Supreme Court ruled that the Cherokees had legal title to their lands in the South, President Andrew Jackson forcibly evicted them and forced them to walk a thousand miles in midwinter from Carolina and Georgia to Oklahoma. Four thousand died in this forced march. The Native Americans had been promised that the land they settled in the Indian territory would never be made part of a state; yet this area became part of Oklahoma in 1907.

As the population of European origin in the United States began to surge west of the Mississippi in the late 1800s, there was increasing pressure on the recently removed groups, such as the Cherokee and the Sioux to give up large amounts of land traditionally under their control. Some of this further expansion was accomplished in a relatively peaceful manner through treaties, and some was accomplished through violent military confrontation. The lands reserved for Native Americans were generally regarded as the least desirable by Whites and were almost always located far from major population centers, trails, and transportation routes that later became part of the modern system of metropolitan areas, highways, and railroads. In sum, for most of the nineteenth century the policy of the U.S. government was to isolate and concentrate Native Americans in places with few natural resources, far from contact with the developing U.S. economy and society (Sandefur, 1989).

Brian Gable, *The Toronto Globe* (October 1992). Reprinted by permission.

In 1871 all Indians were made wards of the federal government and were placed on federal reservations on lands considered of little value. As wards, Native Americans had no control of their communities and no power to effect federal policies over them. They were under the jurisdiction of the Bureau of Indian Affairs, which decided "what they would eat, where they would live, and ultimately what style of living they would adopt" (Luhman and Gilman, 1980:37). Thus, they were stripped of their political rights and even of their culture.

Native Americans were first granted U.S. citizenship and the right to vote in 1924. Some states, including New York and North Carolina, disputed their right to vote even into the 1970s. Recent legislation and court decisions have restored some rights and powers to Native American tribes. This legislation is significant in two major respects. First, various tribes are claiming in the courts that they have the legal rights to millions of acres of land. Second, Indian lands are teeming with riches that the Indians also claim. According to Cook:

> It is one of history's more stunning ironies. The 51.9 million acres in the U.S. reserved for the Indians were lands the white man could not see any conceivable reason to reserve for himself. They were too wet or too dry, too barren or too remote. Now, at a time when the U.S. seems to be running out of practically everything, the 272 federally recognized Indian reservations constitute one of the largest and least known mineral repositories on the continent—nearly 5 percent of the U.S.'s oil and gas, one-third of its strippable low-sulfur coal, one-half of its privately owned uranium. (Cook, 1981:108)

We do not yet know how the powerful will decide on these claims. If history is a guide, Native Americans will not receive their share.

The treatment of Native Americans throughout their history of contact with Europeans and White Americans has been brutal. At the time of Columbus, the

Native Americans are the poorest racial/ethnic group in the United States.

size of the American Indian population was somewhere between 2 to 5 million individuals. By 1890, the size of the American Indian population had dwindled to 228,000. Historians are fairly certain that a critical reason for this dramatic decline was the introduction of diseases such as smallpox and measles, to which the native population had never been exposed. This population decline led to changes in social structure and to a decline in the ability of the native groups to defend themselves against military attacks by the French, Spanish, English, and other European colonizers, which, in turn, led to even further destruction of the Indian population (Sandefur, 1990:38).

This population decline contrasts with the population recovery that has occurred during this century. Experts who used to forecast the extinction of the American Indian are now revising their predictions as the U.S. population increases and becomes even more diverse. Important changes occurred in the social and economic well-being of the Native American population from 1960 to the present. At the time of the 1970 census, American Indians were the poorest group in the United States, with incomes well below those of the Black population. By 1980, despite the high poverty rates on many Indian reservations, poverty among American Indians had declined and real incomes had risen to a level exceeding the real incomes of Blacks. By the standards of White Americans, Native Americans are not well educated, they are marginally attached to the labor force, and they do work that is not highly valued; and the consequences of these liabilities are poverty and economic hardship (cited in Sandefur, 1990:39). Economic conditions are particularly bad on many Indian reservations, where poverty can reach as high as 60 percent.

Despite these patterns, a renaissance is occurring in American Indian communities. In 1990 almost 2 million people claimed American Indian as their race. More than 7 million people claim some Indian ancestry. That is about one person in thirty-five. American Indians still feel strong bonds to their native cultures. This cultural resurrection has brought education and economic gains to many Indians living on and off reservations. A college-educated Indian middle class has emerged. American Indian business ownership has increased, and some tribes are creating good jobs for their members (Fost, 1991:26).

African Americans, Latinos, Asian Americans, and Native Americans remain subordinated. Some important characteristics help explain their continued secondary status in U.S. society. Each group is set apart from the majority on the basis of race—a characteristic that has social and political rather than biological significance. The next section elaborates on the explanations given for this phenomenon.

Explanations of Racial and Ethnic Inequality

Why have some racial and ethnic groups been consistently disadvantaged throughout American history? Some ethnic groups, such as the Irish and Jews, have experienced discrimination but have managed to overcome their initial disadvantages (Sowell, 1981). Others, such as the Blacks, Chicanos, and Native Americans, have not been able to cast off their secondary status. Three types of theories have been used to explain why some groups are consistently singled out for discrimination: deficiency theories, bias theories, and structural discrimination theories. (The following discussion is adapted from Barrera, 1979:174–219.)

Deficiency Theories

A number of analysts have argued that some groups are inferior in society because they *are* in fact inferior. That is, when compared with the majority, they are deficient in some important way. There are two varieties of deficiency theory.

Biological deficiency.   This classical explanation for the inferiority of certain groups maintains that their inferiority is the result of flawed genetic—and, therefore, hereditary—traits. This is the position of Arthur Jensen and Richard Herrnstein, (as we discuss in Chapter 6)—that Blacks are mentally inferior to Whites. Despite the work of these and other theorists, there is no definitive evidence for the thesis that racial groups differ in intelligence. Biological deficiency theories are generally not accepted in the scientific community.

Cultural deficiency.   Many varieties of explanations for racial subordination center on cultural characteristics thought to be inherited from the past and handed down from generation to generation. Cultural differences treated as cultural deficiencies are the reason that racial minorities are disproportionately found in subordinate positions. Cultural deficiency explanations argue that some flaw within the minority way of life is responsible for that minority group's secondary status.

From this perspective minorities are culturally disadvantaged because of their heritage and customs. For example, some analysts have argued that Chicano culture has held members of this group back (Kluckhohn and Strodtbeck, 1961; for the opposing position, see Baca Zinn, 1981, 1982). From this perspective, Chicanos are viewed as disadvantaged because their culture values the present rather than the future, dependency rather than independence, and low rather than high motivation for achievement. These traits, coupled with the difficulty that many have with the English language, mean that Chicanos will be less likely to be successful in Anglo schools and Anglo work settings.

Cultural deficiency provides the basis for the famous 1967 report of Daniel Patrick Moynihan. He charged that the tangle of pathology within Black ghettos was rooted in the deterioration of the Negro family (U.S. Department of Labor, 1965). High rates of marital dissolution, female-headed households, out-of-wedlock births, welfare dependency, and the resulting family structure were explained as the residuals of slavery and discrimination, a complex web of pathological patterns passed down through successive generations. This work was guided and shaped by assumptions about poverty that found cultural patterns of the poor to be defective and self-perpetuating.

The Moynihan report was widely criticized for contending that deviant family forms are part of Black culture rather than being an adaptation to socioeconomic conditions. The main objection to the Moynihan report is that it is a classic case of blaming the victim. It locates the cause of pathology within Black Americans, not in the racially stratified society.

In effect, culture deficiency theorists blame the victim and ignore the structural constraints that deny certain groups the same opportunities that other groups have. During the 1960s and 1970s there was extensive refutation of cultural deficiency theories. Many scholars documented various strengths within minority communities and showed how their unique ways of life were adaptations to the conditions of poverty and racism. Recently, however, a revival of cultural deficiency has occurred to explain rising poverty and the growth of female-headed households in U.S. inner cities. According to some scholars, policy makers, and social commentators, declining economic conditions in Black ghettos are created by culture, the deteriorating family, and welfare. We return to this theme in the last section of this chapter.

Bias Theories

The deficiency theories just discussed blame the minorities for their plight. Bias theories, on the other hand, blame the members of the majority—in particular, they blame the prejudiced attitudes of majority members. Gunnar Myrdal, for example, argued in his classic *American Dilemma* that prejudiced attitudes are the source of discriminatory actions, which, in turn, keep minorities subordinate (Myrdal, 1944). The inferior status of minorities reinforces negative stereotypes that, in turn, justify the prejudice of the majority; the process is a vicious cycle that perpetuates the secondary status from generation to generation.

David Wellman has made an extensive critique of bias theories and presented an alternative (Wellman, 1977). He has raised a number of objections to the traditional view that the attitudes of White Americans are the major cause of racism. The typical view is that Whites, particularly lower-class Whites, have hostile feelings toward and make faulty generalizations about minorities.

Minorities are thus prejudged and misjudged by the majority, and the result is discrimination.

Prejudiced attitudes, however, do not explain the behaviors of unprejudiced Whites who defend the traditional arrangements that negatively affect minorities. Unbiased persons fight to preserve the status quo by favoring, for example, the seniority system in occupations, or they oppose affirmative action, quota systems, busing to achieve racial balance, and open enrollment in higher education. As Wellman has argued:

> The terms in which middle-class professionals defend traditional institutional arrangements are, strictly speaking, not examples of racial prejudice. They are neither overtly racial nor, given these people's *interests*, misrepresentations of facts. However, while the sentiments may not be prejudiced, they justify arrangements that in effect, if not in intent, maintain the status quo and thereby keep blacks in subordinate positions. (Wellman, 1977:8)

Thus, to focus strictly on prejudice is to take too narrow a view. This focus presents an inaccurate portrayal of racism because it concentrates only on the bigots and ignores the discriminating acts of those who are not prejudiced.

Moreover, according to Wellman, prejudice is not the cause of discrimination. Rather, it is the racial organization of society that is the cause of people's racial beliefs. The determining feature of majority-minority relations is not prejudice but, rather, the superior position of the majority and the institutions that maintain this superiority. "The subordination of people of color is functional to the operation of American society as we know it and the color of one's skin is a primary determinant of people's position in the social structure" (Wellman, 1977:35). Thus, institutional and individual racism generates privilege for Whites. Discrimination provides the privileged with disproportionate advantages in the social, economic, and political spheres. Racist acts, in this view, are not based on hatred, stereotyped conceptions, or prejudgment but are rational responses to the struggle over scarce resources by individuals acting to preserve their own advantage.

Structural Discrimination Theories

Critics of the deficiency and bias theories argue that these explanations focus, incorrectly, on individuals—on the characteristics and attitudes of the prejudiced majority and the flaws of the minority. Both kinds of theories ignore the political economic system that dominates and oppresses minorities. Parenti has criticized people who ignore the system as victim-blamers: "Focusing on the poor and ignoring the system of power, privilege, and profit which makes them poor, is a little like blaming the corpse for the murder" (Parenti, 1978:24). Structural discrimination theories correct this error by focusing on institutionalized patterns of discrimination that operate independently of people's attitudes. These themes are based on the power, domination, and conflict that are institutionalized in the U.S. racial order.

Institutional racism refers to the established, customary, and respected ways in which society operates to keep the minority in a subordinate position. For Carmichael and Hamilton (1967) there are two types of racism—individual and institutional. **Individual racism** consists of overt acts by individuals that harm other individuals or their property. This type of action is usually publicly decried and is currently on the increase in the United States. Institutional racism is more injurious than is individual racism to more minority group members, but it is not recognized by the dominant-group members as racism. Carmichael and Hamilton illustrated the two types as follows:

> When a black family moves into a home in a white neighborhood and is stoned, burned or routed out, they are victims of an overt act of individual racism which many people will condemn—at least in words. But it is institutional racism that keeps black people locked in dilapidated slum tenements, subject to the daily prey of exploitative slumlords, merchants, loan sharks, and discriminatory real estate agents. . . . Respectable individuals can absolve themselves from individual blame: *they* would never plant a bomb in a church: *they* would never stone a black family. But they continue to support political officials and institutions that would and do perpetuate institutionally racist policies. Thus *acts* of overt, individual racism may not typify the society, but institutional racism does.
> (Carmichael and Hamilton, 1967:4–5)

We have noted that some individuals and groups discriminate whether or not they are bigots. These individuals and groups operate within a social milieu that is also discriminatory. The social milieu includes laws, customs, religious beliefs, social stratification, the distribution of power, and the stable arrangements and practices through which things get done in society. These social arrangements and accepted ways of doing things may consciously or unconsciously disadvantage some social categories while benefiting others. The major sectors of society—the system of law and the administration of justice, the economic system, the formal educational structure, and health care—are all possible discriminators. Thus, the term *institutional discrimination* is a useful one. As Knowles and Prewitt have said, the institutions of society

> have great power to reward and penalize. They reward by providing career opportunities for some people and foreclosing them for others. They reward as well by the way social goods and services are distributed—by deciding who receives training and skills, medical care, formal education, political influence, moral support and self-respect, productive employment, fair treatment by the law, decent housing, self-confidence, and the promise of a secure future for self and children. (Knowles and Prewitt, 1965:5)

Analysts of society, pursuing the phenomenon of discrimination, need to ask, How are things normally done in the society? Who gets preferential treatment under these normal arrangements? Who is automatically excluded because of these arrangements? The answers to these questions are not always easy because the arrangements are natural and the discrimination often unintentional or disguised. The task is especially difficult because the exact placement of responsibility is often impossible to pinpoint. Who is responsible for the low scores of ghetto children on standard IQ tests? Who is responsible for residential segregation? Who is responsible for the high unemployment rate of minority group members?

There are four basic themes of institutional discrimination (Benokraitis and Feagin, 1974). First is the importance of history in determining present conditions and affecting resistance to change. Historically, institutions defined and enforced norms and role relationships that were racially distinct. The U.S. nation was founded and its institutions established when Blacks were slaves, uneducated, and different culturally from the dominant Whites. From the beginning Blacks were considered inferior (the original Constitution, for example, counted a slave as three-fifths of a person). Religious beliefs buttressed this notion of the inferiority of Blacks and justified the differential allocation of privileges and sanctions in society. Laws, customs, and traditions usually continue to reinforce current thinking. Institutions have an inertial quality: once set in motion, they tend to continue on the same course. Thus, institutional racism is extremely difficult to change without a complete overhaul of society's institutions.

The second theme of institutional discrimination is that discrimination can occur *without* conscious bigotry. All it takes for institutional discrimination to continue is for employers to insist that prospective employees take aptitude or IQ tests that are based on middle-class experiences, or for decisions on who must be fired in times of financial exigency to be based on seniority, or for employers to stress educational requirements for hiring. These conditions, seemingly fair and neutral, are biased against minorities.

Institutional discrimination is also more invisible than is individual discrimination. Institutional discrimination is more subtle and less intentional than are individual acts of discrimination. As a result, establishing blame for this kind of discrimination is extremely difficult.

Finally, institutional discrimination is reinforced because institutions are interrelated. The exclusion of minorities from the upper levels of education, for example, is likely to affect their opportunities in other institutions (type of job, level of remuneration). Similarly, being poor means that your children will probably receive an inferior education, be propertyless, suffer from bad health, and be treated unjustly by the criminal justice system. These inequities are cumulative. As Benokraitis and Feagin have argued:

> Once a minority is excluded from one institution, chances are greater that it will also be excluded from other institutional privilege. Thus, institutional racism theorists agree that once, historically, institutions have evolved differential opportunities for wealth, power, prestige, privilege, and authority based on racial criteria, unequal resources will produce unequal qualifications to compete for goods and services, unequal qualifications will limit access to goods and services and unequal access to goods and services will result in unequal resources. (Benokraitis and Feagin, 1974:6)

Let us examine some illustrations of how various aspects of the society work to derogate minority groups, deny them equality, and even do them violence. Institutional derogation occurs when minority groups and their members are made to seem inferior or to possess negative stereotypes through legitimate means by the powerful in society. The portrayal of minority group members in the media (movies, television, newspapers, and magazines) is often derogatory. Only recently has there been an effort to thwart the negative images of minorities in the media. The "Amos n' Andy" radio program that was popular in the 1940s and 1950s used almost all the Black stereotypes—and people laughed. The early Shirley Temple movies had an adult Black by the name of Stepin Fetchit whose role was to be more childlike than Miss Temple. The traditional roles of Blacks, Native Americans, and women in movies and novels and on television have typically focused on the negative stereotypes of these groups. These stereotypes are similarly reinforced in textbooks.

The system (customs, practices, expectations, laws, beliefs) also works to deny equality to minority group members—most often without malicious intent. Because it is the system that disadvantages, discrimination would continue even if tomorrow all people in the United States were to awake with all animosity toward minority groups obliterated from their hearts and minds. All that is needed for minorities to suffer is that the law continue to favor the owners of property over renters and debtors. All that is needed for job opportunities to remain unequal is for employers to hire people with the most conventional training and experience and to use machines when they seem more immediately economical than manual labor. All that is needed to ensure that poor children get an inferior education is to continue tracking, using class-biased tests, making education irrelevant in their work, rewarding children who conform to the teachers' middle-class concepts of the good student, and paying disproportionately less for their education (buildings, supplies, teachers, counselors) (Steinberg, n.d.:3). In other words, all that is needed to perpetuate discrimination in the United States is to pursue a policy of business as usual.

Skolnick has described institutional discrimination as it applies to Blacks, but the same could be said for the treatment of other minority groups as well:

> It is theoretically possible to have a racist society in which most of the individual members of that society do not express racist attitudes. A society in which most of the good jobs are held by one race, and the dirty jobs by the people of another color, is a society in which racism is institutionalized, no matter what the beliefs of its members are. For example, the universities of America are probably the least bigoted of American institutions. One would rarely, if ever, hear an openly bigoted expression at schools like Harvard, Yale, the University of Chicago, the University of California. At the same time, university faculties and students have usually been white, the custodians black. The universities have concerned themselves primarily with the needs and interests of the white upper middle and upper classes, and have viewed the lower classes, and especially blacks, as objects of study rather than of service. In this sense, they have, willy-nilly, been institutionally "white racist." (Skolnick, 1966:180)

One structural theory, colonial theory, directly addresses the question of why some ethnic groups have overcome their disadvantaged status whereas others have not. This issue is important because it challenges the myth that the United States is a melting pot. Colonial theory argues that there are fundamental differences between the experiences of racial ethnics and European ethnics. Racial ethnics were colonized within the boundaries of the United States, but Europeans immigrated to this society. Internal colonialism determined the asymmetrical relations of people of color within the dominant society, and it shaped their continuing experiences in the United States. Using this framework, we can see that despite certain similarities (such as poverty and discrimination) the experiences of racial minorities contrasted sharply with those of European immigrants. These conditions make assimilation into the larger society a myth for people of color because the colonial experiences embedded them in a system of racial domination. The key ingredient in internal colonialism is that the racial control that began as the result of conquest is institutionalized in social, economic, and political spheres.

The colonial model assigns fundamental importance to the labor that people of color did when they were brought into the United States. European ethnics began work mostly in industry, or at least in industrial sectors of the economy, where they could move about as families or individuals in response to the needs of an industrializing economy. In contrast, Blacks and Chicanos were forced into certain types of work. Blauner has noted the consequences of preindustrial work:

> Like European overseas colonialism, America has used African, Asian, Mexican, and to a lesser degree Indian workers for the cheapest labor, concentrating people of color in the most unskilled jobs, the least advanced sectors of the economy and the most industrially backward regions of the nation. In an historical sense, people of color provided much of the hard labor (and the technical skills) that built up the agricultural base and the mineral-transport-communications infrastructure necessary for industrialization and modernization, whereas the Europeans worked primarily within the industrialized, modern sectors. The initial position of European ethnics, while low, was therefore strategic for movement up the economic and social pyramid. The placement of nonwhite groups, however, imposed barrier upon barrier on such mobility, freezing them for long periods of time in the least favorable segments of the economy. (Blauner, 1972:62)

Today, the labor market continues to trap minority group members. Job opportunities are segmented in U.S. society into a dual labor market. (The following discussion is adapted from Moore, 1978:27–34.) There are essentially two types of employers, with the labor market operating differently for each. Employers in the primary core enterprises are heavily capitalized and unionized; they offer jobs with relatively high wages, good working conditions, security, fringe benefits, and the chance for advancement. The other type, the marginal employers, pay the lowest wages and often have deplorable working conditions (such as in the garment industry, restaurants, and farming). These jobs require few skills. Employers are interested in workers who will make minimal demands. Workers who agitate for better wages and working conditions are soon replaced because they have no job security and there is generally a large pool of persons available to take over their jobs (teenagers, ex-convicts, recent migrants from rural areas, recent immigrants, and the poor).

Very few people at the bottom of the labor market ever have access to the jobs considered part of the American dream—those with security, good pay, and chances for advancement. Low educational attainment and lack of skills keep minority group members in jobs that are unstable, below average in wages, and a dead end. The poor Black or Chicano is most likely to end up in these jobs because the institutions of society are programmed for sifting and sorting individuals, usually according to predetermined categories such as age, race, sex, and socioeconomic background (see Chapter 14).

Structural theories view race as a basis for the formation of power and resource inequality. Most structural theories recognize that class discrimination and racial discrimination work with and through each other to produce social inequality. The roots of racial discrimination lie deep within the U.S. economy. Racial stratification theories emphasize the deep roots of racial and ethnic inequalities in the U.S. economy. **Assimilation** theories tend to neglect these economic issues. (Assimilation is the process by which individuals or groups voluntarily or involuntarily are incorporated into society.) These theories are concerned primarily with how minorities adapt in the larger society. Assimilation theories see the situations of Blacks and other non-Whites as similar to those of earlier White immigrants. However, racial ethnics were placed in the larger society in ways that precluded their assimilation. The U.S. economy did not provide equal opportunities for them. Racial stratifications exists because certain segments of society benefit from it. The capitalist class benefits from it. Employers can turn racism into higher profits by paying lower-than-average wages to people of color.

In 1980 employers' direct gain from wage discrimination—the extra money they would have to pay if Black workers earned the same as Whites—reached $25 billion, a substantial fraction of corporate profits. Employers also benefit indirectly when they are able to keep a divided labor force in a weak bargaining position. This situation, however, harms White workers as well as Black workers.

Nevertheless, White workers also benefit from racism. If there is a certain amount of unemployment to be shared by workers, and a given number of good jobs to go around, White workers benefit from their relatively lower unemployment, their better access to good jobs, and a higher income relative to workers who face discrimination (Zarsky and Bowles, 1986:54).

Discrimination against Blacks and Hispanics: Continuity and Change

The treatment of Blacks and Hispanics has been disgraceful throughout U.S. history. Members of each category have been denied equality in money, jobs, services, housing, and even the right to vote. Since World War II, however, under pressure from civil rights advocates, the government has led the way in breaking down these discriminatory practices. The 1960 civil rights movement overturned segregation laws, opened voting booths, created new job opportunities, and renewed hope for racial equality. Public policies and economic growth improved the situation of racial minorities. However, most of the gains made by civil rights legislation, increased education opportunities, affirmative action programs, and increased Black political participation have been short-lived. Although many well-educated people of color in the past three decades have made considerable gains, large gaps between the well-being of racial minorities and Whites remain. There is continuing evidence of the second-class status of African Americans and Latinos.

A comprehensive four-year National Research Council study on the state of Black America during the past fifty years has found that there is a continuing gap in status between Blacks and Whites in the United States. The 1989 report revealed that on virtually every indicator of well-being—income and living standards, health and life expectancy, and residential opportunities, as well as political and social participation—Blacks remained substantially behind Whites (Jaynes and Williams, 1989). Hispanics,* too, fall well behind Whites on most indicators of status. Even though levels of well-being vary widely among Hispanic groups, they face common obstacles to becoming incorporated into the economic mainstream of society. The basic point of the next subsection is that racial

*Unless otherwise noted, this section uses statistics on Hispanics rather than on Chicanos. Lumping Hispanics into one group obscures diversities within this category. However, the data supplied by the government provide information only on the total Spanish-speaking population. Hispanics, although they share the Spanish language and Catholicism, vary in many respects, so that few generalizations are possible.

minorities face inequalities that reflect the routine operation of the political economy and the basic patterns of institutional discrimination.

Income

Table 7.1 shows that the average income for White families is greater than the average income of Black and Hispanic families. In 1990, the median income of Black families was $21,423, about 58 percent of the White median family income of $36,915. Hispanic median family income was $23,431, (or 63 percent of the median income of White families) (U.S. Bureau of the Census, 1991d:56). Even though the median income for Blacks is still below that of Hispanics, per-person income for Hispanics is actually lower because Hispanics tend to have larger families.

Racial differences in poverty have persisted in recent years. Although most poor people are White, Blacks remained disproportionately poor, followed by

Table 7.1   Median family income by race: 1972–1990

Year	White	Hispanic	Black
1972	$25,107	$17,790	$14,922
1973	25,777	17,836	14,877
1974	24,728	17,594	14,765
1975	24,110	16,140	14,835
1976	24,823	16,390	14,766
1977	25,124	17,141	14,352
1978	25,606	17,518	15,166
1979	25,689	18,255	14,590
1980	24,176	16,242	13,989
1981	23,517	16,401	13,266
1982	24,603	16,227	13,598
1983	25,837	16,930	14,561
1984	27,686	18,822	15,431
1985	29,152	19,027	16,786
1986	30,809	19,995	17,604
1987	32,274	20,306	18,098
1988	33,915	21,769	19,329
1989	35,975	23,446	20,209
1990	36,915	23,431	21,423

Sources: U.S. Bureau of the Census, "Money Income and Poverty Status of Families and Persons in the United States: 1981," *Current Population Report,* Series P–60, no. 134 (July 1983), Table 3; U.S. Bureau of the Census, *Current Population Reports,* Series P–60, no. 154, "Money, Income and Poverty States of Families and Persons in the U.S.: 1985 (advance data from the March, 1986 Current Population Survey)," U.S. Government Printing Office, Washington, D.C., 1986, Table 2, p. 9; U.S. Bureau of the Census, "Money Income of Households, Families, and Persons in the United States: 1987," *Current Population Reports,* Series P–60, No. 162, Table 9, p. 32; U.S. Bureau of the Census, "Money, Income and Poverty Status in the United States, 1988," (advance data from the March 1989 Current Population Survey) U.S. Government Printing Office, Washington, D.C., 1989 Table A, p. 3.; U.S. Bureau of The Census, "Money, Income of Households, Families, and Persons in the United States: 1990 *Current Population Reports,* Series P–60, no. 174, Table 13, pp. 52–54.

Hispanics and then Whites. In 1991, the poverty rate for Whites was 11.2 percent compared with 32.7 percent for Blacks and 28.7 percent for Hispanics (Pear, 1992:A1). For Hispanics, these percentages represent the highest number of people living in poverty since the Census Bureau began collecting figures on Hispanics in 1972. In recent years, the poverty rate of Hispanics has risen more rapidly than that of Whites or Blacks. However, poverty rates differ greatly among Hispanic groups. Among Puerto Ricans, poverty has hovered at a rate of 40 percent in the last several years. Recent evidence suggests that economic conditions in areas where Hispanic groups are concentrated account for the difference in their economic well-being. Puerto Ricans are concentrated in major cities of the eastern end of the Snowbelt states, where larger economic changes have affected less-skilled workers (Aponte, 1991). If overall Hispanic poverty patterns continue, Hispanics will emerge as the nation's poorest racial ethnic group of the 1990s.

The relationship between poverty rates for Whites and Blacks and Hispanics generally holds true regardless of age. For example, for children younger than eighteen, the poverty rate in 1990 was 12.3 percent for White children, 38.8 percent for Black children, and 31 percent for Hispanic children (Usdansky, 1992b:3A).

Poverty is especially prevalent in families headed by females. In these families, race and gender inequalities combine to produce extreme hardships. Almost half of the Black and Hispanic families headed by women in 1990 had incomes below the poverty level.

Black and Hispanic women maintaining families had lower labor force participation rates and higher unemployment rates than did White women maintaining families. These data give one explanation for the high incidence of poverty in families maintained by women. Thus, feminization of poverty is important in explaining some kinds of poverty, but it does not explain the persistent pattern of widening income inequality in minority families with a man and a woman present. A two-parent family is no guarantee for racial minorities to escape poverty. Many young children in a married-couple home are in the lowest income tier—two in ten White children, three in ten Black children, and four in ten Hispanic children (Ahlberg and De Vita, 1992:38).

Many factors explain the difference in White and minority earnings. Racial-ethnics are concentrated in the South and Southwest, where incomes are lower for everyone. Another part of the explanation is the differing age structure of minorities. They are younger, on average, than is the White population. A group with a higher proportion of young people of working age will have a lower average earning level, higher rates of unemployment, and lower rates of labor force participation.

Looking at racial inequalities by age also reveals another disturbing pattern. The degree of inequality increases after the teenage years. Racial disparities become greater in peak earning years. This result suggests that another part of the explanation for racial inequalities in earnings lies in the lack of education and skill levels required to move out of poor-paying jobs. All of these explanations leave a substantial amount of inequality unexplained (Currie and Skolnick, 1988:151–155). Minorities at all levels of employment and education still earn less than do Whites owing to current racial discrimination in the labor force.

The gap between minority and White earnings has increased in recent years. On the average, Blacks still earn about 56 cents for every dollar earned by Whites, a drop of about 5 percentage points in the last decade (Williams, 1987:56).

Education

Educational progress for Blacks and Hispanics followed the civil rights era, but those gains in educational attainment have not closed the gap. Chapter 12 discusses racial inequality in education. Low educational achievement has been a major barrier to the advancement of minorities. Many minority group members are becoming part of the U.S. underclass, eligible for little more than low-paying jobs or welfare. The relatively low level of educational attainment for Hispanics and Blacks is the result of several factors, including language differences, malnutrition, drug abuse, teenage pregnancy, and lack of family support. Yet many of the problems have less to do with minority students themselves and more to do with discrimination in the schools. According to the National Coalition of Advocates for Students, a child who is poor, Black, or Hispanic is much more likely to be physically disciplined, suspended, expelled, or made to repeat a grade—all practices shown to increase the likelihood that a child will drop out of school. A minority child is three times as likely as a White child to end up in vocational education or in classes for the mildly mentally retarded. In effect, minority children are being "pushed out" of schools (*U.S. News & World Report,* 1987:66).

Despite similarities in the educational experiences of minority students who are poor, Hispanic students are more segregated today than are Black students. A study of school enrollment by the University of Chicago revealed that the percentage of Hispanic students who attend predominantly minority schools is higher now than it was twenty years ago. Nationwide, the percentage of Hispanic students attending schools in which minorities made up more than half the student body increased from 54.8 percent in 1968 to 71.5 percent in 1986. The percentage of Blacks attending predominantly minority schools fell from 76.6 percent in 1968 to 63.3 percent in 1986 (Fiske, 1987:1.15). This growing isolation from middle-class society will further disadvantage Hispanic youth.

The changing demography of race will have far-reaching effects on schools as they adjust to a student body that is more diverse than ever. By 2010, 38 percent of people in the United States under the age of eighteen will be Black, Asian, or other minority. In the most populous states—California, New York, Texas, and Florida—minority children will be a majority by the year 2010 (Schwartz and Exter, 1989:34).

Several additional trends are creating problems for minority students. The general movement against increased taxes hurts public schools, especially the costly programs for the disadvantaged (e.g. bilingual education and Head Start.) Inner-city schools, where minorities are concentrated and which are already understaffed and underfinanced, face even greater financial pressures because of the current trend to reduce federal programs to aid the disadvantaged.

Another trend that may reduce the number of minorities attending college is the increased cost of higher education. Because they are more likely to be poor than are Whites, minorities are less able to afford college. This decline should accelerate as the costs of education rise.

These pessimistic trends are compounded by the reality that minority members, regardless of their level of education, are underpaid compared with Whites of similar education. Many of the disadvantaged, knowing that race is the significant variable keeping minorities down, have little motivation to do well in school because they regard education as having no payoff.

At each education level, there is a significant difference in income between Blacks, Hispanics, and Whites. Yet education alone is not the answer. Two examples reinforce this point: Black high school graduates are more likely to be unemployed than are Whites who drop out of high school; and for Blacks who earn a college degree, they can expect to earn almost $5,000 less annually than will White college graduates (Wickham, 1989:A10). Given the persistence of discrimination in U.S. society, education by itself cannot eliminate the income gap between racial minorities and other people in the United States.

Unemployment

Unemployment rates have consistently varied by race. The National Research Council study on the status of Blacks found that the unemployment level of Blacks and Whites has increased since 1954, when the Supreme Court outlawed school segregation. The jobless rate of Blacks is usually double the national rate, and the jobless rate of Hispanics is commonly 40 to 50 percent higher than the overall employment rate.

Since the 1970s, there has been a growing gap in the unemployment rates of men and women of color relative to the rates for White men and women. Although the official unemployment rate for May 1992 was 7.5 percent, the rate for Blacks was 14.7 percent, more than double the 6.5 percentage rate for Whites. The rate for Hispanics was 11.3 percent (*USA Today,* 1992:2B). These government rates are misleading, however. They count as employed the almost 6 million people who work part-time because they cannot find full-time jobs, and they do not count as unemployed the discouraged workers, numbering more than 1 million, who have given up their search for work. Given the low pay for jobs that minorities receive if they can find work, more of them than Whites would likely become discouraged enough to stop looking for a job.

The existence of pockets of disproportionately high minority unemployment suggests great potential for social problems. Minorities from urban slums are most affected by few job opportunities. High levels of unemployment for Black and Hispanic teenagers lead to rising crime rates and out-of-welock births (Wilson, 1987).

Type of Employment

African Americans and Latinos have always been important components of the U.S. Labor force. But their jobs prospects are different from those of other people in the United States. Not only are minorities twice as likely as Whites to be unemployed, but those who do work are also overrepresented in jobs for which the pay, power, and prestige are low. Many more Blacks and Hispanics than Whites are blue-collar and service workers, whereas Whites hold a majority of the white-collar jobs, which are physically safer, better paying, more stable, and offer more chance for advancement.

Although minorities are working in the least rewarding jobs, there have been positive changes since 1960. Because of greater educational attainment and affirmative-action programs, non-Whites hold a greater number of management, white-collar, and upper-level, blue-collar jobs than before. Despite these gains, however, a huge gap remains.

The transformation of the U.S. economy from one based on manufacturing to one based on information and services is having devastating effects on minority communities across the country. The effects of economic and industrial change are most visible in three areas: (1) the trend toward unemployment, (2) the changing distribution and organization of jobs, and (3) the tendency for the jobs created to be relatively low paying. Hispanics and Blacks have suffered disproportionately from industrial job loss and declining manufacturing employment. Their employment status, which is declining in all regions, is worse in areas of industrial decline. For Blacks the lowest employment rates are in the Midwest and Great Lakes region, that is, in the old industrial heartland. The labor market status of Whites has also been lowered in these areas, but the level of racial inequality has increased to scandalous levels. In Swinton's words,

In such cities as Detroit, Buffalo, Chicago, and Cleveland, the gap between the labor market position of blacks, especially black males, and whites probably exceeds the highest levels that ever existed in the most racist of the South's cities. (Swinton, 1987:68)

The new economy will increasingly be made up of people of color. According to the U.S. Department of Labor, one out of every three new entrants to the labor force by the year 2000 will be non-White (Harrison, 1990:65).

Contemporary Trends and Issues in U.S. Race and Ethnic Relations

Growing Racial Diversity

For much of the nation's history, national demographic trends were largely a result of trends in the White population. The 1990 census confirmed that the United States is now one-fourth minority and that the non-Hispanic population no longer unerringly reflects the nation's character (Frey, 1991:6). New social challenges are posed by the demographic shift from an Anglo White society to a society with three large racial ethnic minorities, each of them growing in size while the White majority declines in population (Riche, 1991:26) (see Figure 7.2.) Five facts illustrate the magnitude of this demographic transformation.

One-fourth of the people in the United States are Black, Hispanic, Asian, or Native American. Fourteen percent of residents speak a language other than English at home; 19.8 million are foreign born.

Racial minorities are increasing faster than the majority population. During the 1980s the number of Asians more than doubled from 3.5 million to 7.3 million, and Hispanics grew from 14.6 to 22.4 million. The increase in the number of Blacks was from 16.5 to 30.0 million (Frey, 1990:6). The result of these trends is that whereas Whites in 1980 were 80 percent of the population, they will be only 70 percent by 2000 (Population Reference Bureau, 1989:10). "By 2056, when someone born today will be 66 years old, the "average" U.S. resident, as defined by Census statistics, will trace his or her descent to Africa, Asia, the Hispanic world, the Pacific Island, Arabia—almost anywhere but White Europe" (Henry, 1990:28).

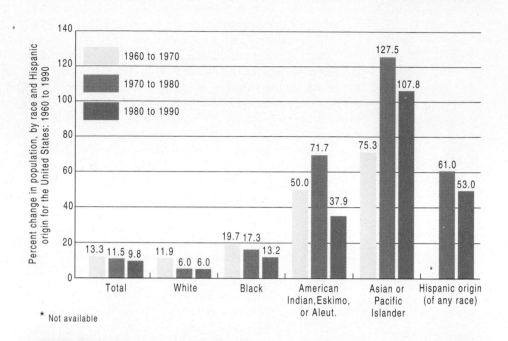

Figure 7.2   Percentage change in population by race and Hispanic origin for the United States: 1960 to 1990

Source: U.S. Bureau of the Census, 1990 Census Profile. "Race and Hispanic Origin," (June 1991):1.

Blacks are losing their position as the most numerous racial minority. In 1990, for the first time, Blacks were less than half of all minorities, "a precursor of the flip flop expected by 2010, when Hispanics replace them as the largest minority" (Usdansky, 1992:B1).

Immigration now accounts for a large share of the nation's population growth. The largest ten-year wave of immigration in U.S. history occurred during the 1980s with the arrival of almost 9 million people. More immigrants were admitted during the 1980s than during any decade since 1900–1910 (Miles, 1992:68). Legislation enacted in 1986 and 1990 ensures that this record high number will easily be surpassed in the 1990s (Portes, 1992). By 2020, immigration will have more impact on U.S. population growth than will natural increase (Waldrop, 1990:23).

New patterns of immigration are changing the racial composition of U.S. society. Among the expanded population of first-generation immigrants, "the Asian-born now outnumber the European-born. Those from Latin America—predominantly Mexicans—outnumber both" (Barringer, 1992a:2). This contrasts sharply with what occurred as recently as the 1950s, when two-thirds of legal immigrants were from Europe and Canada.

A disproportionate number of racial/ethnic minorities work at jobs with low status, poor pay, and few, if any, benefits.

These trends signal a transformation from a White majority to a multi-racial/multicultural society. Old definitions of minority groups are becoming meaningless as thc share of Black, Hispanics, Asians, and other groups continue to gain on the White majority.

New Racial Divisions

As the United States faces the economic and social challenges posed by the growth of minority populations, there is ongoing polarization between racial ethnics and the White population. In addition, interethnic tensions are also emerging in many inner cities.

Geographic differences and disparities are pervasive. Several recent studies using data from the 1980 and 1990 U.S. Censuses have confirmed that the distribution of Whites in the United States across geographic regions and metropolitan areas is becoming increasingly dissimilar to that of the faster-growing minorities (Frey, 1991; Gilmour and Doig, 1992). Minorities have always had a high degree of concentration, and the recent increase in the size of minorities in certain areas has accentuated this trend.

Racial segregation is most apparent at the neighborhood level. More than 30 percent of Blacks live in all-Black neighborhoods, and two-thirds of Whites also live in racial isolation. The most segregated cities are in northern industrial areas such as Detroit. Sunbelt cities such as Miami are more integrated, partly because Hispanics and Asian Americans are integrating into both Black and White neighborhoods (Gilmour and Doig, 1992:48). Residential segregation is found in middle-class suburbs as well as in impoverished inner cities. An important obstacle to social mobility, residential segregation persists simply because of racial discrimination in housing (Usdansky, 1991:2A).

These trends are accompanied by a massive rollback of economic, social, and political gains for minorities. Conservative economic strategies during the Reagan and Bush administrations dramatically accelerated the economic decline of people of color. The Reagan administration played a crucial role in dividing the United States along lines of race. Tax policies that have redistributed income from the poor to the wealthy, the shift in U.S. government spending, and the deliberate shrinking of the public sector have all had a disproportionate impact on minorities. Among the most telling changes is the dismantling of civil rights legislation that has taken place under Reagan and Bush Supreme Court appointees.

Divisions between the races have emerged on a host of fronts. Race-infused conflicts heightened during the 1980s. Race itself acquired new meaning within the political climate of the times. Often "when the official subject was presidential politics, taxes, welfare, crime, rights, or values, the real subject was race" (Edsall and Edsall, 1991:53). Along with the new politics of race in the United States; racial and ethnic confrontations and battles in other parts of the world are leading to increased violence.

- The Boston police department, which averaged about 150 race-related crimes annually from 1986 to 1988, had 202 in 1989.

Racial bigotry is rising in the United States.

- In New York City, such crimes were up 14 percent for the first four months of 1990 as compared with 1989.
- For 1989, the Anti-Defamation League recorded the highest number of "bias crimes" in eleven years (Goldman, 1990:1).
- White supremacist groups with such diverse elements as the Ku Klux Klan, Nazi-identified parties, and skinheads have expanded across the country (Langer, 1990). These groups are up 27 percent from a decade earlier (Mayfield, 1992).

Recent headlines about racism on college campuses have surprised many people in the United States, although campus racism appears to be widespread. From MIT to the University of California, Berkeley, and on campuses throughout the nation, racial attacks on Blacks, Hispanics, and Asians are revealing an extensive problem of intolerance in settings where tolerance is essential to the pursuit of knowledge.

Racial violence is often associated with deteriorating economic conditions—lack of jobs, housing, and other resources—that lead to minority scapegoating on the part of Whites (reported in *USA Today,* 1989a:1). In Florida and many parts of the West and Southwest, perceptions that Cubans, Mexicans, and other Hispanics are taking jobs from Anglos have touched off racial tensions.

Many problems of class are leading to interethnic strife. The 1992 Los Angeles riot spotlighted tensions between Hispanics and Blacks. Although Latinos were overlooked by media coverage during the riot, they played a dominant role in riot-related incidents, accounting for half of the 8,700 people arrested during the violence (*U.S. News & World Report,* 1992:40). Economic deprivation of both Blacks and Latinos led to rioting. Mounting tensions in South Central Los Angeles between Latino immigrants from Central and South America and Blacks contributed to the rampage (Miles, 1992; Mydans, 1992).

Urban Black Poverty: Culture or Structure?

What accounts for persistent poverty in U.S. inner cities? One answer is that racial minorities themselves are responsible for declining conditions; that broken families and lack of motivation in finding jobs have prevented the people from taking advantage of the opportunities made by antidiscriminatory legislation. This cultural explanation is in error on many counts. It relies too heavily on cultural traits to explain poverty. It falls back on blaming the victim in order to explain patterns that are actually rooted in social structure. Economic changes in society have removed jobs and other opportunities from inner-city residents, and their families have been severely affected. This is a better explanation of persistent and concentrated poverty among Blacks.

This explanation is detailed in William J. Wilson's compelling book, *The Truly Disadvantaged* (1987). According to Wilson, all of the social problems of the ghetto are outgrowths of joblessness, which is due to fundamental transformations of the larger economy and the class structure of ghetto neighborhoods. The movement of middle-class Black professionals from the inner city has left behind a concentration of the most disadvantaged segments of the Black urban population. Meanwhile, the shift of jobs from central cities to suburbs and from the Rustbelt to the Sunbelt continues to isolate and increase the unemployment of urban

Blacks. These forces have led to more unemployment, more poverty, and more female-headed households among Blacks, not a deviant culture, as so many would argue.

Wilson (1987) provides evidence that jobs influence the likelihood of marriage among Blacks. He suggests that increasing male joblessness is a major underlying factor in the increase of the number of Black single mothers and female-headed households. Wage discrimination also works against marriage. Wilson found that men with higher incomes are more likely to be married than are men with lower incomes. The underclass is largely the result of a long-term decline in the proportion of Black men, and particularly young Black men, who are in a position to support a family. These structural conditions make it necessary for many Black women to leave a marriage or to forgo marriage altogether. Adaptations to structural conditions leave Black women disproportionately divorced and responsible for their children. The Black inner city is not destroying itself by its own behaviors and culture, but is being destroyed by economic forces.

CHAPTER REVIEW

1. Racial and ethnic stratification are basic features of U.S. society. These forms of inequality are built into normal practices, and they exclude people from full and equal participation in society's institutions. Racial and ethnic stratification exist because they benefit certain segments of society.

2. Race is a social category that serves as a basis for differential treatment. The concept of race is socially rather than biologically significant. Racial groups are set apart and singled out for unequal treatment.

3. An ethnic group is culturally distinct in race, religion, or national origin. That group has a common culture that is distinct from the culture of the majority. Some ethnic groups such as Jews, Poles, and Italians have distinguishing cultural characteristics that stem from religion and national origin. Because racial groups also have distinctive cultural characteristics, they are referred to as racial-ethnics.

4. Racial and ethnic groups are systematically disadvantaged by society's institutions. Both race and ethnicity are traditional bases for systems of inequality, although there are historical and contemporary differences in the societal placement of racial-ethnics and White-ethnics in this society.

5. Racial-ethnic groups that have difficulty escaping devalued states became part of the United States involuntarily and were forced into preindustrial work that was low in pay, status, and chances for upward mobility. Blacks, Chicanos, Asian Americans, and Native Americans are four such groups.

6. Blacks came to the United States involuntarily as slaves. Following the Civil War, they were freed from slavery but remained oppressed by the economic, legal, and social practices of the majority.

7. Chicanos became part of the United States involuntarily as a result of military conquest and a change in political boundaries. With few exceptions they were dispossessed of power and property. They became the major source of cheap labor in the Southwest. They continue to be the objects of discrimination today.

8. Asian Americans are more diverse than the other prominent racial minorities in the United States. Their characteristics vary according to their national origins, time of entry into the United States, and, for the more recent immigrants, social class background.

9. The lands of the Native Americans were taken by the Europeans and their descendants by force and fraud. The Native Americans were made wards of the federal government and placed on reservations. Today, the Native American population is increasing in numbers and becoming more diverse.

10. Deficiency theories maintain that some groups are unequal because they lack some important feature common among the majority. These deficiencies may be biological (such as low intelligence), structural (such as weak family ties), or cultural (such as the culture of poverty).

11. Bias theories place the blame for inequality on the prejudiced attitudes of the members of the dominant group. These theories, however, do not explain the discriminatory acts of the unprejudiced, which are aimed at preserving privilege.

12. Structural theories argue that inequality is the result of the politicoeconomic system that dominates and oppresses minorities. There are four main features of institutional discrimination: (1) the forces of history shape present conditions; (2) discrimination can occur without conscious bigotry; (3) this type of discrimination is less visible than individual acts of discrimination; and (4) discrimination is reinforced by the interrelationships among the institutions of society.

13. The segmented labor market is a structural source of inequality. There are two kinds of jobs: those that are secure, pay well, have fringe benefits, and offer a chance for advancement; and those that are unstable, poorly paid, and a dead end. Large numbers of minorities are found at the bottom of the labor market because of institutional discrimination, particularly in the educational and economic sectors.

14. The assimilation model—that minorities will eventually become part of the mainstream once they give up their distinctive ethnicity and learn the skills required by society—is not applicable to colonized people of color. The colonization of people means their subordination in all spheres—social, economic, and political. The superordinate group exploits the colonized people for its own advantage. This exploitation traps the minority in a subordinate status.

15. Civil rights legislation improved the status of some racial-ethnics, yet the overall position of Blacks and Hispanics relative to Whites has not improved. Large gaps remain in work, earnings, and education. Changing conditions in the economy have contributed to the persistent poverty in U.S. urban centers.

16. The racial demography of the United States is changing. Immigration and high birth rates among minorities are making this a multiracial, multicultural society. These trends are also creating new forms of racial segregation and racial conflict.

KEY TERMS

Majority.   A dominant group in society.
Minority.   A subordinate group in society.

Racial stratification.   A system of inequality in which race is the major criterion for rank and rewards.

Minority group.   A group dominated by a more powerful group and, as a result, singled out for differential and unfair treatment.

Racial group.   A group socially defined and singled out for differential treatment.

Ethnic group.   A social group with a common culture, distinct from the culture of the majority because of race, religion, or national origin.

Ethnicity.   Culturally distinctive characteristics based on race, religion, or national origin.

Racial ethnic group (or **racially defined ethnic group**).   A group with a common ancestry based on racial discrimination.

Institutional racism.   The established and customary social arrangements that exclude on the basis of race.

Individual racism.   Overt acts by individuals that harm members of another race.

Assimilation.   The voluntary or involuntary incorporation of groups or individuals into society.

FOR FURTHER STUDY

Margaret L. Andersen and Patricia Hill Collins. *Race, Class, and Gender: An Anthology.* Belmont, Calif.: Wadsworth Publishing Company, 1992.

Elijah Anderson. *Street Wise: Race, Class, and Change in An Urban Community.* Chicago: University of Chicago Press, 1990.

Andrew Hacker. *Two Nations: Black and White, Separate, Hostile, Unequal.* New York: Scribners, 1992.

Gerald David Jaynes and Robin M. Williams, Jr. *A Common Destiny: Blacks and American Society.* Washington, D.C.: National Academy Press, 1989.

Louise Lamphere, ed. *Structuring Diversity: Ethnographic Perspectives on the New Immigration.* Chicago: University of Chicago Press, 1992.

Edwin Melendez, Clara Rodriguez, and Janis Barry Figueroa, eds. *Hispanics in the Labor Force.* New York: Plenum Press, 1991.

William O'Hare and Judy Felt. *Asian Americans: America's Fastest Growing Minority Group.* Washington, D.C.: Population Reference Bureau, 1991.

Michael Omi and Howard Winant. *Racial Formation in the United States.* New York: Routledge & Kegan Paul, 1987.

Alejandro Portes and Ruben G. Rumbaut. *Immigrant America.* Berkeley: University of California Press, 1990.

C. Matthew Snipp. *American Indians: The First of This Land.* New York: Russell Sage Foundation, 1989.

Studs Turkel. *Race: How Blacks and Whites Think and Feel about the American Obsession.* New Press, 1991.

William J. Wilson. *The Truly Disadvantaged: The Inner City, the Underclass, and Public Policy.* Chicago: University of Chicago Press, 1987.

Norman R. Yetman, ed. *Majority and Minority: The Dynamics of Racial and Ethnic Relations.* 5th ed. Boston: Allyn and Bacon, 1991.

FORUM

HOW SOCIAL RESEARCH COULD INFORM DEBATE OVER THE LOS ANGELES RIOTS

On May 5, *The New York Times* reported: "The White House said today that the riots last week in Los Angeles were a result of social welfare programs that Congress enacted in the 1960's and 1970's." And the next day another *Times* article stated: "In a counterattack on the Bush Administration, Governor Bill Clinton said yesterday that the riots in Los Angeles resulted in part from " '12 years of denial and neglect' of festering social problems under Presidents Bush and Reagan."

So even as the rubble was being swept from the streets, the event was being appropriated to aid familiar ideological agendas.

Disillusioned academics and political commentators already are suggesting that Americans will fail to learn from this tragedy, just as we failed to learn from the Watts riots. Yet over the past 25 years, and in the past five years especially, much research has been done into the frustrations of inner-city life, which ought to have raised the debate to a much higher level of sophistication. Some studies have shown the long-term value of child development programs, for instance, and how to design job training more effectively. Other research has shown how the decline of manufacturing in the inner city affects both unemployment and marital stability. Various studies have refuted simplistic arguments that welfare fosters dependency. Why did this academic research have so little influence?

Americans respect science and like to believe that their society is adept at practical problem solving, without the ideological prejudices of more class-divided industrial societies. Yet American culture also idealizes dreaming. The word "dream" appears everywhere as a substitute for ambition, hope, or achievement, with the implicit or explicit message that anything can be achieved, whatever the obstacles, if only Americans remain faithful to their desires.

The very qualities that give social research its scientific authority—its systematic objectivity, its disavowal of value judgments—are particularly incompatible with dreams. Evidence tends to confirm the intransigence of mundane obstacles to success. Thus social research about poverty is, for the most part, telling both ordinary people and political leaders what they do not want to hear—that policies are not working, that dreams are naïve, that they share the blame.

To inspire other, more realistic policies, research has to become engaged with the moral issues that its findings address, such as racial and gender discrimination, inequality of opportunity, and what responsibility our society should take for political and economic decisions that affect our most vulnerable citizens. But social scientists often are uncomfortable with this, because it seems to compromise the conventions of objectivity in which they have been trained, and from which they derive their legitimation.

Practicality has its own illusions, however, especially the illusion that research, done without preconceptions, will tell you what to do. But research must begin and end, at a time and a place, with a particular set of questions and observations. The framework for any research shapes its meaning and how its results may relate to policy. The framework implies concerns about how human beings should act by the questions it asks and the context in which it asks them.

For instance, if you ask what are the characteristics of poor neighborhoods, you will notice an association among welfare dependency, crime, and large numbers of minority-group members. But because most poor people do not live in such neighborhoods, but are distributed throughout urban and rural areas, if you ask what are the characteristics of poor people in general, you are more likely to see an association with divorce and the low wages earned by women. Further, you will get different answers depending on whether you study a sample of poor people at a particular moment or over a period of time. If a researcher ignores what happens over time and in a variety of settings, the characteristics of a small minority of poor people can be misrepresented as typical. If the researcher does not present these limitations or restrictions explicitly or convincingly, the work is likely to be ignored or misrepresented by others to suit their own agendas.

Social scientists are not taught the elements of dramatic structure in presenting their research findings—such as where to begin and end a story or how to build to a climax—which might help to make their research and its conclusions more compelling to policy makers and the people the research is designed to help. Even thinking about their work in these terms offends their conception of science. In a world of policy debate where politicians, community leaders, newspaper commentators, and the fellow standing next to you in the bar have no such inhibitions, the stories told by social scientists tend to come across as too technical, obscure, tentative, and highly qualified.

This does not bother other academics. In fact, few academics in social research are rewarded with promotion or tenure because their work is relevant to policy or interesting to a lay public. Prestige comes from writing in journals read by their peers, where the admired qualities are analytical sophistication and conceptual innovation. Reputations are made on the skill with which a conceptual idea is promoted and defended or critically attacked. And these controversies tend to frame research in an intellectual context very remote from action.

In 1987, for instance, the Rockefeller Foundation made substantial grants to the Social Science Research Council to encourage research into persistent poverty, out of concern that a new "underclass" was becoming established in the United States, one permanently excluded from the opportunities for advancing in society. As the foundation's guidelines for grants were translated into research ideas, academics' impetus toward conceptual controversy thrust the word "underclass" into the center of the debate: Was it an appropriate concept? How do you define it? How do you measure it?

Much time and intellectual energy were absorbed in defending or challenging the validity of the concept. The problem is not that this was all a waste of time: The debate raised important questions about what was happening to the inner city and what characteristics its residents did or did not share. But it was remote from the way that people who were trying to intervene in the inner city thought about the problems. At the same time as it financed research, the Rockefeller Foundation also financed six community-planning and action programs in inner cities. But the language and preoccupations of the people running those programs were profoundly different.

They hoped to make local governments and government agencies more aware of the needs of poor people and more open to innovative ways of serving them better. They had no use for the word "underclass," which sounded like a denigration of the people they were trying to help. They translated "persistent poverty" into interventions to improve child development and health, as well as education and training; such programs were at once less stigmatizing and more hopeful.

So although the academic researchers and the community reformers were inspired by the same underlying concerns, they did not provide each other with much guidance.

Each group was asking a different kind of question, which required a different kind of answer. If you are asking how to understand the persistence of poverty and frustration in the inner city, the answers tend to refer to large-scale changes in the world economy and the demographic shifts that accompany them. Such explanations often are called "structural," because they can be represented as a structure of relationships among social, economic, and governmental factors that together determine the impoverishment of inner-city neighborhoods.

But if you are asking what we can do, now, about this impoverishment, structural explanations are not very helpful, because they offer no point of intervention. For people trying to make changes, the way relationships are reproduced—in the running of a school or the hiring of employees or the recruitment of a gang of drug dealers—is crucial. Both kinds of answers are, in the end, attempts to grasp the same pattern of relationships. But to the reformers, the academics often seem remote and daunting, preoccupied with their theoretical controversies. The academics find the ideas of the reformers superficial, narrow, or naïve.

Some profound inhibitions exist, then, on the influence of social research: They lie partly in the rewards and concerns of the academic profession, and partly in the ambivalence of society at large toward the findings of social science. There are always some scholars with the skill and intellectual self-confidence to overcome these limitations, such as Mary Jo Bane, David Ellwood, Herbert Gans, William Julius Wilson, Frances Fox Piven, and Richard Cloward, to mention only a distinguished few. But a mass of knowledge circulates within academe that is only very slowly and partially absorbed into the wider public debate, if at all.

What can we do about this, apart from trying to create more occasions where academics and reformers meet to try to understand each other?

We can begin to try to change the academic reward structure so that scholars' research is more respected and honored if it is useful and accessible. We can train social scientists to write better, with a larger sense of constituency.

We also need, I think, a profession of social-science journalism, equivalent to scientific journalism, whose practitioners are expert enough to understand research on its own terms and able to translate it for a wider audience of policy makers, community workers, and the general public—including the communities the research is designed to help.

The potential contribution of such a profession, both to politics and the intellectual life of America, is profound. It could at once inform the discussion of policy and reconnect sociology to its roots in social idealism and reform. A sociology department that encouraged its best students to believe that social-science journalism could be the career for them would be a very stimulating, and influential, intellectual community.

Source: Peter Marris, "How Social Research Could Inform Debate over Urban Problems." *The Chronicle of Higher Education* (May 20, 1992): A40. Reprinted by permission.

Women have made great strides during the past two decades. Nevertheless, gender bias is a social problem affecting more than one-half of the population in one way or another.

The much-publicized Tailhook scandal in which Naval officers allegedly assaulted 26 women (many of them fellow officers) and the Senate's insensitive handling of Anita Hill's allegations against Clarence Thomas have brought to light some of the problems women face in its most cherished institutions.

Some examples of the dimensions of gender inequality are:

- Most women remain concentrated in female-dominated fields, where earnings traditionally have been low and remain so.
- More women are entering high-paid, traditionally male professions, but they are typically paid less than their male counterparts.
- Median earnings for full-time women workers are less than 70 percent of earnings for their male counterparts.

Drawing by Cheney; © 1992 The New Yorker Magazine, Inc.

- Women college graduates who work full-time have earnings roughly on a par with fully employed male high school dropouts.
- Women head an ever-growing proportion of poor households.

The United States, like all other societies, places women and men unequally at many different levels of social organization. From the macro level of the societal economy, through the institutions of society, to small groups and the individual, women and men are differently placed and differently rewarded. In other words, social organization is gendered. **Gendered** refers to distinguishing between and differentially evaluating males and females. Virtually everything social is gendered.

Until recently, the social division of labor by sex seemed natural. However, gender differentiation is not natural at all but is actually a product of social organization. **Gender stratification** refers to the ranking of the sexes in such a way that women are unequal in power, prestige, and presumed worth. At the same time, both women and men are denied the full range of human and social possibilities. The social inequalities created by gender differentiation have enormous consequences for society at large.

This chapter examines gender inequality in U.S. society at both structural and individual levels of social organization. Taking a **feminist approach** (one in support of women's equality), the theme of the chapter is that social rather than individual conditions are responsible for gender inequality and its problems.

The Roles and Ranking of Women and Men

Women's and men's roles are not the same throughout the world; every society has certain ideas about what women and men should be like as well as ways of producing people who are much like these expectations. The concept of role is borrowed directly from the theater and is a metaphor intended to convey the idea that conduct adheres to positions (statuses) in a social system. The social system that assigns roles to women and men is the gender system. This system consists of two complementary, yet mutually exclusive, categories in which all human beings are placed.

Gender is a socially constructed experience, not a biological imperative. Sociologists distinguish between the terms *sex* and *gender* to emphasize this point. **Sex** refers to one's biological identity as male or female. **Gender** is the cultural and social definition of feminine and masculine. It is a learned identity based on one's sex. Because it is embedded in social structures, it cannot be understood at the individual level alone (Andersen and Collins, 1992:51).

Are Gender Roles Based on Physiological Differences?

A controversy among scientists concerns the basis for gender roles. One school argues that there is a biogenetic foundation for the observed differences in male and female behavior, but their counterparts are convinced that the differences are explained largely by differential learning. We know that there are biological differences between the two sexes. The key question is whether these unlearned differences in the sexes contribute to the gender role differences found in societies. To answer this question, let us first review the evidence for each position.

The biological bases for gender roles.   Males and females are different from the moment of conception. Chromosomal and hormonal differences make males and females physically different. These differences, for example, give the female health superiority. At every age, from conception until old age, more males than females get sick and die. Approximately 120 males are conceived for every 100 females, yet there are only 105 live male births for each 100 female births, meaning that fetuses spontaneously aborted (miscarried) or stillborn are typically males. Various studies have shown that males are more susceptible than females to respiratory, bacterial, and viral infections, hepatitis, and childhood leukemia. The explanation for females being the healthier sex is that they have twice as many of a group of genes that program the production of immunological agents. Thus, females, compared with males, produce larger amounts of antibodies to combat a number of infectious agents.

Hormonal differences in the sexes are significant. The male hormones (androgens) and female hormones (estrogens) direct the process of sex differentiation from about six weeks after conception throughout life. They make males taller, heavier, and more muscular. At puberty they trigger the production of secondary sexual characteristics. In males the secondary characteristics include body and facial hair, a deeper voice, broader shoulders, and a muscular body. In females puberty brings pubic hair, menstruation, the ability to lactate, prominent breasts, and relatively broad hips. Actually, males and females have both sets of hormones. It is the relative proportion of androgens and estrogens that gives a person masculine or feminine physical traits.

These hormonal differences may explain in part why males tend to be more active, aggressive, and dominant than are females. Studies in animals provide some evidence for this assertion. Castrated rats and monkeys, deprived of the sex hormones created by the testes, have decreased levels of aggression. When testosterone is injected into these castrated males, their aggression levels increase (Quadagno, Briscoe, and Quadagno, 1977). However, critics of the biological determinist approach have argued that research on animals is irrelevant for human beings because of the importance of socialization and culture.

Biological differences that do exist between women and men are only averages, and they are often influenced by other factors. For example, although men are on the average larger than women, body size is influenced by diet and physical activity, which in turn may be influenced by culture, class, and race. Greater variation exists within one sex than between the sexes. The sociocultural variation of gender suggests that pressures of society are more important than are innate physiological conditions.

The social bases for gender roles.   Gender roles are not uniform throughout the world. Every society has certain expectations for both women and men, as well as elaborate ways of producing people who are much like these expectations. The cross-cultural evidence shows a wide variation of behaviors for the sexes. Table 8.1 provides some interesting cross-cultural data from 224 societies on the division of labor by sex. This table shows that for the majority of activities societies are not uniform in their gendered division of labor. Even activities requiring strength, presumably a male trait, are not strictly apportioned to males. In

Table 8.1   Gender allocation in selected technological activities in 224 societies

Activity	Number of Societies in Which the Activity Is Performed by:					
	Males Exclusively	Males Usually	Both Sexes Equally	Females Usually	Females Exclusively	% Male
Smelting of ores	37	0	0	0	0	100.0
Hunting	139	5	0	0	0	99.3
Boat building	84	3	3	0	1	96.6
Mining and quarrying	31	1	2	0	1	93.7
Land clearing	95	34	6	3	1	90.5
Fishing	83	45	8	5	2	86.7
Herding	54	24	14	3	3	82.4
House building	105	30	14	9	20	77.4
Generation of fire	40	6	16	4	20	62.3
Preparation of skins	39	4	2	5	31	54.6
Crop planting	27	35	33	26	20	54.4
Manufacture of leather products	35	3	2	5	29	53.2
Crop tending	22	23	24	30	32	44.6
Milking	15	2	8	2	21	43.8
Carrying	18	12	46	34	36	39.3
Loom weaving	24	0	6	8	50	32.5
Fuel gathering	25	12	12	23	94	27.2
Manufacture of clothing	16	4	11	13	78	22.4
Pottery making	14	5	6	6	74	21.1
Dairy production	4	0	0	0	24	14.3
Cooking	0	2	2	63	117	8.3
Preparation of vegetables	3	1	4	21	145	5.7

Source: Adapted from George P. Murdock and Caterina Provost, "Factors in the Division of Labor by Sex: A Cross-Cultural Analysis," *Ethnology* 12 (April, 1973):207. Reprinted by permission of the publisher.

fact, activities such as burden bearing and water carrying are done by females more than by males. Even an activity like house building is not exclusively male.

Although there is a wide variety in the social roles assigned to women and men, their roles "do not vary randomly" (O'Kelly, 1980:41). In most societies of the world the domestic and familial is the world of women and the public and political is the world of men.

The Differential Ranking of Men and Women

Male dominance refers to the beliefs, values, and cultural meanings that give higher value and prestige to masculinity than to femininity, that value males over females, and men over women, and to the male control of and privilege access to socially valued resources. **Patriarchy** is another term used for forms of social organization in which men are dominant over women.

A central issue in the study of gender has been whether male dominance is universal, found in all societies across time and space. Some scholars have adopted this position, claiming that all societies exhibit some forms of patriarchy in marriage and family forms, in division of labor, and in society at large, (Rosaldo, 1974). More recently, however, scholars have challenged the universality of patriarchy by producing cases that serve as counterexamples (Shapiro, 1981). Today, the thinking in anthropology tends to follow the latter course. Sexual differentiation, it seems, is found in all societies, but it does not always indicate low female status (Rogers, 1978). Gender stratification, male dominance, and female subordination are not constants. They vary from society to society. They also vary within a given society. In the United States gender has always been race-specific and class-specific. It is important to keep in mind that although women may be subordinate, they are not always the passive victims of patriarchy. Like other oppressed groups, they have created various survival strategies and have often engaged in political struggles to end discrimination.

To explain gender inequality, sociologists turn to the surrounding systems that affect all human behavior. Most theories highlight the institutional structures that assign women and men different positions, different roles, and consequently different behaviors. The most compelling explanations of gender inequality are materialist theories that use cross-cultural data on the status of women and men (Chafetz, 1984; Blumberg, 1984).

Materialist theories explain gender inequality as an outcome of how women and men are tied to the economic structure of society (Nielson, 1990:215). Such theories stress control and distribution of valued resources as crucial facts in producing stratification. They point out that women's roles of mother and wife, although vital to the well-being of society, are devalued and also deny women access to highly valued public resources. They point out that gender stratification is greater where women's work is directed inward to the family and men's work is directed outward to trade and the marketplace. The division between domestic and public spheres of activity is particularly constraining to women and advantageous to men. The domestic and public spheres of activity are associated with different amounts of property, power, and prestige. Women's reproductive roles and their responsibilities for domestic labor limit their association with the resources that are highly valued (Rosaldo, 1980). Men are freed from these responsibilities. Their economic obligations in the public sphere assure them of control of highly valued resources and give rise to male privilege.

In capitalist societies the domestic-public split is even more significant, because highly valued goods and services are exchanged in the public, not the domestic, sphere. Women's domestic labor, though important for survival, ranks low in prestige and power because it does not produce exchangeable commodities (Sacks, 1974). Because of the connections between the class relations of production (capitalism) and the hierarchical relations of its society (patriarchy) (Eisenstein, 1979a, b), the United States is a **capitalist patriarchy,** where male supremacy keeps women in subordinate roles at work and in the home.

Socialization versus Structure: Two Approaches to Gender Inequality

In examining gender inequality in the United States, we must distinguish between (1) a gender roles approach, which focuses on learning behaviors that are defined as masculine or feminine, and (2) a structural approach, which focuses on features of social organization that produce sex inequality. The difference between the two approaches lies in whether the individual or the society is the primary unit of analysis.

The **gender roles approach** emphasizes characteristics that individuals acquire during the course of socialization, such as independent or dependent behaviors and ways of relating. The **structural approach** emphasizes factors that are external to individuals, such as the social structures and concrete settings that are themselves gendered, that shape gendered interaction, and that locate and reward women and men differently.

These approaches tend to differ in how they view the sexes, in how they explain the causes and effects of sexism, and in the solutions they suggest for elimination of inequality. Both individual and structural approaches are necessary for a complete understanding of sexism. This chapter places primary emphasis on social structure as the cause of inequality. Although gender roles are learned by individuals and produce differences in the personalities, behaviors, and motivations of women and men, gender stratification is essentially maintained by societal forces.

Learning Gender

The most complex, demanding, and all-involving role that a member of society must learn to play is that of male or female. "Casting" for one's gender role

> takes place immediately at birth, after a quick biological inspection; and the role of "female" or "male" is assigned. It is an assignment that will last one's entire lifetime and affect virtually everything one ever does. A large part of the next 20 years or so will be spent gradually learning and perfecting one's assigned sex role; slowly memorizing what a "young lady" should do and should not do, how a "little man" should react in each of a million frightening situations— practicing, practicing, playing house, playing cowboys, practicing—and often crying in confusion and frustration at the baffling and seemingly endless task. (David and Brannon, 1980:117)

From infancy through early childhood and beyond, children learn what is expected of boys and girls, and they learn to behave according to those expectations.

The characteristics associated with traditional gender roles are those valued by the dominant society. Keep in mind that gender is not the same in all classes and races. However, most research on gender socialization reflects primarily the experience of White middle-class persons—those who are most often the research subjects of these studies. How gender is learned depends on a variety of social conditions affecting the socialization practices of girls and boys. Still, society molds boys and girls along different lines.

The Child at Home   Girls and boys are perceived and treated differently from the moment of birth. Parents describe newborn daughters as tiny, soft, and delicate, and sons as strong and alert (Richardson, 1981:48); and they interact differently with newborn daughters and sons.

How parents treat their children may be the most important factor in the creation of sex stereotypes. When one compares the life of the young girl to that of the young boy, a critical difference emerges: she is treated more protectively and is subjected to more restrictions and controls; he receives greater achievement demands and higher expectations. Girl infants are talked to more. Girls are the objects of more physical contact such as holding, rocking, caressing, and kissing (Lewis, 1972). We also know that fathers, especially working-class fathers, are more concerned than are mothers about their young children engaging in behaviors considered inappropriate for their sex.

Research has compared the influence of mothers, fathers, and peers in rewarding and punishing gendered behavior in three- and five-year-old children (Langlois and Downs, 1980). Fathers provided the strongest pressures for gender-specific behavior. In addition, they used different techniques with daughters and sons: They rewarded their daughters and gave them positive feedback for gendered behavior. With their sons they used more negative feedback and punished them for gender-inappropriate behavior. Mothers were more likely to reinforce behavior of *both* boys and girls with rewards and positive feedback. Peers, in contrast, were more likely to use punishment on both sexes. The researchers concluded that the combined pattern of the three socializing agents provided a

Parents play an active role in reinforcing conformity to society's gender demands.

finely tuned system in which fathers, mothers, and peers each make a unique contribution in reinforcing gendered behavior (Langlois and Downs, 1980). Recent research by Jacqueline Eccles has found that parents uphold sex stereotypes more today than they did in the 1970s, when she began her research (cited in Keegan, 1989:26).

In addition to the parents' active role in reinforcing conformity to society's gender demands, a subtler message is emitted from picture books for preschool children that parents select for their children. A classic study of eighteen award-winning children's books from 1967 to 1971 found the following characteristics (Weitzman et al., 1972):

- Females are virtually invisible. The ratio of male pictures to female pictures was 11:1. The ratio of male to female animals was 95:1.
- The activities of boys and girls varied greatly. Boys were active in outdoor activities, whereas girls were passive and most often found indoors. The activity of the girls typically was that of some service for boys.
- Adult men and women (role models) were very different. Men led, women followed. Females were passive and males active. Not one woman in these books had a job or profession; they were always mothers and wives.

An update of this study has found important changes in how girls and women are portrayed in the Caldecott books. Females are no longer invisible; they are as likely as males to be included in the stories, and they have begun to move outside the home if not into the labor market. In many respects, however, female storybook characters remain consistent with traditional culture. No behavior was found to be shared by a majority of the females, whereas all of the males were portrayed as independent, persistent, and active. Girls expressed no career goals, and there were no adult female role models to provide any ambition. The researchers found that only one woman in the entire 1980s collection of twenty-four books had an occupation outside of the home, and she worked "as a waitress at the Blue Tile Diner" (Williams et al., 1987:155).

Two books by the same author best illustrate how children's books are biased toward traditional occupational roles apportioned by sex. The first, *What Boys Can Be,* lists fourteen occupations: fireman, baseball player, bus driver, policeman, cowboy, doctor, sailor, pilot, clown, zoo manager, farmer, actor, astronaut, and president (Walley, n.d.). The book *What Girls Can Be* also lists fourteen occupations: nurse, stewardess, ballerina, candyshop owner, model, actress, secretary, artist, nursery school teacher, singer, dress designer, bride, housewife, and mother (Walley, n.d.).

Even the television show *Sesame Street* is sexist! Although it is one of the best shows on television for small children, and the adult characters of the show are balanced, the puppet stars of the show are gendered. Bert, Ernie, and most of the major animal characters are male. The female puppets always play children while the male puppets play adult parts (Heiman and Bookspan, 1992:30).

Before formal schooling, parents often send their child to day-care centers and nursery schools. The teachers there serve as surrogate parents, also reinforcing traditional gender roles. A study of fifteen preschools found that teachers act and react in quite different ways to boys and girls. The teachers, for example, responded more than three times as often to males as to females who hit or broke things. Boys were typically punished by a loud public reprimand, but girls were taken aside for a soft rebuke. In task-learning situations boys were twice as likely as girls to receive individual instructions on how to do things. Summarizing their study, the researchers noted that

> as nursery-school children busily mold clay, their teachers are molding behavior. Unwittingly, teachers foster an environment where children learn that boys are aggressive and able to solve problems, while girls are submissive and passive. The clay impressions are transient, but the behavioral ones last into adulthood and present us with people of both sexes who have developed only parts of the psychological and intellectual capabilities. (Serbin and O'Leary, 1975:57)

Differences can be found even where gender roles are changing and socialization is becoming more flexible or androgynous. **Androgyny** refers to the integration of traditional feminine and masculine characteristics. Jeanne Brooks-Gunn at The Educational Testing Service in Princeton, New Jersey, conducted a study of "masculine," "feminine," and "androgynous" mothers. The androgynous mothers were self-reliant as well as tender, affectionate as well as assertive. Although they encouraged nurturing and independent behavior in their daughters, they did not promote nurturing in their sons. One can thus speculate that in the next generation some females will be androgynous but men will still be socialized in the traditional way (Shreve, 1984:43).

The Child at Play

The rules of gender are learned in small groups and collectivities. Children's play groups stress particular social skills and capabilities for boys and others for girls. Janet Lever's research on fifth graders found that boys, more than girls, (1) played outdoors, (2) played in larger groups, (3) played in age-heterogeneous groups, (4) were less likely to play in games dominated by the opposite gender, (5) played more competitive games, and (6) played in games that lasted longer (Lever, 1976).

These differences in play by sex reinforce the traditional roles: boys play at competitive games that require aggressiveness and toughness whereas girls tend to play indoors with dolls and play-acting scenarios of the home.

Toys play a major part in gender socialization. Toys entertain children; they also teach particular skills and encourage children to explore through play a variety of roles they may occupy as adults. By providing girls and boys with different types of toys, we are essentially training them for separate (and unequal) roles as adults. Today, most toys for sale are gender-linked. Toys for boys tend to encourage exploration, manipulation, invention, construction, competition, and aggression. In contrast, girls' toys typically rate high on manipulability, creativity, nurturance, and attractiveness. Playing with gendered toys may be related to the development of differential cognitive skills and social skills in girls and boys (Renzetti and Curan, 1992:66–67).

Bipolar gender experiences may be more characteristic among White middle-class children than among children of other races. An important study on Black adolescent girls by Joyce Ladner has shown that Black girls develop in a more independent fashion (Ladner, 1971). Other research has also found that among African Americans, both girls and boys are expected to be nurturant and expressive, emotional as well as independent, confident, and assertive (McAdoo, 1988; Stack, 1990).

Formal Education   Congress outlawed sex discrimination in 1972 through Title IX of the Educational Amendments Act. Nevertheless, formal education remains a central conduit for gender inequality. A recent report released by the American Association of University Women (1992) offers compelling evidence that girls are not receiving the same quality or even quantity education as boys. Whether one looks at achievement scores, curriculum design, or teacher-student interaction, schools shortchange girls. Let us examine the following areas: course offerings, textbooks, teacher-student interactions, sports, female role models, and counseling.

Curriculum.   Schools are charged with the responsibility of equipping students to study subjects (e.g., reading, writing, mathematics, and history) known collectively as the formal curriculum. But schools also teach students particular social, political, and economic values that constitute the so-called hidden curriculum operating alongside the more formal one. Both formal and informal curricula are powerful shapers of gender (Renzetti and Curan, 1992:75).

The AAUW Report offers the following findings (taken from the AAUW Report Executive Summary, 1992):

- Differences between girls and boys in math achievement are small and declining. Yet, in high school, girls are still less likely than boys to take the most advanced courses and to be in the top-scoring math groups.
- The gender gap in science, however, is *not* decreasing and may, in fact, be increasing. One-fourth of boys take physics in high school in contrast to 15 percent of girls.
- The *evaded curriculum* is a term coined in the AAUW report to refer to matters central to the lives of students that are touched on only briefly, if at all, in most schools. Students receive inadequate education on sexuality, teen pregnancy, the AIDS crisis, and the increase of sexually transmitted diseases among adolescents.

Teacher-student interactions.   Even when girls and boys are in the same classrooms, they are educated differently. Girls receive significantly less attention from classroom teachers than do boys. A large body of research indicates that teachers give more classroom attention and more esteem-building encouragement to boys.

In a study conducted by Myra and David Sadker, boys in elementary and middle school called out answers eight times more often than girls. When boys called out, teachers listened. But when girls called out, they were told to "raise your hand if you want to speak" (cited in AAUW Report, 1992). Even when boys do not volunteer, teachers are more likely to encourage them to give an answer or an opinion than they are to encourage girls.

Teachers are now being advised to encourage cooperative cross-sex learning, to monitor their own (teacher) behavior to be sure that they reward male and female students equally, and actively to familiarize students with gender atypical

Studies show that teachers treat boys differently than girls, thus reinforcing traditional gender roles.

roles by assigning them specific duties as leaders, recording secretary, and so on (Lockheed, 1985, cited in Giele, 1988).

Textbooks.   The content of textbooks transmits messages to readers about society, about children, and about what adults are supposed to do. For this reason, individuals and groups concerned about the potential for sexist bias in schools have looked carefully at how males and females are portrayed in textbooks assigned to students. Their findings provide a consistent message: textbooks commonly used in U.S. schools are overtly and covertly sexist. Sexism has become a recent concern of publishers, and a number have created guidelines for creating positive sexual and racial images in educational materials.

Despite these efforts, the AAUW study reports that the contributions of girls and women are still marginalized or ignored in many textbooks used in our nation's schools (1992). When women are mentioned, it is usually in terms of traditional feminine roles, such as for nursing, Florence Nightengale; for sewing, Betsy Ross; and Dolly Madison and Jackie Kennedy Onassis for being married to famous men (Renzetti and Curran, 1992:83).

An extensive survey of the words used in elementary texts revealed that *he* occurred three times as often as *she,* and that *boy* occurred twice as often as *girl.* In an interesting switch, however, *wife* was found three times more than the word *husband.* This pattern is not necessarily inconsistent, because the emphasis on wife suggests that society heavily stresses that role, whereas the husband's role is not as important.

Textbooks, then, have given official sanction to the subordinate roles that society imposes on women in real life.

The reinforcement of gender in school sports.   Sports in U.S. high schools and colleges have historically been almost exclusively a male preserve (this section is dependent on Eitzen and Sage, 1993). The truth of this observation is clearly evident if one compares by sex the number of participants, facilities, support of school administrations, and financial support.

Such disparities have been based on the traditional assumption that competitive sport is basically a masculine activity and that the proper roles of girls and women are as spectators and cheerleaders. What is the impact on a society that encourages its boys and young men to participate in sports while expecting its girls and young women to be spectators and cheerleaders? Sports reinforce societal expectations for males and females. Males are to be dominant and aggressive—the doers—while females are expected to be passive supporters of men, attaining status through the efforts of their menfolk.

An important consequence of this traditional view is that approximately one-half of the population was denied access to all that sport has to offer (physical conditioning, enjoyment, teamwork, goal attainment, ego enhancement, social status, and competitiveness). School administrators, school boards, and citizens of local communities have long assumed that sports participation has general educational value. If so, then girls and women should also be allowed to receive the benefits.

In 1972 passage of Title IX of the Educational Amendments Act required that schools receiving federal funds must provide equal opportunities for males and females. Despite considerable opposition by school administrators, athletic directors, and school boards, major changes occurred over time because of this federal legislation. More monies were spent on womens' sports, better facilities and equipment were provided, and women were gradually accepted as athletes. The most significant result was an increase in female participation. The number of high school girls participating in interscholastic sports increased from 294,015 in 1971 to 1,836,356 in 1987. By 1988, 35 percent of all high school participants were female, and the number of sports available to them was more than twice the number available in 1970. Similar growth patterns occurred in colleges and universities.

On the positive side, budgets for women's sports improved dramatically, from less than 1 percent of the men's budgets in 1970 at the college level to approximately 35 percent of the men's budgets in 1989. On the negative side, budgets for women's sports will stay at about that level because football is so expensive and it is exempt from the equation. Thus, womens' sports remain and will remain unequal to men's sports. This inequality is reinforced by unequal media attention, the scheduling of games (men's games are always the featured games), and the increasing lack of women in positions of power. One ironic consequence of Title IX has been that as opportunities for female athletes increased and programs expanded, many of the coaching and administration positions formerly held by women are being filled by men. In the early 1970s most coaches of women's intercollegiate teams were women. By the late 1980s, however, the majority were men. This trend is also true at the high school level. Also, whereas women's athletic associations at the high school and college levels were once controlled by women, they have now been subsumed under male-dominated organizations. Thus, females who aspire to coaching and athletic administration have fewer opportunities, girls and women see fewer women as role models in such positions, and inequality is reinforced as women are dominated by males in positions of power. Thus, even with federal legislation mandating gender equality, male dominance is maintained.

Female role models in education.   A subtle form of gender role reinforcement in education is found in the types of jobs held by men and women. The pattern is the familiar one found in hospitals, business offices, and throughout the occupational world: women occupy the bottom rungs, and men are in the prestigious and decision-making positions. Women make up a large percentage of the nation's classroom teachers but a much smaller percentage of school district superintendents. In 1989 women comprised 83.3 percent of all elementary school teachers, more than half of all secondary school teachers (51.8 percent), and 41.4 percent of all school administrators (U.S. Bureau of the Census, 1991:395).

As the level of education increases, the proportion of women teachers declines. In 1990, eighteen years after the Office of Civil Rights issued guidelines spelling out the obligations of colleges and universities in the development of affirmative action programs, women represented only 27 percent of the full-time faculty (American Association of University Professors, 1990). In the academic world a definite prestige and pay pyramid extends from lowly instructorships to full professorships. Women tend to be lower in academic rank than men, make less money (even when statistically controlling for academic level), are less likely to have tenure, and are underrepresented in administrative positions.

In 1991 at the University of Michigan, the first university to incorporate an affirmative action plan for the hiring and promotion of women, the distribution of women among faculty ranks remained distinctly pyramidal: only 8 percent of professors and 28 percent of assistant professors were women (Nazario, 1991:B4).

Counseling.   A fundamental task of school guidance personnel is to aid students in their choice of a career. This function involves testing students for their occupational preference and aptitude and advising them on course selection and what kind of post-high-school training they should get. The guidance that students receive on career choice tends to be biased.

High school guidance counselors may channel male and female students into different (i.e., gender stereotyped) fields and activities. There is evidence that gender stereotyping is common among counselors and that they often steer females away from certain college preparatory courses, especially in mathematics and the sciences (Renzetti and Curran, 1989:93).

In the past, aptitude tests have themselves been sex-biased, listing occupations as either female or male. Despite changes in testing, counselors may inadvertently channel students into traditional gendered choices.

Socialization as Blaming the Victim

The discussion so far shows clearly the many ways in which gender differences are learned. Thus, socialization appears useful for explaining women. However, the socialization perspective on sexism can be misused in such a way that it blames women themselves for inequality. A critique of the socialization perspective by Linda Peterson and Elaine Enarson contends that when used uncritically, socialization diverts attention from the oppression imposed by the dynamics of contemporary social structure:

> Misuse of the concept of socialization plays directly into the Blaming the Victim ideology; by focusing on the victim, responsibility for "the woman problem" rests not in the social system with its sex-structured distribution of inequality, but in socialized sex differences and sex roles. (Peterson and Enarson, 1974:8)

Not only is the cause of the problem displaced, the solutions are also:

> Rather than directing efforts toward radical social change, the solution seems to be to change women themselves, perhaps through exhortation ("If we want to be liberated, we'll have to act more aggressive . . . "), or, for example, changing children's literature and mothers' child rearing practice. (Peterson and Enarson, 1974:8)

This issue raises a critical question: If the socialization perspective is limited and perhaps biased, what is a better way of analyzing gender inequality? In answering this question, let us look at the ways in which male dominance affects our society.

The Reinforcement of Male Dominance

Male dominance is both a socializing and structural force. It exists at all levels of society, from the interpersonal interactions of women and men, to the patterning of gender that is found in all cultural forms and social institutions. This section describes the interpersonal and institutional reinforcement of gender inequality.

Language

Language perpetuates male dominance by ignoring, trivializing, and sexualizing women. Use of the pronoun *he* when the sex of the person is unspecified and of the generic term *mankind* to refer to humanity in general are obvious examples of how the English language ignores women. Common sayings like "that's women's work" (as opposed to "that's men's work!"), jokes about women drivers, phrases like "women and children first" or "wine, women, and song" are trivializing. Women, more than men, are commonly referred to in terms that have sexual connotations. Terms referring to men (*studs, jocks*) that do not have sexual meanings imply power and success, whereas terms applied to women (*broads, dogs, chicks*) imply promiscuity or being dominated. In fact, the term *promiscuous* is usually applied only to women, although its literal meaning applies to either sex (Richmond-Abbott, 1992:93). Terms such as *dogs* and *chicks* tell us a great deal about how women are regarded by society. The cumulative effect of such language is illustrated in the following passage:

> In her youth she is a "chick" and then she gets married and feels "cooped up" and goes to "hen parties" and "cackles" with her women friends. Then she has her "brood" and begins to "henpeck" her husband. Finally, she turns into an "old biddy." (Nilson, quoted in Richmond-Abbott, 1992:93)

Interpersonal Behavior

Day-to-day interaction between women and men perpetuates male dominance. Gender differences in conversational patterns reflect differences in power. Women's speech is more polite than men's. Women end statements with tag questions ("don't you agree?" "you know?") (Lakoff, 1975). According to sociolinguist Deborah Tannen (1990) women and men have different styles of communication and different communication goals. Women and men speak different "genderlects." Like cultural dialects, these differences sometimes lead to miscommunication and misunderstanding. Tannen argues that men in conversations seek to dominate whereas women seek to connect.

Research has found that in conversations, men are more direct, interrupt more, and talk more, notwithstanding the stereotype that women are more talkative. Men also have greater control over what is discussed (Parlee, 1979). Another indication of women's lack of power lies in the work they do to keep conversations going. Fishman studied male-female conversations and found that women work harder in conversations, even though they have less control over the subject matter (Fishman, 1978). Males typically initiate interaction with women; they pursue, while females wait to be asked out.

Male dominance is also sustained by various forms of nonverbal communication. Men take up more space than women, touch women without permission more than women touch men. Women, in contrast, engage in more eye contact, smile more, and generally exhibit behavior associated with low status. These behaviors show how gender is continually being created in various kinds of social interaction that occurs between women and men. Candace West and Don Zimmerman call this "doing gender" (1987). It involves a complex of socially guided interactional activities that cast certain behaviors as expressions of masculinity and femininity. Doing gender takes place in specific social settings and legitimates gender inequality.

Mass Communications Media

The mass media (television, newspapers, magazines, and movies) reflect society's assumptions about gender. Thus, since the 1950s women's portrayal in magazines has become less monolithic. With the rise of feminism, many magazines devoted attention to women's achievements. Alongside these magazines for the new woman are many ladies magazines, which continue to define the lives of women in terms of men—husbands or lovers. Many newspapers have refused to treat women on their own terms. Only in 1986 did the *New York Times* use the title *Ms.* in its pages.

Women are 52 percent of the U.S. population, but this fact is not obvious when reading most newspapers or watching network news. A 1989 study of the front pages of ten large daily newspapers found that 11 percent of the people mentioned in articles were women, 27 percent of articles were written by women, and 24 percent of photographs were of women, usually with a spouse or children. The study also looked at network newscasts and found that women reported 22 percent of the stories on CBS, 14 percent on NBC, and 10 percent on ABC. Women were the focus of 13 percent of the stories on ABC, 10 percent on CBS, and 8 percent on NBC (*USA Today,* 1989b:2B).

Studies have continually demonstrated that highly stereotypic behavior characterizes both children and adult programming as well as commercials. Male role models are present in greater numbers than are female, with the exception of daytime soap operas, in which men and women are equally represented. The imbalance has also been found with respect to occupations of men and women. Males are represented as occupying a disproportionately high percentage of the work force, a greater diversity of occupations, and higher-status jobs. Sex typing of behavior and personal characteristics during prime-time television has also been found.

Images of women on television have improved in recent years. Working women have enjoyed a positive decade on entertainment television. A report by the National Commission on Working Women has found increasing diversity of characters portraying working women as television's most significant improvement in the past decade. In serials such as *L.A. Law* and *The Cosby Show,* women do play strong and intelligent roles. but in most shows, men are still the major characters and women are cast as glamorous objects, scheming villains, or servants. And for every contemporary show that includes more positive images of women, there are numerous other shows in which women are sidekicks to men, sexual objects, or helpless imbeciles (Andersen, 1993:54).

Television commercials also present the sexes in stereotyped ways. A review of the research on television advertising has shown, for example, that (1) almost all commercials with voice-overs are spoken or sung by men; (2) men have a wider variety of roles than do women; (3) the roles depicted for females are typically family roles; (4) women tend to be doing activities in the home that benefit men; (5) women tend to be inside the home and men outside; (6) women are younger than men; and (7) in commercials during children's programming, women and girls are seen less often than are men and boys (see Butler and Paisley, 1980:103–314).

The sexism prevalent in advertising can be very subtle, as Erving Goffman has noted:

> (1) Overwhelmingly a woman is taller than a man only when the man is her social inferior; (2) a woman's hands are seen just barely touching, holding or caressing—never grasping, manipulating, or shaping; (3) when a photograph of men and women illustrates an instruction of some sort the man is always instructing the woman—even if the men and women are actually children (that is, a male child will be instructing a female child); (4) when an advertisement requires someone to sit or lie on a bed or a floor that someone is almost always a child or a woman, hardly ever a man; (5) when the head or eye of a man is averted it is only in relation to a social, political, or intellectual superior, but when the eye or head of a woman is averted it is always in relation to *whatever* man is pictured with her; (6) women are repeatedly shown mentally drifting from the scene while in close physical touch with a male, their faces lost and dreamy, "as though his aliveness to the surroundings and his readiness to cope were enough for both of them"; (7) concomitantly, women, much more than men, are pictured at the kind of psychological loss or remove from a social situation that leaves one unoriented for action (e.g., something terrible has happened and a woman is shown with her hands over her mouth and her eyes helpless with horror). (Goffman, 1979:viii)

The advertising industry has been slowly modifying this image, since it has realized the potential buying power of larger numbers of working women, who have become targets of advertising campaigns designed to sell a wide variety of products. The underlying message is that women were discriminated against in the past but that mistake has been remedied (Gordon, 1983). One cigarette advertiser directed an entire campaign to such a segment of the market with a slogan ("You've come a long way, baby")intended to reach the "new woman." Such advertising actually exploits women, though, by masking their position in society (women, as we discuss, have not come such a long way), by trivializing them ("baby"), and by fostering excessive consumption.

The advertising aimed at the "new woman" places additional stresses on women and at the same time upholds male privilege. Television commercials that show women breezing in from their jobs to sort the laundry or pop a roast in the oven reinforce the notion that it is all right for women to pursue careers as long as they can still handle the housework. Advertising aimed at career women sends the message that they should be superwomen, managing multiple roles of wife, mother, and career woman and be glamorous as well. Such multifarious expectations are not imposed on men. A cologne advertisement illustrates well the new expectations placed on employed women. Appealing to the "24-hour woman," the advertisement suggested that she "bring home the bacon, fry it up in a pan, and never let him forget he's a man." Under the guise of liberation, advertisers contribute to gender inequality by reinforcing the notion that domestic labor, child rearing, and pleasing men are women's responsibilities.

Religion

The customs, beliefs, attitudes, and behaviors that discriminate against women are reinforced by organized religion. Despite important differences in religious doctrines, there are similarities in views about gender. Limiting discussion to the Judeo-Christian heritage, let us examine some teachings from the Old and New Testaments regarding the place of women. The Old Testament clearly established male supremacy in a number of ways. To begin, God is believed to be a male. Women were obviously meant to be second to males because Eve was created from Adam's rib. According to the Scriptures, only a male could divorce a spouse. A woman who was not a virgin at marriage could be stoned to death. Girls could be purchased for marriage. Employers were enjoined to pay women only three-fifths the wages of men: "If a male from 20 to 60 years of age, the equivalent is 50 shekels of silver by the sanctuary weight; if it is a female, the equivalent is 30 shekels" (Leviticus 27:4). As Gilman notes,

> the Old Testament devotes inordinate space to the listing of long lines of male descent to the point where it would seem that for centuries women "begat" nothing but male offspring. Although there are heroines in the Old Testament—Judith, Esther and the like—it's clear that they functioned like the heroines of Greek drama and later of French: as counterweights in the imaginations of certain sensitive men to the degraded position of women in actual life. The true spirit of the tradition was unabashedly revealed in the prayer men recited every day in the synagogue: "Blessed art Thou, O Lord . . . for not making me a woman." (Gilman, 1971:51)

The New Testament generally continued the tradition of male dominance. Jesus was a male. He was the son of a male God, not of Mary, who remained a virgin. All the disciples were male. The great leader of the early church, the Apostle Paul, was especially adamant in arguing for the primacy of the male over the female. According to Paul, "the husband is supreme over his wife," "woman was created for man's sake," and "women should not teach nor usurp authority over the man, but to be silent."

Contemporary religious thought reflects this heritage. Some conservative denominations severely limit or even forbid women from any decision making. Others allow women to vote but limit their participation in leadership roles.

There are, however, some indications of change. Recently, the National Council of Churches called for elimination of sexist language and the use of "inclusive language" in the Revised Standard Version of the Bible. Terms such as *man, mankind, brothers, sons, churchmen,* and *laymen* would be replaced by neutral terms that include reference to female gender.

Women are pursuing equal rights in all denominations and faiths, and the sexual revolution is causing upheaval and resistance at every level of organized religion. The number of U.S. women ordained to full ministry, that is, preaching the word and administering the sacraments, nearly doubled in the past decade. Women in 1987 made up almost 8 percent of the clergy in denominations ordaining women (Cornell, 1989:106). The number of female rabbis in the nation has grown, climbing to 130 in 1986 (Goldman, 1986:E6). The number of women enrolled in seminaries and divinity schools had increased from 10 percent in 1972 to 29 percent in 1989 (Renzetti and Curan, 1992:295). Despite reluctance of established churches, women are making advances in religious status and changing the face of the ministry.

The Law

That the law has been discriminatory against women is beyond dispute. One need only recall that women were specifically denied the right to vote prior to passage of the Nineteenth Amendment. Less well known, but very important, was the 1824 Mississippi Supreme Court decision upholding the right of husbands to beat their wives (the U.S. Supreme Court finally prohibited this practice in 1891). Another interesting case that shows the bias of the legal system is *Minor* v. *Happerset* (1874). Here, the Supreme Court ruled that the "equal-protection" clause of the Fourteenth Amendment did not apply to women. Another ruling by the Supreme Court, at the time of early feminist Susan B. Anthony, ruled that women are entitled to counsel, but that it must be male counsel.

During the past three decades, legal reforms and public policy changes have attempted to place women and men on more equal footing. Some laws that focus on employment include the 1963 Equal Pay Act, Title VII of the 1964 Civil Rights Act, and the 1978 Pregnancy Discrimination Act. The 1974 Educational Amendments Act calls for gender equality in education. Other reforms have provided the framework for important institutional changes. For example, sexist discrimination in the granting of credit has been ruled illegal; discrimination against pregnant women in the work force is now prohibited by the law. Affirmative action has remedied some kinds of gender discrimination in employment; sexist discrimination in housing is prohibited; and the differential requirements by gender as traditionally practiced by the airline industry have been eliminated. The force of these new laws, however, depends on their enforcement as well as on the interpretation of the courts when they are disputed.

Legal discrimination remains in a number of areas. There are still problems with Social Security and other pension programs (see Chapter 9). State laws vary considerably concerning property ownership by spouses, welfare benefits, and the legal status of homemakers. Many legal reforms are greatly threatened. Recent Supreme Court decisions in the areas of abortion and affirmative action are chipping away at women's basic rights. In 1989 and 1992, the Supreme Court narrowed its 1973 landmark *Roe* v. *Wade* decision that had established the right to abortion. *Roe* v. *Wade* was a major breakthrough for women, giving them the ultimate right

Lee Judge, The Kansas City Times.

to control their bodies. The 1989 and 1992 decisions make it easier for the states to restrict women's reproductive freedoms at any stage of pregnancy, including the first three months. These decisions threw the future of abortion rights in limbo. By moving the abortion battleground to federal and state legislatures, the Supreme Court withdrew the rights it granted in 1973. The Court's growing conservative majority may not bode well for women's rights (Lacayo, 1992:16).

However, President Clinton has begun reversing Republican policy limiting abortion. One of Clinton's first acts in office was to sign five executive orders lifting restrictions on access to abortion. Among the most important reversals is a rule restricting abortion counseling at federally funded clinics. Despite these reversals, Supreme Court decisions continue to be important in determining the future of abortion rights.

Other Supreme Court decisions have also contributed to the dismantling of progressive legislation for women. In the Civil Rights Act of 1964, the Court had upheld affirmative action programs to end race and sex discrimination in employment. A series of recent rulings, however, place the burden of proof on the individuals who file bias suits. By shifting the burden of proof to women and minorities, discrimination will be difficult to abolish.

Politics

Women's political participation has been different from that of men. Women received the right to vote in 1920, when the Nineteenth Amendment was ratified. Although women make up a very small percentage of officeholders, 1992 was a turning point for women in politics. Controversies such as Anita Hill's sexual

The 1992 election resulted in the number of women senators increasing from two to six. Barbara Boxer and Diane Feinstein are the two new senators from California.

harassment allegations, the abortion rights battle, and the lack of representation at all levels of politics propelled women into the political arena. Eleven women ran for the Senate and another 106 competed in House races. Widely touted as the year of women in politics, 1992 ushered into Congress the biggest influx of women (and minorities) in history. The new Senate has 6 women (up from 2), and the new House of Representatives includes 47 women (up from 28).

Despite these gains, the United States ranks among the worst in according women access to political leadership. See "Other Societies, Other Ways," the chart on "Women Members of National Legislative Bodies." It bears repeating that in the country's 200-year history, there has never been a woman president, only one vice-presidential candidate from a major party, and only one female justice of the Supreme Court. Before 1992, only fourteen women had ever served in the U.S. Senate, and the majority of them inherited their husbands' seats or were appointed for limited terms (Kaminer, 1992).

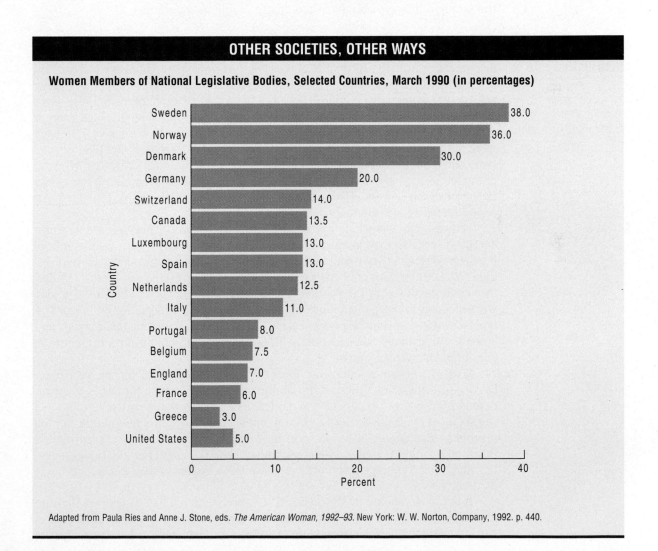

OTHER SOCIETIES, OTHER WAYS

Women Members of National Legislative Bodies, Selected Countries, March 1990 (in percentages)

Country	Percent
Sweden	38.0
Norway	36.0
Denmark	30.0
Germany	20.0
Switzerland	14.0
Canada	13.5
Luxembourg	13.0
Spain	13.0
Netherlands	12.5
Italy	11.0
Portugal	8.0
Belgium	7.5
England	7.0
France	6.0
Greece	3.0
United States	5.0

Adapted from Paula Ries and Anne J. Stone, eds. *The American Woman, 1992–93*. New York: W. W. Norton, Company, 1992. p. 440.

Voting studies of national elections since 1980 demonstrated that women voted differently from men. The gender gap refers to measurable differences in the way women and men vote and view political issues. This gap continues today. Women tend to vote for liberal candidates and issues more than men do. Women in politics also differ from their male counterparts. They are more likely to focus on women's rights, child care, health care, and family concerns (Center for the American Woman and Politics, Rutgers University, cited in Quindlen, 1992:E19). (See the forum at the end of this chapter.)

Structured Gender Inequality

In this discussion of structured gender inequality, we examine specific processes that limit women's access to highly valued resources and thereby place them in subordinate roles and activities. Gendered work patterns in the labor force and the family reinforce each other and create problems for women.

Occupational Distribution

In the past five decades the proportion of women in the labor force has changed dramatically. In 1940 less than 20 percent of the female population age sixteen and older was in the labor force. By 1991, the figure had risen to 57 percent. This means that women make up nearly half of the work force (45 percent of the work force is female.) In 1989, 58.7 percent of Black women (6.6 million), 57.2 percent of White women (46.4 million), and 53.5 percent of Hispanic women (3.6 million) were in the labor force (U.S. Bureau of the Census, 1991b:384). Since 1980 women have taken 80 percent of the new jobs created in the economy. Yet their growing presence in the labor force has created new tensions and disputes. When Anita Hill confronted Clarence Thomas, the nation was forced to confront the problem of sexual harassment in the workplace.

Who is today's working woman? She may be, whatever her age, a nurse or a secretary or a factory worker or a department store clerk or a public school teacher. Or she may be—although it is much less likely—a physician or the president of a corporation or the head of a school system. Hers may be the familiar face seen daily behind the counter at the neighborhood coffee shop, or she may work virtually unseen, mopping floors at midnight in an empty office building. The typical woman worker is a wage earner in clerical, service, manufacturing, and some technical jobs that pay poorly, give her little possibility for advancement, and little control over her work.

Women's surge into the labor force has taken place in the so-called pink-collar occupations, those that are predominantly female. The economy's growing demand for workers in service and clerical jobs has been met by women. In 1989 the six most prevalent occupations for women were, in order of magnitude, school teachers, (excluding those teaching in colleges and universities), semi-skilled machine operators, managers and administrators, retail and personal sales workers, and bookkeepers and accounting clerks (U.S. Department of Labor, Women's Bureau, 1990:2).

A study conducted by the National Research Council has concluded that the overall degree of sex segregation has not changed much since 1900 (Reskin and Hartmann, 1986). This is surprising in light of the enormous changes that have taken place in the structure of the economy (see Chapter 2). Some characteristics of women's participation remain amazingly resistant to change: their concentration in sex-typed jobs, their disproportionate share of low-ranking positions, and their low earnings relative to those of men with similar training and experience.

Media coverage of women's gains in traditionally male jobs is often misleading. Between 1970 and the late 1980s small reductions occurred in the overall extent of sex segregation in the labor force. For example, in blue-collar fields gains look dramatic at first glance, with the number of women in blue-collar jobs rising by 80 percent in the 1970s. But the increase is so high because women were virtually excluded from these occupations until then. In 1989, only 3 percent of machinists, 1.2 percent of carpenters, and 0.7 percent of auto mechanics were women (U.S. Bureau of the Census, 1991b:397).

The years 1970 to 1990 found more women in the fields of law, medicine, journalism, and higher education. Today, women fill one-third of all management positions (up from 19 percent in 1972). Despite recent progress in the prestige professions, there are fewer women in these jobs than men. In 1989, only 22 percent of lawyers, 17 percent of doctors, and 38 percent of university or college teachers were women (U.S. Bureau of the Census, 1991a:395). Although women have made inroads in the high-paying and high-prestige professions, they still occupy the least professional specialties and they face barriers to their entry into and advancement through the professions.

As the economy is being transformed from its traditional manufacturing base to a base in service and high technology, men and women are affected differently. Industrial jobs are taken away from men, and more women are employed in service jobs. The Bureau of Labor Statistics expects that through 1995 nearly 75 percent of new jobs will come from service-producing sectors of the economy.

Along with service work, clerical work is projected to increase at faster rates than all other occupational categories. The explosion of services would appear to benefit women by expanding employment opportunities as keypunchers, sales-clerks, food service workers, secretaries, and cashiers. But the full effect of economic restructuring on women must take into account the low wage levels and the limited opportunities for advancement that will characterize service work in the new economy.

Women often seek part-time work as a way of combining earning a living and raising a family. Yet three-fourths of women who work part-time are in low-paying sales, service, and clerical occupations (Rix, 1987:134).

Earnings Discrimination

The earnings gap between women and men has been widely documented. Although there has been a slight narrowing of the earnings difference during the past ten years, women workers do not approach earnings parity with men even when they work in similar occupations (see Table 8.2).

In 1990 the average working woman earned 71 cents for every dollar earned by a man. In 1980, it was 59 cents on the dollar. This means that women's overall pay relative to men's has increased by about a penny a year in the past ten years (Woller, 1991:4B). The earning gap persists for several reasons:

Table 8.2   Unequal pay

Occupation	Women	Men	Gap
Graphic designer	$19,812	$32,032	38.1%
Insurance underwriter	25,116	38,532	34.8
Financial manager	29,016	43,524	33.3
Buyer, wholesale or retail	20,436	30,212	32.4
Personnel manager	31,408	45,812	31.4
Property/real estate manager	19,916	26,884	25.9
Attorney	45,500	61,256	25.7
Accountant/auditor	25,116	33,488	25.0
College professor	32,240	42,016	23.3
Editor/reporter	23,504	30,576	23.1
Public administrator	28,548	36,920	22.7
Educational/vocational counselor	29,276	36,140	19.0
Physician	41,704	50,856	18.0
Computer systems analyst	34,372	41,548	17.3
Public-relations specialist	27,248	32,396	15.9
Teacher	26,260	30,888	15.0
Psychologist	26,728	31,460	15.0
Secretary	17,732	20,124	11.9
Engineer	38,272	42,744	10.5
Advertising salesperson	24,804	27,196	8.8
Police/detective	25,116	26,624	5.7
Mechanic	23,868	24,804	3.8
Registered nurse	31,616	32,032	1.3
Postal clerk	29,068	28,392	+2.4

1990 median salaries.

- Women are concentrated in lower-paying occupations.
- Women enter the labor force at different and lower-paying levels than men.
- Women as a group have less education and experience than men; therefore, they are paid less than men.
- Women tend to work less overtime than men.

These conditions explain only part of the earning gap between women and men. They do not explain why women workers earn substantially less than men workers with the same number of years of education and with the same work histories, skills, and work experience.

Two research scientists at the University of Michigan have examined the income gap to determine if it can be explained by differences in job qualifications of men and women. Although findings do reveal some differences between the sexes in accumulated job experiences, taken together, they account for only about one-third of the existing wage gap. Corcoran and Duncan found that a large part of the wage gap can be explained by institutional sex discrimination in the labor market that obstructs women's access to the better-paying jobs through hiring or promotion or simply paying women less than men in any job (*ISR Newsletter,* 1982).

Differential earning can be found even within occupational classifications. Fully employed women when compared with fully employed men are consistently underpaid by thousands of dollars when equal in type of occupation.

Double Discrimination: Race and Gender

If women are disadvantaged due simply to their sex, minority women are doubly disadvantaged. In 1988, White women who worked full time had median weekly earnings of $318, approximately 68 percent of the $465 median earning of full-time working White men. Black and Hispanic women fared even worse, earning, respectively, only 62 percent and 56 percent of what White men earned (Rix, 1990:360). Black and Hispanic women are overrepresented in low-paying, low-status jobs. They tend to have few fringe benefits, poor working conditions, high labor turnover, and little chance of advancement. Black and Hispanic women are clustered in service jobs such as cooks, dishwashers, food counter and fountain workers, cleaning service workers, waitresses, nurses' aides, and child care workers. Because of their race, Black and Hispanic women are crowded into society's dirty work sectors. The gender system works with and through the system of racial stratification to place women of color at the bottom of the work hierarchy (see Table 8.3).

Pay Equity

Pay inequality creates serious problems for women. A record number of women are now in the work force, and many are the sole providers for their children. Most low-income families rely on the wages of both spouses to stay above the poverty line, and there are more children in poverty than ever before, most of them living in households with only their mothers. Given these trends, it is essential that women be able to earn as much as men for work of comparable value.

Considerable evidence suggests that traditionally female jobs pay less because women rather than men who do them. Nevertheless, the law does not presently view such differences as discrimination. Beginning in the early 1980s, a number of state and local governments began addressing the pay gap issue by instituting pay equity policies in the public sector. **Pay equity** policies are designed to bring the pay levels of women in closer alignment with those of men. Their immediate aim is to increase the salaries of women in undervalued female-dominated jobs; their broader aim is to reduce the male/female earnings disparity.

Raises would be accomplished by subjecting jobs to a rational evaluation that would assess their so-called worth in terms of skills and responsibilities of the work itself. Because **pay equity** calls for jobs of comparable value to be paid the same, it is also called *comparable worth* (Hacker, 1986; Sociologists for Women in Society, 1986).

Table 8.3 Women as a percentage of all civilian employees in selected occupations by race, 1990

Occupation	Percentage Female All Races	Percentage White Female	Percentage Black Female	Percentage Hispanic Origin Female
Secretaries	99.0	89.5	7.5	5.1
Textile sewing machine operators	89.2	66.5	14.6	18.0
Health aides, except nursing	84.8	65.6	17.0	4.7
Waitresses	80.8	74.2	3.3	4.3
Production inspectors, checkers, and examiners	52.2	42.4	7.9	4.5
Bus drivers	51.5	42.4	8.6	2.3
Financial managers	44.3	41.3	1.8	1.0
Assemblers	43.5	34.1	7.3	5.6
Computer programmers	36.0	30.6	2.4	1.0
Precision food	32.7	25.3	6.7	3.1
Insurance sales	32.6	29.3	2.6	1.3
Stock handlers and baggers	25.0	21.9	2.2	2.3
Farm workers	21.0	19.0	1.3	4.2
Physicians	19.3	16.2	0.5	0.5
Laborers, except construction	18.7	14.4	3.7	1.9
Police and detectives	13.9	9.8	3.9	0.8
Electrical and electronic equipment repairers	8.7	6.5	1.8	0.3
Engineers	8.0	7.0	0.1	0.3
Construction trades	1.9	1.7	0.1	0.1
Total, all occupations	45.4	38.7	5.0	3.0

Source: U.S. Bureau of Labor Statistics, unpublished data, 1990. Adapted from Paula Ries and Anne J. Stone, eds. *The American Woman, 1992–93.* New York: W. W. Norton, Company, 1992.

How would employers use sex- and race-neutral criteria to set equal wages for workers in different but equally demanding occupations? Employers would set their own pay scales, but pay scales would be based on the work itself. The pay scales would be set up by using *job evaluation systems.* In job evaluation the employer and employees (and union, when there is a collective-bargaining agreement) select the criteria on which wages should be based—such as skill, effort, responsibility, working conditions—and decide how much to weigh each factor. Points are assigned for every job in a company according to its evaluation system, so that a job's total score represents its worth to the employer. Very different jobs in the same company may have similar scores. These scores are used to set *salary ranges* for each job, so that jobs with the same score fall into the same salary range. The idea of job evaluation is not new; at present, about two-thirds of all U.S. workers are employed in establishments that use some form of job evaluation to set wages. However, employers often use separate wage scales for predominantly male and predominantly female jobs (Sociologists for Women in Society, 1986).

FACTS ABOUT PAY EQUITY

Sociologists for Women in Society

Is pay equity fair? The point of pay equity is not to eliminate inequality in wages, but to eliminate wage inequality that is based on sex or race. Jobs that are more difficult or valuable should be rewarded accordingly. However, job evaluation studies by employers and state civil service systems have repeatedly shown that women's jobs are underpaid relative to their evaluation scores. Basing wages on workers' personal characteristics rather than on the worth of the job is unfair.

Will pay equity cost so much it will weaken the economy? Implementing pay equity will cost less than many fear. For example, the cost of doing so in Minnesota was less than 4 percent of the state's payroll budget. Moreover, taxpayers already share the cost of women's artificially low wages. A Department of Labor study calculated that about half of the families living in poverty would not be poor if their female wage-earners were paid as much as similarly qualified men. Pay equity will save tax dollars spent assisting employed women and minorities whose wages are lowered by discrimination.

Will pay equity mean government interference in private firms? Pay equity would *not* require national or state-wide wage-setting systems. Employers would continue to set wages, but they would have to do so in a nondiscriminatory way according to their own job evaluation systems.

Will implementing pay equity lower white men's wages? Under the Equal Pay Act and Title VII, courts have consistently held that an employer may not lower any employee's pay to eliminate wage discrimination. Pay equity will mean raises for *all* workers who work in occupations that have been underpaid. Since these tend to be women, pay equity will reduce the wage gap between predominantly male and female occupations.

Why don't women and minorities change to higher paying jobs? Race and sex discrimination continue to exclude women and minorities from many jobs. Moreover, jobs traditionally reserved for white men could not begin to absorb the millions of women and minorities who work in sex- and race-segregated jobs. Even if enough jobs existed, many mature workers lack the credentials or specific skills they require. Schools and the media continue to channel young people into occupations that have been labelled "appropriate" for their sex and race.

What can you do to promote pay equity?

Inform yourself. . . . Work to inform others, in the classroom, through letters to the editor, and talks to community groups. Write your legislators, supporting your opinions with facts.

If you do research on race or sex segregation or wage differences, share your findings with the public legislators.

Organize workshops, conferences, letter-writing campaigns.

Press for job evaluation studies and pay equity on your job, in your union or employees' organization, and in your city and state government.

Contact and support labor, women's and civil rights organizations working for pay equity. These include the American Association of University Women; the American Civil Liberties Union; the American Federation of State, County and Municipal Employees; the Business and Professional Women's Foundation; the Coalition of Labor Union Women; the League of Women Voters; the Mexican-American Women's National Association; the National Conference of Puerto Rican Women; the National Education Association; the National Organization for Women; 9 to 5; the National Association of Working Women; the Service Employees International Union.

These and other groups belong to the National Committee of Pay Equity (N.C.P.E.), (1201 Sixteenth Street, N.W., Washington, D.C. 20036, 202/822–7304).

Source: "Facts about Pay Equity," Sociologists for Women in Society, (April 1986). Reprinted with permission from Sociologists for Women in Society.

male and predominantly female jobs (Sociologists for Women in Society, 1986). See the Observation about pay equity.

A decade of lobbying for pay equity has brought women and minorities in the public sector more than $450 million in wage and salary gains. According to the National Committee on Pay Equity, twenty state governments have negotiated pay increases. The prospects for achieving further increases for women and minorities in the 1990s are bright because these groups will represent the majority of new entrants into the job market (*USA Today,* 1989c:1). In 1990, Bethlehem Steel Corporation reached a $3,000,000 out-of-court settlement with the United Steelworkers of America in an equal pay lawsuit. The union sued after discovering that female clerical workers were paid an average of $200 a month less than men doing the same work (Woler, 1991).

The Organization and Operation of Work

The conventional wisdom is that women's low status in the labor force is a problem of their own making—that is, a result of their socialization, their low aspirations, and their greater commitments to family than to work. New sociological research has found that structural conditions, not individual characteristics, account for gender differences in the workplace. Let us examine the organization of the labor force that assigns better jobs and greater rewards to men and positions of less responsibility with lower earnings to women.

The differential placement of women and men stems from forces in the U.S. economy. The capitalist labor market is divided into two separate segments with different characteristics, different roles, and different rewards. The primary segment is characterized by stability, high wages, promotion ladders, opportunities for advancement, good working conditions, and provisions for job security. The secondary market is characterized by low wages, fewer or no promotion ladders, poor working conditions, and little provision for job security.

Women's work tends to fall in the secondary segment. Clerical work, the largest single occupation for women, has many of the characteristics associated with the secondary segment. The office provides a good example of segmentation by gender. According to Glenn and Feldberg:

> We observe two separate groups of office jobs, divided by sex. Some jobs are clearly "female" (typists, secretaries, key punchers); others are clearly "male" (vice president, product manager, sales manager). Furthermore, groups of jobs are organized into a hierarchy and the "clerical" staff is a largely female hierarchy. Each hierarchy is made up of jobs graded by level representing steps in a career. When a person takes a job she/he occupies not only that particular job, but also a step on a particular career ladder. A person who starts on the clerical career ladder may move up the ranks as she/he gains experience, but she/he rarely is allowed to cross over into a different ladder. Occasionally one hears of a clerk or secretary who becomes an officer in a company. Such stories generate excitement precisely because each is a freak occurrence. (Glenn and Feldberg, 1984:314)

Today's office is in the midst of change, described variously as "office automation," "the electronic office," and "the office of the future." Women are an overwhelming majority of office workers—workers in the occupation group identified as "administrative support, including clerical"—and they are particularly affected by changes in this workplace. Advances for business are not always advances for women, though, whose work is becoming more repetitious and subject to impersonal supervision. Machung has described word processing and the deskilling of clerical work:

> Working face to face with a T.V. screen all day long, operators, especially those in large centers, have few social contacts, except with each other. Unlike secretaries who are highly visible at front desks, word processing operators are virtually invisible. Isolated from the rest of the corporation by their dress (frequently more casual), their age (frequently younger), and their race (frequently minority), they work anonymously under fluorescent lighting in crowded back offices and windowless rooms. A supervisor usually handles all contacts with areas of the center; operators never see the person whose letter or paper they have typed. . . . Unlike secretaries who are known by their first names and friendly manners, word processing operators are virtually unknown. Many have taken the jobs to escape the stigmatization and subordination of secretarial work, only to find themselves even more faceless and nameless. (Machung, 1984:129)

Gendered work can be found even in the professions. In medicine women may no longer be concentrated in the low-prestige specialties such as pediatrics and obstetrics/gynecology; but except for general surgery, their numbers are not increasing in the more prestigious areas of medicine. Women lawyers are engaged in low-prestige specialties with a large proportion of female clients.

Although women are increasingly entering managerial and administrative jobs in private industry, they tend to be clustered in areas more traditionally open to females: public relations, personnel, and other staff jobs; consequently, they earn less than men with the same background.

Structural changes now occurring within the professions are creating a split between prestige jobs and a new category of more routinized jobs that are "professional" in name only. Carter and Carter have shown that women are concentrated in the new, more routinized sectors of professional employment, but the upper tier of relatively autonomous work continues to be male-dominated, with only token increases in female employment (Carter and Carter, 1981).

Changes in the organization of three professions—medicine, college teaching, and law—have degraded women's work. In medicine, the growth of hospital-based practice has paralleled women's admission to the profession. Women doctors are more likely than men to be found in hospital-based practice, which provides less autonomy than the more traditional office practice. In college and university teaching, demand is greatest in two-year colleges with heavy teaching responsibilities that leave little time or energy for writing and publishing—the keys to academic career advancement. And in law, women's advancement to prestigious positions is being eroded by the growth of the legal clinic, where much legal work is routinized.

Women have made important inroads into the professions. But because of structural changes occurring in many professions, the occupations to which women have gained access in recent years no longer have the same meaning in terms of economic or social status that they once possessed. Although they require a fair amount of formal schooling, many professional positions have become low paying, routine, and dead-end, much like other occupations employing larger numbers of women.

People have long assumed that women's and men's behavior in work settings is different and that women's behavior accounts for their lack of career advancement. Men are thought to be more ambitious, task-oriented, and work-involved; women are considered less motivated, less committed, and more oriented to work relationships than to work itself. Recent research, however, has pointed to the importance of the effect of people's location or placement in work settings and its effect on behavior.

Rosabeth Moss Kanter's important research on men and women in the corporate world reveals that structural position can account for what appear to be sex differences in organizational behavior. Hierarchical structures of opportunity and power shape women's and men's work behavior. People in low-mobility or blocked situations (regardless of their sex) tend to limit their aspirations, seek satisfactions in activities outside work, dream of escape, and create sociable peer groups in which interpersonal relationships take over other aspects of work. The jobs held by most women workers tend to be associated with shorter chains of opportunity. What has been considered typical women's behavior can be explained by their structural position (Kanter, 1977:129–163).

Just as hierarchical structures track women and men, other processes contribute to gender stratification. In the professions, for example, sponsor-protégé systems and informal interactions among colleagues limit women's mobility. Cynthia Epstein points to the importance of sponsorship in training personnel and

Males dominate decision-making at the highest levels of business. Here, the heads of the three automotive firms and the president of the United Auto Workers meet with President-elect Clinton and Vice President-elect Gore.

ensuring leadership continuity. Women are less likely to be acceptable as pro-
tégés. Furthermore, their sex status limits or excludes their involvement in the
buddy system or the old-boy system (Epstein, 1970). These informal interactions
create alliances that can further chances for social mobility, but they are systematically blocked for women.

Women and Men in Families

Women's status in the family parallels their status in other social institutions. The
gender-structured family assigns maintenance work (work with no identifiable
product) to women. In the roles of wife and mother a woman earns no money for
her household chores of cleaning, ironing, cooking, sewing, and caring for the
needs of the household members. Although this work is necessary, it is low in
prestige and it is unpaid. Apportioning domestic labor and child rearing to women
upholds male privilege by freeing men from such responsibilities. Like most
women in most regions of the world, U.S. women spend as much time working as
do men when unpaid labor is taken into account.

Although many wife-husband relationships are moving toward equality, men
continue to exercise greater power within the family. A cycle of power relations
connects work and family. The higher the husband's occupational status, the
greater his power. Such resources are acquired outside of the family. We have
seen that women's opportunities to acquire these resources are much more limited than are those of men: U.S. families are still patriarchal. Family life tends to
be subordinate to demands of the male-husband role.

The Costs and Consequences of Sexism

Who Benefits?

Clearly, gender inequality enters all aspects of social life in the United States. This
inequality is profitable to certain segments of the economy, and it also gives privileges to individual men.

Capitalists derive extra profits from paying women less than men. Women's
segregation in low-paying jobs produces higher profits for certain economic sectors, namely, those in which most of the labor force is female. Women who lack
the economic support of husbands and who are in the wage labor force on only a
temporary basis have always been a source of easily exploitable labor. These
women provide a significant proportion of the marginal labor force capitalists
need to draw on during upswings in the business cycle and to release during
downswings (Edwards, Reich, and Weisskopf, 1978:333).

Gender inequality is suited to the needs of the economy in other ways as well.
Capitalism involves not only the accumulation of capital but also the maintenance
of labor power. The physical and emotional labor of maintaining wage workers
must be done. The unpaid work that women do inside the home keeps capitalism
going, servicing its workers both physically and emotionally. Women do domestic labor and child rearing, but they also do the emotional work, building and
maintaining interpersonal relationships and ensuring the stability of children and
men so that they can function in the economy.

Because domestic work and emotional work are assigned to women, individual men gain leisure and service and the opportunity to pursue their own interests

or careers. If women tend to men's "existence needs," such as cooking and taking care of clothing, men gain time at women's expense. Newton observes:

> He reads the evening paper and his wife fixes dinner. He watches the news or an informative television show and she washes the dishes. He retires to his study (or his office or his shop or a soft chair) and she manages the children. Men gain leisure time at the expense of the oppression of women. This is a very

ANOTHER SOCIETY, ANOTHER WAY

EQUALITY BETWEEN MEN AND WOMEN IN SWEDEN

Swedish equal opportunities policy is fundamentally concerned with the ability of each individual to achieve economic independence through gainful employment. This also means that it must be possible for everybody, regardless of sex, to develop and participate in all aspects of community life, according to his or her capabilities.

The development towards equality has been made possible by a substantial demand for labour, which has been mainly due to the expansion, in the 1960s and 70s, of the public sector, and by consistently pursued reforms in the field of economic, social and family policy. The introduction of separate taxation for husbands and wives, and amendments to matrimonial legislation that clearly uphold the economic independence of all adults, have done much to transform attitudes concerning the traditional role of men and women. These reforms have in turn generated other changes, for instance the expansion of child-care facilities and parental benefits which have been important preconditions for the combination of gainful employment and parenthood.

In the work of reform in Sweden, the women's organizations—both political and independent ones—have played a vital role. There is a general consensus on the principles of equality in Sweden and they are also incorporated in the Swedish Constitution.

A number of public bodies and organizations in Sweden, each in its different field, are actively pursuing the objective of equality. It has also been made a guiding principle for government policy.

Promotion of equality at government level. All government ministers are required to pay regard to aspects concerning equality between men and women in the fields for which they are responsible. The overall responsibility for equality affairs rests, however, with the Deputy Minister of Public Administration, also called Minister for Equality Affairs.

The Equal Opportunities Commission is a special body which, pursuant to the Equal Opportunities Act and at the request of the Ombudsman, can order an employer to take active measures to promote equality between the sexes at workplaces.

Legislation. A major safeguard against discrimination on the basis of sex is to be found in the Swedish Constitution.

The Equal Opportunities Act. The main statute governing the practical realization of the principle of the equality of women and men in Sweden is restricted to working life. The purpose of the Act on Equality between Women and Men at Work or Equal Opportunities Act, which came into force in 1980, is to promote equal rights for women and men with respect to employment, working conditions, and opportunities for development at work. The Act consists of two main parts. One part contains rules prohibiting an employer from discriminating against a person because of his or her sex. The other makes it incumbent upon an employer to take active measures to promote equality at work. The ban on discrimination does not apply, however, if the employer can show that the decision was not founded on the person's sex but that it constituted part of a conscious effort to promote equality at work. Exceptions are also made for the furtherance of ideological or other special interests. An employer who contravenes the ban can, in certain cases, be sentenced to payment of compensation for the moral or other injury. Disputes about discrimination on grounds of sex are tried by the Labour Court.

A person who claims to have been a victim of sex discrimination does not have to refrain from taking action on economic grounds. An employee can, first and foremost, obtain help from his/her trade union. Job applicants and employees who are not union members, or who do not receive sufficient help from their union, can apply to the Equal Opportunities Ombudsman, whose services are free of charge.

The obligation of an employer to take active measures to promote equality means that the employer shall make planned and goal-oriented efforts to promote equality at his/her place of work and in proportion to available resources. The rules on active measures can, however, be replaced or supplemented by collective agreements between trade union and employer organizations at the national confederation level. Such central agreements now exist for practically the entire labour market.

Equality in working life. Sweden has a population of 8.5 million, with an active working population of 4.4 million. Women make up more than half of the population and almost one-half of the labour force. Slightly more than 82 percent of all women and 90 percent of all men are gainfully employed. During the period 1975–85, the number of women in the labour force grew

fundamental privilege which accrues to the division of labor (or lack of division) in the home. (Newton, 1973:121)

This domestic division of labor, in turn, can limit women's occupational participation and advancement. Women burdened with domestic duties have less time or energy left over to devote to careers. This upholds mens occupational superiority (for an alternative system, see "Another Society, Another Way" about Sweden).

by almost 350,000. This increase consists to a great extent of women with small children. At the same time, the number of men in the labour force declined somewhat, owing mainly to a lowering of the retirement age. There has thus been a convergence in the employment participation rate of men and women. Women previously had a slightly higher unemployment rate than men, but in 1987 the rate for women and men was the same, namely 1.9 percent.

Even if Swedish women have almost the same employment participation rate as men, they are employed on different terms. Women have the legal right to employment in all occupations (for example, in the armed forces) but even so they are employed in a more restricted sector of the labour market than men and in occupations which are less well paid. Women and men also have different hours of work. In spite of being gainfully employed, women still do most of the work in the home and assume most of the responsibility for caring for the children. In 1985, 44 percent of the gainfully employed women worked part-time as against 6 percent of the men. Most of the women who work part-time do so in order to be able to combine economic activity and caring for their children. The women who worked part-time increased their working hours during the 1970s and 1980s.

The principle of equal pay for equal work has long since been agreed upon in Sweden. This principle has also been laid down in collective agreements on equal opportunities between men and women.

Pay differentials between men and women are small in Sweden compared with many other countries. There are still, however, differences in male and female earnings, with women earning on average less than men. Men and women are employed in different sectors of the labour market; typical women's jobs are paid less than those where men predominate.

The greatest differences between the sexes in incomes are due to women being so extensively employed part-time. They also have a smaller share of overtime pay and shift-work bonuses.

Plan of action for equality. In June 1988, Parliament adopted a Government Bill on Equality Policy to the Midnineties. The Bill contains a five-year Plan of Action wherein the sights have been set much higher than formerly regarding its goals for the equal-

ity policy. Furthermore, a substantial amount of money is being allocated for various equality measures over the five-year period.

The plan comprises five different sectors, specifies concrete goals for equality that are to be attained by certain dates and describes the measures that are to be taken in order to reach the goals. The sectors taken up in the plan are: the role of women in the economy, equality on the labour market, equality in education, equality in the family and, finally, the influence of women.

Some examples of the goals to be reached before 1993 are:

- At least ten occupational fields should have an even-sex distribution (from today's four).
- The proportion of women engaged in routine work in one occupational field should not be greater than the proportion of women employed in that field.
- The proportion of women in senior posts and those doing qualified work should also be at least as large as the proportion of women employed in that field.
- Neither sex should fill less than 40% of the places on education and training courses.
- More men must make use of the availability of parental benefit.
- The proportion of men working in public child care must increase.
- By 1992 the representation of women in public bodies is to have increased to 30 percent and by 1995 to 40 percent. If 30 percent is not reached by 1992, the Government will consider legislation in this field.

Various measures are now being undertaken to reach the goals set up in the plan. They include projects, action programmes, support measures, the compilation of statistics, research, instructions to various national agencies and other bodies, etc., in all the fields covered by the plan.

Source: Adapted from "Equality between Men and Women in Sweden," *Fact Sheets on Sweden* (Stockholm, The Swedish Institute.) September 1989:1–4.

**Social and
Individual Costs**

Gender inequality generates benefits for certain segments of society, but ultimately society and individual women and men pay a high price. Sexism diminishes the quality of life for all people in the United States. Our society is deprived of one-half of our human potential. By keeping women from jobs requiring leadership, creativity, and productivity, the economy will suffer. The pool of talent consisting of half the population will continue to be underutilized and underproductive.

Sexism also produces suffering for millions of people. We have seen that individual women pay for economic discrimination. Their children pay as well. Women and children are swelling the ranks of the poor at a great cost to society. Households headed by women account for 83 percent of all AFDC (Aid to Families with Dependent Children) recipients, 70 percent of all food stamp households, 60 percent of those using Medicaid, 66 percent of households using subsidized housing, and 67 percent of all legal service clients (Stallard, Ehrenreich, and Sklar, 1983:47).

All women pay a psychological price for sexism. The devaluation of women by society can create identity problems, low self-esteem, and a general sense of worthlessness, particularly as women age. Middle-aged and older women in U.S. society face two problems from which men are relatively exempt. The first problem is the loss of sexual attractiveness. The second problem is the loss of their primary role—the bearing and raising of children.

Given the occupational patterns of our society, men generally gain in prestige and power as they age. They therefore tend to retain or even enhance their attractiveness to women. The reverse, however, is not the case (Bell, 1979). The result is that widowed or divorced men tend to remarry younger women. Widowed or divorced women either remain single or marry older men. Consequently, although the male-female ratio is approximately 1:1 in the forty-five to sixty-four age bracket, there are three times as many single, divorced, and widowed women as there are single, divorced, and widowed men in that age category. Those women who worked inside the home for husbands and children can become displaced homemakers through the death, separation, or divorce of a husband.

Sexism also denies men the potential for full human development. Occupational segregation by sex denies employment opportunities to men who wish to enter such fields as nursing, grade school teaching, or secretarial work. Eradication of sexism would benefit such males. It would benefit all males who have been forced into stereotypic male behavioral modes. In learning to be men, boys express their masculinity through physical courage, toughness, competitiveness, and aggression. Expressions typically associated with femininity, such as gentleness, expressiveness, and responsiveness, are seen as undesirable for males. In rigidly adhering to gender expectations, males pay a price for their masculinity. As Pleck puts it:

> The conventional expectations of what it means to be a man are difficult to live
> up to for all but the lucky few and lead to unnecessary self-deprivation in the
> nest when they do not measure up. Even for those who do, there is a price: they
> may be forced, for example, to inhibit the expression of many emotions. (Pleck,
> 1981:69)

Male inexpressiveness can hinder communication between husbands and wives, between fathers and children; it has been labeled a "tragedy of American society" (Balswick and Peck, 1971). Certainly, it is a tragedy for the man himself, crippled by an inability to show the best part of a human being—his warm and tender feelings for other people (Balswick with Collier, 1976:59).

Ideally, men and women should be able to integrate traditionally feminine and traditionally masculine traits. Such flexibility of gender, or androgyny, would permit all people to be either rational or emotional, either assertive or yielding, depending on what is appropriate to the situation.

Fighting the System

Feminist Movements in the United States

Gender inequality in U.S. society has led to feminist social movements. Three stages of feminism have been aimed at overcoming sex discrimination. The first stage grew out of the abolition movement of the 1830s. Working to abolish slavery, women found that they could not function as equals with their male abolitionist friends, and they became convinced that women's freedom was as important as freedom from slavery. In July 1848 the first convention in history devoted to issues of women's position and rights was held at Seneca Falls, New York. Participants in the Seneca Falls convention approved a declaration of independence, asserting that men and women are created equal, and that they are endowed with certain inalienable rights.

During the Civil War feminists for the most part turned their attention to the emancipation of Blacks. After the war and the ratification of the Thirteenth Amendment abolishing slavery, feminists were divided between those seeking far-ranging economic, religious, and social reforms and those seeking voting rights for women. The second stage of feminism gave priority to women's suffrage. The women's suffrage amendment, introduced into every session of Congress from 1878 on, was ratified on August 26, 1920, nearly three-quarters of a century after the demand for women's suffrage had been made at the Seneca Falls convention. From 1920 until the 1960s feminism was dormant. "So much energy had been expended in achieving the right to vote that the woman's movement virtually collapsed from exhaustion" (Hole and Levine, 1979:554).

Feminism was reawakened in the 1960s. Social movements aimed at inequalities gave rise to an important branch of contemporary feminism. The civil rights movement and other protest movements of the 1960s spread the ideology of equality. But like the early feminists, women involved in political protest movements found that male dominance characterized even movements seeking social equality. Discovering injustice in freedom movements, they broadened their protest to such far-reaching concerns as health care, family life, and relationships between the sexes.

Another strand of contemporary feminism emerged among professional women who discovered sex discrimination in earnings and advancement. Formal organizations, such as the National Organization of Women, evolved seeking legislation to overcome sex discrimination (Freeman, 1979).

These two branches of contemporary feminism gave rise to a feminist consciousness among millions of U.S. women. As a consequence, during the 1960s and early 1970s many changes occurred in the roles of women and men. However, periods of recession, high unemployment, and inflation in the late 1970s fed a backlash against feminism. The contemporary women's movement may be the first in American history to face the opposition of an organized antifeminist social movement. From the mid-1970s a coalition of groups calling themselves profamily, prolife, and anti-ERA emerged. These groups have drawn from right-wing political organizations and the Moral Majority to oppose feminist gains in reproductive, family, and antidiscrimination policies (Sapiro, 1986:972). In addition, many gains were set back by President Reagan's opposition to affirmative action programs and other equal-rights policies. Political, legal, and media opposition to feminism continue to undermine women's equality (Faludi, 1991).

Social Structure and Equality

Is gender equality compatible with present political economic conditions? We have seen gender inequality at all levels of U.S. society. Because structural problems are largely invisible, we must understand how individual lives are bound up with structural events. Individual women and men seeking change will continue to discover that no matter how they struggle for equality, the gender hierarchy that is embedded in our society will continue to affect them. Thus, the insights of sociology have become increasingly significant in the continuing struggle for women's equality.

CHAPTER REVIEW

1. U.S. society, like other societies, ranks and rewards women and men differently.
2. Gender differentiation is not natural but is instead a product of social organization.
3. Many sociologists have viewed gender inequality as the consequences of behavior learned by individual women and men. More recently, sociologists have explained gender inequality as a consequence of social structure.
4. Gender inequality is reinforced through language, interpersonal behavior, mass communication, religion, the law, and politics.
5. The occupational concentration of women in a few gendered occupations contrasts with that of men, who are distributed throughout the occupational hierarchy; and women, even with the same amount of education and when doing the same work, earn less than men in all occupations.
6. Labor market segmentation is the basic source of gender inequality in the labor force. Work opportunities for women tend to concentrate in a secondary market that has few advancement opportunities, fewer job benefits, and lower pay.
7. The position of women in families parallels their status in the labor force. Their responsibility for domestic maintenance and child care frees individual men from such duties and supports the capitalist economy.

8. Gender inequality deprives society of the potential contributions of half of its members, creates poverty among families headed by women, and limits the capacities of all women and men.
9. Feminist movements aimed at eliminating gender inequality have created significant changes at all levels of society. But because inequalities are deeply embedded in the social structure, its elimination will require a fundamental transformation of U.S. society.

KEY TERMS

Gendered.   The differentiation of women's and men's behaviors, activities, and worth.

Gender stratification.   The ranking and rewarding of the sexes in such a way that women are unequal to men in power, prestige, and presumed worth.

Feminist Approach.   View in support of equal relations between women and men.

Sex.   The biological fact of femaleness and maleness.

Gender.   The cultural and social definition of feminine and masculine.

Patriarchy.   Forms of social organization in which men are dominant over women.

Capitalist patriarchy.   A condition of capitalism in which male supremacy keeps women in subordinate roles at work and in the home.

Gender roles approach.   Males and females differ because of socialization. The assumption is that males and females *learn* to be different.

Structural approach.   Males and females differ because of factors external to them.

Androgyny.   The integration of traditional feminine and masculine characteristics.

Pay equity.   Raising pay scales according to the worth of the job instead of the personal characteristics of the workers.

FOR FURTHER STUDY

Joan Acker. *Doing Comparable Worth.* Philadelphia: Temple University Press, 1989.

Teresa L. Amott and Julie A. Matthaei. *Race, Gender, and Work.* Boston: South End Press, 1991.

Margaret L. Andersen. *Thinking about Women.* 3rd ed. New York: Macmillan, 1993.

Ann Bookman and Sandra Morgan, eds. *Women and the Politics of Empowerment.* Philadelphia: Temple University Press, 1988.

Patricia Hill Collins. *Black Feminist Thought.* Cambridge, Mass.: Unwin Hyman, 1990.

Susan Faludi. *Backlash, the Undeclared War against American Women.* New York: Crown Publishers, 1991.

Judith Lorber and Susan A. Farrell, eds. *The Social Construction of Gender.* Newbury Park, Calif., Sage Publications, 1991.

Joyce McCarl Nielsen. *Sex and Gender in Society.* Prospect Heights, Ill.: Waveland Press, 1990.

Barbara F. Reskin and Patricia A. Roos, eds. *Job Queues, Gender Queues.* Philadelphia: Temple University Press, 1990.

FORUM

DO WOMEN OFFICEHOLDERS MAKE A DIFFERENCE?

Women are the "new kids on the block" when it comes to political power in the United States. Shut out of even the right to vote until well into the twentieth century, women generally had no choice during the first two-thirds of our nation's history but to use the tactics and strategies of outsiders if they wanted to influence government action on issues about which they cared. Many of the early women reformers held firm convictions born of religious, political, and social values that championed human rights and decried injustice.

Why should we care whether women have parity with men in holding public office? One good reason is that the under-representation of women among our public leaders symbolizes the failure of American society to provide equality of opportunity for all its citizens. Another is that the under-representation of women means that half the nation's talent remains largely untapped—a waste in any era, and particularly costly today, when raid change and complex, almost insurmountable problems face us locally, nationally, and globally.

A third—and very significant—reason that we must be concerned with women's under-representation in elected positions is that the presence of women in public office promises something new in policymaking—new and valuable perspectives and priorities that might otherwise be ignored because they are not typically the perspectives and priorities men have brought to public office.

Is public policy different because women hold public office? Would policy change if those women were replaced by men? Not so long ago, those who believed that the answer to both these questions is "yes" had to rely largely on isolated examples and general impressions to support their claim. In recent years, however, scholars at the Center for the American Woman and Politics (CAWP) and elsewhere have been systematically gathering and analyzing information about women in public office. Since 1975, CAWP has conducted four national surveys of elected officials; these—and especially the most recent of them—furnish broad-based evidence that, when it comes to poli-

cy and to leadership more generally, the perspectives that women bring to public office ten to differ in important respects from those of men.

On the surface, elected women and men in the last several decades may seem to be much alike. By and large, elected officials of both sexes come from the middle class, are middle-aged, fairly well-educated, Caucasian, and Protestant. The majority are married and have had children.

However, there are also some suggestive gender differences among public officials. For example, elected women are less likely than elected men to be *currently* married or to be the parents of *young* children. Elected women are also more likely than elected men to say that the age of their children influenced their timing in running for office. Considering these differences, as well as the fact that it is women who are the more likely to have had the daily responsibility of caring for children, elderly relatives, or other family members and friends, the implications are clear: elected women are more likely than their male counterparts to have had the hands-on responsibility of family caregiving and to have had to make trade-offs when family responsibilities and public life conflict.

The occupational and employment experiences of female officials also tend to be quite different from those of their male colleagues. For example, a smaller proportion of the women than of the men have law degrees. A smaller proportion of the women than of the men are employed for pay while holding elective office. And the elected women who are employed are much more likely than their male colleagues to work in traditionally female occupations—nursing, social work, teaching, secretarial work.

In part because of such differences in life experience, women and men typically come into elective offices by different routes, bringing with them the influences not only of their different occupational backgrounds and employment histories, but also of their different informal networks, organizational memberships, and campaign constituencies.

Understanding that women come to public office with life experiences very different from those of their male colleagues is key to understanding why the priorities and attitudes of women in public office often differ from those of men.

There is good reason to believe that women officeholders might make government more sensitive to the special concerns of women if only because they themselves are more sensitive to these issues. For example, while an official of either sex may be concerned about crime and violence, a woman is more likely to understand the gravity of rape. Because a woman is more likely than a man to be a family caregiver, she is more likely to have seen firsthand the economic and health care problems of the aged. She may also identify with the aged more closely than a man does, since such a large proportion of the frail elderly are of her sex. And, while both male and female public officials are likely to be parents, women are more likely to know from their own experience about the need for child care and parental support systems.

In the past 20 years, every election cycle has brought an increase in the numbers of women winning office, especially in state legislatures.

Elected women themselves generally believe that they are making a difference, as do their male colleagues. This is all the more remarkable in light of the still small proportion of women among officeholders.

We will have to wait until the numbers of women and men in office are more evenly distributed across the board before we can really begin to understand the full consequences of gender-balanced public leadership in the United States.

Source: Excerpted from Ruth B. Mandel and Debra L. Dodson, "Do Women Officeholders Make a Difference?" in *The American Woman, 1992–93.* New York: W. W. Norton, Company. 1992. pp.148–177.

SENIOR·POWER·DEMAND
ACTION·NOW· No· TIME
LIKE· THE· PRESENT

The thesis of this chapter is that old people constitute a minority group in our youth-worshipping society, with a highly visible trait—an aged body—that makes them different from the majority. They are relatively powerless. Their behavior and traits are stereotyped and regularly depreciated and devalued by the dominant group. And, most important, because of their age, the elderly are singled out for differential and unfair treatment.

There are several cultural reasons the aged are stigmatized and oppressed in U.S. society. One is that the members of our society are obsessed with youth. We have traditionally associated a number of highly valued traits with youth: beauty, health, sexual vigor, happiness, usefulness, and intelligence. One consequence is that people who are considered old are typically believed to be physically unattractive, sickly, asexual, useless, and incompetent.

Second, in our rapidly changing, highly technical society, old people are considered to be unnecessary. Their wisdom represents another age that is irrelevant now. By contrast, in simpler societies where tradition is paramount, the elderly are highly respected, admired, and even revered because they are the repositories for the group's accumulated wisdom. They serve as memories for the group, passing on to the next generation the cherished values, myths, and skills necessary for survival and success.

The elderly constitute a surplus population in another way: they are nonproducers in a society in which production translates into value. As Gornick puts it:

> America is one of the worst countries in the world in which to grow old. This is a country in which the only value of a human being is the ability to produce. If you can produce you are respected and have power; if you can't, you are despised and shunted aside. (Gornick, 1976:32)

Not only are the elderly devalued for their lack of productivity, but they also are often viewed as social leeches living off the production of the young. They are targets of possible increased resentment as their members grow and, thus, their cost to society increases.

Parenti has summarized why the elderly constitute an oppressed minority group in U.S. society:

> The very old suffer from natural disabilities when attempting to compete for social outputs. In a society that places a premium on beauty, youth, energy, speed, earning power, aggressive drive, and productivity, the old and infirm are easily deprived of their place in the sun. When one's status and security is [sic] determined by one's ability either to control wealth or sell one's labor on the market, the superannuated are a surplus people of little use to the productive system, to their families and, as often happens, to themselves. The deference accorded a person of years in more traditional societies is replaced with impatience, patronization, neglect, and finally incarceration in a nursing home. As the elderly are given more years to live, they are given [fewer] reasons to live. (Parenti, 1978:68)

The Social Definition of Old

Aging is a relentless biological imperative that begins with birth. No one escapes it. In the process of aging the skin wrinkles, powers of seeing and hearing diminish, hair turns white and is gradually lost, reflexes slow, and the body's organs deteriorate. These effects of physical aging are already noticeable when one is thirty to forty years of age. They are demonstrated vividly in the decline and eventual retirement or dismissal of star athletes. But the aging process is a highly individual phenomenon. Genetic differences among people and variances in life experiences cause body wear and tear to be highly variable. So when is a person old?

Even though the aging process itself varies with the individual, society tends to accept an arbitrary chronological age as the social determinant of being old (this is what is meant by the **social definition of old**). We believe that age sixty-five is the line of demarcation separating the old from the nonold. But why sixty-five? In 1889 Otto von Bismarck, the chancellor of Germany, pushed a historic piece of legislation through the German Reichstag. The legislation represented the first time a government of the Western world assumed an obligation for the support of its older citizens. That legislation specified sixty-five as the age at which benefits for the elderly would begin. The number could have been fifty-five, sixty-two, or any other number, for that matter. Bismarck himself was seventy-four when he promulgated the legislation. Certainly sixty-five was a more realistic cutoff point in 1889 than now, since the average life expectancy has almost doubled in the intervening years. This arbitrary age, set in the previous century, was the precedent for the Social Security legislation passed in the United States in the 1930s. It has also been widely accepted by various levels of government, scientists, statisticians, insurance companies, theaters, and other people who offer special services or rates to the elderly.

Every day in the United States some 5 thousand people reach the age of sixty-five. On that day they are not any different physically or mentally than the day before, but now they are assumed by their employers, the government, and others to be old. They have entered a stage that some have called "statutory senility." Yet the use of age sixty-five as a benchmark has little relevance, for there is too much individual variance in mental capacity, physical endurance, and organ deterioration. So reaching sixty-five is a convenient but frequently inaccurate indicator of being old. It is significant, however, because it labels people. People expect certain behaviors of others depending on their stage in the life cycle. If people define sixty-five as old, then they treat those who are sixty-five as old. In this way the expectations of society become a self-fulfilling prophecy.

This use of an arbitrary chronological definition of age lumps together as aged a very heterogeneous category of individuals: people who are vigorous and others who are decrepit, people who are mentally sharp and those who are not. This single categorization for a heterogeneous group causes tensions because of its underlying assumption that everyone reaching a certain chronological age shares similar levels of social competence and biological and intellectual capacities.

Who is elderly and who is not is socially defined. Therefore, who is thought of as old varies from society to society. Among primitive societies where few people reach sixty-five, for example, fifty-year-olds are considered old. (The following examples are adapted from de Beauvoir, 1973:57–131.) Among the Siriono of

Bolivia, life is so harsh that those who survive to forty are worn out and considered old. Eskimos recognize that people age at different rates and assume that someone is old when he or she is not productive and becomes a burden to the group. That person is expected to die for the good of the group. While this practice may seem brutal and uncaring to us, it is accepted by young and old alike as appropriate in that cultural setting. The Ainu of Northern Japan, in contrast, neglect their elderly without compassion, allowing them to live, but in utter disrespect and impoverishment. Among the Aranda of Australia, the elderly are revered, for only they know the great secrets (when to plant, how to detect underground water, how to treat the sick). They pass on the sacred traditions and are believed to have magical powers. Elderly men in this tribe reach the highest authority when they become decrepit. In this state, because they are closest to the next world, they are believed to have supernatural powers.

These examples show the diverse definitions of old, how the elderly are treated, and the variance in respect for the old among the traditional societies of the world. Simone de Beauvoir provides this commentary:

> The practical solutions adopted by primitive peoples to deal with the problems set by their old people are very varied: the old are killed; they are left to die; they are given a bare minimum to support life; a decent end is provided for them; or they are revered and cherished. . . . What are called civilized nations apply the same methods: killing alone is forbidden, unless it is disguised. . . . Moreover, by the way in which a society behaves towards its old people it uncovers the naked, and often carefully hidden, truth about its real principles and aims. (de Beauvoir, 1973:131)

While U.S. society legally sets sixty-five as the age dividing the old from the nonold, there are differences in the social definition of age by sex. Women are thought to age earlier than men; they are considered old ten or fifteen years sooner. In short, the cultural definition of aging is a double standard, giving men decided psychological, sexual, and economic advantages over women.

In U.S. society the physical symptoms of aging are believed to make women sexually unattractive much earlier than men. Typically, women's sexual value is based on physical attractiveness; men's is defined much more by intelligence, earning power, and social position. Thus, women are much more likely than men to try to disguise the aging process by dyeing their hair, having their faces lifted, and dieting. Bell tells us:

> The multimillion dollar cosmetics advertising industry is dedicated to creating a fear of aging in women, so that it may sell them its emollients of sheep's fat, turtle sweat, and synthetic chemicals that claim, falsely, to stem the tide. "Did you panic when you looked in the mirror this morning and noticed that those laugh lines are turning into crow's feet?" "Don't let your eyes speak your age!" "What a facelift can do for your morale!" (Bell, 1976:150)

Dramatic proof of different age definitions for men and women is seen in the norms governing the appropriate age of marriage partners. Mature men find it acceptable, even desirable, to marry a women twenty years younger, but the reverse is clearly unacceptable. Thus, widowhood comes to be an expected role, but not widowerhood; and a widowed or divorced woman will have a much more difficult time remarrying than will a man.

The double standard for age also hurts women economically. Older women seeking jobs are discriminated against because male employers consider so many so-called female jobs to be reserved for the young and attractive. Summing up this dilemma, Bell said:

> The differential definition of age in men and women represents a palpable advantage to men at the expense of women. It multiplies the options for emotional satisfaction on his side while it diminishes them on hers. It raises his prestige and self-esteem at the expense of hers. All men in our society benefit to some degree from this custom, while not a single woman who lives into middle age escapes bearing some of the cost. If we are ever to restructure this society into one of true equality for both sexes, this is one of the crucial points at which we must begin. (Bell, 1976:161–162)

An arbitrary age to denote the elderly is important in establishing age legally for entitlement programs (e.g., Social Security, Medicaid). A standard age permits both the government and individuals to plan rationally. The issue, through, is, What is an appropriate age? Because life expectancy has risen, should not the chronological age determining the elderly also rise? If, for example, the age were put at ten years before death, the age denoting who is old would vary with life expectancy. Given present life expectancy, the arbitrary line determining "old" should be seventy-six, since the average seventy-six-year-old can expect about ten more years of life.

The Demographics of Aging

To understand the nature and scope of the discrimination that the elderly experience in our society and to appreciate the special problems they face, we need, first, to examine the population statistics.

Number

The most striking feature about the aged in U.S. society is their past and projected future growth in numbers and proportion. The separate demographic trends converge to produce the rapid growth of the elderly population (Dychtwald and Flower, 1990):

- *The senior boom.* In the United States, people are living longer than before, and they are healthier than any older generation in history.
- *The birth dearth.* Since 1980 the birth rate in the United States has been at or near an historic low point. In other words, the increase in the number of elders is not being offset by an increase in the number of children.
- *The aging of the baby boom.* The oldest baby boomers are now over forty-five. As this generation passes age sixty and then seventy, the numbers in the elderly category will jump dramatically.

Figure 9.1 shows that the older population (using the arbitrary age of sixty-five) has grown steadily as a share of the total U.S. population, from 3.1 million in 1900 to 31.5 million in 1990. Along with the numbers, the proportions have also shifted—the people over sixty-five constituted 4.1 percent of the population in 1900, 12.6 percent in 1990. The average life expectancy in 1900 was forty-nine years, and in 1990 seventy-five and six-tenths. But even as the average life expectancy gradually levels off, the number of elderly will continue to swell, as Figure 9.2 shows. Moreover, the proportion of elderly will grow steadily—to an estimated 21.8 percent in 2030. A surge in the number and proportion of elderly will occur between 2010 and 2025, when the **baby-boom generation** (those born in the fifteen-year period following World War II) reaches retirement age (Uhlenberg 1992:452–453).

Composition by Sex

In contrast to the gender split in lower age categories, the majority of older people in the United States are women (in 1990, 18.7 million women and 12.7 million men). The pattern shows a progressive decline for males, from a small excess among young children to a large deficit in extreme old age. Currently, there are only 68.6 males for every 100 females age sixty-five and over. With increasing age the disparity increases—at age seventy-five and over there are only 56 men for every 100 women.

A combination of biological advantages for women and social reasons explains this difference. The secondary status of women in U.S. society has provided them with extra longevity. Traditional gender roles have demanded that men be engaged in the more stressful, demanding, and dangerous occupations. It will be interesting to note whether there are any effects on female longevity as women receive a more equal share of all types of jobs. Meanwhile, though, the current situation creates problems for the majority of elderly women, who are often widows and have low incomes. Whereas about three-fourths of men over sixty-five are living with their spouses, only one-third of the women of this age are.

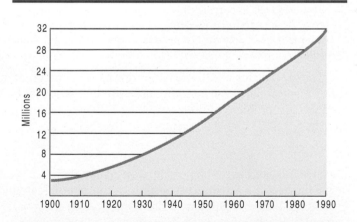

Figure 9.1 U.S. population, age sixty-five and over, for 1900–1985

Source: Bureau of the Census, "Historical Statistics of the United States: Colonial Times to 1970"; *Current Population Reports,* Series P–25, No. 704; "Projections of the Population of the United States: 1977–2050"; *Statistical Abstract of the United States* 1990, 110th ed. (Washington, D.C.: Government Printing Office, 1990), p. 16.

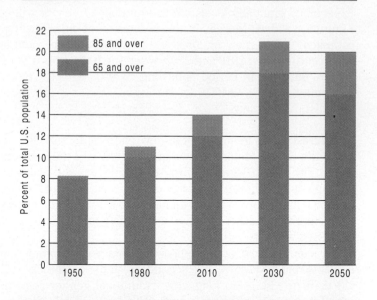

Figure 9.2 Older population as percent of total U.S. population: 1950–2050

Source: Beth J. Soldo and Emily M Agree, "America's Elderly," *Population Bulletin* 43 (September 1988), p. 8.

The gender differential in widowhood is pronounced throughout later life: at ages 65 to 69, 34 percent of women are widowed; for men, the figure is 7 percent. At ages 75 to 79, 60 percent of women are widowed but only 18 percent of the men; and at age 85+, 82 percent of women but only 43 percent of men are widowed. (Bengtson, Rosenthal, and Burton, 1990:270)

These statistics are the result of two factors: the greater longevity of women and the social norm for men to marry younger women. Thus, to the extent that isolation is a problem of the aged, it is overwhelmingly a problem for the female elderly.

Racial Composition   Because Blacks have a lower life expectancy than do Whites (about six years less), they form a smaller proportion of the elderly category than of other age groups. In 1990, 8.2 percent of Blacks were sixty-five years of age and over (9.2 percent of Black females and 7.0 percent of Black males, compared with 12.8 percent of Whites (14.6 percent of White females and 10.9 percent of White males) (U.S. Bureau of the Census 1991c:19). The percentage for the population of Latino origin (1989) was even lower—5.0 percent—although there was wide variation within this category, ranging from only 3.3 percent of Central and South Americans to a high of 17.1 percent for Cubans (U.S. Bureau of the Census 1991b:40).

In the United States, women, on average, outlive men by about seven years.

Geographic Distribution

The states with the largest numbers of elderly people are Florida with 3.4 million, California with 3.2 million, and New York with 2.3 million as of 1990. Other states with more than 1 million people age sixty-five and older are Pennsylvania, Illinois, Texas, New Jersey, Michigan, and Ohio. In 1990 five states had 14 percent or more elderly (Florida had the highest concentration, with 18 percent). Many states with a high concentration of elderly are rural states, where there has been a large outmigration of young people.

The Sunbelt states, especially Florida, California, Arizona, Nevada, and Texas, have experienced a tremendous growth in elderly citizens because of favorable climate. It is important to note that the elderly who migrate to the Sunbelt states are not representative of people over sixty-five. They tend to be younger and more affluent. Thus, they benefit their new communities by broadening the tax base through home ownership, strong purchasing power, and not burdening the local job market. The communities they left in the Snowbelt are negatively affected. The elderly who remain are disproportionately older and poorer and thus require more public assistance but from a lower community tax base.

Labor Force Participation

The percentage of men over sixty-five who work in the labor force has been declining—from 48 percent in 1947 to 16.6 percent in 1989. The proportion of older women in the labor force, however, has remained relatively unchanged—from 8 percent in 1947 to 8.4 percent in 1989. By age seventy only 10.4 percent of men and 4.3 percent of women are in the labor force (Soldo and Agree, 1988:24).

Educational Attainment

The educational attainment of the elderly is well below that of adults in general. The proportion of the aged who have graduated from high school is only about 54.9 percent, compared to 76.9 percent of the entire population age twenty-five years and over. The reasons for this gap are, first, that a relatively high proportion of the aged (15 percent) are foreign-born. Second, the socioeconomic status of people in the United States has risen rapidly since World War II, giving each age cohort greater educational opportunities than the previous one. This second trend means that the educational attainment of the elderly will rise substantially, narrowing the gap with the other adults, as we move into the next century.

Wealth, Income, Poverty, and Cumulative Advantage or Disadvantage

The net worth of householders differs according to marital status and gender. Elderly married couples in 1988 had a median net worth of $124,419 ($45,890 excluding home equity). Households maintained by unmarried elderly males had a median net worth of $48,883 ($15,914 excluding home equity); and households maintained by unmarried elderly women had a median net worth of $47,283 ($10,693 excluding home equity) (U.S. Bureau of the Census, 1991a:23). Home equity is significant because it gives older people who bought their first homes in the 1950s and 1960s a distinct advantage. Homes then, compared to the 1970s and 1980s, were inexpensive, with interest and mortgage payments low relative to wages. This has meant that 85 percent of current homeowners sixty-five or older own their homes outright, debt free (Peterson, 1991). Subsequent generations as they become old will be much less likely to own their homes and thus will have substantially lower net worth than those who are old now.

Personal income is usually reduced by one-third to one-half after retirement. In 1990 the median income for men age sixty-five and over was $13,107, and for women in that age category was $7,655 (Crooks, 1991).

Social Security benefits, which are indexed to offset inflation, have lowered the proportion of the elderly in official poverty status (12.4 percent in 1991, compared to 13.9 percent in 1978 and more than 33 percent in 1959). However, certain categories of older people in the United States are disproportionately poor—unmarried women, minorities, and the physically disabled. As Soldo and Agree have stated,

> At the extremes of poverty are those who suffer the cumulative effects of being old, female, and a member of a minority group—60 percent of black women 65 and older, not living in families, were below the poverty line in 1986. These official estimates would be higher still if they included the "hidden poor"—older persons whose low incomes force them to live with younger relatives. (Soldo and Agree, 1988:26)

Typically, we assume that economic inequality narrows after age sixty-five, when benefit programs replace work as principal income sources (the following is taken from Crystal and Shea, 1990). This, however, is not the case; the inequalities from income and privilege tend to be magnified among elderly people. People who are initially advantaged, for example, are more likely than their less fortunate counterparts to receive good educations and obtain good jobs with better health and pension benefits, which lead to higher savings and better postretirement benefit incomes. Crystal and Shea (1990) present data to support this contention:

- For every dollar the bottom 20 percent receive in Social Security income, the top 20 percent receive $1.72.
- For every dollar the bottom 20 percent receive in pension income, those in the upper quintile receive almost $16.
- For every dollar of dividend income received by persons in the lowest 20 percent, those in the upper 20 percent receive almost $90.

Most noteworthy, the government is partly responsible for these skewed advantages to the affluent. The relatively affluent are encouraged by the government, because of tax incentives, to invest in retirement income programs such as IRAs (Individual Retirement Accounts), Keough plans, or other tax-deferred programs. Thus, the already advantaged are given preferential tax treatment, which amounts to tax subsidization, thereby increasing their economic advantage over the disadvantaged after age sixty-five.

Discrimination Against the Elderly

Ageism refers to the systematic stereotyping of and discrimination against people because they are old. Ageism is a real phenomenon in U.S. society, as Sharon R. Curtain asserts:

> People who manage to survive to old age know that the present system is destroying them. They experience discrimination, intolerance and isolation based on the sole fact that they are old. Their oppression stems from an irreversible biological condition, as surely as the black person faces oppression because of color and a woman experiences oppression based on sex. (Curtain, 1972:193)

This section enumerates some of the ways in which individuals and society discriminate against the elderly.

Negative Stereotypes

One theme in Simone de Beauvoir's classic *The Coming of Age* is that the worst thing about getting old is not getting sick but receiving dehumanizing looks from other people (de Beauvoir, 1973). These looks (and actions) by the nonold imply that the old are unattractive, worthless, worn out, and in the way. These expressions of disdain are the consequence of commonly held **stereotypes** about the elderly. (A stereotype is an exaggerated generalization of a category of people that persists regardless of the evidence). The old are believed to be unfortunates—poor, isolated, neglected, sickly, senile, and depressed. These notions are based only partly on fact. For example, as we have seen, a disproportionate number of the elderly are poor. For the most part, however, the stereotypes do not fit the majority of the elderly. Let's look at these negative stereotypes, how they are reinforced, and the facts (Kart, 1981:7–15).

All elderly people are alike. This prejudice, according to expert Bernice Neugarten, is the most insidious stereotype of all for the aged. It puts

> the old (or, for that matter, the young or the middle-aged) into a distinct category or a distinct group. There is, in truth, no such thing as "the" young, or "the" old. People *do* differ; they also become increasingly different over time, as each

person accumulates an idiosyncratic set of experiences and becomes committed to a unique set of people, things, interests, and activities. . . . To put the same point another way, calendar age or chronological age is a poor basis for grouping people who have attained biological maturity. Study after study of the happiness, intelligence, personality, or health of adults has shown that age is a poor index of the differences between people. (Neugarten, 1980:323–324)

Most of the aged are disabled. This stereotype is contradicted by the facts: 89 percent of all men and women over sixty-five live in a community and are self-sufficient.

The aged are not capable of or interested in sexual activity. Because many elderly are widows and without sexual partners, this statement (in terms of sexual activity) is essentially correct, but for social not physiological reasons. Approximately 60 percent of married couples remain sexually active to age seventy-five. Evidence shows that the capacity for sexual response does slow down gradually, along with the other physical capacities, but it sometimes continues beyond age eighty.

As people age, their intelligence declines. Evidence from longitudinal studies (that is, observations of a single group of subjects over a period of years) contradicts this stereotype. The stereotype is usually based on the common belief that the aged are senile. The fact is, however, that mental faculties stay clear and sharp until very late in life. A minority of older people suffer from memory lapses, forgetfulness, and confusion, conditions that result from diseases such as hardening of the arteries.

The elderly are isolated, neglected, and sickly. Bernice Neugarten examined a number of studies using large and representative samples of older people and found

> that they do not become isolated and neglected by their families . . . [and] are not dumped into mental hospitals by cruel or indifferent children. They are not necessarily lonely or desolate if they live alone. Few of them ever show overt signs of mental deterioration or senility, and only a small proportion ever become mentally ill. (Neugarten, 1980:323)

Negative images of the old rise from a variety of sources. Most important, the views that individuals have toward the old are shaped by the ideals of the culture in which they live. Because U.S. society denigrates the traditional and highly values youth, old age is unlikely to be given high prestige.

A more explicit denigration of the elderly is found in various forms of humor. Another source of such negative stereotypes is the image of the elderly in literature, movies, television, and advertisements. Another reason for the maintenance of negative beliefs about the elderly is the infrequency of attempts by the media to use their persuasive powers to change such beliefs.

Advertising in the media invariably correlates desirable traits with youth (vigor, sexuality, cleverness, beauty). Advertising also tells us "that we should quickly remove all telltale signs of approaching old age, and even of middle age. We are told to disguise the gray in our hair, to use wrinkle creams, and even to get our faces lifted and our hair transplanted" (Henslin, 1976b:148).

A final source of misconceptions about the old is the early gerontological research, which was based largely on institutionalized older people and therefore was not representative of the entire population of the aged.

There are some serious consequences of negative stereotypes of the elderly. First, they support ageism—discriminatory attitudes and behaviors such as mandatory retirement. As long as it is commonly accepted that senior citizens are unhappy, rigid, cantankerous, and confused, then their second-class citizenship would appear to be deserved. Second, people fear aging. As Neugarten has put it, "most people see aging as alien to the self and tend to deny or repress the associated feelings of distaste and anxiety. We have an irrational fear of aging and, as a result, we maintain a psychological distance between ourselves and other persons" (Neugarten, 1980:322).

Another and related consequence of the negative stereotypes is the possibility that they are also believed by the aged themselves. The result is a self-fulfilling prophecy. If the aged believe, say, that sex is an exclusive activity of the young, they might refrain from it because it is abnormal. Moreover, the widespread denial of sexuality in older people

> has a harmful influence that goes far beyond its effect upon an individual's sexual life. It makes difficult, and sometimes impossible, correct diagnoses of medical and psychological problems, complicates and distorts interpersonal relations in marriage, disrupts relationships between children and parents thinking of remarriage, perverts the administration of justice to older persons accused of sex offenses, and weakens the whole self-image of the older man or woman. (Rubin, 1976:438)

Finally, the negative stereotypes common in U.S. society do actual *physical* harm to the aged. Alexander Comfort, a noted authority on the aged, claims that

> physical aging accounts for perhaps 25 percent of the picture of aging that we see in American society. Seventy-five percent is accounted for by another type of aging, *sociogenic aging,* which has no physical basis. It is the role which our folklore, prejudices, and misconceptions about age impose on "the old." (Comfort, 1976:4)

Suppose that instead of treating older people as asexual, unemployable, and crazy, we held them in high esteem and let them continue to be productive citizens. Would those people live longer? Would fewer of them exhibit symptoms of senility? These questions cannot be answered with certainty, but there is evidence from other societies that if the elderly are held in high esteem, they live longer. Societies whose inhabitants have extraordinary longevity have one thing in common: social status is positively age-dependent. The older the person, the higher is the regard members of society have for him or her. The consequence of such high esteem is a very long and productive life.

The Bias in the Social Security Program

Social Security is the only source of income for about half of retired people and a major source of income for 80 percent of the elderly in U.S. society. Since the 1930s, the amount paid per person annually has steadily increased, as have the number of workers eligible to receive benefits. Certainly, Social Security is better than no program at all, but several serious problems with the system place a burden on certain categories of the elderly and on some portions of the workers paying into the program.

An immediate problem is that not all workers are covered by Social Security. Some groups of workers are unable to participate because they work for states with alternative retirement programs. Other workers, however, are covered by neither Social Security nor other pension programs. Legislation has specifically exempted certain occupations (such as agricultural workers) from the Social Security program.

For workers who are eligible for Social Security, there are wide disparities in the benefits received. The amount of benefits depends on the length of time workers have paid into the Social Security program and the amount of wages on which they paid a Social Security tax. In other words, low-paid workers receive low benefits at retirement. Thirty percent of the elderly who depend almost exclusively on Social Security benefits have incomes below the poverty line. These elderly typically are people who have been relatively poor during their working years or are widows.

The Social Security system also is biased against women. Ruth Sidel has summarized the inequities.

> Social Security benefits—tied to income—vary widely depending upon the individual's gender, work history, and marital status. Benefit levels are higher for men than for women; for individuals who are part of a two-worker couple than for those who are not; for white couples than for black couples; for white women than for black women. Benefit levels are least favorable for widows and, particularly, for divorced women. (Sidel, 1986:162)

Let us examine some of the specific provisions of Social Security benefits that disadvantage women.

- Social Security recognizes only paid work. Thus, a woman who has worked as a homemaker receives no personal credit for her work. She receives a spouse benefit equal to half of the benefit her husband receives.
- A divorced woman receives half of her former husband's benefit if they had been married at least 10 years. If the divorce occurs before being married 10 years, then she receives nothing.
- Where wife and husband are both employed, the wife will receive pension benefits for her work only if her benefits exceed those earned by her husband.
- A woman who is widowed will not receive any Social Security benefits until age sixty unless she has a child under sixteen or an older disabled child or she herself is disabled.
- Retired women workers receive lower monthly Social Security benefits than retired men workers. This is because women are usually paid less than men and they spend more time out of the workforce—an average of eleven years—usually to care for children. In 1989 the average monthly payment for retired men was $639, while only $488 for retired women (Crooks, 1991:284).

Criticizing Social Security, a publication by the Older Women's League stated that

> Social Security and pension systems benefit male work patterns. Designed when lifestyles were dramatically different, Social Security best serves 'traditional' families that consist of a lifelong breadwinner, a lifelong homemaker, and two children. Less than 10 percent of American families fit that definition today; even fewer will fit in the future. . . .
>
> As long as women continue to assume greater child and elder care responsibilities, are paid less than men, and live longer, these biases will take an enormous toll on women's retirement income. (Cited in Crooks, 1991:284)

The Social Security system is financed through taxes on wages and salaries. From a payroll tax of 2 percent on the first $3000 of earnings when it began in the 1930s, the rate has increased substantially over the years. The 1990 rate was 15.3 percent, with the cost being split between the worker and the employer, but most economists agree that the burden of the tax is on the employee because employers finance their share by paying their employees that much less.

The method of financing Social Security is not equitable, because it disproportionately disadvantages lower-income wage earners. In other words, the tax is regressive: it takes a large percentage from people with the lowest incomes. The Social Security tax has the following negative features:

- It is levied at a constant rate (everyone, rich and poor, pays the same rate).
- It starts with the first dollar of earned income, offering no allowances or exemptions for the very poor.
- It applies only to wages and salaries, thus exempting income typical for the wealthy, such as interest, dividends, rents, and capital gains.
- It is imposed up to a ceiling ($51,300 in 1990). Thus, in effect, in 1990 a worker making $51,300 and an executive making a $350,000 salary paid exactly the same Social Security tax.

Other Problems of the Elderly

Aside from discrimination and degradation, the elderly face additional problems because of their age. This section focuses on the problems of four categories of the old: the elderly in general, the elderly in poor health, the elderly poor, and the special problems of the institutionalized elderly.

Typical Problems   Two common problems of the elderly are role loss and learning a new role. **Role** refers to the behavioral expectations and requirements attached to a position in a social organization. (The following discussion is adapted from Riley and Waring, 1976; and Bengtson, 1985.) Becoming old means facing a time of transition: most elderly people are giving up a comfortable role for one that is essentially devalued in society. In essence, becoming old is being demoted, a personal condition that is unsettling and threatening. Becoming old involves role loss in retirement, the loss of norms that influence many of our actions, the loss of a spouse, and the loss through death of friends and relatives. Thus, it is a stage of life that increases the likelihood of psychological problems of low self-esteem and depression.* These problems can be tempered by adequate social support for the individual; friends, fellow workers, family, and neighbors can ease the burden. But being cut off from work (retirement), from children (who live far away, a high probability in our mobile society), and from a spouse (widowhood), the chances of personal trauma increase manyfold. In addition to the role transition of old age, three role shifts within old age itself are especially traumatic: retirement, widowhood, and death.

Retirement, whether forced or not, involves the loss of a valued role. As Riley and Waring have put it:

---

*The elderly have the highest suicide rate of any age group in U.S. society.

In many societies, including our own, performance in a work role bears witness to the traditional ethic of work, and therefore commands respect. When that role is given up, respect diminishes. There may be residual esteem for past performance, but the base for generating new esteem is largely lost. Other gratifications are also removed. Apart from pension and Social Security payments, income derived from the role is gone. The comradeship and personal support of fellow-workers is left behind. A familiar, day-long routine has disappeared. Competencies of long standing no longer have a focus. . . . It is not surprising that a good many face retirement with dismay and disorientation rather than happy anticipation. (Riley and Waring, 1976:392)

The transition from wife to widow (the typical case, because men tend to die first) or from husband to widower is an especially difficult change for the individual. As well as the loss of a loved one, there are the problems associated with taking on a new role—widow—that is negatively valued by society and by the individual. The widow is especially vulnerable to loneliness because she lives alone and lacks opportunities for interpersonal involvement. Studies have shown what meager social support widows experience; they "have fewer contacts with children, greater unhappiness, and higher rates of suicide and death than do married persons of similar age" (Riley and Waring, 1976:391). Widowed males are more fortunate than widowed females, because they are more likely to remarry.

The anticipation of death is the last role transition people face. As one might suppose, this stage is especially traumatic. Riley and Waring observe:

Compared to other transitions, the passage to death is especially devoid of social supports. In America, this lack of support is partly attributable to an historical change in the locus of death, from the home to the hospital. Hospitals are geared to saving lives, not to presiding over death. In contrast to earlier times, the dying person today is rarely given center stage. Caretakers for the dying are now typically recruited from overdemanded health professionals rather than from close relatives and friends. The lack of support may result from the fact that, with increased longevity, most deaths now occur among the old. The old, sometimes viewed as repugnant, sometimes as having had their chance at life, often receive a low priority for care and attention. The relative inadequacy of professional support derives further from the frequent discomfort of the well in the presence of the dying. . . . Not infrequently, pretense characterizes interactions between the dying person and others, as doctors, nurses, and even family members and friends pretend not to know. The dying person who correctly senses the gravity of his or her condition may also feign ignorance. Such cover-ups and brave fronts only add to the strains, in some cases diverting energies better used in support of the dying person and the significant others. (Riley and Waring, 1976:392–393)

Problems of the Elderly Poor

In 1991, 12.4 percent of people age sixty-five and over were poor. This proportion is relatively low (the overall poverty rate in 1991 was 14.2 percent) because Social Security benefits are indexed for inflation. This poverty rate, slightly below the poverty rate for the nation as a whole, is perceived typically as a success. However, 3.5 million elderly were poor, and another 30 percent of the elderly were in the "economically vulnerable" category—that is, they had incomes between one and two times the official poverty rate.

The elderly poor spend almost half of their income for food. Thus, they are especially affected by inflation at the grocery store. The only recourse for the poor in inflationary times, when their incomes do not increase with spiraling costs, is either to eat less or to eat cheaper, less nutritious food.

The elderly poor spend about 20 percent of their incomes on energy for heat and electricity. These costs are especially vulnerable to inflation. Those on fixed incomes are likewise negatively affected by inflationary increases in the cost of rents, taxes, and health care. The last is a special burden for the old who are poor. Health costs for the elderly are almost four times those for people under sixty-five. The result is that the elderly poor tend to live in substandard housing, receive inadequate medical care, and have improper diets.

If the poor and the old are doubly cursed, then the elderly poor who are members of a racial or ethnic minority group experience a triple disadvantage. Individual and institutional sources of discrimination coalesce to make these people's lives especially miserable and problematic. The higher probability of older Blacks' being poor is a direct consequence of their relatively low status throughout life. With average incomes only about 60 percent those of Whites, they have little chance of building a nest egg to supplement their pension incomes. Blacks are also more likely than Whites to have worked at jobs that do not qualify for Social Security (prior to 1974, for example, only 80 percent of elderly Blacks received some Social Security benefits, compared with 90 percent of older Whites). If they have worked at jobs qualifying for Social Security, minority members usually are eligible only for lower benefits because of their lower wages.

These related problems reflect the discrimination in the job market and unfair legislation directed at minorities. Clearly, equity in Social Security benefits will not occur until Blacks and Whites experience similar work careers and compensation. The result is that one-third of elderly African Americans and one-fourth of elderly Latinos are below the poverty line.

After a lifetime of lower earnings and receiving small or no pensions, the elderly minorities must live in substandard housing. They are much more likely than elderly Whites to live in deteriorated housing with inadequate plumbing, heating, and sewage disposal. Similarly, minority aged suffer more health problems than do majority senior citizens. For instance, among all minority aged the prevalence of chronic disabilities is twice as high as among the White elderly.

Health Care Problems

Most older people are in reasonably good health. Of all age groups, however, the elderly are the most affected by ill health. Health problems occur especially from age seventy-five onward as the degenerative processes of aging accelerate (see Figure 9.3).

Here are some facts:

- Although the elderly comprised 12.6 percent of the population in 1990, they represented one-third of the hospital population.
- Prescription drugs represent the largest out-of-pocket health-care expense for 75 percent of older people. The problem is that the costs of these drugs are rising much faster than inflation.

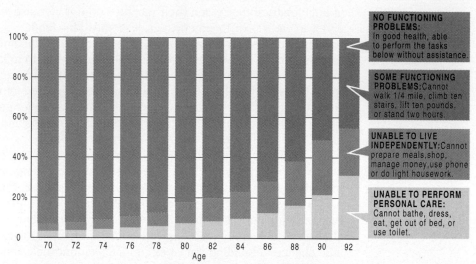

Most people in their 70s are healthy enough to live independently; by their 80s, however, many need help. About 42% of 70-year-olds live to be 85. But only one-quarter of 85-year-olds are in good health.

Figure 9.3   Which problems hit at which age

Source: Brian O'Reilly, "How to Take Care of Aging Parents," *Fortune* (May 18, 1882), p. 110. © 1992 Time Inc. All rights reserved.

- Their medical expenses are three times greater than those of middle-aged adults, yet their incomes are typically much less.
- Although Medicare helps with the medical costs of the aged, on the average the elderly still pay one-fourth of their medical expenses.

Late in 1987 Congress improved the Medicare coverage for the 31 million beneficiaries by protecting them against the costs of catastrophic illness. The bill put limits on the amount patients must pay for hospital costs and doctors' services. Not included, however, was comprehensive coverage for extended nursing home stays, which are the greatest source of catastrophic costs for the elderly. A congressional survey revealed that half of the couples with one spouse in a nursing home become impoverished within six months and 70 percent of single elderly patients reach the poverty level after only thirteen weeks in a nursing home. This problem is compounded by the cost of insurance to cover nursing home care. A study by Families USA found that only one out of six older people in the United States can afford such insurance. The typical policy for someone sixty-five years old in 1990 cost $1,255 a year. The average premium was $1,808 for someone at age seventy, $2,879 at seventy-five and $3,860 at age seventy-nine. People eighty and older are ineligible for this type of insurance (reported in *Denver Post,* 1990).

Between 4 and 5 percent of people age sixty-five and over are confined to nursing homes and other extended-care facilities.

Problems of the Institutionalized Elderly

In 1990 about 1.3 million patients resided in 15,000 nursing homes. The data indicate that at any one time between 4 and 5 percent of people age sixty-five and over are confined to nursing homes and other extended-care facilities. This low figure is misleading, however. It does not mean that only 4 to 5 percent of the aged ever will be confined to a nursing home. At age sixty-five a person may have no need for such a facility, but at eighty-five it may be a necessity.

The residents of nursing homes are typically over seventy-five-years old (81 percent), female (74 percent), White (93 percent), and widowed (69 percent) (Curran and Renzetti, 1987:268). Conspicuously absent are racial minorities, as Curran and Renzetti note:

> The general absence of minorities in nursing homes is the result of several factors. First, nonwhites are concentrated in areas of the country—the Southern states, for example—which have low overall institutionalized rates. Additional evidence indicates that elderly minorities are the victims of racial discrimination in nursing home admissions. Blacks and other minorities tend to be channeled into other types of institutions, such as state mental hospitals, or they are admitted to nursing homes that have low quality-of-care ratings. (Curran and Renzetti, 1987:268)

The economically advantaged elderly are less likely than their less wealthy age cohorts to be institutionalized, and if institutionalized, they are apt to be found in private nursing homes and to receive better care. Kosberg compared the nursing homes for private residents with those for welfare recipients and found the former decidedly superior in staffing, freedom, pleasantness of surroundings, cleanliness, patient communication, and meals. Kosberg found homes for the affluent old tend to provide **therapeutic care** (the approach that focuses on meeting the needs of patients) and treatment, whereas homes housing welfare recipients tend to receive **custodial care,** (the approach in a health facility that focuses on meeting the needs of the institution, rather than those of the patients). This distinction is an important attitudinal difference; custodial "patients are conceived of in stereotyped terms as categorically different from 'normal' people, as totally irrational, insensitive to others, unpredictable, and dangerous. . . . Custodialism is saturated with pessimism, impersonalness, and watchful mistrust" (Kosberg, 1976:427–428). This finding has implications for the federal law that states that patients must use all of their savings before receiving Medicaid. Because nursing-home care costs about $25,000 a year, long-term care results in many patients' spending themselves into poverty. Does this also result in a change from therapeutic care to custodial care? Previous research indicates that it does.

There are two extreme points of view concerning the functions of nursing homes. One view is that such homes are necessary places for the elderly who need extensive health care. Obviously, such facilities are needed for people suffering from Alzheimer's disease or for people paralyzed from strokes.

The opposing view sees nursing homes as dumping grounds or repositories for getting rid of people who represent what we do not want to be or see. As Henslin has said, nursing homes

> are the places in which we lock up our old and sick. We put them out of sight and out of mind. Just as we do with our prisoners, we do with the unfortunate old—but we call their prisons nursing homes, instead of jails. In our nursing homes, we deposit those on the journey of no return—those who have not broken the law, but who carry a stigma so great that others feel they might catch it if they get too close to those who have it. (Henslin, 1976b:150)

Whatever one's views on these institutions, one fact is pertinent: although many nursing homes provide good environments for their patients, there are serious problems in others (see the Observation on Nursing Home abuses). The problem is that there are no federal standards that nursing homes must meet for the health and safety of their patients. The standards are left to the individual states, and they vary in their standards and rigor in enforcing them.

Some examples of the problems in some states from a 1990 federal report:

- In Michigan, 33 percent of skilled nursing homes, which care for the frailest patients, did not serve patients' bathroom needs. Nationally, 18 percent did not meet federal standards.
- In New Jersey, 60 percent of skilled homes did not follow doctors' orders on drugs. Nationally, 24 percent flunked that test.
- In Washington state, 67 percent did not provide adequate personal hygiene or encouragement of patients to care for themselves. Nationally, 26 percent failed.
- In Alabama, 62 percent failed to handle food under sanitary conditions. Nationally, 36 percent did not make the grade.

■ Across the USA, 21 percent of skilled homes did not follow appropriate procedures to prevent the spread of infection; 12 percent did not treat bedsores properly, and 15 percent did not provide patients with privacy during treatment or
personal care. (cited in *USA Today,* 1990b:10A)

Common problems in nursing homes with a custodial style are the overuse
and misuse of drugs. Drugs can be used for a host of therapeutic reasons, but one
common use is not healthful—drugging an individual to control behavior. The use
of tranquilizers, for example, keeps people from complaining and from asking for
service. This procedure minimizes disturbances, thereby requiring fewer personnel, and so increasing profits. Of course, the quality of life for the patients is diminished and even their lives may be broken.

> The scenario is all too familiar. An elderly woman goes into a nursing home suf-
> fering from a broken hip, but is otherwise alert and continent. A few months
> later, she is depressed, drooling, incontinent, unable to remember things or fol-
> low simple conversation. When her children ask what happened, they discover
> their mother has been placed on psychoactive drugs. They ask why and are told
> that she was "agitated." She withdraws still further and spends her remaining
> months of life effectively warehoused, an empty, broken shell of a person.
> (Beck, 1990:77)

The nursing home business is big business. Two factors make the profit
potential especially great: (1) the elderly population is growing at a 2 percent
annual rate, and (2) the government pays for much of the care. One consequence
of these factors is the proliferation of private nursing homes (about 75 percent are
private) organized to generate profits. Many of these facilities provide excellent
care for their patients, but others have shown that their interest in profit exceeds
their interest in clients.

Not all nursing homes are unnecessary, and not all owners and personnel are
greedy and uncaring. Many older people benefit from a sheltered environment,
and doubtless many thousands of the 15,000 nursing homes in the United States
are patient-oriented and provide adequate—perhaps even superior—services to
their clients. But we must also acknowledge that there are widespread abuses in
U.S. nursing homes.

What is the effect of institutionalization on the patients? Obviously, it will vary
according to the facilities and treatment philosophy of a particular nursing home.
But all institutions (including prisons, mental hospitals, and nursing homes) must
be wary of depersonalizing individual clients. In the name of efficiency, people eat
the same food at the same time, wear the same type of clothing, perform the same
chores in the prescribed manner, watch the movies provided them, and live in
rooms with identical dimensions and decor. The widespread use of tranquilizers
compounds this depersonalization. The result is that docility and similarity
abound, which makes management happy but obviously overlooks the individual
needs of the elderly patients. Hendricks and Hendricks have summarized the
problem:

> As a consequence of what is sometimes referred to as *psychological railroading*
> within highly routinized environments, some older residents are prone to a kind
> of *institutional neurosis.* Chief among its symptoms is a gradual erosion of the
> uniqueness of one's personality traits so that residents become increasingly

OBSERVATION

NURSING HOME ABUSES

An investigation into the deaths of two Pennsylvania nursing home residents has led to charges of involuntary manslaughter against four officials at two West Philadelphia nursing homes.

"We allege that each of the victims died from massive and infected bed sores that resulted from criminally negligent and grossly incompetent care," says Pennsylvania Attorney General Ernie Preate. "The victims were in these nursing homes because they required skilled care," he explains. "Instead, they allegedly were neglected, mistreated and forced to suffer greatly prior to their deaths."

Margaret White lived at Care Pavilion nursing home in Philadelphia, from June 1988 until her death on November 29, 1991 at the age of 75. Elizabeth Ellis was admitted to Cobbs Creek nursing home in Philadelphia in August 1986 and died at a Philadelphia hospital on September 1, 1990 at the age of 69.

According to Preate, his office, which routinely investigates Medicaid fraud charges, launched the investigations as a result of complaints he had received about the level of care provided to Medical Assistance recipients at Care Pavilion. Preate says the investigation is continuing, with as many as five additional deaths to be examined.

According to the attorney general, state law holds nursing home administrators responsible for enforcing state regulations pertaining to the health care and safety of patients and for the protection of patients' personal and property rights. The law also makes the director of nursing responsible for the activities of the nursing services staff. The charges allege that while the nursing home employees in question were aware of White's and Ellis' conditions, they failed to act to ensure that the women received adequate care at their respective facilities.

The attorney general says his office also filed criminal charges, including counts of involuntary manslaughter, against GMS Management of Philadelphia, alleging that the corporation failed to discharge its duty under the law to provide adequate care for patients. GMS is a subsidiary of Geriatric and Medical Centers, Inc., which operates the nursing homes under a contract with Resource Housing of America in Atlanta, the owner of the homes, according to state officials.

"The grand jury found that GMS Management's alleged failure to correct continuing deficiencies in management and staffing of the homes contributed to the deaths and constituted criminal behavior," Preate says. In a statement, GMS counters that it "strongly denies these allegations and is confident it will prevail when all of the facts are presented."

The attorney general's charges against GMS Management include a count of Medicare fraud, based on the nursing homes' alleged failure to provide White and Ellis minimal accepted levels of care required by state law. According to Preate, because both White and Ellis were Medical Assistance recip-

---

dependent on staff direction for even the most mundane needs. Visitors often complain about the sense of distance between themselves and the resident or the latter's seeming lack of attendance to events outside the institution. It isn't necessarily that personnel in the institution are insensitive to the older person's plight; rather, that the operational procedures themselves bred a kind of docility leading in turn to a leveling of character attributes. (Hendricks and Hendricks, 1977:284–285)

Noninstitutionalized Care of the Elderly by Their Children　Two demographic trends mentioned earlier in this chapter—the decline in fertility and an increased life expectancy—impact the patterns of taking care of the elderly by family members (the following is from Bengtson, Rosenthal, and

ients, the homes billed the state Medicaid program for the care the women received.

The complaints note that the grand jury reviewed reports about White and Ellis from health care experts, including Dolores M. Alford, a gerontic nurse consultant. Alford's report states that her review of White's records "tells the story of a frail woman who went to Care Pavillon because she was in need of care and compassion. That she did not get. She was sorely abused physically and mentally by a most incompetent and uncaring staff, who willfully and wantonly destroyed her body. Mrs. White had to die to get some relief."

Alford's report on Ellis states that the staff at Cobbs Creek "willfully and callously disregarded the basic needs of a human being for food, water, and personal care." Alford concludes that the staff at Cobbs Creek "made her [Ellis] into a living cadaver. This staff did not afford her the dignity of a humane life."

At a news conference, Preate said that, "one sore was so deep it penetrated the victim's internal organs and her bowels drained out of her hip." Medical experts told the grand jury that bed sores—technically known as decubitis ulcers—result from the failure of the nursing care providers to reposition bedridden patients regularly and from inadequate food and water. Such sores can be prevented, and, when they do develop, can be cured, by proper medical treatment, the experts testified.

White and Ellis also developed other health problems while at their respective nursing homes, according to the charges. Ellis, for example, developed severe contractures of her limbs. According to an affidavit of probable cause filed with the complaints, "her arms and legs were contracted up into her body. Her left arm was twisted and contorted in a fashion such that her hand was pressing into her armpit. The flesh at her left wrist was ruptured open and the bone was protruding."

Janet Wells, editor of Quality Care Advocate, a publication of the Washington, D.C.-based National Citizens Coalition for Nursing Home Reform, says that the deaths of White and Ellis are part of "a repeated pattern of deficiencies" in nursing home care in the United States. She contends that poor conditions in U.S. nursing homes are due in part to the failure of the federal government to enforce federal standards for care in nursing homes. According to Wells, since the Nursing Home Reform Act was passed in 1987, no federal enforcement regulations have been implemented to guaranteed humane care to nursing home residents.

Source: Russell Mokhiber, "Nursing Home Abuses," *Multinational Monitor* 13 (October 1992), p. 6. Reprinted with permission from Multinational Monitor, P.O. Box 19405, Washington DC 20036. Individual subscription $25/yr.

Burton, 1990; and Bengtson, Marti, and Roberts, 1991). First, multigeneration kinship patterns unlike anything existing earlier have emerged. There is what is known as the **beanpole family structure,** where the number of living generations within lineages increases, but there is an intragenerational contraction in the number of members within each generation.

In the decades to come, individuals will grow older having more vertical than horizontal linkages in the family. For example, vertically, a four-generation family structure has three tiers of parent-child relationships, two sets of grandparent-grandchild ties, and one great-grandparent–great-grandchild linkage. Within generations of this same family, horizontally, aging individuals will have fewer brothers and sisters. In addition, at the level of extended kin, family

The trend is for larger numbers of the young-old (those around 65) to care for their old-old parents (those 85 and older).

members will have fewer cousins, aunts, uncles, nieces, and nephews. (Bengtson, Rosenthal, and Burton, 1990:264)

Second, family members will spend more time occupying intergenerational family roles than ever before. In other words, we will spend more years both as parents and as children of aging parents than any earlier generation.

Third, there is an increased likelihood that family members will be involved in longer periods of elder-caregiving. At the extreme, this means that the young-old (those around sixty-five) will care for their parents who are old-old (those eighty-five and older).

Finally, because there are fewer siblings in families, the caretaker responsibilities in a particular family will be concentrated in a few (usually daughters or daughters-in-law) rather than shared among many. This is significant, because an estimated 5 million people provide care for elderly family members (Blieszner and Alley, 1990).

Battered Elders

In the 1960s child abuse gained attention as a serious family problem. Then, spouse abuse received focus in the 1970s. Unnoticed until recently, though, has been the problem of the battered elderly. The problem, although certainly not new, has become more of a problem because people are living longer (in 1900 the average life expectancy was fifty years, and now it exceeds seventy-five) and the numbers of elderly are increasing. Thus an ever-larger number of adult children must assume a caretaker role for their own parents. It is in the context of this care-taker role that physical abuse can occur.

We examine the type of elderly abuse that occurs when elderly persons live with their children. The forms that this abuse can take include the following:

- Physical abuse: hitting, slapping, shoving, use of physical restraints, as well as the withholding of personal care, food, medicine, adequate medical attention, and the like.
- Psychological abuse: verbal assaults, threats, fear, and isolation.
- Drug abuse: encouragement by doctors and families to take too many drugs, which serves the families by keeping the elderly manageable.
- Material abuse: the theft or misuse of money and other personal property owned by the elderly.
- Violation of rights: forcing a parent into a nursing home, for instance.

Accurate information on how many elderly persons are subjected to these abusive acts is impossible to obtain. The elderly victims are in a double-bind situation that traps them in an abusive situation in which they feel that they cannot notify the authorities. According to Steinmetz,

> the abuser is providing financial and other resources necessary for the victim's survival. Thus, the [elderly victim recognizes his or her dependency on the] abusing caretaker. These battered parents, whose attacks cover an even wider range of abuse than that perpetrated upon children, often refuse to report the abuse for fear of retaliation, lack of alternative shelter, and the shame and stig-ma of having to admit that they reared such a child. Paralleling the battered wife, these abused old people prefer the known, even when it includes physical abuse, to the unknown, if they seek to leave the situation. (Steinmetz, 1978:55)

Despite these problems with underreporting, some experts have estimated conservatively that one out of every ten elderly persons living with a family mem-ber has been subjected to some form of abuse. The House Committee on Aging's subcommittee on health and long-term care reported in 1990 that an estimated 1.5 million elderly are abused each year, up from 1 million victims annually in 1980 (reported in Associated Press, 1990a).

The problem seems to occur in situations in which the adult child is over-whelmed by the role of taking care of his or her parent(s). The costs (emotional, physical, and financial) can be enormous. Hospital and other medical costs are extremely expensive for the elderly because they are more prone to illness. The obvious additional food and housekeeping costs may be a problem. Furthermore, the timing of the additional financial burdens may be especially difficult because it is likely to coincide with higher expenses for their children (college, wedding, helping them buy their first home).

Parents living with their adult children cause stress and resentment in a num-ber of other ways as well. The household is more crowded, necessitating differ-ent sleeping arrangements and causing overcrowded bathrooms, shortages of hot water, and the like. The caretaking responsibility will likely be assumed by the wife, and she may resent the parents because of the extra work, the intrusion into her privacy, and the excessive demands on her time. Of course, as parents age and disabilities become more pronounced, the care they need can become overwhelming. The wife may be especially hostile to the parents because she is losing the freedom she expected to have once her children were gone—freedom to travel, to go back to school, or to take a job. But with elderly parents to restrain her, she is back to the parental role.

Parents living with an adult child can cause special problems when they have not resolved their problems from an earlier time. The parents may continue to treat their adult child as a child, taking over or trying to take over the decision-making role. Or the hostile feelings generated when the child was an adolescent return to haunt both parties. Clearly, there is tension when the behaviors and values of the adult child do not coincide with those of the elderly parent. They may differ on political issues, religious issues, how the grandchildren should be raised, and what television programs to watch.

The adult child may also resent parents living in his or her home because the adult feels forced into the situation. Perhaps the other children live in different communities, and so the parents, no longer able to live alone, move in with the child living in their community. The hostile feelings increase if the adult child feels that other relatives are not sharing the burden, at least financially.

All of these factors can contribute to interpersonal problems between spouses and between generations. Thus, stresses and tensions are inevitable. For some families the results are actual physical and mental abuse of the elderly. The psychological and social factors related to child and spouse abuse are also pertinent for the abuse of the elderly. One additional catalyst that must be considered is the ageism prevalent in society. Ageism provides an atmosphere in which the elderly are devalued, negatively stereotyped, and discriminated against. To the extent that older people accept these negative definitions of the aged, they may view abusive treatment as deserved or at least unavoidable. Similarly, if their children accept tenets of ageism, they are likely to assume that the elderly deserve their mistreatment.

Responses of the Elderly to the Devalued Role

Being old is a difficult stage in life for individuals. Elderly people are the victims of discrimination. People who were once attractive, active, and powerful may no longer be so. They must live on restricted incomes that become more constricted by inflation. They must face health problems and impending death. Some elderly, especially the poor and those in many nursing homes, live lives of desperation and hopelessness. What are the characteristic coping responses of the elderly to these psychological and social conditions?

After studying the aged for fifteen years, Bernice Neugarten and her associates have found that four major personality types prevail among people age seventy and over; these types are essentially extensions of the middle-age coping patterns. (The following material is adapted from Neugarten, 1980.) The majority of elderly people retain *integrated* personalities. They function well, are intellectually able, and have competent egos. Another category, the *defended,* are achievement-oriented people who continue working hard. They fight the aging process by not giving in to it and by remaining very active. *Passive-dependent* people, in contrast, have essentially given in to the inevitability of aging. They become inactive and depend on others. Finally, a relatively small proportion are the *disinterested* (disorganized) elderly. These people have experienced a deterioration of their thought processes. They may be confused, disoriented, forgetful, childish, and paranoid.

These personality types reflect responses to being old, a devalued status in U.S. society. Being considered old by society and by oneself is a catalyst that provokes the individual to respond in characteristic ways. But—and this is the central point—the elderly are reacting to socially structured inequalities, not to age as such. In a cultural setting in which status increased with age, observers might find different personality types and responses.

Some researchers have argued that senior citizens respond to the aging process by retreating from relationships, organizations, and society (called **disengagement**). This behavior is considered normal and even satisfying for the individual, because withdrawal brings a release from societal pressures to compete and conform. Other researchers have quarreled with disengagement theory, arguing that many elderly people are involved in a wide range of activities.

The majority of the elderly do remain active until health problems curtail their mobility. A striking number of them are becoming more politically active in an attempt to change some of the social conditions especially damaging for them. Faced with common problems, many are joining in a collective effort. Several national organizations are dedicated to political action that will benefit the elderly, including the following: the American Association for Retired Persons (AARP), with 33 million members and growing by 8000 every day (it is the nation's largest special-interest organization); the National Committee to Preserve Social Security and Medicare; the National Council of Senior Citizens; the National Council on Aging (a confederation of some 1400 public and private social welfare agencies); the National Caucus on Black Aged; and the Gerontological Society. Collectively, these organizations have many millions of members. They work through lobbyists, mailing campaigns, advertising, and other processes to improve the lot of the elderly in U.S. society.

Just how effective these organizations are is unknown. But as the elderly continue to increase in numbers, their sphere of influence is likely to increase as well. Because they now account for about 15 percent of the voting public, elderly citizens could be a significant voting bloc if they developed an age consciousness and voted alike. Politicians from states with a high concentration of old people are increasingly aware of their potential voting power, and legislation more sympathetic to the needs of the elderly may be forthcoming. It is probably only a matter of time before the elderly will focus their concerns and become an effective pressure group that demands equity.

One of the more interesting organizations for the elderly is the Gray Panthers. Founded in the early 1970s by Maggie Kuhn, this organization of 70,000 elderly activists seeks to bring together a political coalition of all age groups to fight ageism in society. The Gray Panthers is a militant organization similar in many respects to radical activists' groups of the 1960s. It was organized to redress specific grievances of the elderly, and it uses a variety of protest tactics. Because of these tactics, many elderly people are reluctant to join or support the organization. They prefer to work through prescribed channels. Any student of history knows, however, that almost without exception minority groups remain powerless and discriminated against until they confront the people in power with their own power. Whether the Gray Panthers or some similar organization will gain a broad base of support depends on the willingness of the powerful in society to redress the real and serious grievances of this ever-expanding age category.

Future Prospects

As we approach the end of the twentieth century, the aged will be an ever larger proportion of the population. Will they continue to be neglected? Will the increased costs to government reduce even further the services provided for the elderly?

Demographers can accurately predict the population of the aged for the year 2000 because the projection depends on death rates, not birth rates. By 2000 the number of people sixty-five and over will be about 35 million, an increase of 3.5 million from 1990. Figure 9.4 depicts the population pyramids from 1960 through 2030. These shapes graphically show how the age structure of U.S. society is changing, with the elderly becoming an ever larger proportion of the population.

As the aged population grows in size, societal problems of providing for the needs of the elderly will be heightened. Older people have specialized medical problems that are expensive to treat. They are retired, so they must live on pensions. And the problems of financial support are exacerbated as the nonold become proportionately smaller, creating a "piggyback" problem of too many non-productive people being supported by too few productive workers. As the number of elderly increases, the tax burden on the nonold will be extremely high—or benefits to the aged will decrease dramatically. How will the old react to the increased strain and pressure on the community and institutional social service delivery systems? Will they increase political pressures on the government? But the burdened nonold may also pressure politicians to reduce services to the elderly. One expert has suggested that the gap between the federal government's policy for providing services to older persons and its capacity to implement such a policy will become enormous. This gap is likely to increase political activity and age consciousness among older people.

Because of the current dramatic growth of the elderly age group, the next twenty-five years or so are critical in establishing appropriate policies and adequate funding to supply the necessary services and resources for the aged population. These policies will set the stage for massive growth in about 2010, when the baby-boom generation begins reaching old age. At a minimum, these policies must be directed toward the following concerns:

- *Adequate health care.* Although it will be expensive, a national health care system is necessary for people of all ages to provide greater equity in health delivery to all segments of society. Today's coverage for the elderly pays only half of medical expenses.
- *Adequate pensions.* With 12.4 percent of the elderly in the United States living below the poverty line, the current pension system is clearly inadequate.

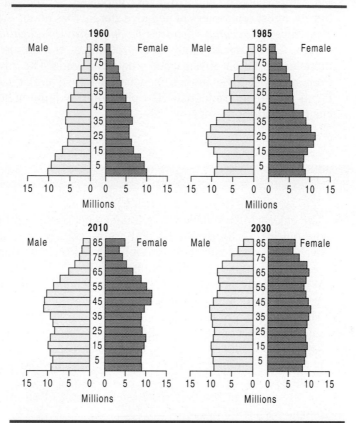

Figure 9.4 Age and sex composition of the U.S. population: 1960, 1985, 2010, and 2030

Source: Beth J. Soldo and Emily M. Agree, "America's Elderly," *Population Bulletin* 43 (September 1988), pp. 10–11.

Social Security is especially unfair to widows and to workers in low-paying jobs or exempt occupations. Somehow, payments must be more equitable and provided with cost-of-living increases to withstand the inroads of inflation. The problem of financing Social Security is extremely difficult. As a beginning, future revisions should eliminate the system's regressive features by accelerating the rates as incomes increase and by raising or getting rid of the ceiling. The entire tax structure needs enormous reform, which if successful could eliminate the loopholes for the well-to-do and divert monies to the elderly and other groups in need of equity. Another possibility is to increase private retirement pension plans to supplement Social Security. Tax-deferred annuity programs are now available to individuals wishing to plan and provide for their retirement.

■ *Flexible retirement.* Retirement should be voluntary for the worker unless he or she is judged incompetent by objective observers. Allowing employees to work beyond age seventy would reduce the financial burden on pension plans. Even more important, the elimination of compulsory retirement would reduce one of the strongest reinforcers of negative stereotypes about the elderly.

■ *Provisions for adequate facilities for the institutionalization of the elderly who require those services.* Many elderly people at some time will need a nursing home to meet their physical and emotional needs. The government must, however, supervise these homes to ensure that the overall quality of life for the residents is more than adequate. The philosophy of nursing homes must shift from custodial care to therapeutic care.

CHAPTER REVIEW

1. The elderly in U.S. society constitute an oppressed minority group. They are the objects of discrimination and are negatively stereotyped; they are relatively powerless; and they have a highly visible trait that makes them different from the majority—an aged body.

2. Who is elderly and who is not is socially defined. Thus, who is considered old varies from society to society.

3. The proportion of the U.S. population age sixty-five and over is growing. In this category women outnumber men, and minorities are underrepresented. Although the elderly as a category are *not* disproportionately poor, the elderly who are women, minorities, and those who live alone *are* disproportionately poor.

4. *Ageism* refers to the systematic stereotyping of and discrimination against people because they are old.

5. The negative stereotypes of the elderly have some serious consequences: (a) they support discrimination, especially in the job market; (b) they cause people to fear aging; (c) they can be self-fulfilling; and (d) they can do physical harm through sociogenic aging.

6. The Social Security program is biased in several ways: (a) some workers are not included; (b) people with low career earnings receive fewer benefits; (c) women (homemakers, divorced, and widowed) are disadvantaged; and (d) the tax is regressive.

7. There are several key role changes, each involving role loss, that occur with being old—retirement, widowhood, and impending death.

8. At any one time only about 5 percent of people age sixty-five and over are confined in nursing homes. These homes have important functions for those needing their services, but abuses are associated with some of these operations: patients are given custodial care, drugged, and provided with inadequate nutrition.

9. As many as 1.5 million elderly people in the United States are abused physically by relatives annually. Most commonly, abuse occurs when the adult child is overwhelmed by the role of taking care of his or her parent(s).

10. The elderly may respond to their devalued status in several characteristic ways. They may withdraw from social relationships; they may continue to act

as they have throughout their adult lives; or they may become politically active to change the laws, customs, and social structures that disadvantage them.

11. The numbers and proportion of the elderly in the U.S. population will increase. This aging population will create a difficult burden for the young, who, through taxes, will be required to finance pension plans and other assistance for the elderly. If the gap between the needs of the elderly and the benefits they receive widens, political activity and age consciousness among older people are likely to increase.

KEY TERMS

Old (social definition).   The arbitrary designation by society of what age divides the old from the nonold.

Baby-boom generation.   The term referring to people born in the fifteen-year period following World War II, when an extraordinary number of babies were born in the United States.

Ageism.   The systematic stereotyping of and discrimination against people because they are old.

Stereotype.   An exaggerated generalization of a category of people that persists regardless of the evidence.

Role.   The behavioral expectations and requirements attached to a position in a social organization.

Therapeutic care.   The approach in a health facility that focuses on meeting the needs of patients.

Custodial care.   The approach in a health facility that focuses on meeting the needs of the institution, resulting in poor quality care for the patients.

"Beanpole family structure."   Where the number of living generations within lineages increases, but there is an intragenerational contraction in the number of members within each generation.

Disengagement.   The response by some people to the aging process of retreating from relationships, organizations, and society.

FOR FURTHER STUDY

Simone de Beauvoir. *The Coming of Age.* New York: Warner Paperback Library, 1973.

Robert H. Binstock and Linda K. George, eds. *Handbook of Aging and the Social Sciences.* San Diego, Calif.: Academic Press, 1990.

Karen A. Conner. *Aging America: Issues Facing an Aging America.* Englewood Cliffs, N.J.: Prentice-Hall, 1992.

Jerry Gerber, Walter Klores, Janet Wolff, and Gene Brown. *Lifetrends: The Future of the Baby Boomers and Other Aging Americans.* New York: Macmillan, 1990.

Richard J. Margolis. *Risking Old Age in America.* Boulder, Colo.: Westview Press, 1990.

Linda G. Martin. "The Graying of Japan." *Population Bulletin* 44 (July 1989): entire issue.

Karl Pillemer and Kathleen McCartney, eds. *Parent-Child Relations throughout Life.* Hillsdale, N.J.: Lawrence Erlbaum Associates, 1991.

Barbara Boyle Torrey, Kevin Kinsella, and Cynthia M. Taeuber. *An Aging World.* International Population Reports Series P–95, No. 78. Washington, D.C.: Bureau of the Census, 1987.

FORUM

DOES THE GOVERNMENT PROVIDE SPECIAL ADVANTAGE TO THE ELDERLY?

We have an excessive sense of entitlement to the elderly, which means that the needy in other social categories receive less than their share.

Richard D. Lamm

Progressivity in taxation—the idea that those who earn more should pay more of the costs of government—is an old idea that has found new vigor.

The Congress, insistent on taxing the rich, has just passed a budget that gives approximately 60 percent of our Federal social spending to just 12 percent of our citizens: Americans over 65. Yet, the elderly have the highest disposable income and the lowest rates of poverty of any group in America. They own one-third of all household assets and 40 percent of all financial assets.

Poverty in America is more likely to wear diapers than a hearing aid. Nevertheless, Congress in 1987 spent $10,010 per capita on the elderly and only $854 per child. We may want to tax the rich, but we also distribute our Federal largesse not on the basis of who needs it but on who has the political power. There's little question that the elderly are the most politically powerful group in America. It's highly questionable whether they are the most deserving.

To be sure, there are many poor Americans over 65, and I'm very proud that my Democratic Party pioneered Social Security and Medicare, which were invaluable in lifting many of the elderly out of poverty. But today there are many retirees receiving overgenerous Federal transfer payments who just don't need them. For example, through Medicare we are paying the health costs of hundreds of thousands of elderly millionaires, while 20 percent of America's kids don't have all their vaccinations and 600,000 American women give birth every year without adequate or any prenatal care. We have recently amended Medicare to pay for heart transplants, yet 31 million Americans go without health insurance. We have a life expectancy rate of 80 years, the highest in the world, yet we rank 18th in infant mortality.

Even programs designed specifically for the poor are being slanted toward the elderly. Medicaid, a program aimed originally at poor women and children, today devotes 27.6 percent of its funds to long-term care for the elderly. While this money does go toward the poor elderly, it is nevertheless symbolic of how our limited resources are being taken away from the majority of the population. Public policy should transfer money from the rich to the poor, not from the young to the old.

We have created an excessive sense of entitlement in the elderly, and they are vociferous in defending and enlarging their benefits. Our political establishment, supposedly trained to meet new needs with new spending, finds it impossible to reallocate existing spending. But there is not enough new wealth being created to solve all our new challenges. New needs, to some degree, will have to come from reallocated resources.

In short, we cannot make fiscal sense of our future without eventually taking on entitlements for the elderly. Moreover, if we are to leave a sustainable nation for our children, we have to spend more money on the next generation and less money on the last one. It is not good public policy to transfer federal monies to the millionaire elderly while less than 30 percent of our children in need have access to Headstart programs.

If we are going to initiate a luxury tax, why don't we further tax Social Security and Medicare for those seniors who are in the high income brackets? If we are going to tax the rich, we should at the very least have the backbone to look at "progressivity" on the spending side of government.

The elderly are blamed unfairly for a number of social ills for doing precisely what they have been asked to do by their employers and their government.

Robert C. Atchley

The infamous March 28, 1988, cover of *The New Republic* showed a cartoon phalanx of older people with golf clubs and gardening trowels menacingly bearing down upon the viewer. The caption above the drawing read "Greedy Geezers." Inside was a four-page article by contributing editor Henry Fairlie, who depicted retired people as a selfish lot who are threatening the economic security of today's younger generations by their callous efforts to secure ever-increasing public benefits. Fairlie is not alone in this assessment. Since the early 1980s, numerous articles have appeared in the popular press and in professional journals asserting that the cost of pensions and health care for the retired is an intolerable drain on national resources and that older people owe it to younger generations not to demand so much. In my opinion, this recent flurry of "retiree bashing" misrepresents the economic situation and demands of retirees, uses retired people as scapegoats for a wide variety of social ills that are in fact caused by shifting economic circumstances and political philosophies, and castigates retirees for doing precisely what they have been asked to do by their employers and their government.

Research indicates that retirees are neither selfish nor particularly demanding. Only a very small minority of retirees are affluent people who "still have the first nickel they ever made" and who aggressively pursue every additional nickel they see an opportunity to acquire. About 60 percent of retired Americans feel that they are financially okay now and are not pressing for increases in Social Security or Medicare. In large part these people are economically okay because they have paid off their homes and they deferred wages in the past to pay for pensions to supplement their Social Security. They rightly feel vulnerable should they need long-term care, which is not currently covered by Medicare except in a small minority of cases, and, like most of us, they resist taking cuts in income. A large

minority, perhaps 35 percent of retirees, cannot secure adequate food, clothing, shelter, and health care with the retirement incomes they currently have. Most retirees with inadequate retirement incomes were employed steadily from entry into the labor force until retirement and seem justified in refusing to quietly acquiesce to a life of poverty.

A second theme of retiree bashing is that the delivery of lavish Social Security retirement benefits is responsible for a wide variety of current economic ills, including the rising national debt and poverty among children. These charges have no basis in fact.

In the first place, Social Security retirement benefits are hardly lavish. The average Social Security retirement benefit was only $5,870 in 1987. Only a small proportion of retired couples have Social Security pensions that replace above 65 percent of preretirement earnings. Social Security earnings replacement rates for retired individuals average under 40 percent. Those with truly high retirement incomes get most of their income from sources other than Social Security—sources such as income from assets or employer pensions.

In the second place, Social Security is paying its own way. It has not added one dime to the national debt. In fact, the surplus currently being amassed to fund retirement benefits for the baby boomers represents a large pool of funds that can only be lent to the federal government, thus reducing government competition with private borrowers for private investment capital. The real cause of the massive national debt run up during the Reagan administration was its policy of cutting taxes and increasing defense spending. In his book, *Came the Revolution,* Daniel Patrick Moynihan contends that the Reagan administration intentionally ran up huge deficits in order to produce fiscal pressures which could then be used as justification for scaling back social programs, including Social Security. In this context, retiree bashing can be seen as part of a conservative rhetoric designed to undermine the legitimacy of Social Security.

Retirees have also been blamed for inadequate funding of education and a growing proportion of American children living in poverty. In fact, the dismal situation for young Americans, mostly those in minority groups, is the result of an administration philosophy that poverty and education are local problems that are not the business of national government. Congress did not override President Reagan on his cutbacks either in programs designed to aid the poor or in education. Retirees did not create these policies. They were created by a President and Congress elected by American voters. Retirees are simply scapegoats for consequences of our own voting behavior that some of us would rather not acknowledge.

Retiree bashing seems all the more unjust because most retirees are simply being good citizens and following the life-course program laid out for them many years ago. Since the 1950s, retirement at or near age 65 has been expected of older Americans, and with every passing year a growing proportion are meeting that expectation. For much of their working lives, today's retired people were told that retirement at 65 was not just available, it was expected. Many private pension plans required retirement around age 65. Social Security provisions contained economic disincentives for employees to remain on the job past age 65. In the national press the virtues of an independent life in retirement were extolled and the need to make way for younger workers was stressed. By the early 1960s a large majority of Americans had internalized the notion that retirement was both needed by society to curb unemployment among youth and desirable for the aging individual as a reward, in the form of freedom and autonomy, for lengthy service in the labor force. Now retired people are being told repeatedly in the media that they are being selfish and inconsiderate for doing what was expected of them and for asking that their government keep its end of the Social Security bargain.

Source: Robert C. Atchley, "Retiree Bashing: No Good Deed Goes Unpunished," *Generations* 13 (Spring 1989), pp. 21–22. Reprinted with permission from *Generations,* 833 Market St., Suite 512, San Francisco CA 94103. Copyright 1986 ASA.

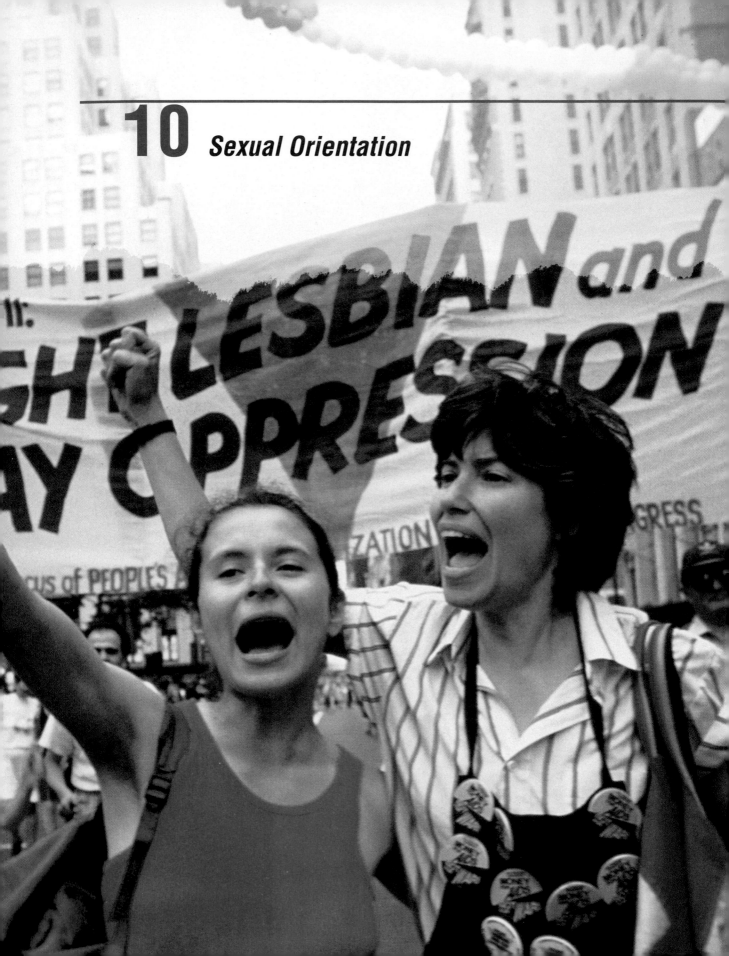

10 *Sexual Orientation*

The previous four chapters examined four categories of people designated as minorities in society because of their impoverishment, race/ethnicity, gender, or age. The members of these social categories suffer from powerlessness, negative stereotypes, and discrimination. This chapter looks at another type of minority group. Unlike the other four minorities, which are disadvantaged because of economic circumstances or ascribed characteristics, the minority group examined in this chapter—homosexuals—is the object of discrimination because it is defined by the majority as different and, therefore, deviant. It is important to underscore a crucial point—*homosexuality is not inherently deviant but it is defined and labeled as deviant.*

The chapter is divided into four sections. The first section examines the concept of deviance and its implications. The next section presents what is known about homosexuals. The third section describes the various forms of discrimination faced by gay men and lesbian women in the United States. The final section describes the coping strategies of gays and their political activities aimed at changing the societal structures unfair to them.

Social Deviance

Most of us conform to the norms of society most of the time. Similarly, most of us on occasion violate minor social norms, and these violations are usually tolerated or even ignored. An occasional breech of etiquette, participation in a riotous celebration after an important sports victory, or loud chatter in a theater, may bring some minor social disapproval to the violators but no serious punishment. The social deviance that most interests sociologists concerns offenses that are seriously disapproved of by many people and therefore evoke serious social consequences for the violators. The following discussion examines some important principles that help us understand social deviance in general and a sexual orientation that is defined as deviant in particular.

Because **deviance** is behavior that does not conform to social expectations, *it is socially created* (Becker, 1963:8–9). Societies create right and wrong by originating norms and saying that failure to follow the rules constitutes deviance. Whether an act is deviant depends on how other people react to it. As Kai Erikson has put it; "Deviance is not a property *inherent* in any particular kind of behavior; it is a property *conferred upon* that behavior by the people who come into direct or indirect contact with it" (Erikson, 1966:6).

Even though sexuality has a biological base, it is also a social construction. Society impinges on this intensely private form of intimacy to shape our ideas about what is erotic, to define what is taboo, and to determine who are appropriate sexual partners. The social context of parents, peers, community, church, school, media, and government thus condition, constrain, and socially define sexual behavior (Ross and Rapp, 1983:53). In contemporary U.S. society **heterosexuality** (opposite-sex eroticism) is the expected—actually, demanded—sexual orientation. In fact, most people in the United States believe that **homosexuality** (sexual preference for someone of the same sex) or **bisexuality** (attraction to both sexes) is evidence of moral weakness or pathology. Thus, society has *created* homosexuality as deviance.

Because deviance is not a property inherent in any particular kind of behavior, *deviance is a relative, not an absolute, notion.* Evidence for its relativeness is found in the wide variation of definitions of deviance from society to society and from one historical period to another. Homosexuality is deviant in the United States, but is not a universally deviant form of sexuality. One anthropological study of 190 societies found that two-thirds of them accept homosexuality for certain individuals or for specific occasions. Among the 225 Native American tribes, more than half accepted male homosexuality and 17 percent accepted female homosexuality (Pomeroy, 1965). In ancient Greece homosexual relationships between men were considered the supreme intellectual and spiritual expression of love (Crooks and Baur, 1987:310). Men in ancient Greece and Rome were regarded as naturally bisexual, as Lawrence Stone notes:

> No distinction was made between the love of boys and the love of women. This was simply a question of taste, about as significant as preferring coffee or tea for breakfast. The crucial distinction in law and morality was between those who took the active roles and those who took the passive roles—the penetrators as opposed to the penetrated. This concept effectively degraded submissive boys, women, and slaves of both sexes, and elevated active men, regardless of their gender preference. (Stone, 1985:27)

Stone, in his review essay of twenty-six books and articles on the history of sexuality in Western civilization, concluded:

> What is absolutely certain . . . is that over the long history of Western civilization, there has been no such thing as "normal sexuality." Sexuality is a cultural artifact that has undergone constant and sometimes dramatic changes over time, and there is every reason to suppose that there are still more surprising transformations in store for us in the not too distant future. (Stone, 1985:37)

Erikson has summarized the relative nature of the concept of deviance:

> Definitions of deviance vary widely as we range over the various classes found in a single society or across the various cultures into which mankind is divided, and it soon becomes apparent that there are no objective properties which all deviant acts can be said to share in common—even within the confines of a given group. *Behavior which qualifies one man for prison may qualify another for sainthood, since the quality of the act itself depends so much on the circumstances under which it was performed and the temper of the audience which witnessed it.* [Italics added.] (Erikson, 1966:5–6)

An important insight is that deviance is an integral part of all societies. According to Emile Durkheim, deviant behavior actually has positive consequences for society because it gives the nondeviants a sense of solidarity. By punishing the deviant, the group expresses its collective indignation and reaffirms its commitment to the rules. Durkheim explains:

> We have only to notice what happens, particularly in a small town, when some moral scandal has just been committed. They stop each other on the street, they

visit each other, they seek to come together to talk of the event and to wax indignant in common. From all the similar expressions which are exchanged, for all the temper that gets itself expressed, there emerges a unique temper . . . which is everybody's without being anybody's in particular. That is the public temper. (Durkheim, 1960:102)

Thus, when individuals in an organization condemn a homosexual colleague, they are reaffirming that their sexuality—heterosexuality—is the only legitimate option. The negative sanctions applied to the deviant (gossip, avoidance, exclusion) serve to enforce conformity in the group by restraining other people from deviating.

Whoever holds the power determines who or what is deviant. Power is a crucial element in deciding who or what is deviant. Certain social groups have relatively greater power and resources than others in getting their definitions of deviance to prevail. The major religious bodies in the United States, for example, have taken a strong position against homosexuality, and their opposition has influenced the laws and community norms. And occasionally, even deviants can mobilize power to change a discriminatory situation. As we discuss later in this chapter, homosexual activists were able to mobilize enough political power to persuade the psychiatric community no longer to consider homosexuality as a mental disorder.

The status of a person is an identification. An individual has many statuses—male, student, adolescent, sociology major, Hispanic, athlete, son, and brother. When one status dominates the others in an interaction, it is called a **master status.** The status that defines one as a minority (race/ethnicity, gender, age, deviance) tends to be a master status because it is the one that determines how you are evaluated and treated by other people. As Edwin Schur has said, "Sex is one of the several 'master status-determining traits.' Sexual orientation goes to the very heart of social and personal identity" (Schur, 1965:98). A male physician, for example, who is known to be gay will find that his status of gay male supersedes his other statuses in the eyes and behaviors of other people in straight society.

This discussion leads to a final insight about deviance—that violators of important social norms are **stigmatized.** That is, deviants not only differ from so-called normals in behavior but also are set apart by being socially disgraced. The society—through the church, medical community, and the law—stigmatizes gays as sick, sinful, criminal, and despicable (Humphreys, 1972). In the community they are pejoratively labeled as "queers," "fags," and "fairies." This societal/community reaction to gays has several consequences for them that are considered later in this chapter. The extremely negative reaction to gays may keep many of them invisible, will drive those open about their sexuality into gay ghettos, and may cause extreme personal distress. In the latter instance, gays experiencing the disgust that so-called "normals" have toward them may accept society's negative label and consider themselves as sinners, criminals, and sick—and therefore in need of help. The opposite may also occur: persons labeled as outsiders may reject the dominant rules and regard those who judge them so harshly and unfairly as the problem.

The Gay and Lesbian Community: An Overview

An immediate issue is whether homosexuality has genetic or social origins. There is a growing scientific literature that provides evidence for a biological basis for homosexuality (LeVay 1991; for summaries, see Burr 1993; Gelman 1992; Gorman 1991a; Angier 1991). If biology is destiny and homosexuality is genetic, then it is natural rather than an aberration that results from choice or seduction. Such a finding has profound implications:

> Many gay men said they welcome proof that might convince mainstream, straight society of what they themselves have always believed: that their sexuality is profoundly inscribed in their being, and is not a perversion brought on by willful disregard of social norms, a sordid upbringing or too much time spent playing with dolls. Above all, they say, it is certainly not a condition they can be cured of or cajoled out of, any more than devout heterosexuals can be persuaded to change their erotic ways. (Angier, 1991:El)

The scientific evidence, however, so far is inconclusive. Some researchers are convinced that an area of the brain, the hypothalamus, is responsible. Others find that the size of the anterior commissure of the brain makes the difference. Other researchers remain unconvinced, given the complexity of biology and environmental factors on individual behavior. This ambiguity is expressed by John D'Emilio, a historian of sexuality:

> There's a tremendous amount of evidence in history and cross-cultural studies to suggest that human sexual behavior and desire are enormously malleable, not just from culture to culture or from time period to time period, but in an individual's life. I'm not willing to say that there isn't a biological component, but there's too much else we haven't explored (quoted in Wheeler 1992:A9)

Whatever its origins, homosexuality is defined by many people as deviant, and because of this homosexuals are the objects of discrimination.

The numbers of gay men and lesbian women are unknown and probably unknowable because many never reveal their sexual orientation, living lives that appear heterosexually oriented. There are also problems of definition, as Hess, Markson, and Stein note:

> Is homosexuality to be defined strictly in terms of behavior, or is self-definition the key? Many people who are attracted to persons of their own sex do not act on these feelings. Conversely, many people who have had homosexual relations continue to define themselves as basically heterosexual. (Hess, Markson, and Stein, 1988:306)

The common estimates by researchers range from 4 to 10 percent of adults in the United States are exclusively or substantially homosexual. (The following discussion is adapted from Baca Zinn and Eitzen, 1990:409–441). These people constitute a sizable minority, from 10 to 20 million. There have been several major studies on homosexuals by social scientists. Pioneering research by Alfred Kinsey and his associates—first on men, in 1948, and then on women, in 1953—made it clear that homosexuality was much more common than anyone had suspected. Since then, several scientists have been interested in studying gay life-styles (e.g., Bell and

Weinberg, 1978; Peplau, 1981; Harry, 1983). Their conclusions about sexual relationships point to a number of similarities and differences between homosexuals and heterosexuals and between gay men and lesbian women, some of which contradict the prevailing stereotypes. Alan Bell and Martin Weinberg (1978) studied 979 Black and White, male and female homosexuals. On the basis of interviews and questionnaires, they formulated five categories of homosexuals:

1. *Closed couples.* These homosexual couples were "closely bound together" and looked to each other rather than to outsiders for sexual and interpersonal satisfaction. They described themselves as "happily married."
2. *Open couples.* These couples were living with a special sexual partner but "not happy with their circumstances" and tended to seek satisfaction with people outside their partnership.
3. *Functionals.* These men and women tended to organize their lives around their sexual experiences. They engaged in a wide variety of sexual activity.
4. *Dysfunctionals.* This group conformed to the stereotype of the "tormented homosexual." They reported many problems due to their homosexual orientation.
5. *Asexuals.* These women and men were lonely, less overt about their sexual orientation, and had few friends.

Gays are similar to heterosexuals in their desire for an intimate relationship with one special person. Because homosexuals are denied marriage by law, homosexual couples must turn to cohabitation relationships. Approximately three-fourths of lesbian couples live together, compared with somewhat more than half of all gay male couples (Harry, 1983:225). Blumstein and Schwartz (1983) found that lesbian couples and gay male couples faced many of the same issues confronting heterosexual couples who live together, married or not. They must work out issues related to the division of household labor, power and authority, and emotional obligations.

Homosexual couples also face additional problems. Because of the general antipathy toward homosexuality in U.S. society, gay men and lesbian women are not encouraged to be open about their sexual preferences and their relationships. Hence, they may feel restricted in showing public affection toward their lover. They are seldom extended such commonplace courtesies as having a partner invited to an office party or to a retirement banquet. Even heterosexuals who might like to welcome a gay friend's partner may not know how to go about doing so. Blumstein and Schwartz contend that the "couple" status of homosexuals is always in jeopardy:

> The problem with gay male culture is that much of it is organized around singlehood or maintaining one's sexual marketability. Meeting places like bars and baths promote casual sex rather than couple activities. The problem with the lesbian world is quite different. Women are often in tight-knit friendship groups where friends and acquaintances spend so much intimate time together that, it seems to us, opportunities arise for respect and companionship to turn into love and a meaningful affair. (Blumstein and Schwartz, 1983:322–323)

Gender is important in defining homosexual relationships. According to Letitia Peplau, the fact of being a man or a woman often exerts greater influence on relationships than does sexual orientation. Gay men in Peplau's study (1981) were much more likely than lesbians to have sex with someone other than their steady partners. This issue of sexual exclusivity is often a major source of tension in male homosexual relationships. Charles Silverstein has suggested that "at some point in the life of every gay couple, the monogamy battle will be fought" (Silverstein, 1981:140). The tendency for gay men to be less sexually exclusive than lesbian women parallels the difference in heterosexual males and females. And this difference is related to gender role socialization in society where "males are socialized to engage in sexual behaviors both with and without affection while women are expected to combine the two" (Harry, 1983:226).

In a major departure from the heterosexual pattern, homosexual couples tend to be egalitarian. Heterosexual couples, whether in cohabitation or marriage relationships, tend to accept the traditional gender roles for men and women. In contrast, homosexual couples are much more likely to share in the decision making and in all of the household duties. There are three likely reasons for this difference from the heterosexual pattern. One is the conscious effort by homosexuals to reject the dominant marriage model that prescribes specific and unequal roles. Another reason is that in same-sex relationships the partners have received the same gender role socialization. Another source of equality in gay relationships is that there tends to be little income difference between the partners, a condition rare in heterosexual relationships. Most homosexual couples are dual-income units. And because both partners in a homosexual relationship are of the same sex, they are subject to the same degree of sex discrimination in jobs and income (Harry, 1983:219).

An important implication of the equality found in homosexual relationships is that, contrary to the stereotype, the partners do not take the role of either "husband" or "wife." The prevailing assumption is that one takes the masculine role and is dominant in sexual activities and decision making while the other does the "feminine" household tasks and is submissive to the first. Research consistently refutes this so-called butch/femme notion, noting that only a small minority of couples reflect the stereotype. Those relatively few couples who conform to the stereotype generally are composed of individuals who are older, from lower socioeconomic levels, newcomers to the homosexual community, and male (Bell and Weinberg, 1978; Peplau, 1981).

A final stereotype about gays and lesbians is that their homosexuality is a master status *for them.* That is, there is the widespread belief that being homosexual is such a powerful identity that it overrides every other aspect of a person. But according to Hess, Markson, and Stein,

> this is not necessarily the case. Just as heterosexuality does not obsess most men and women, coloring their every thought and act, the homosexual's choice of sex partner is only one part of a complex social person. The problems of daily life—work, leisure, comfort and safety, companionship, death, and taxes—beset the gay as well as the straight, and in many ways, they are harder for the homosexual to resolve because of discrimination and stigmatization. (Hess, Markson, and Stein, 1988:308)

Discrimination

Variance from the societal norm of heterosexuality is not a social problem; *the societal response to it is.* Society has defined what is appropriate sexual behavior and orientation. Consequently, people who differ from the approved orientation are objects of derision and contempt by members of society and are discriminated against by individuals and by the normal way that the institutions of society operate. In short, their different sexual orientation makes homosexuals a minority group.

Gays confront three types of oppression: (1) ideological, in which their behaviors are defined and stigmatized as immoral; (2) legal, where their activities are defined as illegal or they are treated unfairly by the courts and other agents of control; and (3) occupational, where jobs, advancement, and income are restricted or denied. This section examines each of these manifestations of institutional discrimination that homosexuals experience.

Ideological Oppression

There is a long tradition of fear and hatred of homosexuality in Western society, termed **homophobia.** Gays are considered by the majority as outsiders. Homosexuals are targets of ridicule, restricted from social interaction, and stigmatized. Public opinion polls show the intolerance toward gays that is common in society. For example, a 1992 *Newsweek* poll found that only 41 percent of people in the United States believed that homosexuality is an acceptable alternative lifestyle. Moreover, only 35 percent approved of legally sanctioned gay marriages (Turque, 1992:36–37). Certain categories of persons are especially intolerant of gays: the poor, Blacks, people over age fifty, and non-high school graduates.

For many people, the homosexual individual is an outcast. Gays are seen as an aberration, perhaps even a dangerous deviation, from so-called normal sexuality. Because people believe that gays are immoral, they belittle their life-style, tell jokes about "queers," deny their rights to housing, jobs, and memberships in organizations, and even engage in hostile acts (verbal and physical assaults) such as gay bashing by adolescent males. These homophobic attitudes and behaviors cause many homosexuals to have personal problems with self-concept and other adjustment problems. As Long and Sulton have argued; "We wish to suggest that many of the problems of adjustment that may be experienced by some homosexuals do not result directly from being homosexual, but are created by the way society views homosexuality" (Long and Sulton, 1987:227). The way that society views homosexuality is shaped significantly by our religious heritage and the views of the medical community.

Religion. The Judeo-Christian tradition considers homosexual behavior a heinous sin. The Old Testament approves of sexual intercourse only within marriage and for the purpose of procreation. Homosexuality has, therefore, been expressly forbidden. Crooks and Baur comment:

> Many religious scholars believe that the condemnation of homosexuality stems from a reformation movement beginning in the seventh century B.C., through

which Jewish religious leaders wanted to develop a distinct, closed community that was different from others of the time. Homosexual activities were a part of the religious services of many groups of people, including the Jewish people, in that era. Rejecting religious rituals involving homosexual activities that had previously been considered sacred was one way of establishing the uniqueness of a religion. Homosexual behaviors were then condemned as a form of pagan worship. Strong prohibitive biblical scriptures were written: "You shall not lie with a man as one lies with a female, it is an abomination" (Leviticus 18:22). (Crooks and Baur, 1987:308)

The New Testament continued this tradition. The early Christians strived for human perfection unencumbered by the desires of the flesh—celibate religious leaders, sexual intercourse only within marriage, and condemnation of homosexuality. Speaking of homosexuality, the Apostle Paul, for example, considered lustful behavior between men and between women as "vile passions . . . against nature" (Romans 1:26). Paul in Corinthians also wrote that homosexuals along with fornicators, idolaters, adulterers, and thieves would never inherit the kingdom of God. Summarizing the Judeo-Christian theology condemning nonprocreative sex, Meredith Gould has said:

> The Scriptures are a powerful body of myth, legend, and divine law which have significantly shaped the ideology of Western Civilization. The portion of the code regulating sexuality is firmly entrenched in the assumption, indeed the prescription, that sexual intercourse is for procreation; only through reproduction can sexual activity of any sort be condoned. Consequently, masturbation, cunnilingus, fellatio, and anal intercourse are fundamentally heretical, threatening the natural order established by a stern, moralistic God. Anything other than penis-vagina coitus is condemned as sinful and morally rank according to the Christian church. (Gould, 1979:51–52)

Contemporary Christian churches and denominations have varied in their response to the homosexual issue. Some, perhaps the majority, reject homosexuality and consider it a sin. This position is consistent with Christian history, where for centuries the church ostracized homosexual people and gave its blessing to civil persecutions. The current expression of this position continues the heritage of moral condemnation and punitiveness toward gays. The Reverend Jerry Falwell, fundamentalist preacher and founder of the Moral Majority, for example, called the outbreak of AIDS among homosexuals as a "form of judgment of God upon a society" (cited in Crooks and Baur, 1987:312). A Gallup poll found that 60 percent of the people who were pro-school prayer and antiabortion felt that AIDS was God's punishment for immoral sexual behavior (reported in *Newsweek,* 1988:7).

As an example of the thinking of fundamentalists on homosexuality, Pastor Peter J. Peters asserts, "The truth is, the Bible advocates discrimination against, intolerance of and the death penalty for homosexuals" (Peters, 1992:i).

In 1986 the Vatican's doctrinal congregation issued a directive, approved by Pope John Paul II, to all Roman Catholic bishops around the world. This directive ordered all bishops to withdraw support from any organization that opposed the church's teaching that homosexual behavior is sinful. This meant that gay liberation groups and organizations such as Dignity, which is an explicitly gay organization for Catholics, would no longer be able to meet in Catholic churches or

An opponent of the Gay Rights Bill uses religion to support his strong feelings against homosexuals.

schools (Ostling, 1988). In 1992 the Vatican issued a document that condoned the discrimination against homosexuals in employment, housing, and the adoption of children.

> Sexual orientation does not constitute a quality comparable to race, ethnic background, etc. in respect to non-discrimination. Unlike these, homosexual orientation is an objective disorder. There are areas in which it is not unjust discrimination to take sexual orientation into account, for example, in the placement of children for adoption or foster care, in employment of teachers or athletic coaches and in military recruitment. (quoted in *Rocky Mountain News,* 1992:3)

Many congregations and denominations are more accepting of homosexuality. Some maintain that homosexuality must be condemned but, because of God's grace, homosexuals must not be condemned. Others are even more accepting, ranging from the acceptance of gay Christians as members to the ordination of gays as ministers. The Quakers have adopted a full acceptance of gays:

> One should no more deplore homosexuality than left-handedness. . . .
> Homosexual affection can be as selfless as heterosexual affection, and therefore we cannot see that it is in some way morally worse. (Quoted in Crooks and Baur, 1987:310)

But the full acceptance of homosexuals in churches is relatively rare. Even among the more liberal congregations and denominations division has occurred on such issues as the acceptance of believers of whatever sexual preference, the marriage of gay couples, the ordination of gay ministers, and the formation of explicit homosexual Christian groups (such as Lutherans Concerned, Evangelicals Concerned and Dignity, for Roman Catholics; and Integrity, for Episcopalians).

Even in a relatively liberal denomination like the Methodists, there is not full acceptance of homosexuals. In 1987 a Methodist minister, Rose Mary Denman, revealed that she was a lesbian. In a church trial she was found to have violated church law and was suspended from the ministry (Morris, 1987). The Methodists are split on this issue, and it is hotly debated at each annual conference.

Medicine. The beliefs that people in the United States have about homosexuals has been shaped by religion, as we have seen, and also by the prevailing views of the medical community. Whereas religious ideology tends to view homosexuality as a sin, psychiatric theory, until 1973, considered homosexuality as an illness. As an illness, it could be cured, and many techniques were tried, including prefrontal lobotomies, crude forms of conditioning (such as drugs that induce a sensation of suffocation or emetics to induce vomiting), and even castration. These and more moderate strategies of psychoanalysis were singularly unsuccessful in treating this so-called malady.

The American Psychiatric Association publishes the *Diagnostic and Statistical Manual* (see Chapter 16), which defines officially the conditions considered mental illnesses. In the first edition, homosexuality was labeled as a mental illness. Some mental health professionals held the minority view that this label was wrong. Dr. Robert Spitzer, for example, said:

> With the exception of homosexuality, all other disorders were associated with impairment in general, occupational or social functioning, or inherently caused some distress. . . . The argument the gay activists were making was that any distress was a reaction to social pressure. (Cited in Mach, 1987:44)

In 1973, after years of lobbying by gay activists and the efforts of other people, the American Psychiatric Association by a majority vote of its membership declassified homosexuality as a mental disorder; homosexual behavior was henceforth to be regarded simply as a manifestation of a preference, not as mad or bad. Although this enlightened view is not universally held in the psychiatric community, it does prevail officially. Most psychiatrists seem to agree with Dr. Stephen Morin, who says:

> Gay people need psychotherapy for the same reasons straight people do. You need psychotherapy when you have a significant problem that interferes with your social or occupational functioning. But you don't need therapy because you happen to be gay. (Cited in Mach, 1987:48)

As Morin implies, many gays and lesbians do have problems, but their problems do "not result directly from being homosexual, but are created by the way society views homosexuality" (Long and Sulton, 1987:227). Homosexuals are more likely than other people to have problems with guilt, anger, and self-esteem owing to the prevailing religious views, occupational discrimination, and the rejection they experience because they differ from the sexual norms of society.

Legal Oppression: The Law, the Courts, and the Police

In fourteenth-century Europe the common punishment for homosexuality was burning at the stake. The Puritans in the colonies continued the death penalty for this "crime." Around the time of the American Revolution, Thomas Jefferson and some liberal reformers of the day proposed changing Virginia law, replacing the death penalty for homosexuality with castration (Tivnan, 1987).

The legal status of homosexuals has progressed considerably since the days of death and castration, but they are still not treated equally because of their sexual orientation. For example, the marriage of homosexuals is not recognized by the state. In addition to losing the symbolic importance of having a union legitimated by the state, gays experience other negative consequences. Gould elaborates:

> While heterosexuals enjoy many rights and privileges by virtue of marriage, homosexuals in similar long-term relationships forfeit legal and financial protections such as community property rights, inheritance, tax breaks, and insurance premium reductions. (Gould, 1979:63)

This section begins by surveying the major developments in the law in three areas of great concern to the gay community: sodomy laws, discrimination against gays by the military, and family rights for homosexuals (the following is taken from Leonard, 1990).

Sodomy laws. Prohibitions against **sodomy** (oral or anal sex) were universal in the United States until 1961, when Illinois became the first state to repeal its sodomy law. Other states followed, and now only twenty-four states still have sodomy laws. In 1986 there was a constitutional challenge to sodomy laws. The argument in this challenge was that sexual activity between consenting adults in private is not questioned, let alone regulated, even in states with laws prohibiting sodomy, *provided the adults are heterosexual*. In short, sodomy laws are used to harass homosexuals, especially gay men, because women in general and lesbians in particular are socially invisible in society. Gould notes, "Homosexual men, in contrast, routinely encounter blatant and humiliating invasions of privacy and freedom which lesbians have been spared—such is the bitter irony of a sexist society" (Gould, 1979:53).

In *Bowers* v. *Hardwick* (1986) the Supreme Court reversed the U.S. Court of Appeals decision, ruling by a five-to-four vote that states had the right to prohibit sodomy. Justice Byron White's opinion "characterized as 'facetious' the argument that gay people have a 'fundamental right' to engage in consensual sex." (Leonard, 1990:12).

The military. The armed forces have always discriminated against gays and lesbians. From 1982 to 1992 about 14,000 people have been discharged from the military as homosexuals. According to Defense Department statistics, women are three times more likely to be removed for homosexuality than are men "with 16 of every 10,000 women on active duty expelled compared to five of every 10,000

Fred Seltzer, Richard Kirton, and Robert Matt have said that they are gay. President Clinton, in opposition to popular opinion, has argued that they and other gays should be allowed remain in the military.

men" (cited in Atkins, 1989:16). These discharges have led to many lawsuits. The decisions consistently reaffirm the military's right to purge homosexuals from its ranks. In 1990 the Supreme Court refused to hear two challenges to the Pentagon regulation that homosexuality is incompatible with military service. In doing so, the Supreme Court upheld this rule, although by not hearing the case, the court did not set a precedent affecting future cases. President Clinton has vowed to change the regulations so that homosexuals will not be discriminated against in the military.

Family rights.   No state permits marriage between members of the same sex (indeed, no industrial nation, except for Denmark, which permits "registered partnerships," gives official recognition to homosexual marriages). No state recognizes (although sixteen counties and cities do, including San Francisco, Seattle, Santa Cruz, West Hollywood, and Madison, Wisconsin) "legal domestic partners." The San Francisco law defines domestic partners as "two people who have chosen to share one another's lives in an intimate and committed relationship" (quoted in Bishop, 1989:All). These laws permit homosexuals to register their relationships formally. They do not, however, permit a next-of-kin relationship that the state will enforce. Aside from the emotional benefits of marriage, significant marriage benefits are denied to homosexuals: coverage under their spouses' health and pension plans, rights of inheritance and community property, and potential savings from joint tax returns. The courts have ruled consistently to deny these benefits to homosexuals in long-term relationships.

There is one recent exception, however. In 1989 the New York Supreme Court ruled in *Braschi* v. *Stahl Associates* that surviving partners of AIDS victims, threatened with eviction from rent-regulated apartments in New York City by landlords wanting to gain rent increases on vacancy, should be treated as family members and thus guaranteed the same rents as their partner.

Another court case, regarding the guardianship of Sharon Kowalski, is significant. Two lesbians, Sharon Kowalski and Karen Thompson, had lived together in a committed relationship for four years. A car accident left Sharon Kowalski brain-damaged and a quadriplegic. A battle ensued between her partner and her parents over guardianship. A Minnesota court ruled in favor of her parents, but in 1991 the Minnesota Court of Appeals in a unanimous decision overturned that decision. This important decision gives legal protection for homosexual couples (for a summary of this and other relevant court decisions, see Hunter, 1991).

Parenthood has become the newest battleground for lesbian and gay rights. Lesbian mothers are rarely given custody of children in divorce cases because "it tends to be considered sufficient evidence that the mother is an unfit parent" (Lewin and Lyons, 1982). One consequence of this bias by the courts is that lesbian mothers may forgo child support payments from the father if he agrees to her having custody of the children.

Homosexuals also find it nearly impossible to adopt a child. As an example of this bias against gays, a presidential advisory group in 1987 argued that the federal government should not preclude individuals from consideration as adoptive parents because of marital status, age, or handicap. However, it could *not* support homosexual adoption (*New York Times,* 1987a).

An interesting contemporary phenomenon is the "lesbian baby boom." More and more lesbian couples are deciding to have children. A common practice is for one partner to be artificially impregnated with the sperm of a male relative of her partner so that the child will be genetically related to both partners. In 1992 lesbians were raising an estimated 10,000 children conceived through artificial insemination (Turque, 1992:39). Legal problems arise when a lesbian relationship breaks up and the birth mother tries to limit her former partner's contact with the child. In this case the courts have generally ruled that where there is a blood connection, it overrides other considerations. Another set of cases occurs when the birth mother dies and the surviving woman's right to keep the child is challenged. Courts in Florida and Vermont have recognized the parental status of the nonbirth mother in this situation, finding that she has rights superior to grandparents and other genetic relatives.

Now, let's consider police action. Although the rate and kind of harassment vary from jurisdiction to jurisdiction, the police use a variety of techniques to harass homosexuals. They may use questionable means to apprehend and arrest homosexuals (e.g., film sexual interactions through one-way mirrors installed in public rest rooms, wiretaps of telephones, and the use of decoys to entrap). Bars where homosexuals gather are frequently raided for suspected violation of the sodomy laws. Patrons in these raids may be photographed and fingerprinted, which is particularly frightening to people who wish to keep their homosexual orientation private. The owners of these establishments are harassed by public authorities who may, for example, revoke their liquor license or issue citations for inconsequential or even nonexistent building code violations. In effect, the agents of social control in many communities have an unofficial policy that encourages the harassment of deviant groups, of which homosexuals are considered by many to be the most abhorrent.

A third police action, actually inaction, that negatively affect gays is their response to gays as victims of violence. The National Institute of Justice commissioned a study from Abt Associates, a private consulting firm, which found that homosexuals were probably the most frequent victims of hate-motivated violence (assault, verbal intimidation, and vandalism), more so than Blacks, Hispanics, Southeast Asians, or other minority group. The study found that "the vast majority of police departments and district attorney's offices around the country have failed to address the problem of hate-motivated violence" (Freiberg, 1987b:10). Only a few police and sheriff's departments have made bias crime a priority, and even fewer have expanded their jurisdiction to include antigay violence (San Francisco, Boston, and New York City are three prominent exceptions). The majority, however, reveal a bias against gays by their selective inattention to the crimes against homosexuals.

Occupational Discrimination

The exact amount of job discrimination against homosexuals is unknown primarily because the government does not provide employment discrimination statistics, as it does for women, Blacks, and other minorities. The two elements of discrimination that confront homosexuals in the workplace are anticipated discrimination and actual discrimination.

Many homosexuals fear that they will lose their jobs if their sexual orientation is revealed. Or if not fired, they may experience other forms of discrimination, such as being passed over for deserved promotions, being given relatively low salary raises, and being harassed. One study of 203 lesbians from New York City revealed that three-fifths of the women expected discrimination if their sexual orientation were discovered. Of this number, two-thirds expected to be fired and 90 percent predicted their coworkers would harass them with taunts, ostracism, and even violence (Levine and Leonard, 1984).

These fears are likely based on reality. The New York State Health Code includes a section, for example, that states that employees can be fired for moral turpitude (which includes homosexuality as such a case). Because few legal protections are available to homosexuals, especially in the private sector, and because homophobic attitudes are common, homosexuals have little choice in many cases but to hide their sexual orientation.

After employment, the hidden homosexual, knowing that retention and promotion depend on keeping the secret, must use a number of ploys to appear heterosexual. The strategies include bringing someone of the opposite sex to company social events, telling appropriate sexual jokes, and wearing appropriate clothing (Stewart, 1991). But as Levine observes, "Needless to say, passing causes psychological problems, feelings of being on stage, anxiety over exposure and subsequent sanctions, strain from artificial behavior and talk" (Levine, 1979:156).

Actual discrimination against known homosexuals occurs frequently in the workplace. Table 10.1 presents data from a Gallup poll on the hiring of homosexuals in selected occupations. Although the data from this table indicate a trend toward greater tolerance by the public, many employers, personnel directors,

Table 10.1 Percentage who feel homosexuals should be hired, by occupation and year

Occupation	1977	1982	1987	1989	1992
Salespersons	68%	70%	72%	79%	82%
Armed forces	51	52	55	60	57
Doctors	44	50	49	56	53
Clergy	36	38	42	44	43
Elementary school teachers	27	32	33	47	41

Sources: Data from "Homosexuality," *The Gallup Report,* No. 258 (March 1987), pp. 12–18; "Homosexuality," *The Gallup Report,* No. 289 (October 1989), p. 12; and *The Gallup Poll Monthly,* No. 321 (June 1992), pp. 2–6.

school boards, and other people involved in hiring do not hire homosexuals. They may not hire gays and lesbians because they are bigoted or because they feel the community or clients may object. Or they may feel that the exclusion of gays is justified because they believe that homosexuals are neurotic, morally degenerate, sexually dangerous to youth, a medical danger because of AIDS, or the like.

The process of applying for a job is more problematic for homosexuals than it is for other people. The application form may ask if the applicant has ever been arrested, and if so, why. Because the laws criminalize homosexuality in many jurisdictions, homosexuals are more likely than heterosexuals to have a police record. Gays and lesbians are thus caught in a double bind. If, on the one hand, they disclose their arrest for homosexual behavior, they will be denied a job. On the other hand, if they conceal this fact, they will be fired for lying, because most companies check information on application forms against official records. A similar situation occurs when the form asks about one's military service. Known homosexuals will have been dishonorably discharged, which is an obvious excuse for not hiring them. Finally, if applicants voluntarily disclosed their homosexuality on the application, they are not likely to be hired (Levine, 1979:154).

About 300 occupations require that practitioners be certified by a government agency or board of professionals (e.g., architect, teacher, doctor, and barber). Applicants who possess a criminal record—which, as noted above, is a relatively high probability for homosexuals—will not receive the license. Nor will they if there is evidence of supposedly bad moral character. Similarly, some jobs in government and private industry require a security clearance because of access to classified information. Homosexuals are typically denied this clearance because it is assumed that they are susceptible to blackmail.

For all of these reasons, a sexual orientation that deviates from what is considered normal jeopardizes employment. Beyond the obvious impact on income, there are other serious consequences from this form of discrimination, as Levine observes:

> Job discrimination strikes at the core of one's existence. In modern society, occupation is the pathway to sustenance, self-realization, income, and self-esteem. By segregating gay men [and lesbian women] into less desirable and less remunerative positions, employment discrimination seriously reduces

[their] life chances. The practice also diminishes their potential contribution to society. Owing to job discrimination, many talented and qualified gays are working in positions beneath their capabilities. . . . Such victimization clearly violates long cherished American beliefs. (Levine, 1979:161–162)

A few employers are taking the lead in breaking down discrimination in the workplace. One important example is Lotus Development Corporation, which offers all family benefits to gay and lesbian employees and their partners (Horn, 1991). Thus, Lotus employees and their partners receive medical and dental care, vision and hearing coverage, bereavement leave, as well as coverage for natural or adopted children, or children of whom one partner has legal custody. Other progressive corporations, albeit few, provide diversity training to demystify homosexuality and to encourage gay and lesbian groups within the organizations.

Fighting the System

The chapter up to this point has documented the hostility, anger, and abhorrence aimed at homosexuals in U.S. society. These reactions occur at the societal level through court actions that discriminate and in punitive religious ideology that condemns homosexuals' immorality. At the personal level hostility occurs with looks, taunts, ostracism, and even violence. The objects of this assault—individual lesbian women and gay men—experience great personal stress as a result. According to Patton,

the stress of being a lesbian or gay man is enormous. Worrying about self and friends, and constructing elaborate shields against discovery and persecution occupy a great deal of time for the individual lesbian or gay man. There are virtually no local or social remedies for the organized and systematic attacks on individuals and the community by police, ministers, doctors, politicians, and the average citizen and his/her rude comments and [hostile] methods. (Patton, 1985:14)

Homosexuals use two basic strategies for living in a society hostile to their sexual orientation. One is to conceal their sexual orientation from straights to avoid stigmatization, harassment, and discrimination. These **secret gays** segregate their lives into gay and straight activities. When in the straight world, they conceal their sexual orientation from family, friends, coworkers, and other associates. Those most likely to stay in the closet are from the working class. The structural and personal pressures against coming out are much greater for them than for those from the middle and upper classes.

Gay liberationists identify themselves openly as homosexuals. Rather than evade the efforts of straights to stigmatize them, they challenge society in an effort to transform it (Persell, 1987:544). The gay men and lesbian women who confront society are the focus of this section.

The negative sanctions from society, employers, friends, and family have kept homosexuals for most periods of U.S. history from organizing to change a repressive situation. A few homosexual organizations were formed (the first in 1925 and others in the 1950s) for mutual support, but only a relatively few homosexuals were willing at the time to declare publicly their deviance from the norm of heterosexuality.

The 1960s provided a better climate for change when youths, Blacks, women, pacifists, and other groups questioned the norms and ideologies of the dominant society. This decade clearly was one of heightened awareness among the oppressed of their oppression and of the possibility that through collective efforts they could change what had seemed to be unchangeable.

The precipitating event for homosexual unity occurred at 3 A.M. on June 28, 1969, when police raided the Stonewall Inn of New York's Greenwich Village. But instead of dispersing, as homosexuals had always done in similar situations, the 200 homosexual patrons threw objects at the police and set fire to the bar. The riot lasted only forty-five minutes, but it gave impetus to a number of collective efforts by gays to publicize police harassment of the gay community, job discrimination, and other indignities they face. Gay liberation groups emerged in many cities and on university campuses. Many neighborhoods in major cities became openly homosexual—most notably the Castro district in San Francisco, New Town in Chicago, and Greenwich Village in New York City. These communities included gay churches, associations of professionals, health clinics, and networks of gay-owned businesses to supply the gay community's needs. The proliferation of these organizations for homosexuals has provided a supportive climate allowing many of them to come out of the closet. By 1992 there were 1,580 gay and lesbian organizations, including political, social, activist, and student groups (Cohn 1992:39).

The increased numbers of public homosexuals have provided the political base for changing the various forms of oppression that homosexuals routinely experience. The Gay Media Task Force promotes accurate and positive images of gays in television, films, and advertising; the Gay Rights National Lobby promotes favorable legislation; the Gay Men's Health Crisis helps gays deal with the reality of AIDS; and the National Gay Task Force serves to further gay interests by attacking the minority group status of homosexuals in a variety of political and ideological arenas.

Two countervailing forces in the 1980s impacted the gay rights movement. The election of Ronald Reagan and his conservative agenda along with the surge of Christian fundamentalism inhibited the movement's momentum in the first part of the decade. The AIDS epidemic acted to propel the movement in the late 1980s. As it became clear that AIDS endangered the lives of more and more gay males, the sense of a shared danger and the realization that they needed to prod the government into action quickly inspired unity. More organizations formed, some directed specifically at the health needs of AIDS patients and other people aimed at lobbying Congress and state governments for legislation important to gays.

On October 11, 1987, the largest gay rights demonstration occurred when several hundred thousand lesbians, gay men, and their supporters marched in Washington, D.C. They held a parade, had a huge marriage ceremony to mock the laws forbidding the marriage of gays, mourned their comrades who had died of AIDS, staged a mass civil disobedience action at the U.S. Supreme Court to protest the 1986 decision upholding state sodomy laws (840 were arrested), and joined with other activist groups. Rev. Jesse Jackson spoke at the rally:

We are together today to say we insist on legal protection under the law of every American . . . for workers' rights, for civil rights, for the rights of religious freedom, the rights of individual privacy, for the rights of sexual preference. We come together for the rights of the American people. (Quoted in Freiberg, 1987a:15)

The leaders of the march identified the unfinished agenda—the structural changes needed for equality—in their formal demands (Freiberg, 1987a:16):

- Legal recognition of gay relationships.
- The repeal of all laws that made sodomy between consenting adults a crime.
- A presidential order banning antigay discrimination by the federal government.
- Passage of the congressional gay rights bill.
- An end to discrimination against people with AIDS, ARC, HIV-positive status, or people perceived to have AIDS.
- A massive increase in funding for AIDS education, research, and patient care.

By 1992, twenty years after Stonewall and two decades of change, homosexuals had made some modest gains. Some court decisions, some new laws by progressive legislatures and city commissions, some religious leaders and a few congregations accepting gays and lesbians, and changing attitudes had helped move homosexuals closer to the mainstream of society. But huge obstacles remain. Most religious groups are unyielding. The military openly discriminates. Many employers subtly discriminate. The Supreme Court remains unsympathetic.

Since the Stonewall Inn incident in 1969, gays and lesbians have organized protests to highlight their oppression and fight for equal rights policies.

There are renewed pressures from conservatives to roll back some of the gains of the last twenty years. The Republican Party during the 1992 election made thinly veiled attacks on homosexuals in their "family values" rhetoric (Painton, 1992). In short, homosexuals still remain a target. As Brownworth notes,

> gay men and lesbians are the only minority in the country . . . that it is still safe to scapegoat. . . . In Philadelphia, where a gay rights bill was adopted more than nine years ago, a recent study . . . found that a majority of gays and lesbians felt the law did not protect them or that they had no recourse against discrimination. A recent report by the National Gay and Lesbian Task Force, citing several university-based studies, finds that anti-gay violence is on the rise, and that gay men and women are four to seven times as likely to be victims of violence as any other group. . . . Rampant discrimination and the lack of legal recourse remain compelling reasons for many to stay in the closet, reaffirming homophobia. Twenty years after Stonewall, we have not gained acceptance or legal protections. (Brownworth, 1989:5–6)

CHAPTER REVIEW

1. Homosexuals are a minority group in U.S. society. They are relatively powerless and the objects of negative stereotypes and discrimination.
2. Unlike the status of most minorities, the minority status of homosexuals is based on deviance from society's norms rather than on ascribed characteristics. There are several important characteristics of social deviance: (a) it is socially created; (b) it is a relative, not an absolute, concept; (c) it is found universally in societies; (d) it serves society by reaffirming the rules; (e) it allows the powerful to determine who or what is deviant; and (f) it creates an atmosphere in which deviants can be stigmatized for their disreputable behavior.
3. The response to homosexuals varies by society and historical period. Although homosexuality is considered deviant behavior in contemporary U.S. society, it was not so considered in ancient Greece and Rome. Nor is it deviant among some Native American tribes.
4. The identification as homosexual is a master status superseding other characteristics for most heterosexuals. Because this status is stigmatized, the accomplishments of gays do not negate their powerful but negative master status in the opinions of other people.
5. Although the proportion of the population that is homosexual is not known and is probably unknowable, the best estimate is 10 percent. About three-fourths of lesbian couples live together, as do about half of gay male couples. Gay men are more likely than lesbian women to have sex with someone other than their steady partners, a similarity shared with heterosexual males. Homosexual couples are much more likely than heterosexual couples to be egalitarian. Contrary to the common stereotype, homosexual couples are not composed of a "male" partner and a "female" partner. Finally, being a homosexual is not necessarily a master status for the person involved.
6. Variance from the societal norm of heterosexuality is not a social problem; the societal response to it is. Gays confront three types of oppression: (a) ideological, stemming from traditional homophobic beliefs, especially religious and

medical; (b) legal, stemming from the law, court decisions, and behaviors by society's social control agents; and (c) occupational, where jobs, advancement, and income are restricted or denied.

7. Homosexuals use two basic strategies to cope with living in a society hostile to their sexual orientation. One is to conceal their homosexuality from heterosexuals. The other is to identify openly as a homosexual. Gay liberationists, of course, are in this latter category. Rather than evade the efforts of straights to stigmatize them, they challenge society in an effort to transform it.

8. The challenge to change society's oppression of homosexuals began with the Stonewall Inn riot in 1969. Since then, homosexuals have organized communities, organized protests, and formed self-help and political lobbying organizations.

KEY TERMS

Deviance.   Behavior that does not conform to social expectations.

Heterosexuality. Opposite-sex eroticism.

Homosexuality.   Sexual preference for someone of the same sex.

Bisexuality.   Sexual preference for or attraction to both sexes.

Master status. A position so important that it dominates all other statuses.

Stigma.   A powerful negative social label that affects a person's social identity and self-concept.

Homophobia.   Fear or hatred of homosexuality.

Sodomy.   Oral or anal sex.

Secret gays.   Homosexuals who conceal their sexual orientation.

Gay liberationists.   Homosexuals who openly identify themselves as such and challenge society in an effort to eliminate the stigma and discrimination they face.

FOR FURTHER STUDY

Dennis Altman. *The Homosexualization of America, the Americanization of the Homosexual.* New York: St. Martin's Press, 1982.

Alan P. Bell, Martin S. Weinberg, and Sue Kiefer Hammersmith. *Sexual Preference: Its Development in Men and Women.* Bloomington: Indiana University Press, 1981.

John D'Emilio. *Sexual Politics, Sexual Communities: The Making of a Homosexual Minority in the United States 1940–1970.* Chicago: University of Chicago Press, 1983.

Celia Kitzinger. *The Social Construction of Lesbianism.* Newbury Park, Calif.: Sage, 1988.

Eric Marcus. *Making History: The Struggle for Gay and Lesbian Rights, 1945–1990.* New York: HarperCollins, 1992.

Randy Shilts. *And the Band Played On: Politics, People, and the AIDS Epidemic.* New York: St. Martin's Press, 1987.

FORUM

WHAT SHOULD COLLEGES AND UNIVERSITIES DO ABOUT GAY OPPRESSION ON CAMPUSES?

Institutions of higher education must devise a set of policies that guarantee equal treatment. Professor D'Emilio presents such a set that many people in campus communities will find controversial and other people will accept as necessary to insure fairness.

John D'Emilio

Being openly gay on campus still goes against the grain. Despite the changes in American society in the last two decades, gay people are still swimming in a largely oppressive sea. Most campuses do not have gay student groups. Most gay faculty members and administrators have not come out. Even on campuses that have proven responsive to gay and lesbian concerns, progress has often come through the work of a mere handful of individuals who have chosen to be visible. And, although I do not have statistics to measure this precisely, I know that there are still many, many campuses in the United States where no lesbian or gay man feels safe enough to come out. From a gay vantage point, something is still wrong in the academy.

Oppression in its many forms is still alive, and the university is not immune to it. Indeed, as the gay population has become a better organized and stronger force in the 1980s, we have also become easier to target. In recent years, harassment, violence, and other hate-motivated acts against lesbians and gay men have surfaced with alarming frequency on campuses across the country. Institutions such as the University of Kansas and the University of Chicago, to name just two, have witnessed campaigns of terror against their gay members. At Pennsylvania State University, a report on tolerance found that bias-motivated incidents most frequently targeted gay people.

Unlike many other groups—women and African Americans, for instance—in which one's identity is clear for the world to see, most gay men and lesbians have the option to remain invisible. I cannot fault individuals who choose that path: the costs of visibility often can be high. Yet the fear that compels most gay people to remain hidden exacts a price of its own. It leads us to doubt our own self-worth and dignity. It encourages us to remain isolated and detached from our colleagues and peers, as too much familiarity can lead to exposure. And it often results in habitual patterns of mistrust and defensiveness because anyone, potentially, may cause our downfall. Hence, speaking about gay oppression involves not only addressing injustice in the abstract but also acknowledging the emotional toll it levies on particular individuals and the institutions of which they are a part.

For reasons that I cannot quite fathom, I still expect the academy to embrace higher standards of civility, decency, and justice than the society around it. Having been granted the extraordinary privilege of thinking critically as a way of life, we should be astute enough to recognize when a group of people is being systematically mistreated. We have the intelligence to devise solutions to problems that appear in our community. I expect us also to have the courage to lead rather than follow.

Although gay oppression has deep roots in American society, the actions that would combat it effectively on campuses are not especially difficult to devise and formulate. What sort of policies would make a difference? What would a gay-positive institution look like?

One set of policies would place institutions of higher education firmly on the side of equal treatment. Gay faculty, administrators, staff, and students need to know that their school is committed to fairness, to treating us on the basis of our abilities. At a minimum that would mean:

A nondiscrimination policy, formally enacted, openly announced, and in print wherever the institution proclaims its policy with regard to race, gender, and religion. Such a policy would apply to hiring, promotion, tenure, admissions, and financial aid. Because of the history of discrimination in this country, it is not enough for an administration to claim that it subscribes to the principle of fairness for everyone. Sexual orientation, sexual preference, sexual identity, or whatever term one chooses to adopt, needs to be explicitly acknowledged.

Spousal benefits for the partners of gay men and lesbians, at every level of institutional life and for every service that is normally provided to husbands and wives. These benefits include health insurance, library privileges, access to the gym and other recreational facilities, listings in school directories if spouses are customarily listed, and access to married students' housing for gay and lesbian couples.

An approach to gay student groups that is identical to that for all other groups with regard to recognition procedures, funding, and access to facilities. Administrators who place obstructions in the way of these groups are doing a costly disservice to their institutions since courts have uniformly sustained the rights of gay students to organize.

Subscribing to the above policies would simply place lesbians and gays in a *de jure* position of parity. Implementing these measures would go a long way toward alleviating the fears that we live with, integrating us fully into the life of the campus, and letting us know that we are valued and "welcomed."

The university's responsibility towards its gay members goes well beyond these elementary procedures of fairness, however. Administrators will need to take an activist stance to counteract the misinformation about gays and lesbians that many members of the university community have, the cultural prejudices that are still endemic in the United States, and the growing problem of hate-motivated incidents. The following areas need attention:

1. One of the prime locations where harassment occurs is in residence halls. Dormitory directors and their assistants need to be sensitized about gay issues and trained in how to respond quickly and firmly to instances of oppressive behavior and harassment. In an age when heterosexual undergraduates routinely hold hands, walk arm-in-arm, and engage in other simple displays of affection, lesbian and gay students need to know that they will not have their rooms ransacked, or their physical safety endangered, for doing the same. They also

need reassurance that campus activism on gay issues will not come back to haunt them when they return to their dorms each night.

2. Student affairs programming is an important tool in fostering toleration, understanding, and enthusiasm for differences in culture and identity. Resources should be made available to sponsor special gay awareness week events, as well as to integrate gay films, public lectures, and other events and activities into the regular programming.

3. Late adolescence is an especially stressful time for gay men and lesbians. These may be the years when they become sexually active, form their first relationships, and grapple with issues of identity. School counseling services need personnel who are sensitive to these issues and who can foster self-acceptance and self-esteem rather than reinforce self-hatred.

4. Because the issues and situations affecting lesbians and gay men range widely across the structure of large and medium-size campuses, hiring an "ombudsperson" for gay and lesbian concerns makes good institutional sense. Someone who can think expansively about these issues, provide a resource where needed, and intervene decisively in emergencies can move a whole campus forward.

5. When hate-motivated incidents occur—and the evidence of the last few years suggests that they happen with greater frequency than we care to admit—the *highest* officers of the university need to exercise their *full* authority in condemning the attacks and correcting the underlying problems which encourage such incidents. Bias-motivated incidents are awful, but they also offer a unique opportunity for raising consciousness and for shifting the climate of opinion on a campus.

6. An institution that prohibits discrimination against gays ought not to countenance the presence on campus of institutions and organizations that engage in such discrimination. The government intelligence

agencies and the military are the most egregious perpetrators of anti-gay bias. Recent actions by the military against its gay and lesbian personnel amount to a form of terrorism. Military recruiters and ROTC programs ought to be banned from American campuses until the armed forces change their policies.

7. Last, but not least, is the issue of research. The 1980s have witnessed an efflorescence of scholarship on gay and lesbian issues in several disciplines.

Yet many topics go begging for researchers because faculty members know that prejudiced department heads and tenure committees will label such work trivial and insignificant. Gay scholarship, opening as it does a new window on human experience, must be encouraged.

Source: John D'Emilio, "The Campus Environment for Gay and Lesbian Life," *Academe* 76 (January/February 1990), excerpts from pp. 16–19. Reprinted with permission.

n the 1992 presidential campaign, the words *family values* blasted out from podiums and headlines. The nation was caught up in a debate about the U.S. family. Family patterns of the 1990s were said to be symptoms of decline and decay. This attack on the family was based on the myth that immoral behaviors cause social problems. The family is an easy target for people who blame social decay on bad people doing bad things. The commonly held belief is that when the family fails, the rest of society fails. This view of the world is flawed in two fundamental respects. First, it reverses the relationship between family and society by treating families as the building blocks of society rather than as a reflection of social conditions. Second, it ignores the structural reasons for family breakdown.

Some social problems have their locus in family settings. Although many of these problems are rooted in developments outside of the family, in social, economic, and demographic trends, they become family problems that affect growing numbers of children and adults. This chapter examines the family as a social institution and the social problems that have their locus in family life. The chapter is divided into five parts. The first demythologizes the family by showing the gap between the idealized image of the family and family life as it actually is experienced in this society. The remaining four sections examine representative family-based social problems: the economic disadvantages for the members of some families and how they are perpetuated, inadequate child care, divorce, and domestic violence.

The Mythical Family in the United States

Family life is difficult to think about objectively. Our perceptions are clouded by our own family experiences and by cultural ideals about family. Critics decrying the breakdown of the family contrast a lost golden past of family togetherness with an unhappy present. But this is based on nostalgic and false images of the past:

> The image of a warm secure stable family life in past times that serves as a backdrop to most discussions of family change is deeply at odds with the findings of recent research in the history of the family. Nostalgia devotees, in particular, seem unaware of the disruptive impact of high mortality rates on families in past times, or of how close to the margin of survival most people lived before the twentieth century. (Skolnick, 1991:xviii).

Paradoxically, the very familiarity of family life can cloud reality. Because the family is familiar, we tend to take it for granted, to view it as natural. Other obstacles have handicapped the study of the family: "It is morally sacred, and it is secret" (Skolnick, 1983:33). The family is not merely a social institution; it is associated with a larger societal morality of good and right. It is, at the same time, the most private of all society's institutions. The norm of privacy gives the family a secret quality that exists alongside its familiarity. To a greater extent than before, family life goes on behind closed doors (Laslett, 1977). The family is a **backstage** area where people can be relaxed and behave in ways they would not in public

(Goffman, 1959). According to Arlene Skolnick, this privacy accounts for the deceptive quality of family life:

> Privacy results in pluralistic ignorance—we have a backstage view of our own families, but can judge others only in terms of public presentation. The gap between public norms and private behavior can be wide; marital relationships tend to be even more private and invisible than those between parents and children. (Skolnick, 1983:300)

We have little direct knowledge of what goes on behind closed doors, but we do know what family life *should* be. Family in U.S. society is a symbol, a visual image of adults and children living together in mutually satisfying and harmonious ways. Family evokes warmth, caring, and physical and psychological nurturance apart from the troubled world. This image characterizes the family as a refuge from an impersonal world, a place of intimacy, love, and trust where individuals can escape the competition of dehumanizing forces in modern society. Lasch (1977) named this image a "haven in a heartless world" and described it as a glorification of private life made necessary by the deprivations experienced in the public world. In this image family and society are set apart. Relations inside the family are idealized as nurturant, and those outside the family, especially in business and work, are seen as competitive.

Relationships between husbands and wives and between parents and children are especially idealized in the family image. The ideal states that families are formed in the marriage of one man and one woman who will satisfy each other's emotional and physical needs till death do them part. When children are added to this exclusive dyad, then parenting becomes the natural extension of the husband and wife relationship. Parents mold and shape happy children (who will become successful adults) by providing proper child care (Birdwhistell, 1980).

This view assumes a division of labor based on sex: "a breadwinner husband, freed for and identified with activities in a separate sphere, and a full-time mother defined as the core of the family" (Thorne, 1992:4). It also assumes a single uniform family experience for all members of society.

This image of the family bears little resemblance to present family situations. Mothers are likely to be employed outside of the home, and many family forms are common: single-parent families (resulting either from unmarried parenthood or divorce), remarried couples, unmarried couples, stepfamilies, foster families, extended or multigenerational families, and the doubling up of two families within the same home (Ahlburg and De Vita, 1992:2). Half of marriages end in divorce, and one-half of all children will spend at least part of their childhood in a single-parent family (90 percent with their mothers).

And what of the supposedly perpetually happy family set apart from the harsh realities of the world? This myth ignores the persistent effects of economic conditions (e.g., poverty or near poverty, unemployment or underemployment, downward mobility or the threat of downward mobility). It ignores the social inequalities (racism, sexism, ageism) that prevent certain kinds of people from experiencing the good things in life. This erroneous view also masks the inevitable problems that arise in intimate settings (tensions, anger, and even violence in some instances). The family ideal implies a private, autonomous retreat

The composition of a family unit takes many forms, including the single parent family.

set apart from society. This image obscures the real relationship between families and the economy. A better way of understanding the interconnections is to distinguish between family and household. A **family** involves blood ties among husbands, wives, and children; a **household** is a coresidential economical unit. Households vary in membership, composition, and the resources they have for family living, a fact not recognized by the concept of family. As an ideology of family relations, family implies a single form, but the reality is that households are diverse. A good example of the importance of distinguishing between family and household is the restructuring of family obligations and household composition after divorce (Ferree, 1991:107).

Households are defined by the U.S. Census Bureau as taking one of three general forms: family, nonfamily, and single-person household. Family households consist of two or more persons living together who are related through marriage, birth, or adoption. The most common family household is a married couple with or without children in the home. A single parent with one or more children also comprises a family household. Nonfamily households consist of two or more unrelated individuals who share living quarters. They can be nonmarried couples of the same or opposite sex. Single-person households are individuals who live alone in their own separate residential units.

Over the years, U.S. households have changed in several important ways. Average household size fell from 2.76 members in 1980 to 2.63 people in 1990. Households continue to shrink with increases in the number of single-parent families, childless married couples, and people living alone (Waldrop and Exter, 1991:35). Between now and the year 2000, households made up of married couples will increase only slightly in number, while other types of households will increase dramatically. Fewer households will have children present. No one household arrangement will be typical. Instead, a very diverse world of households, families, and individual life histories is emerging. These changes in the distribution of households by family and nonfamily status are the results of changing preferences that show a reduced commitment to the conventional nuclear family and to married life as the preferred arrangement (Wetzel, 1990:5)

Stratification and Family Life: Unequal Life Chances

Previous chapters examine growing inequalities in the distribution of resources and rewards. The stratification hierarchies—class, race, and gender—are changing and reshuffling families and individuals. In this section, we examine the effects of social class on families in the United States.

Families are embedded in a class hierarchy that is "pulling apart" to shrink the middle class while more families join the growing ranks of the rich or the poor (Usdansky, 1992a). This movement creates great differences in family living and no longer guarantees that children's placement in the class system will follow that of their parents. Still, a family's location in the class system is the single most important determinant of family life.

Households in different parts of the class structure have different connections with the outside economy and different ways of acquiring the necessities of life. They do so through inheritance, salaries, wages, welfare, or various involvements with the hidden economy, the illegal economy, or the irregular economy. Families with more secure resources conform more closely to the nuclear family ideal of self-support. In a stratified society, family structures differ because households vary systematically in their ability to hook into, accumulate, and transmit wealth, wages, or welfare (Rapp, 1982). This variation is closely related to the connections that households and families have with other social institutions. The social networks or relationships outside the family—at work, school, and church—voluntarily produce differential access to society's resources, and they produce class and racial differences in families.

Among the middle class, households are based on a relatively stable and secure resource base. When exceptional economic resources are called for, nonfamilial institutions usually are available in the form of better medical coverage, expense accounts, and credit at banks (Rapp, 1982:181).

These links with nonfamily institutions are precisely the ones that distinguish life in middle-class families from families in other economic groups. The strongest links are with the occupations of middle-class family members, especially those of the husband-father. Occupational roles greatly affect family roles and the quality of family life (Schneider and Smith, 1973). Occupations are part of the larger opportunity structure of society: occupations that are highly valued and carry high income rewards are unevenly distributed. The amount of the paycheck determines how well a given household can acquire the resources needed for survival and perhaps for luxury. (See Table 11.1 for a breakdown of median income by race and type of family.) The job or occupation that is the source of the paycheck connects families with the opportunity structure in different ways.

In the working class, material resources depend on wages acquired in exchange for labor. When such hourly wages are insufficient or unstable, individuals in households must pool their resources with other people in the larger family network. The pooling of resources may involve exchanging baby-sitting, sharing meals, or lending money. Pooling is a way of coping with the limited resources that families need to survive. Pooling requires that the boundaries of the family be expanded. In effect, a wider network of people become part of the family, as they share what little they have. The lower a person moves in the class

Table 11.1   Median income by race and type of family

Race and Family	Median Income
All Races	
Married couple families	$39,895
Wife in labor force	46,777
Male householder, no wife present	29,046
Female householder, no husband present	16,932
White	
Married couple family	40,431
Wife in labor force	47,247
Male householder, no wife present	30,570
Female householder, no husband present	19,528
Black	
Married couple family	33,784
Wife in labor force	40,038
Male householder, no wife present	21,848
Female householder, no husband present	12,125
Hispanic	
Married couple family	27,996
Wife in labor force	34,778
Male householder, no wife present	22,744
Female householder, no husband present	11,914

Source: Department of Commerce, U.S. Bureau of the Census, "Money, Income of Households, Families, and Persons in the United States: 1990," *Current Population Reports*, P–60, No. 174 (March 1991).

structure, the more uncertain and difficult survival through wage work becomes and the more important the kin network becomes in providing subsistence over time. Much has been written about these networks among poor Black families: "extremely flexible, and fluctuating groups of people committed to resource pooling, to sharing, to mutual aid, who move in and out from under one another's roofs" (Rapp, 1982:177).

The fluctuating boundaries of these families do not make them unstable. Instead, this family flexibility is a way of sustaining the limited resources that result from their place in the class hierarchy. Even the Black single-parent family, which has sometimes been criticized as being disorganized or even pathological, is often embedded in a network of sharing and support. Latino families also exhibit strong and persistent kinship bonds that provide socioeconomic and emotional support. In fact, most racial ethnic families are characterized by the presence of extended kinship and network of support spread across multiple households. Looking at these families without racist assumptions, we see that variation in family organization is a way of adapting to a society where racial stratification shapes family resources and family structures (Baca Zinn, 1990).

What is most important about the differences in family boundaries is that they arise out of different kinds of linkages with institutions that are *consequences* of class position, not causes of that position. Lacking economic resources to purchase services from specialists outside the family, poor people turn to relatives and exchange these services. This family network then becomes a crucial institution in both the working class and the lower class.

Middle-class families with husbands (and perhaps wives) in careers have both economic resources and built-in ties with supportive institutions such as banks, credit unions, medical facilities, and voluntary associations. These ties are intrinsic to some occupations and to middle-class neighborhoods. They are structurally determined. Yet the middle class is shrinking, and many middle-class families are without middle-class incomes because of changes in the larger economy. Changes in family structure have also contributed to the lowering of family income. High divorce rates, for example, create many more family units with lower incomes.

In contrast to the economic autonomy of the middle class, many blue-collar jobs lack ties that would link family with work and other institutions. The boundaries of the middle-class family are more circumscribed because institutional ties allow these families to be independent from kin. But the stable working class is also threatened because millions of manufacturing workers continue to be the victims of deindustrialization. Kin have become the lifeline for millions of families with displaced workers.

Turning to the upper class, we find that family boundaries are more open than are those of the middle class, even though class boundaries are quite closed. Among the elite, family constitutes not only a nuclear family but also the extended family. The elite have multiple households (Rapp, 1982:182). Their day-to-day life exists within the larger context of a network of relatives (Dyer, 1979:209).

The institutional linkages of the elite are national in scope. Families in various sections of the country are connected by such institutions as boarding schools, exclusive colleges, exclusive clubs, and fashionable vacation resorts. In this way the elite remains intact, and the marriage market is restricted to a small (but national) market (Blumberg and Paul, 1975:69).

Family life is privileged in every sense, as Stein, Richman, and Hannon report:

> Wealthy families can afford an elaborate support structure to take care of the details of everyday life. Persons can be hired to cook and prepare meals and do laundry and to care for the children. (Stein, Richman, and Hannon, 1977:9)

The vast economic holdings of these families allow them to have a high degree of control over the flow of rewards and resources of society. They enjoy freedoms and choices not normally available to other families in society. These families maintain privileged access to **life chances** (the chance throughout one's life cycle to live and experience the good things in society) and life-styles.

Kinship ties, obligations, and interests are more extended in classes at the two extremes than they are in the middle (McKinley, 1964:22). In the upper extreme and toward the lower end of the class structure, kinship networks serve decisively different functions. At both extremes they are institutions of resource management. The kin-based family form of the elite serves to preserve inherited wealth. It is intricately tied to other national institutions that control the wealth of society. The kin-based family form of the working and lower classes is a primary institution through which individuals participate in social life as they pool and exchange their limited resources to ensure survival. It is influenced by society's institutions, but it remains separate from them.

Structural Transformation and Family Life

The transformation of the economy brought about by new technologies, the globalization of the economy, capital flight, and deindustrialization has widened the gap between high and low wage earners. This has profoundly affected families and will continue to do so in the foreseeable future. As the need for certain kinds of labor diminishes, more working-class and middle-class families are the victims of economic dislocation. Families are affected when their resources are reduced, when they face economic and social marginalization, and when family members are unemployed or underemployed. (This section is adapted from Baca Zinn and Eitzen, 1990:151–152.)

What does **downward mobility** (the movement to a lower social class) mean for families? Katherine Newman describes the experience of the downwardly mobile middle class:

> They once "had it made" in American society, filling slots from affluent blue collar jobs to professional and managerial occupations. They have job skills, education, and decades of steady work experience. Many are, or were, homeowners. Their marriages were (at least initially) intact. As a group they savored the American dream. They found a place higher up the ladder in this society and then, inexplicably, found their grip loosening and their status sliding. Some downwardly mobile middle-class families end up in poverty, but many do not. Usually they come to rest at a standard of living above the poverty level but far

below the affluence they enjoyed in the past. They must, therefore, contend not
only with financial hardship but with the psychological, social, and practical consequences of "falling from grace," of "losing their proper place" in the world.
(Newman, 1988:8)

Downward mobility is devastating in U.S. society not only because of the loss
in economic resources but also because self-worth is so closely connected to
occupation. Loss of occupational status also ravages the people affected because
people in the United States tend to interpret this loss as the fault of the downwardly mobile.

Downward mobility also occurs within the stable working class whose link
with resource-granting opportunity structures has always been tenuous. Many
downwardly mobile families find successful coping strategies to deal with their
adverse situations. Some families develop a tighter bond to meet their common
problems. Others find support from families in similar situations or from their personal kin networks. For many families, however, downward mobility adds tensions that make family life especially difficult. Family members experience stress,
marital tension, and depression. Newman has suggested that these conditions are
normal given the persistent tensions generated by downward mobility. Many families experience some degree of these pathologies and yet somehow endure. But
some families disintegrate under these pressures, with serious problems of physical brutality, incapacitating alcoholism, desertion, and even suicide (Newman,
1988:134–140).

The new technology may affect families in other ways. The redistribution of
jobs has displaced many workers and placed many millions of people in low-wage,
service jobs, often without traditional benefits (see Chapter 14). These kinds of
jobs include contingent work such as part-time work, temporary work, and home-
based work—jobs disproportionately held by women. We focus here on women
working for pay in their homes (the following discussion is from Christensen,
1988).

Home-based work includes word processing, typing, editing, accounting, telemarketing, sewing, laundry, and child care. Women often opt for home-based
work because the flexibility permits them to combine work and family obligations.
Employers contract women to do work at home because they pay only for work
delivered, they avoid unions, and they do not pay for benefits such as health insurance, paid leaves, and pensions.

There are positive and negative consequences of home-based work. On the
positive side, home-based work allows flexibility and independence not found in
most jobs. On the negative side, the pay is typically low, and the strains engen-
dered from combining the work and parent roles may be overwhelming. Children,
spouses, neighbors, the telephone, household tasks, and other home distractions
hinder productivity—and pay. "Working at home eliminates the boundary
between work and family so that women often find they never leave their work"
(Christensen, 1988:5). Thus, the combination of work and family in the home setting engenders a form of claustrophobia for some people. This feeling is exacerbated by the common problem of isolation. Working alone and doing work for
powerful other people mean that home-based workers are denied the fair pay and
appropriate fringe benefits that most other workers receive.

**The Consequences
of Social Class
Position**

Perhaps Karl Marx was right that the key to the class structure is economics. The extent of one's wealth is the determining factor in a number of crucial areas, including the chance to live and the chance to obtain those things (e.g., possessions, education) that are highly valued in society (life chances). This experience is dependent almost exclusively on the economic circumstances of the family into which one is born. Gerth and Mills have contended that life chances refer to

> everything from the chance to stay alive during the first year after birth to the chance to view fine art, the chance to remain healthy and grow tall, and if sick to get well again quickly, the chance to avoid becoming a juvenile delinquent— and very crucially, the chance to complete an intermediary or higher educational grade. (Gerth and Mills, 1953:313)

U.S. households have widely diverse income levels. Demographer Judith Waldrop used the 1989 Current Population Survey (CPS) to construct a portrait of U.S. households (Waldrop, 1990) (see Table 11.2). In Table 11.2, U.S. households are divided into three income categories—upscale, midscale, and downscale. Upscale households have incomes of $50,000 or more; midscale households have incomes of $25,000 or more; and downscale households have incomes of below $25,000. In 1988, 20 percent of all households were upscale, 33 percent were midscale, and 46 percent were downscale.

Waldrop's findings included the following:

- Downscale households are split into two groups—the youngest and the oldest households.

Table 11.2 From the richest to the poorest: A portrait of households in the United States

(Selected characteristics of households by income groups)	Total	Less than $25,000	$25,000 to $49,999	$50,000 and over
Total households (in thousands)	92,830	42,569	30,927	19,332
Percent of all households	100.0%	45.9%	33.3%	20.8%
Median household income*	$27,200	$12,900	$35,500	$66,300
Family households	70.9%	56.9%	79.1%	88.7%
Married couples	56.1%	36.6%	66.9%	82.0%
Female-headed families	11.7%	17.5%	8.5%	4.1%
With children under 18	36.1%	29.2%	41.6%	42.7%
One person in household	24.5%	39.5%	15.4%	5.9%
Two or three persons in household	49.8%	44.2%	54.6%	54.6%
Four or more persons in household	25.7%	16.4%	30.0%	39.5%
Median age of householder	49	51	41	42
Percent high school graduates	75.8%	61.0%	85.1%	93.3%
Percent with four or more years of college	22.3%	9.7%	23.7%	47.5%
Black	11.4%	16.4%	8.2%	5.4%
Hispanic	7.1%	8.7%	6.6%	4.4%

*Income figures from the 1989; Current Population Survey are for 1988.

Souce: American Demographics' tabulations of the Census Bureau's March 1989 Current Population Survey. Cited in Judith Waldrop, "Up and Down the Income Scale," *American Demographics* (July, 1990):24–30. Reprinted with permission © American Demographics.

- Minorities make up only a small portion of downscale households.
- Midscale households are not the most family-oriented households.
- Level of education is strongly connected to household income.
- Marital status is also connected to household income.

This portrait of households in the United States reveals important patterns associated with income level.

In reality, most family incomes are highly variable. A rapid rise or drop in living standard is not unusual. Life-cycle events have profound effects on family well-being. Research conducted by the University of Michigan's Panel Study of Income Dynamics has discovered dramatic shifts in income as individuals move through life. Seven key events accounted for the variability in family living standards: divorce or separation from a spouse, the death of a spouse or parent, becoming a family head or spouse, unemployment, work loss due to retirement, a reduction in the work hours of a wife, and a reduction in the work hours of other family members. Three quarters of people in the United States experience at least one of these events in a decade. The events that occur to individuals in their prime working years are the most likely to be involuntary and unpredictable. Because these losses are unexpected, they are more harmful to the families that experience them than are the planned losses experienced by older people (Duncan, 1987:9).

Parents and Children

Since World War II, economic roles within the family have shifted significantly. One of the most important changes has been the increase in married-couple families in which both spouses are in the labor force, or **dual-worker families**. In 1950, one out of every eight married women with a child under age six was in the labor force; now the proportion is more than one out of every two women. Regardless of the presence of children, including infants, wives are now more likely to work outside of the home than to work solely as homemakers. Fifty-eight percent of mothers with preschool children are now in the labor force.

Dual-worker families are now the dominant family model among workers in the labor force. The number of single-parent families maintained by women has also grown—from about 5 percent of all families in 1965 to around 10 percent in 1988. (Hayghe, 1990:14).

As so-called traditional working arrangements of parents have shifted, U.S. families have become more diverse. New patterns of parents' employment have produced massive changes in children's living arrangements. Half a century ago, the overwhelming majority of children lived in families in which the father was in the labor force and the mother maintained the home. This model is now the exception rather than the rule.

Working mothers in both categories—single and married—share similar problems, such as juggling the demands of a job, housework, and parenting, as well as finding good child care. However, one critical difference is that single mothers tend to raise their children with inadequate financial resources, whereas married mothers in the work force often have a stronger financial base.

Social Supports for Working Parents

Dual-earner families and single-parent families share a common problem—the lack of adequate social supports in the community and workplace to ease the strains of their dual roles of workers and parents. In general, U.S. society is unresponsive to the needs of working parents. (This section is adapted from Baca Zinn and Eitzen, 1993:177–178.)

Among the many problems facing working parents, two are critical: obtaining job-protected leaves for family emergencies including birth; and finding satisfactory care for their children while they are at work. In both instances, the policies of the federal and state governments lag behind the child support policies of other Western nations.

Parental leave.   Some businesses provide generous parental leave policies for their employees so that parents can have children, remain at home for some time after the birth of children, or meet the emergency health needs of their families without losing their jobs, benefits, or sometimes even wages. Other employers have less generous programs or no programs at all for their employees. For example, a survey of the nation's largest companies found that only 52 percent had some form of maternity leave with an associated job guarantee (Phillips, 1990). Some states have such provisions—twenty-six states in 1990 required leaves extending from four weeks to six months (Aldous and Dumon, 1991:475).

Until recently, the United States and the Union of South Africa were the only two industrial nations to have no family leave legislation. Virtually all other industrialized countries provide some form of family leave. The two biggest economic competitors of the United States, Japan and Germany, each guarantee at least three months of paid leave with additional unpaid leave if desired (Shanker, 1990a). The Family and Medical Leave Act signed by President Clinton in 1993 is an important victory on a major social issue. After eight years of effort in Congress and two vetoes by former President Bush, the new law provides twelve weeks of unpaid leave per year from work for the birth or adoption of a child, for the care of a seriously ill child, spouse, or parent, or for a serious illness affecting the employee. Employers must guarantee that a worker can return to the same or a comparable job. Although this is an important advance on the family policy front, the new law is greatly limited. It applies only to companies with fifty or more employees. This means that half of the U.S. work force will not be affected.

Child care.   Probably the biggest problem facing working parents is finding accessible and acceptable child care. (The following is from Baca Zinn and Eitzen, 1993:178–179.) *Accessible* refers to cost, proximity, and compatibility with work schedules. *Acceptable* refers to various dimensions of adequacy, such as sanitation, safety, stimulation, and caring supervision. Each of these variables is important, but the most immediate concerns are availability and cost. Child care is very expensive; it is the largest single work-related expense for working mothers (Aldous and Dumon, 1991:475). "In-home care runs about $8,000 a year. Top quality care outside the home is estimated to be $5,000 a year, and acceptable care in licensed pre-schools averages $3,500" (Christensen, 1988:165). This means, of course, that the more affluent parents are able to take advantage of higher-quality facilities that emphasize child development and other learning opportunities. Parents who are less well off are more likely to use child care facilities that are overcrowded, unlicensed, and perhaps even unhealthy.

Some parents may opt out of employment because they do not have the resources for adequate child care. Research also suggests that the lack of good child care often confines women to part-time or home-based work. The result, as Elliott Currie and Jerome Skolnick argue, is that "inadequate child care helps trap many women in low-paying, dead-end work or joblessness" (Currie and Skolnick, 1988:229).

The United States has no comprehensive child care system. This lack of a system differentiates us from the other industrialized nations. (See "Another Society, Another Way" about France.)

> For decades, other countries have recognized that children are valuable societal resources, and they have provided families with a broad base of support. Sixty-seven countries, including all developed nations except the United States, provide family or child allowances in the form of cash benefits to supplement the incomes of those raising children. In addition, most European countries guarantee jobs, seniority, and pension entitlements to parents who leave work for an average of six months to one year at the time of childbirth. Most also provide some cash benefit through the social security system as wage replacement dur-

ANOTHER SOCIETY, ANOTHER WAY

CHILD CARE IN FRANCE

Why do we have to have such a lousy system of child care? Working parents who agonize over finding decent and affordable child care often have to settle on something that may not be decent. And if that's hard on the parents, just think of the kids! It's not that we're too poor, either. Some countries no wealthier than we are have excellent child-care systems that are even publicly financed. How do they do it?

A group of specialists who recently went to France to examine its system of child care gives some answers to this question in *A Welcome for Every Child: How France Achieves Quality in Child Care* (New York: The French-American Foundation, 1989). The visitors found a comprehensive, generously financed national system that includes public and private schools for preschoolers, a range of child-care options for younger children and free preventive health care for children under six.

French children don't have to attend preschool, but almost all of the country's three- to five-year-olds do—85 percent in public schools and 13 percent in private schools. Since only about 46 percent of French mothers are in the workforce, the high percentage of kids in school demonstrates how satisfied parents are with the system. And they are right. French census data show that children who attend preschool increase their chances of passing first grade, no matter what their socioeco-

nomic background, and this in turn is a good predictor of success later in school.

The quality of French preschool teachers undoubtedly has something to do with the quality of the system. Unlike their wretchedly paid and often poorly trained American counterparts, these teachers must have the equivalent of a master's degree in their field, and they are paid accordingly. The government works hard to get good people into the profession and keep them there by giving them a free education and a modest living allowance while they study. In return, the new teachers promise to teach for five years after graduation.

Child-care programs for younger French children offer the choice and flexibility Americans like to talk about and with a much higher level of quality than we manage. There are the familiar options of child-care centers and home care. And there are child-care networks of 6 to 35 individual home-care providers who are recruited, trained and monitored by central administrations.

The child-care centers and the networks are supervised by pediatric nurses with specialties in child development, so the kids get highly professional care. Even individual home-care providers are far more likely to be licensed and supervised than the ones in this country. In fact, the figures are staggering.

ing the leave period. All now provide additional unpaid leave from six months to three years.

The United States is thus the only industrialized nation that fails to provide workers with comprehensive health-care services, maternity benefits, paid or unpaid leaves, or job guarantees. Although the infrastructure to support a vastly expanded child-care industry is now emerging . . . no national child-care policy currently exists to guide its formation. Of all the nations in the world, only four lack a family policy: South Africa, New Guinea, the Sudan, and the United States. (Lubeck and Garrett, 1988:31; see also Kamerman and Kahn, 1988)

Currently, the federal government is involved in providing for child care through three programs. First, it permits the deduction of child care payments on income tax returns. This amounts to about a $4 billion tax credit, which is considerable. The problem, however, is that by being tied to taxes, it benefits the most affluent families and has negligible effects on the poor. Second, Congress passed the Child Care and Development Block Grant, which authorized $2.5 billion for the states over three years, beginning in 1991 ($731.9 million for that year). Under this legislation, the states are required to use three-quarters of the grant to help eligible families pay for care or for activities to increase the availability and quality of care. The remaining 25 percent is reserved for quality improvements, early childhood education, and school-age child care programs (Children's Defense Fund, 1991:46–49).

According to the report, 75 percent of all French home-care providers are licensed, in comparison with as few as 10 percent here.

One reason for this contrast is the French government's determined use of incentives. Parents get special tax deductions when they hire a licensed child-care giver rather than an unlicensed one. And when care givers become licensed, they are eligible for fringe benefits that other French workers get: retirement and disability benefits, unemployment insurance, paid maternity leave and paid sick and vacation leave—all financed by the government. They also are entitled to a minimum wage, although they may bargain with their employers for more.

As a result, the French can set and maintain a decent standard for people who take care of children in their homes. Parents know that the people they employ have met certain requirements and have agreed to be advised and monitored by pediatric nurses who visit their homes at least every three months and more often if needed. Parents don't need to fly blind, the way we often do here. And they don't have to accept something that is not acceptable because that's all there is.

The universal preventive health service is another piece of the French child-care system. It actually begins before children are born with free prenatal care for their mothers and continues with free examinations throughout early childhood and preschool. The system offers parents incentives to get preventive care for their children by linking examinations with admission to and continuance in child-care programs and by giving allowances to parents who take advantage of the services.

What kinds of lessons can we draw from the child-care system in France? *A Welcome for Every Child* doesn't suggest that we adopt the French system. But it makes French child care a mirror in which we can see our own shabby practice. We talk vaguely about being a child-centered society and come up with half-funded programs that serve a tiny fraction of our children. The French believe society is responsible for giving *all* children a good start—for "awakening" and "welcoming" them. And they act on their belief by spending $7.12 billion a year, or about $130 per capita, on their child-care program.

Why shouldn't we do as much? We are not a poor nation by any means; in 1985, the income of the average American citizen was nearly twice that of the average French citizen—$16,494 compared to $9,251. In failing to care for all our children, we are cheating them and, ultimately, ourselves.

Source: Albert Shanker, "The French System of Child Care: A Welcome for Every Child," *New York Times* (November 11, 1990):E7. Reprinted with permission.

Third, in addition to the Child Care and Development Block Grant, $300 million a year for each of five years will be available to states for families who are at risk of becoming welfare dependant and who need child care in order to work. In order to receive these funds, each state must match the amount provided by the federal government.

In particular, those who are powerful in the states will vary in political views about child care. Some will take the politically conservative position that the government should not interfere with parents' decisions regarding their children. The assumption is that parents (and particularly mothers, because child care is also viewed primarily as a woman's job) will find their own arrangements for care and will come up with the money to pay for them (Currie and Skolnick, 1988:231). Other parents strongly oppose the traditional laissez-faire government attitude regarding day care. Day-care centers, it is argued, must be provided as the rights of parents and children and as the obligation of society.

Aside from the issue of availability of good child care, there is the crucial question of the effects of child care on children. The common assumption is that a preschool child deprived of maximum interaction with its parents, especially the mother (maternal deprivation), will be harmed. Because this belief is widely accepted, many working parents feel guilty for their assumed neglect.

> Many modern mothers share [the] conviction that a mother should not give her infant to a substitute caretaker. In violating that natural obligation, she believes she is not only placing her child's development at risk but also increasing the likelihood that she will produce a socially disruptive adult. (Kagan, 1978:91)

The relationship between child care and child development is complex, involving sources within the child (for example, temperament, impairment), factors in the child's immediate environment (such as the quality of relationships with parents), and factors in the child's larger social environment (for example, neighborhood and the broader culture). Although this complexity prevents us from gaining a full understanding of the relationships between child care and child development, the cumulative evidence from empirical studies does permit us to draw some conclusions (the following is from a thorough review of the research by a panel on child care of the National Research Council as reported in Hayes, Palmer, and Zaslow, 1990:47–144; see also Belsky, 1991).

1. Young children need to develop enduring relationships with a limited number of specific individuals, relationships characterized by affection, reciprocal interaction, and responsiveness to the individualized cues of young children.
2. There is a normal tendency for children to form multiple, simultaneous attachments to caregivers.
3. Children can benefit from "multiple parenting" *if* it provides affection, warmth, responsiveness, and stimulation in the context of enduring relationships with a reasonably small number of caregivers (usually assumed to be five or fewer).
4. For children beginning child care after their first year in life, there is little indication of differences in the mother-child relationship. Children beginning full-time child care within the first year, however, increase the risk of insecurity in

their attachments to their mothers than children at home full-time with their mothers.

5. Children reared in child care orient more strongly to peers and somewhat less strongly to adults than do their home-reared counterparts.

6. Child care does not negatively impact the cognitive development of middle-class children, and it has positive consequences for the intellectual development of low-income children (if the child care programs emphasize cognitive enrichment, as Head Start does).

7. The overall quality of child care (group size, caregiver/child ratio, caregiver training, and educational material available) is associated with children's cognitive as well as social development.

8. The children who experience quality care in their families and child care environments have the strongest development. Children from low-income families are the most likely to be found in lower-quality care settings; thus, they experience the double jeopardy from encountering stresses at home and stress in their care environments.

Single Parents and Their Children

In 1990, some 15.9 million children under the age of eighteen lived in one-parent households, and another 1.8 million lived with neither parent. The increase in one-parent families has been dramatic in recent years, from 20 percent of all families with children under age eighteen in 1980 to 25 percent in 1990 (for the distribution by race, see Table 11.3). About nine out of ten single-parent households are currently headed by a woman with no husband present. This is a consequence of the high divorce rate (which has doubled in the past fifteen years), the relatively high rate of never-married mothers (which also has doubled in the last fifteen years) and the strong tendency for divorced and separated women to have custody of the children.

The important question to answer concerning this trend is, what are the effects on children of living in mother-only families? Research has shown consistently that children from single-parent homes are more likely than children from intact families to have behavioral problems such as mental illness, drug abuse, and delinquency. McLanahan and Booth's (1991) review of the recent research on

Table 11.3 Percentage of children under 18 living with one parent by race ethnicity: 1960, 1970, 1980, 1990

Race/Ethnicity	1960	1970	1980	1990
White	7.1	8.7	15.1	19.2
Latino	(NA)	(NA)	21.1	30.0
Black	21.9	31.8	45.8	54.8

Source: Bureau of the Census, "Marital Status and Living Arrangements: March 1990," *Current Population Reports,* Series P–20, No. 450 (May 1991), p. 5.

children from mother-only families, compared to children from two-parent families, shows that:

- They have poorer academic achievement. This relationship is even more negative for boys than for girls.
- They are more likely to have higher absentee rates at school.
- They are more likely to drop out of school.
- They are more likely to marry early and to have children early, both in and out of marriage.
- If they marry, they are more likely to divorce.
- They are more likely to commit delinquent acts and to engage in drug and alcohol use.

Because 90 percent of one-parent families are headed by a woman, the common explanation for the disproportionate pathologies found among the children of single parents has been that the absence of a male adult is detrimental to their development (Davidson, 1990). The evidence is not clear on this, except for one point. The absence of a spouse makes coping with parenting more difficult. Coping is difficult for any single parent—female or male—because of three common sources of strain: (1) responsibility overload, in which single parents make all the decisions and provide for all of their family's needs; (2) task overload, in which the demands of work, housekeeping, and parenting can be overwhelming for one person; and (3) emotional overload, in which single parents must always be on call to provide the necessary emotional support. Clearly, when two persons share these parental strains, it is more likely that the needs of the children will be met.

While the factors just described help to explain the behavioral differences between parents from one-parent and two-parent homes, they sidestep the major reason—a fundamental difference in economic resources. As Andrew Cherlin has argued, "it seems likely that the most detrimental aspect of the absence of fathers from one-parent families headed by women is not the lack of a male presence *but the lack of a male income*" (Cherlin, 1981:81; emphasis added). In 1989, for example, 32 percent of single-mother families were below the poverty line compared to only 5.6 of two-parent families (U.S. Bureau of the Census, 1989). The reasons are obvious. First, many divorced or separated women have not been employed for years and find it difficult to reenter the job market. Second and more crucial, jobs for women, centered as they are in the bottom tier of the segmented job market, are poorly paid; women (*women,* we must underscore again) presently earn less than 70 cents for every dollar earned by men. And, third, half of the men who owe child support do not pay all they owe, and a quarter of them do not pay anything; women who do receive child support find that the amount covers less than half the actual cost of raising a child. Thus, as a study in California indicated, one year after divorce, the woman's income drops by 73 percent while the man's rises by 42 percent (Weitzman, 1985).

The economic plight of single-parent families is much worse for families of color. Females of color who head households have the same economic problems as White women who are in the same situation plus the added burdens of institutional racism. In addition, they are less likely to be receiving child support (their husbands, unlike White husbands, are much more likely to be poor), and they are more likely to have been high-school dropouts, further reducing their potential for earning a decent income.

The financial plight of women head of households is sometimes alleviated in part by support from a kinship network. Relatives may provide child care, material goods, money, and emotional support. But for many, kin may not be near, and for others, there may be a reluctance to seek help.

Public assistance programs, particularly, Aid to Families with Dependent Children and food stamps, have helped women-headed families in the past to provide a modest level of support. However, these governmental programs were reduced considerably during the 1980s, adding significantly to the numbers who live in poverty and lowering their already meager standards of living even further.

Children's poverty has also increased in two-parent families. According to Harvard researchers Mary Jo Bane and David Ellwood (1989), poverty among two-parent families was a substantial component of children's poverty in the 1980s. Poor two-parent families are often part of the "working poor." Stagnation in the wages of male workers during the 1980s contributed to poverty even in families in which full-time work is the norm.

Children's economic status can be precarious in a variety of family forms. In 1992, an estimated 20 percent of all children in the United States lived in poverty. Striking racial differences in the poverty rates of children have increased in the last decade. Black and Latino children are more likely to be poor than are White children in both one-parent and two-parent families.

(The following discussion is adapted from Baca Zinn and Eitzen, 1993: 165–167.) That one in five children in the United States is living in poverty raises serious policy questions. Recent public policy has shifted away from children. While the situations of children should be improving relative to other social categories, socioeconomic indicators suggest the opposite. The elderly are increasing in numbers (an increase of 54 percent from 1960 to 1980), while numbers of children are decreasing (a loss of 7 percent at that time). This change would appear on the surface to benefit children, with more societal and family resources per child, better pupil-teacher ratios, and the like. Similarly, it would seem that the elderly would be especially disadvantaged by their own high numbers because of fewer societal resources, overcrowded nursing homes, and too few medical resources. In actuality, however, the opposite has occurred (the following is dependent on Preston, 1984).

The clearest evidence for the shift in support away from children and toward the elderly involves the changing proportion in poverty. In 1970, the proportion of elderly in poverty was double the national average, yet by 1990 the poverty rate among the elderly was below the national average (12.2 percent compared to the national rate of 13.5 percent). The poverty rate for children under age fourteen in 1970 was more than one-third lower than that for the elderly. By 1990 this rate had changed, with 20.6 percent of children living in poverty.

In effect, since 1970 the proportion of children living in poverty has increased while the proportion of elderly living in poverty has decreased below the national average (certain categories of older people are still disproportionately poor, however—women, racial minorities, and people living alone). During the last twenty years, federal benefits to the elderly have risen from one-sixth of the federal budget to one-fourth (to about $300 billion annually). This increase has occurred because federal policymakers have expanded Social Security benefits by indexing the benefits to offset inflation. These decisions have benefited the elderly.

Conversely, however, these same decision makers did not provide adequately for needy families with children. The divorce rate has risen dramatically since 1970, resulting in many female-headed families. These families, for the most part, do not receive adequate child support from fathers, and if the mothers work, they receive relatively low wages. While the proportion of these families was expanding, the government actually reduced the programs targeted to benefit children (e.g., the children's share of Medicaid, Aid to Families with Dependent Children, Head Start, food stamps, child nutrition, and federal aid to education).

Childhood poverty is especially acute for racial minorities. In 1990, for children under age eighteen, 44.8 percent of Blacks and 38.4 percent of Latinos were below the poverty line, compared to 15.9 percent of Whites (U.S. Bureau of the Census, 1991:4). The bias against children in federal programs is heightened for minority children. Senator Daniel Patrick Moynihan has pointed out that there are two ways the federal government provides benefits to children in single-parent families. The first is Aid to Families with Dependent Children. The majority of the children receiving this type of aid are Black or Hispanic. Since 1970 the government has *decreased* the real benefits by 13 percent. The other form of assistance is Survivors Insurance (SI), which is part of Social Security. The majority of children receiving SI benefits are White, and these benefits have *increased* by 53 percent since 1970 (adjusted for inflation). Moynihan, whose previous work on Black families has blamed them for their disadvantage, sees the structure as the source of the problem in this instance. In his words:

> To those who say we don't care about children in our country, may I note that the average provision for children under SI has been rising five times as fast as average family income since 1970. We do care about some children. Majority children. It is minority children—not only but mostly—who are left behind. (Moynihan, 1988:5)

The decisions to help the elderly disproportionately reflect the power that the elderly have compared to the young. The elderly have electoral power. They are organized, with several national organizations dedicated to political action that will benefit their interests (the American Association of Retired Persons, for example, is the nation's largest special interest organization, with 33 million members and growing by 8,000 daily). As 15 percent of the voting public and much more in areas with high concentrations of old people (e.g., Florida), politicians tend to pay attention to their special needs. Children, on the other hand, have no electoral power and few advocates (an exception is the Children's Defense Fund). Their parents, especially those who are poor, are not organized. So, in a time of fiscal austerity the priorities of children—prenatal care for poor women, nutritional and health care, day care, and better schools—are underfunded. The irony here is that the political right wing, which claims to be profamily, limits its political agenda to antiabortion legislation and court cases and ignores or fights governmental assistance to needy children and their struggling parent(s).

The argument here is *not* that the elderly and the young should compete for scarce resources and that one or the other should win. It is not a matter of "day care or wheelchair . . . toddlers vs. totterers" (Reeves, 1988:3H). Rather, both age groups are U.S. dependents and are in need. The test of a civilization is the condition of its dependents. So far the United States has opted to care moderately well for one and not at all for the other. (See the Observation on moments in the United States.)

Divorce

Most people in the United States marry, but all marriages do not last forever; some eventually are dissolved. Recent divorce rates show that the chances of a first marriage in the United States ending in divorce are about one in two. One expert (Bumpass, 1990) argues that if current levels persist, 60 percent of recent marriages will end in divorce. The U.S. divorce rate is the world's highest—more than triple the Japanese rate and at least double the divorce rates in other major industrial democracies except England.

OBSERVATION

MOMENTS IN AMERICA

Every 35 seconds an infant is born into poverty.

Every 2 minutes an infant is born to a mother who received late or no prenatal care.

Every 2 minutes an infant is born at low birthweight (less than 5 pounds, 8 ounces).

Every 11 minutes an infant is born at very low birthweight (less than 3 pounds, 8 ounces).

Every 14 minutes an infant dies in the first year of life.

Every 31 seconds an infant is born to an unmarried mother.

Every 55 seconds an infant is born to a mother who is not a high school graduate.

Every 21 seconds a 15- to 19-year-old woman becomes sexually active for the first time.

Every 32 seconds a 15- to 19-year-old woman becomes pregnant.

Every 64 seconds an infant is born to a teenage mother.

Every 5 minutes an infant is born to a teenage mother who already had a child.

Every 74 seconds a 15- to 19-year-old woman has an abortion.

Every 14 hours a child younger than 5 is murdered.

Every 5 hours a 15- to 19-year-old is murdered.

Every 2 hours a 20- to 24-year-old is murdered.

Every 2 seconds of the school day a public school student is suspended.

Every 4 seconds of the school day a public school student is corporally punished.

Every 10 seconds of the school day a student drops out of school.

Source: The State of America's Children 1991, copyright 1991, Children's Defense Fund.

Demographics of Divorce

Divorce and marital separation are not evenly distributed through the population but vary according to social and economic characteristics. The following list gives some generalizations about divorce in the United States.

- Half of all divorces occur during the first seven years of marriage.
- The divorce rate is related to economic conditions: the rate increases during prosperity. Apparently, this increase is due to unwillingness to break up a marriage when wives and children will need greater economic support.
- The younger the age at marriage of the partners, the greater is the likelihood of divorce. Martin and Bumpass (1989) conclude that age at first marriage is the strongest predictor of divorce in the first five years of marriage. "Men and women who are under the age of twenty when they first marry are two to three times more likely to divorce than their counterparts who first marry in their twenties" (Price and McKenry, 1988:17).
- The higher the income, the less is the likelihood of divorce.
- The higher the education for males, the lower the incidence of divorce. In contrast to males, a more complicated pattern is found for women. The highest rate of divorce is found among the least educated women, followed by those with postgraduate degrees. The lowest rates were found for those women with high school and college educations.

Half of all divorces occur during the first seven years of marriage.

- The divorce patterns for Blacks and Hispanics differ significantly from those of Whites. Data from 1960 through 1990 show that White and Hispanic marriages are the most stable, with the divorce rate for Blacks more than twice as great as that for Whites and Hispanics.
- About four out of every five people who obtain a divorce will remarry, with men more likely than women to do so.

There are many reasons for the increased divorce rate, including increased independence (social and financial) of women; deindustrialization that eliminates many jobs for men and makes women's employment necessary; women's inequality; greater tolerance of divorce by religious groups; and reform of divorce laws, especially the adoption of no-fault divorce in many states (that is, one spouse no longer has to prove that the other was at fault in order to obtain a divorce). An important reason is the striking change in public attitudes toward divorce. Divorce is a difficult step and one that commands sympathy for the partners and children. But as Goode observes, "It is no longer considered a violation of public decency. Whether the individual is viewed as the sinner or as sinned against, divorce is generally accepted today as one possible solution for family difficulties" (Goode, 1976:529).

The Consequences of Divorce

Divorce is an intensely personal event, and this intensity makes the breakup a painful experience, even when both parties want the marriage to end. In this section we scrutinize the personal side of divorce—the consequences for ex-wives and ex-husbands and for their children. (This section is adapted from Baca Zinn and Eitzen, 1993:378–385.)

"His" and "her" divorce.   Both partners in a divorce are victims. Each is affected, in the typical case, by feelings of loneliness, anger, remorse, guilt, low self-esteem, depression, and failure. Although ex-spouses tend to share these negative feelings, the divorce experience differs for husband and wife in significant ways because of the structure of society and traditional gender inequality.

"His" divorce.   Ex-husbands have some major advantages and a few disadvantages over their ex-wives. On the advantage side, they are almost always much better off financially. Typically, they were the major income producers for their families, and after the separation their incomes stay disproportionately with them. A ten-year study in California, for example, found that men after divorce were much better off than were women. The study found that in Los Angeles County the income of divorced men jumped 42 percent in the first year after divorce while their former wives suffered a 73 percent financial loss (Weitzman, 1985).

A second benefit that men have over women after divorce is greater freedom. If children are involved, they usually live with the mother (about 90 percent do), so most men are free not only from the constraints of marriage but also of child care. Thus, they are freer than ex-wives to date, travel, go to school, take up a hobby, or work at a second job. Especially significant is sexual freedom, because males tend to have more money and leisure time. Moreover, because older men in U.S. society are considered more attractive to younger women than are older women to younger men, men have a much wider selection of new potential spouses than do women.

The experience of ex-husbands on some counts, however, is more negative than that of ex-wives. Many divorced men, especially those from traditional marriages, experience initial difficulty in maintaining a household routine. They are more likely to eat erratically, sleep less, and have difficulty with shopping, cooking, laundry, and cleaning. And because ex-wives usually have legal custody of the children, ex-husbands are able to see their children only relatively rarely and at prescribed times. Thus, they may experience great loneliness because they have lost not only a wife but their children as well. Some fathers are so frustrated and distraught by this situation that they kidnap their own children.

The image of liberated ex-husbands as swinging bachelors does not fit many men. Some find dating difficult because they have not done it for many years. They find that women in general have changed or that they have changed. Many men withdraw from relationships because of their fear of rejection (Mariani, 1980). These fears, along with the loss of wives and children, are aggravated by the traditional male gender role, which discourages them from sharing their pain with others (Keen, 1991).

"Her" divorce.   The benefits of divorce for women are few. To be sure, many ex-wives are relieved to have ended an onerous relationship, and some are even freed from a physically abusive one. Some are now liberated from a situation that stifled their educational and career goals. Of course, divorce also frees spouses to seek new and perhaps more fulfilling relationships.

But the negatives of divorce clearly outweigh the positives for women. Women, especially those oriented to traditional gender roles, often feel helpless and experience a loss of identity associated with their husbands' statuses. Divorced mothers who retain sole custody of their children often feel overwhelmed by the demands of full-time parenting and economic survival. The emotional and time overloads that usually accompany solo parenting leave little time for personal pursuits. The result is that divorced women often experience personal and social isolation, especially the feeling of being locked into a child's world. Also White women cope less well with divorce than do African American women (Price and McKenry, 1988:63). Presumably, this is because Black women have better social supports (extended family networks and friendship and church support networks) than do White women (Taylor et al., 1991:280–281).

Both ex-husbands and ex-wives tend to lose old friends. For the first two months or so after the divorce, married friends are supportive and spend time with each of the former mates. But these contacts soon decline because, as individuals, divorced people no longer fit into couple-oriented activities. This disassociation from marital friends is especially acute for women (Goetting, 1983:369).

Those few women who give up custody of their children face a two-edged sword. On the one hand, they have lost their children, and on the other, they face society's double standard—it is appropriate for divorced men to give custody of their children to their children's mothers but not for women to let fathers have custody. By giving up their children they experience social ostracism as unfit mothers.

The biggest problem facing almost all divorced women is a dramatic decline in economic resources (see Holden and Smock, 1991). As Leonore Weitzman argues, for most women and children

> divorce means precipitous downward mobility—both economically and socially. The reduction in income brings residential moves and inferior housing, drastically diminished or nonexistent funds for recreation and leisure and intense pressures due to inadequate time and money. Financial hardships in turn cause social dislocation and a loss of familiar networks for emotional support and social services, and intensify the psychological stress for women and children alike. On a societal level, divorce increases female and child poverty and creates an ever-widening gap between the economic well being of divorced men on the one hand, and their children and former wives on the other. (Weitzman, 1985:323)

Divorce has drastic social and economic effects on women and their children. It is a major social problem created by institutions that perpetuate gender discrimination and by divorced fathers who do not contribute to the support of their children (Arendell, 1990:493).

Children and divorce. Approximately 60 percent of divorcing couples have children. This means that about one in every three White children and two in every three Black children by age sixteen will experience the permanent disruption of their parents' marriage. Most of them will remain with their mothers and live in a fatherless home for at least five years (Thornton and Freedman, 1983:8). Some are twice cursed by the broken relationships of their parents; about one-third of White children and one-half of Black children whose mothers remarry will experience a second divorce before the children reach adulthood (Bumpass, 1983).

The crucial question is, What are the consequences of divorce on children? There is clearly the possibility of emotional scars from the period of family conflict and uncertainty prior to the breakup, when children may be caught in the middle and even "exploited by the parents, unwittingly or not, in their relationship with each other during this period" (Bumpass and Rindfuss, 1979:50–51). Children will be affected by the permanency of divorce and the enforced separation from one of the parents. As the extreme, Frank Furstenberg has found that one-half of children of divorce had not seen their father in at least a year (cited in Press, 1983:42). There are the possible negative effects of being raised by a single parent who is overburdened by the demands of children, job, economics, and household maintenance.

Negative consequences also may result from the sharp decline in resources available to the family when the parents separate. This decline may require the family to move to a different home and school, reducing the probability of a college education, and may cause other alterations in life-style. All of these possible outcomes of divorce mean that children may experience behavioral problems, decline in school performance, and other manifestations of maladjustment. Before discussing these problems, however, we must note that the long-term effects of divorce are difficult to measure. We simply cannot know, for example, how the children from a particular family would have fared if the parents had stayed together. In fact, there is evidence that children may be better off with one parent than with two feuding ones (Santrack, 1972).

Violence in U.S. Families

The family has two faces. On the positive side, it is a haven from an uncaring, impersonal world, a place where love and security prevail. The family members love each other, care for each other, and accept each other under all circumstances. However, there is another side to the family. The presence of tension and discord can be found in all families at various phases in the family life cycle. The intensity that characterizes intimate relationships can give way to conflict. Some families resolve the inevitable tensions that arise in the course of daily living, but in other families conflict gives way to violence.

Family Organization and Violence

Although the family is based on love among its members, the way it is organized encourages conflict. First, the family, like all other social organizations, is a power system; that is, power is unequally distributed between parents and children and between spouses. It is essential to see violence in the broader social context of power relations and gender inequalities. A feminist perspective views violence as a symptom of a greater problem—that is, a systematic set of gendered structures that produce violence against women (Breines and Gordon, 1983). Gender differences may not present a problem in some homes, but for many couples these problems can become a constant source of stress.

Unlike most organizations, in which activities and interests are relatively narrow, the family encompasses almost everything. Thus, there are more events over which a dispute can develop. Moreover, there is a vast amount of time during each day when family members can interact. Extensive exposure increases the probability of disagreements, irritations, violations of privacy, and the like, which increase the risk of violence.

Family privacy is another characteristic that enhances the likelihood of violence. The rule in our society that the home is private has two negative consequences. First, it insulates the family members from the protection that society could provide if a family member becomes too abusive. And second, the rule of privacy often prevents the victims of abuse from seeking outside help.

Wife Abuse

The family is a major location of violence in society. One-fourth of all the murders in the United States involve the killing of spouses, parents, and children. The most common request for police help is for domestic disturbances. More police personnel are killed (22 percent) trying to settle family fights than in any other line of duty. Millions of wives and children are regularly assaulted by husbands and parents. Even the elderly are sometimes physically abused by their adult children. Here, we consider only one form of family violence—husbands physically abusing their wives.

Wife abuse is "the use of physical force by a man against his intimate cohabiting partner" (Bograd, 1988:12). Domestic violence is the leading cause of injury and death to U.S. women, causing more harm than vehicular accidents, rapes, and muggings combined. Even though there are some causes of domestic violence in which the wife is the abuser as well as problems of abuse among gay couples, in the overwhelming majority of cases, women are the victims at the hands of men (Brody, 1992:B6). Terms such as *family violence* or *spouse abuse* do not adequately identify the nature of wife abuse because these terms "obscure the dimensions of gender and power that are fundamental to understanding wife abuse" (Bograd, 1988:13). Men use violence as a way to control female partners. This makes male-female relations central to the analysis of interpersonal violence (Kurz, 1989:489).

The actual statistics on battered wives are impossible to obtain. The reasons are fairly obvious. Foremost, the events generally take place in private, with no witnesses other than family members. Battered women are often attended by physicians who treat their wounds either without asking embarrassing questions or, if they know the cause, without reporting the abuse to the authorities. The victims, most commonly, lie about the causes of their injuries because of shame or fear. Finally, many victims do not go to public agencies for help because they have often found them to be unresponsive. Unresponsiveness is especially true of the police and the courts, because these agencies typically feel that most domestic violence is a private affair and none of their business. Also, the situation often comes down to the wife's word against her husband's, leaving prosecution difficult if not impossible.

Understanding the limitations of the data on spouse abuse, we can examine some estimates of the frequency of its occurrence:

- Each year, an estimated 6 million women are beaten by the men they live with, and 30 percent of women who become homicide victims die at the hands of men with whom they have a family relationship.
- At some point in their married lives, 25 to 50 percent of wives are physically assaulted by their husbands.
- Wife beating, occurring once every eighteen seconds, is estimated by the FBI to be the most frequently occurring crime in the country (Shapiro, 1987; Bukovinsky, 1982).
- In 3 percent of divorce actions husbands mentioned the wife's physical abuse as a reason for seeking a divorce; 37 percent of wives in divorce actions mentioned their husband's physical abuse as a reason (Steinmetz, 1977:65).

These statistics, although imprecise, reveal that wife abuse is a fairly common practice. We do know some facts about the conditions under which this phenomenon occurs. Foremost, although they are found in all social strata, battered women tend to be found primarily in families threatened by economic hardships. Ursula Dibble and Murray Straus (1980:77) found from their study of 2143 U.S. couples that violence against spouses decreases as income increases. They reason that increased wife abuse occurs in poor families because

> low income husbands are less in a position to live up to their role obligations as providers than are middle-class husbands. Their wives are, therefore, less likely to recognize the male as the head of the house than are their middle-class coun-

Each year an estimated six million women are beaten by the men they live with, and 30 percent of female homicide victims die at the hands of the men with whom they have a "family" relationship.

terparts. When such recognition and other resources are lacking, husbands may, in turn, use force to control their wives. . . . In contrast . . . high-income husbands have economic and prestige resources which let them control their wives without the need to use force. (Dibble and Straus, 1980:79)

Pregnancy seems to be a time when wives are most vulnerable to attack. The National Institute of Mental Health has found that one-quarter of battered women were victims while pregnant (Steif, 1979:76).

Research on husbands known to be abusers of their wives has tended to find that these men are underachievers when compared with their wives. They may be less intelligent, less successful in their jobs or schools, or lower in certain status characteristics compared with their wives. The inability to be superior to one's wife in a male-oriented society apparently leads to the desire to prove one's superiority over her in physical ways. Summarizing this, Gelles and Straus say, "perhaps the most telling of all attributes of the battering man is that he feels inadequate and sees violence as a culturally acceptable way to be both dominant and powerful" (1988:89).

The most common trait associated with wife abuse is the excessive use of alcohol. The problem with assuming a relationship between alcohol abuse and wife abuse is that the relationship is not causal but contributory. All major theorists point to the excessive use of alcohol as a key element in the dynamics of wife beating. However, it is not clear whether a man is violent because he is drunk or whether he drinks to reduce his inhibitions against his violent behavior. Battered women frequently report their husbands appear to use their drunkenness as an excuse for their violence by not remembering the violent incident or pleading for forgiveness because they did not know what they were doing. It may be that the same causal factors that propel a man to drink, low frustration tolerance, for example, are also variables that propel him to beat his wife (Labell, 1979:264).

Wife beating is also generated by a number of problems facing the husband in his marriage, his work, or other situation. The problems may include financial difficulties, sexual dysfunction, and jealousy.

A major contributing factor to being violent in a family situation is coming from a family that was itself violence-prone. Husbands who batter their wives most often come from homes in which they were beaten by their parents or in which they had observed their own fathers beating their mothers. Even though there is a relationship, "this does not predetermine that all those who experience violence will grow up to be abusers" (Gelles and Strauss, 1988:91).

The key determinant, then, is the dominance of males throughout society—in politics, the media, the economic system, the schools, and all other institutions—that makes women supposedly inferior. The secondary status of women makes them subject to those with power. One response for men, when faced with threats to their dominance, is to use physical force. Thus, the reduction and eventual elimination of sexism throughout society will be a major step in solving the problem of wife beating.

Child Abuse and Neglect

Gelles and Straus have concluded that "with the exception of the police and the military, the family is perhaps the most violent social group, and the home the most violent social setting, in our society" (Gelles and Straus, 1979:15). Of the various forms of family violence, violence by parents toward their children is the most prevalent. This problem is reviewed here, focusing on the definition, incidence, causes, and consequences of child abuse. (The following discussion is adapted from Baca Zinn and Eitzen, 1993:347–350.)

Definition and incidence. What constitutes child abuse? (See especially Giovannoni and Becerra, 1979.) The extreme cases of torture, scalding, beatings, and imprisonment are easy to place in this category. But there are problems in determining whether many other actions are abusive. For example, one definition of child abuse is violence "carried out with the intention of, or perceived as having the intention of, physically hurting the child" (Gelles and Straus, 1979:136). This definition includes everything from spanking to murder. The problem is that spanking is used by nine out of ten parents and is considered legitimate and acceptable behavior. At what point does appropriate punishment become excessive? This is an important question for which there is, as yet, no universally accepted answer. However, counselors, social workers, health practitioners, and the courts must agree on a definition because the consequences for the children and parents are enormous. To have a definition that is too lax imperils the health and safety of children, and to have one that is too stringent jeopardizes parents who might incorrectly receive the label of child abuser, have their children taken from them, and even be imprisoned.

Perhaps the most useful definition, focusing on violence, is that child abuse occurs when there is a nonaccidental physical injury requiring medical attention. But this definition omits the area of child neglect. Neglect involves a range of behaviors, including the inadequate feeding of a child or lack of provision of sanitary living conditions. Neglect may be just as damaging to children, physically and mentally, as is physical aggression. The problem is complicated because children may or may not be willfully neglected by their parents.

Given these problems with defining **child abuse**, we have chosen an all-inclusive definition: "The distinctive acts of violence and nonviolence and acts of omission and commission that place children at risk" (Gelles, 1976:136). We should not be misled, in using this broad definition, into thinking that all the forms of child abuse and neglect are essentially alike, caused by the same sources, and subject to a uniform treatment (Gelles, 1976). We generalize about this problem, but the reader is warned that it is, like all social problems, very complex.

The precise extent of child abuse and neglect is impossible to know for two reasons. First, studies of the phenomena have not used uniform definitions; and second, the issue is extremely sensitive to the persons involved. To be the perpetrator or victim of child abuse is generally something for which people are stigmatized. Acts of violence and neglect are hidden from society because they occur in private. When asked by a survey researcher if they have ever physically abused their children, abusing parents will most likely deny such an act. Thus, many statistics are taken from police, teachers, social workers, and medical personnel who must *assume* that the children were victims of abuse. Obviously, such subjective observations are subject to error. As one illustration of the problem of subjectivity, we can note that the parents and children of the middle and upper classes are commonly viewed quite differently by authorities than are those from the lower classes. Trained personnel are more likely to assess a poor child with a black eye as a victim of child abuse than a child from a rich family. Also, of course, many cases of abuse and neglect are never seen by authorities. Official statistics, then, always underreport the actual incidence.

In terms of the actual number of cases reported, a total of 2.4 million children were reported as abused or neglected in 1989 (a 10 percent increase over the 1988 number) (Children's Defense Fund, 1991:24). About half of the reported cases involve neglect. Although the extent of neglect is impossible to determine, most professionals agree that it is probably six times more frequent than abuse (Bybee, 1979:6).

Causes.   The reasons for the abuse and neglect of children by parents are complex and varied, involving personal, social, and cultural factors. The most commonly assumed cause for abusive behavior toward children is that the perpetrators are mentally ill. This assumption, however, is a myth that hinders the understanding of child abuse (Gelles, 1976:138). In the view of experts only about 10 percent of maltreating parents have severe personality disorders or psychoses. This is not to say that personal factors are unimportant. Obviously, abusive parents let their aggressive feelings go too far. There are several possible reasons that they do. One important reason is that abused children have a higher probability of becoming abusive parents than do nonabused children. In short, violence tends to beget violence. Abused children may take their parents as models for their own parenting behavior, or they may harbor unusual hostility because of their negative experiences. The failure to learn parenting skills may also be the reason that there is a tendency for children who have lost a parent, been separated from their mothers, or come from a disrupted home to become abusing parents themselves.

Abusive parents, for whatever reason, tend to be more demanding than are other parents. Goode observes that

> abusing parents demand far higher performance from their children than ordinary parents. What they demand is beyond the capacity of their children even to understand, much less perform. Typically they become angry because the child will not stop crying, eats poorly, urinates after being told not to do so, and so on. In fact, they feel righteous about the punishments they have inflicted on their children. They avoid facing the degree of injury they have caused, but they justify their behavior because they feel their children have been "bad." (Goode, 1971:633)

A relatively common trait of abusing parents is chronic alcohol consumption. This activity reduces the normal restraints inhibiting aggression in the individual. Chronic alcoholism is also associated with a number of other factors that produce strain and disruption in stable family patterns—greater unemployment, poor health, low self-esteem, isolation, and preoccupation with self (Macmurray, 1979).

A number of social factors have also been found to be related to child abuse, probably because they increase stress in individuals. The data from a number of studies indicate that child abuse is more likely to occur in families of low socioeconomic status. We must be careful in interpreting these data, because wealthier families are simply better able to hide abuse (e.g., they go to private physicians who may be more reluctant to report signs of abuse in their respectable clients than are the doctors ministering to the poor in general hospitals). Nonetheless, the generalization is appropriate that children of the poor are more likely to be abuse victims (Gelles and Straus, 1979:30; see also Giovannoni, 1971; Pelton, 1981).

Unemployment is another condition associated with child abuse. Unemployment may lead to poverty, low self-esteem (because of being a failure in a success-oriented society), and depression. The unemployed are also homebound, increasing their interaction with children. Gelles and Straus (1979:31) found, for example, that the rate of physical abuse to children in families in which the husband was unemployed was 22 percent; families with an employed husband had a rate of 14 percent. From 1981 to 1982 the reported instances of child abuse rose 10 percent in the United States. According to Anne Cohn, director of the National Committee on Child Abuse, this increase was directly related to the concomitant rise in national unemployment (cited in Atwater, 1983). Similarly, Richard Krugman, director of the C. Henry Kempe National Center for the Prevention and Treatment of Child Abuse and Neglect, attributed, at least in part, the 20 percent increase in reported child abuse cases in Colorado from 1981 to 1982 to the doubling of the unemployment rate in the state (cited in Lindsay, 1983).

The lack of social supports is also related to child abuse. The research by Gelles and Straus found that the most violent parents had lived in the community less than two years; belonged to few, if any, community organizations; and had little contact with friends and relatives.

> The social isolation cuts them off from any possible source of help to deal with the stress of intimate living or economic adversity. These parents are not only more vulnerable to stress, their lack of social involvement also means that they

are less likely to abandon their violent behavior and conform to community values and standards. (Gelles and Straus, 1988:87–88)

Men are much more likely than women to be the assailants in all forms of family violence except child abuse, where women are the perpetrators as often as men. But even this fact reveals that women are much less likely than men to be violent even though they may have greater reason to be. Women are almost always the parent interacting most with children. Women are much more likely than men to be in stressful economic situations (to head households alone, to be in poverty, and to do less fulfilling and economically rewarding work). Because she is the primary parent, a mother also feels more responsibility and guilt than does the father for the failures of her children. Given all of these differential pressures on women, it is impressive that women commit only 50 percent of child abuse (Breines and Gordon, 1983:504).

Gertrude Williams (1980:597) has argued that there are some additional gender-related issues that also promote child abuse by women. In her opinion, the primary reason for child abuse is the pronatalist bias in society. This bias is the widespread belief that a woman's only fulfilling activity is motherhood. This ideology forces many women into a role that they may not want. They are also forced into the mother role by the lack of interesting and well-paid work options and by unwanted pregnancies from inadequate contraceptive methods and beliefs opposing abortion. Unwanted children born to a woman in a marginal economic situation are prime candidates for abuse and neglect.

Consequences.   Many consequences of child abuse are obvious. There can be physical injuries to the child, such as fractures, burns, internal damage, and neurological dysfunctions, which may lead to permanent damage or even death. The physical disabilities and/or mental anguish resulting from abuse may lead to problems with learning, speech, and acceptable behavior patterns for the victims. Psychological problems are another obvious consequence from the trauma of being abused by one's parents.

Parental abuse has also been found to be a fundamental reason for a child running away from home. Incest and other forms of child abuse have been found responsible for about half of runaways. Running away during childhood or adolescence generally has additional negative consequences—a higher incidence of malnutrition, health problems, being victims of assault, and criminal activity, especially prostitution, both male and female.

Adults who were mistreated as children have a greater tendency to be violent when compared with those who are not mistreated. As noted earlier, they are more prone to be child abusers themselves. The best estimate of this rate of intergenerational transmission of violence is about 30 percent (Gelles and Conte, 1991:328–329).

Violence in the family presents the ultimate paradox—the physical abuse of loved ones in the most intimate of social relationships. The bonds between wife and husband, parent and child, and adult child and parent are based on love, yet for many people these bonds represent a trap in which they are victims of unspeakable abuses.

The organizing principle for this chapter is the interaction of the family in two major life-cycle stages (the third, old age, is covered in Chapter 9). The first family relationship is the married couple; like other family relationships, marriage involves intense interaction in a wide range of areas. It often produces strong emotions such as love and sometimes hate. We usually ignore the hate/violence side of marriage, but it is real for many couples who have not learned to manage their emotions. The result is often spouse abuse. The second stage of the life cycle after marriage is parenting, with the intensity of emotions between a parent and child leading some parents to abuse their children physically beyond the societal norms.

Although it is impossible to know the extent of battering that takes place in families, the problem these forms of violence represents is not trivial. The threat of violence in intimate relationships exists for all couples and for parents and children. For people who do not cope well, the result is the abuse by the strong of the weak. But violence in the family is not only a problem of family units. It represents an indictment of society, its institutions, and the cultural norms that support violence.

CHAPTER REVIEW

1. The family is one of the most idealized of all of society's institutions. There are disparities between the common images of the family and real patterns of family life.
2. Families are embedded in class and race hierarchies. This gives them different connections with institutions that can provide resources for family support. It also creates variation in household and family structure. Class and race are important determinants of the quality of family life.
3. The changing nature of work has a direct impact on the family life in several significant ways: (a) as the need for skilled labor has diminished, many blue-collar families have experienced unemployment or underemployment; (b) both spouses working outside the home has become an economic necessity for many families; and (c) some forms of work have moved into the home with mixed consequences for women.
4. A major demographic trend since World War II has been the sharp rise in mothers with young children who work outside the home. Thus, a critical need has emerged in society for accessible and acceptable child care. In general, U.S. society has been unresponsive to this need.
5. About one-fourth of all households with children are single-parent families; more than one-half of all Black families, one-third of Hispanic families, and one-fifth of White families are in this category. In 90 percent of the cases these families are headed by a woman. Single-parent families have a number of unique problems, the most prominent being a lack of economic resources.
6. Twenty percent of all children in the United States live in poverty.
7. The economic situation of children has worsened relative to the elderly.
8. The divorce rate in U.S. society is the highest in the world. The reasons for this high rate are the increased social and financial independence of women, increased affluence, greater tolerance of divorce by religious groups, passage of no-fault divorce laws, and a more lenient public attitude toward divorce.

9. There are several important consequences of divorce: (a) males and females experience divorce differently, with males having more advantages than females; (b) the economic resources ("life chances") to children are reduced; and (c) the trauma for children is heightened for young children, for boys, for large families, and for children whose mother goes to work for the first time after divorce.

10. Key researchers on family violence have concluded that the family is among the most violent social groups and that the home is among the most violent settings in U.S. society. The forms of domestic violence are wife beating, child abuse and neglect, incest, and elderly abuse (a topic discussed in Chapter 9).

11. Wife beating is the most frequently occurring crime in the United States. This abuse is most common when husbands (a) are facing economic problems, (b) are underachievers, and (c) have grown up in violent families. What is most important is that wife beating occurs in a society that supports such violence. A key societal support of wife beating is the dominance of males throughout society.

KEY TERMS

Backstage behavior.   Erving Goffman's term that people act differently in private than they do in public because of fewer constraints.

Family.   Social arrangements whereby persons related by ancestry, marriage, or cohabitation live together, form an economic unit, and often raise children.

Household.   Residential unit in which members share resources. These units vary in membership and composition. A household is not always a family (parents and children), and a family is not always a household (because it may be separated geographically).

Life chances.   Opportunities throughout one's life cycle to live and to experience the good things in society.

Downward mobility.   The movement to a lower social class.

Dual-worker families.   Families in which both spouses are in the labor force.

Wife abuse.   The use of physical force by a man against his intimate cohabiting partner.

Child abuse.   The distinctive acts of violence and nonviolence and acts of omission and commission that place children at risk.

FOR FURTHER STUDY

Dennis A. Ahlburg and Carol J. DeVita. *New Realities of the American Family.* Washington, D.C.: Population Reference Bureau, August 1992.

Maxine Baca Zinn and D. Stanley Eitzen. *Diversity in Families.* 3rd ed. New York: HarperCollins, 1993.

Suzanne M. Bianchi. *America's Children: Mixed Prospects.* Washington, D.C.: Population Reference Bureau, June 1990.

David T. Ellwood. *Poor Support: Poverty in the American Family.* New York: Basic Books, 1988.

Frances K. Goldscheider and Linda J. Waite. *New Families, No Families? The Transformation of the American Home.* Berkeley: University of California Press, 1991.

Arlie Hochschild. *The Second Shift.* New York: Viking, 1989.

Lillian Breslow Rubin. *Worlds of Pain: Life in the Working-Class Family* (with a new introduction). New York: Basic Books, 1976.

Arlene Skolnick. *Embattled Paradise: The American Family in an Age of Uncertainty.* New York: Basic Books, 1991.

Judith Stacey. *Brave New Families.* New York: Basic Books, 1991.

Patricia Voydanoff and Linda C. Majka. *Families and Economic Distress.* Newbury Park, Calif.: Sage Publications, 1988.

Work and Family: Policies for a Changing Work Force. Washington, D.C.: National Academy Press, 1991.

FORUM

IS THE FAMILY IN DECLINE?

According to sociologist David Popenoe, today's societal trends are bringing to an end the cultural dominance of the traditional nuclear family.

I believe that we are now witnessing the end of an era. Today's societal trends are bringing to an end the cultural dominance of what historians call the modern (I will use the term "traditional") nuclear family. By traditional family I mean: a family situated apart from both the larger kin group and the workplace, focused on the procreation of children, and consisting of a legal, lifelong, sexually exclusive, heterosexual, monogamous marriage, based on affection and companionship, in which there is a sharp division of labor (separate spheres) with the female as full-time housewife and the male as primary provider and ultimate authority. Lasting for only a little more than a century, this family form emphasized the male as "good provider," the female as "good wife and mother" and the paramount importance of the family for childrearing. (Of course, not all families conformed to these cultural ideals.) During its cultural heyday, the terms "family," "home," and "mother" ranked extraordinarily high in the hierarchy of American cultural values.

In terms of its distribution across the population, this family form had reached its apogee by the middle of the twentieth century. In the 1950s—fueled in part by falling maternal and child mortality rates, greater longevity, and a high marriage rate—a higher percentage of children than ever before were growing up in stable, two-parent families. Similarly, this period witnessed the highest-ever proportion of women who married, bore children, and lived jointly with husbands at least until age 50.

But beginning in the 1960s, four major social trends emerged to signal a widespread "flight" from both the ideal and the reality of the traditional nuclear family. These trends are: rapid fertility decline, the sexual revolution, the movement of mothers into the labor force, and the divorce revolution.

These trends in family decline are all interrelated. They are evident, in varying degrees, in every industrialized society. They are based, therefore, not in particular political or economic systems, but in the broad cultural shifts that have accompanied industrialization and urbanization.

Fundamentally, what emerges from these cultural shifts is an ethos of radical individualism in which personal autonomy, individual rights, and social equality have gained supremacy as cultural ideals. In keeping with these ideals, the main goals of personal behavior have shifted—from obligation and commitment to social units (families, communities, religions, nations) to personal choices, life-style options, self-fulfillment, and personal pleasure.

The greatest negative effect of recent family trends, in the opinion of nearly everyone, is on children. Because children represent the future of a society, any negative consequences for them are especially significant. There is substantial, if not conclusive, evidence that, due to family changes, the quality of life for children in the past twenty-five years has worsened.

Much of the problem is of a psychological nature and thus difficult to measure quantitatively. Perhaps the most serious problem is a weakening in many families of the fundamental assumption that children are to be loved and valued at the highest level of priority.

Source: Adapted from David Popenoe, "The Family Transformed," *Family Affairs* Vol 2, No. 2–3 (Summer/Fall 1989):1–2. Published by Institute for American Voters, New York.

Sanford M. Dornbusch of The Stanford Center for the Study of Families, Children and Youth, does not agree that the family is in decline.

I agree with David Popenoe that family life is changing: I don't agree that the family is in decline. Whenever social institutions shift their functions and structure, the usual perception is of decay. We shouldn't exaggerate the pleasures associated with an earlier world. The family life of the 1950s was neither as monolithic as is often portrayed, nor was it as happy. There are major differences between current family problems and those of earlier generations, but little is gained by viewing the current situation as unprecedented.

I recently edited a book whose title, *Feminism, Children and the New Families,* expresses some of my central concerns. First, the term "new families" emphasizes that our society must take on the difficult task of assisting numerous types of families, not just those that fit the traditional male-breadwinner/female-homemaker model. Dr. Popenoe is correct in stressing socially responsible action to help the new families.

The term "feminism" brings to mind the central changes in women's roles. Dr. Popenoe is right in noting the relatively brief hegemony of a family form we think of as traditional. Women are in the labor force to stay; our social institutions cannot continue to view working mothers with alarm and do so little to help them. Men also have a role to play. Few men have increased their efforts at home to reflect the double duty faced by so many women.

With respect to "children," it is politically easier to mobilize our society to assist them than to assist working women or families in the abstract. The feminist movement would be well advised to fight for children, whose welfare is inextricably linked to that of their parents. What helps children helps families.

"What do families do best?" We must recognize those key interpersonal functions that are best performed one-on-one in an atmosphere of warmth and caring. Families are still essential; there is no cost-effective substitute. Strengthening the new families is not an option; it's a necessity for our society's survival.

Source: Adapted from "The Family Transformed," *Family Affairs* Vol. 2, No. 2–3 (Summer/Fall 1989):3. Published by Institute for American Voters, New York.

12 Education

This chapter examines one of society's basic institutions—education. We discuss how schooling is organized to perpetuate the existing distribution of power. The chapter is divided into four sections. The first describes the characteristics of U.S. education. The second focuses on how corporate society reproduces itself through education—in particular, how the schools socialize youth in accordance with their class position and point them toward factory, service, bureaucratic, or leadership roles in the economy. The third section describes the current role of education in perpetuating inequality in society. The concluding section describes alternatives to eliminate the race and class biases in education.

The Characteristics of Education in the United States

Education as a Conserving Force

The formal system of education in U.S. society (and in all societies) is conservative, because the avowed function of the schools is to teach newcomers the attitudes, values, roles, specialties, and training necessary to the maintenance of society. In other words, the special task of the schools is to preserve the culture, not to transform it. Thus, the schools indoctrinate their pupils in the culturally prescribed ways. Children are taught to be patriotic. They learn the myths and the superiority of their nation's heritage; they learn who are the heroes and who are the villains. Jules Henry has put it this way:

> Since education is always against some things and for others, it bears the burden of the cultural obsessions. While the Old Testament extols without cease the glory of the One God, it speaks with equal emphasis against the gods of the Philistines; while the children of the Dakota Indians learned loyalty to their own tribe, they learned to hate the Crow; and while our children are taught to love American democracy, they are taught contempt for the totalitarian regimes. (Henry, 1963:285–286)

There is always an explicit or implicit assumption in U.S. schools that the American way is the only really right way. When this assumption is violated on the primary and secondary school level by the rare teacher who asks students to consider the viability of world government, or who proposes a class on the life and teachings of Karl Marx or about world religions, then strong enough pressures usually occur from within the school (administrators, school board) or from without (parents, the American Legion, Daughters of the American Revolution) to quell the disturbance. As a consequence, creativity and a questioning attitude are curtailed in school, as Parenti points out forcefully:

> Among the institutions . . . , our educational system looms as one of the more influential purveyors of dominant values. From the earliest school years, children are taught to compete individually rather than work cooperatively for common goals and mutual benefit. Grade-school students are fed stories of their nation's exploits that might be more valued for their inspirational nationalism than for their historical accuracy. Students are instructed to believe in America's global virtue and moral superiority and to fear and hate the Great Red Menace. They are taught to hold a rather uncritical view of American politico-economic institutions. One nationwide survey of 12,000 children (grades two

to eight) found that most youngsters believe "the government and its representatives are wise, benevolent and infallible, that whatever the government does is for the best."

Teachers concentrate on the formal aspects of representative government and accord little attention to the influences that wealthy, powerful groups exercise over political life. Teachers in primary and secondary schools who wish to introduce radical critiques of American politico-economic institutions do so often at the risk of jeopardizing their careers. High school students who attempt to sponsor unpopular speakers and explore dissident views in student newspapers have frequently been overruled by administrators and threatened with disciplinary action.

School texts at the elementary, high-school, and even college levels seldom give but passing mention to the history of labor struggle and the role of American corporations in the exploitation and maldevelopment of the Third World. Almost nothing is said of the struggles of indentured servants, of Latino, Chinese, and European immigrant labor, and of small farmers. The history of resistance to slavery, racism, and U.S. expansionist wars is largely untaught in American schools at any level. (Parenti, 1988:37–38).*

Mass Education

People in the United States have a basic faith in education. This faith is based on the assumption that a democratic society requires an educated citizenry so that individuals can participate in the decisions of public policy. For this reason they not only provide education for all citizens but also compel children to remain in school at least until the eighth grade or until age sixteen (although the law varies somewhat from state to state).

It is hard to quarrel with the belief that all children should be compelled to attend school, since it should be for their own good. After all, the greater the educational attainment, the greater is the likelihood of larger economic rewards and upward social mobility. However, to compel a child to attend school for six hours a day, five days a week, forty weeks a year, for at least ten years, is quite a demand. The result is that many students are in school for the wrong reason. The motivation is compulsion, not interest in acquiring skills or curiosity about their world. This involuntary feature of U.S. schools is unfortunate because so many school problems are related to the lack of student interest.

As a result of the goal of and commitment to mass education, an increasing proportion of persons have received a formal education. In 1940, for example, 38 percent of people in the United States age twenty-five to twenty-nine had completed high school. This proportion increased to 74 percent in 1970 and 86 percent in 1990 (U.S. Bureau of the Census, 1991b:4).

Local Control of Education

Although the state and federal governments finance and control education in part, the bulk of the money and control for education comes from local communities. There is a general fear of centralization of education—into a statewide educational system or, even worse, federal control. Local school boards (and the commu-

---

*Copyright © 1988 from *Democracy for the Few*, Fifth Edition, by Michael Parenti. Reprinted with permission of St. Martin's Press, Incorporated.

Children are taught to be patriotic as part of their cultural indoctrination.

nities themselves) jealously guard their autonomy. Because, as is commonly argued, local people know best the special needs of their children, local boards control allocation of monies, curricular content, and the rules for running the schools, as well as the hiring and firing of personnel.

There are several problems with this emphasis on local control. First, tax money from the local area traditionally finances the schools. Whether the tax base is strong or weak has a pronounced effect on the quality of education received (a point we return to later in this chapter). Second, local taxes are almost the only outlet for a taxpayers' revolt. Dissatisfaction with high taxes (federal, state, and local) on income, property, and purchases is often expressed at the local level in defeated school bonds and school tax levies. Third, because the democratic ideal requires that schools be locally controlled, the ruling body (school board) should represent all segments of that community. Typically, however, the composition of school boards has overrepresented the business and professional sectors and overwhelmingly underrepresented blue-collar workers and various minority groups. The result is a governing body that is typically conservative in outlook and unresponsive to the wishes of people unlike themselves.

Fourth, local control of education may mean that some communities will opt for the banning of books considered classics by most educators (favorite targets are, for example, *The Catcher in the Rye* by J. D. Salinger and John Steinbeck's *Grapes of Wrath*). A University of Wisconsin survey of 6600 secondary schools nationwide examined 739 book and magazine challenges to school libraries between 1987 and 1990 (reported in Associated Press 1992b; see also Mydans 1989). The study found that (1) publications that drew objections from parents and organizations were removed 26 percent of the time and restricted by age and grade 22 percent of the time; (2) the smaller the community, the more likely that materials will be successfully challenged; and (3) the most frequently questioned book was *Forever* by Judy Blume and the most challenged magazine was the annual swimsuit issue by *Sports Illustrated.* Similarly, the local school boards may use textbooks that support religious fundamentalism or some other narrowly shared belief.

A final problem with local control is the lack of curriculum standardization across the nation's 15,000 school districts and 50 states. Arguing for a common curriculum, Albert Shanker, the president of the American Federation of Teachers, states:

> A common curriculum means that there is agreement about what students ought to know and be able to do and, often, about the age and grade at which they should be able to accomplish these goals. . . . In most countries with a common curriculum, linkage of curriculum, assessment and teacher education is tight. . . . In the U. S., we have no such agreement about curriculum—and there is little connection between what students are supposed to learn, the knowledge on which they are assessed, and what we expect our teachers to know. (Shanker 1991:E7)

The lack of a common curriculum has at least two negative consequences. First, there is a wide variation in the preparation of students. Second, because families move on the average of once every five years (and the rate is probably higher for families with school-age children), there are large numbers of children each year who find the requirements of their new schools different, sometimes very different, from their previous schools.

The Competitive Nature of U.S. Education

Not surprisingly, schools in a highly competitive society are competitive. Competition extends to virtually all school activities. The compositions of athletic teams, cheerleading squads, pompom squads, debate teams, choruses, drill teams, bands, and dramatic play casts are almost always determined by competition among classmates. Grading in courses, too, is often based on the comparison of individuals (grading on a curve) rather than on measurement against a standard. To relieve boredom in the classroom, teachers often invent competitive games such as "spelling baseball" or "hangman." In all these cases the individual learns at least two lessons: (1) your classmates are enemies, for if they succeed, they do so at your expense; and (2) you'd better not fail—fear of failure is the great motivator, not intellectual curiosity or love of knowledge.

The "Sifting and Sorting" Function of Schools

Schools play a considerable part in choosing the youth who come to occupy the higher-status positions in society. Conversely, school performance also sorts out those who will occupy the lower rungs in the occupational-prestige ladder. Education is, therefore, a selection process. The sorting is done with respect to two different criteria: a child's ability and his or her social class background. Although the goal of education is to select on ability alone, ascribed social status (the status of one's family, race, and religion) has a pronounced effect on the degree of success in the educational system. The school is analogous to a conveyor belt, with people of all social classes getting on at the same time but leaving the belt in accordance with social class—the lower the class, the shorter the ride.

The Preoccupation with Order and Control

Most administrators and teachers share a fundamental assumption that school is a collective experience requiring subordination of individual needs to those of the school. U.S. schools are characterized, then, by constraints on individual freedom. The school day is regimented by the dictates of the clock. Activities begin and cease on a timetable, not in accordance with the degree of interest shown or whether students have mastered the subject. Another indicator of order is the preoccupation with discipline (i.e., absence of unwarranted noise and movement, and concern with the following of orders).

In their quest for order, some schools also demand conformity in clothing and hairstyles. Dress codes are constraints on the freedom to dress as one pleases. School athletic teams also restrict freedom, and these restrictions are condoned by the school authorities. Conformity is also demanded in what to read, where to set the margins on their word processors, and how to give the answers the teacher wants.

The many rules and regulations found in schools meet a number of expressed and implicit goals. The school authorities' belief in order is one reason for this dedication to rules: teachers are rated not on their ability to get pupils to learn but, rather, on the degree to which their classroom is quiet and orderly. The community also wants order.

The paradoxes listed below indicate the many profound dilemmas in U.S. education. They set the foundation for the remaining sections of this chapter, which deal with the crises facing education and with some alternative modes.

- Formal education encourages creativity but curbs the truly creative individual from being too disruptive to society.
- Formal education encourages the open mind but teaches dogma.
- Formal education has the goal of turning out mature students but does not give them the freedom essential to foster maturity.
- Formal education pays lip service to meeting individual needs of the students but in actuality encourages conformity at every turn.
- Formal education has the goal of allowing all students to reach their potential, yet it fosters kinds of competition that continually cause some people to be labeled as failures.
- Formal education is designed to allow people of the greatest talent to reach the top, but it systematically benefits certain categories of people regardless of their talent: the middle- and upper-class students who are White.

The Political Economy of Education in Corporate Society

People in the United States want to believe that their society is a meritocratic one in which the most intelligent and talented people rise to the top. Because public schools are free and available to everyone, individuals can go as high as their ability and drive will take them. In this view education is the great equalizer, providing opportunities for everyone to develop his or her full potential. This section and the next argue that this belief is a myth. The truth is that schools reinforce inequality in society. (The discussion in this section is adapted from Spring, 1972; Bowles and Gintis, 1973; Carnoy, 1975; and Bowles, 1977). This belief, besides being a myth, has an especially negative outcome: it tends to blame or credit individuals for their level of failure or success without considering the aspects of the social structure that impel or impede their progress (another instance of blaming the victim). Thus, it results in praise of the system and condemnation of individuals who are defined as losers.

The Role of Education in Corporate Society

The schools perform several vital functions for the maintenance of the prevailing social, political, and economic order. Education, along with the institutions of the family and religion, has a primary responsibility for socializing newcomers to the society. A second function of education is the shaping of personalities so that they are in basic congruence with the demands of the society. In other words, one goal of the educational system of any society is to produce people with desired personality traits (such as competitiveness, altruism, bravery, conformity, or industriousness, depending on the culture and organization of the society). A third function is preparing individuals for their adult roles.

In U.S. society schools prepare individuals for the specialized roles of a highly complex division of labor. They also prepare youngsters for life in a rapidly changing world. Early in American history the primary aims of schooling were teaching the basics of reading, writing, spelling, and arithmetic, so that adults in an agrarian society could read the Bible, write letters, and do simple accounting. Modern society, however, demands people with specialized occupational skills, with expertise in narrow areas. The educational system is saddled with providing these skills in addition to the basics. Moreover, the schools have taken over the teaching of citizenship skills, cooking, sewing, and even sex education—skills and knowledge that were once the explicit duty of each family to transmit to its offspring.

Contemporary schools go beyond these functions, however. They exist to meet the needs of the economy by providing employers with a disciplined and skilled labor force and a means to control individuals in order to maintain political stability. A review of the changing role of the school in American history can make this function clear (Bowles, 1977).

When most Americans were farmers and artisans, the schools had a relatively simple task because the skills society required were essentially unchanged from generation to generation and were generally learned at home. As the economy changed to a factory system in urban settings, the family became less important as an agent of economic socialization, and the school grew in importance. Work became specialized, technology changed rapidly, and work was done in large organizations with rigid authority structures. The workers were no longer in control of their own labor but were controlled by the owners of the factories. Thus, workers were placed in potentially oppressive and alienating work situations. This condition was a concern to capitalists because the workers might unite to challenge the existing system. Stability was also threatened by the rising number of immigrants who entered the United States to live in urban centers and work in factories.

According to radical educational historians, mass public education was perceived by the people in power as the answer to these problems in a changing society, for the church and family were no longer effective in teaching the skills and uniformity in belief necessary for an effective and tractable work force. According to Bowles, an ideal preparation for factory work was found in the social relations of the school: specifically, in its emphasis on discipline, punctuality, acceptance of authority outside the family, and individual accountability for one's work. The social relations of the school would replicate the social relations of the workplace, and thus help young people adapt to the social division of labor. Schools would further lead people to accept the authority of the state and its agents— the teachers—at a young age, in part by fostering the illusion of the benevolence of the government in its relations with citizens. Moreover, because schooling would ostensibly be open to all, one's position in the social division of labor could be portrayed as the result not of birth, but of one's own efforts and talents. (Bowles, 1977:139)

Social Class Biases of the Educational System

Through their curricula, testing, bureaucratic control, and emphasis on competition, the schools reflect the social class structure of society by processing youth to fit into economic slots quite similar to those of their parents. As the educational system rapidly expanded during the nineteenth and early twentieth centuries, a system of class stratification emerged within the schools (Katz, 1968). As the high schools opened to youth of all social classes, the older curriculum, which provided a standard education for all, was supplanted by the progressive notion that school should be tailored to meet the individual needs of each child. Although individual tailoring makes obvious sense, in effect the new curriculum tended to provide vocational school tracks for children of working-class families and preparation for college for children of professionals. Such a division was not blatant, because supposedly objective tests were used to decide the program for each child. Though seemingly fair, these tests were biased. The IQ test, for example, is clearly biased to reward children who have had middle-class experiences (Kagan, 1973). Thus, they unfairly legitimate a hierarchical division of labor by separating individuals into different curricula, with different expectations, which in turn then fulfill the prophecy of the original test scores. Moreover, they serve to reconcile people to their eventual placement in the economic system (Bowles and Gintis, 1976:74).

The amount of schooling one has is directly correlated with economic success in society. Thus, schools act as society's gatekeepers. But how the schools work biases the outcome, as we have seen. Two rules-of-the-school games serve to buttress this bias further. The first rule is that

excellence in schooling should be rewarded. Given the capacity of the upper class to define excellence in terms on which upper class children tend to excel (for example, scholastic achievement), adherence to this principle yields inegalitarian outcomes (for example, unequal access to higher education) while maintaining the appearance of fair treatment. Thus the principle of rewarding excellence serves to legitimize the unequal consequences of schooling by associating success with competence. At the same time, the institution of objectively administered tests of performance serves to allow a limited amount of upward mobility among exceptional children of the lower class, thus providing further legitimation of the operations of the social system by giving some credence to the myth of widespread mobility. (Bowles, 1977:148)

The second rule of the game is the principle that elementary and secondary schooling should be financed largely from local revenues. This principle is supported on the seemingly logical grounds that the local people know what is best for their children. The effect, however, is to perpetuate educational inequalities.

The next section catalogs the reasons for this perpetuation and the many other ways in which education reinforces inequality.

Education and Inequality

Education is presumed by many people to be the great equalizer in U.S. society—the process by which the disadvantaged get their chance to be upwardly mobile. The data in Table 12.1 show, for example, that the higher the educational attainment, the higher the income. But these data do not in any way demonstrate equality of opportunity through education. They show clearly that Blacks and Latinos with the same educational attainment as Whites receive lower economic rewards. For example, the median income for White males who have an eighth-grade education is *more* than the median income for Latino males who have one to three years of high school and within fifty dollars of Black males with a high school degree. Similarly, there are significant differences between males and females *of the same educational level.* Interestingly, while there is a wide difference in income for males by race and education, the gap is much narrower for females by race and education. These differences reflect discrimination in society, not just in schools. This section examines the ways that the schools help to perpetuate class and race inequities.

As we have seen, a fundamental function of the schools is to "sift and sort" their products. Those who succeed in school will occupy the higher-status positions in society. Conversely, school performance also sorts out those who will occupy the lower rungs in the occupational-prestige ladder.

Education is therefore a selection process. The sorting is done with respect to two different criteria: the child's ability and his or her social class background. Although the goal of education is to select on ability alone, ascribed social status

Table 12.1   Median earnings by years of school completed for full-time workers, 18 years and over, by race and sex: 1989

| | Median Income | | | | | |
| | White | | Black | | Hispanic | |
Highest Educational Attainment	Male	Female	Male	Female	Male	Female
8 years	$18,676	$11,618	$14,903	—	$16,291	$10,579
1–3 yrs. high school	19,801	12,474	15,884	11,424	15,684	11,555
High school grad.	24,396	15,752	18,702	14,781	19,637	14,808
1–3 yrs. college	28,228	18,934	23,291	18,363	22,304	19,686
College grad.	35,472	23,789	29,715	23,229	26,532	23,495
5 or more years	41,713	28,852	34,825	26,653	36,193	25,589

Source: Bureau of the Census, "Educational Attainment in the United States: March 1989 and 1988," *Current Population Reports,* Series P–20, No. 451 (August 1991), pp. 67–71.

(the status of one's family, race, and religion) has a pronounced effect on the degree of an individual's success in the educational system.

To document this assertion and analyze its consequences, this section examines two factors: the comparison of school performances by socioeconomic background, and how the educational system tends to reinforce the socioeconomic status differentials in performance.

The Relation between School Success and Socioeconomic Status

The evidence that educational performance is linked to socioeconomic background is clear and irrefutable. The advantages of the children of the relatively affluent over those of the poor are enormous, as seen in the following illustration from a study by the Carnegie Council on Children:

> Jimmy is a second grader. He pays attention in school, and enjoys it. School records show he is reading slightly above grade level and has a slightly better than average I.Q. Bobby is a second grader in a school across town. He also . . . enjoys school and his test scores are quite similar to Jimmy's. Bobby is a safe bet to enter college (more than four times as likely as Jimmy) and a good bet to complete it—at least twelve times as likely as Jimmy.
>
> Bobby will probably have at least four years more schooling than Jimmy. He is twenty-seven times as likely as Jimmy to land a job which by his late forties will pay him an income in the top tenth of all incomes. Jimmy has one chance in eight of earning a median income.
>
> These odds are the arithmetic of inequality in America. . . . Bobby is the son of a successful lawyer whose annual salary of $35,000 puts him well within the top 10 percent of the United States income distribution in 1976. Jimmy's father, who did not complete high school, works from time to time as a messenger and a custodial assistant. His earnings, some $4,800, put him in the bottom 10 percent. (Kempton, 1979:8–9)

The research of Bowles and Gintis also makes the point that socioeconomic background determines how much education one receives. They found that people in the lowest 10 percent in socioeconomic background *with the same average IQ scores* as people in the highest 10 percent will receive an average of 4.9 fewer years of education (Bowles and Gintis, 1976:31).

Christopher Jencks and his associates have added to the work of Bowles and Gintis, providing the most current and methodologically sophisticated analysis of the determinants of upward mobility in their book *Who Gets Ahead?* (Jencks et al., 1979). Among their findings is that educational attainment, especially graduation from college, is very important to later success; but it is not so much what one learns in school as the obtaining of the credentials that counts. Most important, the probability of high educational attainment is closely tied to family background.

Inequality in education occurs also along racial lines (which is closely related to socioeconomic status). In 1989, for example, 78.4 percent of adult Whites were at least high school graduates, compared to 76.1 percent of Asians and Pacific Islanders, 64.6 percent of African American adults, and 50.9 percent of Latino adults (U.S. Bureau of the Census; 1991b:2–3). The Coleman report, an analysis of all third-, sixth-, ninth-, and twelfth-grade pupils in 4000 schools, noted that Whites surpass Blacks in various achievement areas and that the gaps increase the longer they remain in school (Coleman et al., 1966). Clearly, the school is to blame, for in no instance is the initial gap narrowed. Moreover, the increasing gaps are *understated,* because there is a greater tendency for the people of lowest aptitude among the minority groups to drop out of school.

William Ryan has summarized the situation as follows:

> The school is better prepared for the middle-class child than for the lower-class child. Indeed, we could be tempted to say further that the school experience is tailored for, and stacked in favor of, the middle-class child. The cause-and-effect relationship between the lack of skills and experiences found among lower-class children and the conditions of lower-class life has yet to be delineated. So far, explanations of this relationship have been, at best, sketchy and have been based on casual observation. We know poor and middle-class children exhibit certain differences in styles of talking and thinking, but we do not know yet why or how these differences occur.
>
> We do know, however, that these differences—really differences in *style* rather than ability—are not handicaps or disabilities (unlike barriers to learning such as poor vision, mild brain damage, emotional disturbance or orthopedic handicap). They do represent inadequate *preparation* for the reality of the modern urban school. They are, in no sense, cultural or intellectual defects. (Ryan, 1976:35–36)

How is the educational system stacked in favor of middle- and upper-class children and against children from the lowest classes?* At least four interrelated factors explain why the education system tends to reinforce the socioeconomic status differentials in the United States: finances, curriculum, segregation, and personnel. We examine the first three factors in the following subsections. The next section discusses school finances.

Finances. Though not a guarantee of educational equality, if schools spent approximately the same amount of money per pupil, they would be taking a significant step toward meeting that goal. Equal financing has not been accomplished nationwide, because wealthier states are able to pay much more per pupil than are poorer states. In 1990, for example, the top five states in per-pupil spending were New Jersey ($8,439), New York ($8,094) Connecticut ($7,934), Alaska ($7,252) and Rhode Island ($6,523). The five states with the lowest per pupil spending were Utah ($2,733), Idaho ($3,037), Mississippi ($3,151), Arkansas ($3,272), and South Dakota ($3,312) (U.S. Bureau of the Census, 1991b:149). Because the federal government provides only about 6 percent of the money for public schools, equalization from state to state is impossible as long as the states vary in wealth and commitment to public education.

The disparities in per-pupil expenditures within a given state are also great, largely because of the tradition of funding public schools through local property

---

*We have phrased the question to focus on the system, not the victims, contrary to the typical response, which is to focus on the **cultural deprivation** of the poor. That approach attacks the home and culture of poor people. It assumes that these people perform inadequately because they are handicapped by their culture. Observers cannot, however, make the value judgment that a culture is deprived. They can note only that their milieu does not prepare children to perform in schools geared for the middle class. In other words, children of the poor and/or minority groups are not nonverbal—they are very verbal, but not in the language of the middle class.

taxes. This procedure is discriminatory because rich school districts can spend more money than poor ones on each student, and at a *lower* taxing rate. Thus, suburban students are more advantaged than are students from the inner city; districts with business enterprises are favored over agricultural districts; and districts with natural resources are better able to provide for their children than are districts with few resources. (See the Observation for a discussion of the unequal financing of urban schools.)

Texas has the greatest disparity in spending for each pupil by district. The spending ranges from $3,190 in the poorest schools to $11,801 per pupil among the richest schools (Cellis, 1992).

The U.S. Supreme Court in *San Antonio* v. *Rodriquez* (1973) ruled that while there were unequal expenditures in Texas, these disparities did not violate the U.S. Constitution. In effect, the Court ruled that this was matter for the individual states to decide.

Several states, led by California, have made strides to right inequities in school financing. In 1976 the California Supreme Court declared in *Serrano* v. *Priest* that the state's system of school finance violated the state and federal constitutional guarantees for the right of citizens of equal protection under the law. By 1988 California had equalized finances so that "95.6 percent of all students attend districts with a per-pupil revenue limit within an inflation adjusted . . . band [$238] of the statewide average for each district type (Wise and Gendler, 1989:15). Gradually, the courts in other states have ruled that their school financing needs revamping. In 1989, the Texas Supreme Court ruled unanimously that the state's

Students in wealthy school districts enjoy the advantages of extensive libraries, and computers as well as a wide choice of language, science, mathematics, and social science course offerings.

unequal method of school finance was unconstitutional. In 1992 twenty-three states were in court, accused of having illegal school spending plans.

If the equalization of finances were equalized it would have significant consequences.

> It equalizes the capacity of poor districts to secure the services of a sufficient number of teachers, even to bid for the services of highly qualified teachers. It permits schools from poor districts to exercise the same choices—Shall we offer Latin or Russian? Shall we buy computers or microscopes?—that schools from wealthy districts now enjoy. It ensures, to the extent that is possible, that educational opportunity is independent of the wealth of one's parents and neighbors.

> Improving education for children in poor school districts would benefit them and the nation. A future physicist is as easily born in Jersey City as in Princeton, a future pianist in Edgewood as in Alamo Heights. But it is not only potential luminaries that are lost; it is part of an entire generation of citizens whose potential contributions are stunted by the inadequacy of the education they are provided. School finance reform cannot solve all of the problems of education, but it can equalize the opportunities that the state provides. To continue to distribute better education to children in rich districts and worse education to children in poor districts is only to exacerbate the inequalities that children bring to school. To equalize educational opportunity is to redress some of the accidents of birth. (Wise and Gendler, 1989:37)

As an example, African Americans and Latinos are overrepresented in the poorest school districts. One consequence is that they will less likely be computer

---

OBSERVATION

THE UNEQUAL FINANCING OF URBAN SCHOOLS

Poor children live in a societal context that seriously disadvantages them. Because of unhealthy living conditions (exposure to toxic chemicals, pollution, and inadequate diets and housing) and lack of immunizations and no health insurance, they are at high risk for infant mortality, infectious diseases, and even brain damage.

Only about one in four eligible children is able to participate in Head Start, even though this program has been shown to increase school success and improve eventual employability (Schorr, 1988). This program is underfunded because it receives a relative low priority by the federal government.

School funding is based on the wealth of local districts. This places urban schools at a disadvantage, compared to their suburban neighbors. The cities are disproportionately the home of the poor and the near poor, who pay little taxes and require many services. The cities have a disproportionate number of tax-free institutions such as churches, colleges, hospitals, and art museums. Cities must pay a relatively large part of their limited tax revenues on police matters (because of a relative high rate of street crime in inner cities) and fire department costs (due to an unusual number of fires because of substandard wiring, dilapidated housing, and abandoned warehouses).

Ironically, the tax treatment of property taxes for schooling promotes inequality in education. Consider the argument by Jonathon Kozol:

> Because the property tax is counted as a tax deduction by the federal government, home-owners in a wealthy suburb get back a substantial portion of the money that they spend to fund their children's schools—effectively, a federal subsidy for an unequal education. Home-owners in poor districts get this subsidy as well, but, because their total tax is less, the subsidy is less. The mortgage interest that home-owners pay is also treated as a tax deduction—in effect, a second, federal subsidy. These subsidies, as I have termed

literate (which has serious implications for their job prospects) than their White counterparts. The data show that 60.9 percent of White students in grades kindergarten through eight had used computers in 1989, compared with 38.4 percent of Blacks and 42.7 percent of Latinos. The problem is compounded by a similar finding for the availability of computers in homes (see the next section): 35.8 percent of White households had computers in 1989, compared to 15.3 percent of Black households and 14.3 percent of Latino households (Kelly, 1992B).

Family economic resources. The College Board reported that the average combined SAT scores for youth from families whose annual income was $70,000 or more was 997, compared to an average score of 768 for youth from families whose incomes is $10,000 less (reported in *Harper's*, 1992:13). How are we to explain this difference of 229 points on the SATs? Among the reasons are the benefits that come from economic privilege (this section is dependent on Children's Defense Fund, 1989b:68–77). Poor parents, most without health insurance, are unable to afford prenatal care, which increases the risk of babies being born at low birthweight, a condition that may lead to learning disabilities. As these poor children age, they are less likely to receive adequate nutrition, decent medical care, and a safe and secure environment. These deficiencies increase the probability of their being less alert, less curious, and less able to interact effectively with their environment than are healthy children.

Children of the affluent are also advantaged by being more likely to attend early childhood development programs, which prepare children for school. "In

them, are considerably larger than most people understand. In 1984, for instance, property-tax deductions granted by the federal government were $9 billion. An additional $23 billion in mortgage-interest deductions were provided by home-owners: a total of some $32 billion. Federal grants to local schools, in contrast, totaled only $7 billion, and only part of this was earmarked for low-income districts. Federal policy, in this respect, increases the existing gulf between the richest and the poorest schools. (Kozol, 1991:55)

Added to these inequities is the actual amount spent per pupil, comparing rich school districts with poor school districts. Kozol presents some examples (1991:236–237):

- In 1989, Chicago spent $5,265 per student compared in $9,371 in Niles Township High School.

- In 1989, the Princeton district in New Jersey spent $7,725 per pupil while the Camden district spent $3,538.
- In 1987, New York City spent $5,585 compared to $11,372 in Manhasset, $11,325 in Jerico, and $11,265 in Great Neck,]

Actually, these gaps are wider than they appear because the poorer urban schools spend a smaller proportion of their budget on instruction than do the suburban schools. This is because dilapidated schools require more maintenance and higher fuel costs than do newer, fuel-efficient buildings.

The result is that poor urban children enter school with a disadvantage, and the unequally financed schooling they receive compounds that disadvantage. The system, in effect, condemns these children to unequal lives.

Source: D. Stanley Eitzen and Maxine Baca Zinn, *In Conflict and Order,* 6th ed. (Boston: Allyn and Bacon, 1993), p. 492. Reprinted with permission.

1986, for example, two out of three four-year-olds in families with annual incomes of $35,000 or more were enrolled in some type of preschool program, compared with only four out of ten four-year-olds in families with incomes less than $10,000" (Children's Defense Fund, 1989b:73).

Poor children are more likely than the children of the affluent to attend schools with poor resources, which, as we have noted, means that they are less likely to receive an enriched educational experience. Similarly, most poor young people live in communities where

> opportunities to apply academic skills and build new ones are either not available or not accessible. The lack of community resources is especially destructive during the summer months, the time when children doing least well in school (a group that is disproportionately poor) slide backward the farthest. Recent research shows that most of the learning gap between poor and nonpoor children is due to this summer learning loss. (Children's Defense Fund, 1989b:74)

Poor teens are more likely than their wealthier peers to fall behind in school. Among sixteen-year-olds who have lived at least half of their lives below the poverty line, 40 percent have repeated at least one grade, a rate twice as great as for children whose families had never lived in poverty (Children's Defense Fund, 1989b:69).

The level of affluence also affects how long children will stay in school, because schools, even public schools, are costly. These financial demands pressure youngsters from poorer families to drop out of school prematurely to go to work. The children from the middle and upper classes, not constrained by financial difficulties, tend to stay in school longer, which means better jobs and pay in the long run. Because minorities are overrepresented among the poor, their dropout rate is disproportionate to that of Whites—in 1991 the dropout rate for Latinos was 35.3 percent, 13.6 percent for African Americans, and 8.9 percent for Whites (U.S. Department of Education, reported in Associated Press, 1992f).

> These children [dropouts]—most of them poor, Black or Hispanic—are America's educational underclass. While middle-class kids enjoy gleaming laboratories and computers, these children struggle in an educational Third World where supplies are shoddy, teachers are baffled by a barrage of different languages, and discrimination handicaps even the brightest and most willing child. From this classroom ghetto, it's a short journey to the world of adults trapped in joblessness and poverty. (Horn, 1987:66)

The affluent also give their children educational advantages such as home computers; travel experiences abroad and throughout the United States; and visits to zoos, libraries, and various cultural activities. Another advantage available to the affluent is the hiring of tutors to help children having difficulty in school or to transform good students into outstanding ones. One tutor in the state of Washington said, "One hundred percent of the children I tutor are from wealthy families. I charge $40 an hour" (quoted in Warren, 1988:24).

The well-to-do also have the option of sending their children to private schools (about 12 percent of U.S. children attend these schools). Parents offer several rationales for sending their children to private schools. Some do so for religious reasons. Another reason is that private schools, unlike public schools, are selective in whom they accept. Thus, parents can ensure that their children will interact with children similar to theirs in race (some private schools were expressly created so that White children could avoid attending integrated public schools) and social class. Similarly, private schools are much more likely than public schools to get rid of troublesome students (i.e., behavioral problems and low-achievers), thereby providing an educational environment more conducive to learning and achievement. A final reason for attending private schools is that the most elite of them provide a demanding education *and* an entree to the most elite universities, which, in turn, lead to placement in top positions in the professional and corporate occupational worlds.

Obtaining a college degree is a most important avenue to later success. One's family finances are directly related to whether one attends college and, if so, what type. The cost of higher education, always out of reach of the poor, rose twice the rate of inflation during the 1980s. The result was that by 1990 the full costs at a private college were $14,326 per student (about 40 percent of a family's median income) and $6,671 at a public college (almost 20 percent of median-family income) (Gwynne, 1988). These high costs, which continue to rise, coupled with declining scholarship monies, preclude college attendance not only for the able poor but also increasingly for children of the working and lower middle classes.

The ability to pay for college reinforces the class system in two ways. We have just seen that the lack of money shuts out the possibility for some students. For students who do attend college, money stratifies. The poorest, even those who are talented, are most likely to attend community colleges, which are the least expensive; they emphasize technical careers and are therefore limiting in terms of later success (in 1991 some 43 percent of the nation's college students attended community colleges). Students with greater resources are likely to attend public universities. Finally, students with the greatest financial backing are the most likely to attend elite and prestigious private institutions, where the annual cost exceeds $20,000. A study by two economists found that the proportion of middle-class youth attending these elite schools is diminishing—students from families with earnings between $40,000 and $65,000 made up only 18 percent of private-college enrollment in 1989, compared to 27 percent in 1982 (cited in Toch, 1991). It is important to note that it is not ability that places college students in this stratified system, although ability is an important variable, but money. For example, "some less qualified students from upper-class families are able to attend elite universities because of admission programs that favor the children of alumni and the children of big contributors to the university's fund-raising campaigns" (Coleman and Cressey, 1990:103).

Minorities and higher education. Because racial minorities are much more likely than Whites to be poor or near poor, they are underrepresented in having a college education. The following facts make this point.

First, even though more minorities are attending college than ever, they continue to be underrepresented in higher education. In 1990, racial minority students were 17 percent of total college enrollments (about 1 million students), much below their proportion in the general population.

As reported by the American Council on Education, in 1990, 39.4 percent of White eighteen- to twenty-four-year-old high school graduates were in college, compared to 33 percent of Blacks and 29 percent of Latinos (reported in Kelly,

1992a:Dl). The proportion of Black and Latino men is especially low (Scarpitti and Andersen, 1992:581).

Second, racial minorities are more likely than Whites to attend community colleges and schools that are less well funded (Ramirez, 1992). Third, the minority students who attend college are less likely than Whites to graduate. Table 12.2 provides these data.

Fourth, the disproportionate low number of college degrees earned by minorities is reflected in the relatively low number of students who attend and graduate from graduate school. This, of course, results in a low proportion of minority professions in the near future. The problem can be seen in the current racial composition of full-time faculty in higher education: White (88.5 percent), African American (4.5 percent), Latino (2.0 percent), Asian American (4.7 percent), and Native American (0.3 percent) (Mullins, 1992).

Curriculum.   U.S. schools are essentially middle or upper class. The written and spoken language in the schools, for example, is expected to be middle class. For children of the poor, however, English (at least middle-class English) may be a second language. English is clearly a second language for many Hispanic youngsters, making their success in U.S. schools especially problematic. Standardized tests often ask the student to determine how objects are similar. For students whose first language is Spanish, this task presents a problem. "Spanish, which separates words into masculine and feminine categories, tends to emphasize the differences between objects. This interferes with tasks that require the subject to describe how objects are similar" (Philippus, 1989:59). The schools, in general, have failed to recognize the special needs of these and other bilingual students, which results in their overall poor student performance.

In these and other matters the curriculum of the schools does not accommodate the special needs of the poor. To the contrary, the schools assume that the language and behaviors of the poor are not only alien but wrong—things to be changed. This assumption denigrates the ways of the poor and leads to loss of ego strength (a trait already in short supply for the poor in a middle-class world).

Table 12.2   Educational attainment for people 25 and over by race: 1989

Race	Percentage with 4 or More Years of College
White	21.8
Black	11.8
Latino	9.9
Cuban	19.8
Central/So. American	17.5
Puerto Rican	9.8
Mexican	6.1

Sources: Bureau of the Census, "Educational Attainment in the United States: March 1989 and 1988," *Current Population Reports,* Series P–20, No. 451 (August 1991), p. 2; Bureau of the Census, "The Hispanic Population in the United States: March 1989," *Current Population Reports,* Series P–20, No. 444 (May 1990), pp. 8–9.

Racial minorities are underrepresented among college students.

The curriculum also is not very germane to the poor child's world. What is the relevance of conjugating a verb when you are hungry? What is the relevance of being able to trace the path of how a bill becomes a law when your family and neighbors are powerless? Irrelevancy for the poor is also seen in the traditional children's primers, which picture middle-class surroundings and well-behaved blond children. There is little effort at any educational level to incorporate the experience of slum children in relation to realistic life situations of any kind. Schools also have a way of ignoring real-life problems and controversial issues. Schools are irrelevant if they disregard topics such as race relations, poverty, and the distribution of community power.

The typical teaching methods, placement tests, and curricula are inappropriate for children from poor families. This factor, along with the others mentioned earlier, results in failure for a large proportion of these youngsters. They perceive themselves (as do others in the system) as incompetents. As Silberman has put it,

> Students are not likely to develop self-respect if they are unable to master the reading, verbal, and computational skills that the schools are trying to teach. Children must have a sense of competence if they are to regard themselves as people of worth; the failure that minority-group children, in particular, experience from the beginning can only reinforce the sense of worthlessness that the dominant culture conveys in an almost infinite variety of ways, and so feed the self-hatred that prejudice and discrimination produce. Chronic failure makes self-discipline equally hard to come by; it is these children's failure to learn that produces the behavior problems of the slum school . . . and not the behavior problems that produce the failure to learn. (Silberman, 1970:67)

Silberman's discussion of the problems of minority group children can be broadened to include all poor children (who are, after all, also a minority group). The poor of all races experience prejudice and discrimination. They quickly learn that they are considered misfits by the middle class (teacher, administrator, citizen).

Segregation

U.S. schools tend to be segregated by social class, both by neighborhood and, within schools, by ability grouping. Schools are based in neighborhoods that tend to be relatively homogeneous by socioeconomic status. Racial and economic segregation is especially prevalent at the elementary school level, carrying over to a lesser degree in the secondary schools. Colleges and universities, as we have seen, are peopled by a middle- and upper-class clientele. Thus, at every level, children tend to attend a school with children like themselves in socioeconomic status and race. This results most often in unequal facilities, because rich districts provide more than poor districts do for their pupils. Moreover, within districts, the schools labeled *lower class* tend to get a disproportionately smaller slice of the economic pie than do middle-class schools.

Tracking and Teachers' Expectations

Although segregation according to the socioeconomic composition of neighborhoods is by no means complete, the tracking system within the schools achieves this to a large extent. **Tracking** (also known as ability grouping) sorts students into different groups or classes according to their perceived intellectual ability and performance. The decision is based on grades, teachers' judgments, and primarily on standardized tests. The result is that children from poor families and from ethnic minorities are overrepresented in the slow track while children from advantaged backgrounds are disproportionately in the middle and upper tracks. The rationale for tracking is that it provides a better fit between the needs and capabilities of the student and the demands and opportunities of the curriculum. Slower students do not retard the progress of brighter ones, but teachers can adapt their teaching more efficiently to the level of the class if the students are relatively homogeneous in ability. The special problems of the different ability groups, from gifted to retarded, can be dealt with more easily when groups of students share the same or similar problems.

Although these benefits may be real, tracking is open to serious criticisms. First, students in lower tracks are discouraged from producing up to their potential. They tend to be given repetitive and unchallenging tasks. Students labeled as *low-ability* tend to be taught a curriculum empty of ideas (Rachlin, 1989). They are given low-level work that increases the gap between them and students in the higher tracks. Rather than seeing the remedial track as a way to get students up to speed, many "teachers see themselves as weeders, getting rid of the kids who can't make it, rather than nurturers trying to make all grow to their potential" (Rachlin, 1989:52).

Second, students in the upper track develop feelings of superiority while those in the lower track tend to define themselves as inferior. As early as the second grade students know where they stand on the smart or dumb continuum, and this knowledge profoundly affects their self-esteem (Tobias, 1989:57). These psychological wounds can have devastating effects. Third, the low track students are tracked to fail. The negative labels, low teacher expectations, poor education resources (the highest track is much more likely to have access to computers, for example), and the fact that teachers typically do not want to teach these classes (there is a subtle labeling among teachers regarding who gets to teach what level) all lead to a high probability of failure among students assigned to the lowest tract. Given all of these negatives, it is not surprising that students who are discipline problems or who eventually drop out come disproportionately from the low track.

Fourth, the tracking system is closely linked to the stratification system—that is, students from low-income families are disproportionately placed in the lowest track, resulting in a reinforcement of the social class structure. If this criticism is correct, the tracking system so prevalent in U.S. schools denies equality of educational opportunity and thus is contrary to the ideal of the school system as open and democratic.

Finally, and most telling, recent research calls into serious question whether tracking has educational value. Research at Johns Hopkins University found, for example, that "given the same curriculum in elementary and middle-grade schools, there is no difference in achievement between advanced students in a tracked school and students in the top third of a class made up of students with varying abilities" (cited in Rachlin, 1989:52). The Carnegie Corporation, in a report assessing the state of middle-grade schools, advocated "abolishing tracking on the grounds that it discriminates against minorities, psychologically wounds those labeled slow, and doesn't work" (cited in Rachlin, 1989:51).

The tracking system appears not to accomplish its educational goals, but it is powerful in its negative effects. There are four principal reasons this system stunts the success of students who are negatively labeled (see the Forum at the end of this chapter).

Stigma.   Assignment to a lower track carries a strong **stigma.** Such students are labeled as intellectual inferiors. Their self-esteem wanes as they see how other people perceive them and behave toward them. Thus, individuals assigned to a track other than college prep perceive themselves as second class, as unworthy, stupid, and in the way. Clearly, assignment to a low track is destructive to a student's self-concept.

The self-fulfilling prophecy.   A self-fulfilling prophecy is an event that occurs because it is predicted and people after their behavior to conform to the prediction. This effect is closely related to stigma. If placed in the college-prep track, students are likely to receive better instruction, have access to better facilities, and be pushed more nearly to their capacity than are students assigned to other tracks. The reason is clear: the teachers and administration *expect* great things from the one group and lesser things from the other. Moreover, these expectations are fulfilled. Students in the higher track do better, and those in the lower track do not. These behaviors justify the greater expenditures of time, faculties, and experimental curricula for those in the higher track—thus perpetuating what Merton has called a "reign of error" (Merton, 1957:421–436).

An example comes from a controversial study by Rosenthal and Jacobson (1986). Although this study has been criticized for a number of methodological shortcomings, the findings are consistent with theories of interpersonal influence and with the labeling view of deviant behavior. In the spring of 1964, all students in an elementary school in San Francisco were given an IQ test. The following fall the teachers were given the names of children identified by the test as potential academic spurters, and five of these children were assigned to each classroom. The spurters were chosen by means of a table of random numbers. The only difference between the experimental group (those labeled as spurters) and the control group (the rest of the class) was in the imaginations of the teachers. At the end of the year all the children were again tested, and the children from whom the teachers expected greater intellectual gains showed such gains (in IQ and grades). Moreover, they were rated by their teachers as being more curious, interesting, happy, and more likely to succeed than were the children in the control group (Rosenthal and Jacobson, 1968).

The implications of this example are clear. Teachers' expectations have a profound effect on students' performance. When students are overrated, they tend to overproduce; when they are underrated, they underachieve. The tracking system is a labeling process that affects the expectations of teachers (and fellow students and parents). The limits of these expectations are crucial in the educational process. Yet the self-fulfilling prophecy can work in a positive direction if teachers have an unshakable conviction that their students *can* learn. Concomitant with this belief, teachers should hold *themselves,* not the students, accountable if the latter should fail (Silberman, 1970:98). Used in this manner, the self-fulfilling prophecy can work to the benefit of *all* students.

Future payoff.   School is perceived as relevant for students going to college. Grades are a means of qualifying for college. For the non-college-bound student, however, school and grades are much less important for entry into a job. At most, students need a high school diploma, and grades really do not matter as long as one does not flunk out. Thus, non-college-bound students often develop negative attitudes toward school, grades, and teachers. These attitudes for students in the lower tracks are summed up by sociologist Arthur Stinchcombe:

> Rebellious behavior is largely a reaction to the school itself and to its promises, not a failure of the family or community. High school students can be motivated to conform by paying them in the realistic coin of future advantage. Except perhaps for pathological cases, any student can be motivated to conform if the school can realistically promise something valuable to him as a reward for working hard. But for a large part of the population, especially the adolescent who will enter the male working class or the female candidates for early marriage, the school has nothing to offer. . . . In order to secure conformity from students, a high school must articulate academic work with careers of students. (Quoted in Schafer, Olexa, and Polk, 1972:49)

As we have seen, being on the lower track has negative consequences. Lower-track students are more rebellious both in school and out and do not participate as much in school activities. Finally, what is being taught is often not relevant to their world. Thus, we are led to conclude that many of these students tend to feel that they are not only second-class citizens but perhaps even pariahs. What other interpretation is plausible in a system that disadvantages them, shuns them, and makes demands of them that are irrelevant?

The student subculture.   The reasons given above suggest that a natural reaction of persons in the lower track would be to band together in a student subculture that is antagonistic toward school. This subculture would quite naturally develop its own system of rewards, since those of the school are inaccessible. David Hargreaves, in *Social Relations in a Secondary School,* (described in Schafer, Olexa, and Polk, 1972), showed this to be the case in an English secondary school that incorporated tracks (or "streams," as they are called in England): boys in the high stream were drawn to the values of the teachers, while lower-stream boys accorded each other high status for doing the opposite of what the teacher wanted.

These factors show how the tracking system is at least partly responsible for the fact that students in the lower tracks are relatively low achievers, unmotivated, uninvolved in school activities, and more prone to drop out of school and to break school or community rules. To segregate students either by ability or by future plans is detrimental to the students labeled as inferior. It is an elitist system that needs to be reevaluated and changed. Tracking is a barrier to equal educational opportunity for lower-income and other minority students who are disproportionately assigned to the lowest track. It is an elitist system that for the most part takes the children of the elite and educates them to take the elite positions of society. Conversely, children of the nonelite are trained to recapitulate the experiences of their parents. In a presumably democratic system that prides itself on providing avenues of upward social mobility, such a system borders on immorality (Oakes, 1985).

The conclusion is inescapable: inequality in the educational system causes many people to fail in U.S. schools. This phenomenon is the fault of the schools, not of the children who fail. To focus on these victims is to divert attention from the inadequacies of the schools. The blame needs to be shifted. As Ryan notes,

> we are dealing, it would seem, not so much with culturally deprived children as with culturally depriving schools. And the task to be accomplished is not to revise, and amend, and repair deficient children but to alter and transform the atmosphere and operations of the schools to which we commit these children. Only by changing the nature of the educational experience can we change its product. (Ryan, 1976:60)

Possible Ways to Promote Equality of Opportunity

A fundamental tenet of U.S. society is that each individual, regardless of sex, race, ethnicity, religion, age, and social class, has the opportunity to be unequal on her or his own merits. In other words, the system must not impede individuals from reaching their potential and from gaining the unequal rewards of an unequal society. The data presented in this chapter show that U.S. schools tend to block the chances of minority and poor children in their quest to be successful in society. This section outlines several programs that schools and society could adopt to promote equality of opportunity for all children.

We must realize at the start that if the situation for poor and minority children is difficult now, it will worsen significantly if changes are not made. This assertion is based on two facts. The first, documented throughout this book, is that the gap between the affluent and poor is widening. The number of poor families is increasing. The number of children being raised in poverty is increasing. Moreover, the localities in which the poor are clustered are increasingly poor, which means that the services provided by local governments, including education, will be less and less able to provide for their citizens.

The second fact that will negatively impact the educational opportunities of minorities unless changes are made is that the number of racial minorities is increasing. Moreover, racial and ethnic minorities are concentrated in poor states (the South and Southwest) and poor geographical regions (Appalachia and the Ozarks) and in poor sections of cities. This is significant because racial/ethnic minorities have higher rates of poverty than do the majority and have less stable family lives, more unemployment, and lower educational attainment than do the more fortunate majority. In effect, under current policies, children from minorities are disadvantaged economically and are at greater risk of educational failure. So, wherever these children are overrepresented, there will be disproportionately less local money to meet their educational needs (because of the lower tax base). Moreover, because they are disadvantaged, they will need extra services, which, of course, are costly.

Looking first at demographic projections, by 1995, African Americans will constitute 16.2 percent of the student population (age five to seventeen), Latinos some 11.4 percent, and Asians and others about 3.5 percent. Whites are projected to be 69 percent of the school enrollment. But somewhere early in the next century U.S. minorities will become the majority of students in school (*Newsweek,* 1990a:74,85). Minorities already are a majority in many school districts.

Reforming the Financing of Education

There must be a commitment to a free education for all students. Presumably, public education at the elementary and secondary levels is free, but this assumption is a fallacy, as discussed earlier. Although circumstances vary by district, typically children must pay for their supplies, textbooks, laboratory fees, locker

The widening gap between the poor and the affluent is especially evident in the difference in money spent for the education of the children in each group.

rental, admission to plays and athletic events, insurance, transportation, meals, equipment for extracurricular activities, participation in extracurricular activities, and the like. Some districts waive these costs for poor families. But waivers do not occur uniformly across school districts, and the procedures for granting these waivers are often degrading (i.e., done in such a way that other people know who receive the handouts). These costs are regressive because they take a larger proportion of the poor family's budget, thereby increasing the pressure to withdraw the child from school, where he or she drains the family resources.

By making education absolutely free to all children, communities could reduce dropout rates among the poor. As mentioned in Chapter 6, a program of greater scope would also provide a living allowance for each child from a poor family who stayed in school beyond the eighth grade. This program would be analogous to the GI Bill, which provided similar benefits to soldiers returning after World War II. Special care must be given to provide these benefits, as did the GI Bill, without making their acceptance degrading.

Obtaining a college diploma is an important avenue to later success. The poor are severely disadvantaged by the U.S. system of higher education in two ways. First, their taxes help subsidize public higher education (typically, at least one-third of the average college student's costs are subsidized by states); yet—and this is the second way in which the poor are disadvantaged—their children are likely to find the costs of higher education prohibitive. These costs are high and rising faster than is inflation, making college attendance by children of the poor and even the not-so-poor more and more unlikely. An indicator of this trend is the declining enrollment of Blacks in colleges. As Taylor observes:

> Behind the decline is a shortage of money. Since 1980, while college costs have outstripped the inflation rate, requirements for financial aid have tightened. A decade ago, most black students who needed money could get government grants covering nearly 75 percent of their college costs. Now, most aid is in the form of loans. Grants, on average, cover only 45 percent of the costs, which in some schools run to $15,000 to $20,000 a year. (Taylor, 1987b:75)

Thus, an important way to produce equal opportunity is to provide a free college education to all students who qualify. This means the elimination of tuition and fees and an allowance for books for everyone, plus grants and loans for students in need to pay for living expenses while attending college.

The federal government now provides about 6 percent (down from 8 percent in 1971) of the monies for elementary and secondary education in the United States. The federal government should engage in four programs to promote equal opportunity for the disadvantaged. First, the government should provide national education standards, a national curriculum, and national tests. There are 40.7 million students, 15,500 school districts, and 83,000 schools in the United States. We must require that each school district and school, rather than acting on its own, meet specific standards for school achievement agreed to by a national consensus among educational leaders. The minimum result of this would be that students, whether growing up in Nebraska or New York, would learn the same basic materials. This also means that as students move with their families from one locality to another, they would not be at a disadvantage because of the esoteric schooling they had received. (See Another Society, Another Way for a comparison of our system with other nations.)

Such a plan goes against the time-honored belief that the essential decisions about curriculum and standards must be locally determined. There is evidence, however, that people are ready for such a change. In 1989 the Gallup organization polled people in the United States, with the following results:

Asked "would you favor or oppose requiring the public schools to conform to national achievement standards and goals?", 70 percent of Gallup's respondents were in favor, 19 percent opposed.

Asked "would you favor or oppose requiring the public schools in this community to use a standardized national curriculum?", the responses were 69 percent yes, 21 percent no.

And asked about "requiring the public schools in this community to measure the academic achievement of students?", the results were 77 percent affirmative, only 14 percent negative. (Reported in Finn, 1989:E13)

The second reform at the federal level would be to spend the federal monies unequally to equalize differences among the states. In effect, the federal government must take the money it receives in taxes, taking disproportionately from the wealthy states, and redistribute it to the poor states. Otherwise, the gap between the rich and poor states will be maintained.

The third effort at the federal level would be to encourage states to distribute their funds to eliminate or minimize disparities between rich and poor districts. This could be done by the federal government's withholding funds from states with discrepancies between their poor and rich districts that exceed federal guide-

---

ANOTHER SOCIETY, ANOTHER WAY

IMPROVING OUR SCHOOLS BY EXAMINING WHAT WORKS IN OTHER SOCIETIES

People who say that U.S. schools are performing better than ever in most respects are correct. Today, our schools are educating more students and more difficult students to levels that once were attained only by a small and favored group. The trouble is, these levels are below what we need to maintain or improve our standard of living. And they do not compare well with the achievement of students in competitor nations. . .

Here are some of the important differences between their traditional schools and ours:

- Schools in these countries are run by professionals, with relatively little interference by lay persons.
- Schools are financed nationally or regionally. As a result, the disparity between wealthy and poor schools that is so destructive and shocking in the U.S. does not exist.
- For the most part, there is a national curriculum. Teacher training, textbooks, and assessments are geared to this curriculum. If students move from teacher to teacher or school to school, there is continuity.
- Assessments are curriculum-based and challenging. Teaching to the test is something positive when you have really good test results.

- These countries produce a higher percentage of students at top levels of achievement. Also, teaching is a relatively prestigious—in Japan, very prestigious—profession, so they can guarantee that all classrooms have teachers who have attained high levels of excellence.
- Like us, these countries track their students . However, we begin as early as first grade and they hold off until later. This means that all their kids get a more or less equal start. Ours don't.
- All these countries have clearly visible consequences for student performance. There are strict college-entry standards and clear employment standards. Students work hard, and their teachers and parents push them because success is rewarded in all tracks.
- Schools are relatively safe and free from disruption because the legal system supports school regulations needed to maintain a proper educational atmosphere.

Source: Albert Shanker, "Improving Our Schools," *New York Times* (May 17, 1992), p. E7.

lines. In such cases, the federal government could channel its monies directly to the poorer districts within the offending states.

Fourth, the federal government must increase its funding for programs such as Head Start and must continue such compensatory programs through at least kindergarten and first grade.

> Head Start has become the one Big Government social program everyone is allowed to like. It has been praised by George Bush, protected by Ronald Reagan, adored by Jimmy Carter; it was proudly fathered by Lyndon Johnson. Head Start puts poor 3- to 5-year-olds in preschool and hits all the right political buttons along the way. Who can object to a program that helps the most innocent (and adorable) of the poor, encourages preventive health care and gets parents more involved in their child's education?
>
> Yet despite the universal adoration, only 48 percent [other estimates are as low as 20 percent] of eligible children benefit from Head Start for even one year—and until this year no administration and no Congress has ever proposed fully funding it. Which leads to a difficult riddle: if the federal government so easily spends lots of money on stupid things, why hasn't it been able to spend enough on the one program that seems so meritorious? (Waldman, 1990:78)

Clearly, the federal government must reorder its priorities if poor and minority children are to be given a chance to succeed in school and later in society.

At the state level, monies must be equalized across the districts. Nationwide, the traditional property tax system of raising money for education locally is under assault. The supreme courts in various states are ruling in case after case that the states are failing the children in the poorer districts. In effect, they are saying that the state should collect monies from the rich districts and redistribute them to the poor districts. This, of course, is often fought by the advantaged. For instance, Roy LeBlanc, Louisiana Board of Elementary and Secondary Education, has argued that

> you can't penalize parents whose parish [county] happens to have a better tax base. It's not the responsibility of parents that have a better tax base to support the parishes that don't have the tax base. (cited in *USA Today,* 1990a:8A)

If that logic prevails, then the cycle of poverty is perpetuated.

Finally, at the state and district levels, special efforts should be made to increase the racial/ethnic diversity of teachers. Now, about 90 percent of all public school teachers are White.

> The issues regarding the impact of minority teachers in the classroom are complex. Some advocates believe minority students should have minority teachers, but clearly not all can unless the number of minority students in teaching rises dramatically. Many agree that in the multi-cultural society of the U.S., it is beneficial for *all* students—regardless of race or ethnic heritage—to be exposed during their early educational careers to teachers and role models from a variety of racial, ethnic, and cultural backgrounds.
>
> There is no conclusive evidence that minority teachers can teach minority students any more successfully than nonminority teachers, although there is evidence that teachers of high socioeconomic status (regardless of race) have greater difficulty teaching poor or disadvantaged minority students. (Griffith, Frase, and Ralph, 1989:16)

Special Programs for the Disadvantaged

The most important variable affecting school performance is not race but socioeconomic status. Regardless of race, children from poor families tend to do less well in school than do children from families who are better off. Compensatory programs such as Head Start and Follow Through are predicated on the assumption that if children from lower-class homes are to succeed in middle-class schools, they must have special help to equalize their chances.

California has initiated an innovative program to eliminate the learning gap between middle-class and lower-class children. This program is for all youngsters from kindergarten through the third grade and aims at having every youngster reading and writing, computing, and excited about school by the time he or she is eight years old. This goal is accomplished through parent involvement and individualized instruction. Using parent volunteers, paid aides, and teachers reduces the adult-pupil ratio to 1:10. Early results show that although all students benefit from this plan, children from schools in lower-class areas are gaining faster than are those in other schools. The plan is expensive, but administrators hope that the costs will be offset by great reductions in expenditures for remedial work for older students. The payoff for the children is enormous: the program allows them to be normal participants in school and to avoid the stigma of failure.

The problem with compensatory programs is that they blame the victim. The effort is to change the individual so that he or she will adapt to society. As noted in this and earlier chapters, these programs are based on the assumption that the individual is culturally deprived and needs extra help. By blaming the individual, well-meaning people direct attention away from the schools and society—the real sources of the problem. The two types of programs described next focus on the reformation of the school and society.

Reforming Schools to Allow Each Individual to Realize Her or His Potential

The California experiment mentioned above is an attempt to change the schools to minimize the differences between the children of the advantaged and disadvantaged. But this plan, like most, does not question the structure and philosophy of the educational system, which opponents argue essentially stifles children in attaining their potential. In the view of the critics, the system itself is wrong and the generator of many profound problems. These critics want to reconstruct the entire educational enterprise along very different lines. This demand for change is based on three related assumptions. The first is that the school is a microcosm of the larger society. Because society is too competitive, repressive, inhumane, materialistic, racist, and imperialist, so, too, are the schools. Changing society entails changing the schools.

The second assumption of the radical critics of education is that the process of public education as it currently exists damages, thwarts, and stifles children. The schools somehow manage to suppress the natural curiosity of children. They begin with *inquisitive* children and mold them into *acquisitive* children with little desire to learn.

Third, the educational system is a product of society and hence shapes its products to meet the requirements of society. The present system is predicated on the needs of an industrial society in which citizens must follow orders, do assigned tasks in the appropriate order and time span, and not challenge the status quo. But these behaviors will not be appropriate for life in the near future or perhaps even the present. The future will likely require people who can cope with rapid turnover—changes in occupations, human relationships, and community ties. Moreover, the citizens of the future (present?) must be able to cope with a myriad of choices. Does an educational system built on order, a rigid time schedule, and the lecture method adequately prepare youngsters for life as it is and will be?

The proponents of these and other alternatives are critical of U.S. education. They conclude that schools are failing not only children from the ghettos of large cities but also suburban and small-town youngsters. The schools fail because they treat children as miniature adults; because they treat children as a group rather than as individuals; because they stifle creativity; because they are repressive; and because they fail to allow children to reach their potential. This situation is not new, though. As Peter Drucker stated,

> today's school does no poorer a job than it did yesterday; the school has simply
> done a terribly poor job all along. But what we tolerated in the past we no
> longer can tolerate. . . . The school has suddenly assumed such importance for
> the individual, for the community, for the economy and for society, that we can-
> not suffer the traditional, time-honored incompetence of the educational system.
> (Drucker, 1972:49)

This approach makes the revolutionary assumption that the success or failure of the child lies with the school, not the child. The child is innately curious. If he or she is apathetic, then it must be the fault of the school. Because the self-fulfilling prophecy is such a powerful factor, teachers should hold *themselves,* not their students, responsible if the students do not learn. Middle-class bias in all its forms (e.g., teacher expectations for behavior and class-bias tests) must be eradicated from schools because it ensures the failure of the lower-class child.

Restructuring Society

The approaches to equality described above focus on changing either individual students or the schools. But if equality of opportunity is truly the goal, education cannot accomplish it alone. The problem is not in the individual or in the school but in the structure of society. As Bowles has argued,

> the burden of achieving equality of educational opportunity . . . cannot be borne
> by the educational system alone. The achievement of some degree of equality of
> opportunity depends in part on what we do in the educational system but also,
> to a very large degree, in what we do elsewhere in the economy, in the polity,
> and in the society as a whole. (Bowles, 1969:121)

Closing the achievement gap between advantaged and disadvantaged students cannot be accomplished without a societywide assault on racism and poverty. Christopher Jencks and his associates maintain that this assault requires fundamental changes in the system of societal rewards: a redistribution of wealth through equalizing occupational rewards, a minimum income for all members of society, and a reduction in the ability of parents to transmit their economic advantages and disadvantages to their offspring (Jencks et al., 1972). After a thorough investigation of inequality in our society, they concluded that inequality in the U.S. schools is not the major cause of economic stratification among adults. Poverty can be eliminated only through fundamental revisions in the economic and familial institutions. This is not to say that reform of the schools should be ignored. Efforts to improve our schools should parallel attempts to restructure the other institutions of society.

CHAPTER REVIEW

1. The system of education in the United States is characterized by (a) conservatism—the preservation of culture, roles, values, and training necessary for the maintenance of society; (b) belief in mass education; (c) local control; (d) competition; (e) reinforcement of the stratification system; and (f) preoccupation with order and control.

2. The belief that our society is meritocratic, with the most intelligent and talented at the top, is a myth. Education, instead of being the great equalizer, reinforces social inequality.

3. Schools perform a number of functions that maintain the prevailing social, political, and economic order: (a) socializing the young, (b) shaping personality traits to conform with the demand of the culture, (c) preparing for adult roles, and (d) providing employers with a disciplined and skilled labor force.

4. The curricula, testing, bureaucratic control, and emphasis on competition in schools reflect the social class structure of society by processing youth to fit into economic slots similar to those of their parents.

5. The schools are structured to aid in the perpetuation of social and economic differences in several ways: (a) by being financed principally through property taxes, (b) by providing curricula that are irrelevant to the poor, and (c) by tracking according to presumed level of ability.

6. The tracking system is closely correlated with social class; students from low-income families are disproportionately placed in the lowest track. Tracking thwarts the equality of educational opportunity for the poor by generating four effects: (a) a stigma, which lowers self-esteem; (b) the self-fulfilling prophecy; (c) a perception of school as having no future payoff; and (d) a negative student subculture.

7. Equality of educational opportunity must begin with the reform of educational finance in order to equalize the budgets of schools regardless of the wealth of individual districts.

8. The federal government could promote equality of opportunity by (a) providing national educational standards, a national curriculum, and national tests; (b) distributing money unequally to the states according to need; (c) encouraging states to minimize economic disparities among their school districts; and (d) increasing funding for Head Start and other compensatory programs.

9. Compensatory programs have achieved some success in narrowing the gap between children of the poor and of the affluent. The problem with these programs is that they blame the children for not measuring up to society's standards. Thus, this approach diverts attention away from the schools and society—the real sources of the problem.

10. Radical critics of the educational system argue that the schools fail all children, whether they are from the ghettos or suburbs. Schools, as they are presently structured, damage, thwart, and stifle children. Inquisitive children become acquisitive children with little desire to learn. Schools shape children to fit into a society where citizens follow orders and do assigned tasks without questioning.

11. The restructuring of schools will not meet the goal of equality of educational opportunity, radical critics argue, unless the society is also restructured. This change requires a societywide assault on racism and poverty and a redistribution of wealth to reduce the inequalities that result from economic advantage.

KEY TERMS

Cultural deprivation.   The erroneous assumption that some groups (e.g., the poor) are handicapped by a so-called inferior culture.

Tracking. Ability grouping in schools.

Stigma.   A powerful negative social label that affects a person's social identity and self-concept.

Self-fulfilling prophecy.   An event that occurs because it is predicted. That is, the prophecy is fulfilled because people alter their behavior to conform to the prediction.

Student subculture.   The members of the disadvantaged band together in a group with values and behaviors antagonistic toward school.

FOR FURTHER STUDY

Samuel Bowles and Herbert Gintis. *Schooling in Capitalist America: Educational Reform and the Contradictions of Economic Life.* New York: Basic Books, 1976.

Peter W. Cookson, Jr., and Caroline Hodges Persell. *Preparing for Power: America's Elite Boarding Schools.* New York: Basic Books, 1985.

Jeanne E. Griffith, Mary J. Frase, and John H. Ralph. "American Education: The Challenge of Change." *Population Bulletin* 44 (December 1989): entire issue.

Christopher Jencks et al. *Who Gets Ahead? The Determinants of Economic Success in America.* New York: Basic Books, 1979.

Jonathan Kozol. *Savage Inequalities: Children in America's Schools.* New York: Crown, 1991.

Elizabeth Kamarch Minnich. *Transforming Knowledge.* Philadelphia: Temple University Press, 1990.

Newsweek. "How to Teach Our Kids." *Newsweek,* special issue (Fall/Winter 1990): entire issue.

William Noble. *Bookbanning in America.* Middlebury, Vt.: Paul S. Eriksson Publisher, 1990.

Jeannie Oakes. *Keeping Track: How Schools Structure Inequality.* New Haven: Yale University Press, 1985.

Mike Rose. *Lives on the Boundary.* New York: Penguin Books, 1989.

Lois Weis, ed. *Class, Race, and Gender in American Education.* Albany: University of New York Press, 1988.

Anne Wheelock. *Crossing the Tracks: How "Untracking" Can Save America's Schools.* New York: The New Press, 1992.

FORUM

ABILITY GROUPING IN SCHOOLS

Let's detrack schools. The evidence is that these practices have a negative impact on most children's school opportunities and outcomes.

Jeannie Oakes and Martin Lipton

During the past decade, research on tracking and ability-grouped class assignments have provided striking evidence that these practices have a negative impact on most children's school opportunities and outcomes. Moreover, the negative consequences of these practices disproportionately affect low-income, African-American, and Latino children.

Increasingly, this research evidence is triggering responses from reform-minded policy makers and educators. The National Governors' Association has recommended detracking as part of its strategy for meeting the national education goals; the Carnegie Corporation endorses detracking in *Turning Points,* its report on reforms for the middle grades; and the College Board's report, *Access to Knowledge: An Agenda for Our Nation's Schools,* identifies tracking as a barrier in many students' paths to college. After vigorous discussion, the National Education Association resolved to eliminate tracking as it is now practiced. Across the country, local educators and policy makers are questioning their own local practices, and many are moving toward alternatives. . . .

Tracking structures are firmly grounded in widespread and historically rooted beliefs about human capacity and about individual and group differences. Tracking is also supported by outmoded conceptions that intelligence is global (i.e., a single entity that can be measured and reported as an I.Q. score), that it is fixed quite early (either before birth or soon thereafter), and that learning is the accumulation of a sequence of knowledge and skills.

If the *capacity to learn* is understood as unalterable and the range in capacity among school children is perceived to be great, then tracking must appear sensible. In this view, schools accommodate differences by separating students according to their measured ability and be adapting curriculum and instruction accordingly. The fact that learning capacity seems to be unevenly distributed among groups—with disadvantaged members of minority groups exhibiting less capacity to learn—appears to be beyond the control of the school. Thus schools typically conclude that the disproportionate assignment of low-income and minority students to low-track classes is an appropriate, if regrettable, response.

Alternatives to tracking begin to make sense when schools seriously entertain other conceptions of intelligence and learning: when detracking is not merely a response to an abstract sense of fairness but is also a practical way to act on new knowledge about intelligence and learning. A number of educators have told us that their views have been dramatically altered by the work of Howard Gardner and of Robert Sternberg, both of whom argue compellingly that intelligence is multifaceted and developmental and that learning is a complex process of constructing meaning. Serious consideration of their work has enabled these educators to invest new meanings in such popular notion as "all children can learn," rather than simply to mouth them as meaningless, if well-intentioned, slogans. And when they no longer interpret such statements to mean that all children can achieve their very different "potentials," educators can let go of the belief that children of "like potentials" must be grouped together.

These shifting conceptions of intelligence and learning have enabled a number of schools to support detracking by setting up heterogeneous classrooms in which instruction challenges the sense-making abilities of all capable (if different) children and in which differences become assets rather than liabilities. For example, Susan Benjamin of Highland Park (Illinois) High School described the values underlying classrooms in her school. "In the English Department," Benjamin wrote in the March 1990 *English Journal,* "the basic philosophy is that diversity within the classroom enriches the learning environment."

But powerful beliefs about the purposes of schooling also support tracking. For example, most Americans believe that schools should transmit the essential knowledge and values of the culture to all students as well as prepare a highly productive work force. While the first part of this belief argues for common schooling experiences, the second often provides a rationale for tracked schools with differentiated curricula that prepare students for different types of jobs. When schools explicitly acknowledge these seemingly contradictory purposes, they are likely to find that *all* students benefit from the diversity of learning experiences previously reserved either for college-bound or work-force-bound students.

Detracking, then, seems to involve a critical and unsettling rethinking of fundamental educational norms. This rethinking asks people to challenge their entrenched views of such matters as human capacitates, individual and group differences, the purposes of schooling, and the ever-present tensions between the norms of competitive individualism and the more democratic norms of support and community. As Paula Hatfield of the J. A. Leonard Middle School in Old Town, Maine, observed, "Simply eliminating tracking will not cure all of the ills of schooling and society. However, it may set off a powerful synergistic reaction requiring other institutional changes, changes in how teachers teach, how students relate to teach other, and how the school hierarchy operates. Most important, it may liberate students' and teachers' beliefs about who should and could achieve."

Source: Jeannie Oakes and Martin Lipton, "Detracking Schools: Early Lessons from the Field," *Phi Delta Kappan* 73 (February 1992), excerpts from pp. 448–454. Reprinted with permission.

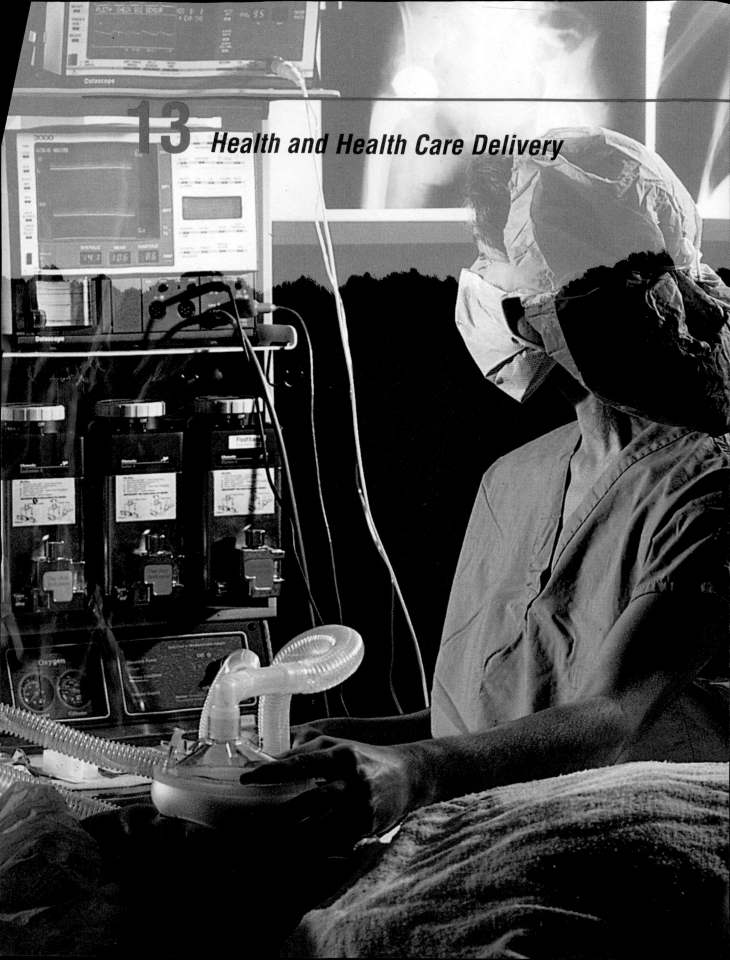

13 Health and Health Care Delivery

T he United States spends more for health care, both in total dollars and percentage of gross national product, than any other industrialized nation. The country's health care system is also the most technologically sophisticated with the best-trained practitioners. But apparently the United States is not getting a good return on its health investment: in 1989 the country ranked twentieth in the world in infant mortality and sixteenth in the world in life expectancy. The problem is that health care in the United States is rationed on the basis of ability to pay; that is, the system is superb for people who can afford it and falls woefully short for those who cannot. For the affluent, the best physicians, surgeons, hospital care, and the latest technology are available. Among the impoverished and near poor, however, approximately 37 million people are uninsured, which means that they are essentially left outside the health care system. Another 50 million are underinsured, which leaves them exposed to large financial risks or excludes coverage for certain medical problems. In short, the health delivery system in the United States and the health of people in the country are maldistributed.

The three sections of this chapter examine health and inequality: (1) health care and inequality, looking at the U.S. health care system by class, race, and gender; (2) the high cost of medical care and the reasons for these costs; and (3) the examination of some alternatives.

Health, Health Care Delivery, and Inequality

As we examine the structure of society and any of its institutions, we ask; who benefits and who suffers from the way it is organized? When health care delivery is the focus, the answer to this question is clear: there are glaring inequities that result in some categories of people being less healthy than others. Our examination of this structural inequity focuses on the three fundamental structures of inequality: class, race, and gender, which are key determinants of health (i.e., the distribution of health and disease) and health care delivery (i.e., the distribution of treatment). These structures of inequality make a difference, not surprisingly, with the advantaged being advantaged and the disadvantaged being disadvantaged.

Social Class

Economic disadvantage is closely associated with health disadvantages. Put another way: "How people live, get sick, and die depends not only on their race and gender, but primarily on the class to which they belong" (Navarro, 1991:2). The poor are more likely than the affluent to suffer from certain forms of cancer (cancers of the lung, cervix, and esophagus), and from hypertension, low-weight birth, hearing loss, diabetes, and infectious diseases (especially influenza and tuberculosis). The well-to-do live longer, and when stricken with a disease they are more likely to survive than are the poor. For example, a study of 4750 women with breast cancer found that those without insurance or on Medicaid were more likely to be diagnosed with cancer after it had progressed beyond a curable stage than were women with private insurance. "But even when it is detected in earlier, treatable stages, uninsured women are 66 percent more likely to die of the disease than women with private insurance. The increased risk for women on Medicaid is

40 percent (reported in the *Wall Street Journal*, 1992:B1). Similarly, the American Heart Association has found that the higher the income, the lower the risk of dying of coronary diseases such as heart attacks, strokes, and hypertension (Stewart, 1989).

The physical health of poor persons is more likely to be impaired than is the health of the more well-to-do because of differences in diet, sanitation, shelter, exposure to pollution, work conditions, and medical treatment. The focus here is on differences in medical care.

There are two government health programs—Medicare for the elderly and Medicaid for the very poor. Virtually all of the elderly population have at least some health care coverage through Medicare. The same is not true for the poor who are not covered by insurance and should be covered by Medicaid (Brown and Dallek, 1990). Medicaid is funded jointly by the federal government and each state. Each state administers its version of Medicaid with few federal guidelines. Thus, Medicaid varies from state to state in quality, eligibility of patients, coverage, and the adequacy of fees for the services of physicians and hospitals. In short, "State-by-state differences make obtaining Medicaid services a function of residency, not poverty level or need" (Brown and Dallek, 1990:379).

In 1992 about 18 million poor people in the United States were treated under Medicaid, but there are serious problems with this program.

> Medicaid is a system in breakdown, overloaded with patients and facing hundreds of millions of dollars in cost overruns—a system in which doctors increasingly refuse to treat patients because states often pay only half what private insurers pay. (Vilbig, 1992:4)

Because many physicians refuse to treat Medicaid patients, the poor often delay seeking medical attention, and when they do they typically go to hospital emergency rooms, where they cannot be turned away. This overburdens hospitals and postpones treatment as patients often must wait many hours before being seen by a physician. Often the examination is superficial and the treatment careless because the attending physicians are overwhelmed by the numbers of patients.

Other people must fend for themselves with some form of medical insurance. The problem is that many people cannot afford such insurance, resulting in some 37 million people younger than age sixty-five, 18 million of whom were children under age thirteen, who had no medical insurance (Children's Defense Fund, 1989a:2). More than three-fourths of the noninsured in 1987 were workers and their families. Some were self-employed and went without coverage because it was too expensive. Others worked for employers who did not provide any health benefits or who did not provide benefits for the dependents of their workers. The working poor are the hardest hit because the restrictive eligibility requirements for Medicaid eliminate them from the program because, although poor, they earn too much money to qualify.

The uninsured, of course, cannot afford the costs for physicians, dentists, and hospitals, so they often do without. Poor pregnant women (26 percent of women of childbearing age have no maternity coverage), as a result, often do not receive prenatal and postnatal health care. The consequences are a high maternal death rate (typically from hemorrhage and infection) and a relatively high **infant**

The poor and uninsured use hospital emergency rooms for routine medical treatment. Thus, they endure longer waits and receive more impersonal care than those who can afford their own doctors.

mortality rate, which is the number of deaths per 1000 live births (see Table 13.1). If the U.S. rate of 10 infant deaths per 1000 live births were equal to Japan's much lower rate, more than 17,000 infant lives would be saved annually.

Surviving infants are apt to have low birthweights and other complications. A study reported in the *New England Journal of Medicine* of 146,000 births in the San Francisco Bay area in 1982, 1984, and 1986 found that babies whose parents had no health insurance were about 30 percent more likely than those from insured families to die or be seriously ill at birth (reported in Associated Press, 1989). (A cautionary note: This finding should not be interpreted to mean that the lack of insurance is the sole cause of adverse health outcomes, but rather that poor health is a combination of diminished access to health care together with other factors related to poverty.)

Even when the poor do go to physicians and clinics, they are more likely than the more affluent to receive inferior services. This results from several factors. First, the poor often are served by understaffed clinics and public hospitals, which means that their visits often require long waits and hurried attention by overworked health practitioners. Second, there are disproportionately fewer physicians in poor urban and poor rural areas than in affluent urban and suburban areas (a consequence of physicians' tending to cluster where their practices will be the most lucrative). For example, in 1991 there were only 97 doctors for every 100,000 rural residents compared to 225 per 100,000 urban residents (Walmer, 1991). We should not infer from these data that all urban areas are well staffed with physi-

Table 13.1 Infant mortality rates, by country, 1987–1989

Rank in 1987	Country	Infant Deaths per 1,000 Live Births		
		1987	1988	1989
1	Japan	5.0	4.8	4.4
2	Taiwan	5.3	6.1	6.0
3	Sweden	6.1	5.8	5.7
4	Finland	6.2	6.1	5.8
5	Switzerland	6.8	6.8	7.3
6	Canada	7.3	7.2	–
7	Hong Kong	7.4	7.4	–
7	Singapore	7.4	7.0	7.5
9	Netherlands	7.6	6.8	6.8
10	France	7.8	7.8	7.5
11	Ireland	7.9	9.2	–
12	Denmark	8.3	7.6	8.4
13	Norway	8.4	8.0	–
14	East & West Germany	8.4	7.6	7.4
15	Spain	9.0	–	–
16	United Kingdom	9.1	9.0	8.5
17	Belgium	9.4	9.2	–
18	Australia	9.8	9.2	7.7
19	Austria	9.8	8.1	8.3
20	Italy	9.8	9.5	8.9
21	New Zealand	10.0	10.8	10.2
22	United States	10.1	10.0	9.7

(–) indicates data not available.

Source: Carl Haub and Machiko Yanagishita, "Infant Mortality: Who's Number One?"
Population Today 19 (March 19, 1991):6.

cians. Consider the possible disparity in physicians practicing in, for example, the Upper East Side of New York City compared to the rate in Harlem or the Bronx. And, third, the inferior service that the poor tend to receive is a consequence of their relative passivity in the patient-physician relationship.

The common belief is that the poor are accountable for their health deficiencies. Their lack of education and knowledge may lead to poor health practices (diet, exercise, preventive health care). They may, for example, be unaware of the dangers of lead in old paint where their children play or not know that excessive sodium in diets is a major contributor to hypertension. The poor, from this perspective, have cultural norms that differ from the majority. Their life-style is less likely than the life-style of the more affluent to include proper exercise for a healthy heart. Their diets are more likely to contain relatively high amounts of fat. They are more likely to smoke cigarettes and to abuse drugs. The children of the poor, for instance, are more likely than the children of the affluent to be born addicted to crack (somewhere between 100,000 and 350,000 crack babies are born each year in the United States) (Anderson, 1990) and to be victims of fetal alcohol syndrome.

The essence of this argument is that the problems of ill health that beset the poor disproportionately are a consequence of their different life-style. In short, this line of reasoning blames the poor for their failure to follow healthier life-styles.

This approach, however, ignores the fundamental realities of social class. Williams (1990), in his comprehensive review of the social science literature on socioeconomic status and health, argues that privilege in the social stratification system translates both directly and indirectly into better health in several major ways.

First, the privileged live in home, neighborhood, and work environments that are less stressful. The disadvantaged, on the other hand, are more subject to the stresses (and resulting ill health) from high crime rates, financial insecurity, marital instability, death of loved ones, exposure to unhealthy work conditions where they are exposed to hazardous risks and toxic substances, and exposure to pollution and toxic wastes in their neighborhoods (Elson, 1990). Poor workers are more likely than the nonpoor to be in jobs with low job security. The poor have more stress and hypertension (high blood pressure) because of living in crowded conditions and worrying about having enough resources for food, utilities, and rent. The poor also may not have adequate heat, ventilation, and sanitation, which means that they are more susceptible to infectious and parasitic diseases. See the Observation on the health of migrant workers.

Second, the privileged have more knowledge of positive health habits (adequate sleep, refraining from smoking, drinking moderately or not at all, maintaining normal weight, physical exercise, and monitoring cholesterol and blood pressure levels) and the resources to implement them.

Third, the children of privilege have healthier environments in the crucial first five years of life. Many adults from disadvantaged backgrounds suffer throughout their lives because of an unhealthy environment in their formative years.

Fourth, the privileged have better access to and make better use of the health care system (the primary subject of this chapter). Early intervention at the onset of a disease and medical management of a chronic illness affect both the survival rates and the quality of life. The fewer the economic resources, the less likely a person will receive preventive care and early treatment. This is because medicine in U.S. society is a market commodity and thus is dispensed unequally to the people who can afford it.

Physicians and private hospitals treat people who can afford their services, often leaving aside those who cannot. This practice is called **patient dumping.** For-profit hospitals either turn away patients who cannot afford their services, or they tend to switch them to public hospitals as soon as possible, or they keep the poor away by not providing the services they most require (e.g., an emergency room). These practices help the hospital's bottom line but they do not help the poor who need specialized care. Also, patient dumping decreases the quality of care at public hospitals because it increases overcrowding and increases the demand on the limited resources of public hospitals. The practice of patient dumping also indirectly increases the profits of private hospitals by increasing the

OBSERVATION

THE HEALTH OF MIGRANT WORKERS

There are about 4 million migrant farm workers in the United States, mostly African Americans and Latinos. These workers and their families follow the fruit and vegetable harvests. Typically, they live in housing supplied by their employers. Their living conditions are often overcrowded and dirty. Sanitation is often below standard. Water is sometimes contaminated. Their work is difficult, requiring stooping, climbing, and heavy lifting. Migrant workers work long days exposed to the sun and to the pesticides and herbicides that saturate the fields where they work. More than 90 percent of migrant farm workers live at or below the poverty level. Because they move from locality to locality and from state to state, they do not receive the benefits that many employees typically receive. Moreover, they are not always eligible for state and federal welfare programs.

As a result of these conditions, the health of migrant workers and their families is similar to what might be found in a Third World country. Some facts (these are from Walmer, 1990):

- Life expectancy is well below average (49 years compared to 75.2 years).
- Parisitic infections among children is 10 times greater than in the general population.

- Migrant workers are three times more likely to get urinary tract infections than nonmigrant workers.
- Infant mortality is high (12.1 per 1000 compared to 9.7).
- Tuberculosis is a special problem for migrant workers. One study in the *Journal of the American Medical Association* reported active tuberculosis in 0.47 percent of Latino farm laborers and 3.6 percent of U.S.-born Blacks. Moreover, the prevalence of TB infection (i.e., positive tuberculin skin tests) was 37 percent in Latinos, 62 percent in U.S.-born Blacks, and 76 percent among Haitians (Snider, Seggerson, and Hutton, 1991).

In sum, Nancy Foote, who has run clinics for farmworkers for eight years, says that her clients bring with them the ills of the developing world—parasites, tuberculosis, poor nutrition. To these they add injuries from difficult physical work and farm accidents, as well as headaches, nausea and sinus problems, some of which may come from the mix of chemicals that most workers inhale or get on their skin each day. (quoted in *The Economist* 1992e:29)

---

desire of many of the affluent to choose them over public hospitals. The rationale is provided by Lekachman:

> One of the tribulations of hospitalization is the sort of people one meets. In the next bed may restlessly toss someone of the wrong color, occupation, life style or income. Privatization promises better company. Treatment in a strategically located Humana hospital warrants continuation in sickness as in health of safe, middle-class suburban life. Your fellow patients fit snugly into your own class niche. Their education, jobs, income, and opinions are just like those you encounter in your car pool or on the commuter train. Critics of corporate hospitals justifiably complain that they cream the population, consigning difficult people and their complicated ailments to public and voluntary units. Of course. The critics have identified the major attraction of private hospitals to those creamed. Who prefers skimmed milk to cream? (Lekachman, 1987:303)

As strong as the case is for providing equal access to medical care to all people, it is not the most fruitful approach to correcting the differences in health by socioeconomic class. The answer, most fundamentally, is to reduce the inequalities of class (and race and gender) that perpetuate poor health among the disadvantaged. According to Williams,

> the available evidence suggests . . . that equality in the health care delivery system [while a legitimate and desired goal] will not eliminate inequality in health status . . . if the inequalities remain in the fundamental reward structures of society. The point here is neither that changes in health care delivery will make no difference nor that the determinants of inequality are static. What is implied is that inequality will persist in a variety of social indicators as long as the basic reward structures remain unequal. (Williams, 1990:95)

Race

Nonwhite people in the United States are disproportionately poor (e.g., about one-third of all Blacks and nearly 30 percent of all Hispanics are below the poverty line). This fact combined with racial discrimination leads to unfavorable patterns of health and health care delivery for them. Let us examine some of these health differences by race.

Life expectancy.   Perhaps the best illustration of the difference that race makes on health is in life expectancy. The 1990 estimates revealed that the difference between White males and Black males was 5 years, and the difference between White females and Black females was 4.6 years (U.S. Bureau of the Census, 1991C:73).

The discrepancy is even wider for Native Americans, who have the poorest health of any racial category in the United States. Their life expectancy is ten years below that of the nation as a whole. "Their mortality rates are one and a half times higher than those of the general population and, in the period from 1980 to 1982, 37 percent of Native American deaths occurred among those under age 45, compared with 12 percent of deaths at this age in the general population" (Scarpitti and Andersen, 1992:337).

Infant mortality.   The rate of infant mortality in the United States reveals striking differences by race. According to the National Center for Health Statistics, the infant mortality rate for Whites in 1989 was 8.1 deaths per 1000 births, while the rate for Black babies was more than twice as high at 18.6 per 1000 live births (reported in Leigh, 1992:49). Since 1970 the rate has been halved for Whites and Blacks, but, obviously, the gap between Whites and Blacks remains, and the evidence is that this gap is no longer narrowing (National Center for Health Statistics, 1990b:3). Most significant, in the racial ghettos of some of the nation's inner cities the infant mortality rate is as high as that of some of the poorest Third World countries.

Maternal mortality.   The leading causes of maternal death are preventable. Statistics reveal that the deaths of Black and non-White mothers is much higher than that of White mothers.

In 1986 black and all nonwhite mothers were substantially more likely (3.8 and 3.3 times, respectively) than white mothers to die of pregnancy-related causes. The maternal mortality rates for black and all nonwhite women were 18.8 and 16.0 deaths per 100,000 live births, respectively, compared with 4.9 for white women. (Hughes et al., 1989:10)

Prenatal care.   In 1988, one birth in seventeen was to a mother who did *not* receive prenatal care until the last three months of pregnancy, or not at all. By race, the breakdown was that 5 percent of White mothers had not received any prenatal care, compared to 10 percent of Black mothers, and 12.1 percent of Latino mothers (see Table 13.2).

Low birth weight.   In 1988 Black children were twice as likely to be born with a low birth weight (less than 5 pounds, 8 ounces) as were White children and Latino children. Specifically, the rates were 5.6 percent of White babies were born weighing less than 2,500 grams, 6.2 percent of Hispanic babies, and 13.0 percent of Black babies (see Table 13.2). These proportions by race have remained about the same since 1960. The difference noted is *not* completely attributable to a higher proportion of young mothers among Blacks. Older Black mothers are more likely to have low birth weight babies than are older White mothers (Miller, 1987:506).

Heart disease.   Middle-age Black men have more than double, and Black women more than triple, the rate of death from heart disease than do middle-age White men and women.

Cancer.   The death rate from cancer is about three and one-half times greater for Black males than for White males. The rate for Black women is also higher than it is for White women. The problem, generally, is that Blacks (and Latinos) are more likely to be diagnosed with cancer in its later stages, making survival less

Table 13.2   Live births, by race on selected characteristics: 1988

Race	Percentage of Mothers Beginning Prenatal Care During		Percentage of Births with Low Birth Weight
	First Trimester	Third Trimester or No Care	
White	79.4	5.0	5.6
Black	61.1	10.0	13.0
Latino	61.3	12.1	6.4
Mexican	58.3	13.9	5.6
Puerto Rican	63.2	10.2	9.4
Cuban	83.4	3.6	5.9
Central and So. American	62.8	12.5	5.6

Source: U.S. Bureau of the Census, *Statistical Abstract of the United States 1991*. Washington, D.C.: U.S. Government Printing Office, 1991:66.

likely. This, of course, is not because of race *per se* but because of the greater like-lihood of Blacks and Latinos to be poor and without adequate medical insurance.

The cancer rate is higher for Blacks than Whites for all cancers except stomach cancer and breast cancer. The latter anomaly may be explained by the apparent fact that the younger a mother at the birth of her first child, the lower the breast cancer risk, and Black women tend to have children at younger ages. Once cancer is detected in both Blacks and Whites, Whites have a much higher survival rate.

Vision problems.   More than 9 million people in the United States have visual impairment caused usually by glaucoma, diabetes, and retinal diseases. Black adults are nearly twice as likely as Whites to be legally blind or vision impaired, according to a study in the *Archives of Ophthalmology* (reported in Goldfarb, 1990). African Americans are six times more likely to have glaucoma than are Whites and four times more likely to be blinded by it. These high glaucoma rates for Blacks are attributable to their relative lack of access to medical care and their high rate of high hypertension (Atkins, 1991). Hispanic Americans are more likely than Whites to be blind, primarily because of complications from diabetes, a disease they are three times more likely than Whites to have (Altman, 1991b).

Communicable diseases.   The diseases especially found among the poor (e.g., influenza, pneumonia, and tuberculosis) are disproportionately found among non-Whites because they are disproportionately poor. Hispanics, for instance, are four times more likely to contract tuberculosis than are Whites. Native Americans are four times more likely to die from tuberculosis and dysentery than are non-Native Americans.

The reasons for these racial disparities in health are varied and complex. Some biological differences account for a few differences. Some Blacks, for example, are genetically susceptible to sickle cell anemia. As real as this genetic difference is, however, nonbiological influences are much more important. So, too, with hypertension (high blood pressure). Blacks have higher blood pressure than do Whites. Is the reason genetic or social in origin? A study at Johns Hopkins examined this, assuming that if race is the factor leading to hypertension, then the darker the skin of African Americans the higher the blood pressure regardless of income, job status, or education. The findings were, to the contrary, that darker skin people had higher blood pressure only if they also were poor and less educated. Responding to this study, an editorial in the *Journal of the American Medical Association* argued that discrimination rather than genes is the reason for Blacks being at higher risk for hypertension: "A combination of disadvantaged socioeconomic status and a behavior pattern of repressed hostility in a dark-skinned individual may be the marker of the at-risk person" (reported in Friend, 1991:A1).

Cultural or life-style differences offer some explanations. This blaming-the-victim approach argues that racial minorities do not take proper care of themselves. Their diets tend to be high in fat, sugar, and salt. They are more likely to smoke (a fact not lost on the tobacco companies as they target their products and advertising to Blacks and Hispanics). They are less likely than members of the majority to exercise. Thus, Blacks, for example, have a high incidence of obesity, hypertension, and heart disease. Louis Sullivan, Secretary of Health and Human Services in the Bush administration has said in this regard, the top 10 causes of premature death in our nation are significantly influenced by personal behavior and life-style choices. [He has exhorted Blacks to quit smoking, cut down on drinking and lose weight.] Such personal inititive could eliminate up to 45 percent of deaths from percent cardiovascular disease, 23 percent of deaths from cancer and more than 50 percent of the disabling complications of diabetes. (cited in Gorman, 1991:52b)

But even though life-style differences among the races account for some variations in health, other factors are more important.

Economic factors explain much of the variation (this section relies on the insights of Miller, 1987). Minority racial and ethnic groups are disproportionately poor. This means that many of them must live in rat-infested neighborhoods, where they are exposed to diseases carried by these vermin. Their neighborhoods also have high concentrations of lead (in the paint and plumbing), which exposes their children to many health dangers, including brain damage. Living in poverty also means living in inadequate shelter, where exposure to the cold leads to complications such as bronchitis and pneumonia. Living in overcrowded situations leads to the spread of communicable diseases. A low income means reliance on a diet of cheap, fattening, nonnutritious food.

Living in poverty also results in the disruption of social networks and in heightened fears and anxieties caused by arson, drug abuse, and violent crime. Regarding this last point, the Justice Department reported from data covering 1979 through 1986 that Blacks were nearly six times more likely than Whites to be murdered and almost twice as likely to be robbed and that Blacks were raped at a rate nearly double that of Whites (reported in Nichols, 1990:1).

The poor also are less likely to receive adequate medical attention. Many, as noted, do not have medical insurance, and being poor they cannot afford medical care on a regular, preventive basis. The absence of insurance of coverage is related to race: 33 percent of all Latinos in 1990 were without private or public health insurance, compared to 19.7 percent of African Americans and 12.9 percent of Whites (study by the National Council of La Raza and the Labor Council for Latin American Advancement, reported in the *New York Times,* 1992). Thus, they delay going to the physician, dentist, or hospital until the health problem is too serious to ignore. This may mean that the problem is too advanced for a cure.

Blacks are much more likely than Whites to rely on emergency room and hospital outpatient departments rather than on a family physician. The two most important reasons for this are that they cannot afford a family physician, and, if they could afford one, physicians are in short supply where most Blacks live. "As of 1985, for example, one-third of the 750 American counties with the highest proportion of black population had been designated by the federal government as 'critical shortage areas' for primary care physicians; this is half again as common as for all other counties in the country" (Schlesinger, 1987:276).

There are four negative outcomes from this for Blacks. First, they do not meet regularly with a physician who is familiar with their health history (see Table 13.3). Second, the number of hospitals in the poor sections of cities and where rural poverty is prevalent is declining. Third, the federal cutbacks during the 1980s resulted in decreased medical attention for Blacks. And, fourth, even when

Table 13.3 Child health utilization by race

	Race/Ethnicity		
	White	Black	Hispanic
Percent of children under age 17 who have never had a routine physical examination, 1982	3.5	4.2	9.2
Percent of 3- to 16-year-olds who have not had a vision examination in a year, 1982	37.2	42.1	41.6
Percent of 4- to 11-year-olds who have not had a dental visit in a year, 1986	25.7	41.3	40.6
Percent of 5- to 11-year-olds who have never had a dental visit, 1986	10.2	16.9	20.3

Source: Dana Hughes, Kay Johnson, Sara Rosenbaum, and Joseph Liu, *The Health of America's Children* (Washington, D.C.: Children's Defense Fund, 1989), p. 61. Reprinted by permission.

health services are accessible, Blacks may face racial discrimination in attempting to obtain care. "This discrimination may simply be the result of irrational racial prejudice, but it may also reflect a more calculated judgment that Black patients will be more difficult or expensive to treat [i.e., they will not be able to pay their bills]" (Schlesinger, 1987:277).

Thus, a major reason for the high death rate of African Americans from cancer is, as the American Cancer Society has noted, because they often do not have access to quality health care (reported in Cimons, 1989). But the link may be stronger than that—when Blacks (and other racial minorities) have access to good medical care, they do not receive the same treatment as do Whites.

Researchers at Harvard University found that a significantly higher proportion of Whites admitted to Massachusetts hospitals with heart problems undergo coronary bypass operations and cardiac catheterizations than do Blacks. The important finding in this study was that this difference occurred even when the Whites and Blacks were at the same income level, had the same insurance status, or were the same age. The conclusion is inescapable—the difference in treatment was because of the patient's race, with Whites receiving better care than Blacks (reported in Stevens, 1989).

One more finding makes this case even stronger: the recipients of organ transplants are disproportionately White. In 1988, for example, Whites received 97.6 percent of transplanted pancreases. Moreover, according to the U.S. Department of Health and Human Services, Blacks on average wait almost twice as long for a kidney transplant as do Whites (13.9 months versus 7.6 months) (reported in Esters and Seligmann, 1990).

Poverty and its attendant problems are exacerbated by the social inequalities associated with race. Being Black, Hispanic, or Native American means for many people to be considered inferior, even to be despised. Hierarchy creates tensions and stresses.

> For blacks in the United States the sense of economic inequality, social distance, discrimination and hierarchy—of not being accorded full equality—is undoubtedly strong and persisting. . . . Almost any encounter, at whatever level . . . is a confrontation with a hostile environment and represents a potential stress situation above and beyond that which normally exists for whites. . . . The experiences of poverty and inequality and uncertainty about how one is perceived because of one's race is certainly a type of continuing, prolonged stress. Such stress not only makes its victims susceptible to acute illnesses but also harms them socially. (Miller, 1987:511–512)

Blacks, especially low-income Blacks, have higher hypertension rates than do the more well-to-do. This is partially the result of a poor diet. But it also is reasonable to assume that the stress associated with hypertension results from blocked social mobility, anger over perceived and real injustices, fear of crime, and from being treated as a social inferior.

Gender

The health of women and the health care they receive reflect primarily their status in society and only secondarily their physiological differences from men. Women do have significant health advantages over men; for example, their life expectancy exceeds that of males by about seven years. These advantages begin in the womb, where female fetuses have a 10 percent higher survival rate than do male fetuses. These advantages continue after birth and throughout the life cycle as male death rates exceed female death rates at all ages. Women are less likely than men to die from the leading causes of death, including heart disease and cancer or from accidents, suicide, and homicide (the only exception is death from diabetes).

There are both biological and social reasons for some of the health advantages that women have over men. During early childhood girls have biological benefits over boys, as exhibited by their greater resistance to infectious and chronic diseases. As adults women in the past were more protected than were men, at least until menopause, especially from heart disease and hypertension. The gender gap is now closing, however, as many more women are now in the labor force and therefore experience many of the same job-related stresses as do men.

More important, though, than the biological differences between the sexes are the significant social differences that also account for gender differences in health. The adolescent and young adult male gender role includes being assertive and daring. This accounts for the greater likelihood of males being in automobile accidents; driving while drunk; and using more alcohol, illegal drugs, and cigarettes (recently, however, the number of women who smoke is increasing so that the difference between men and women is converging). Males also are more likely than females to work at risky jobs (including military combat).

The female gender role, on the other hand, is more conducive to good health in several ways. Women are expected to be more knowledgeable about health matters and thus to be more aware of changes in their bodies than are men. Women are also more likely to see a physician or be admitted into a hospital than are men (traditional men tend to see this behavior in males as a sign of weakness).

That women receive more health care than men appears to be more than just a manifestation of gender roles. The evidence is that women, despite their greater longevity rates, *are* sick more often than men. As examples, women have fifty bouts with flu for every thirty-seven men have; women are bedridden 35 percent more days than men are; women are fifteen times more likely to have autoimmune thyroid disease and nine times more likely to have lupus; and women visit doctors more often for anemia, constipation, gallstones, arthritis, and bronchitis (Painter, 1992b).

The differences between men and women are explained by Lois Verbrugge:

> In sum, women have more frequent illness and disability, but the problems are typically not serious (life threatening) ones. In contrast, men suffer more from life threatening diseases, and they cause more permanent disability and earlier death for them. One sex is "sicker" in the short run, and the other in the long run. (Verbrugge, 1985:162–163)

This is not to suggest that women are more likely than men to be hypochondriacs. Men, because of gender expectations to be strong and courageous, are more likely than women to deny early warning signs of ill health.

Women on average are less likely than men to have medical insurance. This disadvantage is strongest for women between ages forty-five and sixty-four (before they qualify for Medicare) and especially for Black and Latino women in this age category (about 35 percent of women compared to two-thirds of men) (Barringer, 1992). This is because women are more often employed in part-time work, work at low-wage jobs, and work for small businesses. Also, as noted in Chapter 9, insurance coverage for women stops under their husbands' policies when they are widowed or divorced.

Women face two major health risks. One is childbearing, which can be unhealthy, even deadly for mothers. The other health risk is a consequence of traditional gender roles. Because women in U.S. society are evaluated by their physical appearance, they are much more likely than men to suffer from anorexia nervosa and bulimia (conditions that result when individuals take extraordinary measures to lose weight).

Women are also much more likely than men to risk surgery for cosmetic reasons (tummy tucks, liposuction, breast implants or reduction, and face lifts), which may have negative health effects. Since 1963, when the first breast implant operation was performed, about 2 million U.S. women have used this procedure (85 percent for cosmetic reasons and 15 percent for reconstruction after surgery for breast cancer). This operation, while usually successful, can have side effects, such as scarring, firmness of the implant, leakage, and a loss of sensation. There is also the question of the long-term safety of silicon in the body.

The advantage women have over men in mortality rates is overshadowed by the advantages men receive from the medical profession. First, the medical profession is dominated by males—about 83 percent of physicians are male (although now about 40 percent of first-year medical students are female) (Angier, 1992); 81 percent of all medical school faculty members are male (Bickel, 1990). Women in medicine, on the other hand, are vastly overrepresented in the nurturant, supportive, underpaid, and relatively powerless roles of nurse and aide.

Second, much medical research has excluded women as subjects. For example, the major study on whether taking daily doses of aspirin can reduce the risk of a heart attack used 22,071 subjects—all men. In most cases, a drug proved effective in men is also effective for women. But the differences in hormone proportions and the menstrual cycle can make a difference. In the aspirin study it would have been useful to determine whether taking aspirin prevents heart attacks in premenopausal women, in only postmenopausal women, or not in any women. Another study used 12,866 male subjects to explore the links between heart disease and high cholesterol, lack of exercise, and smoking. By excluding women from the study, the medical profession has no clear scientific proof whether the linkages among these variables found for men also occur for women (Purvis, 1990).

The National Women's Health Resource Center has noted that other major health studies have overlooked women. As in the aspirin and heart disease study, research using only male subjects has studied diet, exercise, and cholesterol, "Type A" behavior and heart disease; and alcohol and blood pressure (Silberner 1990).

Third, research appears to put women's health priorities second to men's. For example, the National Institutes of Health spends only 13 percent of its research budget on women's health care issues (Sperling, 1990). Perhaps this explains why medical research has yet to come up with an acceptable, safe, and effective male contraceptive. This deficiency has meant that women have had to bear the responsibilities and health risks of contraception. Other examples of research on women that have been minimized are breast cancer, osteoporosis, and hormone replace-

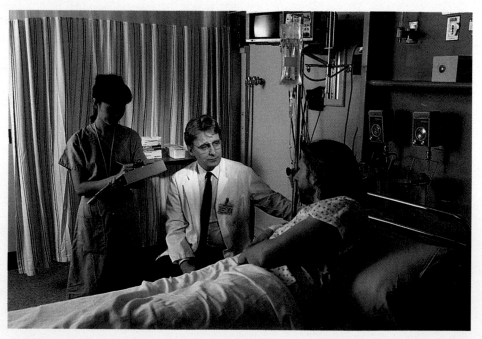

The most prestigious positions within the medical profession are dominated by white males.

ment after menopause. In response to this relative lack of research on women's health, the National Institutes of Health issued a report in 1992 that posed many gender-related health issues and challenged medical researchers to fill the gap between what is known about men and what is known about women.

Fourth, women patients interacting with male physicians encounter a number of sexist practices. These include paternalistic attitudes (use of first names, for instance), insensitivity toward the special problems of women surrounding the menstrual cycle and menopause, siding with husbands who were leary of vasectomies and performing, rather, tubal ligations on wives, even though the cost and medical risk were much greater, and requiring more specific tests for men than for women during diagnostic examinations. Another example of male physicians' insensitivity to women often occurs during an unwanted pregnancy. Many male physicians often consider women's interests secondary to fetal survival. For a final example of paternalism, see the Observation about women in coma.

Fifth, women are discriminated against in the treatment they receive or do not receive. Two recent examples make this point. A study reported to the American Heart Association found that men were twice as likely as women to receive newer, life-saving treatments for heart attacks such as clot-busting drugs or angioplasty (reported in Altman, 1991a). Another study found that among cancer patients under age fifty, women were twice as likely as men the same age to receive less potent pain medication for the pain they suffer (reported in Snider, Healy, and Miller, 1992).

The High Cost of U.S. Health Care

The U.S. medical bill in 1992 was about $817 billion, which is 14 percent of the nation's gross national product (GNP). No other nation spends as much on health (see Other Societies, Other Ways). Medical costs in 1991 rose 11 percent a year— at a time when overall inflation was around 3 percent. The result is that in 1935 medical costs amounted to only 3 percent of the GNP, in 1960 costs were up to 6 percent, and in 1985 they had risen to 10 percent. It is projected that medical costs, if left to continue as in the past, will reach an estimated $1,616 billion in the year 2000, which is 16.4 percent of GNP (Faltermayer, 1992:47).

The problems with these high and rising medical costs correspond with who pays them. The private sector (businesses providing benefits for their employees) pay about one-fourth of the total U.S. health bill, governments (federal, state, and local) pay two-fifths (using tax dollars), and individuals pay about one-third, either through direct payments as patients or through private insurance premiums (Maher, 1989).

The private sector is feeling an enormous financial strain as its medical costs escalate. In 1991, for example, the health care costs of employers rose 12.1 percent to $3605 per employee (Freudenheim, 1992). This cost is passed on to the consumer, with General Motors adding, for instance, about $900 to the cost of each car in 1992 for the medical costs of its employees.

The second problem is that these rising costs of health care are straining public finances (e.g., government monies for Medicare and Medicaid, which are indexed to rise with inflation). The cost of Medicaid (federal and state monies for

OBSERVATION

BIGOTRY AGAINST WOMEN EXTENDS EVEN TO THOSE IN COMA

Scientist Estelle Ramey, citing the use of prenatal diagnosis to detect and abort female fetuses, once wondered aloud whether being born female could now be considered a genetic disease.

She knew, of course, that wasn't the real disease. It is the deep-seated belief, learned by all of us from infancy through a million clues, that women are not just different but inferior.

I've written and spoken thousands of words about this epidemic, but it wasn't till I read a recent research paper that I realized bigotry toward women even threatens their right to die in dignity.

Lawyers Allison August and Steven Miles, in the journal *Law, Medicine and Health Care,* say they examined the 22 "right-to-die" cases that have been decided by appeals courts in 14 states.

In each case, the patient was a permanently unconscious adult who hadn't left written directions, either in a Durable Power of Attorney for Health Care or a "living will." In each case, a doctor or a relative asked a court to intervene.

The cases go back as far as Karen Quinlan, whose parents fought to release her from artificial support in the mid-1970s, and got the rest of the nation talking about the taboo issue of death. The cases are as recent as the 1988 Missouri case (but not the more recent U.S. Supreme Court decision) of Nancy Cruzan, now in her seventh year of persistent vegetative state. [Nancy Cruzan was allowed to die in December 1990 after a county judge gave her parents permission to remove the artificial life support system.]

The courts went at the problem in two different ways: Some tried to reconstruct what the patient would have wanted. In this approach, the judges were respecting the autonomy of the patient and his or her right to refuse treatment even when unable to speak.

Some judges designated a substitute to make the decision on the basis of what he or she thought was best for the patient—not what the patient would have wanted.

In some of these latter cases, the designated decider was a family member or guardian, the doctor or even the hospital.

Can you guess, in our patchwork of state laws, where there was consistency in these cases?

It was this: In 75 percent of the men's cases, the judges took the first approach, trying to find out what the patient would have wanted. In 85 percent of the women's cases, the judges took the second approach—designating a "father knows best" decision-maker. In only 14 percent of the cases did the court try to find out what the woman would have wanted.

Miles and August found that in justifying these decisions, the judges described the male patients' reported wishes as "reaching a judgment," being "very serious," having beliefs "deeply held"—a "solemn, intelligent determination."

But the judges called the women's past wishes "casual," "emotional," a mere "distaste" for prolonged treatment, a "wish" to die.

A judge dismissed Cruzan's reported wishes as "informally expressed reactions," which by definition couldn't be considered an informed refusal of treatment.

Wait. There's hope.

Quinlan's trial judge, years later, officially apologized for not taking seriously her reported requests. And just weeks ago, the U.S. Supreme Court, in aggregate only inches to the left of Jesse Helms, sent Cruzan's case back for a retrial that began last week.

The justices said Cruzan has a right to have her past requests heard, even if she's now in a coma. And even if she is a woman.

Source: Bruce Hilton, "Bigotry against Women Extends Even to Those in Coma," *Rocky Mountain News* (November 15, 1990), pp. 52, 55. Reprinted with permission from The San Francisco Examiner. © 1990 San Francisco Examiner.

the poor) rose from $2.3 billion in 1967 to $158 billion in 1991, providing health care to 27.3 million people in the United States. Similarly, Medicare, which provides health care for the elderly, rose from a $5 billion program in 1965 to one that cost $110 billion in 1991 (Castro, 1991:37–38).

The third problem is described in the first section of this chapter. Some persons and families do not have resources to afford sufficient medical insurance or to pay for necessary health care. There has always been a mismatch between the resources of the poor and the cost of medical care, but in recent years this disjuncture has increased markedly. This section examines the reasons health care in the United States is so expensive. We want to go beyond the obvious reasons such as demographic trends (e.g., more old people who have greater health needs than do younger people) and inflation. We examine, rather, the forces within the structure of U.S. medicine that cause the ever higher prices.

The Method of Payment

The cost for health services in the United States is determined by the people who provide the services—physicians, therapists, hospitals, clinics, and laboratories—with little outside interference. Physicians, for example, are, for the most part, independent, fee-for-service, entrepreneurs. Patients have little power to complain or go elsewhere because physicians and hospitals have so much more knowledge and power and because fees tend to be relatively standardized within a community or region. This means, in effect, that health providers are able to increase their profits because there are few incentives to control consumer costs and few controls to limit abuses. The more that physicians, for example,

OTHER SOCIETIES, OTHER WAYS

The Cost of Health Care for the United States and Selected Countries, 1990

1990 Figures	Life Expectancy Male/Female	Infant Mortality Rate*	Per Capita Health Expenditures**	Health Expenditures as a % of GDP	Doctors per 1000 People	Average Days In-Patient Care[1]
Japan	75.9 / 81.8[1]	4.6[1]	$1,171	6.5%	1.6[2]	51.4
Canada	73.0 / 79.7[3]	7.2[1]	$1,730	9.0%	2.2	13.0 ·
Britain	72.8 / 78.4[1]	7.9	$974	6.2%	1.4[1]	14.8
France	72.7 / 80.9	7.2	$1,543	8.9%	2.6[1]	12.8
Italy	72.6 / 79.1[1]	8.5	$1,234	7.7%	1.3[1]	11.7
Germany	72.6 / 79.0[1]	7.5[1]	$1,487	8.1%	3.0	16.2
U.S.	72.1 / 79.0	9.2	$2,566	12.4%	2.3	9.2

* Per 1,000 live births.
** Adjusted for purchasing power, 1990 U.S. dollars.
[1] 1989.
[2] 1988.
[3] 1986.

Source: Fortune, "Comapring Health Care," (July 27, 1992), p. 80. © 1992 Time Inc. All rights reserved.

have their patients visit them for checkups and treatments, the more money they make. Also, patients cannot purchase prescription drugs without the physician's prescription. This permits a physician to see dozens of patients a day for the normal office call fee (typically $25 to $35) in order to write the prescription. Also, in some cases, the physician shares in the profits with the pharmacist. Similarly, the more tests that a hospital performs on patients and the longer the patients stay, the more profitable is the hospital. Probably most treatments by physicians and tests by hospitals are necessary, but the profit-enhancing system encourages the likelihood of such abuses as excessive inpatient care and unnecessary tests.

This problem of increasing costs has been exacerbated by the rise of the third-party system of funding—payments by insurance companies or by the government (Medicare and Medicaid). In 1965 Congress created programs to provide medical benefits for specific categories of people in the United States. **Medicare** was created to provide partial coverage of medical costs primarily for people over age sixty-five. This program cost the government $95 billion in fiscal 1990. **Medicaid** is a government health program for poor people. These two programs were organized so that physicians and hospitals are reimbursed for their costs. This practice encourages hospitals, nursing homes, and physicians to order excessive and, therefore, more expensive treatment. The irony is that about one-fourth of the people in the United States still do not receive enough medical care (especially the working poor, who often are excluded because they do not qualify for Medicaid); and some people receive more care than is sometimes necessary.

Typically, consumers pay only about one-third of physician's fees and about one-tenth of hospital bills. The remainder is paid by insurance or government programs. This third-party system encourages high health costs in two ways, depending on the source of payment. Health insurance limits payments to inpatient care by physicians and to hospital-related expenses, both of which inflate expenses by encouraging these activities even when they may not be needed.

Especially costly is the incentive (for the profit of physicians and hospitals) for using a variety of laboratory tests, the use of elaborate and expensive technology for diagnostic tests (e.g., computerized tomography—CT scanners—or magnetic resonance imaging—MRI machines), and elaborate new surgeries such as heart bypass and organ and bone-marrow transplants. Even though these procedures are sometimes successful, they are usually very expensive. Economists have estimated that these heroic medical efforts cost about $13.2 billion in 1990 (Eugene *Register-Guard,* 1990). Tim Wise has summarized the problem:

> Under fee-for-service, hospitals and physicians have been paid on a cost-plus basis, much like defense contractors. They set their fees to cover costs and guarantee a profit, then send the bill to the insurer. Private insurers guarantee payment, build in their own profit margins, and pass the costs on in higher premiums. Neither the provider nor the insurer has much incentive to hold down costs. (Wise, 1989:6)

Administrative Costs

About one-fifth of medical costs—$163 billion in 1992—goes for administrative costs. *Consumer Reports* estimates that at least $70 billion is wasted in administrative inefficiency.

Projecting from 1991 estimates by the General Accounting Office, the U.S. could save roughly $70 billion this year by switching from our fragmented and inefficient insurance system to a single-payer system—one in which all citizens receive health care from private doctors and hospitals that are paid by a single insurance entity. (*Consumer Reports,* 1992a:437)

The primary reason for the current administrative inefficiency is that there are more than 1200 private health insurance companies. Private physicians must hire office help to cope with the regulations and paperwork demanded by the various insurance companies and by the government.

Hospitals in the U.S. spend fully 20 percent of their budgets, on average, on billing administration—compared to only 9 percent for Canadian hospitals. To run a health plan covering 25 million people, Canada employs fewer administrators than Massachusetts Blue Cross, which covers 2.7 million. (*Consumer Reports,* 1992a:448)

Private For-Profit Hospitals

Traditionally, hospitals in the United States have been nonprofit organizations run by churches, universities, and municipalities. Since the mid-1960s, however, private profit-oriented hospitals and hospital chains have emerged, and more than 20 percent are now owned privately. The impetus for this shift toward privatization was the federal government's Medicare and Medicaid programs along with the insurance industry's open-ended system of payout, which virtually gave hospitals and nursing homes the power to determine how much their product was worth.

According to the basic tenet of capitalism, competition should lead to efficiency and reduced costs; but this has not happened. The findings from two representative studies support this claim. One study compared the charges at 280 California profit and nonprofit hospitals. This study found that the profit hospitals charged an average of 47 percent more per admission (reported in Dallek, 1990:20).

The second study, reported in the *New England Journal of Medicine,* found that profit hospitals charged 22 percent more per admission than did their not-for-profit counterparts. Of special interest was the finding that nearly 90 percent of this difference in daily charges was because the for-profit hospitals charged significantly more for ancillary services such as X-ray, operating, and recovery rooms, tests, and medications. The authors concluded, "these results strongly suggest the existence of a strategy by the investor-owned chain hospitals of setting competitive prices for the more visible room and board services while setting higher prices for ancillary services which are less easy to compare from hospital to hospital" (quoted in Tatge, 1986:E1–2). Thus, as hospitals have become increasingly owned by private profit-seeking interests, the cost of medical care has increased.

Hospitals attract patients (and profits) in several ways. First, they seek the well-insured population by projecting an upscale image, and by providing amenities such as cable TV and gourmet menus. A second tactic is to woo doctors who typically decide when and where their patients will be hospitalized. Most private hospitals provide financial concessions and incentives to attract doctors and, as a

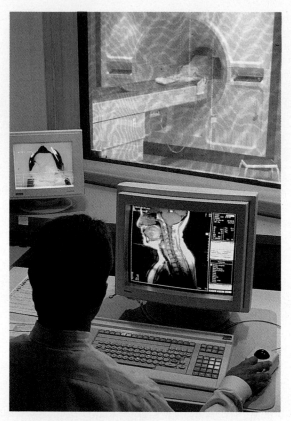

A Magnetic Resonance Image (MRI) of a patient's brain. This expensive technology is one example of why medical costs are so high.

consequence, their patients. Doctors may receive free office space, special facilities in the hospital, subsidies for equipment, financial support for the physician and his or her staff, and offers of potentially lucrative investments (Paton, 1992:I5).

Hospitals profit the longer patients are hospitalized. One study by a health care consulting firm found that 53 percent of all hospital days were not necessary, including all the days spent in the hospital by the 24 percent of patients who did not need to be there in the first place (reported in *Consumer Reports,* 1992a:442).

The Fear of Malpractice Lawsuits and Defensive Medicine

There has been a sharp rise in the past decade or so in the number of malpractice lawsuits brought by patients against physicians, other health practitioners, and hospitals for alleged mistakes, incompetence, and fraud. These lawsuits or the fear of them has driven up health costs in two ways. First, there is the high cost of malpractice insurance, which is passed on to the consumer. These costs can be enormous (as much as $100,000 annually) depending on the medical specialty and location of the practice (e.g., urban physicians pay much more than those practicing in rural areas). The second reason for possible malpractice causing higher costs to patients is the practice of **defensive medicine.** Physicians, in order to protect themselves from possible future blame, often require patients to undergo a range of tests beyond the reasonable. These tests are expensive and usually unnecessary. The American Medical Association has estimated that the total cost of malpractice insurance and defensive medicine is about 17 percent of physicians' earnings (reported in *Consumer Reports,* 1992a:443).

Fraud

Some of the information noted above has implied fraud on the part of physicians and hospitals. That is, we have discussed that medical practitioners sometimes require unnecessary tests or have padded their bills to insurance companies and to the government in order to receive extra compensation.

Some people in the medical profession commit the crime of fraud. This problem is not trivial, with estimates running as high as $80 billion in year in just false billings to insurers and to the government (*U.S. News & World Report* 1992:34). Such a charge runs counter to the common belief that physicians are more virtuous and law abiding than other people. Of course, most people in the medical profession are ethical; but some are not. Let us examine four examples of medical fraud—unnecessary surgery, conflict of interest, kickbacks, and overbilling—and the high costs that result.

Unnecessary surgery.   "With so many incentives to overtreat patients, it seems inevitable that a sizable fraction of American medical care must be simply unnecessary, if not downright harmful" (*Consumer Reports,* 1992a:439). Research by the Rand Corporation suggests that as much as 34 percent of the surgical and medical procedures in the United States are unnecessary and have a cost of $50 billion (reported in Jasinowski, 1990). Five unnecessary surgeries most commonly prescribed are coronary bypasses, hysterectomies, Caesarean deliveries, radical mastectomies, and carotid endarterectomies (note that three of these surgeries affect women only).

The Rand Corporation has found that 50 percent of Caesarean section births were unnecessary, as were 27 percent of hysterectomies, 20 percent of pacemaker implantations, 17 percent of surgeries for carpal tunnel syndrome, 16 percent of tonsillectomies, and 14 percent of laminectomies (the most common type of back surgery) (reported in *Consumer Reports,* 1992a:440–441, 447).

A government-sponsored study provides further evidence that some, perhaps many, physicians allow their financial interests to override the health concerns of their clients. One study compared government employees covered by Blue Cross health insurance, which pays physicians on a fee-for-service basis, with a group belonging to a health maintenance organization (HMO), which pays physicians a flat salary, regardless of the number of services performed. The group covered by Blue Cross had twice as many surgeries as the group covered by the health maintenance organization (reported in Coleman, 1989:113–114). In Coleman's words, "the conclusion seems inescapable that the more money physicians make from a medical procedure, the more often they perform it" (Coleman, 1989:114).

The result, of course, is higher cost. *Consumer Reports* estimates that at least 20 percent of the amount that actually goes for patient care ($130 billion) is spent on procedures and services that are clearly unnecessary (*Consumer Reports,* 1992a:436). In the words of criminologist Jeffrey Reiman, "This gives us yet another way in which we are robbed of more money by practices that are not treated as criminal than by practices that are" (Reiman, 1990:66). Moreover, there are the physical costs. Again, consider Jeffrey Reiman's estimate:

> In 1986, the FBI reported that 3,957 murders were committed by a 'cutting or stabbing instrument.' Obviously, the FBI does not include the scalpel as a cutting or stabbing instrument. If they did, they would have had to report that between 15,957 and 19,957 persons were killed by 'cutting or stabbing' . . . . No matter how you slice it, the scalpel may be more dangerous than the switchblade. (Reiman, 1990:65)

Conflict of interest.   Some physicians prescribe drugs and laboratory tests when they benefit financially from such procedures. For example, a study comparing the practices of the same physicians before and after a bonus program was instituted at a for-profit health clinic revealed that the financial incentives meant many more tests and X-rays. Prior to the bonus program, the physicians were paid a flat hourly rate. Under the bonus program, they were paid the same rate or a percentage of the gross monthly charges they generated, whichever was higher. With the incentive program, physicians ordered 23 percent more lab tests per patient visit and 16 percent more X-rays, compared with the period before the bonus program. Also, patient visits increased 12 percent, with the average charge per visit rising 7 percent (Winslow, 1990). (See the Observation on doctors.)

A study of the health insurance claims for 65,000 patients by University of Arizona researchers found that doctors who had diagnostic imaging equipment in their offices ordered four times more imaging exams than did physicians who referred patients elsewhere for tests (reported in *Consumer Reports,* 1992a:439).

When physicians also are owners of pharmacies or laboratories, there is a clear conflict of interest. A 1989 government report revealed that 12 percent of the physicians who treat Medicare patients refer them to laboratories and clinics in which the physicians have financial interests (Johnson, 1989). Although this practice is legal, there is a **conflict of interest,** and the potential for unnecessary testing and for inflated bills. As evidence, the inspector general of the Department of Health and Human Services in the above report stated,

> patients of referring physicians who own or invest in independent clinical laboratories received 45 percent more clinical laboratory services than all Medicare patients in general, regardless of service. . . . Similarly, patients of physicians who have a financial interest in physiological labs, for radiology, computer scanning and magnetic resonance imaging, used testing services 13 percent more frequently than Medicare patients in general. (cited in Johnson, 1989:1)

Also, when physicians sell their own products there is a problem. Some repackage drugs purchased from other manufacturers, put on their own labels, and charge exorbitant markups. Another example of conflict of interest is from the study of ophthalmologists that found that doctors who sold glasses prescribed glasses 83 percent more than did the ophthalmologists who did not (reported in Coleman, 1989:114).

Government studies reveal that more than 10 percent of the nation's physicians have invested in businesses to which they refer patients. This practice of self-referral results in extra procedures that are medically unnecessary and thus add to health costs (Pear and Eckholm, 1991).

Kickbacks. Kickback schemes occur throughout the medical industry. Pacemaker manufacturers, for example, may make arrangements to pay cardiologists a percentage of the cost of each pacemaker purchased. Similar arrangements occur when ophthalmologists steer their patients to certain companies that manufacture and service products for the eye. Another practice is **fee splitting**, where physicians refer patients to other physicians, laboratories, or pharmacies and receive a portion of the fee in return, without the patient's knowledge.

Overbilling.   Some physicians bill insurance and Medicaid programs for services never performed. One practice—ganging—occurs when a physician treats and bills all members of a family present when only one is actually ill. Another tactic is to walk through a nursing home, for example, saying "Hi" to the patients, counting each salutation as a physician's official visit and billing the government accordingly (Pepinsky and Jesilow, 1985:49–50).

In one celebrated case Dr. Richard Kones pleaded guilty to defrauding the government and health insurance companies of $500,000 under the Medicare program. From 1977 to 1980 he submitted more than $1.5 million in false claims for services never performed (reported in Hagan, 1990:366).

The *New York Times* investigated psychiatric hospitals operated for profit and found that one chain of hospitals

- Inflated bills for medications and services—$1,100 a person for three hours of group therapy, or $4.15 for a single Advil tablet, which costs 11 cents in drug stores.
- Billed for services never rendered, as in the case of a woman who says she was charged for group therapy at $80 an hour when she was at lunch, at dinner, or was being inspected for lice.
- Altered diagnoses and treatments to match insurance coverage.
- Admitted children to psychiatric hospitals even though experts say they do not need hospitalization. (Kerr, 1991:l)

The General Accounting Office estimates that fraud and billing abuse account for 10 percent of medical expenditures in the United States (Leary, 1992).

Toward a Better Health Care System: Some Alternatives

The United States, as we have stated, spends much more for health care, both in total dollars and as a percentage of its gross national product, than any other nation. Overall, we do not get a very good return on this investment. All major indicators of national health show that other nations are getting more for their health dollars than is the United States. The reason for the relatively high rates in infant mortality and low rates for longevity is that so many people in the United States do not receive adequate care because they cannot afford it. At the other end of the resource hierarchy, however, the U.S. health care system is superb, with

OBSERVATION

DOCTORS FEEL PRESSURE TO KEEP THEIR HOSPITALS FINANCIALLY HEALTHY

Derry, N.H.—When six people were hurt in a car wreck a few years ago, the surgeon on duty at nearby Parkland Medical Center knew his small emergency room would be overwhelmed by all the cuts and broken bones.

So Dr. Paul Harper made a quick decision: Ambulances should carry the victims to three other hospitals besides Parkland. Spreading the carnage around meant the injured would get help more quickly. The doctor felt it was best for the patients.

But in this case, what was best for the patients was not necessarily best for the hospital. Parkland lost business.

"I caught it for that," Harper recalled. "The patients were supposed to come to Parkland, even though [it] couldn't handle them. The head nurse told me the administration was mad and I shouldn't do that again."

Such vignettes are common. Hospitals need patients. Doctors who send them away for any reason, even for better care, risk rebuke: A gentle scolding, perhaps. A quiet lecture about hospital economics. Or worse.

In Harper's case, what came next was much worse. His career is in ruins. Once he performed 350 operations a year, making him the hospital's busiest surgeon. Now, he performs a dozen.

Harper has filed a lawsuit claiming the hospital engineered a slander campaign that destroyed his reputation and made doctors afraid to send him patients. Richard V. Wiebusch, the hospital's attorney, counters that Harper is in trouble because he is an incompetent doctor, not because he is a financial liability.

Such open warfare between doctors and hospitals still is unusual, but the rules of conduct are changing. Many fear that blunt coercion is becoming more customary as more hospitals press doctors to practice a style of medicine that puts the health of the institution first.

Usually, hospitals try to keep doctors in line through more subtle means: Nurses, who lose their jobs when hospital beds stand empty, cajole doctors to admit more patients. Many hospitals post the names of those who fail to discharge elderly, low-paying Medicare patients quickly enough. Physicians who don't get the message may suddenly stop receiving referrals from the emergency room, an important source of new patients.

But gentle persuasion can turn harsh. Some doctors complain that they have been dogged by crudely planted rumors of incompetence, that hospital administrators have ordered other doctors to stop sending them patients or that their tiniest medical misjudgments are scrutinized by hospital review committees.

The worst of these abuses do happen, said Dr. Howard L. Lang of Kentfield, Calif., chairman of the American Medical Assn.'s Hospital Medical Staff Section.

"It's not a daily occurrence," he said, "but it is occurring enough that it is not rare. We are not talking about a few whining malcontents. There are real problems out there."

In general, hospitals want their doctors to bring in lots of patients. They want them to order plenty of X-rays and tests when the sick are covered by generous private insurance plans. And they want them to do just the opposite when Medicare picks up the tab.

Hospitals lose money when the elderly ill linger too long. Medicare categorizes virtually all old people into DRGs, or diagnosis-related groups. The DRG classification for a particular illness pays a single flat fee for all patients, no matter how sick they are or how long they stay in the hospital.

all the wonders of high-technology medicine and the most qualified (and expensive) physicians available. At present the U.S. health care system is rationed according to ability to pay (either from one's own resources or through one's insurance). This section examines some alternatives to the present system of health care in the United States. These alternatives are (by increasing scale of dif-

"DRGs encourage the hospitals to keep their costs down, and yet the physician controls what the hospital bill will be," said Dr. E. Haavi Morreim of the University of Tennessee. "The hospitals have had to do something to bring the physicians under the same incentive. Many hospital administrators have felt the necessity for some sort of system of carrots and sticks, either formal or informal."

Perhaps the most feared and effective of these sticks is peer review. This process is the main way doctors watch over the competence of their hospital colleagues.

Critics complain the system is sometimes perverted into a way of punishing those who are economic threats to the hospital or to other doctors. At its most extreme, doctors lose the right to admit patients or to perform specific tests, procedures and operations.

"There is overwhelming economic motive to eliminate doctors who cost the hospital money," said Dr. Verner S. Waite of Downey. "Doctors who complain about unethical billing practices, unnecessary tests, using items the hospital can charge for that are not necessary, are all at great risk of a peer review."

Waite has formed an organization to fight abuses of peer review. He and many others believe that instead of weeding out bad doctors, the system sometimes may protect dangerous hacks who are financially and politically powerful because they admit lots of patients.

"When they want to get you, they get you good. They blackball you," said Dr. David M. Freedman. "They will take away privileges for nothing, when another doctor can murder someone and, because he's in good standing, they don't bother him."

Freedman works with Harper at Parkland Medical Center, an 86-bed community hospital owned by Hospital Corporation of America, the nation's largest for-profit hospital chain.

Freedman believes his own practice has suffered because he refused an order from a hospital administrator to stop referring patients to Harper for surgery. Harper claims many other doctors in this distant suburb of Boston also were warned not to send him patients, in large part because he went against the hospital's financial interests.

Sometimes, a hospital can get rid of someone it considers a financial nuisance simply by giving another physician the sole right to perform that doctor's medical specialty.

Ohio cardiologist Dr. Efraim Montesinos contended he was forced to move his busy heart surgery practice from Toledo Hospital because his patients often ran up bigger bills than were covered by Medicare's flat-fee DRG system, which began in 1984.

Said Dr. Peter Overstreet, one of Montesinos' supporters: "Before DRGs, he was a hero. Since DRGs, he is a villain. It's the same guy."

Montesinos said he cared for a large number of very sick patients. They often took longer than usual to get better, so the hospital lost money. "I am in the service of my patients," he said. "I am not in the service of the hospital or the insurance company."

Last year, the hospital decided to give an exclusive contract to a single heart surgery group. Montesinos, who could have bid for the job, believes the exclusive contract was a ploy "to get me out of the hospital." He moved his practice to the nearby Medical College of Ohio.

Dr. John Gibbs, the hospital's director of medical affairs, acknowledged finances played a role in the decision to change surgeons.

Source: Fred Bayles and Daniel Q. Haney, "Doctors Feel Pressure to Keep Their Hospitals Financially Healthy," *Los Angeles Times* (November 4, 1990), pp. A26-A28. Reprinted by permission of Associated Press.

ficulty to attain) (1) reforms within the health care system, (2) alternative national health insurance plans, and (3) societal changes that indirectly affect the health of its citizens.

Reforms within the Medical Community

A number of reforms within the medical community could spread the benefits of health care to more people and also could reduce costs. These reforms require changes in philosophy at the governmental and personal levels about when life ends; decisions by medical schools and medical associations; better overseeing by the government, insurance companies, and the medical profession over medical practices; and changes in philosophy by the government and insurance companies on which medical activities are appropriate and which are not. The following list is not comprehensive, but it is a start:

- Spend more money on basic medicine and less, much less, on heroic medicine. As Richard Lamm has pointed out, "we keep people alive for whom there is no happy outcome, yet we do not vaccinate kids. There is a woman in Washington, D.C., who has been comatose, with no reasonable hope of recovery, since 1953. Yet in that same city the infant mortality rate is greater than in many Third World Countries" (Lamm, 1989b:59).
- Society needs more accessible physicians. This means two things: (a) colleges of medicine must train *more* physicians who practice family medicine, pediatrics, and internal medicine and *fewer* specialists (only 10 percent of U.S. physicians are general practitioners, compared to 50 percent of the physicians in Canada); and (2) the number of physicians and other health care practitioners should be redistributed so that they work in appropriate numbers in rural areas and in inner cities.
- Spend more money on preventive medicine. At present, insurance programs and government health programs emphasize treating people who are sick rather than trying to keep them healthy (Deets, 1989). Periodic health examinations with counseling regarding diet and exercise would cost much less in the long run. **Health Maintenance Organizations (HMOs)** operate on this philosophy. In these programs, all health services are provided to members at a fixed, prepaid annual rate, regardless of cost. Just like an insurance company, the HMO assumes that overuse of health services will be balanced by underuse. To insure this, HMOs emphasize wellness programs and preventive care.
- Reform the tort system of law (civil law regarding one party suing another) so that there would be reasonable limits on malpractice suits. This would reduce the cost of the insurance physicians and hospitals must pay and would lessen the perceived need for defensive medicine, which is also so costly.
- There is a need for medical boards that would stem the waste of billions of dollars spent on unnecessary or counterproductive medical tests and procedures. Meanwhile, the government and insurance programs must insist on paying only specified amounts for specified medical services deemed necessary from second opinions from reputable physicians or from a medical board.
- There needs to be stronger enforcement against medical fraud. Peer review committees within the medical profession are not effective at policing their own members. Individual states and the federal government need to pass stricter

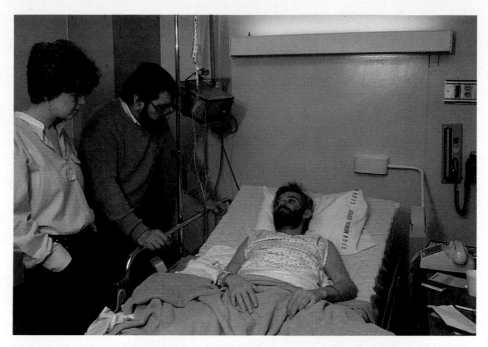

The federal and local governments must deal with the expense of treating AIDs patients, which averages $38,000 each.

laws concerning the questionable conduct of physicians and then to use their criminal justice systems to investigate and punish violators.

National Health Insurance

The United States and South Africa are the only major industrial countries that do not have universal, government-paid medical program for residents. Rather, the United States distributes health care by the ability to pay. This system leaves the uninsured and the underinsured, who are disproportionately non-White, women, and children, with inadequate health care. The results are a relatively high infant mortality rate, a higher rate of disability for youth, a greater likelihood of premature death and lingering illnesses for adults, and, in general, a poorer quality of life.

Should the United States provide basic health protection for *all* residents? Public opinion surveys reveal that people in the United States favor a fundamental change in our health care system; 61 percent would prefer a health system like that in Canada to ours (Deets, 1989). Such a plan, however, is vigorously opposed by the American Medical Association (A.M.A.), the nation's largest association of physicians (approximately 300,000 members). This association has always resisted a national, comprehensive medical insurance program because it does not want government intruding into the professional lives of physicians. Its position is that even though the U.S. health care system needs improvement, it basically works. The A.M.A.'s answer is to force more employers to provide health insurance and to expand Medicaid coverage for the poor (Toufexis, 1990b).

There are more than 200 health-related political action committees (PACs) representing the A.M.A. and other physician organizations, for-profit hospitals, and pharmaceutical firms that contribute money to congressional candidates (more than $60 million between 1980 and 1991) and additional monies to the political parties. In essence, this money is being spent to block health care reform. As Tom Goodwin, public affairs director of the Federation of American Health Systems, which represents some 1400 for-profit hospitals, said, "We spend our money on those members. . . most interested in maintaining the current system" (quoted in Kemper and Novak, 1992:9).

Societal Changes   The Canadian system or some variation of a national and universal health insurance is a must if the United States is to be a more just society. (See "Another Society, Another Way" explaining the Canadian system of health care. Also, see the Forum at the end of this chapter.)

ANOTHER SOCIETY, ANOTHER WAY

THE CANADIAN NATIONAL HEALTH CARE SYSTEM

Unlike the private enterprise model, which is the foundation of the U.S. health care system, Canada has a health care system based on different principles (*Consumer Reports* 1992b:579):

1. Universality. Everyone is covered.
2. Portability. People can move from province to province and from job to job or be unemployed and they will still be covered.
3. Comprehensiveness. The plan covers all medically necessary treatment.
4. Public administration. The system is publicly run and publicly accountable.

Since 1947 Canada has had a tax-supported health care system in which every Canadian is covered for the costs of all medically necessary services. Under this plan each citizen is issued a health card by the government, which is presented when health care is received. Using tax money the government reimburses physicians and hospitals based on a fee schedule determined by the government, not the market. The keys are that the health services are paid for by the government and all Canadians have equal access to the care they need. Canadians can select any doctor they like. The plan is a "single payer" plan with the doctors billing the provincial insurance plans directly (the government of each Canadian province pays the medical bills of its citizens). For patients, there are no bills, claim forms, fees, and long waits for reimbursement from insurance carriers.

The key difference between the Canadian system and that in the United States is that "in Canada health care is considered a social right, while in the United States it is treated more like a commodity" (Farnsworth, 1992:C8).

The usual arguments against such a plan are that it is inefficient and costly. In Canada's case, health care is administered more efficiently, at less cost, and with better results, than the health care system in the United States. The results, as measured by infant mortality and life expectancy, show that Canada is ahead of the United States. Administrative costs are less in Canada (about one-fourth of U.S. administrative expenses for physicians, hospitals, and insurance companies). In terms of cost, health care in Canada takes a much smaller fraction of GNP than it does in the United States (Currie and Skolnick, 1988:295).

A common argument against the Canadian plan is that it is "socialized medicine."

Canada does not have "socialized medicine." Medicare, as Canada's health-care system is called, is simply a social insurance plan, much like Social Security and Medicare for older people in the U.S. Canada's doctors do not work on salary for the government. (*Consumer Reports* 1992b:579)

The Canadian health care system is not perfect. Canadians have less access than Americans to the latest technological innovations. There may be waits for those not needing immediate surgeries. But despite some glitches, most Canadians like their health care system. A Gallup Poll in 1991 revealed, for example, that 91 percent of Canadians rated their health care system better than that in the United States, compared to only 26 percent of Americans who felt their system was superior to that in Canada (Hugick, 1991:2).

More than this is necessary, however, if we are to have a more healthful society. U.S. society must cooperate with other nations to make our fragile environment safer and healthier. This commitment to the environment must also be shared by the U.S. business community and all people. Also, the business community, monitored by the government, must provide work environments safe from hazards such as toxic chemicals, polluted air, and risky work conditions.

Moreover, there should be educational campaigns against eating unhealthful foods (e.g., fats, sugars, and chemical additives) and against using dangerous drugs (e.g., illegal as well as legal drugs). The effort to reduce smoking, for example, has had dramatic and positive effects. Most important, though, if U.S. society is committed to the better health of its people, would be the elimination of poverty.

We have seen that poverty is directly related to higher rates of illness and to higher mortality rates. These are the results of poor diets, living in overcrowded rooms in dilapidated, ill-heated housing, and living in unsanitary conditions. The quality of the health of poor people is also diminished because of the greater likelihood of having to live where the pollution is the worst and having to work where dangerous conditions are most likely to prevail. The point is that even if there were a universal health program in which the poor received adequate medical attention, the existence of poverty would still make the poor more prone to illness and disease. Thus, a commitment to a society in which *all* members have the right to an appropriate health standard requires both universal health care *and* the elimination of poverty. At a minimum this means that all people should be brought above the poverty line. This action would improve the health (and other aspects of well being) for the millions of poor people, who are disproportionately Black, Hispanic, and Native American, and who are disproportionately single women, and disproportionately children. The important issue is whether the people of the United States will make such a commitment. Obviously, it is a matter of priority, and so far the nation has given the health and welfare of its poorest citizens a low priority.

CHAPTER REVIEW

1. The U.S. health care system is rationed according to ability to pay for services. For people who can afford it, the United States provides the most advanced medical technology and the best trained medical personnel in the world. For those who cannot (about one-fourth of the population), medical care is poor in quality and quantity.

2. Economic disadvantage is closely related to health disadvantages. The poor are much more likely than the affluent to die in infancy, to suffer from certain diseases, and as adults to die sooner. They are less likely to receive medical attention because of being uninsured (37 million) or underinsured (50 million), and when they do receive medical care, to receive inferior service.

3. The most commonly held explanation for the strong relationship between social class and health is that the poor are responsible for their disproportionate ill health because of ignorance or neglect. This approach blames the victim because it ignores the primary role that privilege plays in health and

the lack of privilege in poor health. The fundamental solution for reducing socioeconomic differences in health is to reduce the inequalities in society that perpetuate poor health among the disadvantaged.

4. Race is also related to health, with non-Whites disadvantaged by a combination of economic disadvantage and racial discrimination.

5. Health and ill health are also related to gender differences. Women have health advantages over men because of their physical differences and differing gender expectations. Women are placed at risk, however, by childbearing, the greater likelihood of unnecessary surgery such as hysterectomies, the relative lack of medical research using women as subjects, and the still common sexist practices by physicians, who are predominantly male.

6. Health care in the United States is the world's costliest (14 percent of GNP), and the cost continues to rise faster than the rate of inflation. The reasons for this unusually high cost are (a) the method of payment, which allows physicians and hospitals to set the fees; (b) the trend toward the privatization of hospitals; (c) defensive medicine from the fear of malpractice suits; and (d) fraud. In essence, the medical profession in the United States is based on the capitalist model, which works to the advantage of the medical profession and to the disadvantage of consumers.

7. One solution to the problems in the health field is to institute reforms within the medical community. A more extreme solution and one opposed by the majority of physicians is a national, comprehensive health care program. The United States is the only industrialized nation in the Western world without such a program. The Canadian health care system provides an interesting model that some people have suggested should be used in the United States. Their system, which is universally applied to all residents, is more efficient, less costly, and has better medical results than the current U.S. model.

8. A national health program with the goal of bringing all residents up to a minimum acceptable standard must not only include a universal health program but also must eliminate the worst of poverty, because poverty itself is a major contributor to ill health.

KEY TERMS

Infant mortality rate.   The number of deaths per 1000 live births.

Patient dumping.   The practice by physicians and private hospitals of treating only patients who can afford their services.

Medicare.   The government program that provides partial coverage of medical costs primarily for people over age sixty-five.

Medicaid.   The government health program for the poor.

Defensive medicine.   The practice of physicians' requiring patients to undergo a range of tests to protect themselves from blame in possible future malpractice suits.

Conflict of interest.   The situation in which a physician or other health practitioner benefits materially from his or her recommendations to patients.

Fee splitting.   The practice of dividing a fee for professional services between two physicians, as between a specialist and the referring physician, without the knowledge of the patient.

Health Maintenance Organization (HMO).   A health program in which members pay a fixed annual fee in return for all necessary health services.

FOR FURTHER STUDY

Walt Bogdanich. *The Great White Lie: Dishonesty, Waste, and Incompetence in the Medical Community.* New York: Touchstone, 1992.

Children's Defense Fund. *Lack of Health Insurance Makes a Difference.* Washington, D.C.: Children's Defense Fund, 1989.

Consumer Reports. "Health Care in Crisis," 3-part series, *Consumer Reports* 57 (July, August, September 1992).

Dana Hughes, Kay Johnson, Sara Rosenbaum, and Joseph Liu. *The Health of America's Children.* Washington, D.C.: Children's Defense Fund, 1989.

Jonathan Kwitney. *Acceptable Risks.* New York: Poseidon Press, 1992.

Wilhelmina A. Leigh. *A Health Assessment of Black Americans.* Washington, D.C.: Joint Center for Political and Economic Studies, 1992.

Ellen Lewin and Virginia Olesen, eds. *Women, Health, and Healing.* New York: Tavistock, 1985.

National Center for Health Statistics. *Health, United States, 1990.* Hyattsville, Md.: Public Health Service, 1991.

Kathryn S. Ratcliff. *Healing Technology: Feminist Perspectives.* Ann Arbor: University of Michigan Press, 1989.

Michael D. Reagan. *Curing the Crisis: Options for America's Health Care.* Boulder, Colo.: Westview, 1992.

John M. Smith. *Women and Doctors: A Physician's Explosive Account of Women's Medical Treatment—and Mistreatment—in America Today.* New York: Atlantic Monthly Press, 1992.

Paul Starr. *The Social Transformation of American Medicine.* New York: Basic Books, 1982.

U.S. House of Representatives, Select Committee on Children, Youth, and Families. *U.S. Children and Their Families: Current Conditions and Recent Trends.* Washington, D.C.: U.S. Government Printing Office, 1989.

FORUM

SHOULD THE UNITED STATES ADOPT THE CANADIAN MODEL OF HEALTH CARE DELIVERY?

In the absence of market-set prices, waiting lists have emerged as a means of allocating health services in Canada.

Michael Walker

Recent publicity about the problems of Americans who lack health insurance has renewed calls for universal coverage guaranteeing free medical care. But with the British model in disrepute, American proponents of socialized medicine increasingly cite the example of Canada.

In particular, they argue that Canada's apparent success in controlling health-care costs demonstrates the superiority of its system, under which the government regulates and pays virtually all medical fees. On closer examination, however, this interpretation proves shaky.

True, Canada spends 8 1/2 cents per dollar of GNP on health care, a level that has remained basically unchanged since 1978, while medical expenditures have risen to 11 cents per dollar in the United States. But even on its face, this fact does not indicate that Canada's health-care system is preferable to a more market-oriented approach. After all, high fractions of income devoted to housing, recreation, and travel are considered signs of an affluent society. Why shouldn't health-care spending be viewed similarly? Further, the experts bemoan the low share of GNP spent on education in this country. Does it make sense to invest a large percentage of GNP in education—in improving human capital—but not in health care to ensure the proper maintenance of that capital?

Contrary to advocates of the Canadian model, it is by no means clear that spending less on health care is *a priori* a good thing. Indeed, although the United Kingdom spends about half as much per capita on health care as Canada does, no one therefore infers that British patients are better off. (In fact, the reverse is true.)

So we cannot safely conclude that Canada's health-care system works better than its American counterpart based merely on the difference in cost. To determine whether American patients are truly being bilked in comparison to their northern neighbors, it is necessary to measure performance more directly.

That is the aim of an ongoing study by the Fraser Institute, a public policy think tank in Vancouver. Although the final results are not in, the evidence so far suggests that Canadian health-care consumers get what they pay for: fewer facilities and longer waits for diagnostic services and surgical procedures.

The study's preliminary findings indicate that Canada's lower health-care costs are accompanied by a lower level of service. For example:

- The entire province of British Columbia has fewer CAT scanners than the city of Seattle.
- There are more magnetic-resonance imaging machines in Michigan than in all of Canada.
- With a population of 570,000, the province of Newfoundland has only one functioning CAT-scanner team, so patients must wait two months for a scan. Pap-smear tests also take two months or longer. The waiting period for mammograms is two-and-a-half months; for bone scans, 90 days; and for myelograms, three to four months.
- Throughout Canada, there are long delays for hip replacement (6 to 10 months), cataract removal (2 months or more), and coronary bypass surgery (up to a year).
- According to a February 13 cover story in *Maclean*'s magazine, six heart patients died last year waiting for surgery at Winnipeg's Health Sciences Centre. The article reported that about 1,000 people in Toronto were being compelled to wait as long as a year for bypass operations and that two had died since December. Delays at the city's Hospital for Sick Children are so bad that in January the facility sent home 40 children in need of heart surgery.
- Administrators at a major metropolitan hospital in British Columbia estimate average waiting periods of six weeks for orthopedic surgery and four weeks for both elective and urgent general surgery.

By contrast, critics of the U.S. health-care system complain not of shortages but of excess capacity. For insured American patients, waiting lists are virtually unheard of.

The types of problems brought to light by the Fraser Institute may not be apparent to most Canadians, since the waiting lists are confined to services beyond those provided by general practitioners. But the shortcomings found by the study should nevertheless give pause to those inclined to imitate Canada's health-care system.

In the absence of market-set prices, waiting lists have emerged as a means of allocating services. By mandating fees, Canada's universal, government-provided health insurance in effect restricts the supply of medical care. Moreover, health-care costs are covered primarily with general tax revenue; there is little connection between insurance premiums and actual expenditures. Because the consumers are not the buyers, their influence on the service providers is limited.

Indeed, the Canadian government discourages physicians from accommodating patients dissatisfied by service under the state-funded system. User fees and extra billing are prohibited, and doctors are not permitted to serve both publicly insured and private patients.

In the United States, because government plays a smaller role, patients have more options. And since the buyers of insurance bear the burden of rising costs, there is a strong incentive for innovations such as health-maintenance organizations, which help control general medical costs by increasing competition.

Under the U.S. system, of course, not everyone has equal access to health care, since millions of Americans are uninsured. A closer look at Canada's system, however, reveals that it does not provide equal access, either, since waiting periods for medical services vary from one part of the country to another.

In any case, the issue of uninsured citizens should be dealt with as an income problem rather than a deficiency in the health-care system. People who have difficulty paying health-insurance premiums may also have difficulty buying food. We do not therefore conclude that something is wrong with the food-distribution system, nor do we heavy-handedly interfere with industry to solve the problem.

While government may choose to supplement the incomes of the poor so they can afford a minimum level of health care, it is folly to insist on the same standard for all, regardless of their means. In Canada, those with higher incomes are effectively prevented from obtaining better health care by paying more for it. The rationale is that enforcing one standard gives everyone an interest in resisting attempts to cut back funding for the system. But because the best cannot be made available to everyone, such an arrangement results in a lower quality of health care overall. Rather than throw a group of drowning people life preservers, the government sinks a yacht so they can cling to the wreckage.

Source: Reprinted with permission, from the December 1989 issue of *Reason* magazine. Copyright 1989 by the Reason Foundation, 2716 Ocean Park Blvd., Suite 1062, Santa Monica, CA 90405.

14 *Work*

Work is central to the human experience. Societies are organized to allocate work in order to produce the goods and services needed by the society and its members for sustenance, clothing, shelter, defense, and even luxury. Work provides individuals with their social identity, economic resources, and social location. Work dominates their time and is a primary source of life's meaning because it constitutes their contributions to other people.

The world of work also has a dark side, however. The structure of work is a major source of social problems. Work is alienating for many people. The organization of work sometimes exploits, does harm to workers, and often dehumanizes them. The distribution of work and how it is rewarded are major sources of inequality in society.

This chapter focuses on the social problems generated by the social organization of work. The chapter is divided into four parts. The first part examines the problems common to the experience of the U.S. work world: the control of workers, alienated labor, the hazards in the workplace, the inequality generated by a segmented labor market and capitalist patriarchy, and unemployment. The second part of the chapter describes the structural transformation of the U.S. economy as it shifts from an industrial society to an information/service economy. The third part examines the job-related problems posed by the structural transformation of the society. And the final part focuses on the inequality generated by these massive structural changes in the economy.

The Problems of Work

Work is a universal human activity. People everywhere engage in physical and mental activities that enhance the physical and social survival of themselves and others. Although people universally must work to meet their material needs, the way work is structured varies by society. This section examines the problems created from the way work is structured in U.S. society.

The Control of Workers

With the advent of the Industrial Revolution more and more families left agrarian life, moved to cities, and worked in factories. Work in these factories was sometimes difficult, often tedious, and usually boring. There was always the threat of lowered productivity and worker unrest under these adverse conditions. The factory owners and their managers used several tactics to counteract these potential problems and especially to maintain high productivity—scientific management, hierarchical control, technical control, and extortion.

Scientific management (called *Taylorization,* after its founder, Frederick Taylor) came to the fore in U.S. industry around 1900. The emphasis was on breaking down work into very specialized tasks, the standardization of tools and procedures, and the speeding up of repetitive work. These efforts to increase worker efficiency and therefore to increase profits meant that workers developed a very limited range of skills. Instead of a wide knowledge of building cars or furniture, their knowledge was severely curtailed. This specialization had the effect of making the workers highly susceptible to automation and to being easily replaced by cheaper workers. But this scientific management approach also had a contradictory effect. In its attempt to increase efficiency by having workers do ever more compartmentalized tasks, it increased the repetition, boredom, and meaninglessness of work—hence, the strong tendency for workers to become alienated and restless. Consider the description by George Ritzer:

> [The assembly line] is clearly a dehumanizing setting in which to work. Human beings, equipped with a wide array of skills and abilities, are asked to perform a limited number of highly simplified tasks over and over. Instead of expressing their human abilities on the job, people are forced to deny their humanity and act in a robot-like manner. People do not express themselves in their work, but rather deny themselves. (Ritzer, 1993:26)

Closely related to scientific management is the use of bureaucracy to control workers. Work settings, whether in factories, offices, or corporations, are organized into bureaucratized hierarchies. In this hierarchy of authority (chain of command) each position in the chain gives orders to those below, taking responsibility for their actions and following orders from above. The hierarchical arrangement controls workers by holding out the possibility of advancement, with more prestigious job titles, higher wages, and greater benefits as one moves up the ladder. Those who hope to be upwardly mobile in the organization must become obedient rule followers who do not question authority.

Similarly, work organized along an assembly line permits maximum control over workers. "Workers must do the tasks that are required of them when they

The assembly line is a dehumanizing setting in which to work.

are necessary. It is immediately obvious when a worker fails to perform the required task on time" (Ritzer, 1993:26).

Workers are also controlled by management's use of technology to monitor and supervise them. Some businesses use lie detectors to assess worker loyalty. Telephone taps have been used to determine whether workers use company time for personal use. Closed-circuit television, two-way mirrors, and other devices have been used by management to determine whether workers are using their time most productively. The most common contemporary technology for worker control is the computer. The computer can count keystrokes, time phone calls, monitor frequency of errors, assess overall employee performance, and even issue warnings when the employee falls short of the ideal. The National Institute of Occupational Safety and Health estimates that two-thirds of video display terminal operators are monitored (reported in National Association of Working Women, 1986:3).

A final management tool to control workers is extortion. If workers become too militant in their demands for higher wages, safe working conditions, or benefits, management can threaten them with reprisals. In the past owners threatened to hire cheaper labor (new immigrants, for example) or to use force to end a strike. Today, the most common and successful management tool is the threat to move the plant to a nonunion state (or even outside the United States if the union does not reduce its demands) or to replace the workers with robots or other forms of automation.

Alienation

Alienation refers to the separation of human beings from each other, from themselves, and from the products they create. In capitalism, according to Karl Marx, worker alienation occurs because the workers do not have any control over their labor, because they are manipulated by managers, because they tend to work in large, impersonal settings, and because they work at specialized tasks. Under these circumstances workers use only a fraction of their talents and have no pride in their own creativity and in the final product. Thus, we see that worker alienation is linked with unfulfilled personal satisfaction. As Blauner has described it,

> Alienation exists when workers are unable to control their immediate work processes, to develop a sense of purpose and function which connects their jobs to the overall organization of production, to belong to integrated industrial communities, and when they fail to become involved in the activity of work as a mode of personal self-expression. (Blauner, 1964:5)

Put another way, this time by philosopher Albert Camus: "Without work all life goes rotten. But when work is soulless, life stifles and dies" (quoted in Levitan and Johnson, 1982:63).

In the absence of satisfaction and personal fulfillment, work becomes meaningless. When this meaninglessness is coupled with management's efforts to control workers, the repetitious nature of the work, and the requirement of punching a time clock, many workers feel a profound resentment. This resentment may lead workers to join together in a union or other collective group to improve their working conditions. For many workers, though, the alienation remains at a personal

"Thanks guys. Looks great!"

Drawing by M. Twohy; © The New Yorker Magazine

level and is manifested by higher worker dissatisfaction, absenteeism, disruption in the workplace, and alcohol or other drug abuse on the job.

Alienation is not limited to manual workers. The work of white-collar workers such as salesclerks, secretaries, file clerks, bank tellers, and keypunchers is mostly routine, repetitive, boring, and unchallenging. These workers, like assembly line workers, follow orders, do limited tasks, and have little sense of accomplishment.

Studs Terkel, in introducing his book *Working,* summarized the personal impact of alienating work:

> This book, being about work, is, by its very nature, about violence—to the spirit as well as to the body. It is about ulcers as well as accidents, about shouting matches as well as fistfights, about nervous breakdowns as well as kicking the dog around. It is, above all (or beneath all), about daily humiliations. To survive the day is triumph enough for the walking wounded among the great many of us.
>
> It is about a search, too, for daily meaning as well as daily bread, for recognition as well as for cash, for astonishment rather than torpor; in short, for a sort of life rather than a Monday through Friday sort of dying. Perhaps immortality, too, is part of the quest. To be remembered was the wish, spoken and unspoken, of the heroes and heroines of this book.
>
> For the many, there is a hardly concealed discontent. The blue-collar blues is no more bitterly sung than the white-collar moan. "I'm a machine," says the spotwelder. "I'm caged," says the steelworker. "A monkey can do what I do,"

says the receptionist. "I'm less than a farm implement," says the migrant work-er. "I'm an object," says the high-fashion model. Blue collar and white call upon the identical phrase: "I'm a robot." (Terkel, 1975:xiii–xiv)

Dangerous Working Conditions

In a capitalist economy workers represent a cost to profit-seeking corporations. The lower that management can keep labor costs, the greater will be their prof-its. Historically, low labor costs meant that workers received low wages, had infe-rior or nonexistent fringe benefits such as health care, and worked in unhealthy conditions. Mines and factories were often extremely unsafe. The labor move-ment early in this century gathered momentum because of the abuse experienced by workers.

After a long and sometimes violent struggle the unions were successful in raising the wages for workers, adding fringe benefits, and making the conditions of work safer. But the owners were slow to change; and worker safety was, and continues to be, one of the most difficult areas. Many owners of mills, mines, and factories continue to consider the safety of their workers a low-priority item, pre-sumably because of the high cost.

Despite the owners' reluctance to make industry safer, there have been some improvements. The probabilities of cave-ins, fires, and other plant disasters are much less now than in the days before unionization. However, significant occu-pational dangers still exist. The dangers today are invisible contaminants such as nuclear radiation, chemical compounds, dust, and asbestos fibers in the air. These dangers from invisible contaminants are increasing because the production of synthetic chemicals has increased so dramatically.

According to the Labor Department, approximately 10,000 workers are killed each year in industrial accidents and 70,000 are permanently disabled (reported in *Multinational Monitor,* 1991:5). Most significant, "30 percent of industrial accidents are caused by illegal safety violations" (*Multinational Monitor,* 1990:6).

The extent of job-induced illnesses is much more difficult than the number of job-related accidents to determine exactly, primarily because for some diseases it takes many years of exposure to affect the skin, lungs, blood chemistry, nervous system, or various organs. Russell Mokhiber's estimate, after reviewing the evi-dence, is that in the workplace there are

> at least 100,000 worker deaths each year from exposure to deadly chemicals
> and other safety hazards; and 390,000 new cases of occupational disease. Of the
> 38 million workers in manufacturing industries, 1.7 million are exposed to a
> potential carcinogen each year. Workplace carcinogens are believed to cause an
> estimated 23 to 38 percent of all deaths resulting from cancer each year.
> (Mokhiber, 1988:16–17)

The following examples describe the specific risks of continued exposure to dangerous chemicals in certain industries:

- Workers in the dyestuffs industry (working with aromatic hydrocarbons) have about thirty times the risk of the general population of dying from blad-der cancer.

According to the Labor Department, each year approximately 10,000 workers are killed in industrial accidents and 70,000 are permanently disabled.

- About 10 percent of coal miners suffer from black lung, caused by years of breathing coal dust in areas with inadequate ventilation.
- Migrant farm workers have a life expectancy thirty years below the national average. This low rate is a consequence of living in poverty or near-poverty and, most significant, of the exposure to herbicides and pesticides sprayed on the fields where they work.
- The California Division of Labor has found that among the state's 64,000 semiconductor workers, 21 percent had job-related ailments in 1985 from exposure to acids, gases, and solvents used in chip manufacturing (cited in Bock, 1987:51).
- Pregnant operators of video display terminals have disproportionate numbers of miscarriages or babies with birth defects, apparently from exposure to nonionizing radiation (Pinsky, 1987).
- In 1949 the Manville Corporation conducted a study of its workers and found that 534 of the 780 asbestos workers studied had lung changes. Despite this study and others documenting the dangers of exposure to asbestos, Manville continued to manufacture and sell the product. The current prediction is that 240,000 of the million people in the United States who have worked with

asbestos will die from asbestos-related cancer within thirty years (Mokhiber, 1988:284). This number does not include other workers exposed to asbestos, especially those who remove asbestos from the buildings to make them safe for inhabitants.

The record of industry has often been one of ignoring the scientific data (as the example of Manville demonstrated) or of stalling through court actions rather than making plants safer. Most important, some companies have not informed workers of the dangers.

The lack of concern for the safety of workers in the asbestos industry is typical of other industries as well. Safety regulations for cotton dust have been fought by the textile industry. As usual, the claims were that it would cost billions to clean up the mills, jobs would be lost, and prices to consumers would rise dramatically.

This discussion raises a critical question: At what point are profits more important than human life? Speaking of the cotton industry, which is representative of the other industries, one observer has argued that

> in a society in which profits did not take precedence over people . . . the finer points of byssinosis [brown lung disease] would have been considered tangential long ago and the road to its prevention would now be clear: Better air filtration systems would have been installed and other capital expenditures made. But in the United States, where society is tuned to a different chord, the present delay over preventive measures, like the oblivion which preceded it, is rooted not in science and technology but in economics and politics—in the callous traditions of the cotton industry and in government's compromising ways. (Schinto, 1977:28)

Who is to blame for the 100,000 people who die annually in the United States from occupational-related diseases? One observer, Joel Swartz, has argued that although corporate executives make the decisions, the guilt does not stop with them:

> In the long run it is not the outright deception, dishonesty and cunning of corporate executives, doctors and bureaucrats which is responsible for the problem. Rather, the general functioning of the system is at the heart of the problem. . . . The tremendous toll in occupational illnesses results from the oppression of one class by another. The people who own corporations try to exact as much wealth as they can from the workers. Improvements in working conditions to eliminate health hazards would eat into the profits that could be exacted. . . . In particular the asbestos industry would rather spend millions of dollars trying to prove that asbestos is safe, than spend the money necessary to eliminate exposures. In oil refineries many of the exposures to chemicals result from inadequate maintenance of plant equipment. Maintenance costs come to 15 percent of total refinery costs, but these costs are considered controllable. In other words, skipping on maintenance is a good way to cut costs. Only the worker suffers. (Swartz, 1975:19–20)

Unions and Their Decline

Historically, labor unions have been extremely important in changing management-labor relations. Joining together workers challenged owners to increase wages, add benefits, provide worker security, and promote safety in the work place. Through the use of strikes, work slow downs, public relations, and political lobbying, working conditions improved and union members, for the most part, prospered. (See the Observation on the benefits of union membership.) But unions have lost their power since about 1980 as membership declined from 34 percent of the nonagricultural labor force in 1955 to about 16 percent in 1991. With such small and dwindling numbers, labor unions are in danger of becoming irrelevant.

The reasons for the decline in union membership (and clout) are several. First, there was a direct assault against unions by Republican presidents Reagan and Bush. Both of these administrations were unsympathetic with strikes and

OBSERVATION

THE BENEFITS OF UNIONS

Empowering workers constitutes the first step toward a stronger economy and a stronger citizenry. It is a vital step toward overcoming inequality in American society. During the 1980s, the need for better wages for all workers increased as women, traditionally secondary earners, assumed greater responsibility for their own and their children's well-being. Yet the ability to move families to a decent living standard through wage work decreased; real wages fell for most workers. And the Federal Government enacted no new policies to facilitate the integration of work and family, as working women and working families suffered a loss in political power as well.

Low-wage employment falls disproportionately on women of all races and nonwhite men, significantly reducing their chances of earning a wage sufficient to support a family of four above the poverty level. Even when women and minority men have educational background and work experience comparable to white men, they are more likely to be low-wage workers.

Women of color are four times as likely to be low-wage workers as are white men with comparable skills and experience. White women are more than three times as likely as white men to be low-wage workers, and men of color more than one-and-a-half times as likely. More than half of all low-wage workers are the only wage workers in their families (or live alone).

Employment no longer provides an escape from poverty. More than eight million *working* adults are poor; two million of them work full-time, year-round.

More than seven million poor children have at least one working parent. When that one working parent is a low-wage worker, the children have no better chance of escaping from poverty than if the parent were not working at all; more than two-fifths of such children are poor.

What can be done to restore the rewards to work?

Government programs to supplement the income of the working poor are desirable, but the ability to increase such programs may be limited, given the Federal budget deficit, the savings-and-loan bailout, and U.S. military involvement in the Middle East. The intervention of the Persian Gulf has silenced virtually all discussion of the "peace dividend."

Even if generous income assistance were available, the wages *employers* pay would be held to a minimum. In addition, policies such as tax credits for working parents do nothing to increase the political power of working women and men.

Our research shows that unionization is among the most effective strategies for raising pay, especially for women and minority men. Being a union member, or being covered by a collective-bargaining agreement, raised 1984 wages by $1.79 per hour for Hispanic men, $1.32 for black men, $1.26 for Hispanic women, $1.01 for black women, $0.68 for white women, and $0.41 for white men, when all other factors (such as occupation, industry, firm size, education and experience) were held constant. In percentage terms, the union increase was more than 15 percent for blacks and Hispanics, 11 percent for white women, and 4 percent for white men.

sometimes used federal leverage to weaken them. Similarly, their appointees to the post of Secretary of Labor and the National Labor Relations Board (NLRB) were probusiness rather than prolabor. Long delays in decision making at the NLRB and their anti-union rulings have resulted in management sometimes firing pro-union workers with impunity. In effect, the NLRB from 1981 on reversed its previous policies of protecting worker rights (Novak ,1991).

Second, public opinion has turned against unions because some of them are undemocratic, scandal-ridden, and too zealous in their demands. Public opinion has also turned against organized labor because of a probusiness, procapitalist

Union membership also translates into political power that can be used to promote policies that improve the quality of life. Along with women's groups, labor unions have strongly supported such policies as family and medical leave and subsidies for child care. Unions have also strongly supported civil-rights legislation and pay equity, policies that contribute to equalizing incomes. And for many, union membership provides and extended community and a social support network that assists families in times of need.

But the proportion of the work force that is unionized has fallen, especially since 1970. Employers are on the offensive against collective bargaining; the number of workers fired illegally for union activity has increased dramatically in the same period. (The number of workers fired illegally each year is approximately equal to one-fourth the number who vote for a union in a representation election.) Union-representations elections are still won by unions in about the same proportions as formerly, but fewer and fewer organizing campaigns reach the election stage.

A worker's *right* to collective representations is guaranteed by the Wagner Act of 1935, but that right is not backed up by meaningful penalties against employers who knowingly violate the Act. It is time to restore a more equal playing field.

While labor unions have not always exhibited adequate flexibility, foresight, or inclusiveness, the labor movement today is responding to industrial change, shifting economic growth, and a changing work force. Women and minorities make up a dis-

proportionate share of new union members; unions are organizing in new industries among new constituencies.

Unions are an important force for wage equality, since they tend to bring up the wages at the bottom more than those at the top, just as they help minorities and women more than white men.

Rising real wages and a more equal income distribution are also key to a strong economy—an economy that produces real economic growth (not paper growth based on junk-bond mergers) and real goods and services that its workers can afford to buy. Just as Henry Ford thought, high wages create a stable domestic market. High wages also lead employers to make productivity-enhancing investment decisions. High wages can be as much the *spur* to sound economic growth as the by-products of that growth.

We have witnessed a decade of skewed national priorities, in which Congress and the White House provided tax breaks for the rich and cut spending programs for the poor. We also "invested" in the most expensive peacetime arms build-up in U.S. history. We are paying dearly for the de-democratization of both our economy and polity.

To redemocratize, we must restore the power of working people.

Source: "Heidi Hartmann and Roberta Spalter-Roth." Restoring Rewards to Work," *The Progressive* 54 (November 1990), pp. 26–28. Reprinted by permission from *The Progressive,* 408 East Main Street, Madison, WI 53703.

bias that increased during the era of supply-side economics that dominated the Reagan and Bush administrations and much of Congress during that time.

A major reason for the decline of union strength is the transformation of the economy (discussed later in this chapter). Manufacturing jobs, which are in decline, have historically been pro-union while service jobs, which are increasing, have been typically nonunionized. Many businesses, faced with stiff competition from low-wage economies, have insisted on reducing wages and/or worker benefits or said they would go bankrupt or move overseas themselves. The increased use of microchip technology threatens jobs with increased automation in the factory (robots to replace assembly-line workers) and in the office (computers to displace typists and file clerks). Similarly, the advent of computers, modems, and fax machines has increased the number of workers who work at home, as temporaries, and part-time. These workers are the least likely to join unions.

These forces have given the strong advantage to management. This trend has several negative consequences. First, faced with the threat of plants closing or moving to nonunion localities or to low-wage nations, unions have chosen, typically, to give back many of the gains they made during the 1960s and 1970s. Thus, workers have lost real wages and benefits.

A second consequence of union decline is that the work place may be less safe.

> Some of the most injury-prone industries, like food processing and textiles, have clustered in right-to-work [i.e., nonunion] states across the South, where labor organizers get the kind of welcome that used to greet Freedom Riders. (Lacayo, 1991:29)

A major consequence of union decline is the further dwindling of the middle class. In the words of Albert Shanker, president of the American Federation of Teachers,

> the union movement took a lot of workers who were relatively unskilled and turned them into middle class people who educated their children and supported the United States economy. Now, we've got businesses turning their employees into third-world workers. (Shanker, 1992c:E9)

Implied in this statement is a related consequence: if businesses turn their employees into third-world workers, then they will not be able to purchase enough goods and services to encourage economic growth and societal-wide prosperity. As Norman Birnbaum has said, "nations with strong unions and social contracts have the highest living standards" (Birnbaum, 1992:319).

A final consequence points to a possible contradiction—the precipitous decline in unions may actually lead to labor's regeneration. As the unions decline, with workers poorly compensated and ever fearful of losing their jobs, with management becoming more arrogant and demanding, the situation may get bad enough that there will be a turnaround—a surge in union membership and worker militancy. This could lead not only to a stronger collective voice in the work arena but also in the nation's politics. In this latter regard, Robert Kuttner has pointed out that unions have always had a social democratic conception of society:

> The labor movement sought not only gains for organized workers but embodied a broader moral authority as the advocate of society's nonrich, as the constituency for universalistic social insurance, full-employment policies, and distributive justice. (Kuttner, 1986:33)

Of course, the above scenario may not occur. Unions may continue to decline in size and influence; the pay and benefits to workers may continue to erode; and workers will be fragmented rather than united (see Salvatore, 1992).

Discrimination in the Workplace: The Perpetuation of Inequality

Women and minorities have long been the objects of discrimination in U.S. industry. Currently (and we have progressed mightily), approximately fifty thousand charges of discrimination by organizations are filed annually with the U.S. Equal Opportunity Commission. The charges now and in the past have centered on hiring policies, seniority rights, restricted job placement, limited opportunities for advancement, and lower pay for equal work. A number of court suits (and those settled out of court) illustrate that discriminatory policies have been common among such major corporations as AT&T, General Motors, and Northwest Airlines and in such industries as banking and steel.

There are two mechanisms operating in the U.S. economy that perpetuate inequalities in the job market by social class, race, and gender—the segmented labor market and capitalist patriarchy.

Segmented labor market. The capitalist economy is divided into two separate sectors that have different characteristics, different roles, and different rewards for laborers within each (Piore, 1975; Bonacich, 1976; Gordon, Edwards, and Reich, 1982). This organization of the economy is called the **segmented labor market**, or the **dual labor market**. The primary sector is composed of large, bureaucratic organizations with relatively stable production and sales. Jobs within this sector require developed skills, are relatively well paid, occur in good working conditions, and are stable. Within this sector there are two types of jobs. The first type, those in the upper tier, are high-status professional and managerial jobs. The pay is very good for the highly educated persons in these jobs. They have a high degree of personal autonomy, and the jobs offer variety, creativity, and initiative. Upward mobility is likely for those who are successful. The second type, the lower-tier jobs within the primary sector, are held by working-class persons. The jobs are either white-collar clerical or blue-collar skilled and semiskilled. The jobs are repetitive, and mobility is limited. The jobs are relatively secure because of unionization, although they are much more vulnerable than those in the upper tier. When times are difficult, these workers tend to be laid off rather than terminated.

The secondary economic sector is composed of marginal firms in which product demand is unstable. Jobs within this sector are characterized by poor working conditions, low wages, few opportunities for advancement, and little job security. Little education or skill is required to perform these tasks. Workers beginning in the secondary sector tend to get locked in because they lack the skills required in the primary sector and they usually have unstable work histories. A common interpretation of this problem is that secondary-sector workers are in these dead-end jobs because of their pathology—poor work history, lack of skills, and lack of motivation. Such an explanation, however, blames the victim. Poor work histories

Most work settings are characterized by male dominance.

tend to be the result of unemployment caused by the production of marginal products and the lack of job security. Similarly, these workers have few, if any, incentives to learn new skills or to stay for long periods with an employer because of the structural impediments to upward mobility. And unlike workers in the primary sector, workers in the secondary sector are more likely to experience harsh and capricious work discipline from supervisors, primarily because there are no unions.

The significance of this dual labor market is threefold. First, placement in one of these segments corresponds with social class, which tends to be perpetuated from generation to generation. Second, employment in the secondary sector is often so inadequately paid that many full-time workers live in poverty, as noted in Chapter 6. And third, the existence of a dual labor market reinforces racial, ethnic, and gender divisions in the labor force. White males, while found in both segments, tend to predominate in the upper tier of the primary sector. White females tend to be clerks in the lower tier of the primary sector, and White ethnics tend to be clerks in the lower tier of the primary sector. Males and females of color are found disproportionately in the secondary sector. These findings explain why unemployment rates for Blacks and Hispanics are consistently much higher than the rate for Whites. They explain the persistent wage differences found by race and gender.

These findings also explain the vast overrepresentation of people of color and women living in poverty. Referring to women, Ehrenreich and Stallard have argued that occupational segregation makes a crucial difference:

> For women, employment is not necessarily an antidote to poverty. The jobs that
> are available to us are part of the problem. The list is familiar—clerical work,
> sales, light manufacturing, and the catchall category, "service work," which

includes nurse's aides and grade-school teachers, waitresses, and welfare case-workers. Only 20 out of 420 listed occupations account for 80 percent of employed women, and it is this occupational segregation that accounts for women's low average earnings. In general, "women's work" not only pays less than men's but is less inflation proof. . . . The extreme occupational segregation of women in our society makes for a crucial difference between women's poverty and men's. For men, poverty is often a consequence of unemployment, and is curable by getting a job. But for women, concentrated in the low-wage stratum of the work force, a job may not be a solution to poverty. According to the National Advisory Council on Economic Opportunities, "poverty among hundreds of thousands of women already working underlines the failure of the 'job' solution." (Ehrenreich and Stallard, 1982:220)

Similarly, people of color are doubly disadvantaged. As Baron observes,

the combination of racial [disadvantage] with the primary-secondary segmentation compounds the immobility, low wages, and poor working conditions of the large number of black workers [and we would add Hispanics, Native Americans, and others of color] who participate in the secondary labor market. On the whole they are considerably worse off than the white poor and the near poor who work in the secondary sector. (Baron, 1975:205)

Capitalist patriarchy. Closely tied to segmented labor markets is the phenomenon of **capitalist patriarchy.** Although male supremacy (patriarchy) existed before capitalism and is found in noncapitalist societies today, a strong relationship between the two helps explain the present oppression of women in U.S. society (Eisenstein, 1979b). The concept refers to male dominance in work-related roles. This dominance is reflected in two ways—males tend to make the rules and enforce them and males receive unequal (i.e., greater) rewards.

Current gender inequality results from a long history of patriarchal social relations where men have consciously kept women in subordinate roles at work and in the home. Men as workers consistently have acted in their own interests to retain power and to keep women either out of their occupations or in subordinate and poorly paid work roles. Historically, through their unions, males insisted that the higher-status and better-paying jobs be exclusively male. They lobbied legislatures to pass legislation supportive of male exclusiveness in occupations and in opposition to such equalization measures as minimum wages for women. Also, the male unions prevented women from gaining the skills that would lead them to equal-paying jobs. The National Typographical Union in 1854, for example, insisted not only that women be refused jobs as compositors but also that they not be taught the skills necessary to be a compositor (Hartmann, 1976).

Throughout U.S. history capitalists have used gender inequality in the workplace to their advantage. Women were hired because they would work for less money than men, which made men all the more fearful of women in the workplace. Capitalists even used the threat of hiring lower-paid women to take the place of higher-paid men to keep the wages of both sexes down and to lessen labor militancy.

In contemporary U.S. society capitalism and patriarchy interact to oppress women. Males and females are accorded different, and unequal, positions in religious, government, school, work, and family activities. Looking only at work, women and men do different work both in the family and in the labor force. This division of labor between the sexes preserves the differential power, privilege, and prestige of men (see Chapter 8).

There is a current debate—the **comparable worth** or **pay equity** controversy—that illustrates well the discrimination women face in the labor market. In the state of Washington a judge ruled that the state must give its female employees up to $1 billion in back pay to make up for differentiated pay scales that give typically male jobs much more than jobs where women are found disproportionately.

This situation exists in other states, too. For example, a 1982 study in Minnesota found that registered nurses (mostly female) earned $1732 per month, but vocational education teachers (mostly male) earned $2260. Both jobs, however, were evaluated by experts as comparable. Similarly, in Illinois the predominantly male job of electrician earned $2826 per month, but the comparable female job of secretary earned $1486. The proponents of comparable worth argue that the pay for jobs should be based on amount of training needed, skills, and experience.

Independent experts on occupations have equated some jobs in the state of Washington, yet the male jobs are paid hundreds more per month than are the female jobs. Opponents have argued against comparable pay because it would cost the federal government as much as $10 billion annually and because it would be an unprecedented intrusion of the government in the marketplace. In so doing, of course, the president argued for the status quo, which would retain women at a disadvantage in the labor market with wages about 68 percent of males. In 1985 a district court ruled against the comparable worth argument in the state of Washington case and thus supported, in effect, the principle of capitalist patriarchy.

Unemployment

The Bureau of Labor Statistics supplies the official unemployment statistics. The official unemployment rate in the United States since 1980 has ranged from a high of 9 percent in 1982–83 to a low of 4.8 percent in 1988. In May 1992 the rate was 7.5 percent. These rates are misleading because they *understate,* dramatically, the actual amount of unemployment. Not included in the data are the 60 million or so people who are not in the labor force because they are in school, disabled, retired, homemakers, or not seeking work.

The data are distorted by undercounting the unemployed in two ways. First, persons who have not actively sought work in the four weeks prior to being interviewed are *not* counted in the unemployed category. Typically, there are more than 1 million such **discouraged workers,** most of whom were once employed in the secondary sector of the segmented labor force. Women comprise about two-thirds of these discouraged workers, and racial minorities represent about 30 percent. The rationale of the Bureau of Labor Statistics for excluding dispirited workers is that the function of the statistic is to chart fluctuations in the conditions of the active labor force, not to provide a complete portrait of the jobless. Regardless of the reasoning, the official data of the government, by undercounting joblessness, diminish the perceived severity of unemployment and therefore reduce the zeal to do anything about the problem. The extent to which the public perceive unemployment as a problem is further lessened by the counting as employed anyone who had worked for as little as an hour for pay in the week before being interviewed. Thus, people who subsist on odd jobs, temporary work, or minimal part-time work are counted as *fully* employed by the government.

Even the decidedly understated government figures on unemployment reveal that there are many millions of people who want to work but do not. In May 1992, for example, there were 9.5 million persons officially out of work. If we add the 1 million or so discouraged workers and the people working part time but who would rather work full-time (more than 6 million), the percentage of the labor force experiencing total or partial unemployment would be about 13.7 percent, which is a huge surplus of labor. According to Levitan and Johnson, since World War II

> the demand for labor has failed to keep pace with the supply of job seekers. No doubt, some portion of this unemployment is inevitable in a democratic society, as both employers and workers freely choose to accept or reject work situations. Yet the bulk of unemployment is neither frictional nor voluntary. Due to whatever combination of structural barriers and governmental policies, the economy, though it has continued to expand, has failed to generate sufficient numbers of jobs in the aggregate or to produce a reasonable match between the skills of unemployed workers and the emerging demands of labor. (Levitan and Johnson, 1982:55)

Ironically, there are those who favor having a certain proportion of the population unemployed. English reports that

> economists generally consider 6 to 6.5 percent to be the nation's long-term, underlying jobless rate, below which it is difficult to reduce unemployment without causing inflationary pressures. It is also the level at which every person who can be reasonably expected to hold a job has one, and only those with little education, training or work skills are jobless. (English, 1984:56)

Not only is unemployment commonly believed to be functional for society by reducing inflationary pressures, but it is also kept relatively high by capitalists because high unemployment deflates wages and therefore increases profits. When there are unemployed people willing to work, workers will not make inordinate demands for higher wages for fear that they will be replaced by cheaper labor. Thus, even unionized labor becomes relatively docile when unemployment is high. Feagin has summarized the capitalist argument:

> The . . . unemployed are essential to the operation of the capitalist system because they put downward pressure on wages and provide a reserve labor force that can be drawn back into employment when profit and investment conditions require it. Not only the officially unemployed, but also other groups make up this reserve labor force: discouraged workers, part-time workers, immigrant laborers just over the border, and housewives who might enter the market in the future. (Feagin and Feagin, 1990:83)

This **reserve army of the unemployed** is disproportionately comprised of people of color. In May 1992, for example, when the official unemployment rate was 7.5 percent, the unemployment rate for Whites was 6.5 percent; Latinos, 11.3 percent; and Blacks, 14.7 percent. These proportions by race tend to be relatively constant whether the overall unemployment rate is high or low, whether the economy is in a boom or a slump. Thus, the labor market assigns people of color disproportionately not only to the low-paying jobs but also to jobs that are the most unstable, precisely the situation of the secondary sector in the segmented labor market.

An important consequence of the reserve army of the unemployed being composed primarily of racial minorities is that it inflames racial antipathies against them by people who hold unstable jobs. These job holders perceive their enemy as the people below them who will work for lower wages, rather than as the capitalists who oppose full employment and adequate wages for all people.

We have seen that the number of jobs is less than the number of workers because the government wants to keep inflation in check and because capitalists want to depress wages. Several compelling structural reasons maintain unemployment as well, as we discuss in the next section. But first, let us examine another factor that limits the number of jobs: demographics.

There are clear demographic reasons for the shortage of jobs now and for the near future. In the past twenty-five years or so an unusually large number of women entered the labor force, motivated by the necessity of supplementing family income and the need for self-fulfillment in nontraditional roles. From 1960 to 1990 the proportion of married women with children working outside the home more than doubled from 30 percent to more than 66 percent. The other demographic force behind unemployment pressures were the very large numbers of young people entering the job market during the 1970s. The baby-boom generation—those 10 million more babies born between 1947 and 1957 than in the previous ten years—reached the job-seeking stage in the 1970s. These baby boomers increased the pressure for jobs and depressed the wages of people with jobs. The immense burden they put on jobs, wages, and promotions will affect jobs not only for those preceding them but also most notably for those following them. In the 1970s an astonishing 21 million new jobs were created. But because of the unprecedented number of women and young people entering the job market, the labor force grew by more than 24 million, leaving a shortfall of 3 million jobs. As Kuttner observes,

> this huge bulge in the labor force, of course, is a one-time phenomenon; the baby boom will not be repeated for a very long time; nor can female labor-force participation rates jump to nearly male rates more than once. But it will be thirty years before these effects subside. (Kuttner, 1984:21)

But as important as these demographic trends are in explaining the unemployment problem, they are relatively minor when compared with the effects of the structural transformation that is occurring in the United States economy. This critical shift and the accompanying changes are the subjects of the remainder of the chapter.

The Structural Transformation of the Economy

There have been two fundamental turning points in human history. (The following discussion is adapted from Jones, 1991.) First, the Neolithic Agricultural Revolution began about 8000 B.C., marking the transition from nomadic pastoral life (where the animal and vegetable sources of food were hunted and gathered) to life in settlements based on agriculture. During this phase of human existence cities were built; tools were developed and used; language, numbers, and other symbols became more sophisticated; and mining and metal working were developed.

The second fundamental change began in Great Britain in the 1780s—the Industrial Revolution. This revolution was characterized by the following features:

- Small-scale farming declined and was replaced by large-scale commercial agriculture. One indication of the decade when the Industrial Revolution occurred in a country is when the number of farm workers fell below 50 percent of the labor force: This event happened in Great Britain in 1780, in Belgium in 1850, in the eastern United States before 1860, in Australia before 1870, in Germany in 1875, in France about 1890, and in the Soviet Union in 1947.
- Industry (manufacturing and mining) surpassed agriculture as an employer.
- Employment at home or near home declined and was replaced by work at central locations such as factories and shops.
- Urban populations grew rapidly.
- Intensification of the division of labor occurred, which meant the decline of craftsmen and the rise of specialists trained to do repeated tasks.
- Machines replaced animals as an energy source.
- Life at work became increasingly coordinated and standardized. Factory life was bureaucratized, the clock dominated, and parts became interchangeable.
- New forms of transportation and communication developed to increase geographical mobility and to unify previously isolated regions.
- Wood and animal substances were replaced substantially by iron, coal, petroleum, rubber, and other substitutes.
- The development of mercantile, materialist, and competitive values had a profound effect on politics, culture, science, philosophy, and religion.

The first revolution, the Neolithic Agricultural Revolution, took almost ten thousand years to run its course; the second lasted but two hundred years. The Industrial Revolution really involved three distinct but related technological revolutions, each of which brought a fundamental change in the relationship of people and work. The first phase lasted about sixty years in Great Britain and involved primarily the application of steam power to textiles, mining, manufacturing, and transportation. The second phase of the Industrial Revolution occurred largely between 1860 and 1910 in the United States, Great Britain, and Germany. It was marked by a significant cluster of inventions and discoveries—the use of oil and electricity as energy sources for industry and transportation and the invention and development of the telephone, the telegraph, the automobile, the airplane, and the first plastics. The final stage of the Industrial Revolution is still in progress, although in decline since about 1970. The major scientific technological breakthroughs of this stage were atomic fission and fusion, supersonic aircraft and missiles, television, computers, and biotechnology. This third Industrial Revolution has resulted in a major transformation that sets the stage for a new era, which is referred to as the **structural transformation of the economy**. Whereas employment throughout the Industrial Revolution was characterized by ever greater domination by manufacturing, now employment has begun to shift toward service occupations and the collection, storage, and dissemination of information.

This worldwide trend is confirmed by 1990 data showing that more people are employed in service occupations (such as teaching, office work, banking, insurance, accounting, retailing, government, and mail delivery) than in manufacturing and related industries in the United States, Great Britain, Canada, Australia, New Zealand, Japan, Sweden, Norway, Denmark, Finland, France, Austria, Italy, Switzerland, Germany, the Netherlands, Belgium, and Luxembourg.

The present generation is in the midst of social and technological changes that are more far-reaching and are occurring faster than changes that occurred at any other time in human history. Several powerful forces are converging in the United States to transform its economy, redesign and redistribute jobs, exacerbate inequality, reorganize cities and regions, and profoundly affect families and individuals. Four of these forces are (1) technological breakthroughs in microelectronics, (2) the globalization of the economy, (3) capital flight, and (4) the shift from an economy based on the manufacture of goods to one based on information and services. The following subsections (adapted from Eitzen and Baca Zinn, 1989) look at each force in detail.

The New Technologies Based on Microelectronics

The computer chip is the technology that is transforming the United States toward a service/information economy. Microelectronic-based systems of information allow for the storage, manipulation, and retrieval of data with speed and accuracy unknown just a few years ago. Computer transactions are measured in multiples of picoseconds (ten to the twelfth power). Information can be sent instantaneously via communications satellite throughout the world in microseconds. Parallel processing with supercomputers gives machines the ability to reason and make judgments. These thinking machines come in modules that can be combined into a system of parallel processors. It is predicted that by 1996 a system with 16,000 processors (called a teraflop machine) would be capable of performing 1 trillion scientific calculations a second (Elmer-Dewitt, 1991b). Computer-aided design (CAD) permits engineers to design and modify an incredible array of products in three dimensions very quickly. Computer-aided manufacturing (CAM), or the industrial robot, is replacing conventional machines and workers. The problem with industrial robots is that although they increase productivity, they displace rather than create jobs. Moreover, the robots will replace the higher-paid semiskilled workers, not the unskilled manual workers.

Globalization of the Economy

Because of the size of the domestic market, the relative insulation of the Pacific and Atlantic oceans, and superior technological expertise, the U.S. economy throughout most of this century has been relatively free from competitive pressures from abroad. This situation has changed dramatically in the past twenty years. The United States, once the world's industrial giant, has lost its premier status.

In 1960, the United States led the world in per capita gross domestic product (Gross National Product less income from abroad). By 1980, the United States was eleventh among nonsocialist countries on this measure. In 1990 all commercial television sets purchased in the United States were produced outside the country. Also, the most widely purchased car in the United States in 1990, 1991, and 1992 was the Honda Accord, a Japanese product (actually, the four-door Accord is assembled in Japan and the Accord coupe and wagon are produced in the United States). Alvin Toffler discusses the globalization of the economy as it has related to IBM:

> Twenty years ago IBM had only the feeblest competition and the United States probably had more computers than the rest of the world combined. Today computer power has spread rapidly around the world, the U.S. share has sagged, and IBM faces stiff competition from companies like NEC, Hitachi, and Fujitsu in Japan; Groupe Bull in France; ICL in Britain, and many others. Industry analysts speculate about the post-IBM era. (Toffler, 1990:5)

This competition from abroad means reduced profits to U.S. corporations. Their typical response has been to cut costs by demanding concessions from workers, laying them off, or encouraging early retirements. Many corporations in the hardest-hit areas such as steel shut down plants completely, throwing thousands of employees out of work and the communities in which they were located into difficult dislocations. Another strategy employed by U.S. corporations was to compete as strongly as possible through massive investments in labor-saving devices, such as robots, which, of course, did little to help workers.

Capital Flight

Private businesses, in their search for profit, make crucial investment decisions. The term **capital flight** refers to the investment choices that involve the movement of corporate monies from one investment to another. This movement takes several forms: investment in plants located overseas, plant relocation within the United States, and mergers. While these investment decisions may be positive for the recipients of the move, they also take away investment (disinvestment) from others (workers and their families, communities, and suppliers).

Overseas locations for U.S. firms. U.S. multinational corporations have invested heavily in production of their goods in foreign countries. Corporate capital is invested overseas to increase profit, the increase coming primarily through cheap and nonunionized labor and the relative lack of the type of regulations found in the United States. The companies believe that these regulations—on pollution and worker safety, for instance—are excessive and expensive.

The main reason for overseas location, though, is greater profit from lower wages (see the Observation on Nike's Asian workers). For example, more than 1100 U.S.-owned plants—owned by corporations such as Ford, General Motors, RCA, Zenith, and Westinghouse—are located in Northern Mexico close to the U.S. border (these plants are called *maquiladoras*). U.S. corporations are allowed to ship raw materials, components, equipment, and machinery to Mexico duty-free. They are delivered to factories in Mexico and then assembled by low wage workers. The finished products are then exported back to the United States, with duty paid only on the value added. Obviously, the corporations profit greatly from such an arrangement; U.S. workers do not.

Relocation of businesses. Corporate administrators may decide to move their business to another locality. Such decisions involve what is called plant migration or, more pejoratively, runaway shops. The decision may be to move the plant to

OBSERVATION

NIKE'S PROFIT JUMP ON THE BACKS OF ASIAN WORKERS

Her only name is Sadisah, and it's safe to say that she's never heard of Michael Jordan. Nor is she spending her evenings watching him and his Olympic teammates gliding and dunking in prime time from Barcelona. But she *has* heard of the shoe company he endorses—Nike, whose logo can be seen on the shoes and uniforms of many American Olympic athletes this summer. Like Jordan, Sadisah works on behalf of Nike. You won't see her, however, in the flashy TV images of freedom and individuality that smugly command us to JUST DO IT!—just spend upward of $130 for a pair of basketball shoes. Yet Sadisah is, in fact, one of the people who *is* doing it—making the actual shoes, that is, and earning paychecks such as this one in a factory in Indonesia.

In the 1980s, Oregon-based Nike closed its last U.S. footwear factory, in Saco, Maine, while establishing most of its new factories in South Korea, where Sung Hwa Corp. is based. Sung Hwa is among many independent producers Nike has contracted with. Nike's actions were part of the broader "globalization" trend that saw the United States lose 65,300 footwear jobs between 1982 and 1989 as shoe companies sought non-unionized Third World workers who didn't require the U.S. rubber-shoe industry average of $6.94 an hour. But in the late 1980s, South Korean laborers gained the right to form independent unions and to strike. Higher wages ate into Nike's profits. The company shifted new factories to poorer countries such as Indonesia, where labor rights are generally ignored and wages are but one seventh of South Korea's. (The Sung Hwa factory and others like it are located in Tangerang, a squalid industrial boomtown just outside Jakarta.) Today, to make 80 million pairs of shoes annually, Nike contracts with several dozen factories globally, including six in Indonesia. Others are in China, Malaysia, Thailand, and Taiwan. By shifting factories to cheaper labor pools, Nike has posted year after year of growth; in 1991 the company grossed more than $3 billion in sales—$200 million of which Nike attributes to Jordan's endorsement—and reported a net profit of $287 million, its highest ever.

BULAN	:	APRIL 1992
NAMA	:	SADISAH
R-NO	:	8045
BAGIAN	:	I.PMTGAN
SECTION	:	KOCUPA
PER HARI		2,100
OT(JAM)		63,00
H-KERJA-		24

The words printed on the pay stub are Bahasa Indonesia, a language created by fusing Roman characters with a dominant Malay dialect. The message, however, is bottom-line capitalism. "Per hari" is the daily wage for seven and a half hours of work, which in Sadisah's case is 2,100 Indonesia rupiah—at the current rate of exchange, $1.03 *per day.* That amount, which works out to just under 14 cents per hour, is less than the Indonesia government's figure for "minimum physical need." A recent International Labor Organization survey found that 88 percent of Indonesian women working at Sadisah's wage rates are malnourished. And most workers in this factory—over 80 percent—are women. With seldom more than elementary-school educations, they are generally in their teens or early twenties, and have come from outlying agricultural areas in search of

SUNG HWA CORP.
INDONESIA OPERATIONS

PENDAPATAN		POTONGAN	
BASIC	50,400	PAJAK	0
P.KERJA	0	ASTEK	525
INCENTIVE	0	SPSI	500
HADIR	4,200	MAKAN	3,600
H/BESAR	6,300		
OVER TIME	19,845		
CUTI	0		
TOTAL	80,745	TOTAL	4,625

DITERIMA	76,120

city jobs and a better life. Sadisah's wages allow her to rent a shanty without electricity or running water.

"Pendapatan" is the earnings column, and five lines below the base pay figure for the month (50,400 rupiah) is one for overtime. Sadisah and the other workers in this factory are compelled to put in extra hours, both by economic necessity and by employer fiat. Each production line of 115 workers is expected to produce 1,600 pairs of Nikes a day. According to the column at left, next to "OT (JAM)," Sadisah worked 63 hours of overtime during this pay period, for which she received an extra 2 cents per hour. At this factory, which makes mid-priced Nikes, each pair of shoes requires .84 man-hours to produce; working on an assembly line, Sadisah assembled the equivalent of 13.9 pairs every day. The profit margin on each pair of shoes in enormous. The labor costs to manufacture a pair of Nikes that sells for $80 in the United States is approximately 12 cents.

Here are Sadisah's net earnings for a month of labor. She put in six days a week, ten and a half hours per day, for a paycheck equivalent to $37.46—about half the retail price of one pair of the sneakers she makes. Boosters of the global economy and "free markets" claim that creating employment around the world promotes free trade between industrializing and developing countries. But how many Western products can people in Indonesia buy when they can't earn enough to eat? The answer can't be found in Nike's TV ads showing Michael Jordan sailing above the earth for his reported multiyear endorsement fee of $20 million—an amount, incidentally, that at the pay rate show here would take Sadisah 44,492 years to earn.

Source: Jeffrey Ballinger, "The New Free Trade Need," *Harper's Magazine* 285 (August 1992), pp. 46–47.

Mexico, as we have seen, or to the Caribbean (all baseballs for major league teams, for example, are manufactured in Costa Rica), or to the Far East (where many U.S. plants involved in textiles, electronics assembly, and other labor-intensive industries are located).

U.S. corporations are also moving some of their operations to other English-speaking countries such as Ireland, Barbados, Jamaica, the Philippines, and Singapore, where cheap labor does such tasks as data entry to accounting, medical transcription, airline and hotel reservations, and telemarketing (Wysocki, 1991).

Capital is also moved within the United States as corporations shut down operations in one locality and start up elsewhere. Profit is the motivation for investment in a new place and disinvestment in another. Corporations move their plants into communities and regions where wages are lower, unions are weaker or nonexistent, and the business climate more receptive (i.e., lower taxes and greater government subsidies to the business community).

Regardless of whether plants are moved within the United States or to foreign countries, there are consequences to individuals and communities. Plant closures are devastating. Workers in the affected plants are suddenly unemployed—and so, too, are many people in the affected communities whose jobs were directly and indirectly tied to that plant (such as transportation, supplies, and services). Also, real estate, banking, schools, and other businesses are adversely affected. The local governments can no longer provide the same level of services because of a lower tax base. The recipient communities benefit from the increase in jobs, greater tax revenues, and the image of growth and progress. The boom communities, however, often cannot meet the greater demand for new roads, sewage treatment, schools, hospitals, recreation facilities, and housing that the new plants engender.

Mergers.   Another type of capital flight occurs when corporations use their capital to purchase companies in related or unrelated enterprises rather than to expand and modernize their plants. Perhaps the best recent example of this occurred when U.S. Steel, which was having trouble competing with the modern steel plants in Japan and South Korea, paid $6 billion to acquire Marathon Oil. Obviously, the company could have used this money to rebuild its antiquated plants, but it chose, rather, to buy a profitable company in an unrelated industry.

This trend toward megamergers has at least three negative consequences: (1) it increases the centralization of capital, which reduces competition and raises prices for consumers; (2) it increases the power of the huge organizations over workers, unions, and governments; and (3) it diminishes the number of jobs.

From Manufacturing to Services

Manufacturing, the backbone of the U.S. economy in this century, is no longer dominant. In 1947 employment in the service sector of the economy reached 50 percent, and now it is over 78 percent. Whereas in the past people mostly worked at producing goods, now they tend to be doing work in offices, banking, insurance, retailing, health care, education, custodial work, restaurant work, security, and transportation.

Overall, manufacturing has remained relatively stable, but within this sector about twenty industries have experienced steady declines during the past fifteen years. These **sunset industries** (e.g., steel, tires, shoes) have declined in both output and employment (Kutscher and Personick, 1986). More than 1500 plants in these industries have closed permanently since 1975. And literally millions of jobs have been lost that will not be replaced. "The *Fortune* 500 industrial companies employed 3.7 million fewer workers [in 1991] than the top 500 firms did in 1981, a loss of about one job in four" (O'Reilly, 1992:65). Overall, between 1981 and 1991, a time when the population age sixteen and older increased by 19.4 million persons, *the number of manufacturing jobs shrank by 1.8 million* (Barlett and Steele, 1992:xi).

The **sunrise industries,** which are characterized by increased output and employment, are involved in the production of high-tech products (computers, communications equipment, medical instruments, fiber optics, bioengineering, and robotics). These industries are creating many new and exciting products, and the employees are typically highly skilled. But according to Oxford Analytica, a group of scholars from Oxford, England, commissioned by three major U.S. corporations to project trends in the United States,

> only a very small number of very highly trained workers are needed to provide the technical breakthroughs critical to industry—less than 10 per cent of all jobs through 1995. The rest of the jobs will be routine, and new labor-saving technologies will cause workers to be "de-skilled." (Oxford Analytica, 1986:252)

The production workers in high tech, unlike those in heavy industry, tend to be nonunionized with relatively low wages and benefits.

The third category of manufacturing involves industries that have gained in output but have lost employment (e.g., food processing, metal products, industrial machinery, and automobiles). The source of this seeming incongruity (high productivity with a loss in employment) is automation, a topic we discuss shortly.

To repeat, the manufacturing sector of the economy overall has been relatively stable. But this stability masks a massive redistribution of job opportunities, with declines in some industries (steel, for example) and increases in the high-tech industries. But the redistribution of jobs and opportunities occurs not only within the manufacturing sector. The major change is in the growth of the service sector of the economy.

From 1979 to 1989 some 13.6 million full-time jobs were created. Most of these jobs have been in the service sector—from professional and administrative to clerical and service workers. About one-half of these jobs are bad jobs in the sense that they involve few skills, are poorly paid, have little responsibility attached to them, and provide poor job security. The Census Bureau has determined that 18.9 percent of full-time workers had low-wage jobs in 1979. In 1992 the proportion of low-wage jobs was up to 25.7 percent (O'Reilly, 1992:62). "Although young workers, minorities and women were disproportionately represented among these low-wage workers, nearly three-fourths were non-Hispanic Whites and had graduated from high school" (Moberg, 1992:7).

The government's Bureau of Labor Statistics estimates that from 1988 to 2000 the total number of U.S. jobs will increase by 18 million (Silvestri and Lukasiewicz

1989). Of these jobs, 16.6 million will be in the services-producing industries. Manufacturing jobs, in contrast, are projected to decline by 314,000 workers. Although about 2 million of the new jobs in the service industries will be executive, administrative, and managerial occupations and another 3.1 million in professional specialties, the bulk will be so-called bad jobs, such as clerical (adding 2.5 million jobs), retail sales (3.8 million), food preparation, waiters (1 million), janitors and housekeepers (556,000), cashiers (304,000), receptionists (331,000), and nursing aides and orderlies (378,000). In short, the United States is in the process of becoming a low-wage society.

Another source of low-wage jobs is the proliferation of **contingent employment.** This employment arrangement refers to employees who work for an employer as "temporaries" or "independent contractors."

> Since 1973, the rate of part-time, temporary, and subcontracted employment—what the labor market analysts call "contingent" employment—has grown faster than the rate of full-time work. Nearly one in five workers today works part-time while the temporary help industry is one of the fastest growing sectors in the economy. Close to 30 million people—over a quarter of the U.S. labor force—are working in jobs outside the regular full-time work force. And while a significant number are well-paid freelancers, most contingent workers are women and minorities clustered in low-wage jobs with no benefits or opportunities for advancement. (duRivage, 1992:84)

This trend represents a dramatic change in work. Businesses argue that they need this arrangement for flexibility in a rapidly changing competitive economy. This growing number of workers is not tied to an employer, which makes them free to choose from available work options. The downside, however, is that by classifying workers as "temporary" or as "independent contractor," employers do not provide fringe benefits.

> They can pay workers lower hourly wages, exclude them from better-compensated permanent jobs, save on health and pension costs, weaken labor unions, and, in the case of independent contractors, avoid payroll and unemployment insurance taxes. (duRivage, 1992:84)

In short, this trend has meant the proliferation of marginal jobs, with employers now shifting the burden of fringe benefits to individual workers and their families.

Age of Discontinuity

Every new era poses new problems of adjustment, but this one differs from the agricultural and industrial eras. The earlier transformations were gradual enough for adaptation to take place over several decades, but conditions are significantly different now. The rate of change is phenomenal and unprecedented. In today's global economy communication is instantaneous and capital is incredibly mobile. The types of work and the characteristics of the work force in the United States are changing. These factors, which are discussed in this section, result in considerable discontinuity and disequilibrium. (See the Observation of the future of work.)

Technology and Jobs

Several aspects of technology make this era different from the preceding ones. For example, new technologies, some quite revolutionary, are being developed rapidly. They have potentials that can be positive and negative and many that are unforeseen. Lasers and fiber optics, for instance, have a wide variety of applications as components in telecommunications systems, information processing, and entertainment (three-dimensional television). Fiber optics will increase the capacity of communications networks and made them more efficient. These technologies will generate considerable investment, render other technologies obsolete, generate new jobs, and destroy others.

Biotechnology is just beginning to affect changes in a wide range of industries— foods, agriculture, fuel, pharmaceuticals, chemicals, waste treatment, and natural resource recovery. The changes occurring in biotechnology are rapid and far-reaching. This field has tremendous growth potential, but its future consequences for the economy and jobs are unknown.

Of greatest significance for our purposes are the technological changes directly affecting work and workers. For the most part, the new technologies— especially those related to computers—are reducing jobs and wages. The cost of technology in the microchip field, for example, has fallen dramatically relative to the cost of labor. Jones reports that

> despite inflation and the rising cost of resources, the price of each unit of performance in micro-technology is 100,000 times cheaper than it was in 1960. "Miniaturization" has destroyed the historic relationship between the cost of labor and the cost of technology, permitting exponential growth with insignificant labor output. (Jones, 1991:36)

The declining cost of computing power is illustrated by what has happened in personal computers. A 1977 state-of-the-art personal computer processed 100,000 machine instructions per second and came with 64 kilobytes of main memory and 160 kilobytes of disk storage. A 1992 machine not only costs much less, but also has many thousands of times the processing power, main memory, and disk storage capacity.

The capacity of microchips staggers the imagination. Their capacity to store information on microchips increased 10,000 times between 1971 and 1980, and the pace continues exponentially. Superchips (the size of half a thumbnail in 1991) were capable of storing 4 million bits (4 megabits) of information. This capacity is predicted to rise to 256 megabits by the year 2000 (Markoff, 1991). The incredible storage and speed capabilities of modern computers are almost beyond comprehension.

> Imagine . . . two computers conversing with each other over a period. They are then asked by a human being what they are talking about, and in the time he takes to pose the question, the two computers have exchanged more words than the sum total of all the words exchanged by human beings since *Homo sapiens* first appeared on earth 2 or 3 million years ago. (Simons, 1985:165)

Microprocessors, of course, are programmable, making robots possible. Industrial robots can, for example, cut materials, weld, paint, and assemble. These robots, unlike human workers, do not get bored or tired, go on strike, require cost-of-living increases, or bicker among themselves. Robots are drastically altering the workplace. For example, robots perform more than 98 percent of the spot welding on Ford's Taurus and Sable cars. The result of this trend, of course, is fewer and fewer industrial jobs and, for the workers who remain, less and less leverage in bargaining with management.

Robotics are not just mechanical menials. They can be equipped with a multitude of sensors for vision, touch, and proximity. They can react to these sensory inputs and adapt. What is even more incredible, they can be linked (computer-integrated manufacturing, or CIM) into one comprehensive, integrat-

OBSERVATION

THE FUTURE OF WORK
Robert B. Reich*

It's easy to predict what jobs you *shouldn't* prepare for. Thanks to the wonders of fluoride, America, in the future, will need fewer dentists. Nor is there much of a future in farming. The federal government probably won't provide long-term employment unless you aspire to work in the Pentagon or the Veterans Administration (the only two departments accounting for new federal jobs in the last decade). And think twice before plunging into higher education. The real wages of university professors have been declining for some time, the hours are bad, and all you get are complaints.

Moreover, as the American economy merges with the rest of the world's, anyone doing relatively unskilled work that could be done more cheaply elsewhere is unlikely to prosper for long. Imports and exports now constitute 26 percent of our gross national product (up from 9 percent in 1950), and barring a new round of protectionism, the portion will move steadily upward. Meanwhile, 10,000 people are added to the world's population every hour, most of whom, eventually, will happily work for a small fraction of today's American wage.

This is good news for most of you, because it means that you'll be able to buy all sorts of things far more cheaply than you could if they were made here (provided, of course, that what your generation does instead produces even more value). The result-

*While a professor of political economy at Harvard University, Reich circulated the following memorandum to his undergraduate students. Most significant, he is now Secretary of Labor in President Clinton's cabinet.

ing benefits from trade will offset the drain on your income resulting from paying the interest on the nation's foreign debt and financing the retirement of aging baby boomers like me. The bad news, at least for some of you, is that most of America's traditional, routinized manufacturing jobs will disappear. So will routinized service jobs like keypunching of data transmitted by satellite. Instead, you will be engaged in one of two broad categories of work: either complex services, some of which will be sold to the rest of the world to pay for whatever Americans want to buy from the rest of the world, or person-to-person services, which foreigners can't provide for us because (apart from new immigrants and illegal aliens) they aren't here to provide them.

Complex services involve the manipulation of data and abstract symbols. Included in this category are insurance, engineering, law, finance, computer programming, and advertising. Such activities now account for almost 25 percent of our GNP, up from 13 percent in 1950. They already have surpassed manufacturing (down to about 20 percent of GNP). Even *within* the manufacturing sector, executive, managerial, and engineering positions are increasing at a rate almost three times that of total manufacturing employment. Most of these jobs, too, involve manipulating symbols.

Such endeavors will constitute America's major contribution to the rest of the world in the decades ahead. You and your classmates will be exporting engineering designs, financial services, advertising and communications advice, statistical analyses,

ed manufacturing system. In short, robots and computer-controlled machines will work together to plan, schedule, transport, control inventory, and perform many, if not most, of the manufacturing operations that used to require human skills.

The elimination of jobs because of superautomation is not limited to industrial factories. Offices are increasingly electronic. Engineers and architects now draw three-dimensional designs, update them, test them, and store them almost instantaneously in a computer. Agriculture employs robot fruit pickers and sheepshearers, computerized irrigation systems that use sensors to calculate water and

musical scores and film scripts, and other creative and problem-solving products. How many of you undertake these sorts of jobs, and how well you do at them, will determine what goods and services America can summon from the rest of the world in return, and thus—to some extent—your generation's standard of living. . . .

Person-to-person services will claim everyone else. Many of these jobs will not require much skill, as is true of their forerunners today. Among the fastest growing in recent years: custodians and security guards, restaurant and retail workers, day-care providers. Secretaries and clerical workers will be as numerous as now, but they'll spend more of their time behind and around electronic machines (imported from Asia) and have fancier titles, such as "paratechnical assistant" and "executive paralegal operations manager."

Teachers will be needed (we'll be losing more than a third of our entire corps of elementary- and high-school teachers through attrition over the next seven years), but don't expect their real pay to rise very much. Years of public breast-beating about the quality of American education nonwithstanding, the average teacher today earns $28,000—only 3.4 percent more, in constant dollars, than he or she earned fifteen years ago.

Count on many jobs catering to Americans at play—hotel workers, recreation directors, television and film technicians, aerobics instructors (or whatever their twenty-first-century equivalents will call themselves). But note that Americans will have less

leisure time to enjoy these pursuits. The average American's free time has been shrinking for more than fifteen years, as women move into the work force (and so spend more of their free time doing household chores) and as all wage earners are forced to work harder just to maintain their standard of living. Expect this trend to continue.

The most interesting and important person-to-person jobs will be in what is now unpretentiously dubbed "sales." Decades from now most salespeople won't be just filling orders. Salespeople will be helping customers define their needs, then working with design and production engineers to customize products and services in order to address those needs. This is because standardized (you can have it in any color as long as it's black) products will be long gone. Flexible manufacturing and the new information technologies will allow a more tailored fit—whether it's a car, machine tool, insurance policy, or even a college education. Those of you who will be dealing directly with customers will thus play a pivotal role in the innovation process, and your wages and prestige will rise accordingly.

But the largest number of personal-service jobs will involve health care, which already consumes about 12 percent of our GNP, and that portion is rising. Because every new medical technology is infinitely valuable to those whose lives might be extended—even for a few months or weeks—society is paying huge sums to stave off death. By the second decade of the next century, when my generation of baby boomers will have begun to decay, the

fertilizer needs in different parts of a field, and automated chicken houses. Retail stores, banks, and brokerage houses use on-line transaction processing to obtain instant information and to conduct transactions. Laser scanning and bar codes are transforming the physical handling of goods by retailers and wholesale distributors. A final example of technological change affecting jobs is the widespread use of televisions, telephones, and personal computers for the purposes of home banking and shopping.

Today's technology is different from the technology that developed at other stages in history. We now have "smart machines." As Jones has put it,

bill will be much higher. Millions of corroding bodies will need doctors, nurses, nursing-home operators, hospital administrators, technicians who operate and maintain all the fancy machines that will measure and temporarily halt the deterioration, hospice directors, home-care specialists, directors of outpatient clinics, and euthanasia specialists, among many others.

Most of these jobs won't pay very much because they don't require much skill. Right now the fastest growing job categories in the health sector are nurse's aides, orderlies, and attendants, which compose about 40 percent of the health-care work force. The majority are women; a large percentage are minorities. But even doctor's real earnings show signs of slipping. As malpractice insurance rates skyrocket, many doctors go on salary in investor-owned hospitals, and their duties are gradually taken over by physician "extenders" such as nurse-practitioners and midwives.

What's the best preparation for one of these careers?

Advice here is simple: You won't be embarking on a career, at least as we currently define the term, because few of the activities I've mentioned will proceed along well-defined paths to progressively higher levels of responsibility. As the economy evolves toward services tailored to the particular needs of clients and customers, hands-on experience will count for more than formal rank. As technologies and markets rapidly evolve, moreover, the best preparation will be through cumulative learning on the job rather than formal training completed years before.

This means that academic degrees and professional credentials will count for less; on-the-job training, for more. American students have it backwards. The courses to which you now gravitate—finance, law, accounting, management, and other practical arts—may be helpful to understand how a particular job is *now* done (or, more accurately, how your instructors did it years ago when they held such jobs or studied the people who held them), but irrelevant to how such a job *will* be done. The intellectual equipment needed for the job of the future is an ability to define problems, quickly assimilate relevant data, conceptualize and reorganize the information, make deductive and inductive leaps with it, ask hard questions about it, discuss findings with colleagues, work collaboratively to find solutions, and then convince others. And these sorts of skills can't be learned in career-training courses. To the extent they can be found in universities at all, they're more likely to be found in subjects such as history, literature, philosophy, and anthropology—in which students can witness how others have grappled for centuries with the challenge of living good and productive lives. Tolstoy and Thucydides are far more relevant to the management jobs of the future, for example, than are Hersey and Blanchard (*Management of Organizational Behavior,* Prentice-Hall, 5th Edition, 1988).

Source: Robert B. Reich, "The Future of Work," *Harper's Magazine* 278 (April 1989), excerpt from pp. 26, 28, 30–31. Reprinted by permission.

the new technology, for the first time in human history, does not merely extend or replace physical capacity but may also involve a degree of judgment, like humans. . . . Computers can be programmed to parallel human mental processes—including low-level judgement such as rejecting oranges because of unsatisfactory shape or color.(Jones 1991:37–38)

Throughout history, technological changes have tended to increase overall productivity. Although there were considerable dislocations to workers in some fields, employment actually increased overall. The introduction of machines in the past extended the capacity of the labor force. The machines of the past (e.g., sewing machines, typewriters, telephones, and motor vehicles) were designed to have one operator for each machine. In addition, they required other workers to make, sell, and maintain them. Now, however, there has been a trend toward technology and machines designed to reduce and even eliminate human labor. In Jones's words,

> much technological innovation in the past was "labor-complementing"—it extended the capacity of the existing labor force, and the machines themselves changed the nature of work. *But there has been a significant shift to "labor-displacing" technology where low-cost machines are specifically intended to reduce, if not eliminate labor inputs.* [Italics added.] (Jones, 1991:39)

Superautomation is eliminating jobs.

The Global Economy and Domestic Jobs

The profound transformation in the international economy is another factor making this era in history different from previous transition periods. For thousands of years caravans moved across the land and ships sailed with the winds and currents. People explored, conquered, and exploited other peoples and their resources, but the pace was slow and the interaction among different nations muted by time and space. Now, however, there is instant communication around the globe, and transportation anywhere is only a day away rather than six months or more.

These dramatic advances in communication and transportation have at least two important ramifications. First, technological advances now diffuse rapidly. During the Industrial Revolution technological change was quite slow (although rapid compared with change in previous epochs). The first steam-powered cotton mill in the United States, for example, began in 1847, sixty-three years after its adoption in Britain. Now technological breakthroughs in one country spread rapidly to other nations.

The second consequence of advances in transportation and communications is the enhanced mobility of capital. As Harrison and Bluestone have put it,

> the ability to move managers and key components at nearly the speed of sound by jet, and to move money and the information needed to coordinate production at nearly the speed of light enables capital, as never before, to go anywhere in the world. (Harrison and Bluestone, 1983:43)

Corporations of almost any size now make plans regarding raw materials, workers, and markets across national boundaries. Corporations seek cheap labor, which means a transfer of jobs—millions of jobs—to other nations. People in the United States now buy more foreign goods than foreigners buy ours, driving down the number of U.S. jobs and the wages of U.S. workers. U.S. economic, political, and even military powers, supreme since World War II, are now seriously threatened by the globalization of the economy.

Demography and Jobs

Three population facts—declining overall growth, disproportionate growth by racial minorities, and much greater participation by women in the work force—combine to make this time in economic history different from other stages. In this section we examine each of these trends.

A major source of economic growth during the Industrial Revolution was rapid population growth in the technologically advanced countries. The provision of services, construction, and the like provided a significant source of employment, especially in the rapidly growing urban centers. Since about 1970, however, population growth (births minus deaths) has stabilized in some Western countries and actually declined in others. This trend provides a further impetus for corporations to seek markets and workers in other countries.

The second demographic trend making this era unique is that the fertility rate for Whites has declined significantly in the United States, but the rate for racial minorities has remained about the same. This imbalance, combined with the influx of legal and illegal immigrants, has led to the disproportionate growth of racial minorities and their continuing economic plight. Throughout U.S. history, racial minorities have been denied equality in education and jobs. They have been relegated to the semiskilled and unskilled jobs in agriculture, in the mines, in construction, in packing plants, and on the production line. This bias continues today, at a time when these jobs are declining and becoming obsolete, made unnecessary in a society increasingly committed to knowledge, high technology, and education. Immigrants are thus at a distinct disadvantage, more so than at any time in history. So, too, are the racial minorities already here, who are locked into poverty by institutional racism, relegated to blighted neighborhoods with inferior services (especially education), and given fewer and fewer jobs.

The third major demographic trend contributing to the uniqueness of the present economic transformation is the entry of women into the work force on a massive scale. In 1950 about one-third of women held jobs outside the home; now, more than two-thirds do, and the proportion is growing. This change is directly related to shifts in the economy, especially the expansion of the service sector. Two-thirds of the jobs created in the past decade have been filled by women. In fact, it is precisely this great increase in women's paid work that has been a primary factor in the rise of service jobs. These changes, combined with the economic requirements of families (high cost of housing, education, and the like), have made women's labor force participation a permanent phenomenon and have contributed to their greater autonomy.

The Changing Economy, Demography, and the Future of Work

The demographic facts just described point to some important shifts as the United States moves toward the twenty-first century (the following is taken from Boyd, 1989; Bennett, 1989; Nussbaum, 1988; and Bernstein, 1988). First, because the baby-boom generation, which swelled the labor force for the past two decades, is aging and is being replaced by the baby-bust generation, the supply of workers for good jobs will not meet the demand. "Work-force growth will slump to 1 percent a year in the 1990s, far below the explosive 2.9 percent growth in the 1970s, predicts the Hudson Institute" (cited in Bennett, 1989:A22). Second, one of three new entrants to the labor force by the year 2000 will be non-White. Third, about two-thirds of the new workers will be women. Combining the last two: "White native-born males will make up only 15 percent of the entries to the labor force from now through the next century" (Bennett, 1989:A22). This is a profound shift from the present, when almost half (47 percent) of U.S. workers are White men (Boyd, 1989).

When these trends are combined with technological changes, which are continually upgrading the work required for most jobs, the result is that the United States will be running out of workers with the job skills needed for the 1990s and beyond.

> This emerging "skills gap" threatens to drag down the economy, lower the standard of living, hobble the United States in the competition with Japan and Europe, deepen the isolation and despair of the underprivileged, and leave us a deeply divided society. (Boyd, 1989:B1)

In effect, there is a mismatch between an increasing number of people wanting jobs and the skills required for the new jobs. The Hudson Institute predicts that 41 percent of the jobs created in the 1990s will be "high-skill" ones, compared to 24 percent of the existing jobs in 1989 (cited in Bennett, 1989:A22).

At a time when jobs require higher levels of math, science, and literacy than before, the economy is becoming increasingly dependent on the groups that often receive the poorest education. (Nussbaum, 1988:103)

These trends and their consequences present reasons for hope and despair. On the hopeful side, there will be room for people without privilege (minorities and women) for upward mobility, if they have the skills or demonstrate they have the potential to obtain them. A second reason for hope is that the powerful people in government and business will realize that their past decisions to emphasize technology rather than the maximizing of human capital were wrong and must be rectified. As an article in *Business Week* emphasized,

> while Washington has been hell-bent on throwing incentives at business to increase spending on plant and equipment, outlays for human capital in the past fifteen years have lagged behind. (Nussbaum, 1988:102)

More and more the argument is advanced in the business community that the schools must do a better job of educating *all* students and that businesses must also work at retraining their work force and at training new employees for the skills required for the new technology (see, for example, Bennett, 1989; Nussbaum, 1988; Bernstein, 1988). Also, businesses will have to provide more benefits to workers with families (flexible work schedules, maternity leaves, provision of day care) in order to expand the pool of workers (Bennett, 1989). Thus, there is a chance that class, race, and gender barriers to privilege will be removed, at least to some degree.

As these trends converge, however, there is also a strong negative potential. If history is a guide, the education and business communities will not educate the disadvantaged for highly skilled jobs. The children of the poor will continue to receive inferior educations. Many of them will see no hope in the mainstream of schools and jobs because the rewards are not there (see the Observation on African Americans and education).

If they do not acquire the skills of a high technology workplace, they will have to find work in the secondary sector of the economy, as custodians, guards, migrant workers, restaurant workers, file clerks, and the like. Whereas they once worked on assembly lines, this possibility has been foreclosed, for the most part, by robotics and by having to compete with lower-wage people overseas. They will be competing for a dwindling number of low-skilled jobs, which will drive down their wages. Meanwhile, the demand for higher-skilled jobs will be high, raising the wages of these workers.

> The social consequences of this are clear: Warns Irwin S. Kirsch, a researcher at Educational Testing Service in Princeton, N.J.: "If we don't boost the skills of the bottom ranks of the work force, we'll have an even more divided society than we do now." (Bernstein, 1988:108)

The Transformation of the Economy and the Bifurcation of the United States

There are two contrasting views on the dramatic transformation of the economy. For some people, this change in the work force from blue-collar to white-collar work has great positive potential. They argue, first, that it is a shift from a few huge industrial giants to many smaller technological and service-oriented firms, where innovation will lead to more rapid economic growth. Second, the shift from the old industries to those based on the microchip means a transfer from manual labor to mental labor. Cook argues that "if the old tool industries were an extension of the human hand and back, the new ones are an extension of the human brain and nervous system. The basic thrust of the technology is immaterial, and its productivity potential is enormous" (Cook, 1982:163). Third, as economist Robert J. Samuelson has argued, the expansion of the service sector is a sign of national health, not decay. For him, the shifting of labor from manufacturing to services indicates that fewer workers are needed to produce the goods we need, just as fewer agricultural workers today produce many times the products that it took so many farm workers to do several generations ago (Samuelson, 1984:61). Fourth, because of this trend, the United States is creating jobs at a rapid rate. And finally, jobs in the service category, when compared with those in the industrial category, are safer, cleaner, and less alienating. With machines to do society's dirty work, people will be freed to do the challenging and rewarding work.

Although there is some truth to these claims, the fundamental shift we are experiencing in the economy has a dark side as well. Many observers are alarmed by the real and potential negative consequences of the shifting economy. In sum, they see a number of powerful forces that are shifting the income distribution of people in the United States so that the middle class is declining and the gap between the haves and have-nots is expanding.

The distribution of income is very unequal and is widening. From 1970 to 1990 the income share of the highest quintile rose from 43.3 to 46.6 percent, and the bottom one-fifth fell from 4.1 percent to 3.9 percent of all income. The growing disparity in income and wealth is directly related to the changing job structure as the economy shifts from manufacturing to service.

Many people have experienced a sharp slowdown of income growth. This slowdown has caused a shrinkage of the middle class that is related in large measure to the erosion of middle-income jobs and the emergence of a bipolar wage structure in high-tech and service work. The trend has been a decline in wages over the past two decades.

> Between 1973 and 1989, the median wages of hourly workers (adjusted for inflation) fell by 17 percent among women younger than 25, 19 percent among men ages 25 and older, and a stunning 29 percent among men younger than 25.
> (Children's Defense Fund, 1991a:24)

Put another way, a study by the Economic Policy Institute found that a high school graduate with up to five years work experience in 1989 could expect to make nearly 27 percent less than his or her counterpart ten years earlier (reported in Moberg 1992:7). And, while wages declined, the cost of housing, utilities, clothing, transportation, education, and other goods and services increased.

The first factor that leads to a declining middle class is the loss of jobs in the relatively well paid industrial sector. The jobs being created in services, information, and high technology are at the extremes, with few in the middle. There are first-tier jobs in the primary sector with advancement potential, high pay, and prestige, such as in banking, finance, and engineering. These jobs require considerable education and specialized training. Jobs in the secondary sector of the services industry offer low pay, few benefits, low prestige, and no bridge to the first-tier jobs. These jobs as retail clerks, janitors, fast-food handlers, and health care aides, for example, require little training and not even a high school education. Workers who have lost their middle-income manufacturing jobs are not suited for the first-tier jobs in the service sector. Neither are their children, unless they have graduated from college.

The first-tier jobs offer great opportunities, but the catch is that only about 20 percent of the jobs being created are for the engineers, executives, and other professionals in this category. Four out of five of the new jobs will be in the low-wage, low-prestige, alienating jobs. For people whose industrial jobs were terminated and replaced with these second-tier jobs, the differences in pay are significant.

OBSERVATION

AFRICAN AMERICANS AND EDUCATION: THE WRONG SIGNALS

There has been a lot of recent talk about the importance of education to the future of the U.S. economy. Competing in a high-tech world requires well-educated and highly committed workers, the argument goes, and creating such a workforce by improving our educational system should be a top priority. This is especially true for minority Americans. According to the U.S. Department of Labor, one out of every three new entrants to the labor force by the year 2000 will be non-white.

But in all the debate about educating a new generation of workers, few talk about the signals these workers receive when they enter the labor market. It may be a truism of American culture that the path out of poverty is a good education, which in turn will lead to a good job. But when black children look at their elders, they see disproportionately low wages—even for the best educated.

Together with my colleague Lucy Gorham, I recently compared the wage levels of black and white workers between 1979 and 1987. Our work is based on data from the monthly household interviews conducted by the U.S. Census Bureau, generally considered among the best government surveys in the world. The numbers are deeply disturbing.

The 1980s have not been good for wage earners in general, but they have been especially bad for blacks. For example, between 1979 and 1987, the number of "full-time-equivalent" white workers with wages below the poverty line for a family of four—about $12,000 in 1987 dollars—grew by nearly 31 percent. For blacks, the increase was 44 percent. By 1987, a black worker was three times as likely to earn an income below the poverty line as a white worker. This reverses the trend from 1963 to 1979, when the proportion of low-wage jobs was falling for all racial and demographic groups, and the gap between average black and white wages was narrowing.

Even more alarming are the figures for black men in their late twenties and early thirties—a time when most people are settling into their careers. In the past decade, the number of black men aged 25 to 34 who have found jobs but who still earn a poverty wage increased by 161 percent. And this statistic understates the problem, because it does not count those who haven't found work or who, discouraged by their inability to find a decent job, have dropped out of the active labor force altogether.

The decline in manufacturing that traditionally generated middle-income, blue-collar occupations also has added to the numbers in poverty or near-poverty. This category of the new poor of **displaced workers** (see Chapter 6) is composed of laid-off workers who face never being reemployed at comparable paying jobs because their training and skills have become obsolete. These people typically worked hard and steadily in hard-hat industries, but their skills and experience do not fit in the high-technology sector of manufacturing. Those older workers who were laid off are especially vulnerable, because companies may not be willing to invest in their training.

Throughout the 1980s, some 2.3 million workers have been displaced each year, according to the Bureau of Labor Statistics. Roughly 1 million long-term workers—those on the job three years or more—have been replaced annually. Approximately 30 percent of these lack basic skills—reading, writing, and

But perhaps the most disturbing finding of our study is that higher education doesn't necessarily solve the problem. In 1987, the wages of one out of six white male college graduates were below the poverty line. For blacks, it was one out of three. Among female college grads, three out of eight whites earned poverty-level wages in 1987, versus nearly half the blacks.

The gap between white and black earnings also holds at the upper end of the income scale. Of course, there are many successful black professionals. But the sobering fact is that in 1987, 300,000 *fewer* college-educated black men earned $36,000 or more than earned the equivalent in 1979. The number of black women with the same amount of schooling who earned this much did grow during this period, but only by 15,000. That's a meager 7 percent increase over nearly a decade.

This situation is not only a national disgrace. It is an unaffordable economic waste. The U.S. economy is about to face a serious labor shortage at practically all occupational levels. And corporate managers are saying they desperately need technologically literate employees. In such circumstances, we need to convince a new generation of workers that staying in school will pay off in the labor market.

Some businesses and local governments have begun to grasp the seriousness of this problem. Companies have joined with local school boards to advise on curriculum. Other firms are promising entry-level jobs to kids from poor neighborhoods who stay in school, show a respectable attendance record, and graduate from high school with a "B" average. And city councils and state governments are trying to fill the budgetary chasm created by the federal government's disinvestment in education over the past decade.

But local initiatives cannot substitute for national policies aimed directly at improving work opportunities for minorities: raising the minimum wage, enforcing laws and regulations governing affirmative action and equal employment opportunity, and promoting the kind of economic development that creates new jobs at decent wages. As we plan the radical overhaul of our school systems in the years ahead, we need to pay more attention to the wage incentives provided by employers.

Source: Bennett Harrison, "The Wrong Signals," *Technology Review* (January 1990), p. 65. Reprinted by permission of Bennett Harrison.

arithmetic. Consequently, a third never found new jobs at all. Others found work but at substantially lower pay. (Bernstein, 1988:108)

The old poor are also victimized by the trend toward a service economy. John Kasarda has noted that whereas the central business districts of our large cities once housed factories, warehouses, and allied enterprises with work opportunities for the underclass, they now almost exclusively house "knowledge class" jobs in administration, finance, and the professions (Kasarda, 1983). Thus, the opportunities for the disadvantaged are further diminished.

Many communities have been devastated by the loss of companies employing thousands. When U.S. Steel or some other corporation closes its plants, permanently laying off thousands in a community, individuals and families suffer but so, too, do the communities, with declining real estate values, diminished retail sales, plummeting tax revenues, and severely reduced bank assets. Thus, the standard of living for entire communities is affected.

Finally, even workers who remain in the declining manufacturing industries will experience a decline in their standard of living. Given the triple threats of employers to move the plant to the Sunbelt or overseas, heightened international competition, and more layoffs, the unions have tended to accept steep concessions to stem further job losses. Thus, the wages and benefits of industrial workers decline further, removing them from the middle-class life-style they once enjoyed.

In summary, the problems associated with work in U.S. society are structural in origin. The source is not in unmotivated or unwilling workers. To understand the work setting in our society, we must understand the nature of capitalism, where profit guides managerial decisions rather than the human consequences. And in looking at unemployment, we must, as Currie and Skolnick have argued, "focus our attention on the American labor market itself—on the way our economy produces or fails to produce, enough jobs of sufficient quality to put Americans to work at living wages" (Currie and Skolnick, 1984:306). Finally, in examining this labor market, we must understand that the economy is undergoing a profound transformation. The next few generations will be caught in the nexus between one stage and another, and many will suffer because of the dislocations. So, too, will a society that refuses to plan but, rather, lets the marketplace dictate the choices of economic firms.

CHAPTER REVIEW

1. Societies are organized to allocate work in order to produce the goods and services required for survival. The way work is organized generates important social problems.
2. Owners and managers of firms and factories control workers in several ways: (a) through scientific management, (b) through bureaucracy, (c) by monitoring worker behavior, and (d) through extortion.
3. Blue-collar and white-collar workers in bureaucracies and factories are susceptible to alienation, which is the separation of human beings from each other, from themselves, and from the products they create. Specialized work in impersonal settings leads to dissatisfaction and meaninglessness.

4. A primary goal of business firms in a capitalist society is to reduce costs and thus increase profits. One way to reduce costs is not to provide adequately for worker safety.

5. Labor unions have declined in numbers and power. This has resulted in lower real wages and benefits, less safe work conditions, and a declining middle class.

6. Another work-related problem is discrimination, in which women and minorities have long received unfair treatment in jobs, pay, and opportunities for advancement. Two features of the U.S. economy promote these inequities: (a) the segmented labor market and (b) capitalist patriarchy.

7. The official government data on unemployment hide the actual amount by undercounting the unemployed in two ways: (a) people not actively seeking work (discouraged workers) are not counted; and (b) people who work at part-time jobs are counted as fully employed.

8. Unemployment has positive consequences for some people. Having a certain portion unemployed tends to keep inflation in check, according to some economists. Also, unemployment benefits capitalists by keeping wages down.

9. The economy of the United States is in the midst of a major structural transformation. This fundamental shift is the consequence of several powerful converging forces: (a) technological change, (b) the globalization of the economy, (c) capital flight, and (d) the shift from an industrial economy to a service/information economy.

10. These forces combine to create considerable discontinuity and disequilibrium in society. The trend toward robotics and other forms of superautomation reduces the jobs for the unskilled and semiskilled. This high-tech society, however, creates a need for workers skilled in communication, reasoning, mathematics, and computer programming. The proportion of workers traditionally found in these jobs (White males) is declining, while the proportion of new workers is increasingly non-White. Because non-Whites are disadvantaged economically and educationally, there is a skills mismatch. This skills gap offers the disadvantaged the potential of upward mobility if they, governments, schools, and businesses meet the challenge. If not, the gap between the advantaged and the disadvantaged will continue to widen.

11. Deindustrialization and the shift to a service economy have reduced the number of jobs providing a middle-class standard of living and have expanded the number of lower-standard-of-living jobs. The result is a bifurcation of the labor force into the haves and the have-nots.

KEY TERMS

Scientific management (Taylorization). The efforts to increase worker efficiency by breaking down work into very specialized tasks, the standardization of tools and procedures, and the speeding up of repetitive work.

Alienation. The separation of human beings from each other, from themselves, and from the products they create.

Segmented labor market (dual labor market).   The capitalist economy is divided into two distinct sectors, one in which production and working conditions are relatively stable and secure; the other composed of marginal firms in which working conditions, wages, and job security are low.

Capitalist patriarchy.   Male dominance in work-related roles.

Comparable worth (pay equity).   The attempt to equalize the wages of women's jobs to those of men's jobs, where training, skills, and experience are equal.

Discouraged workers.   People who have not actively sought work for four weeks. These people are *not* counted as unemployed by the Bureau of Labor Statistics.

Reserve army of the unemployed.   Unemployed people who want to work. Their presence tends to depress the wages of workers and keeps those workers from making demands on employers for fear of being replaced.

Structural transformation of the economy.   The fundamental change of the economy resulting from several powerful contemporary forces: technological breakthroughs in microelectronics, the globalization of the economy, capital flight, and the shift from a manufacturing economy to one based on information and services.

Capital flight.   Investment choices that involve the movement of corporate monies from one investment to another (investment overseas, plant relocation, and mergers).

Sunset industries.   Industries declining in output and employment.

Sunrise industries.   Industries characterized by increased output and employment.

Contingent employment.   An employment arrangement where employees work as "temporaries" or "independent contractors" freeing employers from paying fringe benefits.

Displaced workers.   Unemployed workers who face never being employed at comparable paying jobs because their training and skills have become obsolete.

FOR FURTHER STUDY

Barry Bluestone and Bennett Harrison. *The Deindustrialization of America*. New York: Basic Books, 1982.

Harry Braverman. *Labor and Monopoly Capital: The Degradation of Work in the Twentieth Century*. New York: Monthly Review Press, 1974.

Gary Burtless, ed. *A Future of Lousy Jobs? The Changing Structure of U.S. Wages*. Washington, D.C.: The Brookings Institution, 1990.

Business Week. "Human Capital: The Decline of America's Work Force," *Business Week*, Special Report (September 19, 1988) 99–124.

Dissent. "Labor's Future in the United States," *Dissent* 39 (Winter 1992): special issue.

Peter F. Drucker. *Post-Capitalist Society*. New York: HarperCollins, 1993.

D. Stanley Eitzen and Maxine Baca Zinn, eds. *The Reshaping of America*. Englewood Cliffs, N.J.: Prentice-Hall, 1989.

Bennett Harrison and Barry Bluestone. *The Great U-Turn: Corporate Restructuring and the Polarizing of America*. New York: Basic Books, 1988.

Arlie Hochschild. *The Managed Heart: The Commercialization of Human Feeling*. Berkeley: University of California Press, 1983.

Barry Jones. *Sleepers Awake! Technology and the Future of Work,* new ed. New York: Oxford University Press, 1991.

Jacqueline Jones. *Labor of Love, Labor of Sorrow: Black Women, Work, and the Family from Slavery to the Present.* New York: Basic Books, 1985.

Frank Levy and Richard C. Michel. *The Economic Future of American Families: Income and Wealth Trends.* Washington, D.C.: Urban Institute Press, 1991.

Philip Mattera. *Prosperity Lost.* Reading, Mass: Addison-Wesley, 1991.

George Ritzer. *The McDonaldization of Society: An Investigation into the Changing Character of Contemporary Social Life.* Newbury Park, Calif: Pine Forge Press, 1992.

Louis Rukeyser and John Cooney. *Louis Rukeyser's Business Almanac,* rev. ed. New York: Simon and Schuster; 1991.

Juliet B. Schor. *The Overworked American: The Unexpected Decline of Leisure.* New York: Basic Books, 1991.

David R. Simon and D. Stanley Eitzen. *Elite Deviance,* 4th ed. Boston: Allyn and Bacon, 1993.

FORUM

IS FREE TRADE THE WAY TO INCREASE JOBS? THE NAFTA AGREEMENT

Proponents of free trade argue that increased exports translate into more U.S. jobs.
Opponents contend that it will mean fewer jobs, as businesses shift production from the
United States to low-wage societies.

Bill Day

Amid a storm of protest, the leaders of the United States, Mexico and Canada announced on August 12 the conclusion of negotiations over a free trade agreement encompassing the vastly different countries of North America. The Bush administration released a summary of the North American Free Trade Agreement, but declined to release the actual text until it is translated into legal language. The agreement faces perfunctory approval in the Mexican and Canadian legislatures, which are controlled by the same parties which hold those countries' executive positions. In the United States, however the agreement must be ratified by the Democratic controlled Congress, where it is sure to be the subject of heated debate.

While the administration and industry groups boast that NAFTA will create jobs and prosperity, unions, environmental groups and consumer advocates predict it could result in increased pollution, lost jobs, lower wages and contaminated food. Consumer advocate Ralph Nader says that NAFTA was created "of the Du Ponts, for the General Motors, and by the Exxons," benefitting multinational corporations at the expense of labor, health, safety and environmental standards in all three signatory countries.

"We oppose it," says Burnie Bond, a spokesperson for the AFL-CIO. "The agreement does not have adequate protection for labor rights, worker health and safety or the environment." The AFL-CIO estimates that if Congress approves NAFTA, 73 percent of U.S. workers will suffer annual wage losses of approximately $1,000 and 500,000 to 600,000 workers will lose their jobs to lower-paid Mexican workers over 10 years.

In sharp contrast, industry representatives express enthusiasm for the proposed agreement.

Howard Lewis, a spokesperson for the National Association of Manufacturers (NAM), says, "From what we know about it, it appears to be an impressive agreement that will be beneficial to many U.S. companies."

Costing jobs. The central element in the congressional debate over NAFTA is likely to be its effect on employment. Critics of the agreement contend it will cost hundreds of thousands of U.S. jobs, as U.S. businesses shift production from the United States to low-wage Mexico. The United States Trade Representatives (USTR) concedes that some U.S. workers will be displaced as a result of the agreement, but estimates that between 600,000 and one million new jobs will be created by exports to Mexico. The Washington, D.C.-based Economic Policy Institute (EPI), in a recent report authored by Jeff Faux and Thea lee, estimates NAFTA will cost half a million U.S. jobs.

The authors further predict that NAFTA will encourage U.S. industry to move production to Mexico to take advantage of low wage rates and lax industry regulation. As a result, the report says, U.S. workers will lose jobs, or be forced to accept lower wages to compete with cheap Mexican labor. Faux and Lee cite 1990 Department of Labor statistics which list the hourly wage for manufacturing workers as $14.83 in the United States, $15.94 in Canada and $1.85 in Mexico.

"I think that this version of NAFTA will be very hard on working class people," Lee says. She predicts that U.S. workers in several types of industry will suffer: those in industries already moving to Mexico, such as automobiles and auto parts, consumer electronics and apparel, who will be subjected to both job and wage losses; workers employed at small- and medium-sized businesses that cannot relocate and will become unable to compete with corporations in Mexico; and workers in small service businesses, like restaurants, which will undergo hardship when large plants move out of their neighborhoods. Finally, Lee argues, growers of products currently produced by high tariffs, such as winter fruits and vegetables, cotton and peanuts, will suffer when the tariffs are removed by NAFTA.

Faux and Lee point out that blue-collar workers who lost their jobs are unlikely to gain access to the high-skill, high-wage jobs that might be created by increased exports to Mexico.

Lewis counters that U.S. labor must adjust to inevitable changes in the job market. "The era of the low-skill, high-pay job is over," he says, "and we'd better adjust to it. That's not the way the competition is going at this point in the game." Lewis recommends that the way to "adjust" is not to regulate trade, but to invest in education and training.

Faux and Lee assert that Canada's loss of 461,000 manufacturing jobs from June 1989 to October 1991 after adoption of the U.S.-Canada trade agreement is a portent of the likely outcome of the expanded free trade agreement with Mexico. But Malcolm McKechnie, press attache at the Canadian Embassy iis Washington, attributes the loss of jobs to the recession, noting that both exports and the Canadian trade balance have increased since the agreement.

Critics of the agreement argue that corporate flight to Mexico will not benefit Mexico or Mexican workers, since corporations will be moving South precisely to take advantage of the country's low wages, worker rights, safety and environmental standards. NAFTA-induced investments will replicate the record of the string of maquiladoras (foreign-owned plants in Mexico which export to the United States) on the U.S.-Mexican border, where "there is no floor on how low you [can] push wages and no limit on how badly you [can] abuse the environment."

"NAFTA is an extension of the *maquiladora* production system to the entire Mexican economy," Lee says. "The point of the *maquiladora* is to import parts from the United States, assemble them with Mexican labor and export them to the United States." According to Lee, because goods produced in the *maquiladoras* are sold in the United States, corporations have no incentive to pay a living wage. "Very few firms producing in the *maquiladoras* have any intention of selling their goods to the workers who work there. So it doesn't matter if you pay 60 cents an hour, because you know that person isn't going to buy the automobile or refrigerator or bra that you're producing. You've ruptured the connection between production and consumption."

Bond agrees that NAFTA will only further the maltreatment of Mexican workers. "The agreement doesn't do anything to encourage Mexican wage levels to rise. . . . If anything, investments of hundreds of millions of dollars along the border has lowered the standard of living." she says. "There is nothing in this agreement, such as adequate labor standards, to offset the tendency of American corporations to exploit Mexican workers."

Lee says that U.S. corporations have already begun to pursue a policy of "low wage" manufacturing by moving production out of the United States to countries where wages are lower. "It has been happening for a decade or more," she says. "NAFTA takes us several steps further down the path than we've already traveled." She and Faux argue that in addition to its devastating effect on U.S. workers and communities, this strategy will ultimately prove less competitive than one in which industry produces higher quality goods more efficiently by investing in the work force.

FORUM

Lowering standards. Low wages are not the only incentive for U.S. and Canadian corporations to move south, charge environmental critics of NAFTA. Pointing out that Mexico is also notorious for its lack of enforcement of environmental, health and safety regulations, Larry Williams, a spokesperson for the Sierra Club, says, "We do not wish Mexico to become a haven for polluters. We do not wish to set up a situation where it becomes attractive to move to Mexico" in order to evade U.S. and Canadian environmental regulations.

Nader argues that the existing United States-Canada free trade agreement has dragged down both countries' health, safety and environmental standards, enabling corporations to play the two nations off one another. All three countries will suffer far more, he says, from an agreement with Mexico, where industry conditions are far worse. "The differences between standards in General Motors plants and General Motors plants south of the border are staggering," he says.

The USTR refuses to comment on criticisms of NAFTA, but the Canadian government is satisfied with NAFTA's environmental provisions. "Our environment minister says [NAFTA] is an advance because it upholds the principle that environmental laws should not be lowered to attract investment," McKechnie says. However, he does acknowledge that the Canadian administration had hoped to include language in the agreement which would allow lax enforcement of environmental laws to be brought before a dispute resolution panel. "The problem in Mexico is not standards, it's enforcement. We're working with Mexico to improve enforcement." McKechnie says.

Antonio Ocaranza, press attache at the Mexican Embassy in Washington, defends his government's record on environmental enforcement. "We have a new law that sets very tough environmental standards," he says.

Critics also fear that under NAFTA, Mexico could challenge stricter U.S. and Canadian environmental, health, worker safety and food purity standards as unfair barriers to trade. Williams explains that Canada and Mexico could attack U.S. environmental or consumer safety standards as not scientifically justified and unfairly discriminating against their products. Unelected panels of trade representatives would resolve disputes over this sort of issues. "DDT is still in use in Mexico. Mexico could challenge our complete ban on DDT use," says Williams.

The proposed NAFTA raises another important environmental issue: the state of the U.S.-Mexico border. The *maquiladora*-dotted border region is an environmental wasteland, where corporations dump toxic waste, contaminate the water and pollute the air with little inhibition. Environmentalists fear NAFTA will exacerbate the problem by bringing more companies intent on polluting to Mexico. "We do not wish Mexico to become a haven for polluters," says Williams.

The Mexican government claims that its recently stepped-up commitment to environmental enforcement is sufficient to address the border problem. "We have . . . increased the number of inspectors in the border region to 200, a four-fold increase since 1989," Ocaranza says. He also notes that Mexico has appropriated $460 million over three years to clean up the area along the U.S.-Mexican border, pointing out that a proportional fraction of U.S. Gross National Product would be $12 billion.

However, Lori Wallach, an attorney for the Washington, D.C.-based public interest group Public Citizen, estimates that the cost of a complete clean up is $5 billion, far more than the allocated $460 million. Williams says the border will only be cleaned up if NAFTA requires it. and perhaps even imposes a tax to fund the clean-up. "We're not happy that the administration has insisted that the border clean-up be independent of the trade agreement," he says. "Even before the ink was dry [on the agreement], the House of Representatives cut 40 percent out of the EPA [Environmental Protection Agency] budget to clean up the border. What's going to happen three or four years from now?"

Citizen Power.   Linking together the concerns of NAFTA's many critics is a fear that multinational corporations will use the agreement to usurp power from citizens and undercut their standard of living. For Lee, the issue comes down to who will make the decisions that guide the U.S. economy and ensure the health and safety of its citizens: "I think the question really is, 'Can we take back control of the economy and manage the economy in some way to basically put a leash on the behavior of multinational corporations?" she says. "I think it's possible and desirable to do so. The one thing we have to control is access to our market. If we tell multinational corporations they can't sell here if they don't respect the basic principles, they'll have no choice."

Source: Bill Day, "The NAFTA Nightmare," *Multinational Monitor* 13 (October 1992), pp. 24–26. Reprinted with permission from Multinational Monitor, PO Box 19045, Washington, DC 20036. Individual subscription $24/yr.

his chapter examines the nature of crime and how society reacts to criminal behavior in the processing of criminals. These topics are important because they help us understand the role of the powerful in regulating social behavior and the bias of the system against the underclass.

Crime in Society

The people of society are naturally concerned with crime for two reasons: if left unchecked, crime destroys the stability necessary for the maintenance of an orderly society; and the people are the potential victims of criminal activities. Though legitimate, these concerns direct attention away from the deviance that results from the orderly working of society and from crimes that are much more costly than street crimes (which we tend to think are overwhelmingly the greatest criminal danger). These ironies will become apparent as we examine four aspects of crime: its definition, the incidence of crime, the kinds of people arrested, and the various types of criminal behavior.

What Is a Crime?

Groups and individuals within society differ in their definition of **crime.** Some people would equate crime with all antisocial behavior. Others would argue that crimes are acts such as racism, sexism, and imperialism that violate basic human rights. Similarly, some people use moral rather than legal criteria to define what is or is not a crime. For example, Martin Luther King, Jr., and his followers believed that the laws enforcing racial segregation were morally wrong, so to violate them was not a crime but a virtue. There are religious people who regard a behavior as a crime if it meets their criteria for sin, regardless of what the formal law decrees.

Although there is no universally accepted definition, the most common one—the breaking of a law—officially labels people and separates society into criminal and noncriminal categories. In other words, criminality is a social status determined by how an individual is perceived, evaluated, and treated by legal authorities. Generally, the law designates as criminal any behaviors that violate the strongly held norms of society. Everyone would agree, for example, that the law should protect property from theft and vandalism. There would also be universal agreement that society must protect its citizens from bodily harm (rape, assault, and murder). But although there may be consensus in society on certain laws, the political nature of the lawmaking and enforcement process has important negative implications for the individuals caught up in them.

Because law is an inherently political phenomenon, a violation of law means that the crime is ultimately an expression of group conflict and interest (Quinney, 1970). Individuals and groups in power determine what behaviors violate these interests and thus are criminal. Pearl observes that

> if the original colonists had failed in their revolution, they would have been branded criminals and their valor, ritualized for subsequent generations, would instead be denounced. Their motives would have been base, etc. The trade-off between crime and revolution in oppressive societies is vital for political stability.

475

This is not to say that there is no such thing as criminal behavior, but ruling forces' description of all opposition as criminal makes it almost impossible to consider the nature of "true" crime. (Pearl, 1977:50)

Consider, for example, how antiwar protestors were treated by local and federal authorities during the late 1960s and early 1970s. Their behavior was considered violent because it threatened the power structure. What the powerful consider violent depends, in fact, on what they perceive to be the intent of the individuals they observe. U.S. society does not always forbid or condemn some acts of force that injure people or destroy property. Property damage during football games, Halloween, or the Mardi Gras is often overlooked. Even ten thousand beer-drinking, noisy, and sometimes destructive college students on the beaches of Florida during spring break are allowed to go on such a binge because "kids will be kids." But if the same ten thousand college students were to destroy the same amount of property in a demonstration whose goal was to change the system, the acts would be defined as violent and the police would be called to restore order by force if necessary (although the authorities would not define these measures as violence). Thus, violence is condoned or condemned through political pressures and decisions. The basic criterion is whether the act supports or threatens existing social and political arrangements. (See the insert on Emile Durkheim.) If they are not supportive, then by definition the acts are to be condemned and punished.

A related implication of the political nature of crime is that the design of laws is influenced by a class bias. The fact that the powerful can have their interests legitimized by law to the neglect or detriment of the powerless means that the interests of the latter will be considered illegitimate. As Pearl has put it, "The violent poor are somehow a more dangerous lot than the violent wealthy, and the well-established victim is deemed more important than the underclass victim" (Pearl, 1977:52). This view pervades the criminal justice system, as discussed in a later section.

Because the law defines crime, then what is a crime depends on the *current* law. As society changes and as new interest groups become powerful, the laws and interpretations of the laws regarding criminal behavior may also change. Many behaviors once considered criminal no longer are, such as missing church on Sunday, harboring a runaway slave, or selling liquor.

Finally, because crime is defined by the powerful in society, the organization and priorities of society are never regarded as harmful to human life (and therefore a moral crime). Yet the order of society itself can be very destructive to some categories of people, as Carmichael and Hamilton showed in their book *Black Power*. They noted that when White terrorists bombed a Black church in Birmingham, Alabama, and killed five children, the act was deplored by most elements of U.S. society. But when hundreds of Black babies die each year in Birmingham because of the effects of racism, no one in the power structure gets upset and calls this violence. Although high infant mortality and rates of preventable disease, which are perpetuated through discrimination, take many more lives than does civil disorder or street crimes, the term *violence* is not applied to these crimes (Carmichael and Hamilton, 1967:4). Thus, **violence** is defined as an act of force perceived by the powerful as threatening to the status quo.

Emile Durkheim and the Social Functions of Crime

Three nineteenth-century social thinkers— Karl Marx, Max Weber, and Emile Durkheim—have had an enormous impact on contemporary thinking about society and social problems. Of these three, Emile Durkheim (1858–1917) was an especially important influence on people who call themselves functionalists (also called order theorists). The whole of Durkheim's scholarly work centered on the question of what holds society together. For him, even crime plays a vital role in achieving social solidarity.

Durkheim argued that society is based on a common moral order. One indicator of morality, though an imperfect one, is the laws of a society. Criminal laws, for example, express the common will because they provide for the punishment of those who disobey. When a crime is committed there is a widespread sense of public outrage. This outrage at the criminal and his or her deviant behavior reaffirms the underlying principles of the society— morality, order, and protection— all of which promote social solidarity. In this way, Durkheim argued, crime serves a positive function of society by holding it together.

Durkheim's notion is rather easy to grasp when the crime is murder, theft, rape, or treason. But what of lesser crimes such as (depending on the society) public nudism, eating forbidden foods, or irreverent behavior in the presence of a sacred object? These crimes are not physically harmful to society, so why are they labeled as deviant? Such logic misses Durkheim's point: many laws may appear unrelated to social survival, but upholding them is essential because they are addressed to the moral force of the society. As Durkheim put it, "We must not say that an action shocks the common conscience because it is criminal, but rather that it is criminal because it shocks the common conscience. We do not reprove it because it is a crime, but it is a crime because we reprove it."*

*Emile Durkheim, *The Division of Labor in Society,* trans. George Simpson (Glencoe, Ill: Free Press, 1960), p. 81.

Crime Rates

The innately political nature of crime is clearly evident when one examines the official crime rates, which emphasize certain types of crimes (those of the underclass) while minimizing or ignoring others. These discrepancies have profound implications because they mean, in effect, that some categories of people are disproportionately labeled as criminals.

The basic source of crime statistics is the *Uniform Crime Reports,* published yearly by the FBI (see Figure 15.1). The primary problem with these statistics is that they focus on traditional crimes and omit white-collar crimes, corporate crime, organized crime, and political crimes. The FBI statistics (called "Index Crimes") emphasize burglary, larceny, auto theft, robbery, rape, assault, and murder. (See the Observation comparing the United States with other nations on crime statistics.) This focus has the effect of directing public attention almost exclusively to crimes involving violence and property, in which the poor and minorities are thought to be the major perpetrators, and away from the crimes of the affluent.

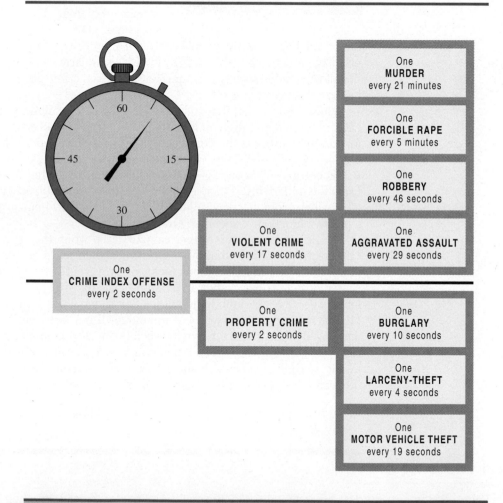

Figure 15.1   Crime Clock 1991

Source: U.S. Department of Justice, *Crime in the United States 1991: Uniform Crime Reports* (Washington D.C.: Government Printing Office, 1992), p. 4.

OBSERVATION

WE ARE NUMBER ONE!

Andrew L. Shapiro (1992) has compared the United States with eighteen other major industrial nations most like us: Australia, Austria, Belgium, Canada, Denmark, Finland, France, Germany, Ireland, Italy, Japan, the Netherlands, New Zealand, Norway, Spain, Sweden, Switzerland, and the United Kingdom. He found that the United States ranked first on a number of crime and criminal justice dimensions (Shapiro, 1992:117–139):

- #1 in percentage of population who have been the victim of a crime (28 percent, compared to a low of 9.3 percent for Japan).
- #1 in murder rate (9.4 per 100,000, compared to a low of 0.7 for Finland).
- #1 in the murder rate of children age 1–19 (3.7 per 100,000, compared to a low of 0.5 for Japan).
- #1 in the number of people killed with a handgun (38.3 per million, compared to a low of 0.1 per million for Japan).

- #1 in reported rapes (114 per 100,000 women age 15 to 59, compared to 4 per 100,000 in Ireland).
- #1 in drug offenders (346 per 100,000, compared to a low of 1 per 100,000 in Ireland and Japan).
- #1 in people killed in car accidents due to drunk driving (8.8 per 100,000, compared to a low of 0.5 in Spain).
- #1 in percentage of households with handguns (28.6 percent, compared to a low of 0.4 percent in the United Kingdom).
- #1 in incarceration rate (426 per 100,000, compared to a low of 40 per 100,000 in the Netherlands).

Source: From *We're Number One* by Andrew L. Shapiro. Copyright © 1992 by Andrew L. Shapiro. Reprinted by permission of Vintage Books, a division of Random House, Inc.

The other obvious problem with the official crime statistics is that they under-report the actual extent of crime because they list only known crimes. Surveys have revealed that about seven out of ten crimes go unreported to police.

Official crime rates are also misleading because they imply that the amount of crime varies a good deal from year to year or from region to region. These changes may occur, but the official statistics make real variations difficult to determine. In some cases the actual incidence of crime may not change, but the accuracy of reports or the increased zeal of law enforcement officials to prosecute criminals may increase.

Despite these problems of accuracy, the official statistics do reflect the actual degree of labeling that occurs, as Hartjen has perceptively argued:

> If crime is defined as a label imposed upon behavior, then crime rates reflect the labeling activity of official agencies. In this respect, crime rates are a perfectly accurate measure of the *amount of social labeling* produced by a population and are not indicative of the number of crimes, in the sense of illegal acts, taking place. (Hartjen, 1978:187)

Realizing that the official statistics are misleading and that they represent the degree of official labeling in society, let us look fat what kinds of people are arrested and labeled for criminal behavior in U.S. society.

Demographic Characteristics of People Arrested for Crimes

The data from official sources clearly indicate that people from certain social categories are more likely than others to be arrested for criminal activities. We examine these categories of sex, age, social class, and race.

Sex.   Street crime as measured by the FBI's *Uniform Crime Reports* has shown a consistently low level of female arrests and, if arrested, a greater likelihood of receiving lighter sentences than males. As Hagan notes,

> The traditional handmaiden of sexism has been paternalism, a sort of noblesse oblige in which males felt that they were responsible for protecting the dependent female. This policy is reflected in the law and its administration, since females generally receive much lighter sentences for the same offense, are viewed more favorably by judges and juries, and seldom receive the death penalty. (Hagan, 1990:84)

The types of crimes committed vary by sex. The sex ratio is 3.2 to 1 (i.e., 3.2 crimes by males for every 1 by a female) for property offenses, but rises sharply to nearly 8 to 1 for violent offenses. The arrest rate for violent crimes has been stable for women over the past twenty years but has increased recently for property crimes. The differences by sex raise two questions: (1) Why is there such an apparent difference in criminal behavior by gender? and (2) Why are women committing more property crimes now?

Explaining the gender gap.   There are three reasons for greater likelihood of male involvement in crime (Sykes and Cullen, 1992:107–108). First, there are biologi-

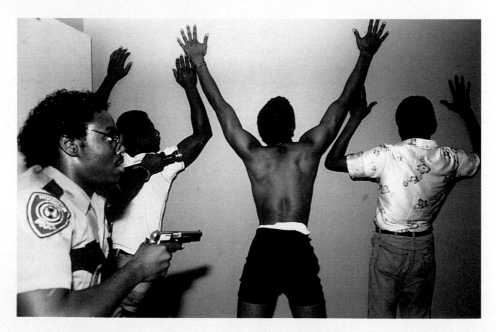

For biological and sociological reasons, males are more likely than females to engage in criminal activities.

cal differences, such as levels of testosterone, which explain why males are more aggressive than females. Second, the gender gap is the result of differences in socialization for males and females. Boys are taught to be aggressive and risk takers, girls are not. Sons are given more freedom by parents, while daughters are typically subject to greater social control.

The third explanation for gender differences in criminal behavior involves structural barriers that limit the possibilities for lawlessness by women. Women, for example, have fewer opportunities than men in employment to embezzle from their employers or to swindle customers. Also, women have few opportunities in organized crime because of institutionalized sexism. "In sum, females' social experiences and social opportunities, legitimate and illegitimate, are likely to limit their criminal involvement" (Sykes and Cullen, 1992:108).

Explaining the rise in female criminality. There is some debate over the source of this recent upswing for property crimes by women. Some people argue that the women's movement for social, political, and economic equality has not only increased gender role equality of women in legitimate ways but has also opened up new opportunities, traditionally reserved for criminal males, in illegitimate and illegal activities. Others argue that the impact of the women's movement on female crime, though real, is less direct. Perhaps, for example, law enforcement agencies have paid more attention to women in general and their criminal activities in particular since the advent of the women's movement. Or possibly, because the present increase in female crime appears limited to property crimes, their increased participation in the labor force has moved many women closer to opportunities to commit certain crimes. More significant, though, is the link between female criminality and greater economic marginality (increasing numbers of women who are dependent on their limited resources for themselves and often for their children (Wilson and Herrnstein, 1985:124).

Age. A disproportionate amount of street crime in the United States is committed by relatively young persons (see Figure 15.2).

> Teenagers and young adults commit crimes at a rate three to five times greater than their proportionate representation in the general population. Those under the age of twenty-five account for 59 percent of arrests made for Crime Index property offenses, and nearly half of the arrests made for violent Index crimes. (Sykes and Cullen, 1992:112)

Social class. The bulk of the people processed by the criminal justice system for committing street crimes are the undereducated, the poor, the unemployed, or those working at low-level, alienating jobs. There are several explanations for this relationship. First, the kinds of crimes listed by the FBI are those of the lower classes (white-collar crimes, for example, are omitted). Second, the police and others in the criminal justice system assume that lower-class persons are more likely to be criminals. Thus, they place more personnel in lower-class neighborhoods, which ensures that they will find more criminal activity. Third, economic deprivation may induce people to turn to crime to ease their situations. The evidence is clear that direct interpersonal types of crime (robbery, larceny, assault)

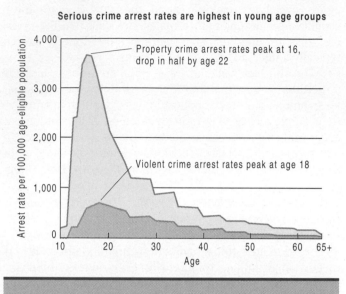

Figure 15.2 Crime arrest rates and age, 1983–85

Source: U.S. Department of Justice, *Report to the Nation on Crime and Justice,* 2nd ed., (Washington, D.C.: U.S. Department fo Justice, 1988), p. 42.

are committed disproportionately by members of the poor. In the words of criminologist Elliott Currie,

> brutal conditions breed brutal behavior. To believe otherwise requires us to argue that the experience of being confined to the mean and precarious depths of the American economy has *no* serious consequences for personal character or social behavior. But this not only misreads the evidence; it also trivializes the genuine social disaster wrought by the extremes of economic inequality we have tolerated in the United States. (Currie, 1985:160)

Social class is also significant at the upper strata of the stratification system. White-collar crimes are committed by those in lofty occupational and political roles. Embezzlement, computer crimes, bribery, manipulation of the stock market, land swindles, and the like involves people at the other end of the social hierarchy. The irony is that while white-collar, political, and corporate crimes do much more harm than do the crimes by the poor, crimes by the poor are seen as *the crime problem.*

Race. People labeled as criminals in the United States are disproportionately people of color—Blacks, Latinos, and Native Americans. The official statistics indicate a Black-to-White crime ratio of over 3 to 1 for all Index crimes and about 5 to 1 for violent crimes (reported in Sykes and Cullen, 1992:110).

Although racial minorities have more contact with the criminal justice system than Whites do, this statistic does not mean that race causes crime. Many crimes on the street are committed by racial minorities because the social conditions of unemployment, poverty, and racism fall more heavily on them. Especially in urban centers there appear to be more and more Blacks living in poverty, jobless, and without hope—"a tangle of social circumstances conducive to high rates of violence" (Sykes and Cullen, 1992:111). Moreover, we should remember that the official statistics reflect *arrest* rates and are not necessarily a true indication of actual rates. The bias of the system against the poor and especially the poor minorities makes the likelihood of their arrest and conviction greater than for well-to-do Whites, as we see in the section on the criminal justice system.

Categories of Crime

The *Uniform Crime Reports* of the FBI focus on traditional types of crime, which tend to be concentrated among the young and the poor. The focus on traditional crime ignores other types that may actually be more costly to society in terms of lives and property—organized, white-collar, corporate, and political crime. Another type of crime—moral order crime—is significant in enforcement costs but not necessarily in human costs.

Traditional street crimes.   Serious crimes against property or violence against people are what many people consider to be the whole of crime. People accused of these crimes are ones who typically clog the courts and jails.

In evaluating this type of crime, we need to consider two types of offenders. One type is habitual offenders, who, for whatever reason, continue their criminal patterns. For all seven major traditional crime categories, the majority of those arrested are repeaters. Obviously, the career criminal must be converted to a new way of life, to a legitimate career that offers all the gratifications received through criminality, if rehabilitation is to be successful.

The other type is one-time-only criminals (accidental or incidental criminals). Liberals maintain that such people should not be punished harshly, for that would be counterproductive. As Pearl puts it,

> The act is idiosyncratic to a life and regardless of the heinousness of the act, there is little to be gained from either punishment or treatment of the offender. Social policy should provide for restitution, if appropriate. Social policy must not encourage accidental criminals to careers in crime (which often happens when such a criminal is stigmatized, forced to associate with career criminals, and is prevented from returning to noncriminal ways). (Pearl, 1977:50)

Conservatives, on the other hand, would argue for swift and severe punishment to deter the person from a life of crime and to reinforce the notion in the rest of society that crime does not pay. Again, to quote Pearl,

> conservatives are moralists with pessimistic notions about *other* human beings. They want criminals to be punished for transgressions. In essence, conservatives propose more support for local police and certain and severe punishment for law violators. Conservatives believe that crime prospers because we are encouraged to commit crime by the shackles put on police by lenient judges, by "bleeding-heart liberal" parole and probation officers, etc. Conservatives believe most people need laws to deter them from misdeeds. Conservative policy, then, is coercive policy. (Pearl, 1977:48)

Crimes against the moral order.   To enforce the morality of the majority, legislation makes criminal certain acts deemed offensive. Violations of these laws are

moral order crimes. Examples of this type of crime are gambling, recreational drug use, and sex between consenting adults. Sometimes these acts that violate the moral order are called **victimless crimes** because even though they may offend the majority they do not harm other people. The argument for such laws is that the state has a right to preserve the morals of its citizens in the interest of promoting social stability and consensus.

Should an individual have the right to choose among alternative forms of behavior without fear of social sanction if that behavior does not harm other people? The answer to this question is not as unqualified as it may seem; many so-called victimless crimes in fact hurt other people at least indirectly. The family members of an alcoholic, drug addict, or compulsive gambler are affected both materially and emotionally by his or her habit. Overindulgence in alcohol or drugs increases the probability of automobile accidents. Prostitution is a victimless crime, except that some people are unwillingly forced to become prostitutes and to live in servitude to a pimp.

A fundamental problem with legislating morality, aside from putting limitations on individual freedoms, is that it labels people as "criminals" on the basis of the tastes of those in power. Thus, secondary deviance may result, not because someone harmed another but because his or her act was presumed by powerful

ANOTHER SOCIETY, ANOTHER WAY

HOLLAND'S TOLERANCE OF DEVIANCE

Holland. Every conservative's nightmare come true. Legal prostitution. Coffee houses that sell marijuana to teen-agers. Free abortions on request. Free needles for heroin addicts. Special rooms for prisoners to conduct liaisons with outside partners, even of the same sex. Euthanasia in hospitals.

To Americans, such policies represent a moral breakdown. They are a prescription for social anarchy: promiscuity, drug addiction, family breakdown, AIDS. To Amsterdam Judge Frits Ruter, such policies are "above all, pragmatic and un-dogmatic." You cannot solve social problems "by making them taboo," he insists.

The Dutch don't drive their human weaknesses underground. Amsterdam's Utopia coffeehouse, where you can choose among 10 kinds of hashish and grass for about $6 a gram, is five doors from the neighborhood police station. The Royal Symphony Hall backs into a red light district that houses not only prostitutes in well-lit windows, but also sex shops that would make Hugh Hefner blush.

The minister of justice of Holland's conservative government explains: The aim is to "prevent as much as possible a situation in which more harm is caused by criminal proceedings than by the (activity) itself."

Legalization allows the government much more flexibility than criminalization. Prostitutes must undergo regular health examinations. One result is an astonishingly low rate of AIDS infection: less than 1 percent, compared to 30–40 percent among America's illegal but probably equally plentiful hooker population. Clean needles for intravenous drug users slow AIDS transmission among a group that now accounts for half the AIDS population in New York. Allowing prisoners sex with loved ones reduces prison tension.

As for drugs, allowing the sale of marijuana gives the government much more credibility when it warns the young about the dangers of hard drugs.

Indeed, says the Dutch secretary of drug policy, "Cannabis used to be the symbol of the youth culture—it was attractive because it was forbidden. Our aim was to turn it into an unsensational item." It worked. The proportion of Dutch teen-agers using marijuana has dropped substantially. It is a fraction of U.S. use. Crack is virtually non-existent.

All Dutch schools teach sex education. A year's worth of birth control pills costs about $10. Yet Dutch girls are no more sexually active than American girls. And 90 percent of those teen-agers who are active use contraceptives. Holland's teen-age pregnancy rate is one-seventh that of America's. American teen-agers have 12 to 14 times more abortions than Dutch teen-agers.

The Dutch treat prostitutes, drug addicts, teen-age pot smokers and the terminally ill with respect. Not surprisingly,

others to be harmful to them (see "Another Society, Another Way" about Holland).

The detection, arrest, and prosecution of victimless criminals is an enormous and expensive task. More than half the arrests and roughly 80 percent of the police work in the United States is related to the regulation of private morals (alcohol abuse, homosexuality, pornography, juvenile runaways, drug use, prostitution, gambling, and the like). Gore Vidal, the successful novelist, argues that such crimes should be abolished:

> Let us remove from the statute books all laws that have to do with *private* morals—what are called victimless crimes. If a man or woman wants to be a prostitute that is his or her affair. It is no business of the state what we do with our bodies sexually. Obviously, laws will remain on the books for the prevention of rape and the abuse of children. . . . Let us end the vice squad. . . . Let us make gambling legal. Those who want to lose their money gambling should have every right to do so. The principal objectors to legalized gambling are the Mafia and the police. *They* will lose money. (Vidal, 1975:63)

Although Vidal's solutions may be too facile, he does raise a number of interesting points. If these private acts were legalized, then the police and the courts would be free for other, more important duties. Formerly illicit activities could

respect breeds responsibility. The addict uses a clean needle. The prostitute does not transmit disease. The teen-ager uses birth control. Doctors assist a patient's death only after a long relationship with that patient.

Where does this sense of mutual respect and collective responsibility come from? Historian Simon Schama looks to Dutch history in "The Embarrassment of Riches." In the 1600s, tiny Holland was the most prosperous nation on Earth. Riches bred a "collective conscience" that demanded generosity for the needy and tolerance for those with different religions and different habits. Obligations to community, to society came first.

Today the Dutch continue that 300-year tradition. They know the most fertile breeding ground for irresponsible behavior is the slum. Thus they offer the world's most comprehensive social support programs. Medical care is free; child care plentiful. Unemployment insurance is nearly forever.

Amsterdam suffers a housing problem incomprehensible to American city planners. Sufficient housing exists for those of modest means, but there's not enough for the rich.

Such generosity of spirit and purse has not undermined Dutch prosperity. They live longer than

Americans. Their economy is robust; their businesses fiercely competitive.

This prosperous country of 14 million has much to teach us, for tolerance has never been an American trait. We have a long history of demanding moral purity of our neighbors and eagerly locking them up if they transgress. We rely on force to solve our social problems, not wisdom. Why we do so is up to the historians and sociologists to ponder. That we do so seems not to be in question. Today America imprisons a larger proportion of its citizens than any country except South Africa, and President Bush now vows to double the number of federal prisoners.

The Dutch watch our descent into social anarchy in amazement. They cannot understand why a nation would willfully destroy itself to control its citizens' personal behavior. After seeing how well tolerance and mutual respect work, neither can I.

Source: David Morris, "Tolerance, Respect Work for Dutch," *Des Moines Register* (October 12, 1989): 3A. David Morris is co-director of the Washington DC-based Institute for Local Self-Reliance.

become legitimate businesses providing tax revenues to local and state governments. Most important, organized crime, which now acquires most of its income from providing illegal goods and services, would no longer be able to hide its investments and profits. Thus, laws against victimless crimes are indirectly responsible for maintaining organized crime.

Moral order crimes also contribute to the corruption of the police and courts. Although many police officers are unwilling to accept bribes from murderers and thieves, they may accept them from the perpetrators of victimless crimes, using the justification that they believe these crimes are harmless and impossible to control anyway. This rationale opens the way for people involved in organized crime to buy protection for their illicit activities.

White-collar crime.   The public, influenced by the media and the FBI reports, focuses its fears on traditional street crimes such as assault and robbery. Even though these are legitimate concerns, crime of the street variety (typically by the young, poor minority person) is much *less* significant in cost and social disruption than are **white-collar crimes** those committed by middle-class and upper-middle-class people in their business and social activities (such as theft of company goods, embezzlement, tax evasion, forgery, passing bad checks, the illicit copying of computer software, movies, and music, and fraudulent use of credit cards, automatic teller machines, and telephones).

Most people have little knowledge of the cost of white-collar crime to the average citizen. As examples, telephone marketing swindlers cheat U.S. consumers out of an estimated $15 billion annually; the "underground economy (i.e., people providing goods and services for cash) avoid paying $200 to $300 billion yearly in taxes; employees embezzle and pilfer an estimated $10 billion from their employers; and time theft by employees (i.e., faked illness, excessive breaks, and long lunches) costs U.S. businesses as much as $200 billion annually.

These cost estimates, however, understate the gap. Even though street crimes sometimes go unreported, there is an even greater reluctance to report white-collar crimes. Also, because many white-collar crimes are attempts at fraud, they are often extremely difficult to detect. Moreover, the victims are often embarrassed at their naivete in having been bilked; whereas if they are victims of a street crime, however, they would not be to blame.

Thus, although we know that white-collar crimes are expensive and extensive, we do not know by how much. Just how many respectable people are guilty of misrepresenting the facts on their income tax returns? How many employees steal from their employers? How many business people deliberately mislead their customers? The answers to these questions, if known, might be staggering, and they would clearly undermine many theories of why people turn to criminal activity.

As we have seen, the criminal activities of the relatively well-to-do are widespread and expensive, but U.S. society is remarkably lenient on such wrongdoers when they are caught. Moreover, those sentenced to prison serve much less time if convicted for white-collar crimes.

Corporate crime.   Business enterprises can also be guilty of crimes, which are known as *corporate crimes*. The list of illegal acts committed in the name of corporate good includes fraudulent advertising, unfair labor practices, noncompliance with government regulations regarding employee safety, price-fixing agreements, stock manipulation, copyright infringement, theft of industrial secrets, marketing of adulterated or mislabeled food or drugs, bribery, swindles, and selling faulty merchandise. The magnitude of such crimes far surpasses the human and economic costs from other types of crime. Here are some representative examples of corporate crime:

- Corporations may continue to produce and sell a product known to be faulty and dangerous. General Motors did so with the Corvair, as did Ford with the Pinto and Audi with its automatic transmission 5000s. Similarly, Firestone continued to manufacture its Firestone 500 radial tire after being warned by its director of development that "we are making an inferior quality radial tire which will subject us to belt-edge separation at high mileage." Despite this memo and others, Firestone made 24 million of these tires, which resulted in at least 41 deaths (*Time,* 1979a). In another infamous case, A. H. Robins sold an intrauterine birth control device—the Dalkon Shield—that caused many miscarriages, made wearers highly susceptible to pelvic inflammatory disease, and was an ineffective contraceptive. After the Dalkon Shield was banned in the United States, Robins continued to sell it abroad. Moreover, Robins deliberately suppressed information about the ineffectiveness and the health dangers of the product (Hausknecht, 1987). (Further examples are detailed in the Observation on corporate crime.)
- Corporations may pollute the environment. For example, the Adolph Coors Co., the company that advertises its beer as coming from pure Rocky Mountain water, paid $650,000 to settle criminal and civil charges that cancer-causing pollutants were pumped from two contaminated springs and dumped illegally into Clear Creek (Newcomer, 1990).
- Corporations may engage in fraud. For example, the government agency in charge of investigating and resolving the Savings and Loan scandal referred more than 1200 cases to the Justice Department for possible criminal prosecution for fraud (Associated Press, 1990d). Another form of fraud involves altering the accounting and falsifying reports. MiniScribe Corporation, a computer-disk-drive company, over a three-year period reported spectacular sales gains (thirteen consecutive record-breaking quarters), resulting in the company's stock quintupling in value in just two years. The problem, however, was that the incredible sales gains had been fabricated. Similar fraudulent schemes have occurred among other companies as well (e.g., Ashton-Tate, DSC Corporation, and Datapoint) (Zipser, 1989).
- Corporations are sometimes guilty of willful negligence in providing for the safety of their employees. For example, the Utah Power and Light Company was cited for 34 safety violations in one of its coal mines. This mine had an underground fire in 1984 that killed 27 miners, and 9 of the violations were linked directly to the ignition and spread of the fire (Franklin, 1987). Similarly, Chrysler was fined $1.5 million for 811 health and safety violations, including the willful exposure of workers to lead and arsenic (Yancey, 1987).
- Corporate policies may discriminate against certain groups in hiring and promotion. A number of corporations—for example, General Motors, AT&T, and Libby-Owens-Ford—have been found guilty of such practices.
- Corporations may misrepresent their products fraudulently. In 1987 Chrysler pleaded no contest to federal charges that it sold several thousand vehicles as new even though they had been driven with disconnected odometers by

company employees. Years earlier, General Motors was found guilty of selling Buicks with Chevrolet engines. On the nutrition front, in 1987 the Beech-Nut Nutrition Corporation pleaded guilty to 215 counts charging that it had mislabeled products purporting to be apple juice for babies with the intent to defraud and mislead the public (Buder, 1987).

■ Corporations may bribe government officials in order to receive special treatment in licensing, zoning, taxation, and the letting of contracts. In New York City, for example, "every $100 million that the city awards in noncompetitive contracts is likely to yield $5 million a year in bribes" (Nossiter, 1986:546). Corporations also bribe foreign politicians in order to receive special favors. In recent years Exxon, Gulf Oil, Mobil Oil, Ashland Oil, Northrop, Lockheed, United Brands, and others have been found to have paid millions to obtain

OBSERVATION

CORPORATE CRIME AND VIOLENCE

In his book, *Agent Orange on Trial,* Peter H. Schuck, a professor of law at Yale University, makes the following observation about the Ford Motor Co. and its decision to market the Ford Pinto—a car with a fuel system that allegedly killed and injured hundreds of Pinto passengers: "Here, as in other such cases, nothing more malicious or reckless on the manufacturer's part was shown than a calculated, conventional decision to design a product in a way that traded safety off against cost and other marketing and engineering considerations."

"Nothing more malicious or reckless . . . than a . . . conventional decision . . . that traded safety off against cost. . . . " The words must ring harshly in the ears of the surviving victims of Agent Orange, the Dalkon Shield, Asbestos, Minamata Disease, Thalidomide, Infant Formula, and Bhopal. In these cases, . . . very calculated and very conventional decisions traded safety for cost. Millions of people were injured and thousands were killed.

For Schuck and others, such "conventional" decisions do not entail a degree of malice or recklessness that demands criminal action, nor do most prosecutors consider criminal prosecution. But the carnage wrought by the criminogenic actions of corporations and their executives is immense.

Over the next 30 years, 240,000 people—8,000 per year, about one every hour—will die from asbestos-related cancer.

Of the 2.8 million U.S. soldiers who served in Vietnam, 40,000 may eventually become ill or die from the effects of Agent Orange and other toxic chemicals dumped on Vietnam and these soldiers may produce 2,000 children with deformities.

The Dalkon Shield intrauterine device seriously injured tens of thousands of women.

One million infants worldwide died in 1986 because they were bottle-fed instead of breast-fed.

In 1984, 2,000 to 5,000 people were killed and 200,000 injured, 30,000 to 40,000 of them seriously, after a Union Carbide affiliate's factory in Bhopal, India released a deadly gas over the town.

In Minamata, a small fishing village in Japan, Chisso Corporation, a chemical company, deposited mercury wastes in Minamata Bay that killed and injured thousands.

Thalidomide, marketed primarily in West Germany, England, and Japan as a sedative, created 8,000 severely deformed babies, some born with shortened or no limbs.

Each of these cases have their own set of disturbing facts, but taken together, they raise an issue of fundamental importance: Why are those responsible for such massive devastation not criminally prosecuted? (Only in the case of Minamata was a successful criminal prosecution brought—and 30 years after the ravages of the disease first appeared, that conviction is on appeal.)

reductions in taxes and to receive exclusive contracts and the like from foreign countries.
- Monopolistic practices allow for excessive prices. A classic example occurred in the heavy-electrical-equipment industry during the 1950s. Twenty-nine companies conspired to fix prices. The government estimated that the loss to the public during a seven-year period was $1.7 billion (the companies were fined $1.8 million, *which they were allowed to write off as a business expense,* and seven company officials were sentenced to thirty days in jail).
- Through intense lobbying and strategic gifts to politicians, corporations may receive lenient government treatment but harm consumers. During the Reagan administration, for example, a Task Force on Regulatory Relief, with Vice President Bush as chairman, was set up to ease the burden on business (there

These corporations and their executives took actions that put thousands at risk and often had direct and deadly consequences. But for too long a double standard has insulated them from criminal sanctions that surely would be imposed had they committed such acts in a non-corporate context.

Reckless disregard of the risks posed by multinational industry demands swift criminal prosecution. In the United States, local and state prosecutors have begun bringing criminal homicide prosecutions against smaller corporations in connection with work and product-related deaths. The obstacles confronting prosecutors contemplating criminal charges against large corporations and multinationals, however, are formidable. Few are in a position to take the political risks involved in bringing such prosecutions. In one notable case, a Republican prosecutor in Indiana decided in 1980 to bring reckless homicide charges against the Ford Motor Company in connection with the fiery deaths of three teenage girls who died when their Ford Pinto exploded after it was hit from behind. Ford, one of the world's largest multinationals, brought significant resources to bear against the local prosecutor, who relied on law students for research. Ford outmaneuvered the prosecution to gain a not guilty verdict. . . .

Traditionally, criminal homicide laws have been the jurisdiction of the states. But corporate crime and violence transcend state borders. The Dalkon Shield, manufactured by the Virginia-based A. H. Robins, killed and injured women throughout the United States and around the world. A chemical plant operated by an Indian subsidiary of Union Carbide released 40 tons of toxic gas and caused the deaths of thousands of people in Bhopal, India. Federal and international criminal law must be restructured with an eye toward multinational corporate criminals. The U.S. Congress could begin this process by passing a tough federal homicide and reckless endangerment statute. Only federal resources can counter those available to multinational corporate defendants.

And if it is true, as Professor Schuck believes, that cases similar to the ones profiled in this issue represent "nothing more malicious or reckless . . . than a conventional decision . . . that traded safety off against cost," then perhaps the conventional has become criminal. If that is the case, then it is time to change the way corporations do business. A good place to begin is by punishing those corporations and their executives who injure and kill others.

Source: Russell Mokhiber, "Corporate Crime and Violence," *Multinational Monitor* Vol. 8, p. 4. Used by permission. This article is reprinted from the *Multinational Monitor,* (April 1987). *Multinational Monitor* is a monthly news magazine published by Essential Information, Inc., P.O. Box 19405, Washington, D.C. 20036. $22 individual.

was a similar commission under President Bush, with Vice President Quayle as chairman). This probusiness task force represented the Republican administration, which had been supported handsomely by the business community (see Chapter 2). Ralph Nader's public interest organization, Public Citizen, issued a report that charged that this task force

> had undermined a system of health and safety standards that has taken America over eighty years to achieve. The record is brutal, indeed. At least 40,000 deaths and one million injuries can be traced to the Administration's delay in requiring air bags and automatic safety belts in cars. Hundreds of thousands of infants were fed nutritionally deficient formula while Bush and the OMB [Office of Management and Budget] delayed rules requiring testing of infant formula, and thousands of babies and young children suffered the serious and often fatal Reye's syndrome disease while the Administration stonewalled rules to place warning labels on aspirin products linked to Reye's syndrome in children. (reported in Mintz, 1991:31)

These examples make two points. First, the goal of profit is so central to capitalistic enterprises that many corporate decisions are made without consideration for the consequences to people. But not only are entrepreneurs indifferent to people; society is also essentially indifferent to certain offenders. The punishments meted out to individual white-collar criminals and especially to corporate officials are incommensurate with their misdeeds.

Political crime.   Any illegal act intended to influence the political system is a political crime. The operant word in this definition is *illegal*. Is it illegal to disobey unjust laws such as laws supporting racial segregation? Is it illegal to oppose tyranny? If the answer to these questions is yes, then Martin Luther King, Jr., and George Washington must be considered political criminals. The definition given above assumes that the political system is always right and that any attempt to change it is wrong. Though antithetical to the heritage of the early American colonists and the Declaration of Independence, such thinking is typical of how those in power interpret any attempt to change the existing political system.

Another way to conceive of political crime is to concentrate on the deviance of the people in power. One example of this type of political crime is the imprisonment or harassment by the powerful of those who act against established authority. Such acts include the jailing of Martin Luther King, Jr., the FBI's infiltration of dissident groups, the Internal Revenue Service's intimidation of people on President Nixon's "enemies list," and the punishment of people involved in providing housing, transportation, and jobs to refugees escaping political repression in Guatemala and El Salvador (the Sanctuary Movement).

The assumption that governments can commit crimes leads to a variety of possible illicit activities. Some examples are the involvement in covert actions to overthrow legitimate governments, such as the Reagan administration's policy to aid the contra effort in Nicaragua; the U.S. attack on Panama in order to capture its leader, Manuel Noriega; the suppression of popular revolts in countries favorable to the United States; secrecy, lying, and deceit; the use of people as unwilling and unknowing guinea pigs in medical experiments; and war crimes (for an elaboration on each of these types, see Simon and Eitzen 1993:251–286).

Organized crime.   Organized crime is a business operation that seeks profit by supplying illegal goods and services such as drugs, prostitution, pornography, gambling, loan sharking, the sale of stolen goods, cigarette bootlegging, and even the disposal of hazardous wastes. In short, persons can and do organize to provide what others want even if it is illegal. In fact, the illegality of what people want ensures that someone will supply the goods or service because the profits are so high.

Several characteristics of organized crime serve to perpetuate it. First, organized crime supplies illegal goods and services that are in great demand. So, one reason for the continued existence of organized crime is that it fills a need. If victimless crimes were decriminalized, organized crime would be left with products and services that could be easily and cheaply supplied by legitimate sources, and its profits and existence might be eliminated.

A second characteristic of organized crime is that it depends on the corruption of police and government officials for survival and continued profitability. Bribery, campaign contributions, delivery of votes, and other favors are used to influence police personnel, government attorneys, judges, media personnel, city council members, and legislators.

Another characteristic of organized crime is its use of violence to enforce conformity with the organization. There are strict rules for conduct and means of enforcing those rules. Individuals who cheat or fail to meet their obligations are disciplined severely. Violence is also used to eliminate competition. When rival organizations vie for the monopoly of a geographic territory or the distribution of a particular service or product, the struggle is often extremely violent.

Finally, organized crime is structured to ensure efficiency. This organization is not just composed of members of a criminal society. There are criminals, of

This is John Gotti, reputed head of a crime family. Crime families, however are not the only perpetrators of organized crime. The coordination, production, and distribution of illegal goods and services is carried out by individuals in government, law enforcement, banking and other institutions.

course, but many of these persons are linked with legitimate members of society as well. Together, the criminal and legitimate elements combine to form networks within cities, regions, and even nations. William Chambliss's field study of organized crime in Seattle led him to conclude that

> there is . . . a loose affiliation of businessmen, politicians, union leaders, and law enforcement officials who cooperate to coordinate the production and distribution of illegal goods and services, for which there is a substantial consumer demand. (Chambliss, 1978:151)

We have seen that there are a number of different types of crimes and criminals. However, the laws and their enforcement apparatus selectively focus on traditional street crimes. The social reaction to these crimes is the subject of the remainder of this chapter.

The Unjust System of Justice

Justice refers to the use of authority to uphold what is lawful in a completely impartial and fair manner. Even though fairness is the goal of the U.S. system of justice, it is far from realized. The law itself, the administration of the law by the police and judges, and the prisons all express bias against certain categories of people. To document this assertion, we must examine the criminal justice system from the labeling perspective, which focuses on the societal reactions to deviation.

This perspective has two emphases: (1) the social processes that create norms, thereby labeling those who behave contrary to the norms as deviants, and (2) the negative reactions (the stigma and segregation) directed at these people, which in turn generate further deviance. From this perspective, deviance is created and sustained at three levels. (The following discussion is adapted from Schur, 1971, 1973.) The first level is that of collective rule making. The rules of society create deviance. What is deviant varies from society to society and from one period to another within a society. Deviance is therefore not inherent in an act itself but only in an act that violates a rule. To assess the fairness of a judicial system, we must know whether its rules are fair. Most important is the question: To what extent do powerful interest groups impose their will in the creation of the laws?

The second level of creating and sustaining deviance is that of interpersonal relations. Becker has suggested that deviance is not a characteristic of individuals but, rather, is a status conferred on the person by an audience or series of audiences (Becker, 1963:9). In a number of studies researchers have determined that many people at various times are involved in serious acts of deviance, yet only a relatively small proportion are labeled deviant. In other words, something other than the commission of the deviant act must differentiate the deviant(s) and those who consistently work to disadvantage certain categories of people. Or is the process impersonal?

Finally, the third level is the formal organizational processing of deviants. Here, the focus is on the public and private agencies that process the wayward—the courts, prisons, and mental hospitals. With reference to those accused of criminal behavior, we need to determine how attorneys are assigned, bail set, juries selected, sentences imposed, and parole granted. Is there a bias at each of these levels that works to the disadvantage of certain types of people? What are the consequences of being legally processed as a criminal? Does the process itself promote the deviance it is created to suppress?

This section, then, examines all phases of the system of criminal justice. Are all people accorded equal treatment under the law? Are the police fair? Are the procedures commonly used in the courts free of bias? As a nation, the United States has always pledged equal and therefore fair treatment to all its residents. This section documents that the reality is far removed from the ideal. There is a systematic bias in the criminal justice system that disproportionately labels members of the underclass as deviants.

The Laws

Of all the requirements for a just system, the most fundamental is a body of nondiscriminatory laws. Many criminal laws are the result of public consensus as to what kinds of behaviors are a menace and should be punished (such as murder, rape, and theft). The laws devised to make these acts illegal and to specify the extent of punishment for violators are nondiscriminatory, because they do not single out a particular social category as the target.*

Other laws, however, do discriminate, because they result from the exertions of special interests to translate their objectives into public policy. In contrast, some segments of society (such as the poor, minorities, youth, renters, and debtors) rarely have access to the lawmaking process and therefore often find the laws unfairly aimed at them. Vagrancy, for example, is really a crime that only the poor can commit.

One example of this interest-group approach to the law is the pre-Civil War and Jim Crow legislation in the South. The majority created laws to keep the races separate and unequal. Here are a few specific examples of the historical bias of the law against Blacks (Burns, 1973:156–166):

- The law played a critical role in defining and sanctioning slavery. For instance, the law made slavery hereditary and a lifetime condition.
- The slave codes denied Blacks the rights to bring lawsuits or to testify against a White person.
- Jim Crow laws codified the customs and uses of segregation.
- After Reconstruction, the grandfather clause, the literacy test, and the poll tax were all legal devices designed to keep Blacks from voting.
- In the nineteenth century the law allowed only White men to sit on juries.

Not only is the formation of the law political; so, too, is its administration. At every stage in the processing of criminals, authorities make choices based on personal bias, pressures from the powerful, and the constraints of the status quo. Examples of the political character of law administration include attempts by the powerful to coerce other people to their view of morality, resulting in laws against homosexuality, pornography, drug use, and gambling; pressure exerted by the powerful on the authorities to crack down on certain kinds of violators, especially individuals and groups who are disruptive (protestors); pressure exerted to keep certain crimes from public view (embezzlement, stock fraud, the Iran-Contra scandal); pressure to protect the party in power, elected officials, and even the

* Although these laws in themselves are not discriminatory, the remainder of this chapter demonstrates that the administration of them is.

police department; and any effort to protect and preserve the status quo. Hartjen has explained why we must conclude that the administration of justice is inherently political:

> Unless one is willing to assume that law-enforcement agents can apply some magic formula to gauge the opinions of the public they serve, unless one is willing to assume that citizens unanimously agree on what laws are to be enforced and how enforcement is to be carried out, unless one is willing to assume that blacks, the poor, urbanites, and the young are actually more criminalistic than everyone else, it must be concluded, at least, that discriminatory law enforcement is a result of differences in power and that actual decisions as to which and whose behavior is criminal are expressions of this power. One need only ask himself why some laws, such as those protecting the consumer from fraud, go largely unenforced while the drug addict, for example, is pursued with a paranoiac passion. (Hartjen, 1978:13)

The Police

Formal law enforcement policy begins with the police. They decide whether a law has been broken. They interpret and judge what behavior is "disorderly," how much noise constitutes a "public nuisance," when a quarrel becomes a "criminal assault," when protest becomes illegitimate, and what constitutes "public drunkenness." Their authority to interpret these questions suggests that the police have great decisional latitude. Unlike other agencies in the criminal justice process, the police in their work often deal with their clients in isolation. Their decisions are rarely subject to review by higher authorities. As Skolnick has said, "police work constitutes the most secluded part of an already secluded system and therefore offers the greatest opportunity for arbitrary behavior" (Skolnick, 1966:14).

Given the great discretionary powers of the individual police, one must determine whether police officers as a group tend to hold particular biases that affect their perceptions and actions. Several characteristics of the job and the types of people attracted to it suggest that certain biases may prevail among this occupational category.

The job itself causes police personnel to develop a distinctive way of perceiving the world. Foremost is that they are given the authority to enforce the law. They have power, even the ultimate power of legitimate force, at their disposal to uphold the law. As authorities sworn to uphold the law, police support the status quo. Naturally, then, they find people who defile the flag or otherwise protest against the system abhorrent.

Second, the danger inherent in their occupation promotes a particular world view among the police. The element of danger tends to make them suspicious of behavior that is nonconforming or otherwise unusual. In the interests of self-defense, they tend to assume the worst of people they believe to be dangerous (minorities, protestors, drug users).

The police also tend to be socially isolated. Because they have actual power to punish other citizens, police personnel are the objects of hostility for many, but especially for minority group members. This hostility is manifested in epithets, ("pigs"), abusive language, spitting, and other forms of harassment. The result, of course, is that the police, even those relatively free of prejudice toward minorities, tend to become hostile themselves over time. The harassment directed toward the police also increases the threat of danger to them. The result is a self-fulfilling prophecy: the police, harassed by victimized categories in societies, in turn harass their tormentors, which leads to charges of police brutality and the justification to be hostile toward them.

This characterization presupposes that the police are relatively free of prejudice, at least at the beginning of their career. This assumption, however, is not always true. Police tend to be recruited from the lower-middle and upper-lower social classes of the community. Research shows that police recruits hold attitudes typical of their working-class origins (respect for authority, belief in the status quo, and hostility toward certain racial and ethnic groups).

In sum, the pressures on the police and the type of people attracted to that role ensure that the incumbents will tend to be politically conservative. Their task is to defend the status quo. Social innovators, therefore, would not find police work compatible with their goals. Moreover, police personnel may harbor negative attitudes toward minorities or be ignorant of the social bases for the hostility of minorities toward themselves and other authorities.

The Judicial Process

This section examines the process by which lawbreakers are prosecuted, convicted, and sentenced and, in particular, the fairness or unfairness of this process in determining guilt and imposing punishment. Given that the courts deal only with those whom the police arrest, clearly the process begins already biased. The question is, do the courts increase the degree of unfairness or not? A related question involves the operation of the principle that individuals brought before the courts are presumed to be innocent: How great is the gap between principle and practice?

To answer these questions, let us examine the formal procedures of the system of justice for the violation of a serious crime. The police arrest the probable offender and bring him or her before a magistrate. The magistrate examines the evidence and decides whether to allow the alleged offender to be free on bail. The case is then turned over to a prosecuting attorney, who formally charges the defendant. This charge is subject to review by a judge at a preliminary hearing or by a grand jury. If the defendant pleads "not guilty," then he or she comes to trial, where the facts of the case are argued by the prosecuting and defense attorneys before a judge and jury. If the jury finds the defendant guilty, he or she is sentenced by the judge to a term in prison or to a term of probation.

The magistrate and the setting of bail. The primary functions of the magistrate are to inform defendants of their right to counsel, to assign them counsel if so requested, to set a date for a preliminary hearing, and to set bail. In the last procedure the magistrate exercises considerable discretion.

Bail is the posting of money by the accused to guarantee that he or she will be present at the time of trial. The Constitution provides the right to bail in noncapital cases. Bail allows accused people to stay out of jail, thereby retaining their family, community, and work responsibilities; most important, it allows them a chance to investigate and prepare their cases.

Several practices in setting bail, however, undermine the principle of treating all people fairly. The primary problem is that the amount of bail to be posted is left to the discretion of the magistrate, who may set high bail to "teach the accused a lesson" or to "protect the community." Magistrates have often taken such an approach when the defendants have been political protestors and minority group members. This practice violates the Eighth Amendment, which specifically forbids the setting of excessive bail; moreover, the concept of preventive detention contradicts the presumption of innocence that is supposed to be at the heart of the judicial process.

The setting of bail is also unfair because magistrates tend to determine the amount of bail by the type of crime alleged instead of by the accused's ability to pay. Moreover, the accused or their families typically obtain bail money from professional bondspersons, who receive 5 to 10 percent of the total as their fee. If the bail were set at $10,000 for everyone accused of a felony and the accused had to pay a bondsperson a fee of $1000, clearly the accused who were poor would suffer the greatest hardship.

The obvious result of the system of setting bail is that the poor remain in jail and the wealthy are released, either because the latter have their own money or bail or because bail bondspersons consider them better risks. This result highlights another problem: the power of bail bondspersons to decide whom they will bond and whom they will not. Of course, the poor are considered more risky. Moreover, bondspersons may refuse to grant bail as a "favor" to the police.

Thus, the biggest problem with the bail-setting practice as it now operates is that it tends to imprison the poor. Time spent in jail before trial varies by locality and by the backlog of pending cases. In some jurisdictions defendants who cannot make bail spend as much as eighteen months in jail awaiting trial. Clearly, this situation violates the principle that the accused person is presumed innocent until proven guilty, for it provides punishment before conviction. And the difference between those who languish in jail before their trial and those who are free is money.

Plea bargaining.   Fewer than 10 percent of the people charged with crimes ever go to trial. The thousands of cases that bypass the trial process do so because either the charges are dropped or the people accused plead guilty to the original or lesser charges. The latter event is called **plea bargaining** because the defendants bargain away their right to a trial in return for their guilty plea and a more lenient punishment than if they were found guilty of the original charge. Plea bargaining has become the rule, not the exception, in the disposition of criminal cases in the United States.

There are many pressures on defendants, lawyers, prosecutors, and judges to encourage plea bargaining. Foremost is the overwhelming caseload facing police, prosecutors, and judges. Without guilty pleas to speed defendants through the system, the criminal justice process could not function because of impossibly crowded courts. One obvious solution is for judges to encourage guilty pleas by implementing the agreements negotiated by prosecutors and defense counsel. Similarly, prosecutors encourage plea bargaining because of their large caseloads. In addition, prosecutors must have a high conviction rate, and plea bargaining achieves this goal at relatively little expense.

Defendants are pressured in several ways to plea bargain. People who are assigned as defense counsel (about half of all felony cases) typically encourage their clients to "cop a plea." One reason they encourage plea bargaining is that assigned counsel receive little compensation, and they would rather return quickly to their more lucrative private practice. Counsel may also feel that plea bargaining is in the best interests of the client, because it will reduce time spent in jail awaiting trial. District attorneys often force plea bargaining on defendants by charging them with more serious crimes (carrying heavier penalties). Compelling defendants to plea bargain has the effect of reducing caseloads. A defendant who refuses faces the possibility of serving a longer sentence and for a more serious offense. Public defenders also encourage plea bargaining to reduce the burden of their large caseloads on their small investigative staffs. They would rather concentrate their efforts on capital crimes.

There are special pressures on defendants who are poor or of moderate means to plead guilty. They will be unable to bear the expense of a lengthy trial. Moreover, those unable to make bail must await trial in jail. These factors deter poor defendants from insisting on their rights.

Although overcrowding in the courts may make it a necessity, plea bargaining subverts the basic foundations of the system of criminal justice. Contrary to the Bill of Rights, the practice operates on an implicit assumption of guilt. It fails to distinguish between the innocent and the guilty, thus penalizing the innocent and rewarding the guilty. Moreover, because it reduces sentences, plea bargaining erodes the elements of deterrence on which criminal sanctions are based. The procedure especially discriminates against the poor. The poor defendant, already in jail, is pressured by court-appointed counsel to bargain from a position of weakness. In a plea-bargaining situation the need for competent and conscientious counsel outweighs all other factors. Yet it is inevitable that a lawyer receiving a handsome fee for his or her services will be more interested in a client's welfare than will an overburdened and undercompensated court-appointed one.

The adversary system.   An intrinsic feature of the criminal justice system is the concept of adversary roles. In the **adversary system,** the state and the accused engage in a public battle to argue and provide evidence before an impartial judge or jury. In order for this principle to work, the adversaries must be relatively equal in ability, incentive, and resources. One obvious indication that the system is unequal is that the defendant in a criminal trial loses about nine times out of ten. The state has enormous resources (police, crime labs, detectives) with which to build its case. The accused, unless he or she is very wealthy, cannot match the resources and expertise of the state.

Poor defendants are especially disadvantaged by the adversary system. They must accept a court-appointed lawyer and must remain in jail if they cannot make bail. Obviously, they cannot pay for detective work and other things necessary to build their case.

Because lawyers for the poor tend to be unequal in resources and expertise to those for the state, the result is higher rates of conviction and more severe sentences for the poor. The adversary process, then, is a relatively fair one for the defendant with large private resources but very unfair for the indigent defendant.

Trial by jury.   Fundamental to a fair system of criminal justice is the right to a trial by a jury consisting of a representative body of citizens. In practice, however, certain categories of persons are underrepresented on juries: minorities, people not registered to vote, students, and occupational groups low in prestige. The result is that the poor, especially the poor from minority groups, are not judged by a jury of their peers.

Blacks do not fare as well as Whites in civil trials. Verdicts go against Blacks more often than against Whites, both as plaintiffs and defendants. Not only do Blacks lose more often than Whites, but when Blacks do win, they win smaller awards than do White plaintiffs.

The failure of juries to reflect communities is significant because the people least represented are those most apt to challenge community norms. This situation puts a special burden on defendants accused of political crimes (such as anti-war and civil rights protest).

In selecting a jury, the attorneys for the state and the accused attempt to choose jurors who are likely to favor their particular side. The selection process tends to be unfair, however. The state, with enormous investigatory and financial resources at its disposal, may use the police and the FBI to investigate minute details about each prospective juror. Unless the accused is very wealthy, the defense usually decides on the bases of intuition and superficial data.

Trial outcomes are also affected to some extent by whether the case is heard by a jury or a trial judge. The research suggests that juries tend to be more lenient than are judges. This points to another inequity of the judicial system: because jury trials increase the probability of acquittal for defendants, they should be equally available to all people.

Judicial sentencing. Until the 1970s judges were given considerable latitude in determining the exact punishment for convicted criminals. The discretion of the judges was almost without limits, and sometimes the results were very inconsistent from judge to judge and even by a particular judge. This discretionary sen-

"Your Honor, we the jury blame the victim."

Drawing by Dana Fradon; © 1992 The New Yorker Magazine.

tencing permitted individualized justice. In other words, the judge could take into account the peculiar factors of the case in her or his decision. Although this ideal is a worthy one, the procedure resulted in a kind of courtroom roulette, depending on the law in the jurisdiction, the ideology of the judge, media attention, and other factors. Most telling among these other factors are the social class and racial characteristics of the defendants, with a strong tendency for middle-and upper-class Whites to receive lighter sentences than do lower-class Whites and non-Whites.

Beginning in the 1970s there was a movement to curb the discretionary power of judges with the passage of mandatory and determinate sentencing laws. **Mandatory sentencing** forced judges to incarcerate violent and habitual criminals. **Determinate sentencing** means that for a given offense, the judge must impose a sentence (sometimes a fixed sentence and sometimes a range, depending on the state), within the guidelines of the law, depending on the crime and the offenders' past record. Typically, a sentencing commission would be appointed in a state to determine these penalties.

The Correctional System

The thesis of this chapter is that the criminal justice system in the United States is biased against the powerless. The obvious result of this process is that a disproportionate number of the poor and minorities are sentenced to prison terms. The annual reports by the Department of Justice confirm this consistent finding. To summarize the situation, the U.S. Department of Justice (1988, 1989, 1992c) has noted:

- Although Blacks constitute 12 percent of the population at large, they account for 47 percent of the state prison population and 42 percent of the jail population. The likelihood that any adult male will have served time in a juvenile or adult jail or prison by age sixty-four is estimated to be 18 percent for Blacks and 3 percent for Whites. In other words, the lifetime chance of incarceration is six times higher for Blacks than for Whites.
- Although Latinos make up 7 percent of the U.S. population, they account for 12.6 of the state prison population and 14 percent of the jail population.
- The median income for both male and female inmates did not exceed the government's poverty level during the year before arrest.
- The highest incarceration rate among U.S. males ages sixteen to sixty-four was among those who were unemployed prior to arrest. Of those inmates who were working prior to arrest, 30 percent were employed outside what they considered their normal occupation. This suggests, very likely, that they were **underemployed** (i.e., employed at a level below which they had been trained).
- The proportion of blue-collar workers in prison was more than double that found in the U.S. population. The reverse was true of white-collar workers, where they constituted less than one-third of their proportion in the U.S. population.
- About 41 percent of all jail and 45 percent of all prison inmates as compared with 11 percent of the U.S. population of males ages twenty to twenty-nine were high school dropouts.

As a final example, as a society the United States has 426 prisoners per 100,000 people (the highest incarceration rate in the world). Even more striking, the number of Black males imprisoned per 100,000 Black males in the United States was 3109, which far surpasses the incarceration rate for Blacks of 729 in the Union of South Africa (Meddis, 1991). In fact, nearly 1 in 4 Black males in the United States age twenty to twenty-nine is either incarcerated, on probation, or on parole.

There are three major reasons for this relationship. First, the crimes defined by official sources as the most important (the FBI's Uniform Crime Index) are the ones most likely to be committed by members of the lower classes. As has already been mentioned, these official data on crimes are biased, and they bias the public, police, juries, and the courts. Because of the official emphasis, we view these crimes as the most threatening, yet in reality the crimes by the powerful (the well-to-do, the corporations, and organized crime) do more harm to people and their property. Second, as we have seen, the criminal justice system is not just. Economic resources make a crucial difference at every stage. And finally, society continues to be racist. Institutional discrimination works to keep racial minorities disproportionately poor, unemployed, and despised. Institutional discrimination has also kept the minorities disproportionately *underrepresented* among police, lawyers, judges, and juries.

Not only are the more well-to-do less likely to receive a prison sentence, but also white-collar and wealthy criminals who are imprisoned receive advantages over the lower-class and minority inmates. The most extreme example of this privilege can be found by examining what type of person actually receives the death penalty—**capital punishment**. (See the Observation on the Supreme Court and racism.)

Who gets parole is another indicator of a bias in the system. **Parole** is a conditional release from prison that allows a prisoner to return to his or her community under the supervision of a parole officer before completion of the maximum sentence. Typically, parole is granted by a board established for each correctional institution or for the state. Often, the parole board members are political appointees without training or experience in criminal justice issues. The parole board reviews the prisoner's social history, past offenses, and behavior in prison and makes a judgment about release. The board's decision is rarely subject to review and can be made arbitrarily or discriminatorily.

The bias that disadvantages minorities and the poor throughout the system of justice continues as parole board members, corrections officers, and others make judgments that often reflect stereotyped notions. What type of prisoner represents the safest risk, a non-White or a White? An uneducated or educated person? A white-collar worker or a chronically unemployed, unskilled worker? Research shows, consistently, that decision makers in these situations typically give preferential treatment to people with the social characteristics more valued in society.

That the members of the disadvantaged in society (the poor and the minorities) are disproportionately represented in the prison population reinforces negative stereotypes already prevalent among the majority of the population. The large number of Blacks and the poor in prison is taken to "prove" that those groups have criminal tendencies.

At least four factors related to prison experiences operate to fulfill the expectation that the poor and the Black will be prone to criminal behavior. The first is that members of the underclass view the entire criminal justice system as unjust. There is a growing belief among prisoners that because the system is biased against them, all prisoners are in fact political. This perception increases their bitterness and anger.

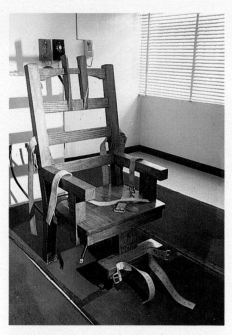

*There is bias in who is sentenced to death
by the state. The race and economic status
of the defendant makes a difference. So,
too, does the race and economic status of
the victim.*

A second reason for the high rate of crime among the people processed through the system of criminal justice is the accepted fact that prison is a brutal, degrading, and altogether dehumanizing experience. Mistreatment by guards, sexual assaults by fellow prisoners, overcrowding, and unsanitary conditions are commonplace in U.S. prisons. Prisoners cannot escape humiliation, anger, and frustration. Combined with the knowledge that the entire system of justice is unjustly directed at certain categories of people, these feelings create a desire for revenge in many ex-convicts.

A third factor is that prisons provide learning experiences in the art of crime. Through interaction with other inmates individuals learn the techniques of crime from experts and develop contacts that can be used later.

Finally, ex-convicts face the problems of adjusting to life without regimentation. More important, because well-paying jobs are difficult for anyone to find, particularly in times of economic recession, ex-convicts, who are automatically assumed to be untrustworthy, must choose between unemployment or jobs nobody else will take.

Nonacceptance by society causes many ex-convicts to return to crime. On the average, previous offenders are arrested for crime within six weeks of leaving prison. This fact, of course, justifies the beliefs of police, judges, parole boards, and other authorities that certain categories of persons should receive punishment but others should not.

OBSERVATION

THE SUPREME COURT, CAPITAL PUNISHMENT, AND RACISM

In 1987 the Supreme Court ruled by a 5–4 vote that a Black Georgia murderer, Warren McCleskey, had not proved that he was discriminated against when the judge in his case sentenced him to die by electrocution. The argument by the lawyers for the defendant was that the judicial system discriminates against Blacks, who constitute 42 percent of the 1900 convicts on the nation's 32 death rows—a proportion far higher than their 12 percent share of the population. One of those involved in trying to persuade the Court of the system's bias, Michael O. Finkelstein, a New York lawyer who teaches statistics at Columbia Law School, wrote the following editorial after the Court's decision against McCleskey.

Warren McCleskey, a black man, was arrested for murdering a white police officer in the course of a robbery. He was tried, convicted and sentenced to death in the Georgia courts. In *habeas corpus* proceedings brought on his behalf, professors David Baldus, George Woodworth and Charles Pulaski introduced an extraordinary statistical study of some 2,500 murder cases that occurred in Georgia during the 1970s. According to the study, the race of the defendant had some effect on sentencing, but the point of greatest concern was the powerful effect of the race of the victim: defendants charged with killing white people received the death penalty in 11 percent of the cases; those charged with killing blacks received the death penalty in only 1 percent of the cases. This finding set the stage for an assault on the Georgia capital punishment law as applied in McCleskey's case.

Under Georgia law a prosecutor who seeks the death penalty must conduct a penalty hearing before the jury. The jury can consider imposing a death sentence only if it finds that the murder was accompanied by at least one of ten statutory aggravating factors. In McCleskey's case the jury found two such factors: the murder was committed during an armed robbery, and its victim was a police officer.

The murder cases studied by the professors all involved statutory aggravating factors and thus could have drawn the death penalty. Nevertheless, the possibility remained that interracial killings involved more such factors than others and that such differences, not race, might account for the higher rate of death penalties in those cases. The authors scrutinized the data to see whether racial factors remained after controlling for differences in the nature of the crimes. Among the variables were the number of statutory aggravating factors, the presence of mitigating factors, and the characteristics of the victim exclusive of race (age, sex, relationship to defendant, etc.).

After controlling for such differences, the study still showed that the victim's race was a crucial element, especially in what Baldus and his colleagues called the middle range of aggravation—neither the most nor the least abhorrent murders. The overall finding was that a defendant who killed a white was 4.3 times as likely to receive the death sentence as one who killed a black. In the middle range of aggravation (McCleskey's was a middle-range case) the study showed that twenty out of every thirty-four defendants convicted of killing white persons

The Unjust Imposition of the Label "Criminal"

The evidence presented in this chapter strongly suggests that the powerless in society (the poor and the minorities) are disadvantaged throughout the criminal justice process. Although the bulk of research has been limited to the poor and Blacks, similar results are found for treatment of other minority groups in the criminal justice system. The results of one study of Native Americans and the system of justice, for example, parallel all the findings comparing Whites and Blacks (Hall and Simkus, 1975).

and sentenced to death would not have received the death sentence if their victims had been black.

In the Supreme Court, where the McCleskey death penalty was allowed to stand, the four dissenters—William Brennan, Thurgood Marshall, Harry Blackmun and John Paul Stevens—found it intolerable under the Eighth and Fourteenth amendments that the decision to impose the death sentence should turn on the irrelevant factor of the victim's race. In the majority opinion, Justice Lewis F. Powell Jr. rejected the study as irrelevant, writing that, to prevail, McCleskey had to prove that the decision-makers in his case intended to discriminate, that the statistical pattern was not enough.

Why not? Justice Powell never made that clear. As Justice Blackmun pointed out in dissent, the statistics demonstrated that because McCleskey's case was in the mid-range in terms of aggravation, it was more likely than not that he would not have received a death sentence if his victim had been black. Powell's majority opinion simply ignores that inescapable conclusion.

Behind the decision of the Court's majority was its unwillingness to ban all capital punishment in Georgia. But, as Justice Stevens pointed out in his dissent, a reversal of McCleskey's sentence on the strength of the statistical evidence would have compelled no such result. The study showed that the racial effects, while highly significant in the mid-range, were small or nonexistent at the extremes. McCleskey's sentence could thus have been reversed without precluding a death sentence in more aggravated cases.

The decision will surely undermine the use of statistical studies in capital punishment litigation, and it casts a disturbing shadow over such evidence in other areas as well. Although formally limited to capital punishment, the majority opinion gives new opportunities for the lower courts to ignore disturbing statistical findings in determining discrimination in particular cases.

Justice Brennan's eloquent dissent closed on the prophetic note sounded by Justice John Harlan, dissenting in *Plessy* v. *Ferguson:*

> Warren McCleskey's evidence confronts us with the subtle and persistent influence of the past. His message is a disturbing one to a society that has formally repudiated racism. . . . Nonetheless, we ignore him at our peril, for we remain imprisoned by the past as long as we deny its influence in the present.
>
> It is tempting to pretend that minorities on death row share a fate in no way connected to our own. . . . the reverberations of injustice are not so easily confined. "The destinies of the two races in this country are indissolubly linked together," and the way in which we choose those who will die reveals the depth of moral commitment among the living.

Warren McCleskey's lawyers say they are planning new appeals, but whether he lives, or dies at the hand of the state, the effect of the Court's opinion will reverberate for a long time to come.

Source: Michael O. Finkelstein, "A Shared Fate," *The Nation* magazine/ © 1987. This article is reprinted from *The Nation* magazine. © The Nation Company, Inc.

That there is a bias is beyond dispute, because the studies compare defendants by socioeconomic status or race, *controlling* for type of crime, number of previous arrests, type of counsel, and the like. These studies, however, do not answer the question so often asked: *Are the poor and minorities more prone toward crime, as the differential arrest rates and composition of the prison population appear to indicate?*

This question is difficult to answer definitively because the crime rate is a function of police activities and does not reflect unreported crimes or activities that are overlooked by the authorities. The actual amount of crime is unknown and probably unknowable. We do know, however, that criminal behavior is found throughout the social structure—by rich and poor, by Whites and Blacks. Businesspeople, for example, are sometimes involved in forms of lawbreaking, such as fraud, misleading advertising, restraint of trade, income tax evasion, bribery, and the like. Studies that ask respondents to report, under the assurance of anonymity, the type and frequency of their criminal acts show that (1) a huge proportion of crimes go undetected; (2) adults and juveniles, regardless of social class, tend to have committed numerous acts for which they could have been adjudicated and imprisoned, if caught; and (3) there is no substantial difference in the *amount* of criminal behavior of middle-class and lower-class respondents.

If criminal activities are common throughout the social structure, then how do certain groups of people avoid the label *criminal* while others do not? The data have shown that the administration of criminal law consistently works to the disadvantage of the poor, minority groups, and others who are powerless. The fact that the system operates with this bias, however, is not proof that there is a conscious attempt to control and punish just certain segments of the population. A number of factors that work to the disadvantage of the powerless help to explain the bias. There is the widespread assumption that the poor and powerless are less trustworthy than the more well-to-do. Thus, their behavior is subject to greater scrutiny, and there is a greater presumption of guilt for them than for the more advantaged in society. This assumption is based on the predominance of members of the underclass in the official crime statistics and in the composition of prison populations and on their high **rate of recidivism** (the percentage of offenders who, after their treatment or punishment has ended, are arrested and convicted of new offenses). Thus, the bias of the system creates a self-fulfilling prophecy and a rationale for citizens, police personnel, judges, jurors, and corrections officers to assume the worst about these types of people.

"Proof" that these people are more criminal-prone is also found in the greater likelihood of their making crime a career. This tendency is the result of crime's being a realistic means for a poor person to achieve material success because attainment through conventional means is virtually impossible for many. Just as important a factor is secondary deviance, the criminal behavior that results from being labeled a criminal. Upon release, the ex-convict returns to a community that is apprehensive and distrustful. Jobs are unavailable or, if available, degrading. The individual is likely to be rejected socially because of the stigma of being a criminal. As Erikson has put it,

> if a returned deviant encounters this feeling of distrust often enough, it is understandable that he too may begin to wonder if the original verdict or diagnosis is still in effect—and respond to this uncertainty by resuming deviant activity. In some respects, this solution may be the only way for the individual and his community to agree on what forms of behavior are appropriate for him. (Erikson, 1962:312)

Thus, if the powerless of society are disproportionately singled out for the criminal label, the subsequent stigmatization and segregation they face results in a tendency toward further deviance—thereby justifying society's original negative response to them. This tendency toward **secondary deviance** is especially strong when the imposition of the label is accompanied by a sense of injustice. Lemert argued that a stronger commitment to a deviant identity is greatest when the individual believes the label (stigma) to be inconsistently applied by society (Lemert, 1967). The research findings presented in this chapter clearly substantiate the existence of such an inconsistency.

Thus, if the powerless do engage in more deviance than do people from the middle and upper classes, they do so largely in response to society's differential treatment, demonstrated at every phase in the process of criminal justice. An excellent statement by Clayton Hartjen summarizes the thesis of this chapter:

> Criminal sanctions are supposedly directed toward a person's behavior—what he does, not what kind of person he is. Yet, the research on the administration of criminal justice . . . reveals that just the opposite occurs. A person is likely to acquire a social identity as a criminal precisely because of what he is—because of the kind of personal or social characteristics he has the misfortune to possess. Being black, poor, migrant, uneducated, and the like increases a person's chances of being defined as a criminal. . . . What I am suggesting here is that the very structure and operation of the judicial system, which was created to deal with the problem called crime, are not only grounded in an unstated image of the criminal but also—merely because the system exists—serve to produce and perpetuate the "thing" it was created to handle. That is to say, the criminal court (and especially the juvenile court) does not exist in its present form because the people it deals with are what they are. Rather, the criminals and delinquents become the way they are characterized by others as being because the court (and the world view it embodies) exists in the form that it does. *The criminal, thus, is a "product" of the structural and procedural characteristics of the judicial system.* (Hartjen, 1978:143–144)

CHAPTER REVIEW

1. Criminality is a social status determined by how an individual is perceived, evaluated, and treated by legal authorities. What is a crime depends on the law, which is created by the powerful. Crime, then, is innately political.
2. Official crime statistics (the FBI's *Uniform Crime Reports*) focus on street crimes against people and property. They omit white-collar crimes, corporate crimes, political crime, and organized crime.
3. According to the official crime statistics: (a) more males than females commit crimes; (b) juveniles and young adults have the highest crime rates; and (c) members of the lower classes and racial minorities are more likely to be criminals.
4. Victimless crimes are private acts designated as criminal by powerful interest groups that are able to legislate morality. Making these acts criminal creates several problems: (a) They are impossible to enforce; (b) they are costly to enforce, and if legal, they would bring in significant tax revenues; (c) they make organized crime profitable; and (d) they contribute to the corruption of the police and courts. Moreover, so-called victimless crimes are rarely victimless—they do harm people.
5. Losses resulting from individual white-collar crime amount to ten times the monetary loss from street crimes. Yet official agencies do not devote as much attention to white-collar crimes, and the few criminals that are apprehended receive relatively light sentences.

6. Corporate crimes are the most dangerous and expensive to society because they involve unsafe working conditions, pollution of the environment, unsafe products, and fraud.

7. Political crimes are of two types: (a) acts that threaten the power structure, and (b) illegal acts by those in power.

8. Organized crime is the second most lucrative business in the United States. Organized crime thrives because of (a) the demand for illegal goods and services, (b) corruption among the police and government officials, (c) violence and intimidation, and (d) its well-organized operation at all levels—locally, regionally, nationally, and internationally.

9. The system of justice is fundamentally unjust. The laws favor the powerful. The Crime Index channels police activities toward certain criminal acts and away from others. The poor are disadvantaged at every stage of the judicial process because lawyers, bail, and an adequate defense are costly. Thus, for similar offenses the powerless are more likely than the powerful to be found guilty, to be sentenced far more harshly, to wait longer for parole, and if sentenced to die, actually to be executed.

KEY TERMS

Crime.   An act that breaks the law.

Violence.   An act of force perceived by the powerful as threatening to the status quo.

Moral order crimes.   Acts that violate laws that enforce the morality of the majority.

Victimless crimes.   Acts that violate moral order crimes; they may offend the majority but they do not harm other people.

White-collar crimes.   Illicit acts committed by middle-class and upper-middle-class people in their business and social activities.

Corporate crimes.   Illegal acts by business enterprises.

Political crimes.   Illegal acts intended to influence the political system. Also, the abuse of authority by those in power. Finally, actions by governments that are illegal or immoral.

Organized crime.   A business operation that seeks profit by supplying illegal goods and services.

Bail. The posting of money by the accused to guarantee that he or she will be present at the trial.

Plea bargaining.   An arrangement between the prosecution and the accused where the latter pleads guilty in return for a reduced charge.

Adversary system.   The U.S. system of justice, whereby the state and the accused engage in a public battle to argue and provide evidence before an impartial judge or jury.

Mandatory sentencing.   By law judges must incarcerate certain types of criminals.

Determinate sentencing.   For a given offense, a judge must impose a sentence that is within the guidelines of the law.

Underemployed.   Employed at a level below which one has been trained.

Parole.   A conditional release from prison in which the former prisoner remains under the supervision of a parole office.

Rate of recidivism. The percentage of offenders who, after their treatment or punishment has ended, are arrested and convicted of new offenses.

Secondary deviance. Deviant behavior that is a consequence of the self-fulfilling prophecy of a negative label.

FOR FURTHER STUDY

Gregg Barak, ed. *Crimes by the Capitalist State: An Introduction to State Criminality.* Albany: State University of New York Press, 1991.

Steven Box. *Power, Crime and Mystification.* New York: Tavistock, 1983.

John Braithwaite. *Corporate Crime in the Pharmaceutical Industry.* London: Routledge & Kegan Paul, 1984.

Elliott Currie. *Confronting Crime: An American Challenge.* New York: Pantheon Books, 1985.

D. Stanley Eitzen and Doug A. Timmer. *Criminology: Crime and Criminal Justice.* New York: Wiley, 1985.

Charles H. McCaghy and Stephen A. Cernkovich. *Crime in American Society.* 2d ed. New York: Macmillan, 1987.

Morton Mintz. *At Any Cost: Corporate Greed, Women, and the Dalkon Shield.* New York: Pantheon Books, 1985.

Russell Mokhiber. *Corporate Crime and Violence: Big Business Power and the Abuse of the Public Trust.* San Francisco: Sierra Club Books, 1988.

Richard Quinney. *The Social Reality of Crime.* Boston: Little, Brown, 1970.

Jeffrey H. Reiman. *The Rich Get Richer and the Poor Get Prison: Ideology, Class, and Criminal Justice.* 3d ed. New York: Macmillan, 1990.

David R. Simon and D. Stanley Eitzen. *Elite Deviance.* 4th ed. Boston: Allyn and Bacon, 1993.

Gresham M. Sykes and Francis T. Cullen. *Criminology.* 2nd ed. Orlando, Fla.: Harcourt Brace Jovanovich.

Doug A. Timmer and D. Stanley Eitzen, eds. *Crime in the Streets and Crime in the Suites.* Boston: Allyn and Bacon, 1989.

Samuel Walker. *Sense and Nonsense about Crime: A Policy Guide.* 2nd ed. Pacific Grove, Calif.: Brooks/Cole, 1989.

James Q. Wilson and Richard J. Herrnstein. *Crime and Human Nature.* New York: Simon & Schuster, 1985.

FORUM

WHAT IS TO BE DONE ABOUT CRIME?

We must forget about the "causes" of crime and go after the criminals.

Alan M. Slobodin

If we are going to stop violent crime, the last thing we need to be doing is spending money to come up with more excuses for criminal behavior.

Trying to look for socioeconomic causes for violent criminal behavior is just another way of looking for excuses not to punish criminals. This is not only foolish but dangerous.

Looking for excuses denies the reality of making moral choices about right and wrong. When socioeconomic causes of violent crime are assumed, it follows that if criminals are not solely responsible for their actions, they don't deserve punishment.

The effect of this excuse-making is pernicious. This kind of thinking has led our criminal justice system to rely heavily on furloughs (a la Willie Horton), probation and parole, insanity defenses, plea bargaining and indeterminate sentences.

As carried out, our criminal justice system does not deter crime because:

- the time between arrest, conviction and punishment is considerable.
- the uncertainty of being caught and punished is great.
- the severity of punishment is too light to matter.

In short, violent crime is increasingly going unpunished. While reported crime rates have risen by more than 24 percent over the last decade, many convicted criminals serve only a small portion of their prison sentences or do not go to prison at all. Those convicted of violent crime typically serve only half their sentences in prison. Overcrowded prisons are turning into a revolving door of crime.

Worse yet, the criminal justice system is overwhelmed with a new, violent criminal who is casual in the commission of his crime. Today's criminals dismiss any suggestion that they ought to feel guilty about their behavior.

Why on earth would we want to continue down the road of not punishing violent criminals?

By not holding them to account, violent criminals sense weakness and a lack of resolve in our society. That will only encourage violent criminals to commit more crime.

Violent crime is escalating not because we have failed to treat the criminal as a victim of some unknown socioeconomic cause but because we haven't cracked down hard enough.

We know there is little doubt that, under proper conditions, punishment deters. What is needed is to increase either the speed, certainty or the severity of punishment, or some combination of all three. We need to deploy our resources in this direction.

We are fighting a crime war in the USA, and the bad guys are winning. Preoccupation with the underlying socioeconomic causes of violent crime will only fly in the face of what needs to be done to murderers, rapists and other violent criminals.

Source: Alan M. Slobodin, "Never Mind 'Causes'; Get after the Criminals," *USA Today* (August 8, 1990), p. 10A. Reprinted by permission of Alan Slobodin, Washington Legal Foundation.

To reduce crime, we must work to eliminate its causes.

USA Today (editorial)

"Friendly neighborhood."

"Safety of your own home."

Cozy phrases being blasted into oblivion by violence.

The mean streets have a way of following people, day and night, indoors and out.

- To a New York apartment Monday, where a sleeping 5 1/2-month-old baby was hit in the head by a stray bullet that tore through the bedroom wall. She is the sixth young child shot in 18 days in the city. Four of them are dead.
- To a Los Angeles Fourth of July celebration, where a 2-year-old was in the line of fire during a drive-by shooting.
- To a Belleville, Ill., tavern, where a man fatally stabbed his estranged wife as horrified patrons watched.
- To a quiet Tulsa, Okla., neighborhood, where a 12-year-old girl was tied up and set on fire by an unknown assailant.

Where do such unspeakable acts come from?

What explains the callousness that drives kids to label stray-bullet victims "mushrooms"?

What makes one teenage gunman's prospects so bleak that, according to his friends, his highest aspiration has been to appear on *America's Most Wanted?*

Why are people so quick to act on anger? Why are they so slow to feel remorse?

To the writer across the page, these questions are too dangerous to ask. He thinks that by trying to answer them, we will wind up excusing instead of punishing criminals.

We need swift and sure justice to protect society from murderous creeps. They must pay for their crimes.

But if we want to reduce the number of criminals there are to punish, we must seek answers to the causes of violent crime. Finding the causes doesn't mean coddling criminals.

Police groups offer one cause—the drugs and guns that flood the streets. The latest FBI crime report counted 21,500 murders last year, with firearms a factor in 62 percent. Drug-related murders increased 50 percent from 1988 to 1989.

Psychologists offer another—the physical and emotional abuse of children that can break their spirits and kill their consciences. Abuse teaches them violence is an acceptable way to resolve conflicts.

Sociologists have another—the poverty and joblessness that destroy any hope of a better life.

We need to commit the money and effort to fight the causes we know about:

- On gun control to remove weapons from the hands of those who are so ready to use them.
- On drug treatment and education to rid bodies and minds of the yearning for these social poisons.
- On prevention of spouse and child abuse, and treatment for abusers, to break the cycle of family violence.
- On job training and education that offer a path out of poverty.

No child should have to sleep barricaded behind furniture to be safe from bullets in his own home. No one should have to scurry for cover at dusk to keep clear of the gunfire that crisscrosses sidewalks.

Punishing violent crimes is good for those of us who survive. Preventing violent crimes is good for those who would be victims.

Source: USA Today, "We Must Get after Violent Crime Causes," *USA Today* (August 8, 1990), p. 10A. Copyright *USA Today.* Reprinted by permission.

16 *Mental Disorder*

T

raditionally, the problems of mental illness have been examined from the context of the presumed threat that the mentally ill posed for society and of the problems caused by the maltreatment of those labeled mentally ill. While these problems deserve attention, this chapter focuses on another set of problems, outlined by these questions: What is mental illness? What is the power of mental health practitioners in the labeling process? Is the treatment of mental disorders strictly a medical issue? What is the role of societal reaction in the development of mental illness careers? How central is the mental health industry to the social control functions of society? Is society mentally ill? This chapter does not provide definitive answers to these questions, for the experts themselves disagree. Rather, the aims are to draw the reader's attention to these issues and the implications of alternatives to some current thinking and to provide *sociological* insights to a subject that is commonly considered a province of psychology.

What Is Mental Disorder?

Mental disorder refers to behavior that exceeds the tolerance of other people. It describes behavior that deviates from what is considered acceptable; it is viewed by other people as bad, criminal, malicious, sinful, idiotic, foolish, or otherwise weird. In other words, what is and what is not a mental disorder depends on a social reaction—observers make a judgment about whether the behavior is seriously abnormal. But because the definition rests on social judgments, the criteria for outlining mental disorders are fuzzy and vary depending on the culture, audience, and situation.

For example, the behavior by itself is not sufficient to inform us whether it is bizarre enough to be considered a mental illness. If a poor woman steals a roast, she is considered a common criminal. Yet if a rich woman were to steal a roast, she would be considered mentally ill—a kleptomaniac. If a woman is sexually promiscuous, she may be considered a nymphomaniac; yet a man exhibiting the same behavior would probably be positively labeled, at least by other males ("Don Juan," "Casanova," "stud," or "swinger"). A man may be quiet, punctual, and obedient during the week but on Saturday afternoons in the fall drink to excess, yell profanities at authorities, and participate in the destruction of property. Is his behavior weird? No, because his actions are acceptable for football fans. But what if he behaved that way at his work or when attending a ballet performance? The context in which behavior is expressed is crucial. So, too, is the culture. In our society shyness in a boy is often considered a problem, but much less so in a girl. Sexual abstinence during the first two years of marriage would be odd in our society (providing legal grounds for annulment), but among the Dani tribe of New Guinea it is required. A Dani who deviated from the societal demand would be labeled a sexual deviant. Time is also a significant variable for defining who is and who is not mentally deviant. Behavior for which one was burned at the stake in Puritan New England might be considered appropriate now. Today, the person who insisted on burning someone at the stake would be considered mentally deranged.

Professionals in the mental health field have developed a classification scheme to provide some order in the diagnosis and treatment of abnormal behavior in U.S. society. The American Psychiatric Association (APA) has developed an official system of classifying psychiatric disorders called the *Diagnostic and Statistical Manual of Mental Disorders (DSM)*. The 1987 revised edition of these guidelines (*DSM III*) provides the current accepted system for classifying mental problems (American Psychiatric Association, 1987):

1. Disorders usually first evident in infancy, childhood, or adolescence such as mental retardation, stuttering, and anorexia nervosa.
2. Organic mental disorders such as senility and brain damage.
3. Substance use disorders such as the abuse of alcohol and/or other drugs.
4. Schizophrenic disorders such as withdrawal from ordinary social interaction and hallucinations.
5. Paranoid disorders involving persistent irrational delusions, such as a fear of persecution.
6. Mood disorders such as depression or exaggerated mood swings.
7. Anxiety disorders such as phobias, panic, extreme anxiety, and stress from traumatic experiences.
8. Somatoform disorders, which are psychological problems manifested as symptoms of physical disease (e.g., hypochondria).
9. Dissociative disorders that occur when the personality is separated from the individual, as in the case of amnesia or multiple personality.
10. Sexual disorders such as transsexualism, exhibitionism, and inhibited sexual desire.
11. Sleep disorders such as insomnia.
12. Disorders of impulse control, which is defined as the inability to control certain undesirable impulses (e.g., pathological gambling and kleptomania).
13. Adjustment disorders, which refers to difficulty in adjusting to the stress accompanying events such as unemployment or divorce.

This classification is widely used, but there are problems with it. Although the *DSM* spells out in detail the symptoms for each classification, the actual diagnosis of patients is not systematic and leads to mislabeling. A reliable diagnostic system has eluded psychiatry since the first systematic efforts at classification. Psychiatrists using a given diagnostic system still find themselves in disagreement, both about *how* to label a particular problem and *what* the label signifies. Traditionally, diagnostic systems have depended on the patient's presenting signs and symptoms, yet their significance to his or her past life or the eventual outcome has been difficult to establish. Moreover, the reported signs and symptoms often vary according to the observer's theoretical stance and depth of knowledge. Further complicating the diagnostician's task is that the signs and symptoms exhibited at the first interview are changeable; a patient who was initially seen as a simple schizophrenic, for example, may look paranoid or hebephrenic after more intensive scrutiny.

More important yet is that the classification keeps changing. In other words, what professionals consider a mental disorder changes with the whim of those making the decisions—or with the impact of special-interest groups.

In 1974, for example, the American Psychiatric Association voted to drop homosexuality from its list of mental disorders. The APA's vote in this case apparently reflected greater tolerance among the general public toward homosexuality. But this action raises a serious question: How can certain behaviors be added or dropped from a mental illness classification system? After all, the classification system developed by professionals should classify behaviors as exhibiting illness or not; and once so defined, they should remain. But that is not how the system works. What is or is not included depends on the public's views, professional fads, and changing governmental policies. In other words, a mental disorder depends on social definitions.

The arbitrariness of the classification system for mental disorders is readily apparent from the controversy that occurred during formulation of the third edition of *DSM*. During the various draft stages of this edition, categories were added and dropped rather capriciously. (The following discussion is adapted from Goldman, 1978.) In the 1978 draft "neurosis" and "hysteria" were eliminated. Many new categories, previously assumed to be human problems but not illnesses, were added. To qualify as a mental disorder in the new edition, a patient's problem must cause him or her distress or disability. On the basis of this definition, the new manual includes cigarette smoking and caffeine addiction under certain circumstances. By this logic, a compulsive cigarette smoker or coffee drinker is not "ill" unless he or she wishes to give up the habit (a consequence of being distressed). The smoker or coffee drinker who continues his or her habit without remorse is not "ill."

DSM now includes considerably more categories than in earlier editions. What is added (or subtracted) is often a consequence of the insistence of a pressure group. Feminists, for example, were appalled by what they considered a male bias in the early drafts. Girls who were "tomboys" were labeled as victims of "gender-identity disorder of childhood." The APA's Committee on Women had the specific clause rewritten to give tomboys a clean bill of mental health.

Insurance companies have lobbied the APA to reduce the number of disorders listed. The reason is purely monetary: insurance companies compensate their clients for recognized illnesses. If a behavioral syndrome is not in the latest edition of *DSM,* then it is not an illness and compensation need not be awarded. Psychotherapists, on the other hand, find it in their interest to include as many behavioral problems as possible. The more categories that exist, the more people there are who will seek treatment. Also, the more categories, the more impressive the statistics on illnesses will be, justifying greater governmental expenditures on mental health.

The tendency for professionals to add categories to *DSM* is a manifestation of what critics have called **psychiatric imperialism** (see Szasz, 1974a). This is the tendency to make mental illness an umbrella concept encompassing more and more behaviors that were once not considered such. Every time the psychiatric establishment officially designates another behavior as an illness, it magnifies the problems of labeling, stigma, and secondary deviance. These issues are being raised again as a committee of the American Psychiartic Association wrestles with what to add to and subtract from the next edition *(DSM IV),* which is scheduled for publication in 1993. Of the ninety-four suggestions for new diagnoses, only twenty are being seriously considered for inclusion (Goode, 1992).

The final—and most fundamental—problem with the official classification scheme is that it assumes mental illness is a disease. Because mental disorder is believed to be an illness, it follows that professionals should be able to distinguish between so-called mentally ill and normal people. An interesting experiment by D.L. Rosenhan (1973) proved this assumption wrong. Rosenhan had eight sane people admit themselves to a psychiatric hospital by complaining that they heard voices. All eight were admitted to different hospitals and diagnosed as schizophrenics. On admission to the hospital each patient then acted perfectly normal. Each requested to be dismissed from the hospital because he or she no longer heard voices. None of the pseudopatients was detected by the professional staff as a fraud. The length of hospitalization lasted from seven to fifty-two days. Each was finally discharged as "schizophrenia in remission."

Rosenhan reported his results to doctors at a university medical center. The doctors scoffed at the results, saying that they reflected incompetence in the staffs at the eight hospitals. Rosenhan countered by saying that within the next three months he would send one or more pseudopatients to their hospital. Every staff member was instructed to look out for phony patients. More than two hundred patients were admitted to that hospital in the next three months. Of these, forty-one were rated by at least one staff member as highly likely to be phonies; twenty-three were suspected by at least one psychiatrist; and nineteen were suspected by at least one staff member and one psychiatrist. Rosenhan had not sent one pseudopatient. This experiment demonstrates that staff members in mental hospitals assume mental illness in the people who are admitted. When this "mental set" is disturbed, they begin to question the mental illness in a substantial minority of the patients.

The Rosenhan study raises some serious questions about the fundamental assumption of psychiatrists that mental illness is a disease. Later, in the section on the medical model, we examine this assumption further.

These criticisms of the official classification system are not meant to convey that society is devoid of people with severe emotional problems manifested in highly unusual behaviors. The criticisms suggest, rather, the following:

- Social definitions determine who is or who is not mentally ill.
- What is officially labeled as a mental illness varies over time.
- What is included or omitted as a mental illness is often decided by the influence of powerful interest groups, not by the realities of human suffering.
- The diagnosis of mental disorders is highly suspect.
- Treatment, because it is based on inaccurate diagnoses, is also problematic.

Mental disorder, then, reflects a social judgment about certain behaviors. It consists of the violation of implicit social norms governing everyday interaction with other people. Talking aloud to oneself, hearing voices, and wearing a business suit but not shoes at a formal dinner are some examples of bizarre behavior. But most of us experience strange thoughts and behave strangely at times. We are sometimes depressed, moody, and aggressive. We daydream and fantasize. Some of us talk to God (though we must not claim to hear God talking back). What, then, distinguishes between the mentally ill and the normal?

There are at least three fundamental distinguishing characteristics. First, one's behavior is normal if it is similar to that of the majority. If, for example, this were a society of atheists, the individual who prayed to God would be considered schizophrenic. This characteristic is the principle of majority rule: no matter how bizarre a behavior may seem to an outsider, it is normal if the majority or the powerful in the society do it. As Kittrie has argued,

> individuals described as mentally disordered are often at variance with the conventions and mores of society. The very symptoms of what we commonly define as mental illness, being primarily behavioral rather than physiological, mark those afflicted by it as socially deviant. Frequently, however, such deviation will be manifested not by violent antisocial or criminal conduct but by eccentric activities and a social withdrawal from common daily functions and responsibilities.
>
> In 1907 a fragile yet determined old lady, who claimed to have founded a new religion, was battling for her liberty from commitment to a mental institution in Pleasant, New Hampshire. Her proclamation of new religious tenets in the modern scientific age was asserted as proof of her mental derangement. Yet

This student at Berkeley went to classes naked. Generally, such behavior would be an indicator of mental illness because it violates the rules that govern normal social behavior. This student, however, claimed to be making a political statement.

> Mary Baker Eddy won her battle and the Christian Science Church now occupies a respectable place among America's more traditional creeds. (Kittrie, 1973:51)

Mental disorder signifies behavior that violates the social norms of a given society. But norms are broken often by individuals, and the label *mentally ill* is not applied. The type of norm broken is crucial. Scheff has argued that the breaking of those rules that govern social interaction ("residual rules") will get the rule breaker labeled as *crazy:*

> Most norm violations do not cause the violator to be labeled as mentally ill, but as ill-mannered, ignorant, sinful, criminal, or perhaps just harried, depending on the type of norm involved. There are innumerable norms, however, over which consensus is so complete that the members of a group appear to take them for granted. A host of such norms surround even the simplest conversation: a person engaged in a conversation is expected to look toward his partner, rather than directly away from him; if his gaze is toward the partner, he is expected to look toward his eyes, rather than, say, toward his forehead; to stand at a proper conversational distance, neither one inch away nor across the room, and so on. A person who regularly violated these expectations probably would not be thought to be merely ill-bred, but as strange, bizarre, and frightening, because his behavior violates the assumptive world of the group, the world that is construed to be the only one that is natural, decent, and possible.
>
> The culture of the group provides a vocabulary of terms for categorizing many norm violations: crime, perversion, drunkenness, and bad manners are familiar examples. Each of these terms is derived from the type of norm broken, and ultimately, from the type of behavior involved. After exhausting these categories, however, there is always a residue of the most diverse kinds of violations, for which the culture provides no explicit label. For example, although there is great cultural variation in what is defined as decent or real, each culture tends to reify its definition of decency and reality, and so provide no way of handling violations of its expectations in these areas. The typical norm governing decency or reality, therefore, literally "goes without saying" and its violation is unthinkable for most of its members. For the convenience of the society in construing those instances of unnamable deviance which are called to its attention, these violations may be lumped together into a residual category: witchcraft, spirit possession, or, in our own society mental illness. (Scheff, 1968:10)

The third element in differentiating the so-called sick from the well is that the former have received the label *mentally ill.* The relation between mental illness and labeling is elaborated later in this chapter.

Given the problems of psychiatric diagnosis and the sociological insight that mental disorder depends on the definition and interpretation of particular audiences (not on trained psychiatrists), we see that it is impossible to know the scope and seriousness of the problem in U.S. society. The only available clues are based on traditional conceptions of mental illness. Recognizing the limitations of the psychiatric perspective, let us examine the data using two different measures.

The first way to understand the size of the problem is to look at the number of persons undergoing psychiatric treatment. Probably about 3 percent of the U.S. population is treated as inpatients or outpatients in county and state mental health facilities in a given year. This measure, however, informs us only of people likely to be the most severely disturbed (and disproportionately those from the lower social classes). It does not include people being treated privately by doctors, for whom data are unavailable. Also not included are people who are troubled but who choose (or their families choose for them) not to seek formal treatment.

Another measure of the extent of mental disturbance in the population comes from the results of studies using random samples. One of the most famous studies took data on a random sample of 1700 New York City adults. Psychiatrists then evaluated the data and classified the respondents. They found that 18 percent of the sample were free of any symptom of psychiatric disorder, 59 percent had moderate or mild symptoms, and 23 percent had marked or severe symptoms of disorder (Srole et al., 1962). Studies of this type have shown widely varying results. When a large number of these studies were reviewed, the median value showed that 15.6 percent of the population was considered mentally ill (Dohrenwend and Dohrenwend, 1969). The National Institute of Mental Health, in the largest and most thorough survey of mental disorder, reported in 1984 that one in five adults suffer from mental problems. Only one-fifth of those affected, however, seek professional help and then usually from general physicians rather than from mental health specialists. Of troubled persons in the United States, 13 million are estimated to be affected by anxiety disorders, 10 million by dependence on alcohol or other drugs, 9.5 million by depression, 1.5 million by schizophrenia, and another 1.4 million by antisocial personalities (Leo, 1984:80).

To reiterate, though, these statistics are misleading and probably conservative. They do not provide an accurate picture of the extent of mental disorder, because they ignore how a person's associates (workers, neighbors, friends, and family) evaluate his or her behavior. Obviously, many people considered strange, even bizarre, by others are never seen by psychiatric personnel. So the diagnostic criteria of professionals are not the ones used by the general public to determine who is and who is not mentally ill. Mechanic observes that "the basic decision about illness is usually made by community members and *not professional personnel* (Mechanic, 1962:69). If these data were available, the proportion of citizens considered "disturbed" would probably be considerably higher than the estimates based on data from the psychiatric profession.

Class, Race, and Gender and the Distribution of Mental Disorders

Researchers have found a relationship between social class and mental disorder. The consistent finding is the inverse relation between social class and reported rate of psychological disorder (i.e., the lower the class, the more likely to have a mental disorder) (for a review of 44 such studies, see Dohrenwend and Dohrenwend, 1969). Despite the universality of this finding, we should remain cautious, however, about this generalization.

First, we should be cautious about cause and effect. In effect, does mental illness cause a person to be lower class, or do the stresses associated with being lower class (discrimination, fear of unemployment and eviction, low wages, no medical insurance, and the like) cause mental disorder? Consider the argument that mental illness is a cause of homelessness. Although many people accept this claim, there are no data to support it. The much stronger argument is that mental illness is a probable consequence of homelessness (Timmer and Eitzen, 1992).

This conclusion is based on the assumption that a stable life leads to mental stability and an unstable one to mental instability. In Jonathan Kozol's words,

> many pregnant women without homes are denied prenatal care because they constantly travel from one shelter to another. Many are anemic. Many are denied essential dietary supplements by recent federal cuts. As a consequence, some of their children do not live to see their second year of life. Do these mothers sometimes show signs of stress? Do they appear disorganized, depressed, disordered? Frequently. They are immobilized by pain, traumatized by fear. So it is no surprise that when researchers enter the scene to ask them how they "feel," the resulting reports tell us that the homeless are emotionally unwell. The reports do not tell us we have made these people ill. (Kozol, 1988:155–156)

A second caution regarding the presumed link between mental illness and lower socioeconomic status is that the lower the economic resources, the more likely the person is to avoid seeking medical attention until the symptoms are severe. Similarly, the lower the economic resources, the more likely the person is to receive medical and psychological attention from a public clinic rather than from private doctors, resulting in a greater likelihood of one's problems becoming public. Finally, there is the possibility that the evaluation of a patient is affected by stereotyped notions of the evaluator.

> Thomas Scheff suggests from his research that the process of psychiatric screening and diagnosis is "more sensitive to economic, political, and social-psychological pressures on the screening agents than to most aspects of the patient's behavior." Inaccurate diagnoses seem most common in situations

Many believe that the major cause of homelessness is mental disorder. But is that the cause of homelessness or is mental disorder the consequence of homelessness?

where the psychological evaluator is superior in social, racial, or gender status to the client. (Feagin and Feagin, 1990:301)

Research also shows that racial minorities appear disproportionately among people diagnosed as mentally ill. The cautions mentioned above are relevant here as well because non-Whites are disproportionately found in the lower-classes. In addition, because African Americans, Latinos, and other racial minorities are the objects of discrimination, they are more likely than members of the racial majority to have feelings of rage, insecurity, depression, hopelessness, persecution, and even self-hate. Table 16.1 shows that racial minorities, who at the time (1986) constituted about 20 percent of the population, were disproportionately admitted to inpatient facilities (25 percent) and admitted to state and county mental hospitals (33 percent).

There are some interesting differences between women and men in the patterns of reported mental disorders. Women, for example, are more often diagnosed as having affective disorders, whereas men have a significantly higher rate of personality disorders. Women are more likely than men to be hospitalized and treated for mental disorders. There are several conflicting interpretations for these findings. The typical interpretation is that the physiological differences between the sexes account for the difference. A second interpretation is that learned gender roles encourage women to seek help more often than men (i.e., traditional men view illness as weakness and thus avoid dealing with problems until they are serious). Summarizing the literature, Scarpitti and Andersen note that

> those who study gender and mental health have concluded that women's higher rates of mental illness stem from their role in society. However, there are different paths to the conclusion. . . . [One] perspective assumes that the experience of living in a male-dominated society makes life more difficult for women, thereby increasing their chances of experiencing mental problems. . . . [Another argument] is that when women do not behave in expected and acceptable ways . . . they are labeled mentally ill. According to this argument, psychiatric diagnoses reflect male definitions of reality; labeling women mentally ill is then a mechanism of social control. . . . Yet another interpretation of the association between mental illness and gender is the argument that mental illness is not more prevalent among women than among men, but that women's learned gen-

Table 16.1 Admissions to all inpatient mental health services and state and county hospitals by race and sex: 1986

Social Category	All Services (%)	State and County (%)
Race		
White	75.4	66.0
All other races	24.6	34.0
Sex		
Male	57.3	62.8
Female	42.7	37.2

Source: National Institute of Mental Health, *Mental Health, United States 1990* (Washington D.C.: U.S. Government Printing Office, 1990):158–159.

der roles encourage them to seek help more often than men might under the same circumstances. (Scarpitti and Andersen, 1992:377)

Related to the above explanations is that women in a male-dominated society are more likely than men to be frustrated, unfulfilled, and unrewarded. In short, like minorities, women have a secondary status in society, and this makes them more likely than men to experience mental disorders.

The Treatment of Mental Disorders

The History of Treatment

The ancient Greeks were probably the first to define madness in medical terms. (The following discussion is adapted from Neaman, 1975; Foucault, 1973; Szasz, 1970). Hippocrates, for example, believed that temperament was determined by the amount, temperature, and color of bile, blood, and phlegm (too much phlegm, for example, resulted in being slow—phlegmatic; black bile caused melancholia; and overheated yellow bile was the source of mania). The treatment for such problems was to change the patient's diet or to supplement it with special herbs in order to restore the proper balance of bile, blood, and phlegm.

A different medical theory postulated that disturbed behavior was caused by an abnormal brain. The cure for madness, then, was to operate on the brain, boring holes in it to clear away the offending obstructions. This practice, although popular in the late Middle Ages, actually dates back to between 1500 and 2000 B.C.

Both of these theories have provided the basic modes for understanding and treating mental disorders throughout much of history. A third strand completes the picture: the tradition of ancient Greeks and later of the Arabs that the physiology of the patient combined with his or her intangible force ("spirit") to cause mental disorder. Thus, treatment included not only attending to the physical sources of the problem but also using psychotherapy (such as having the patient talk about his or her feelings and fears in order to understand and curb the offending behaviors.)

By the medieval period each of these theories had a following among various physicians. Some practiced therapy centering on the use of diet, herbs, and drugs (an early form of chemotherapy); others relied exclusively on surgery; while still others used psychotherapy—all methods in use today.

While medieval physicians typically saw madness as a physical and mental problem, the church provided another explanation for certain behaviors: demonic possession. The medieval church believed that the devil entered certain people, making them rage uncontrollably at times and/or reject the church and its symbols (prayers, Communion, the Bible, and ecclesiastical authority). Thus, the church was able to label pejoratively and therefore discredit people whose actions threatened its power.

This belief in demons was common in the Middle Ages (and later in Puritan New England with the prevalent belief in witches). During this period, flogging, starvation, and burning were used to make the body inhospitable to the devil. In 1484 Pope Innocent VIII appointed two Dominican monks to use the powers of inquisition and excommunication to fight the devils lodged within people. Their resulting treatise on witchcraft, *Malleus Maleficarum,* explained how devils were in league with evil women (witches); it also justified torture as a means of securing a confession (Kramer and Springer, 1942).

The belief in witchcraft continued to be widespread in Renaissance Europe. Led by the church and its rationale, communities severely persecuted witches. Women accused of witchcraft were put in the ultimate double bind: if they confessed to being a witch (because of torture or the threat of death), they fulfilled the group's prophecy and brought total social ostracism on themselves; if they refused to confess, they were put to death. Estimates vary, but historians widely believe that about half a million people were executed in Western Europe for being witches. Although there were dissident voices within and outside of organized religion, the existence of witches was widely accepted by church leaders, including such Protestant leaders as Luther and Calvin.

The important point about witches is that they were not mad. They were people who threatened the power elite (either secular or religious). They were tortured until they admitted to behaviors and experiences that could today be considered signs of madness. Thus, the vast majority of people accused of witchcraft never actually lived what they admitted to under torture. The belief in witchcraft, then, allowed the powerful to control deviants. By admitting to bizarre thoughts and actions, those people labeled as witches admitted to possession by a special form of madness that could be treated only by the church. Consequently, physicians and exorcists faced the problem of distinguishing between forms of possession and forms of insanity. Neaman comments, "only true possession can be treated by an exorcist. The others are recognized today, as they were by the learned in the Middle Ages, as forms of mental illness susceptible to psychotherapy and drug therapy" (Neaman, 1975:36).

The early European colonists of North America brought their belief in witchcraft with them. The most celebrated instance of witch persecution occurred in Salem, Massachusetts, in 1692. There a witchcraft hysteria emerged in which girls and women who acted outside the community norms were accused of being possessed by the devils. The alleged witches were tried, found guilty, and executed (by hanging or being pressed to death under a pile of rocks). As the fear of witches subsided, some accused witches were not killed; but every one of the first twenty-two suspects brought before the court was killed (Erikson, 1966).

The persecution of witches was one way of dealing with deviant persons. A more common approach in early America was to confine the individual to jail so that the public would be safe from his or her threatening behavior. Deutsch reports, "Not infrequently the unfortunate person spent decades incarcerated like a common criminal" (Deutsch, 1949:42).

The first houses of correction in the colonies, established in 1727 in Connecticut, were intended to hold criminals, paupers, and the insane.* The first hospital exclusively for the mentally ill was founded in Williamsburg, Virginia, in

* The first hospital for the insane in Europe was founded much earlier: St. Mary of Bethlehem in London (1547). The name of that hospital was shortened to "bedlam" (a term that today notes great noise and turmoil, apparently depicting the life at St. Mary). Later, mental hospitals were founded in Mexico (1565), Paris (1641), and Moscow (1765).

1773; the second, in 1824 in Lexington, Kentucky. There were no special therapy programs for these patients, only segregation from other types of deviants and from society itself. But the basic assumption for the cause of mental illness had by now shifted from the idea of possession by demons to the view that these people were sick.

The real growth in what were called "insane asylums" occurred in the 1850s (Rothman, 1971). With few exceptions, these hospitals were filthy and their patients abused (overcrowded, chained, beaten, poorly fed). The asylums were obviously custodial rather than therapeutic. Until 1950 or so, public mental hospitals were characterized as "snake pits" because of the inhumane treatment of patients that prevailed there. This situation gradually improved, primarily because of the pioneering efforts of C. F. Menninger and his sons, Karl and Will, of Topeka, Kansas. The Menningers owned a private mental hospital and trained psychiatrists for Topeka State Hospital and, later, for hospitals throughout the nation. These trained physicians, the adverse publicity of the snake pits, and the lobbying efforts of the Menningers changed the funding patterns and the methods of therapy in the hospitals.

Contemporary Treatment

Over the past 200 years asylums have replaced prisons, and hospitals have replaced asylums. Similarly, the treatment of the mentally disturbed has become progressively more humane. The five major forms of treatment for mental disorders today are psychotherapy, awareness, behavior modification, psychopharmacology, and psychosurgery.

Psychotherapy.   Most people believe that talking about one's problems can have a therapeutic effect. Sympathetic listeners allow patients to vent their pent-up feelings or to rid themselves of guilt through confession. They also can guide patients to insights about themselves, thereby helping them to alter their behavior.

The most common form of counseling therapy is called psychotherapy and is based on Sigmund Freud's psychoanalytic theory. Freud believed that mental disorders are really problems of the individual's unconscious. As Draguns and Phillips put it:

> Viewed from Freud's perspective, a person's symptoms are the expression of a
> clash among various incompatible tendencies in his motivational repertoire,
> traceable to crucial parent-child encounters in the first six years of life, and crys-
> tallized in coherent structures geared to wish fulfillment (id), reality adaptation
> (ego), and moral judgment (superego). (Draguns and Phillips, 1971:3)

According to Freud's theory, the ego must deal with the conflicting demands of the id, superego, and society. The particular configurations of these inner conflicts are the bases for all symptoms of mental disorder. Treatment, then, consists of developing a trusting relationship between a therapist and patient. Through extended conversations (sometimes lasting for many years) the therapist attempts to determine such things as the patient's relationship with his or her parents, how the individual fared during the psychosexual stages of development, what he or she dreams about, what he or she fears. By this process the therapist locates the sources of the unconscious conflicts that influence the patient's behavior and interpretation of reality. Through being helped to understand himself or herself, therapists believe, the patient will be able to modify his or her behavior realistically.

There are a number of criticisms of psychotherapy. Most fundamental is that the theory is based on unseen and unmeasurable forces; like religion, it is based on faith rather than on empirical facts. This criticism is significant because some Freudians rely entirely on Freud in interpreting their patient's situations (the assumption being that Freud was and is the fount of all knowledge).

A second criticism is that the treatment is expensive and time-consuming. Third, and most telling, is that research shows that the success rate for people undergoing psychotherapy is not significantly better than for those who received no treatment at all. After examining the research on the effects of psychotherapy, Hans Eyesenck offered the following seven major conclusions:

1. When untreated neurotic control groups are compared with experimental groups of neurotic patients treated by means of psychotherapy, both groups recover to approximately the same extent.
2. When soldiers who have suffered a neurotic breakdown and have not received psychotherapy are compared with soldiers who have received psychotherapy, the chances of the two groups returning to duty are approximately equal.
3. When neurotic soldiers are separated from the service, their chances of recovery are not affected by their receiving or not receiving psychotherapy.
4. Civilian neurotics who are treated by psychotherapy recover or improve to approximately the same extent as similar neurotics receiving no psychotherapy.
5. Children suffering from emotional disorders and treated by psychotherapy recover or improve to approximately the same extent as similar children not receiving psychotherapy.
6. Neurotic patients treated by means of psychotherapeutic procedures based on learning theory improve significantly more quickly than do patients treated by means of psychoanalytic or eclectic psychotherapy, or not treated by psychotherapy at all.
7. Neurotic patients treated by psychoanalytic psychotherapy do not improve more quickly than patients treated by means of eclectic psychotherapy, and may improve less quickly when account is taken of the large proportion of patients breaking off treatment. (Eyesenck, 1970:760–761)

Awareness therapies.   A number of therapies (some of them with very long histories) have recently gained popularity in the United States, among them transactional analysis, est, sensitivity training, primal therapy, biofeedback, transcendental meditation, total awareness, rolfing, yoga, and encounter groups. Although there are differences among them, these therapies generally (1) attempt to focus on immensely powerful but untapped forces within the individual; (2) attempt to resolve individual emotional problems through open, honest, and sometimes painful talk about innermost feelings; and (3) seek to improve the quality of the individual's personal life and interpersonal relationships by helping make them authentic.

There are several problems with these approaches to personal problems. First, they are not appropriate treatment styles for severely disturbed persons.

Second, they tend to provide simplistic answers to highly complex problems. Finally—and this is a criticism applicable to most psychologically based theories—they help people adjust to situations that may themselves be the problems. The focus, in other words, is on the problems of the individual rather than on changing the social conditions that cause people to be disturbed.

Behavior modification.   The fundamental assumption of the behaviorists is that maladusted people have learned or been taught maladaptive behaviors. The solution is for a therapist to teach through positive rewards socially acceptable behaviors to replace the maladaptive ones. This approach deals only with changing behavior and not with the underlying personal or social reasons for the behavior.

Psychopharmacology.   Drug therapy is the most common form of treatment today for mental disturbances, often used in conjunction with other forms of therapy. There are drugs to reduce tension, heighten tension, sedate, inhibit, allay anxiety, maximize pleasure, fortify courage, and the like. For example, one chemical—lithium—is quite successful in combating depression. Other drugs have been helpful in treating schizophrenia, the most stubborn of mental disorders.

The fundamental problem with drug therapies is that they suppress symptoms but do not affect the cause of the symptoms. What they do is important, however. They allow people to leave hospitals for home and work. They eliminate suffering. But they are not cures. They have no effect on the source of the fear, anxiety, or depression that plagues the individual. As a result, the symptoms must be continually curtailed by the drugs, or they will return. Or over time, the drugs lose their ability to affect the symptoms.

The other problem with drugs is that physicians and hospital staffs sometimes use them for social control rather than for therapy. The easiest way to control troublesome patients is to give them a drug. The old method of control was to lock patients away or chain them; now, hospitals accomplish the same effect in a more "humane" way. (See the Forum at the end of the chapter.)

Psychosurgery.   Surgery has been used for centuries in the attempt to cure mental disorders; for example, trephining entailed drilling a hole in the head to provide evil spirits with an escape route. In this century the lobotomy has been an accepted procedure to treat certain mental problems. In this surgical procedure the neural connections in the brain's frontal lobes are severed in order to calm a violent patient. From 1940 to the mid-1950s some fifty thousand lobotomies were performed in this country.

The lobotomy procedure has been refined and expanded in recent years. Now, microelectrodes can be inserted to activate or deactivate certain parts of the brain as necessary. Minute parts of the brain can be treated electrically in the effort to control certain behaviors or relieve pain.

Critics of psychosurgery point to the same problems involved with drug therapy, although the magnitude of the problem is much greater here. The surgery calms the anxious or violent, but it attacks the symptoms rather than the source of the trouble. Psychosurgery is also a most effective way of controlling troublesome people. But although psychosurgery, if successful, is often able to relieve misery and suffering for the patient, there are obvious political and ethical questions related to its use. Its effects are irreversible. It changes people. It may be performed on people against their wishes. It can be used as the ultimate form of social control. Despite these serious implications, though, the tendency has been to increase its use.

Mental Hospitals

The mental hospital is the place society has set aside for people it considers severely disturbed. It serves three functions, either explicit or implicit: (1) to protect the patient from himself or herself; (2) to protect society from potential harm and to isolate and hide troublesome people from the public; and (3) to provide a controlled environment where patients can receive optimal treatment for their problems. But despite humanitarian claims and the reforms that have occurred since the mid-1950s, state mental hospitals are problem-ridden and may even create more problems than they solve.

The fundamental problem stems from the fact that a mental hospital, like an army camp, prison, or convent, is a total institution. It is, according to Erving Goffman, a place of work and residence where a number of relatively powerless people are cut off from the wider society and lead an enclosed, formally administered life (Goffman, 1961). (See the insert on Goffman.) **Total institutions** are characterized by a split between the powerful and the group they manage. The powerless lead a tightly regimented life separated from family, denied heterosexual opportunities, and dehumanized. The inmates cannot escape from the oppression of the powerful.

They are subject to searches. They are forced to take oral or intravenous medications. They are forced to do menial work, and they are stripped of their individuality. They are totally dependent on the institution for all physical needs, and their behavior is tightly controlled. Wing describes the conditions:

> Even the smallest detail, such as when an inmate shall bathe or cut his nails, may be decided for him. Social experience is reduced to a uniform dullness. The inmate is no longer looked upon as a father, or an employee, or a customer, or as a member of numerous specialized social groups, and his ability to play everyday social roles may atrophy from disuse. He does not practice traveling on buses, or spending money, or choosing food or clothes. His relationships with the outside world are reduced to a minimum. (Wing, 1967:220–221)

Goffman noted that patients faced with this oppressive environment tended to adopt one of three coping strategies: total withdrawal (viewed by the powerful as a schizophrenic reaction), conformity to the rules and surrender of personal autonomy (interpreted as "moving toward recovery"), and rebellion against the oppressive system (viewed as obviously needing restraints and more therapy). In short, many patients suffer not so much from the original symptoms for which they were admitted as from a reaction to the depersonalizing effects of the mental hospital itself. As Howard Hills has put it,

> I have known many patients who are alienated and uncooperative in the hospital. Yet, I was convinced that these same people would have been hard-working and responsible if they had had the choice to engage in meaningful, dignified tasks. . . .

Erving Goffman and the Definition of Self as "Sick"

Erving Goffman (1922–1982) a well-known explorer of the meaning of symbols in human interaction, worked as a recreational therapist in a state mental hospital for a year. His book *Asylums,* based on his experiences and observations there, is a classic, with insights especially relevant to labeling theory.

The mental hospital is a total institution (like a prison, a monastery, or a military camp) where patients are segregated from normal society for twenty-four hours a day. Patients are continuously subject to the same monolithic controls. They are assumed to be helpless. They must accept communal living. They are continually reminded that they are sick. They must bend to the routine. They must accept a powerless role. Most significant, they must act out the role of being sick. Goffman has referred to this process of role assignment and role enactment as the "career" of a mental patient. This process is buttressed by the hospital staff's universally held definition of each patient's problem. Because, as Goffman has asserted, the self is a social product, all of these forces cause the individual patients to think of themselves according to the way in which other people interact with and label them. Because of the encapsulization of the total institution environment, patients become habituated to their sick role. The hospital tends to create and maintain dependence and the feeling among patients that they cannot cope with life on the outside. Thus, the social organization of the mental hospital actually creates in patients the behavior it is supposedly designed to cure.

The crisis is one of dignity and identity; of the loss of human sensibilities by patients and staff. The patients are simply not involved meaningfully in their environment. There is no way one can get a handle on a world in which there are no tasks to be performed which reflect personal achievement. Patients are not even engaged in the processes of their own existence. Those who are capable of degrees of independence are forced to share the life-style of those who are not. As a consequence, they are both apathetic and anxious about their condition. They have been removed from all dialogue with their world. They adapt and accommodate, or they resist and suffer. Either way, they withdraw deeper into the one-dimensional world we have created for our mentally ill. (Hills, 1977:3, 5)

Another problem with mental hospitals is that they are understaffed and underfinanced, a situation that inhibits positive therapy. Hills has summarized this problem:

> The history of mental health care in our society is a sad one. Hospitals—state and private—treat only a fraction of those committed to their care. Most hospitalization is custodial in nature, providing only food and shelter, and restraining patients from doing harm to themselves or to others. Because of inadequate budgets, most hospital staffs are so small in relation to hospital population that the notion of meaningful treatment is a permanent joke among those familiar with the problems. . . .
>
> I worked in a hospital that was built ten years after the Civil War. Most of the wards were so crowded and filthy that the staff locked itself away from the patient. Many hospitals cannot find and/or afford doctors, so they hire foreign doctors, who are not licensed in the United States, to work under a licensed director. It is not unusual for these doctors to be unable adequately to communicate with their patients because of a language barrier. . . .
>
> The fact is that mental hospitals simply do not and, because of costs, cannot provide treatment for the thousands of nondangerous people currently being warehoused in our giant institutions. (Hills, 1977:4, 8, 9)

A third problem is the denial of the patients' civil rights. As patients, they have been experimented on without their consent, abused physically (with drugs, physical constraints, or shock therapy), and denied their individuality. They have even been confined against their will, although they were dangerous to no one and able to survive on the outside.

In 1975 a Supreme Court decision—*O'Connor* v. *Donaldson*—changed this practice, restoring to patients at least some of their civil rights (Donaldson, 1976). The case involved a patient, Kenneth Donaldson, who was involuntarily committed at age forty-eight to the Florida State Mental Hospital by his parents. In the hospital he had no privacy (his room contained fifty-nine other patients). He spoke with doctors for only about five hours in fifteen years. For a year he was locked in a kitchen where he worked thirteen hours a day, seven days a week. For fifteen years Donaldson tried to get released from the hospital. On eighteen occasions state and federal judges denied his requests for a hearing, but finally in 1972 a federal court ruled that the hospital staff knew Donaldson was not dangerous to himself or to others and was receiving no treatment other than a prisonlike existence. He was freed and awarded $38,500 in damages. This decision was upheld by the Supreme Court three years later. The Court ruled unanimously—and most significantly—that mental patients cannot be confined in institutions against their will if they are dangerous to no one and can survive on their own.

This landmark case has several implications. First, the court ruled that patients in hospitals are entitled to treatment, not just custodial care. Second, medical opinion is not enough to keep a person in a mental hospital if the patient seeks freedom. Third, hospital care should be supplanted by outpatient care for many. As Hills notes,

> today the hospitals are overflowing with people who could function in the community if the resources spent operating wasteful, old-fashioned hospitals were instead used to provide after-care treatment and support services to released patients in their own dwellings. (Hills, 1977:11)

Finally, the decision implies that the state's medical complex had exceeded the limits within which its actions were compatible with the American heritage of personal liberty.

Despite the fact that mental hospitals may do some patients more harm than good, they have their uses, the most important of which is to provide a therapeutic milieu where patients might, if circumstances were ideal, receive proper treatment to deal with their personal problems.

Because of the patients' rights legal movement, the fiscal pressures facing the states, and the increased use of mood-altering drugs, the hospitalized mental patient population has decreased dramatically—from 560,000 in 1955 to 110,000 in 1986. Many of these former patients successfully returned to family, neighborhood, and work; but many others have not. This trend toward **deinstitutionalization** has created two related problems. First, many people who need care are not receiving it. Lewis Judd, director of the National Institute of Mental Health has observed that "we have 2.8 million people with serious mental illness, and only one in five is receiving adequate care" (quoted in Toufexis, 1990b:58). And, second, some of those people not receiving needed care are living in miserable conditions. Thus, the irony that the movement that led to the release of patients from the restrictive environments of hospitals for humane reasons has resulted in many of them living in inhumane situations.

There are reasons to believe that the trend toward deinstitutionalization may be reversed (causing **reinstitutionalization**). Some states, such as Texas, Washington, and Indiana, have changed their laws to make it less difficult to commit people involuntarily to mental hospitals. The hospitalized population is also expected to increase because of the increased emphasis on treating people who abuse alcohol and drugs. Another reason is that the age group in which schizophrenia is most severe is being swelled by baby boomers (Wines, 1988).

Contrasting Models of Mental Disorder

The forms of therapy for the mentally disordered just described are all based on a common assumption: that mental disorder is an illness that can be treated like any other disease. This medical model prevails among laypersons and professionals alike. Since 1960 or so an alternative set of models that focuses on sociocultural factors has developed a relatively small but vocal following. This section describes and evaluates various aspects of these positions.

The Medical Model   The medical approach to mental disorders views these problems as diseases. The disease, depending on one's orientation, stems from either organic or psychological causes. But in either case, it is a disease—hence, the appropriateness of the term *mental illness* and reference to the sufferer as a *patient,* to his or her therapist as a *doctor,* and to the place he or she is treated in more serious instances as a *hospital.* The APA's *Diagnostic and Statistical Manual* is based on the medical model. Disorders are classified as illnesses, and symptoms are associated with each form.

Medical model purists assume that through systematic observation, description, and classification of disturbed behavior patterns physicians will eventually discover biological sources and cures. Others, such as Freudians, accept the medical model only in a metaphorical way. They do not view mental disturbances as analogous to a physical illness. For them, biology is not the cause of mental illness, but there is an internal structure that accounts for the maladaptive behavior. Among both the biological and psychoanalytic orientations there is a fundamental similarity—they posit "a structural, coherent, organized underpinning responsible for disordered and maladaptive behavior" (Draguns and Phillips, 1971:3). In short, supporters of the medical model assert that the source of mental disorder is almost exclusively within the individual. In McCaghy's words, "The patient needs medical help on an individual basis just as surely as if he or she were suffering from a physical disease against which the body was helpless" (McCaghy, 1976:317).

The medical model very likely has some validity for certain mental disorders. Some mental problems do have an organic origin. As scientists learn more about the brain, they may find that many more problems are organic. For example, we now know that certain parts of the brain affect tension, aggression, feelings of security, and so on. Perhaps, also, chemical imbalances inhibit the transmission and processing of electrical impulses, causing confusion, mood swings, and aggressive or passive behavior.

Certain mental problems may be found to be hereditary. There is evidence indicating that some forms of schizophrenia may have a genetic basis and that the children of schizophrenics therefore have a greater risk of becoming schizophrenics than do the children of nonschizophrenics. This evidence is not conclusive, because the problem may be transmitted socially in these cases rather than genetically. Yet children who are removed from schizophrenic mothers at birth are more likely to be schizophrenic than are children taken from nonschizophrenic mothers at birth. Studies of identical twins also lend some support to the genetic hypothesis. If one twin is schizophrenic, then in 69 percent of the cases the other twin will also be affected. The likelihood that schizophrenia will affect nontwin siblings is only 11 percent. These findings seem to indicate that heredity may predispose some individuals to schizophrenia. But other factors could affect the tendency.

Criticisms of the medical model are numerous and significant. First, there is little empirical evidence supporting it. Actually, very few psychological disorders are of biological origin. Research has shown, for example, that syphilis and other infections can cause emotional instability. We also know that some psychological disturbances can result from tumors and chemical imbalances. Draguns and Phillips, after carefully reviewing the evidence on biologically linked mental disturbances, concluded that

important as these advances are in both scientific and humanitarian ways, they have left untouched the categories that account for the bulk of the identified psychiatrically impaired or incapacitated populations. The yield of medical and biological research on schizophrenia has been described by prominent contributors to this enterprise as inconclusive, although opinions to the contrary continue to be articulately voiced and research animated by organic hypothesis in schizophrenia is vigorously pursued. The evidence of biological correlates in the ambulatory variants of maladaptation, neurosis and characterological disorders, is for the most part fragmentary, controversial, or negative, barring few exceptions, and the thought of equating the entire range of neurosis or character disorder with biological defects is not being seriously entertained. (Draguns and Phillips, 1971:4)

The analogy between physical and mental disorders, despite a few positive findings, is basically not appropriate. The problems that disturbed people identify as the sources of their unhappiness or emotional crisis are generally *not* biological ones but problems of living: job, marriage, children, economic trouble, neighbors, or the threat of nuclear holocaust. Moreover, there are major differences between mental and physical illnesses, including onset, etiology (cause), symptoms, effect, treatment, and cure. Finkel has summarized these differences:

Mental illness usually begins differently, often more gradually, than a physical illness. Mental illness appears to be shaped to a greater extent by significant people, experiences, and social institutions than is typically found to be the case for a physical disorder. Mental disorders have lower cure rates and higher rates of relapse than is the case for physical disorders. (Finkel, 1976:5–6)

For physical problems there is general agreement on the symptoms and diagnosis. Clearly, such agreement does not exist for mental disorders. There is also a general understanding among professionals on how treatment works to cure physical illnesses, but this understanding is also lacking for mental problems. For example, drugs or electroshock have been found to be helpful for alleviating some symptoms, but we do not know why. Finally, a person with a physical problem is generally aware of it and typically seeks help. But a patient with a mental disorder may *insist* that he or she is healthy. As McCaghy has put it,

the majority of persons who become mental patients do so because others—particularly friends and relatives—define them as ill. This is not necessarily inconsistent with the medical model, but it does alert us to an important fact: *the symptoms of mental disorder are forms of social behavior defined by others as deviant.* In short, we are talking about a social phenomenon . . . , the behavior is subject to interpretation by others as to its appropriateness. (McCaghy, 1976:317–318)

One of the medical model's most outspoken and articulate critics, psychiatrist Thomas Szasz, has asserted that

every "ordinary" illness that persons have, cadavers also have. A cadaver may thus be said to "have" cancer, pneumonia, or myocardial infarction. The only illness a cadaver surely cannot "have" is mental illness. Nevertheless, it is the official position of the American Medical Association, of the American Psychiatric Association, and of other medical and psychiatric groups that "mental illness is like any other illness." . . . Bodily illness is something the patient *has,* whereas mental illness is really something he *is* or *does.* If neurosis and psychosis were diseases, like pneumonia and cancer, it should be possible for a person to have *both* a neurosis and a psychosis. But the rules of psychiatric syntax make it absurd to assert such a diagnostic combination. Actually, we use the words "neurotic" and "psychotic" (and other psychiatric diagnostic terms) to characterize persons, not to name diseases. . . .

Disease means bodily disease. Gould's Medical Dictionary defines disease as a disturbance of the function or structure of an organ or a part of the *body*. The mind (whatever it is) is not an organ or part of the body. Hence, it cannot be diseased in the same sense as the body can. When we speak of mental illness, then, we speak metaphorically. To say that a person's mind is sick is like saying that the economy is sick or that a joke is sick. When metaphor is mistaken for reality and is used for social purposes, then we have the makings of myth. (Szasz, 1974a:99, 109)

A final and most critical problem with the medical model is that it ignores social factors. It views individuals experiencing mental problems as acting within a social vacuum. The source of mental disorder is in the individuals. The solution is to find the flaw within them or to segregate them from society for their own and society's protection. To ignore the social forces impinging on individuals and to see the source of the problem as an internal one is a classic example of blaming the victim. Focusing on individual defects deflects attention from a potent source of personal problems. Thus, it protects society from criticism and radical change. This is the point of George W. Albee, past president of the American Psychological Association:

Unfortunately, a defect explanation is less costly to the society than a social-learning explanation of mental disturbance. We can spend a modest amount of public funds supporting biomedical research, looking for the twisted molecule which will explain the twisted behavior. We can promise to develop a pill or injection, an operation, or some other new individual organic treatment which will cure by correcting the defect. Or we can wring our hands at the evidence that certain people are defective (a process called Blaming the Victim) and take no action. Either alternative is relatively inexpensive. If we were to acknowledge that much of the emotional distress and mental disturbance in our society is due to dehumanizing social influences, such a position would call for widespread and expensive social reform. Who will finance the platform for advancing this argument? (Albee, 1975:2)

In short, the medical model, applied to medical illness, has an ideological function. It reaffirms the cultural—and therefore political—status quo of society.

Thus, there are good grounds for questioning the legitimacy and accuracy of the medical model. However, there are two points that should be made in its behalf. First, increasingly sophisticated research may continue to reveal additional ties between biology and mental disturbances. This model may someday be accepted by behavioral scientists as the most effective approach to mental disorder. That time, however, has not yet come. Second, the model should not be rejected just because it does not fit every case. It is valid in limited cases. The problem is that many of the model's adherents tend to want to make it global in its explanatory powers. As long as this tendency prevails, and as long as it fails to take social factors into account, the medical model will remain inadequate to address a majority of mental disorders.

The Sociocultural Approach

Instead of calling mental disorders illnesses and treating them as diseases, the adherents of the sociocultural approaches view them as problems of living. This approach does not deny that people get upset and are sometimes irrational, unable to cope, depressed, or whatever. These behaviors and feelings are real, but they derive not from biology but from the demands of coping with other people in social situations. Not only does this approach focus on the social factors that affect the behavior of people, but it also stresses the factors that affect why some people are labeled *sick, mad,* or *insane* while others are not, and the consequences of such labeling. There are several variants of this approach. We examine two: the labeling perspective and the conflict approach, which includes radical therapy.

The labeling perspective.   The **labeling** approach to mental disorder is entirely different from the medical model. (The following discussion is adapted from Scheff, 1966a, 1974.) Unlike the labeling perspective, the medical model assumes that disease is culture-free: a disease is the same in New York or New Guinea. Instead of conceptualizing mental disturbance as an "illness," with a "patient" in need of "therapy," labeling approach proponents argue that the mentally disrupted are society's rule breakers who have received the label *mentally ill.* Breaking certain rules will get one the label of *criminal* or *addict* or *misfit.* The mentally disordered, in contrast, are people who have broken the normal rules of social interaction. Their behavior is unacceptable because it is so unusual and defies common expectations. Although most of us break such rules (overreacting with anger and abusive behavior, acting sullen and incommunicative) at times, we are not negatively labeled. The label is applied only if we consistently break these rules. Apparently, breaking common rules is intolerable because it indicates a rejection of the social reality as defined by the group.

One other distinction between the labeling perspective and the medical model is that the former does not focus on the rule breaking per se but rather on the reactions of other people (family, neighbors, doctors, society) toward the people whose behavior is defined as deviant. This reaction can include the formal application of the label *mentally ill.* This label is stigmatizing and generally permanent. All past behaviors are now interpreted in the light of this label, a case of re-creating the past to make sense of the present.

The case histories of mental patients provide an example of this process. Psychiatrists and social workers write up a case history that sustains their view of reality. The behaviors that reinforce their diagnosis are included, but past behavior that does not support it is left out. All future behaviors will also be assessed in this way, fulfilling the prophecy and tending to make the label a lifelong one. For example, when it was discovered that Senator Thomas Eagleton had once been subjected to shock therapy to treat depression, he was forced to resign as the Democratic vice-presidential candidate in 1972, something that would not have been considered had he been previously treated for appendicitis or hemorrhoids. The stigma of mental illness dies hard, if it dies at all.

The labeling process is a crucial factor in the formation of a deviant career—the stigma of the label often leads to subsequent deviance. This is what Lemert meant by the concept of secondary deviance. (Lemert, 1967:42–43). **Primary deviance** is the rule breaking that occurs prior to labeling. **Secondary deviance** is behavior resulting from the labeling process. Being labeled *mentally ill* means being rejected by society, by employers, by friends, and even by relatives. There is a high probability that the person negatively labeled will turn to behavior that fulfills the observer's prophecy. People labeled as deviants tend to become locked into a deviant behavior pattern. Thus, secondary deviance further cements the mental disorder "career." Because other people expect the individual to behave in certain ways, the likelihood is that he or she will fulfill the social prophecy. In addition, most people are unwilling to have normal social interaction (as dating partners, as friends, as neighbors, as co-workers) with a person labeled *mentally disturbed.* The individual so stigmatized and isolated may become convinced that he or she is indeed "mad." In other words, the pejoratively labeled person accepts the definitions of others for himself or herself. If they treat the individual as crazy, he or she acts that way. Moreover, powerful others may actually reward the deviant behavior, thus reinforcing it. Cole has provided us with an excellent illustration of this process:

> After someone is labeled as deviant, he often finds it rewarding to accept the label and act deviant. Consider, for example, a patient in a mental hospital who has been diagnosed as a schizophrenic. If the patient refuses to accept the diagnosis, claims that he is not mentally ill, and demands to be immediately released, the staff will consider him to be hostile and uncooperative. He may be denied privileges and treated as hopelessly insane. After all, the person who cannot even recognize that he is ill must be in a mental state in which he has no perception of reality! On the other hand, if the patient accepts the validity of the diagnosis, admits his illness, and tries to cooperate with the staff in effecting a cure, he will be rewarded. He will be defined as a good, cooperative patient who is sincerely trying to get better. Any weird or unusual behavior he engages in will be ignored; after all, he is mentally ill, and such types of behavior should be expected from a person in his mental state. He may even be rewarded for engaging in behavior which is considered to be characteristic of schizophrenia. Such behavior serves to reassure the staff that the patient is indeed mentally ill and that the social organization of the mental hospital makes sense. (Cole, 1975:141–142)

Thomas Scheff has listed nine hypotheses that summarize the labeling theory of mental disorder:

1. Residual rule-breaking [**residual rules** are the rules that govern normal social interaction] arises from fundamentally diverse sources (that is, organic, psychological, situations of stress, volitional acts of innovation or defiance).
2. Relative to the rate of treated mental illness, the rate of unrecorded residual rule-breaking is extremely high.
3. Most residual rule-breaking is "denied" and is of transitory significance.
4. Stereotyped imagery of mental disorder is learned in early childhood.
5. The stereotypes of insanity are continually reaffirmed, inadvertently, in ordinary social interaction.
6. Labeled deviants may be rewarded for playing the stereotype deviant roles.
7. Labeled deviants are punished when they attempt to return to conventional roles.
8. In the crisis occurring when a residual rule-breaker is publicly labeled, the deviant is highly suggestible and may accept the label.

9. Among residual rule-breakers, labeling is the single most important cause of careers of residual deviance. (Scheff, 1975:9–10)

Labeling theory has generated considerable controversy. The critics cite several shortcomings. First, they argue that the theory does not explain the source of the original deviant behavior but, instead, focuses on how the deviant behavior pattern is reinforced by the social reactions to it. Gove (1970) has argued that the labeling approach is wrong in its assertion that societal reaction is the single most important cause of a career of mental illness. He asserts that the individual's behavior, not the reaction to it, is the most important reason:

> The evidence shows that a substantial majority of the persons who are hospitalized have a serious psychiatric disturbance quite apart from any secondary deviance that may be associated with the mentally ill role. Furthermore, persons in the community do not view someone as mentally ill if he happens to act in a bizarre fashion. On the contrary, they persist in denying mental illness until the situation becomes intolerable. Once prospective patients come into contact with public officials, a substantial screening still occurs, presumably sorting out persons who are being railroaded or who are less disturbed. (Gove, 1970:882)

Another criticism is that the labeling theory assumes the individual to be a passive reactor, compelled by social forces and with no autonomy to make choices.

Despite these failings, the labeling approach provides some very important insights about mental disorder. Unlike the medical model, this system views mental disorder as a form of learned behavior. Rosenhan's study of pseudopatients who claimed to hear voices on entering a hospital demonstrates how permanent a label is. No one recognized these patients as sane, and they were all finally discharged as "schizophrenics in remission." Not only is the negative label the fundamental basis on which doctors and nurses interact with the individual, but it also has a profound effect on other interpersonal relationships—independent of behavior. According to Stuart,

> once a negative label has been applied, there is a clear and present danger that the person so identified will be the victim of additional negative inference solely on the basis of his having been designated as a deviant, without reference either to the behavior which culminated in his having been labeled or to any subsequent actions on his part. (Stuart, 1970:104)

The point of the labeling theorists cannot be stressed enough—labeling is inherently dehumanizing. By giving the individual a psychiatric label, the diagnostician molds the patient's behavior to make it conform to the diagnostic stereotypes. Draguns and Phillips conclude "that far from being an objective guide to predicting behavior, diagnosis becomes a self-fulfilling prophecy. People act as they are called; schizophrenic, or sociopathic, or neurotic behavior is stamped in and maintained in this manner" (Draguns and Phillips, 1971:9).

The conflict approach.   At the heart of the **conflict perspective** is the assumption that society is stratified and the powerful people use their power to maintain their power. Mental illness in this view is a label attached by the powerful (and their agents in the medical and legal establishments) to those who threaten the status quo. This labeling takes several forms. First, there are people whose behaviors do not conform to society's norms and who therefore are excluded from full participation in society. Thus, the mental health of people who deviate from the Protestant work ethic, heterosexual relationships, and materialistic life-styles is suspect. By labeling negatively people who deviate from society's dominant norms, the powerful maintain the system that benefits them.

Second, the powerless are disproportionately recipients of negative labels, whether the label be *criminal* or *crazy*. The powerless are not able to defend themselves adequately in the courts and before the medical establishment because they lack economic resources and social power. The result is that women, Blacks and other racial minorities, and the poor are overrepresented in mental hospitals. The disturbed affluent, on the other hand, tend to escape the negative label by seeking private help that is unrecognized in official statistics and by the community.

Another way of interpreting the overrepresentation of the powerless among the mentally disturbed is that their personal troubles result from their being victims of social, political, and economic exploitation. Being a member of a stigmatized, despised, and dispossessed social group is a constant source of alienation, anger, and other forms of stress.

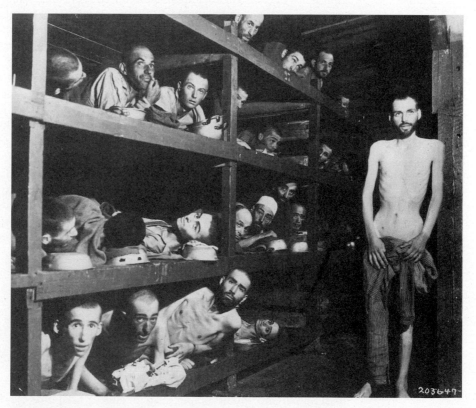

The Nazis attempted to exterminate the Jews, raising the question: Can a society be mentally ill?

Conflict theorists thus assume that society is the root of mental suffering. Rather than focus on the individual and his or her adjustment (although this may be necessary in the short term), which validates and reinforces the establishment system, conflict theorists argue that the only real and lasting form of therapy is a radical transformation of society. The following discussion on radical therapy amplifies this assumption.

The **radical therapists** turn the tables on the medical model. (The following discussion is adapted from Agel, 1971.) For them, society is the problem, not an individual who breaks the residual rules. Mental disorder is viewed as a process that the individual is going through in his or her relationship with the environment; it is the mechanism by which he or she survives in a mad world. Thus, society produces mental aberrations in people because it is mad! How can society be mad? Let's look at some examples.

Perhaps society is ill if it (1) continues to waste finite resources at an astounding rate and is oblivious to the needs of the rest of the world; (2) poisons the air, water, and land; (3) stockpiles enough weapons to kill everyone on earth many times over; (4) oppresses minority groups; (5) allows poverty in the midst of affluence; (6) insists that everyone should work yet continues policies that ensure that millions will be unemployed (sounds schizophrenic, doesn't it?); (7) punishes the relatively small-time street criminal but lets the big-time embezzler off with a suspended sentence; (8) maintains an economic system whose goal is maximizing profit rather than serving people; (9) uses propaganda to get people to stop smoking and at the same time subsidizes tobacco farmers to ensure its continued availability; and (10) has schools that make virtually every activity competitive, sorting students into piles of a few winners and a majority of losers.

Perhaps society is ill if the majority of people within it (1) believe that they can communicate with unseen forces; (2) accept the ideology that women are inferior to men; and (3) obey authority even if it means killing. (R. D. Laing has pointed out that "normal men have killed perhaps 100,000,000 of their fellow normal men in the last fifty years" [Laing, 1967:12].) The thesis of the radical therapists is illustrated nicely by the classic movie *King of Hearts*. During World War I the British sent one of their soldiers to a small French village to find and blow up a bomb that the Germans had left there. The townspeople had fled, and the inmates of the local asylum had taken their places. In the resulting interaction between the soldier and the inmates, the soldier realizes the absurdity of war and begins to wonder which people—the normal people who fight wars or the abnormal people—are really insane. He finally decides that the abnormal are the normal and joins them. The message is that the powerful decide who is well and who is ill. In essence, who is insane depends solely on who has the keys to the asylum.

Another theme of radical therapy is that the goal of the mental health establishment is to focus on the adjustment of individuals so that they will ultimately fit into society. Thus, psychiatry, psychology, and social work validate, enforce, and reinforce the established system. They act as agents of social control to the extent that they testify that prophets, nonconformists, rebels, and other deviants are mentally ill and should be put away in jails or hospitals. So, too, with people who refuse to go to war, the so-called troublemakers who led the civil rights movement in the South, and the student dissenters in the late 1960s. Psychologist Robert

Coles has observed that most people in the United States interpreted the acts of these people as symptoms of something wrong with them (thereby blaming the victim). The students, for example, were thought to be immature, exhibitionists, and unable to handle authority. They were described, typically, as acting out their fantasies, rebelling against authority figures, and letting their ids overrule their egos. The mental health establishment placed the blame for conflict on the people challenging the status quo rather than on the conditions present in society that prompted their actions (Coles, 1970).

People in the United States have castigated the former Soviet Union, and rightly so, for placing its dissidents in mental asylums. The Soviet argument was that anyone who criticizes the state must be irrational, because the state works for the benefit of all. But we should realize that the United States does the same thing, placing its political dissidents in prisons or mental hospitals, with the help of professionals in the medical health field. The American Psychological Association has officially condemned

> the practice, wherever it may occur, of suppressing or neutralizing political dissenters by diagnosing them as mentally ill and committing them to mental hospitals. We consider it the responsibility of individual psychologists to oppose such practices within the organization in which they are employed and, if they do not succeed in changing the practices, to dissociate themselves from personal complicity in them. (American Psychological Association, 1973:1)

A related concern of the radical therapists is the involuntary hospitalization of people diagnosed as mentally ill. They feel that this practice blames the victims and deprives them of their constitutional rights. The person labeled *mentally ill* can be detained involuntarily in a hospital indefinitely, which would not be possible if the individual were a criminal. The state acts on the assumption that society must be protected from dangerous and disruptive individuals, not by punishment but by treatment. This problem is not a minor one; about 42 percent of the patients in institutions are committed involuntarily. However, as McCaghy notes, "it is probably easier in our society to have troublesome individuals committed to a mental hospital than to have them placed in jail. The reason is that in the eyes of psychiatrists and the law, mentally 'ill' persons are seen as incapable of choice, and that is how they are often handled" (McCaghy, 1976:334).

Another tenet of radical therapists is that the mental health establishment and mental hospitals are harmful to people because they place a stigmatizing label on certain people and force them into social roles they do not want. In other words, rather than being beneficial to people, traditional psychiatry is actually harmful because it *creates* mental disorder. In short, according to Anderson, "the whole business of diagnosing, institutionalizing, restraining, drugging and generally doctoring people as insane is simply a bunch of people who see the world one way ganging up on a few people who see it differently" (Anderson, 1973:14).

Such a radical statement actually questions the reality of insanity. The radical therapists consider mental illness a myth. Thomas Szasz, a radical psychiatrist and the prime mover behind this heretical notion, acknowledges that the mental disorders exist but contends that they are not illnesses, only problems of living (Szasz, 1970). They are strategies to cope with difficult or insoluble situations.

They most certainly are not diseases, only difficulties in interpersonal relations that society—through its agents of social control (psychologists and psychiatrists)—labels as a *mental illness*. Szasz concludes that

> the concept functions as a disguise: instead of calling attention to conflicting human needs, aspirations, and value, the concept of mental illness provides an amoral and impersonal "thing"—an "illness"—as an explanation for problems of living. We may recall in this connection that not so long ago it was devils and witches that were held responsible for man's problems in living. The belief in mental illness, as something other than man's trouble in getting along with his fellow man, is the proper heir to the belief in demonology and witchcraft. Mental illness thus exists or is "real" in exactly the same sense in which witches existed or were "real." (Szasz, 1970:21)

Another variant of this "mental illness is a myth" theme comes from social observers such as Carlos Castenada who believe that there is an infinite variety of ways of perceiving and experiencing reality; one is not necessarily better than the other (Castenada, 1972). If Castenada is right, then as Anderson observes,

> the challenge to a democratic society is greater than we had ever suspected. We have to make room for, and recognize the rights of, not only different races and creeds and colors but totally different ideas of reality. We have to consider the possibility that people who cannot get into the state of consciousness we call sanity—the one that makes us all get up in the morning and go to work, the mind-set that Andre Weil in *The Natural Mind* calls "straight thinking"—are not necessarily crazy. We have to consider the possibility that if a person who believes in the Immaculate Conception can be elected president of the United States while a person who claims to see demons is put away in a mental hospital, we do not have separation of church and state after all. (Anderson, 1973:16)

The radical therapists argue for solutions to the dilemma of mentally disturbed people at two levels: personal and societal. Because society is considered the cause of all mental suffering, the only real and lasting form of therapy requires a radical transformation of society. The institutions of society must become just, humane, nonelitist, nonalienating, and nonoppressive.

Because these radical changes are not likely to be forthcoming in the foreseeable future, radical therapists must also focus on the problems of their clients. The goal of radical therapy is not to achieve an adjustment of people to society, as is the case with traditional therapy, but the opposite: to free them from the social conditions that cause psychological distress. People who need the help of a therapist are people who are oppressed and believe the lies they have been socialized to accept. Unlike the conventional therapist, who remains neutral (thus actually siding with the establishment), the radical therapist sides with the client. As Steiner has described it,

> the radical psychiatrist will not look for the wrongness within the person seeking psychiatric attention; rather, he will look for the way in which this person is being oppressed and how the person is going along with the oppression. The only problem that radical psychiatry looks for inside someone's head is how he empowers and enforces the lies of the oppressor and thereby enforces his own oppression. (Steiner, 1974:193)

CHAPTER REVIEW

1. What is and what is not a mental disorder depends on the social judgments of other people. Thus, what is included and what is not varies by the audience, situation, and culture.

2. The classification scheme used by psychiatrists in the United States has changed with each edition of the *DSM*. These changes suggest that what is considered an illness varies with changes in public opinion, professional fads, and the efforts of powerful interest groups.

3. We cannot determine the scope and seriousness of mental disorders in society because of the problems of psychiatric diagnosis and the variation in definitions and interpretations among different audiences.

4. Psychotherapy is based on Freud's assumption that mental disorders are problems of the individual's unconscious. Psychotherapy has shortcomings: (a) the theory is based on unseen and therefore unmeasurable forces; (b) treatment is expensive and time-consuming; and (c) research shows that the success rate of persons treated is not significantly different from those receiving no treatment at all.

5. Awareness therapies focus on authentic relationships, honesty, and capturing one's inner strength. These techniques, however, are inappropriate for the severely disturbed; they tend to give simple answers to complex problems; and they focus on individual rather than social situations.

6. Behavior modification seeks to change the maladaptive behaviors of individuals rather than seeking to change their social environment or their troubled psyches.

7. Drug therapy allows individuals to function by suppressing symptoms, but it does not provide cures. Moreover, doctors and hospital personnel commonly use drugs for social control rather than for therapy.

8. Psychosurgery has a long history. It attacks the symptoms rather than the sources of anxiety and violence. Also, it can be used by people in authority to control troublesome people.

9. Mental hospitals are total institutions, where powerless people are cut off from the wider society and lead an enclosed, formally controlled life. Faced with this oppressive environment, patients tend to adopt one of three coping strategies: withdrawal, conformity, or rebellion. Patients are punished for rebellion because it indicates that they are not willing to accept the role of being sick. Another problem is the denial of a patients' civil rights. A Supreme Court decision—*O'Connor* v. *Donaldson* (1975)—ruled that mental patients cannot be confined in hospitals against their will if they are not dangerous to anyone and can survive on their own.

10. The medical model assumes that mental disorders are diseases with biological sources and cures. Freudians accept the medical model as a metaphor—mental disturbances are analogous to physical illness. The medical model has several problems: (a) there is lack of agreement on the symptoms, diagnoses, and treatments for mental disorders; (b) the source of the illness cannot be located, as it can for physical illness; (c) bodily illness is something a patient

has, but a mental disorder is really something a person is or does; and (d) the medical model ignores social factors.

11. The labeling approach to mental disorder maintains that the mentally disrupted receive the label *mentally ill* because their behaviors exceed the commonly accepted rules of social life (residual rules). Other people in the society respond by assigning a label that is stigmatizing and generally permanent. This labeling encourages continuation of the supposedly bizarre behaviors (secondary deviance) and thus acts as a self-fulfilling prophecy. Critics argue that this approach does not explain the source of the original deviance and that it assumes that individuals are compelled totally by social forces.

12. The conflict perspective assumes that the powerful in society (and their agents in the medical and legal establishments) use the mental illness label to maintain the status quo. The labeling takes two forms: (a) people who deviate from society's norms are considered to be sick, and (b) the powerless disproportionately receive the pejorative label. Conflict theorists thus assume that society, rather than individuals, is the root of mental suffering.

13. Radical therapists assume that society is the problem, not the individuals who break society's rules. Mental disorder is a process that individuals go through in working out their relationship with the environment. It is the mechanism by which they survive in a mad world. From this perspective, the mental health establishment takes the wrong approach because it focuses on getting individuals to adjust to society rather than on trying to change society.

KEY TERMS

Mental disorder. Behavior that exceeds the tolerance of other people.

Psychiatric imperialism. The tendency for the psychiatric establishment to include more and more behaviors under the concept of mental illness.

Total institution. A setting in which individuals are isolated from the rest of society and subjected to the control and manipulation of the powerful.

Deinstitutionalization. The trend to decrease the number of hospitalized mental patients.

Reinstitutionalization. The reversal of the trend to decrease the number of hospitalized mental patients.

Medical model. The application of the terms and assumptions of medicine to a social problem such as mental disorder.

Labeling. The approach to a social problem that emphasizes the power of definition to influence future behavior.

Primary deviance. The rule breaking that occurs prior to labeling.

Secondary deviance. The behavior that results from the labeling process.

Residual rules. Rules that govern normal social interaction.

Conflict perspective. The assumptions that society is stratified and that the powerful people use their power to maintain the status quo.

Radical therapy. Society is the source of all mental suffering, not individuals who are different.

FOR FURTHER STUDY

Jerome Agel, ed. *The Radical Therapist.* New York: Ballantine Books, 1971.

Kai T. Erikson. *Wayward Puritans: A Study of the Sociology of Deviance.* New York: Wiley, 1966.

Michael Foucault. *Madness and Civilization: A History of Insanity in the Age of Reason.* New York: Random House/Vintage, 1973.

Erving Goffman. *Asylums.* New York: Doubleday/Anchor, 1969.

Ann Braden Johnson. *Out of Bedlam: The Truth About Deinstitutionalization.* New York: Basic Books, 1990.

Stuart A. Kirk and Herb Kutchins. *The Selling of DSM: The Rhetoric of Science in Psychiatry.* Hawthorne, N.Y.: Aldine de Gruyter, 1992.

Thomas J. Scheff. *Being Mentally Ill: A Sociological Theory.* New York: Aldine, 1984.

Edwin M. Schur. *Labeling Deviant Behavior: Its Sociological Implications.* New York: Harper & Row, 1971.

Thomas S. Szasz. *The Manufacture of Madness.* New York: Delta Books, 1970.

Thomas S. Szasz. *The Myth of Mental Illness.* Rev. ed. New York: Harper & Row, 1974.

FORUM

ARE DRUGS THE ANSWER TO MENTAL DISORDERS?

According to current research, there appears to be a link between the biochemistry of the brain and abnormal behavior.

William C. Cockerham

The concept of a biochemical cause of insanity goes back to the time of the ancient Greeks and is historically derived from a belief that "poisons" generated within the body are somehow able to affect the mind. At the beginning of the twentieth century, this idea was strengthened by findings demonstrating how syphilis was able to produce infection in the brain and cause manifestly bizarre behavior. Subsequent strategies to locate abnormal biochemical substances in the blood and urine of schizophrenic patients were generally unsuccessful, but there was a major breakthrough in 1952. Two French psychiatrists, Jean Delay and Pierre Deniker, injected chlorpromazine into their patients and soon found that it would activate withdrawn schizophrenics and bring their characteristically flat manner into a relatively normal state. Later, in large controlled studies conducted in the United States, it was confirmed that chlorpromazine produced significant improvements in thought disorder, withdrawal, blunted affect, and autistic behavior.

The focus of biochemical research dealing with behavioral abnormalities has been on the neuronal activity in the central nervous system. This activity consists of signals carried via chemical agents (neurotransmitters) between one neuron and another. How such activity affects behavior is obscure, but the assumption is that the action of the neurotransmitters is very important in mental disorder. It may be that too much or too little of these chemical substances at particular receptor sites produce or fail to produce certain chemical responses that shape behavior. Neurotransmitters may work like keys in a lock; some fit correctly into receptor sites specifically designed to accept them, and others prevent insertion of the correct key. Or, receptor sites may have a selective affinity for some compounds of a given type and a similar affinity for antagonistic compounds which leads to the displacement of one or another substance. Or perhaps some other process is involved. At any rate, chlorpromazine and other drugs of the phenothiazine group are apparently able to block the action of dopamine, a neurotransmitter, whose hyperactivity is thought to be significant in the production of paranoid delusions and auditory hallucinations. An excessive amount of dopamine in brain receptor sites may also be involved in mania, and a deficiency in norepinephrine, another neurotransmitter, might produce depression.

Source: William C. Cockerham, *Sociology of Mental Disorder,* 1981, pp. 80–81. Reprinted by permission of Prentice-Hall, Inc., Englewood Cliffs, N.J.

A skeptic maintains that the prevailing "drugcraft" is merely an extension of the perspective that legitimated witchcraft.

Ronny Turner

The condition and curse of witchcraft, used by humanity for centuries to "explain" aberrant behavior and to justify the execution of over 300,000 people, no longer are accepted in the Western world. They have been replaced by the languages of medicine, psychiatry, and biochemistry. With the increased medicalization of our rhetoric, the curse, sin, and the devil have given way to flawed chemistry—a chemical pathology of the brain.

Chemical imbalance has replaced madness, which earlier replaced badness.

To transform badness into madness reclassifies the problem but contributes nothing to its solution and actively impedes its understanding. The problem, simply stated, is this: the fact that the brain, like every other part of the body, is involved in human conduct does not make deviant behavior a medical problem any more than the fact that nuclear physics may be used in building a bomb makes international diplomatic conflicts problems in physics.

Seeking to explain the causes of deviance in purely biochemical terms is analogous to finding runners (people who have been observed running) and trying to determine what running *is* and what "causes" it by doing biochemical analyses. On the assumption that running lies "in the blood," chemicals are given the runners and scientists observe that running is altered beneficially or deleteriously, depending on the drugs administered; the observation that runners and running are affected by drugs is used as "evidence" that running is caused by chemical elements in the blood. From a social perspective the running is explained in various ways: the person was late for work, exercising for cardiovascular fitness, training for the 100-meter dash, or avoiding a mugger.

Biochemistry cannot explain deviant behavior any more than chemical analysis can differentiate spit from saliva. Spit is saliva that is socially defined as inappropriately placed. There is a difference between tap water and holy water, but the difference exists solely in social definition, not in the chemistry of the water. Deviant behavior is social spit.

If you believe you are Jesus, your assertion is likely to be regarded as a symptom of schizophrenia; if you believe and assert that Jesus was the son of God, then your belief is regarded as a reflection of what you are: Christian. We will discover the chemical cause of schizophrenia when we discover the chemical cause of Christianity.

The biochemical specialist, psychobiologist, psychiatrist dispensing antipsychotic drugs, medical doctors prescribing a vast chemical arsenal—these representatives of science have replaced those who were formerly appointed by authorities to detect witches. In short, drugcraft has replaced witchcraft.

Source: Ronny Turner, professor of sociology at Colorado State University, wrote this essay specifically for the third edition of this book.

17 *Drugs*

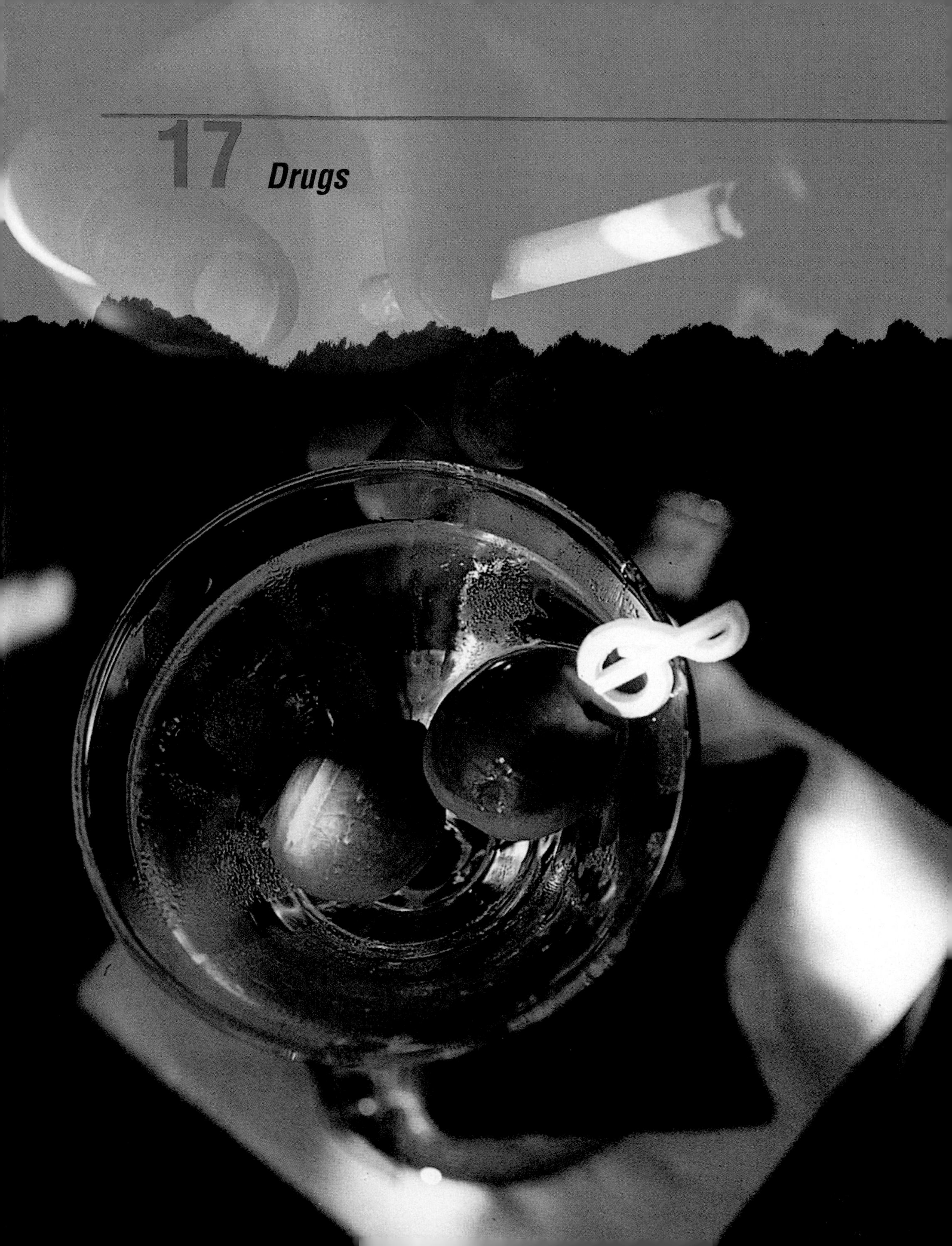

A **drug** is any chemical that causes biochemical reactions in the body when ingested. This definition is very broad and includes such chemicals as aspirin, caffeine, nicotine, and alcohol. Every society accepts some drugs as appropriate and regards others as unacceptable. Some drugs are considered dangerous, and others are harmless. But the definitions vary from society to society, and within U.S. society they are inconsistent and often ambiguous. As Szasz has said,

> There is probably one thing, and one thing only, on which the leaders of all modern states agree; on which Catholics, Protestants, Jews, Mohammedans, and atheists agree; on which Democrats, Republicans, Socialists, Communists, Liberals, and Conservatives agree; on which medical and scientific authorities throughout the world agree; and on which the views, as expressed through opinion polls and voting records, of the large majority of individuals in all civilized countries agree. That thing is the "scientific fact" that certain substances which people like to ingest or inject are "dangerous" both to those who use them and to others; and that the use of such substances constitutes "drug abuse" or "drug addiction"—a disease whose control and eradication are the duty of the combined forces of the medical profession and the state. However, there is little agreement—from people to people, country to country, even decade to decade—on which substances are unacceptable and their use therefore considered a popular pastime, and which substances are unacceptable and their use therefore considered "drug abuse" and "drug addiction." (Szasz, 1975:ix)

Many in the United States are concerned about the drug problem. But what is meant by "the drug problem"? Is drug use equated with abuse? Why is the use of alcohol accepted by society whereas the use of marijuana is not? Is drug use a medical or a criminal problem? These questions are considered in this chapter.

Three points should be made at the outset of this discussion. First, definitions concerning drugs and drug-related behaviors are **socially constructed.** That is, definitions about drugs are not based on some **ontological truth** (a universal and undeniable reality) but rather on meanings that people in groups have imputed to certain things and behaviors. Second, because definitions concerning drugs are socially constructed, members of different societies or groups (e.g., religious and political) within societies will often differ in their social constructions about this phenomenon. And, third, the definition of drugs by the most powerful interest groups in a society will become part of the law and be enforced on others. Thus, the labeling of some drugs as licit and others as illicit involves politics. Therefore, in examining such topics as drug use and abuse, types of drugs, the history of drug laws, and the consequences of official drug policies, this chapter continually refers to the **politics of drugs.**

Drugs in Society

Drugs are used worldwide for conviviality, pleasure, and medicinal purposes. The average U.S. family has about thirty different drugs in its medicine cabinet and numerous alcoholic beverages in its liquor cabinet. Physicians write about 1.5 billion prescriptions for pharmaceutical substances each year. More than 80 percent of the people in the United States are regular caffeine users, two-thirds of adults use alcoholic beverages, and one-third use nicotine regularly (Goode, 1989:15). A 1990 national survey of 11,631 high school students in grades nine through twelve found that almost one-third had used marijuana at least once and 14 percent had used marijuana during the thirty days preceding the survey. That same survey found that 6.6 percent had used any form of cocaine (powder, crack, or freebase) at least once, and 2.1 percent had used cocaine during the thirty days preceding the survey (*Journal of the American Medical Association,* 1991:3266). In short, "ours is a society in which *psychoactive drugs are very important* (McCaghy and Cernkovich, 1987:445)

Types and Effects of Psychoactive Drugs

A **psychoactive drug** is a chemical that alters the perceptions and/or moods of people who take it. There are eleven major categories of psychoactive drugs. This section briefly describes each of them, ranging in order from the least to the most hazardous (Fort and Cory, 1975).

Caffeine.   Probably the most widely used and safest psychoactive drug is caffeine, found most commonly in coffee, tea, chocolate, and cola. It is a stimulant that makes some people more alert and increases their ability to work fast and accurately. There is evidence that caffeine is addictive, because people who normally consume several cups of coffee a day suffer mild withdrawal symptoms when caffeine is eliminated from their diet. Heavy use may cause irritability, insomnia, anxiety, and headache (White, 1991:35).

Marijuana.   Marijuana comes from the hemp plant, *Cannabis sativa.* It is the world's fourth most widely used psychoactive drug (following caffeine, nicotine, and alcohol). In 1988 an estimated 65 million people in the United States had smoked marijuana. The proportion of the population who are current users has declined since the peak use about 1979. Similarly, marijuana use by high school seniors has fallen from a peak of 37 percent in 1979 to 17.4 percent in 1988 (use within the previous month) (National Institute on Drug Abuse, 1989).

The inhalation of marijuana produces a relaxing effect, increases the intensity of sense impressions, and provides a "high" akin to one produced by alcohol. Goode has described the most common effects by users as

> euphoria, relaxation; a sense of one's mind wandering, a kind of stream of consciousness; a sensation that time is slowed down . . . an impairment of one's short-term memory; a feeling of ravenous hunger; a strong increase in the enjoyment of one's senses—food tastes better, music sounds richer, more exciting, touch becomes more sensuous, one's sexual orgasm becomes more intense; one feels far more inclined to find things amusing, silly, uproarious; moving about feels more sinuous, smoother, more graceful and sensuous; one feels a kind of "floating" sensation; there is a reduced and impaired ability to think logically, rationally, in a linear fashion; one finds it difficult or impossible to read well or at all; there is a kind of "eureka" feeling about ordinarily common and usually uninteresting experiences and insights. (Goode, 1973:10)

Marijuana is a widely misunderstood drug. Some people consider pot smokers to be dope fiends. Many consider marijuana addictive, asserting that it creates physiological dependence. Some researchers have argued that it causes lower levels of sex hormones to be produced in males and breaks up chromosomes, causing genetic problems for future generations. These are but a few major problems noted in the media and scientific journals. The current data on marijuana are inconsistent, however, on these and other alleged problems. For example, five research studies done in the 1970s reported that marijuana caused a loss of motivation and the ability to think straight; another five studies reported no such effects.

Although much remains to be learned about the effects of marijuana, three dangers are evident. Marijuana has a negative effect on the lungs; its use increases dangers for people with damaged hearts; and probably 15 percent of automobile accidents in the United States are associated with marijuana intoxication. On the positive side, we know that marijuana is not physiologically addictive; there is no evidence of a lethal dose; and it has been found to have positive effects for certain medical problems, such as migraine headaches, glaucoma, and asthma. Of special note is the successful use of marijuana to reduce or eliminate the nausea that accompanies chemotherapy treatments for cancer. However, the Drug Enforcement Administration in its zeal to fight illicit drugs ruled that it would not reclassify marijuana so that doctors could prescribe it for medicinal use. At that time only 13 people in the United States could legally receive marijuana cigarettes made by the government and dispensed by prescription. In effect, the Drug Enforcement Agency (D.E.A.) ruled out further exceptions.

Inhalants.   The inhalation of certain chemicals found in glue, gasoline, paint thinner, fingernail polish remover, household cement, and the like produce a high, sometimes accompanied by bizarre thoughts, dizziness, loss of judgment, and aggressiveness. Inhalants can be quite dangerous if they replace the oxygen necessary for the brain and other organs to function properly.

Tranquilizers and antidepressants.   Tranquilizers and antidepressants are widely prescribed by physicians and psychologists to aid patients who are troubled by anxiety, insomnia, and depression. Typically, these drugs induce calm without anesthetizing or addicting the individual. There may be side effects, however, such as muscle relaxation, numbness, inability to concentrate, and damage to the liver and bone marrow. Prescriptions for Valium and other tranquilizers peaked in 1975 and have been declining ever since.

Psychedelics.   Also called hallucinogens, psychedelics produce sensory experiences that represent a different reality to the user. The person may react to trivial everyday objects as if they had great meaning. Emotions may be greatly intensified. Among the perceptual phenomena experienced by some people is the feeling that one is looking at oneself from the outside. Hallucinogens occur naturally in the peyote cactus, some mushrooms, and certain fungi and other plants. Bad experiences (or trips) with psychedelics include panic associated with loss of control, the common hallucination that spiders are crawling over the body, paranoia and delusions, and occasionally suicide. The latest psychedelic drug and perhaps the most dangerous is phencycledine (PCP), also known as angel dust. This drug, which is relatively easy to manufacture, can cause psychotic reactions (hallucinations, combative or self-destructive impulses), loss of bowel and bladder control, slurred speech, and inability to walk. Taken in large quantities, it can induce seizures, coma, and death. There is no evidence that physical dependence develops for any of the hallucinogenic drugs. For some people, though, psychological dependence occurs.

Narcotics (opiates).   Narcotics are powerful depressants that have a pronounced effect on the respiratory and central nervous systems. Medically, they are used very effectively to relieve pain, treat diarrhea (paregoric), and stop coughing (codeine). These drugs, which include opium and its derivatives, morphine, and heroin, also produce a euphoria. Many users describe the first "rush" as similar to sexual orgasm, followed by feelings of warmth, peacefulness, and increased self-esteem.

Opiates are addictive. Prolonged users experience severe withdrawal symptoms. Contrary to common belief, however, drugs such as heroin are physiologically harmless. In McCaghy's words,

> in reality, as psychoactive drugs go, heroin is one of the safest—prolonged use results in no disease or damage to organs or cells. There are some minor short-term effects for persons under the drug's influence: diminished sexual potency, menstrual irregularities, constriction of pupils, constipation, and excessive sweating. In the long run, cigarette smoking and alcohol drinking are far more dangerous than heroin—they can kill, heroin cannot.
>
> Furthermore, if the user's primary motivation is to avoid withdrawal distress, he or she can take just enough of the drug to do that and can still behave quite normally; that is, the user can work, drive, and think lucidly, even while using very large dosages. Such would not be the case for the user of alcohol, however. Relatively large doses of alcohol decrease one's mental and physical effectiveness regardless of experience with the drug. (McCaghy, 1976:287–288)

This is not to say that heroin use is safe. It is dangerous for three reasons—each a result of the drug's illegal status, not of the drug itself. First, because the drug is not regulated, it can include harmful impurities. Second, because the drug is injected directly into the veins without medical supervision, there is a constant danger of infection and overdose. The sharing of needles is a major cause of hepatitis and, in recent years, of the fatal disease AIDS. Intravenous drug users are the second-highest (after homosexual males) at-risk category for AIDS. The National Institute on Drug Abuse estimates that there are 1.3 million people taking various illegal drugs intravenously (National Institute on Drug Abuse, 1989).

The third danger associated with heroin is the extremely high cost of purchasing the illegal drug. The users must spend much of their time finding funds to supply their habit. For males finding funds typically means theft; and for females, shoplifting or prostitution—all hazardous occupations. Taken together, then, the criminal activities an addict turns to plus the complications of poor-quality drugs and infection lead to a relatively high rate of deaths. But to repeat McCaghy's point: "The danger of heroin stems not from the drug itself, but from the conditions that its illegality creates" (McCaghy, 1976:288).

Cocaine.   Until 1906, cocaine (a stimulant) was an ingredient in Coca-Cola. Cocaine gives users a euphoric lift, a sense of alertness, a feeling of confidence, and an intensely vivid, sensation-enhancing experience. Fort and Cory have reported that one measure of the drug's appeal is seen in the willingness of laboratory animals to work extraordinarily hard to be rewarded by the drug. When given drug rewards for pushing levers, animals "will push levers up to 250 times in a row for caffeine, 4,000 times for heroin, and 10,000 times for cocaine" (Fort and Cory, 1975:39).

About 22 million people in the United States have used cocaine, and the number of current users (those who have taken the drug in the past thirty days) is about 3 million (National Institute on Drug Abuse, 1989). Cocaine is a popular drug among young adults—12.1 percent of people ages eighteen to twenty-five reported using cocaine at least once in 1988 (National Institute on Drug Abuse, 1989); one in three college students tried cocaine before graduation in 1985 (Meyer, 1986); and nearly 3 percent of junior and senior high school students used cocaine in 1988 (National Institute on Drug Abuse, 1989). The data on cocaine use by young adults and adolescents indicate a downward trend each year since a peak in 1979.

Repeated use of cocaine can produce paranoia, hallucinations, sleeplessness, weight loss, and depression. Because the drug is normally "snorted" (the powder is ingested through the nostrils), use can permanently destroy the mucous membranes and create breathing difficulties. If the user desires a more potent dosage, cocaine can be injected in solution directly into the veins or chemically converted and smoked in the process called freebasing. Cocaine is not physically addictive, but psychological dependence is a problem for many users. Another problem is that cocaine use can lead to the use of sedatives (such as Quaaludes) to calm down after the high in an effort to quell the urge for more cocaine. Another variation is to mix cocaine with heroin, which combines a powerful stimulant with a potent depressant.

A relatively new form of cocaine, crack, is purchased inexpensively in pellets and inhaled as the substance is heated and vaporized in a special smoking device. This potent drug provides an almost instant rush. According to Lamar, "in minutes the flash high is followed by a crushing low that can leave a user craving another hit. But that evanescent electric jolt, priced so that almost anyone can afford it, has made crack the drug of the moment" (Lamar, 1986:16). Approximately 2 million people in the United States used crack in 1989 (National Institute on Drug Abuse, 1989:35).

Inciardi summarizes the use of cocaine:

> Cocaine has become the "all-American drug" and a $30 to $50 billion-a-year industry. It permeates all levels of society, from Park Avenue to the ghetto: lawyers and executives use cocaine; baby boomers and yuppies use cocaine; police officers, prosecutors, and prisoners use cocaine; politicians use cocaine; housewives and pensioners use cocaine; Democrats, Republicans, and Socialists use cocaine; students and stockbrokers and children and athletes use cocaine; even some priests and members of Congress use cocaine. (Inciardi, 1986:79)

Amphetamines. These mass-produced, synthetic stimulants ("uppers") are used to keep people awake and alert. Dieters also use them to decrease appetites. They have been used medically to treat depression, asthma, obesity, hyperactive children, narcolepsy (involuntary sleep), Parkinson's disease, and fatigue.

The effects of amphetamines are euphoria, feelings of self-confidence, alertness, and loss of fatigue. Blood pressure is increased, the bronchial tubes of the lung relax, and with high doses psychotic symptoms such as paranoia, delusions, and hallucinations occur. Physical dependence can occur (White, 1991). A problem with amphetamines is that some people using them find it difficult to calm down and sleep at night, so they take barbiturates ("downers") to help them sleep. Barbiturates, in turn, may make users sluggish and/or depressed in the morning, so they may take an "upper"—and so the cycle goes.

Amphetamines are physiologically and psychologically addictive. Persons who use these drugs intravenously are called speed freaks. They are feared even by other drug users because they are seen as potentially violent, uncontrollable, and dangerous when they are coming down from the effects of the drug. Other problems for the users are undernourishment and dehydration, skin sores, irritability, and hyperexcitability.

Barbiturates.   Barbiturates are depressants that, like alcohol, produce lightheadedness, ease tensions, and reduce inhibitions. They act as sedatives, making the user sleepy. Large doses can slow vital body functions and cause a coma and death. Addiction to these drugs occurs after the user takes larger-than-normal prescription doses for six weeks or more. Addicts undergoing withdrawal may experience hallucinations and convulsions. According to Fort and Cory, "doctors now agree that withdrawal from barbiturate addiction, like withdrawal from alcohol, is far more dangerous than withdrawal from narcotics and ought to take place in a hospital" (Fort and Cory, 1975:4).

The medical uses of barbiturates are for people suffering from anxiety, from insomnia, and for the emergency treatment of epilepsy, tetanus, and cerebral hemorrhage.

Nicotine.   Nicotine is the active ingredient of tobacco. Because the vast majority of smokers smoke fifteen or more cigarettes a day, they are averaging at least one cigarette for each hour they are awake. In this way nicotine "is the only drug that humans use hour by hour, week after week, till death do them prematurely part" (Fort and Cory, 1975:41). Nicotine is a stimulant that raises blood pressure, increases the heart rate, dulls the appetite, and provides the user with a sense of alertness. As a stimulant, nicotine is responsible for a relatively high probability of heart disease and strokes among cigarette smokers.

In addition to the nicotine, smokers inhale various coal tars, nitrogen dioxide, formaldehyde, and other ingredients that increase the chances of contracting lung cancer, throat cancer, emphysema, and bronchitis. Mintz reports that

> well over 400,000 Americans will die prematurely this year from tobacco-
> induced diseases, including about 136,000 from lung cancer, 115,000 from coro-
> nary heart disease, and 60,000 from chronic obstructive lung disease [about 2.5
> million tobacco users will die *worldwide* annually]. (Mintz 1991a:26)

Moreover, as the Environmental Protection Agency reported in 1992, *second-hand smoke* each year causes 3000 lung-cancer deaths, contributed to respiratory infections in babies resulting in 7500 to 15,000 hospitalizations, triggers 8000 to 26,000 new cases of asthma in previously unaffected children, and exacerbates symptoms in 400,000 to 1 million asthmatic children (reported in Cowley, 1992b). Put another way, about 1120 people in the United States die *every day* from prolonged tobacco use.

The smoking of tobacco is declining significantly in the United States (see Figure 17-1). In 1954, for example, 45 percent of adults smoked, compared to 28 percent in 1991. Moreover, people who still smoke are smoking fewer cigarettes than ten years ago (Hugick and Leonard, 1991). Faced with declining sales, the tobacco companies have increased their advertising—from $2 billion in 1982 to $3.2 billion in 1989 (Bass, 1990). This advertising is aimed primarily at African Americans, Latinos, women, youth, and the international market. (Antismoking ads also work; see the Observation on California's Antismoking Program.) The tobacco companies have increased the advertising and sales overseas to compensate for declining domestic sales. In 1989, for example, U.S. manufacturers sent 100 billion cigarettes abroad, more than twice as many as in 1983 (Mintz, 1991a:24).

Nicotine is addictive. Withdrawal symptoms include headache, difficulty in sleeping, problems with concentration, irritability, and anxiety (White, 1991:30–31).

Alcohol.   Alcohol is a relatively safe drug when used in moderation but one of the most dangerous when abused. It is a depressant that directly affects the central nervous system. Alcohol slows brain activity and muscle reactions. Thus, it is a leading cause of accidents:

- More than half of all traffic deaths occurred in alcohol-related accidents. Automobile accidents involving intoxicated drivers is the leading cause of death among teenagers.

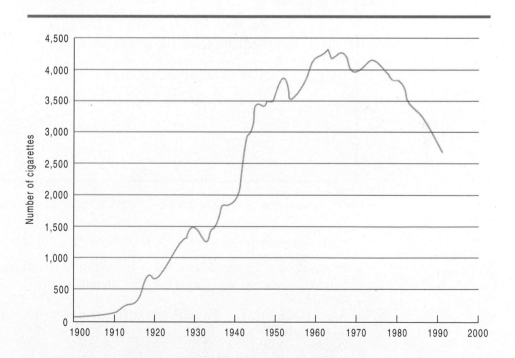

Figure 17.1   Per capita cigarette consumption, United States, 1900–1991

Source: U.S. Department of Health and Human Services, *Smoking and Health in the Americas* (Atlanta, Ga.: U.S. Department of Health and Human Services, Public Health Service, 1992), p. 33.

Mike Peters reprinted by permission of UFS, Inc.

- Alcoholics have a suicide rate six to fifteen times greater than the rate for the general population, and they die in fires ten times more frequently than do non-alcoholics.
- Approximately seven out of ten drowning victims had been drinking prior to their deaths.

  Alcohol consumption is related to other problems as well. Some examples:

- Among those criminals caught, if they used drugs prior to committing a crime, alcohol rather than illicit drugs was much more likely the drug of choice.

CALIFORNIA'S ANTISMOKING PROGRAM

In 1988 California voters passed Proposition 99, an initiative aimed at discouraging smoking and to help people quit. The program has worked, with the rate for adults who smoke dropping from 26.8 percent in 1987 to 22.2 percent in 1991 (a decline of 17 percent, compared to the drop in the national rate of 8 percent over the same period).

Proposition 99 has never cost the state a dime. The 1988 initiative raised cigarette taxes by 25 cents a pack and placed the proceeds in a half dozen dedicated accounts. Most of the $550 million generated each year supports medical services for the poor. But the law reserves 5 percent of the revenue for tobacco-related research and 20 percent for educational programs to discourage smoking. The most visible is a $16 million-a-year media campaign designed to counter the cigarette companies' better-funded promotions. The ads portray the manufacturers as greedy and amoral, accusing them of "the selective exploitation of minorities, the seduction of the young and the promotion of suicide." [While the tax on cigarettes caused some persons to quit, the state's educational efforts also were instrumental in this regard.] According to state Senate staffer John Miller, half of the California survey respondents who quit smoking in 1990 said the ads influenced them and 35 percent cited the ads as their primary motivation. (Cowley, 1992a:54)

- Hundreds of billions of dollars are lost through job absenteeism, lost production, medical expenses, and accidents resulting from alcohol.
- There are intangible and unmeasurable expenses due to disrupted families, spouse and child abuse, and desertion; and countless emotional problems arise from drinking. Most significant, results from a 1992 Gallup poll finds that one in five families reports alcohol as a serious problem in the household (McAneny, 1992:47).
- Among youth (high school and college), excessive drinking is related to vandalism, racist acts, violence, and sexual assault. (See the observation on youth and alcohol).

Continued use of large quantities of alcohol can result in indigestion, ulcers, degeneration of the brain, and cirrhosis of the liver; 14,000 alcoholics die of cirrhosis of the liver each year. Malnutrition is often associated with prolonged use of alcohol; a pint of whiskey provides about half of a person's daily calorie requirements but without the necessary nutrients. Heavy consumption also reduces the production of white blood cells, so alcoholics have a low resistance to bacteria.

Alcoholics, in addition, run the danger of the permanent destruction of brain cells, resulting in memory loss and sometimes psychotic behavior. Chronic use also results in physiological addiction. Withdrawal can be very dangerous, with the individual experiencing convulsions and delirium. The conclusion is inescapable, then, that alcohol is the most dangerous drug physically for the individual and socially for society. In fact, alcohol claims about 100,000 lives a year, twenty-five times as many as all illegal drugs combined.

OBSERVATION

ALCOHOL AND YOUTH

Three studies report heavy drinking among youth.

- A 1992 study by the Surgeon General reported that 8 million of the nation's 20.7 million youths in grades seven through twelve drink alcohol every week. Of those drinkers, 454,000 admit to weekly "binges"—i.e., consuming five or more drinks in a brief time (reported in Elson, 1991:64).
- A 1990 study of high school students in grades nine through twelve by the Centers for Disease Control found that more than one-third (36.9 percent) consumed five or more drinks of alcohol on at least one occasion during the thirty days prior to the survey (*Journal of the American Medical Association,* 1991:3266).
- A Department of Health and Human Services study found that nearly three-fourths of all college students drink at least once a month and that 41 percent of college students drink four or five drinks in a row at least once every two weeks (reported in Elson, 1991:65).

These data contradict two trends: (1) per capita alcohol consumption has been declining in the United States for years; and (2) youth consumption of illicit drugs has been trending down since the 1970s (e.g., while 49 percent of high school seniors had smoked marijuana in 1980, only 27 percent in 1990 had done so).

Why are so many high school and college age youth drinking, some into a stupor?

Boredom, peer pressure, escape from psychological pain and wanting to feel good are the usual answers. Since most of their parents drink, teenagers tend to think of alcohol as a less threatening drug than cocaine or marijuana. Says White House drug czar Bob Martinez: "Adults send a message to their kids that this is acceptable behavior. With marijuana, cocaine and heroin, there is no mixed message. With alcohol there is." To David Anderson, a research professor at George Mason

University's Center for Health Promotion, teenagers who indulge in binge drinking "delude themselves into thinking they can find their identity with alcohol. These kids are in search of community. And they have a quest for intimacy—who can I be at one with?" (Elson, 1991:65)

An extremely important reason is the alcohol industry itself. This industry aims much of its advertising at youth. Paul Wood of the National Council on Alcoholism and Drug Dependence says that alcohol ads, especially those pushing beer "equate being sexy and being powerful and being athletic with the use of alcohol" (quoted in *USA Today,* 1991:15a).

Finally, youth drinking occurs within a pervasive drug culture found in the United States. Eric Sterling, president of the Criminal Justice Policy Foundation, has put it this way:

When we hear the term, "the drug culture," what do we think of? Is it the 1967 "summer of love" in San Francisco, The Doors, Jimi Hendrix, Lenny Bruce, Janis Joplin—people who have been dead for 20 years? This is an anachronism.

You don't think of the Camel "Smooth" Character, "Spuds McKenzie" for "Bud Light," the "Schlitz Malt Liquor Bull," cigarettes "alive with pleasure," "Virginia Slims—you've come a long way baby," "Anacin" for FAST, FAST, FAST Relief," "Midol," because you "don't have time for the pain," . . . "Miller Time," and "the night which belongs to Michelob." That's the drug culture.

The drug culture is instant chemical relief, it is chemical sexiness, chemical camaraderie, chemical sophistication, chemical success and chemical self-esteem. The messages of the drug culture, and the values of the drug culture are created on Madison Avenue and bombarded at us and our children twenty-four hours a day. (Sterling, 1991:627)

In 1992 some 64 percent of the people in the United States polled by Gallup reported drinking alcoholic beverages (see Table 17.1). This is up from the 57 percent who identified themselves as drinkers in 1990 but down from the 70 percent who defined themselves as drinkers in 1981.

Drug Patterns by Class and Race

For whatever reason—perhaps increased awareness of the danger of drugs, renewed health consciousness, or monitoring in the workplace—drug use is declining. This decline is not uniform throughout society, however. The pattern differs significantly by social class. The middle and upper social classes have reduced their drug use, but the poor have not.

The data show consistently that better-educated young people have been reducing their use of marijuana and cocaine and the least educated have not. Actually, with the introduction of crack a few years ago, the consumption of cocaine has increased among the poor, especially the inner-city poor.

Intravenous drug users continue to be found predominantly among the inner-city poor. This practice places them at great risk of exposure to the AIDS virus from the sharing of needles. The common estimate is that about 40 percent of

Table 17.1 Use of alchoholic beverages by sex, age, race, education, and income, 1992

Question: Do you have occasion to use alcoholic beverages such as liquor, wine or beer, or are you a total abstainer?

Catgory	Percent Answering Yes to Alcohol Use
National	65%
Sex	
Male	72
Female	57
Age	
18–29	71
30–49	68
50 & older	56
65& & older	
Race	
Whites	66
Nonwhite	50
Education	
College graduate	78
College incomplete	64
High school graduate	65
Not high school graduate	49
Income	
$50,000 & over	80
$30,000–49,999	63
$20,000–29,000	64
under $20,000	56

Source: The Gallup Poll Monthly, No. 317 (February 1992), p. 46. Reprinted with permission.

diagnosed AIDS cases were Blacks and Hispanics, who constitute the over-whelming majority of intravenous drug users. One devastating consequence: Black babies are twenty-five times more likely to get AIDS than are White babies.

The disproportionate use of drugs by the poor is not limited to illicit drugs. The incidence of cigarette smoking is lower for Whites than for Blacks. This is *not* true for teenagers, however. A nationwide survey of high school students in 1990 found that by race, 41 percent of Whites reported tobacco use, compared to 32 percent of Latinos, and 17 percent of African Americans (reported in Hilts, 1991). Among adults, smoking is inversely related to socioeconomic status (SES)—the lower the SES, the greater the incidence of cigarette smoking.

For alcohol consumption, Blacks, especially Black men, have more alcohol-related problems than do Whites (the information on alcohol and race in this section is taken from the U.S. Department of Health and Human Services, 1991). Age is a significant variable; Whites are more likely to drink than are Blacks as youths, but between thirty and thirty-nine the rates of heavy consumption rise sharply for Blacks, surpassing that for Whites. Gender, too, is relevant, as Black women are much more likely to be abstainers than are White women. Income has an interesting effect—as income rises for Black men, rates of heavy drinking fall; among White men, however, an increase in income is accompanied by an increase in heavy drinking.

Latino males are more likely to have problems related to alcohol abuse than are Black males and White males. Among Latino males, Mexican Americans and Puerto Ricans drink more and have more alcohol related problems than do men in other Latino subgroups (Cubans and men from the countries of Central and South America and the Caribbean). By age, the pattern for Latino men is similar to that of Black men—heavy drinking increases during the thirties and continues into older ages. Latino women tend to abstain or drink infrequently.

Among Native Americans alcohol abuse is a contributing factor in 40 percent of all deaths (accidents, chronic liver disease, homicide, and suicide. The rate of fetal alcohol syndrome, a leading cause of mental retardation, is 6.1 per 1000 for Native American mothers, compared to 2.2 per 1000 in North America. This is despite the fact that Native American women drink considerably less than do men. Alcohol use varies considerably from tribe to tribe. Some tribes have fewer drinking adults than are found in the U.S. population; others have many more drinking adults. Unlike the pattern for Blacks and Latinos, Native American youth in tribes where drinking is heavy, tend to drink heavily.

Alcohol consumption patterns among Asian Americans show that they use and abuse alcohol less frequently than do non-Asians. This holds for people with Chinese, Japanese, Filipino, and Korean heritage, although there are ethnic differences, with the Japanese and Filipinos the most likely to have heavy drinkers. Women drink less than men in all four groups. Combining gender, age, and SES among Asian Americans, the most likely to drink are men under age forty-five who have higher social status.

In general, the poor are more inclined than the rich to use harmful substances. Why? The relative lack of education and therefore a lack of awareness of the dangers is one possibility. With respect to cigarettes and alcohol, another reason may arise from the tobacco and alcohol companies' special efforts to target potential Black consumers for their products: the companies sponsor sports tournaments and music festivals in Black neighborhoods, use highly visible Black entertainers and athletes in commercials, and purchase considerable advertising in Black publications and media outlets. The connection between poverty and using illicit drugs is less clear. One possibility is the irrelevance of the antidrug campaigns, which are implicitly based on the premise that a young person has a lot to lose by using drugs. The young poor who live in situations where jobs and other opportunities for advancement are scarce or nonexistent have nothing to lose by using drugs—they have already lost. The threat of drug-screening programs now increasingly used by employers may constrain people with a chance for a job, but it has no hold on the hopeless. Some observers have theorized that ghetto dwellers are prone to take drugs as an escape from a harsh and painful reality (for a review, see Inciardi, 1986:23–25). Others argue the opposite. Inciardi, considering heroin addicts, has said, "the conduct of most addicts was anything but an escape from life. Much of their time was spent in drug-seeking behaviors, in meaningful activities and relationships on the street . . . surrounding the economic institutions of heroin distribution" (Inciardi, 1986:25).

This discussion may lead to the erroneous conclusion that drug use and abuse are disproportionately lower-class phenomena. This is true for cocaine and heroin, but other drugs are more commonly used by the affluent. Table 17.1

Alcohol is more commonly consumed by Whites than by Blacks, by the educated, and by those with higher incomes.

shows that alcohol, for instance, is more commonly consumed by Whites than by Blacks, by the educated, and by those with higher incomes.

There are more than 2 million barbiturate and tranquilizer addicts in the United States, and they are generally middle- and upper-class Whites. Unlike the poor—who tend to use illicit drugs and, therefore, are hassled by the authorities and treated in prisons and public hospitals—the more affluent tend to use legal and prescription drugs and are treated by private physicians. Thus, their addiction is typically protected and hidden from public awareness.

The Impact of Social Factors on Drug Use

There is a variation in the patterns of use and in the behavioral effects that are caused by social factors. For example, the use of distilled alcohol was unknown to Native Americans prior to its introduction by Europeans. Thus, they had no socially acceptable norms to define its proper use and how to behave under its influence. As a consequence, when they obtained the intoxicant, members of some tribes frequently became drunk and violent. In other tribes, where alcohol was accepted and defined as a way to express happiness, violence from drinking was unknown.

A common belief is that alcohol numbs people's social control so that they behave without inhibition. MacAndrew and Edgerton argue that, on the contrary, the degree of inhibition release depends on the culture of the society, *not* on the amount of alcohol consumed: "Persons learn about drunkenness what their societies impart to them, and comporting themselves in consonance with these understandings they become living confirmations of their society's teachings" (MacAndrew and Edgerton, 1969:172). In other words, the behavior expected of drunks varies from culture to culture, as does their *actual* behavior. Similarly, one learns from others what to experience from a drug. A person's first experience with heroin is likely to produce feelings of fear and sickness rather than pleasure. As McCaghy has put it,

> the reason is that positive responses to the effects of heroin are neither automatic nor inherent in the chemical properties of the drug. One's responses are learned. Most first experiences with heroin occur in the company of others who encourage a favorable interpretation of the drug's effects. This influence may counteract even the most distasteful initiation to heroin. (McCaghy, 1976:284)

So, too, with marijuana. Most users were introduced to marijuana and continue to use it in a group context. They must learn from other user people the proper techniques to maximize the drug's effects, how to perceive the effects and connect them with the drug, and, finally, how to enjoy the effects. Writing of this last stage, Howard Becker has said that the user

> must learn to enjoy the effects he has just learned to experience. Marijuana-produced sensations are not automatically or necessarily pleasurable. The taste for such experience is a socially acquired one, not different in kind from acquired tastes for oysters or dry martinis. The user feels dizzy, thirsty; his scalp tingles; he misjudges time and distance. Are these things pleasurable? He isn't sure. If he is to continue marijuana use, he must decide that they are. . . . In no case will use continue without a redefinition of the effects as enjoyable. This redefinition occurs, typically, in interaction with more experienced users who, in a number of ways, teach the novice to find pleasure in this experience which is at first so

frightening. They may reassure him as to the temporary character of the unpleasant sensations and minimize their seriousness, at the same time calling attention to the more enjoyable aspects. . . .

In short, what was once frightening and distasteful becomes, after a taste for it is built up, pleasant, desired, and sought after. Enjoyment is introduced by the favorable definition of the experience that one acquires from others. Without this, use will not continue, for marijuana will not be for the user an object he can use for pleasure. (Becker, 1963:53–56)

Finally, the new marijuana user must, with the help of the group, set aside his or her conception of morality and decide to continue consciously breaking the law. According to Becker, "a person will feel free to use marijuana to the degree that he comes to regard conventional conceptions of it as the uninformed views of outsiders and replaces those conceptions with the 'inside' view he has acquired through his experience with the drug in the company of other users" (Becker, 1963:78).

Medical and Social Pressures to Use Drugs

In recent times chemists have created numerous synthetic substances that have positive health consequences. Vaccines have been developed to fight illnesses such as polio, mumps, smallpox, diphtheria, and measles. Many of these contagious diseases have been eliminated by the wonders of science. Similarly, antibiotics were created as cures for a number of infectious diseases. The public quickly accepted these drugs as beneficial.

In the early 1950s chemists made a breakthrough in drugs that treated mental disorders such as depression, insomnia, aggression, hyperactivity, and tension. These drugs (tranquilizers, barbiturates, and stimulants) have since been widely prescribed by doctors for these problems. Hills reports that

people are becoming less and less willing to accept psychological discomfort and anguish—the normal trials and tribulations of life—as a natural consequence of human existence. It would appear that much of the medical profession, in fact, has come to view loneliness, anxiety, conflict, or unhappiness as symptoms of "psychic distress," an ailment to be corrected, eliminated, or "cured" with drugs. . . . In the United States, doctor-patient visits reportedly last an average of 14 minutes. In about two-thirds of these contacts, the physician prescribes a drug (one-third of them a mood-altering medication). These statistics would suggest that the medical profession is severely drug-dependent. (Hills, 1980:118–119)

The pharmacological industry works very hard to convince the public to use their products and to convince physicians to prescribe them. Again, we refer to Hills:

Physicians and the pharmacological industry have combined to hold out the promise of putting an end to personal distress through chemistry. Drug manufacturers seeking new markets and bigger profits urge everyone to feel better fast ("relief is only a swallow away"), and attempt to persuade physicians and the public that *unpleasant human feelings are abnormal*—an "illness" that should be corrected with drugs. (Hills, 1980:118)

Thus, physicians and pharmaceutical companies have been instrumental in encouraging the use of drugs. But this encouragement is only part of the reason people in the United States buy drugs. Many people find life so stressful, boring, competitive, and frustrating that they seek drugs for a change in mood or to repress what they do not want to think about. Various pressures cause anxiety, stress, or other symptoms for some individuals. Doctors may prescribe "uppers" or "downers" to help some people relax daily after work. Those who reject reality may even seek to find inner meaning through hallucinogens. Others may find life so harsh that they seek the oblivion that certain drugs can induce.

The pressure to succeed in competitive situations may also encourage some people to take drugs. Individuals who want to be especially alert or calm in order to do well may take a drug to accomplish their goal.

Sports presents an excellent example of drug use to enhance performance. Two types of drugs are used by athletes: **restorative drugs** (to heal a traumatized part of the body) and **additive drugs** (to improve performance). Amphetamines and anabolic steroids are the additive drugs commonly used by athletes. Amphetamines increase alertness, respiration rate, blood pressure, muscle tension, heart rate, and blood sugar. The user is literally "psyched up" by amphetamines. Moreover, these drugs have the capacity to abolish a sense of fatigue. Anabolic steroids are male hormones that aid in adding weight and muscle. If an athlete wants to be a world-class weight lifter, shot putter, or discus thrower, the

Some athletes use additive drugs such as anabolic steroids to add weight, muscle, strength, and speed.

pressures are great to use anabolic steroids: they make the user stronger, and many competitors use such drugs to get the edge on the competition. Football players, even in high school, use these drugs to gain weight and strength in order to be a "star" (various studies report that about 7 percent of high school males take steroids).

The pressures to use drugs are unrelenting. They come from doctors, coaches, parents, advertising, and friends. People may learn to drink in families where social drinking is an integral part of meals, celebrations, and everyday relaxation. Peer groups are also important sources. As mentioned earlier, social groups are important for the entry of the individual into the world of illicit drug use. The person learns from others how to use the drug and how to interpret the drug's effects positively. A person may be part of a subculture (whether in college or in the ghetto) where drug experimentation and regular use are the norms. In situations such as cocktail parties guests are expected to drink alcoholic beverages as part of the social ritual. The hosts continually encourage their guests to drink more. Similarly, marijuana is the "social lubricant" at many social gatherings, and individuals are expected to participate. For people who want to impress others, the pressures to conform are enormous.

The Politics of Drugs

Drugs are a social problem in U.S. society. Yet not all drugs are considered problems, nor are all people who take drugs. Some drugs are legal, and others are not. Some drugs caused problems once but are now considered safe; some that were not considered problems now are. Some drug use is labeled "abuse," but other use is simple use. These inconsistencies demonstrate two central points: (1) the subjective nature of social problems—what is or what is not considered a social problem depends on how other people *interpret* the phenomenon, and this interpretation varies by time, group, and situation; and (2) the politics of social problems—what is a social problem depends on the current law, which reflects the unequal power of pressure groups.

The importance of these two factors is seen vividly in the public's view of drugs and in the official laws governing their use. Ironically, the drugs most objected to and most strictly controlled are *not* those most dangerous to users and society. Marijuana and heroin, though illegal, are *less* dangerous than are barbiturates, alcohol, and nicotine, which can be legally obtained and used indiscriminately. To explain such irrationality, we must understand how drugs and their use came to be considered safe or illicit.

The Historical Legality of Drugs

The definition of drug use and abuse is complicated in U.S. society because different patterns of use are acceptable for different people. Some religious groups forbid the use of any drugs, even for medicinal purposes. Others accept medicines but reject all forms of drugs, including caffeine, for recreational use. At the other extreme are groups that may use drugs in their religious rituals to expand the mind, the better to know the unknowable. Time also changes interpretation. Early in this century, for example, it was socially acceptable for men to smoke tobacco but not for women.

Not only is there variance from group to group within society and from time to time, but there has also been virtually no consistency concerning the legality of drugs historically. The history of the acceptance or rejection of opiates (such as opium, morphine, and heroin) in the United States affords a useful example, for it parallels what happened to public attitudes toward other drugs.

Opiates were legal in the nineteenth-century United States and were widely used as painkillers in the Civil War, with many soldiers becoming addicted. Morphine was legally manufactured from imported opium, and opium poppies were legally grown in the United States. Opium was widely dispensed in countless pharmaceutical preparations. There were five methods for distribution, all of them legal (Brecher, 1972:3):

1. Physicians dispensed opiates directly to patients or wrote prescriptions for them.
2. Drugstores sold opiates over the counter to customers without prescription.
3. Grocery and general stores as well as pharmacies stocked and sold opiates. An 1883–1885 survey of the state of Iowa, which then had a population of less than 2,000,000, found 3000 stores in the state where opiates were on sale, and this figure did not include physicians who dispensed opiates directly.
4. For users unable or unwilling to patronize a nearby store, opiates could be ordered by mail.
5. Finally, there were countless patent medicines on the market containing opium or morphine. They were sold under such names as Ayer's Cherry Pectoral, Mrs. Winslow's Soothing Syrup, Darby's Germinative, Godfrey's Cordial, McMunn's Elixir of Opium, and Dover's powder. Some were teething syrups for young children; some were "soothing syrups"; some were recommended for diarrhea and dysentery or for "woman's trouble." They were widely advertised in newspapers and magazines and on billboards as "painkillers," "cough mixtures," "women's friends," "consumption cures," and so on. One wholesale drug house, it is said, distributed more than 600 proprietary medicines and other products containing opiates.

The only nineteenth-century context in which opiates were declared illegal was one created by anti-Chinese sentiment. The Chinese, who were imported to the West Coast to provide cheap labor to build the railroads, brought opium with them. At first, their opium dens were tolerated. But as the cheap Chinese labor began to threaten the White labor market, there was agitation to punish the Chinese for their "evil" ways. San Francisco and several other West Coast cities passed ordinances around 1875 prohibiting opium dens. These laws were, as Morgan has noted, aimed at the Chinese, not at the drug:

> We conclude that the first opium laws in California were not the result of a moral crusade against the drug itself. Instead, it represented a coercive action directed against a vice that was merely an appendage of the real menace—the Chinese—and not the Chinese per se, but the laboring "Chinamen" who threatened the economic security of the white working class. (Morgan, 1978:59)

The early 1900s were characterized as a period of reform. A number of individuals and groups agitated to legislate morals; the Eighteenth Amendment, which prohibited the sale and use of alcohol, was passed in 1919 as a result of pressure from these reform forces. These groups rallied against psychoactive drugs because they believed them to be sinful. They fought against "demon rum" and "demon seed" as well as against other moral evils such as gambling and prostitution. They believed that they were doing God's will and that, if successful, they would provide a better way of life for everyone. Therefore, they lobbied vigorously to achieve appropriate legislation and enforcement of the laws to rid the country of these immoral influences. In Reasons's words,

> all of these evils violated the ethical and philosophical foundations of the religious and moral culture which dominated political power at that time. Narcotics use, like alcohol use, led to a lack of rationality and self-control which were the cornerstones of proper "WASP" behavior. (Reasons, 1974:388)

As a result of these reform efforts, Congress passed the Harrison Narcotics Act of 1914. This act was basically a tax law requiring people who dispensed opium products to pay a fee and keep records. The law was relatively mild. It did not prohibit the use of opium in patent medicines or even control its use. It did, however, establish a Narcotics Division in the Treasury Department (which eventually became the Bureau of Narcotics). This department assumed the task (which was not specified in the formal law) of eliminating drug addiction. Treasury agents harassed users, physicians, and pharmacists. The bureau launched a propaganda campaign to convince the public that there was a link between drug use and crime. Finally, the bureau took a number of carefully selected cases to court to broaden its powers. In all these endeavors the bureau was successful. The net result was that "what had been a medical problem, if a problem at all, had become a legal one; patients became criminals practically overnight" (McCaghy, 1976:292).

This point cannot be overemphasized: prior to the Harrison Act, drug addicts were thought (by the public and government officials) to be sick and in need of individual help. They were believed to be enslaved and in need of being salvaged through the humanitarian efforts of others. But with various government actions (laws, court decisions, and propaganda) and the efforts of reformers, this image of addicts changed from a "medical" to a "criminal" problem. Reasons observes:

> The addict's image was being transformed rapidly from the "sick" and "repentant" deviant, to the "enemy" deviant. . . . Subsequently the addict would be viewed as the "enemy" deviant, indulging in drugs for his own pleasure in defiance of the values of those in power. Furthermore, he was increasingly perceived in criminal terms as a threat to the personal safety and moral well-being of "good citizens." While the early imagery was primarily one of a moral degenerate, increasing emphasis was being placed upon the user's affiliations with the criminal class. The user of the drugs became associated with the "dangerous classes" and was viewed as manifesting disrespect for the dominant mores and values of society. (Reasons, 1974:397)

Factors Influencing Drug Laws and Enforcement

The previous section shows how differently a drug can be viewed over time. Clearly, current policies regarding opium (most common in the form of heroin) are repressive, but alcohol and tobacco continue to be socially acceptable drugs. These differences, especially given the fact that the laws do not reflect the drugs' relative dangers to users, demonstrate that official drug policies are arbitrary and problematic. What, then, are the factors that affect the focus of our drug laws? We examine two factors: cultural reasons and interest groups.

Cultural reasons.   Drug laws and policies tend to reflect how people typically perceive drug use. Certain drugs have negative stereotypes, and others do not. These stereotypes may have been orchestrated by government or they may be the result of faulty research, propaganda of reformers, negative portrayals in the media, and so on. In the 1940s, for example, most people in the United States shared the assumption that marijuana smokers were "dope fiends." They believed that marijuana users were criminals, immoral, violent, and out of control. Until about 1965 public consensus supported strict enforcement of the marijuana laws. Marijuana was believed to be a dangerous drug associated with other forms of deviance, such as sexual promiscuity and crime. Even college students were virtually unanimous in their condemnation of marijuana smokers as deviants of the worst sort. But the social upheavals of the 1960s included experimentation with drugs and questioning of society's mores. Rapid changes in attitudes and behavior occurred, especially among the young and college-educated. Most significantly, the use of marijuana skyrocketed. In 1965, 18,815 people were arrested for violations of state and local marijuana laws; this number rose to 420,700 in 1973. By 1990 some 18 million people in the United States used marijuana, making it the most widely accepted illegal indulgence since drinking during Prohibition.

Despite these changes in attitudes, public opinion still firmly opposes the legalization of marijuana. Moreover, most people still believe that marijuana is physically addictive and that its use leads to the use of hard drugs. Research has shown both notions to be false. Marijuana is not physically addictive; it does not cause people to use heroin or other, harder drugs. Despite the facts, however, the public generally accepts the negative stereotypes and thus fears the drug and supports strict enforcement.

Some drug use has been interpreted as a symbolic rejection of mainstream values, and in this situation the drug is condemned by those supporting the status quo. Drugs such as alcohol and nicotine do not have this connotation. Because marijuana use was closely associated with the youth protest of the 1960s, many people construed it as a symbol of an alternative life-style—as rejection of the traditional values of hard work, success through competition, initiative, and materialism and as support for socialism, unpatriotic behavior, rejection of authority, and sexual promiscuity. As long as this view prevailed, punitive measures against marijuana users seemed justified to many if not most citizens.

Interest groups.   The approaches for controlling drug use have more to do with the power structure of society than with the inherent characteristics of the substance being controlled (Himmelstein, 1978). There is evidence that elite groups in complex societies ban the use of psychoactive drugs because they link them with subversion. And, in fact, dissident groups often use drug-induced experiences to affirm social solidarity in opposition to the powerful.* Himmelstein has provided examples of this phenomenon from a variety of periods:

*This is not to say that drugs are always used to unify resistance groups. As Himmelstein has shown, some resistance groups reject drug use entirely for two basic reasons. First, they reject drugs *approved* by society because they symbolize the majority's power. Second, radicals claim that drugs dull the revolutionary urge, destroy commitment, and undermine discipline.

We find again and again that elites try to suppress drug use because they link it to subversion and that drugs actually are important elements in many oppositional movements. Egyptian pharaohs (c. 2500 B.C.) fought a continual battle against beer and wine use in the temples of Memphis, which were centers of political unrest. The time-honored image of the coffee house as a center of subversion goes back at least to the sixteenth-century Moslem world, where the death penalty was levied for visiting them. Peyote (in the Native American Church), marijuana (in the Jamaican Ras Tafari movement and of course in the 1960s in the U.S.), and alcohol (in the Afro-Brazilian movement) all have served as the foci for culturally and politically subversive movements. (Himmelstein, 1978:45)

The powerful in society also direct their repression at the drugs used primarily by minority groups, the poor, and criminals (Bonnie and Whitebread, 1974:13–31). Just as the early antiopium laws were aimed at Chinese workers, not at opium itself, so the reform movements aimed at prohibition of alcohol represented retaliation by the old middle class—rural, Protestant, native-born—against the largely Catholic urban workers and immigrants who threatened their privileged status. Himmelstein notes that

in this context, the movement against alcohol turned from reform to prohibition and from concern to moral indignation. Alcohol became a symbol of everything in the new society that threatened the old middle class, and Prohibition became a symbolic way for that class to reassert its cultural and political dominance. (Himmelstein, 1978:46)

The powerful in society direct their repression at the drugs used primarily by minority groups and the poor.

This connection between drug laws and social class is also apparent in the enactment of laws against the opiates. Their change in status occurred as use of the drug shifted from the middle to lower class in the early 1900s (Duster, 1970:9–10). A final example of the relation between social class use and drug policy can be found in the current drive to liberalize marijuana laws. When marijuana was used primarily by the lower class (such as Mexican Americans and deviant groups), the laws against its use were extremely punitive. But in the 1960s middle-class, White, affluent, college youth became the primary users. However much parents may have disagreed with their children's use of marijuana, they did not want them treated as criminals and stigmatized as drug users. The ludicrousness of the gap between the punishments for marijuana use and for alcohol use became readily apparent to the educated. As a result, White, affluent, and powerful people in most communities and states mounted a push to liberalize the laws.

Powerful economic interests promote drug laws favorable to themselves. For example, a significant part of U.S. agriculture and consumer industry is engaged (with government support) in the production and marketing of nicotine and alcohol products. Even though it is well known that tobacco is harmful to users, the government will not ban its use because of the probable outcry from farmers, the states where tobacco is a major crop, the tobacco manufacturers, wholesalers, retailers, transporters, and advertisers. Marijuana, on the other hand, is merchandized and sold illegally, so there is no legitimate economic interest pushing for its legalization. As Etzioni has said, "There are no pot equivalents of tobacco states, wine growers, cigarette manufacturers, and their allies in the U.S. Department of Agriculture or friends on the Hill" (Etzioni, 1974:4).

Similarly, the pharmaceutical industry works diligently to persuade Congress from further restricting amphetamines and other pills. In 1970 Congress, pushed by President Nixon, passed the Comprehensive Drug Abuse Prevention and Control Act. Some forces tried to include amphetamines in the dangerous drug category in that bill, but without success. The law declared marijuana possession a serious crime but did not do the same for amphetamines, despite irrefutable evidence that they are more dangerous to the user. This inconsistency led one observer to conclude: "The end result is a national policy which declares an all-out war on drugs which are *not* a source of corporate income. Meanwhile, under the protection of the law, billions of amphetamines are overproduced without medical justification" (Graham, 1972:14).

The illegal status of some drugs enables illicit economic interests to flourish. Underworld suppliers of drugs oppose changes in the law because legalization would seriously reduce their profits. They therefore promote restrictive legislation. The result is often a strange alliance between underworld economic interests and religious/moral interests seeking the same end—prohibition of the drug—but for opposite reasons. Thus, a member of Congress could safely satisfy religious zealots and organized crime alike by voting for stricter drug laws.

The law enforcement profession is another interest group that may use its influence to affect drug policy. If drugs and drug users are considered threats, then budgets to seize them will be increased. More arrests will be made, proving the necessity of enforcement and, not incidentally, the need for higher pay and more officers. Perhaps the best example of this syndrome is provided by the activity of the Narcotics Bureau, created by the Harrison Act of 1914. As mentioned earlier, the bureau was instrumental in changing the definition of opiate use from a "medical" activity to a "criminal" one. The bureau used a number of tactics to "prove" that its existence was necessary: it won court cases favorable to its antidrug stance; it vigorously used the media to propagate the "dope fiend" mythology; and it used statistics to incite the public or to prove its own effectiveness.

One result of these efforts was the passage of the Marijuana Tax Act of 1937. Although the arguments for enacting the law were based on moral grounds, some observers have suggested that it reflected the bureau's desire to increase its size and importance and that marijuana, which was an unregulated drug at the time, was a convenient tool to accomplish that goal. The head of the bureau, Harry J. Anslinger (who served in that post from 1930 to 1962), led an assault on marijuana in which he depicted the drug as an assassin of youth, leading to heroin addiction. Stories of "marijuana atrocities" by "dope fiends" were supplied to the media. The bureau even sponsored a movie, *Reefer Madness,* which portrayed marijuana users as people who would do anything to obtain the "killer weed." Anslinger's campaign culminated in the passage of the Marijuana Tax Act. There is evidence, however, that Anslinger's crusade was motivated not by the drug but by the fact that Congress had cut the bureau's budget in each of the preceding four years. It is safe to say that the bureau's attack on marijuana was not exclusively based on morality.

To summarize, the current drug laws are illogical. (see the Observation "The War on [Some] Drugs"). Their severity is not related to the danger the drugs pose to individuals and society. Rather, they reflect successful political lobbying by a variety of powerful interest groups, with the less powerful suffering the consequences.

The Consequences of Official Drug Policies

If you were asked to identify the greatest social problems caused by drugs, how would you answer? Certainly, one answer would be crime, on the grounds that addicts commit crimes to support their habits. Another response might be the failure of addicts to function as productive members of society—they are dropouts. But enforcement agencies and Congress have taken the opposite position. As McCaghy has noted,

> With the exception of Prohibition, which was finally repealed, the approach has been unvaried. Pass a law; if that does not work make the sentences harsher, get more policemen, get better detection devices, loosen up the law to make arrests easier, and so on. Whatever you do, refuse to recognize that making some behaviors criminal does not prevent them. (McCaghy, 1976:300)

In short, repressive drug laws are irrational; they achieve not their intended goals but the opposite effect.

The drug laws are intended to deter crime by severely punishing the seller and user. There are three fundamental reasons this approach does not work as intended. First, by making drugs illegal and therefore dangerous to produce, transport, and sell, society pushes the cost to many times what it would be if they were legally available. Thus, heroin users, for example, are often forced into crime to sustain a habit that costs more than $200 a day. Crimes committed to produce money for drugs are typically nonviolent (pimping, prostitution, shoplifting, selling drugs, and burglary), but their cost is enormous. Suppose, for example, that there are 100,000 addicts in New York City with habits each costing $200 daily. If they each steal $1200 worth of goods daily in order to get the $200 (a 6-to-1 ratio is about the way fencing works), *the amount stolen in the city would be $120 million daily, or $43.8 billion a year!*

The necessity of criminal activity to supply an expensive drug habit has another consequence that runs counter to the intent of the law. The addict must devote much—if not all—of his or her time to securing the expensive drug, and this time spent impairs his or her ability to function relatively smoothly in society. As Hartjen has argued,

> when drugs are readily available, addiction apparently had minimal impact on the social functioning of addicts. Little if any serious impairment of marital,

OBSERVATION

THE WAR ON (SOME) DRUGS

Categories often exert a tyranny over our perceptions and judgments. An old joke—perhaps it even happened—from the bad old days of McCarthyism tells of a leftist rally in Philadelphia, viciously broken up by the police. A passerby gets caught in the melee and, as the cops are beating him, he pleads, "Stop, stop, I'm an anticommunist." "I don't care what kind of communist you are," says the cop, as he continues pummeling.

We seem driven to think in dichotomies. Protagoras, according to Diogenes, asserted that "there are two sides to every question, exactly opposite to each other." We set up our categories, often by arbitrary division based on tiny differences; then, mistaking names for moral principles, and using banners and slogans as substitutes for reason, we vow to live or die for one or the other side of a false dichotomy. The situation is lamentable enough when the boundaries are profound and natural; if cows declared war on chickens, we might deplore the barnyard carnage, but at least the divisions would be deep, and membership by birth could not be disputed. But when humans struggle with other humans, the boundaries are almost always fluid and largely arbitrary (or at least a curious result of very recent historical contingencies).

Our current drug crisis is a tragedy born of a phony system of classification. For reasons that are little more than accidents of history, we have divided a group of nonfood substances into two categories: items purchasable for supposed pleasure (such as alcohol) and illicit drugs. The categories were once reversed. Opiates were legal in America before the Harrison Narcotics Act of 1914; and members of the Women's Christian Temperance Union, who campaigned against alcohol during the day, drank their valued "women's tonics" at night, products laced with laudanum (tincture of opium).

I could abide—though I would still oppose—our current intransigence if we applied the principle of total interdiction to all harmful drugs. But how can we possibly defend our current policy based on an absurd dichotomy that encourages us to view one class of substances with ultimate horror as preeminent scourges of life (so heroin joins this group, while chemical cognates no more different from heroin than lemonade from iced tea perform work of enormous compassion by relieving the pain of terminal cancer patients in their last days)—while the two most dangerous and life-destroying substances by far, alcohol and tobacco, form a second class advertised on every neon street corner of urban America.

Former Surgeon General Everett Koop, who was hired by Reagan to be an ideologue and decided to be a doctor instead, properly branded nicotine as no less addicting than heroine and cocaine. Representative Terry Bruce (D-IL) challenged this assertion by arguing that smokers are not "breaking into liquor stores late at night to get money to buy a pack of cigarettes." Koop properly replied that the only difference resides in social definition as legal

occupational, and other role-performances resulted. As long as addicts could secure the drug without difficulty, they were able, for the most part, to live reasonably normal, productive lives. (Hartjen, 1977:95)

The second reason that crime is encouraged by punitive drug laws is that someone has to supply the illicit goods. Legislation does not dry up demand, as was vividly shown during the days of Prohibition. Organized crime thrives in this climate. Illegal drugs are, for the most part, imported, processed, and distributed by organized crime groups. Drug laws, then, have the indirect effect of providing organized crime with its most lucrative source of income.

A third source of crime caused by drug laws is police corruption. Black market activities by organized crime or other entrepreneurs are difficult without the

or illegal: "You take cigarettes off the streets and people will be breaking into liquor stores. I think one of the things that many people confuse is the behavior of cocaine and heroin addicts when they are deprived of the drug. That's the difference between a licit and an illicit drug. Tobacco is perfectly legal. You can get it whenever you want to satisfy the craving."

We do not ponder our methods of classification with sufficient scrutiny—and have never done so. Taxonomy, or the study of classification, occupies a low status among the sciences because most people view the activity as a kind of glorified bookkeeping dedicated to pasting objects into preassigned spaces in nature's stamp album. This judgment rests on the false premise that our categories are given by nature and ascertained by simple, direct observation. Nature is full of facts—and they are not distributed isotropically, so nature does provide some hints about divisions.

But our classifications are human impositions, or at least culturally based decisions on what to stress among a plethora of viable alternatives. Classifications are therefore theories of order, not simple records of nature. More important, since classifications are actively imposed, not passively imbibed, they shape our thoughts and deeds in ways that we scarcely perceive because we view our categories as "obvious" and "natural."

Some classifications channel our thinking into fruitful directions because they properly capture the

causes of order; others lead us to tragic and vicious errors (the older taxonomies of human races, for example) because they sink their roots in prejudice and mayhem. Too rarely, in our political criticism, do we look to false taxonomies, particularly in improper dichotomies, as the basis for inadequate analysis.

Our drug crisis is largely the product of such a false dichotomy. At the moment, hundreds of thousands of drug users live in tortured limbo, driven to crime, exposed to AIDS, and doomed (at least statistically speaking) to early death. Millions of others suffer palpably from the deeds of the addicted— experiencing violence, robbery, or simple urban fear that steals the joy from life. Billions of dollars go down the rathole to enrich the entrepreneurs or to try to stem the plague by necessarily ineffective interdiction. The politics of several nations in our hemisphere are corrupted, the cultures of whole peoples severely compromised.

William Jennings Bryan once argued that we were about to crucify mankind on a cross of gold. Are we not now significantly lowering the quality of American life for everyone, and causing thousands of deaths directly, by basing our drug policy on something even worse—a false and senseless classification?

Source: Excerpts from Stephen Jay Gould, "Taxonomy as Politics: The Harm of False Classification," *Dissent* 37 (Winter 1990), pp. 73–78. Reprinted with permission.

cooperation of police officials or drug enforcement agents, so they are often bought.

The corruption of police officials causes disrespect for the law, another consequence of the unenforceable drug laws. Realization of the arbitrariness of the drug laws (such as the fact that marijuana is illegal but alcohol is legal) is another source of widespread disrespect for the law. A third source of irreverence toward the law is the overzealousness of narcotics agents. In their efforts to capture drug law violators, agents have sometimes violated the constitutional rights of individuals (wire tapping, search and seizure without a warrant, entrapment, use of informants who are themselves addicts, and so on). The use of informants, by the way, has led the Bureau of Narcotics at least indirectly to support "the addiction of some addicts in order to uncover other addicts" (Henslin, 1976a:372). All of these abuses have contributed to an attitude of insolence on the part of many people toward agents of the law.

Criminal laws create crime and criminals. If there were no law regulating a behavior, then there would be no criminal. So it is with drug laws. Prior to 1914, heroin users were not criminals, nor were marijuana users before 1937. The drug laws, then, have created large numbers of criminals. By labeling and treating these persons as criminals, the justice system creates further crime (secondary deviance). In other words, efforts at social control actually cause the persistence of the defiant behaviors they are designed to eliminate. Several interrelated processes are at work here. First, as we note earlier, the drug user is forced to rely on illegal and very expensive sources. This reliance typically forces the user into crime or interaction with the criminal fringes of society. Second, when processed by the criminal justice system, the individual is stigmatized, which makes reintegration into normal society very difficult.

All of these factors encourage those pejoratively labeled by society to join together in a deviant drug subculture. Hartjen has described the effects:

> Probably the most significant consequence of punitive drug policies has been the development of a drug subculture. When drugs were legal and available, it was unnecessary for addicts to associate with other addicts. But when legitimate sources of supply were closed, addicts had two alternatives: (1) either give up drugs or (2) find a new source of supply. For those not willing or able to kick the habit, the illegal nature of drug use led many addicts to seek out and join others of their kind facing similar difficulties. Thus, the emergence of the drug subculture. The subculture offered addicts two advantages. For one, drugs could be secured from other addicts, and contact with other addicts led to the sharing of information on various ways to secure drugs or the resources necessary to do so. At the same time, knowledge of new drugs and techniques to take them could be transmitted. With the growth of the drug subculture, all the elements characteristic of other deviant groups also began to appear. Addicts began to develop a sense of solidarity among themselves, an elaborate ideology justifying addiction, status rankings, and a philosophy that rejected "straight" or "square" society. And, as with other groups, the subculture actively began to recruit new members to its fold. (Hartjen, 1977:94–95)

Thus, official drug policies have been predicated on the assumption that punitive laws and rigorous enforcement were necessary to eradicate the menace of certain drugs. The policies, however, have had just the opposite effect. They have harmed the drug users in a variety of unnecessary ways; they have cost society untold billions of dollars in enforcement costs and have clogged courts; they have resulted in additional indirect and direct crime; and they have kept organized crime very profitable. Are there alternatives to this system that might have positive consequences for individuals and society? The next section explores a variety of possibilities.

Alternatives

The nation's drug laws and policies, as we have seen, are counterproductive. They not only fail to accomplish their goals but in many respects also actually achieve the opposite results. Organized crime flourishes because of official drug policies. Addicts are treated as criminals and must turn to crime to supply their expensive habits. Marijuana smokers are turned into convicts and ex-convicts. Despite vigorous antimarijuana campaigns, marijuana use continues. Users risk their health not just from drug use but also from using adulterated drugs. What can be done to alleviate these problems?

After an exhaustive study of drug use and abuse, Consumers Union suggested a number of ways to counteract the negative outcomes of current drug policies (cited in Brecher, 1972:521–527):

1. *Stop emphasizing measures designed to keep drugs away from people.* Prohibition does not work; furthermore, it raises prices, encourages organized crime, and forces addicts into criminal acts that cost society in dollars and community disruption.
2. *Stop publicizing the horrors of the "drug menace."* Instead of frightening people, scare publicity has publicized and popularized the drugs being attacked.
3. *Stop increasing the damage done by drugs.* The laws encourage the consumption of contaminated and adulterated drugs. Moreover, laws such as those making it a criminal offense to sell or possess hypodermic needles without a prescription encourage the use of nonsterile needles and thus increase the incidence of infection, hepatitis, AIDS, and other diseases.
4. *Stop misclassifying drugs.* Political decisions have labeled some drugs "dangerous and criminal" while ignoring others. The fact that these designations bear no relation to the actual physical damage of the drugs themselves makes the law not only inconsistent but also ridiculous.
5. *Stop viewing the drug problem as primarily a national problem, to be solved on a national scale.* The drug problem is a mixture of local problems. Drug use differs from place to place and from time to time. Therefore, effective solutions vary from community to community.
6. *Stop pursuing the goal of stamping out illicit drug use.* This is an impossible goal.

These practical suggestions would, if implemented, have an immediate impact on the shortcomings of current drug laws and policies. Moreover, they raise the larger issue of exactly what the government's role in the regulation of drugs should be. There are three alternatives. (1) to prohibit trade or use of certain drugs by enacting and enforcing criminal laws; (2) to regulate drug trade or use through licensing and taxation; and (3) to ignore the drugs. The rest of this section examines the three possibilities with the arguments for and against each one.

Prohibition through Criminal Laws and Police Enforcement

Many people who oppose the use of certain drugs on moral or religious grounds advocate that the government take an unyielding stance against drugs and vigorously eliminate their use through coercion (control the smuggling across the borders, drug busts, mandatory and tough sentences). The criminalization of certain drugs, however, has been ineffective, even counterproductive. The failure of Prohibition is evidence enough that legislation and law enforcement do not eliminate a drug problem. To the contrary, Prohibition was costly to enforce, the production and consumption of alcohol continued unabated, and organized crime flourished. Similarly, the current governmental policies and efforts to halt the use of marijuana, cocaine, heroin, and other illicit drugs have failed. The drug war in 1990 at the federal level cost $9 billion, with state and local government's spending another $4 billion to $5 billion. In addition, there are the costs of clogged courts and overpopulated prisons (roughly 10 percent of the inmates in state prisons and one-third of federal prisoners are drug-law offenders).

The proponents of these actions argue that the consumption of drugs is declining as a result. Opponents argue that this policy has decreased neither the number of addicts nor the magnitude of street crime. Moreover, the enforcement of such a policy is very expensive to taxpayers (the costs of a police force, bureaucracy, and overburdening of the courts and jails) and crippling to the users, who are labeled as criminals. Moreover, prohibition of a drug promotes organized crime and criminal behavior by drug users.

Regulation of Trade or Use through Licensing and Taxation

Legalizing a drug but regulating its use, as is now the case with alcohol, tobacco, and prescription drugs, has some obvious benefits:

- It ensures the products' conformity to standards of purity and safety.
- It dries up the black market by channeling profits to legitimate enterprises.
- It provides the government with revenues.
- It keeps drugs away from certain population groups such as youth.

Opponents argue that government regulation would actually condone the use of drugs. This apparent approval together with the easy availability and relatively low prices would promote experimentation and use of the drug. Another objection is that the bureaucracy needed to manage the regulation would be costly.

Under this regulation option the biggest population to deal with would be the heroin addicts. These users are a special problem to themselves and society. Their habits are the most expensive, so of all drug users they are most likely to turn to crime. Their habit also requires almost full-time diligence in securing the drug; and being "strung out," they do not function normally in society. How, then, should the government deal with them? Hard-liners argue that they should be classified as criminals and incarcerated. Other people suggest that addicts could remain in society and be relatively productive if drugs were supplied to them cheaply, under government regulation and medical supervision. Two plans have been used to accomplish this goal: heroin maintenance and methadone maintenance.

The British approach to heroin addiction **(heroin maintenance)** is fundamentally different from the U.S. approach. The object of the latter is to get addicts "off" heroin by drying up their supplies and imprisoning them. Narcotics control, under this plan, is placed under the jurisdiction of law enforcement authorities.

The British plan, in sharp contrast, places control in the hands of medical authorities. Instead of treating addicts as criminals, the British allow physicians to administer drugs to addicts under two conditions: when their complete withdrawal cannot be accomplished, and when they can perform satisfactorily given a controlled dosage. Physicians must notify the British Home Office of all patients under this treatment. When properly registered, addicts are entitled to receive maintenance doses of heroin; if an addict commits a crime, he or she is treated like any other offender. If not registered but in the possession of opiates, the individual is prosecuted for illegal possession of a dangerous drug.

The assumption behind the British approach is that the probability of successfully withdrawing addicts from heroin indefinitely is very small. In short, drug dependence is viewed as irreversible. The idea is that if a society must have addicts, then their addiction should be supervised with proper doses and unadulterated drugs. As Cuskey and Krasner note, the criminal activity of heroin addicts in the United States

> has demonstrated clearly enough that heroin addicts will do almost anything to get their fixes. They risk their lives daily; they will steal relief checks from their own families. Although the drug is soporific, they will drive themselves to violence and killing if the alternative is withdrawal. Some experts believe that, if we cannot escape having addicts and abusers, it might be best if they were addicted to heroin since that would more certainly bring them into the clinics—if maintenance were available. (Cuskey and Krasner, 1973:49)

The British plan has some obvious advantages over the enforcement model in the United States. First, it keeps addicts under medical supervision and functioning in society. Second, it drives the illegal market out of business. If heroin is legalized (by doctors) for addicts and sold cheaply to them, yet remains illegal and punishable (by a strict sentence) to sell or possess, then organized crime will no longer find the business profitable. As Barbara and Morrison have argued, "organized crime's interest in narcotics will vanish only if we stop making criminals out of drug-dependent individuals and start making it possible for persons who need medical treatment to receive it legally" (Barbara and Morrison, 1975:32).

Critics of the British plan point to the increased number of addicts—actually quadrupling in the 1980s (Goode, 1989:267). However, this increase is countered by other facts:

> The statistics on the increase in the number of drug abusers are unreliable. All that is known is that a significant rise in the number of addicts seeking treatment took place. Moreover, according to some estimates, Britain has approximately sixty-two addicts or regular users of heroin per 100,000 population (for a total of 30,000 to 35,000), while the United States has 209 heroin addicts or users per 100,000 population, for a total of 500,000. And very few British heroin addicts engage in serious crime, unlike heroin addicts in America. (Dennis, 1990:130)

In fact, the United States *has* used the British model to treat some of its addicts. Barbara and Morrison report: "In the U.S. the addiction problem has always, in fact, been handled 'the British way' for some addicts, those who are members of the upper class and have the money and the status to be treated as persons with a serious medical problem" (Barbara and Morrison, 1975:169).

A practice similar to heroin maintenance, which the United States has experimented with, is **methadone maintenance.** Methadone is a heroin substitute that can be taken orally. It is just as addictive as heroin, but it is considered safer. Its effects last longer than heroin's, so that an addict needs a fix perhaps once a day rather than three or four times a day. Moreover, the drug does not make the user drowsy. The net effect is that a methadone user can easily continue to be a productive member of society without having to steal for his or her habit.

A strength of both plans is that addicts are not labeled as criminals. They are considered to have a medical, not a moral, problem. Equally important is that addicts remain participating members of the community.

Conservative critics of heroin or methadone maintenance argue that such programs encourage wider use of hard drugs. They also assert that these plans will not be acceptable to most citizens, who will continue to label addicts as criminals and sinful. Liberals, while likely to approve of either plan over the current criminal model, foresee a danger in government control over an addict population dependent on it for drugs. Leroy D. Clarke, former law professor at New York University, has warned, for example, that methadone maintenance may be the ultimate weapon of racial control (quoted in Lewis, 1976:31). Moreover, such programs attack the problem at the individual level (blaming the victim) and ignore the social and cultural sources of drug use.

A most telling criticism of methadone maintenance is that so far the experimental programs have not proved very beneficial. Research on a large New York City program, for example, found that most patients terminated the program before the end of the second year, criminal activity did not decline much, and whatever decline did occur was in drug-related crimes rather than in crimes involving victims (Kleinman, Lukoff, and Kail, 1977). Many of these negative findings may result from addicts' craving for the effects of heroin that are missing in methadone. If this is the case, then heroin maintenance may be the more effective of the two programs.

In sum, these plans have problems but they do have the positive effects of decriminalizing narcotics use, placing addicts under medical supervision, and returning many addicts to a productive life.

Noninterference

Libertarians argue that it is none of the government's business what drugs people put into their bodies. There should be no governmental interference in this private act. Thomas Szasz, for example, argues that all drugs, regardless of their danger, should be legalized:

> I favor free trade in drugs for the same reason the Founding Fathers favored free trade in ideas. In an open society, it is none of the government's business what idea a man puts into his mind; likewise, it should be none of the government's business what drug he puts into his body. (Szasz, 1972:75)

This view, however, does not excuse drug users from their behavior. According to Szasz,

> the right of self-medication should be hedged in by similar limits. Public intoxication, not only with alcohol but with any drug, should be an offense punishable by the criminal law. Furthermore, acts that may injure others—such as driving a car—should, when carried out in a drug-intoxicated state, be punished espe-

cially strictly and severely. The right to self-medication must thus entail unqualified responsibility for the effects of one's drug-intoxicated behavior on others.
For unless we are willing to hold ourselves responsible for our own behavior,
and hold others responsible for theirs, the liberty to use drugs (or to engage in
other acts) degenerates into a license to hurt others. (Szasz, 1972:77)

Proponents of total **decriminalization (legalization) of drugs** argue that all
societies throughout known history have had psychoactive drugs. Legislation and
strict enforcement will not curb the tendency among many people to want to alter
their consciousness artificially. Such acts should be neither penalized or encouraged, because it is none of the government's business what individuals do to themselves.

Critics suggest that decriminalization will encourage the spread of drug use.
Drug use will spread because drugs will be readily available and because commercial interests will see potential profits in these formerly illicit drugs and will
produce them and promote their use. Finally, and perhaps most significant, is the
argument that drug use is not an act in isolation that affects only the user. In short,
although many people believe that drug use is a "victimless vice," there is always
a victim. As Nettler has argued,

> if our spouses wrong *their* bodies, *we* pay a price. If children harm themselves,
> their parents are victims. If parents are dissolute, their children are victims. If
> enough individuals harm themselves, then society is the victim. In brief, there
> can be victimless vice only when no one influences anyone. As long as someone
> pays a price for someone else's action, that action is not victimless. The prices
> paid can be offenses to one's taste or invasions of one's purse. The prices paid
> can be as varied as insults to eye, ear, and nose; to having to wend one's way on
> public streets through prostitutes; to having to pay taxes in support of rehabili-
> tation centers for sick addicts; and so on. (Nettler, 1976:168)

What, then, is the answer to drug use? Probably some combination of these
alternatives makes the most sense. Clearly, the arguments about the solution will
continue to incite passion. There will be people who are concerned with the use
of certain drugs and who feel that society *must control* such deviance. They insist
on imposing their morals on others. At the other extreme are those who are more
concerned with how the laws and their rigorous enforcement *cause* social problems. As the various segments in society continue the debate, legislation will be
proposed and eventually passed. The astute observer should note the role of interest groups in what is decided and also who benefits and who loses by the decision
reached.

The Political Economy of Drugs

Official U.S. policies toward drugs are illogical. They are inconsistent and harmful. As Reasons has argued,

> since the harms produced by illegal drug use in our society—e.g., crime, dis-
> ease, death—are almost entirely a consequence of our drug policy rather than
> the pharmacological effects of such drugs, we must look to the area of social
> policy as a causal factor in the "drug problem." (Reasons, 1974:384)

The inconsistencies and problems inherent in our drug policies are reflections of the political economy of drugs and reveal that the drug problem is really a problem of societal structure.

First, the establishment condones the use of some drugs and condemns the use of others; the danger that the drug poses to the health of the user is not the criterion of legality. In fact, the most dangerous drugs (alcohol, nicotine, amphetamines, and barbiturates) are prescribed by physicians and/or sold legally. Essentially, there are two reasons for this anomaly. Powerful business interests (agriculture, the pharmaceutical industry, tobacco companies, and distilleries) use their clout to maintain the legality of their products. Also, the psychic painkillers of the middle and upper classes are approved, but the psychic painkillers used mainly by the poor, minority groups, immigrants, and criminals are condemned.

The powerful people of society are able to impose their morality on the less powerful through the passage of legislation. According to Yeager,

> if the criminalization of certain drugs constitutes a moral and legal prohibition against self-medication, then it also serves as an instrument of suppression in the conflict over life-styles, moral values, and the prevailing distribution of economic and political power. Many in the dominant order associate illegal drug abuse with hedonism, idleness, sexual promiscuity, and the lack of motivation. Moreover, as a consequence of the turbulent sixties, drug abuse came to be defined "as a basic attack on the traditional values of the dominant groups in society and a deliberate rejection of the respectable conventional world." (Yeager, 1975:159; source of quotation not provided in Yeager.)

Thus, the use of drugs by the lower classes and/or rebellious groups is "naturally" labeled by the powerful as a crime.

This relationship between what kinds of people use a drug and that drug's social respectability is seen clearly in the relaxation of public attitudes and laws regarding marijuana use. The increasing legitimacy of this drug is directly related to its increased use by the sons and daughters of the middle and upper class. Similarly, government officials show much more zeal in cracking down on crack, which is the drug of choice in the poor, predominantly Black areas of the inner city, than for cocaine, which is predominantly a middle- and upper-class drug.

Repressive governmental policies toward the use of certain drugs have created a counterproductive cycle of illegalization, profit seeking, and criminal activity. The law-and-order approach prevalent in the United States since the early 1900s has created a criminal class of drug users (they are considered criminals because they have broken a law, and they are likely to behave criminally in order to support an expensive habit). It has created a lucrative black market with the active involvement of organized crime and the tacit consent of corrupt political and law enforcement officials. The illegality of certain drugs has caused adulterated drugs to be sold and used with unsterile equipment, resulting in more disease and death. As Yeager has put it, "it is indeed one of the paradoxes of the twentieth century that a law which was established, in part, as a reaction to vice and crime, should be so successful in perpetuating the very ills that it set out to eliminate" (Yeager, 1975:161).

The illegality of some drugs has created a subeconomy. The high prices of drugs mean large profits for those willing to take the risks. This situation provides opportunities for status, identity, and wealth for people otherwise without legitimate employment opportunities. In short, by becoming an illegal capitalist, a ghetto resident can become "somebody." Furthermore, the fundamental reason for the continued existence of the drug subeconomy is its profitability to important sectors of the regular economy. Yeager observes that

> society has deemed the preservation of the subeconomy preferable to the establishment of family income guarantees at a level above the poverty line, or the reform of existing employment structures to accommodate the needs of those excluded. In other words, the existence of the subeconomy has helped to thwart dissent among the poor over the existing allocation of legal jobs and opportunities which the dominant society controls. Thus, economist Stanley Friedlander argues that hustling "contributes to the quasi-stable social existence in slum areas capable of exploding from the tremendous economic and social tensions generated by poverty, uncertainty, hunger, disease, and insecurity. . . . Instead of sporadic or permanent explosions, crime, narcotics selling and gambling operate as social depressants built into the life of the ghetto."
> (Yeager, 1975:164–165)

Drug use occurs for a variety of reasons. One is especially important for our purposes, because it points to the inequities in society as a source. According to Michael Tabor, a Black Panther and former heroin addict,

> Our black people, especially our black youth, crave for euphoria, anything that will help to make them oblivious to the squalor, to the abject poverty, to the disease and degradation that engulfs them in their daily existence. And initially the white powdered plague does just that. Under its sinister influence the oppressive, nauseating ghetto prison is transformed into a virtual Valhalla. One becomes impervious to the rancid stench of urine-soaked tenement dungeons, unaffected by the piercing cries of anguish from black folks driven to the brink of insanity by our sadistic and predacious political system, unaffected by the deafening wail of police sirens as they tear through the streets of black hell en route to answer the call of some other police who are in a state of well-deserved distress, unaffected by the trash cans whose decayed, disease-carrying garbage has flowed over to fill the ghetto streets. Under heroin's ecstatic influence one becomes a full-time chartered member of the cloud-nine society and is made oblivious to the ugly social and political realities of life. (Quoted in Kunnes, 1972:94)

In sum, the structure of society, especially economic and political realities, has caused and perpetuated many—if not most—of the problems associated with drugs. Thus, any solution to the country's drug problems must begin with structural changes in society. Using heroin as the example, Kunnes has made this point well:

> Heroin addiction is not a criminal problem, though criminals and crime are involved. Nor is heroin addiction a medical problem, though medical symptoms are produced. Heroin addiction is ultimately a political and economic problem created by, and controlled for, wealthy criminal connections, and corporate officials controlling the priorities of our society. If corporate America remains unchanged, the demand for heroin (or other euphorics) will increase in spite of attempts at its selective suppression and because of attempts to use heroin to suppress selectively, both politically and personally. Heroin manufacturing,

distribution, and usage occur in a well-defined political context. Until that political context is destroyed, heroin and its concomitant diseases and deaths, crime and corruption, will remain part of our daily lives. (Kunnes, 1972:203–204)

CHAPTER REVIEW

1. Some drugs in U.S. society are legal and others are not. The division is based not on their potential for harm to the users or society but on politics—the exercise of power by interest groups and the majority to legislate their views on others.

2. Most people in the United States take some drug on a regular basis. Those drugs considered legal are caffeine, alcohol, nicotine, tranquilizers, amphetamines, and barbiturates. Illegal drugs used by millions of people in U.S. society are marijuana, cocaine, inhalants, psychedelics, and heroin.

3. The prevailing culture, group norms, and social pressures strongly affect the patterns of drug use and their behavioral effects.

4. The pressure to use drugs may come from doctors, coaches, pharmaceutical firms, tobacco and alcohol companies, and one's friends and associates.

5. People in the United States seek and use drugs for a variety of reasons, ranging from medical necessity to desire for a change in mood because life is too boring, stressful, competitive, and/or frustrating.

6. The acceptability of certain drugs such as marijuana or heroin has varied historically. Opiates, once legal in the United States, became illegal for two reasons: (a) members of the White working class on the West Coast felt threatened by cheap Chinese labor and sought coercive measures against those Chinese; and (b) religious groups interpreting opiate use as a moral evil mounted successful pressure. The result was the Harrison Narcotics Act of 1914, which made opiate use a criminal offense. Thus, behavior once considered a medical problem became a criminal problem.

7. Laws defining which drugs are legal and which are not reflect negative stereotypes held by the general public and efforts for control by interest groups (such as religious groups, the pharmaceutical industry, and organized crime) and law enforcement professionals. The result is that current drug laws are illogical. They are not related to the danger of the drugs but reflect the political interests of the powerful.

8. Drug laws promote crime in at least four ways: (a) they create criminals by making possession and use of certain drugs illegal; (b) users often engage in criminal activity because the drugs, being illegal, are so expensive; (c) punitive drug laws encourage organized crime by making importation, processing, and distribution of illegal drugs extremely lucrative; and (d) people selling illicit drugs often corrupt the police.

9. Government can adopt three alternative policies toward drug use: (a) prohibition of trade and use through enforcement of criminal penalties (the current policy); (b) regulation through licensing and taxation; and (c) noninterference (ignoring drugs, because what people do to themselves is not the government's business).

KEY TERMS

Drug.   Any chemical that causes biochemical reactions in the body when ingested.

Social construction of drugs.   Definitions concerning drugs and drug-related behaviors based on the meanings that people in groups have imputed to certain things and behaviors.

Ontological truth.   A universal and undeniable reality.

Politics of drugs.   The labeling of some drugs as licit and others as illicit depends on the definition of drugs by the most powerful interest groups, which are able to get their definitions incorporated into the law.

Psychoactive drug.   A chemical that alters the perceptions and/or moods of people who take it.

Restorative drug.   A chemical that heals a traumatized part of the body.

Additive drug.   A chemical that improves performance.

Heroin maintenance.   The British approach to heroin addiction that treats addicts as sick rather than as criminal; thus, addicts are placed under the jurisdiction of physicians who administer drugs to their patients.

Methadone maintenance.   Similar to heroin maintenance, this provides a heroin substitute (methadone) to addicts under medical supervision.

Decriminalization of drugs.   The legalization of drugs.

FOR FURTHER STUDY

Troy Duster. *The Legislation of Morality: Law, Drugs, and Moral Judgment.* New York: Free Press, 1970.

Erich Goode. *Drugs in American Society.* 3d ed. New York: Knopf, 1989.

James A. Inciardi. *The War on Drugs II: The Continuing Epic of Heroin, Cocaine, Crack, AIDS, and Public Policy.* Mountain View, Calif.: Mayfield, 1992.

Maureen E. Kelleher, Bruce K. Mac Murray, and Thomas M. Shapiro. *Drugs and Society: A Critical Reader.* 2nd ed. Dubuque, Ia.: Kendall/Hunt, 1988.

Larry Sloman. *Reefer Madness: The History of Marijuana in America.* Indianapolis: Bobbs-Merrill, 1978.

Thomas S. Szasz. *Ceremonial Chemistry: The Ritual Persecution of Drugs, Addicts, and Pushers.* Rev. ed. Kalamazoo, Mich: Learning Publications, 1985.

Jason M. White. *Drug Dependence.* Englewood Cliffs, N.J.: Prentice-Hall, 1991.

Larry C. White. *Merchants of Death: The American Tobacco Industry.* New York: Beech Tree Books/Morrow, 1988.

FORUM

SHOULD DRUGS BE LEGALIZED?

Drugs must be prohibited as they are now or else drug use will increase sharply as will the costs to society and individuals.

James Q. Wilson

[In 1972 Milton Friedman, the esteemed economist, proposed the legalization of heroin. He argued that the government had no right to tell people what they should do to their bodies and that the prohibition of a drug imposed much greater costs to society than benefits.]

Suppose we had taken Friedman's advice in 1972. What would have happened? We cannot be entirely certain, but at a minimum we would have placed the young heroin addicts (and, above all, the prospective addicts) in a very different position from the one in which they actually found themselves. Heroin would have been legal. Its price would have been reduced by 95 percent (minus whatever we chose to recover in taxes.) Now that it could be sold by the same people who make aspirin, its quality would have been assured—no poisons, no adulterants. Sterile hypodermic needles would have been readily available at the neighborhood drugstore, probably at the same counter where the heroin was sold. No need to travel to big cities or unfamiliar neighborhoods—heroin could have been purchased anywhere, perhaps by mail order.

There would no longer have been any financial or medical reason to avoid heroin use. Anybody could have afforded it. We might have tried to prevent children from buying it, but as we have learned from our efforts to prevent minors from buying alcohol and tobacco, young people have a way of penetrating markets theoretically reserved for adults. Returning Vietnam veterans would have discovered that Omaha and Raleigh had been converted into the pharmaceutical equivalent of Saigon.

Under these circumstances, can we doubt for a moment that heroin use would have grown exponentially? Or that a vastly larger supply of new users would have been recruited? Professor Friedman is a Nobel Prize-winning economist whose understanding of market forces is profound. What did he think would happen to consumption under his legalized regime? Here

are his words: "Legalizing drugs might increase the number of addicts, but it is not clear that it would. Forbidden fruit is attractive, particularly to the young."

Really? I suppose that we should expect no increase in Porsche sales if we cut the price by 95 percent, no increase in whiskey sales if we cut the price by a comparable amount—because young people only want fast cars and strong liquor when they are "forbidden." Perhaps Friedman's uncharacteristic lapse from the obvious implications of price theory can be explained by a misunderstanding of how drug users are recruited. In his 1972 essay he said that "drug addicts are deliberately made by pushers, who give likely prospects their first few doses free." If drugs were legal it would not pay anybody to produce addicts, because everybody would buy from the cheapest source. But as every drug expert knows, pushers do not produce addicts. Friends or acquaintances do. In fact, pushers are usually reluctant to deal with non-users because a non-user could be an undercover cop. Drug use spreads in the same way any fad or fashion spreads: somebody who is already a user urges his friends to try, or simply shows already-eager friends how to do it. . . .

The notion that abusing drugs such as cocaine is a "victimless crime" is not only absurd but dangerous. Even ignoring the fetal drug syndrome, crack-dependent people are, like heroin addicts, individuals who regularly victimize their children by neglect, their spouses by improvidence, their employers by lethargy, and their coworkers by carelessness. Society is not and could never be a collection of autonomous individuals. We all have a stake in ensuring that each of us displays a minimal level of dignity, responsibility, and empathy. We cannot, of course, coerce people into goodness, but we can and should insist that some standards must be met if society itself—on which the very existence of the human personality depends—is to persist. Drawing the line that defines those standards is difficult and contentious, but if crack and heroin use do not fall below it, what does? . . .

No one can know what our society would be like if we changed the law to make access to cocaine, heroin, and PCP easier. I believe, for reasons given, that the result would be a sharp increase in use, a more widespread degradation of the human personality, and a greater rate of accidents and violence.

I may be wrong. If I am, then we will needlessly have incurred heavy costs in law enforcement and some forms of criminality. But if I am right, and the legalizers prevail anyway, then we will have consigned millions of people, hundreds of thousands of infants, and hundreds of neighborhoods to a life of oblivion and disease. To the lives and families destroyed by alcohol we will have added countless more destroyed by cocaine, heroin, PCP, and whatever else a basement scientist can invent.

Human character is formed by society; indeed, human character is inconceivable without society, and good character is less likely in a bad society. Will we, in the name of an abstract doctrine of radical individualism, and with the false comfort of suspect predictions, decide to take the chance that somehow individual decency can survive amid a more general level of degradation?

I think not. The American people are too wise for that, whatever the academic essayists and cocktail-party pundits may say. But if Americans today are less wise than I suppose, then Americans at some future time will look back on us now and wonder, what kind of people were they that they could have done such a thing?

Source: James Q. Wilson, "Against the Legalization of Drugs." Reprinted from *Commentary,* February 1990, by permission; all rights reserved.

Drug legalization can minimize the risks of enforcement, dramatically reduce the costs of current policies, and directly address the problems of drug abuse.

Ethan A. Nadelmann

Clearly, neither drug legalization nor enforcement of anti-drug laws promises to "solve" the drug problem. Nor is there any question that legalization presents certain risks. Legalization would almost certainly increase the availability of drugs, decrease their price, and remove the deterrent power of the criminal sanction—all of which invite increases in drug use and abuse. There are at least three reasons, however, why these risks are worth taking. First, drug control strategies that rely primarily on criminal justice measures are significantly and inherently limited in their capacity to curtail drug abuse. Second, many law enforcement efforts are not only of limited value but also highly costly and counterproductive; indeed, many of the drug-related evils that most people identify as part and parcel of "the drug problem" are in fact the costs of drug prohibition policies. Third, the risks of legalization may well be less than most people assume, particularly if intelligent alternative measures are implemented.

Few law enforcement officials any longer contend that their efforts can do much more than they are already doing to reduce drug abuse in the United States. This is true of international drug enforcement efforts, interdiction, and both high-level and street-level domestic drug enforcement efforts.

The United States seeks to limit the export of illicit drugs to this country by a combination of crop eradication and crop substitution programs, financial

FORUM

inducements to growers to abstain from the illicit business, and punitive measures against producers, traffickers, and others involved in the drug traffic. These efforts have met with scant success in the past and show few indications of succeeding in the future. . . .

Domestic law enforcement efforts have proven increasingly successful in apprehending and imprisoning rapidly growing numbers of illicit drug merchants, ranging from the most sophisticated international traffickers to the most common street-level drug dealers. The principal benefit of law enforcement efforts directed at major drug trafficking organizations is probably the rapidly rising value of drug trafficker assets forfeited to the government. There is, however, little indication that such efforts have any significant impact on the price or availability of illicit drugs. Intensive and highly costly street-level law enforcement efforts such as those mounted by many urban police departments in recent years have resulted in the arrests of thousands of low-level drug dealers and users and helped improve the quality of life in targeted neighborhoods. In most large urban centers, however, these efforts have had little impact on the overall availability of illicit drugs.

The logical conclusion of the foregoing analysis is not that criminal justice efforts to stop drug trafficking do not work at all; rather, it is that even substantial fluctuations in those efforts have little effect on the price, availability, and consumption of illicit drugs. The mere existence of criminal laws combined with minimal levels of enforcement is sufficient to deter many potential users and to reduce the availability and increase the price of drugs. Law enforcement officials acknowledge that they alone cannot solve the drug problem but contend that their role is nonetheless essential to the overall effort to reduce illicit drug use and abuse. What they are less ready to acknowledge, however, is that the very criminalization of the drug market has proven highly costly and counterproductive in much the same way that the national prohibition of alcohol did 60 years ago.

Total government expenditures devoted to enforcement of drug laws amounted to a minimum of $10 billion in 1987. Between 1981 and 1987, federal expenditures on anti-drug law enforcement more than tripled, from less than $1 billion per year to about $3 billion. State and local law enforcement agencies spent an estimated $5 billion, amounting to about one-fifth of their total investigative resources, on drug enforcement activities in 1986. Drug law violators currently account for approximately 10 percent of the roughly 550,000 inmates in state prisons, more than one-third of the 50,000 federal prison inmates, and a significant (albeit undetermined) proportion of the approximately 300,000 individuals confined in municipal jails. The U.S. Sentencing Commission has predicted that in 15 years the federal prison population will total 100,000 to 150,000 inmates, of whom one-half will be incarcerated for drug law violations. Among the 40,000 inmates in New York State prisons, drug law violations surpassed first-degree robbery in 1987 as the number one cause of incarceration, accounting for 20 percent of the total prison population. In Florida, the 8,506 drug law violators admitted to state prisons in fiscal 1987–88 represented a 525 percent increase from fiscal 1983–84 and 27.8 percent of all new admissions to prison in 1987–88. Nationwide, drug trafficking and drug possession offenses accounted for approximately 135,000 (23 percent) of the 583,000 individuals convicted of felonies in state courts in 1986. State and local governments spent a minimum of $2 billion last year to incarcerate drug offenders. The direct costs of building and maintaining enough prisons to house this growing population are rising at an astronomical rate. The costs, in terms of alternative social expenditures foregone and other types of criminals not imprisoned, are perhaps even more severe. . . .

The greatest beneficiaries of the drug laws are organized and unorganized drug traffickers. The criminalization of the drug market effectively imposes a de facto value-added tax that is enforced and occasionally augmented by the law enforcement establishment and collected by the drug traffickers. More than half of all organized crime revenues are believed to derive from the illicit drug business; estimates of the dollar value range between $10 and $50 billion per year. By contrast, annual revenues from cigarette bootlegging, which persists principally because of differences among states in their cigarette tax rates, are estimated at between $200 million and $400 million. If the marijuana, cocaine, and heroin markets were legal, state and federal governments would collect billions of dollars annually in tax revenues. Instead, they expend billions in what amounts to a subsidy of organized criminals. . . .

[An important connection between drugs and crime] is the violent, intimidating, and corrupting behavior of the drug traffickers. In many Latin American countries, most notably Colombia, this connection virtually defines the "drug problem." But even within the United States, drug trafficker violence is rapidly becoming a major concern of criminal justice officials and the public at large. The connection is not difficult to explain. Illegal markets tend to breed violence, both because they attract criminally minded and violent individuals and because participants in the market have no resort to legal institutions to resolve their disputes. . . .

Repealing the drug prohibition laws clearly promises tremendous advantages. Between reduced government expenditures on enforcing drug laws and new tax revenue from legal drug production and sales, public treasuries would enjoy a net benefit of at least $10 billion per year and possibly much more; thus billions in new revenues would be available, and ideally targeted, for funding much-needed drug treatment programs as well as the types of social and educational programs that often prove most effective in creating incentives for children not to abuse drugs. The quality of urban life would rise significantly. Homicide rates would decline. So would robbery and burglary rates. Organized criminal groups, particularly the up-and-coming ones that have yet to diversify into nondrug areas, would be dealt a devastating setback. The police, prosecutors, and courts would focus their resources on combating the types of crimes that people cannot walk away from. More ghetto residents would turn their backs on criminal careers and seek out legitimate opportunities instead. And the health and quality of life of many drug users and even drug abusers would improve significantly. Internationally, U.S. foreign policymakers would get on with more important and realistic objectives, and foreign governments would reclaim the authority that they have lost to the drug traffickers. . . .

There is no question that legalization is a risky policy, one that may indeed lead to an increase in the number of people who abuse drugs. But that risk is by no means a certainty. At the same time, current drug control policies are showing little progress and new proposals promise only to be more costly and more repressive. We know that repealing the drug prohibition laws would eliminate or greatly reduce many of the ills that people commonly identify as part and parcel of the "drug problem." Yet that option is repeatedly and vociferously dismissed without any attempt to evaluate it openly and objectively. The past 20 years have demonstrated that a drug policy shaped by rhetoric and fear-mongering can only lead to our current disaster. Unless we are willing to honestly evaluate all our options, including various legalization strategies, there is a good chance that we will never identify the best solutions for our drug problems.

Source: Ethan A. Nadelmann, "Drug Prohibition in the United States: Costs, Consequences, and Alternatives," *Science* Vol. 245, pp. 939–947 Sept. 1, 1989. Copyright 1989 by the AAAS.

Bibliography

Ackland, Len. 1990. "Human Guinea Pigs." *The Bulletin of the Atomic Scientists* 46 (September):2.

Acuna, Rudolfo. 1972. *Occupied America.* San Francisco: Canfield Press.

Adams, Terry K., Greg J. Duncan, and Willard L. Rogers. 1988. "The Persistence of Urban Poverty." In *Quiet Riots: Race and Poverty in the United States,* Fred R. Harris and Roger Wilkins (eds.). New York: Pantheon, pp. 78–99.

Agel, Jerome, ed. 1971. *The Radical Therapist.* New York: Ballantine Books.

Ahlburg, Dennis A., and Carol J. De Vita. 1992. "New Realities of the American Family." *Population Bulletin* 47 (August):entire issue.

Ahmad, Eqbal. 1980. *Political Culture and Foreign Policy: Notes on American Interventions in the Third World.* Washington, D.C.: Institute for Policy Studies.

Albee, George W. 1975. "Current Mental Health Models Need a Change." *Rocky Mountain News Trend* (June 29):2.

Albelda, Randy. 1991. "Left in the Dust: U.S. Trails Other Nations in Support for Poor." *Dollars & Sense,* No. 172 (December):20–21.

Aldous, Joan, and Wilfried Dumon. 1991. "Family Policy in the 1980s: Controversy and Consensus." In *Contemporary Families: Looking Forward, Looking Back,* Alan Booth (ed.). Minneapolis: National Council on Family Relations, pp. 466–481.

All Chicago Focus. 1990. "Rich-Poor Income Gap Hits 40-Year High." *All Chicago Focus* (December 1):3.

Allen, James P., and Eugene Turner. 1990. "Where Diversity Reigns." *American Demographics* (August):34–38.

Altman, Lawrence K. 1991a. "Study Finds a Gender Gap in the Treatment of Heart Attacks." *New York Times* (April 13):A12.

Altman, Lawrence K. 1991b. "Many Hispanic Americans Reported In Ill Health and Lacking Insurance." *New York Times* (January 9):A10.

American Association of University Professors. 1990. "Some Dynamic Aspects of Academic Careers." *Academe* (March/April):3–29.

American Association of University Women. 1992. "How Schools Shortchange Girls." Executive Summary, the *AAUW Report,* The American Association of University Women Educational Foundation.

American Psychiatric Association. 1987. *Diagnostic and Statistical Manual of Mental Disorders.* 3d ed., rev. Washington, D.C.: American Psychiatric Association.

American Psychological Association. 1973. *American Psychological Association Monitor* 4 (February):1.

Andersen, Margaret L. 1988. *Thinking about Women.* 2d ed. New York: Macmillan.

Andersen, Margaret L. 1993. *Thinking about Women.* 3rd ed. New York: Macmillan.

Andersen, Margaret L., and Patricia Hill Collins. 1991. *Race, Class, and Gender: An Anthology.* Belmont, Calif.: Wadsworth.

Anderson, Jack. 1990. "Nation Braces for Tragic Effects of Crack Babies." *Rocky Mountain News* (March 24):68.

Anderson, Walt. 1973. "Breaking Out of the Establishment Vice." *Human Behavior* 2 (December):11–16.

Angier, Natalie. 1991. "The Biology of What It Means to Be Gay." *New York Times* (September 1):E1, E4.

Angier, Natalie. 1992. "Bedside Manners Improve as More Women Enter Medicine." *New York Times* (May 7):A8.

Aponte, Robert. 1990. "Urban Hispanic Poverty in the United States." Working Paper, No. 6, Julian Samora Research Institute, Michigan State University.

Aponte, Robert. 1991. "Urban Hispanic Poverty: Disaggregations and Explanations." *Social Problems* 38 (4):516–528.

Appelbaum, Richard P. 1989. "The Affordability Gap." *Society* 26 (May/June):6–8.

Arendell, Terry. 1990. "Divorce: A Woman's Issue." In *Perspectives on the Family: History, Class, and Feminism,* Christoper Carlson (ed.). Belmont, Calif.: Wadsworth, pp. 460–478.

Associated Press. 1989. "Babies of Parents Lacking Insurance Face More Risks." (August 24).

Associated Press. 1990a. "Abuse of the Elderly Increasing but Problem Ignored." (May 1).

Associated Press. 1990b. "Police Chief Assailed over 'Outrageous' Remarks on Drugs." (September 7).

Associated Press. 1990c. "60% of Savings and Loans Failures Linked to Criminal Fraud." (February 28).

Associated Press. 1991. "U.S. Leading Arms Supplier for the World." (August 12).

Associated Press. 1992b. "Censorship Study Worries Library Group." (January 19).

Associated Press. 1992c. "U.S. Children Grew Poorer in '80s." (August 12).

Associated Press. 1992d. "Chrysler Moving Out of Detroit." (September 9).

Associated Press. 1992e. "Color Affects EPA Response, Study Says." (September 14).

Associated Press. 1992f. "Hispanic Dropouts Triple U.S. Average." (September 17).

Atchley, Robert C. 1989. "Retiree Bashing: No Good Deed Goes Unpunished." *Generations* (Spring):1–22.

Atkins, Elizabeth. 1991. "U.S. Blacks More Likely to Contract Glaucoma." *Fort Collins Coloradoan* (December 8):E4.

Atkins, Gary L. 1989. "Lesbians and Gays: Forced March in the Military." *The Nation* (January 2):16–18.

Atwater, Carol. 1983. "Child Abuse Rises 10%." *USA Today* (March 29):D1.

Baca Zinn, Maxine. 1981. "Sociological Theory in Emergent Chicano Perspectives." *Pacific Sociological Review* 24 (April):255–272.

Baca Zinn, Maxine. 1982. "Urban Kinship and Midwest Chicano Families: Evidence in Support of Revision." *De Colores Journal* 6 (Summer):85–98.

Baca Zinn, Maxine. 1990. "Family, Feminism and Race in America." *Gender and Society* 14 (March):62–86.

Baca Zinn, Maxine, and D. Stanley Eitzen. 1990. *Diversity in Families.* 2nd ed. New York: Harper & Row.

Baca Zinn, Maxine, and D. Stanley Eitzen. 1993. *Diversity in Families.* 3rd. ed. New York: HarperCollins.

Baker, Eugene C. 1965. *Mexico and Texas, 1821–1835.* New York: Russell and Russell.

Ballinger, Jeffrey. 1992. "The New Free Trade Heel." *Harper's Magazine* 285 (August):46–47.

Balswick, Jack, with James Lincoln Collier. 1976. "Why Husbands Can't Say 'I Love You.' " In *The Forty-Nine Percent Majority,* Deborah S. David and Robert Brannon (eds.). Reading, Mass.: Addiso–Wesley, pp. 58–59.

Bane, Mary Jo, and David T. Ellwood. 1989. "One-Fifth of the Nation's Children: Why Are They Poor?" *Science* 245 (September):1047–1053.

Banfield, Edward C. 1977. *The Unheavenly City Revisited.* Boston: Little, Brown.

Barbara, John, and June Morrison. 1975. "If Addiction Is Incurable, 'Why Do We Try to Cure It?' A Comparison of Control Methods in the U.K. and the U.S." *Crime and Delinquency* 21 (January):28–33.

Barlett, Donald L., and James B. Steele. 1992. *America: What Went Wrong?* Kansas City: Andrews and McMeel.

Baron, Harold M. 1975. "Racial Domination in Advanced Capitalism." In *Labor Market Segmentation,* Richard C. Edwards et al. (eds.). Lexington, Mass.: Heath.

Barrera, Mario. 1979. *Race and Class in the Southwest: A Theory of Racial Inequality.* Notre Dame, Ind.: University of Notre Dame Press.

Barringer, Felicity. 1992a. "As American as Apple Pie, Dim Sum, or Burritos." *New York Times* (May 3):section 4:2.

Barringer, Felicity. 1992b. "Insurance Gap Is Seen among Older Women." *New York Times* (May 7):A8.

Barry, Tom, Beth Wood, and Deb Preusch. 1983. *Dollars and Dictators.* New York: Grove Press.

Baskir, Laurence M., and William A. Strauss. 1978. *The Draft, the War, and the Vietnam Generation.* New York: Knopf.

Bass, Paul. 1990. "Group Smokes Out Tobacco Investment." *In These Times* (August 29–September 11):9–10.

Bassuck, Ellen L. 1984. "The Homelessness Problem." *Scientific American* 251 (July):40–45.

Beck, Melinda. 1990. "The Goal: A Nurse in Each Nursing Home." *Newsweek* (October 8):77–78.

Becker, Howard S. 1963. *The Outsiders: Studies in the Sociology of Deviance.* New York: Free Press.

Becker, Howard S. 1967. "Whose Side Are We On?" *Social Problems* 14 (Winter):239–247.

Beeghley, Leonard. 1984. "Illusion and Reality in the Measurement of Poverty." *Social Problems* 31 (February):322–333.

Begley, Sharon. 1989. "Teeing Off on Japan's Garbage." *Newsweek* (November 27):70.

Bell, Alan P., and Martin S. Weinberg. 1978. *Homosexualities: A Study of Human Diversity.* New York: Simon & Schuster.

Bell, Inge Powell. 1976. "The Double Standard." In *Growing Old in America,* Beth B. Hess (ed.). New Brunswick, N.J.: Transaction Books, pp. 150–162.

Bell, Inge Powell. 1979. "The Double Standard: Age." In *Woman: A Feminist Perspective,* 2d ed., Jo Freeman (ed.). Palo Alto, Calif.: Mayfield, pp. 145–155.

Belsky, Jay. 1991. "Parental and Nonparental Child Care and Children's Socioemotional Development." In *Contemporary Families: Looking Forward, Looking Back,* Alan Booth (ed.). Minneapolis: National Council on Family Relations, pp. 122–140.

Bengtson, Vern L. 1985. "Loss and the Social Psychology of Aging." In *Aging 2000: Our Health Care Destiny,* Charles M. Gartz, George Niederehe, and Nancy L. Wilson (eds.). New York: Springer-Verlag, pp. 61–73.

Bengtson, Vern L., Gerardo Marti, and Robert E. L. Roberts. 1991. "Age-Group Relationships: Generational Equity and Inequity." In *Parent-Child Relations Throughout Life,* Karl Pillemer and Kathleen McCartney (eds.). Hillsdale, N.J.: Lawrence Erlbaum Associates, pp. 253–278.

Bengtson, Vern L., Carolyn Rosenthal, and Linda Burton. 1990. "Families and Aging: Diversity and Heterogeneity." In *Handbook of Aging and Social Sciences,* 3rd ed., Robert H. Binstock and Linda K. George (eds.). San Diego: Academic Press, pp. 263–287.

Bennett, Amanda. 1989. "Firms Become a Crucial Agent of Social Change." *Wall Street Journal* (June 23):A22.

Benokraitis, Nicole, and Joe R. Feagin. 1974. "Institutional Racism: A Review and Critical Assessment of the Literature." Paper presented at the American Sociological Association, Montreal, August.

Berk, Richard A. 1987. "Anticipating the Social Consequences of AIDS." *The American Sociologist* 18 (Fall):211–227.

Bernstein, Aaron. 1988. "Where the Jobs Are Is Where the Skills Aren't." *Business Week* (September 19):104–108.

Bianchi, Suzanne M. 1990. "America's Children: Mixed Prospects." *Population Bulletin* 45 (June).

Bickel, Janet. 1990. "Women in Medical School." In *The American Woman 1990–91,* Sara E. Rix (ed.). New York: W. W. Norton, pp. 212–221.

Bierstedt, Robert. 1948. "The Sociology of Majorities." *American Sociological Review* 13 (December):700–710.

Billingsly, Andrew. 1987. "Black Families in a Changing Society." In *The State of Black America, 1987.* New York: National Urban League, Inc., pp. 97–111.

Birdwhistell, Ray L. 1980. "The Idealized Model of the American Family." In *Marriage and Family in a Changing Society,* James M. Henslin (ed.). New York: Free Press.

Birnbaum, Norman. 1992. "One Cheer for Clinton." *The Nation* (September 28):318–320.

Bishop, Katherine. 1989. "San Francisco Grants Recognition to Partnerships of Single People." *New York Times* (May 31):All.

Blauner, Robert. 1964. *Alienation and Freedom.* Chicago: University of Chicago Press.

Blauner, Robert. 1972. *Racial Oppression in America.* New York: Harper & Row.

Blieszner, Rosemary, and Janet M. Alley. 1990. "Family Caregiving for the Elderly: An Overview of Resources." *Family Relations* 39 (January):97–102.

Block, Marilyn R., and Jan D. Sinnott. 1979. *The Battered Elder Syndrome.* College Park: University of Maryland, Center on Aging.

Bluestone, Barry, and Bennett Harrison. 1982. *The Deindustrialization of America.* New York: Basic Books.

Blumberg, Paul M., and P. W. Paul. 1975. "Continuities and Discontinuities in Upper-Class Marriage." *Journal of Marriage and the Family* 37 (February):63–78.

Blumberg, Rae Lesser. 1984. "A General Theory of Gender Stratification." In *Sociological Theory,* Randall Collins (ed.). San Francisco: Jossey-Bass, pp. 23–100.

Blumstein, Philip, and Pepper Schwartz. 1983. *American Couples: Money, Work, Sex.* New York: Morrow.

Bock, Gordon. 1987. "Blood, Sweat and Fears." *Time* (September 28):50–51.

Bogdanich, Walt. 1992. *The Great White Lie: Dishonesty, Waste, and Incompetence in the Medical Community.* New York: Touchstone.

Bograd, Michele. 1988. "Feminist Perspectives on Wife Abuse: An Introduction." In *Feminist Perspectives on Wife Abuse,* Kersti Yllo and Michelle Bograd (eds.). Newbury Park, Calif.: Sage, pp. 11–26.

Bonacich, Edna. 1976. "Advanced Capitalism and Black/White Relations in the United States: A Split Labor Market Interpretation." *American Sociological Review* 41:34–51.

Bonacich, Edna. 1989. "Inequality in America: The Failure of the American System for People of Color." *Sociological Spectrum* 9(1):77–101.

Bonnie, Richard J., and Charles Whitebread II. 1974. *The Marijuana Conviction.* Charlottesville: University Press of Virginia, pp. 13–31.

Borkin, Joseph. 1978. *The Crime and Punishment of I. G. Farben.* New York: Free Press.

Bourke, Jaron. 1989. "Mergermania." *The Nation* (October 30):495.

Bouvier, Leon F., and Robert W. Gardner. 1986. "Immigration to the U.S.: The Unfinished Story." *Population Bulletin* 41 (November):entire issue.

Bowles, Samuel. 1969. "Toward Equality of Educational Opportunity." *Harvard Educational Review.* Cambridge, Mass.: Harvard University Press.

Bowles, Samuel. 1972. "Schooling and Inequality from Generation to Generation." *Journal of Political Economy* (May–June).

Bowles, Samuel. 1977. "Unequal Education and the Reproduction of the Social Division of Labor." In *Power and Ideology in Education,* Jerome Karabel and A.H. Halsey (ed.). New York: Oxford University Press, pp. 137–153.

Bowles, Samuel, and Herbert Gintis. 1973. "I.Q. and the U.S. Class Structure." *Social Policy* 3 (January–February): 65–96.

Bowles, Samuel, and Herbert Gintis. 1976. *Schooling in Capitalist America: Educational Reform and the Contradiction of Economic Life.* New York: Basic Books.

Boyd, Robert S. 1989. "U.S. Facing Labor Shortages." *Charlotte Observer* (May 7):B1, B4.

Braithwaite, John. 1984. *Corporate Crime in the Pharmaceutical Industry.* London: Routledge & Kegan Paul.

Brecher, Edward M., and editors of Consumer Reports. 1972. *Licit and Illicit Drugs.* Boston: Little, Brown.

Breines, Wini, and Linda Gordon. 1983. "The New Scholarship on Family Violence." *Signs* 8 (Spring):490–531.

Brenner, M. Harvey. 1973. *Mental Illness and the Economy.* Cambridge, Mass.: Harvard University Press.

Brimelow, Peter. 1992. "The Fracturing of America." *Forbes* (March 30):74–75.

Brody, Jane E. 1992. "Personal Health." *New York Times* (March 6):B6.

Brown, E. Richard, and Geraldine Dallek. 1990. "State Approaches to Financing Health Care for the Poor." *Annual Review of Public Health* 11:377–400.

Brown, Lester R. 1990. "The Illusion of Progress." In *State of the World 1990,* Lester R. Brown et al. (eds.). New York: W. W. Norton, pp. 3–16.

Brownworth, Victoria A. 1989. "Stonewall + 20." *The Nation* (July 3):5–6.

Buder, Leonard. 1987. "Beech-Nut Is Fined $2 Million for Sale of Fake Apple Juice." *New York Times* (November 14):1, 39.

Bukovinsky, Janet. 1982. "A Wife Is Abused Every 18 Seconds, FBI Says." *Rocky Mountain News* (March 9):38, 42.

Bullard, Robert D. 1990. *Dumping in Dixie: Race, Class, and Environmental Quality.* Boulder, Colo.: Westview.

Bullough, Vern L. 1978. "Variant Life Styles: Homosexuality." In *Exploring Intimate Life Styles,* Bernard I. Murstein (ed.). New York: Springer, pp. 245–257.

Bumpass, Larry. 1983. *Children and Mental Disruptions.* Center for Demography and Ecology Work Paper 82–57 (January). Madison: University of Wisconsin.

Bumpass, Larry L. 1990. "What's Happening to the Family? Interactions between Demographic and Institutional Change." *Demography* 27 (November):483–498.

Bumpass, Larry, and Ronald R. Rindfuss. 1979. "Children's Experience of Marital Disruption." *American Journal of Sociology* 85 (July):49–65.

Burnham, Linda. 1986. "Has Poverty Been Feminized in Black America?" In *For Crying Out Loud: Women and Poverty in the U.S.,* Rochelle Lefkowitz and Ann Withorn (eds.). New York: Pilgrim Press, pp. 69–83.

Burns, Haywood. 1973. "Black People and the Tyranny of American Law." *The Annals* 407 (May):156–166.

Burr, Chandler. 1993. "Homosexuality and Biology." *The Atlantic Monthly* 271 (March):47–65.

Business Week. 1992. "The Economic Crisis of Urban America." (May 18):38–43.

Butler, Matilda, and William Paisley. 1980. *Women and the Mass Media.* New York: Human Sciences Press.

Butterfield, Fox. 1991. "Asians Spread across a Land and Help Change It." *New York Times* (February 24):All.

Bybee, Rodger W. 1979. "Violence toward Youth." *Journal of Social Issues* 35 (Spring):1–14.

Cabib, Amalia. 1981. "Indians of the Americas: Refugees in Their Own Land." *Intercom* 9 (June):3.

Cain, Bruce, and Roderick Kiewiet. 1986. "California's Coming Minority Majority." *Public Opinion* (February–March):50–52.

Capitanini, Lisa. 1991. "Sexually Transmitted Diseases: City Losing Battle against Epidemic in Black Communities." *The Chicago Reporter* 20 (November):1, 4–6.

Caplan, Nathan, and Stephen D. Nelson. 1973. "On Being Useful: The Nature and Consequences of Psychological Research on Social Problems." *American Psychologist* 28 (March):199–211.

Caplan, Nathan, and Stephen D. Nelson. 1974. "Who's to Blame?" *Psychology Today* 8 (November):99–104.

Carmichael, Stokely, and Charles V. Hamilton. 1967. *Black Power: The Politics of Liberation in America.* New York: Random House.

Carnoy, Martin, ed. 1975. *Schooling in a Corporate Society: The Political Economy of Education in America.* 2d ed. New York: McKay.

Carpenter, Betsy. 1990. "Faces in the Forest." *U.S. News & World Report* (June 4):63–69.

Carter, Michael J., and Susan Boslego Carter. 1981. "Women Get a Ticket to Ride after the Gravy Train Has Left the Station." *Feminist Studies* 7:477–504.

Castenada, Carlos. 1972. *A Separate Reality.* New York: Pocket Books.

Castro, Janice. 1991. "Condition: Critical." *Time* (November 25):34–42.

Cellis, William III. 1992. "A Texas-Size Battle to Rich and Poor Alike." *New York Times* (February 12):B8.

Chafetz, Janet Saltzman. 1984. *Sex and Advantage: A Comparative Macrostructural Theory of Sex Stratification.* Totowa, N.J.: Rowman and Allanheld.

Chambliss, Lauren, and Sharon Reier. 1990. "How Doctors Have Ruined Health Care." *Financial World* 159 (January 9):46–52.

Chambliss, William. 1978. *On the Take.* Bloomington: Indiana University Press.

Cherlin, Andrew. 1981. *Marriage, Divorce, Remarriage.* Cambridge, Mass.: Harvard University Press.

Chicago Tribune. 1992. "Census Says 1 in 5 Earns Poverty Wage." (May 12):14.

Children's Defense Fund. 1989a. *Lack of Health Insurance Makes a Difference.* Washington, D.C.: Children's Defense Fund.

Children's Defense Fund. 1989b. *A Vision for America's Future.* Washington, D.C.: Children's Defense Fund (entire issue).

Children's Defense Fund. 1991a. *The State of America's Children 1991.* Washington, D.C.: Children's Defense Fund.

Children's Defense Fund. 1991b. *The Nation's Investment in Children: An Analysis of the President's FY 1992 Budget Proposals.* Washington, D.C.: Children's Defense Fund.

Chiswick, Barry R. 1985. "Immigrants in the U.S. Labor Market." In *Majority and Minority,* 3d ed., Norman R. Yetman (ed.). Boston: Allyn and Bacon, pp. 401–407.

Choate, Pat. 1990. "Political Advantage: Japan's Campaign for America." *Harvard Business Review* 68 (September–October):87–103.

Choldin, Harvey. 1985. *Cities and Suburbs.* New York: McGraw-Hill.

Christensen, Kathleen. 1988. *Women and Home-Based Work.* New York: Henry Holt.

Chronicle of Higher Education. 1987a. "Defense Funds to Colleges and Non-Profit Groups Total $2.6 Billion for 1986, Up 7.3 Percent in a Year." (June 10):26.

Chronicle of Higher Education. 1987b. "Hispanics: Some Basic Facts." September 16, A36.

Cimons, Marlene. 1989. "Study Says Poor Die Needlessly from Cancer." *Los Angeles Times* (July 18):1, 16.

Clancy, Paul. 1987. "Recycling Efforts Take Off." *USA Today* (November 16):6A.

Clay, Phillip. 1979. *Neighborhood Renewal.* Lexington, Mass.: Lexington Books.

Cobb, Jean, Jeff Denny, Vicki Kemper, and Viveca Novak. 1990. "All the President's Donors." *Common Cause* Vol. 16 (March/April):21–40.

Cockerham, William C. 1981. *Sociology of Mental Disorder.* Englewood Cliffs, N.J.: Prentice-Hall.

Coffin, Tristram. 1990. "The High Cost of Health Care." *The Washington Spectator* 16 (March 15):1–4.

Cohen, Linc. 1992. "Waste Dumps Toxic Traps for Minorities." *The Chicago Reporter* 21 (April):1, 6–9,11.

Cohn, Bob. 1992. "Discrimination: The Limits of the Law." *Newsweek* (September 14):38–39.

Cole, Philip, and Marlene B. Goldman. 1975. "Occupation." In *Persons at High Risk of Cancer,* Joseph F. Fraumeni, Jr. (ed.). New York: Academic Press, pp. 167–184.

Cole, Stephen. 1975. *The Sociological Orientation: An Introduction to Sociology.* Chicago: Rand McNally.

Coleman, James S. 1961. *The Adolescent Society.* New York: Free Press.

Coleman, James S., et al. 1966. *Equality of Educational Opportunity.* Washington, D.C.: Government Printing Office.

Coleman, James William. 1989. *The Criminal Elite: The Sociology of White Collar Crime.* 2d ed. New York: St. Martin's Press.

Coleman, James William, and Donald R. Cressey. 1990. *Social Problems.* 4th ed. New York: Harper & Row.

Coles, Robert. 1970 "A Fashionable Kind of Slander." *Atlantic Monthly* 248 (November):54–55.

Colosanto, Diane. 1990. "Widespread Public Opposition to Drug Legalization." *The Gallup Poll Monthly,* 292 (January):3.

Comfort, Alexander. 1976. "Age Prejudice in America." *Social Policy* 7 (November/December):4–7.

Common Cause Magazine. 1990. "President Bush's S & L Soft Money." Vol. 16 (July/August):iii.

Commoner, Barry. 1975. "The Energy Crisis—All of a Piece." *The Center Magazine* (March/April):28.

Conklin, Ellis A. 1986. "Immigrant Tide Turns L.A. Area into Alien Stew." *The Flint Journal* (June 16):D5.

Consumer Reports. 1992a. "Wasted Health Care Dollars." 57 (July):435–448.

Consumer Reports. 1992b. "The Search for Solutions: Does Canada Have the Answer?" 57 (September):579–592.

Cook, James. 1981. "The American Indian through Five Centuries." *Forbes* (November 9):108–115.

Cook, James. 1982. "The Molting of America." *Forbes* (November 22):161–167.

Cooper, Matthew. 1991. "The Rich in America." *U.S. News & World Report* (November 18):34–40.

Cornell, George. 1989. "Women in 'Full Ministry' Nearly Double in Decade." *Rocky Mountain News* (May 27):106.

Cowley, Geoffrey. 1990. "AIDS: The Next Ten Years." *Newsweek* (June 25):20–27.

Cowley, Geoffrey. 1991. "Children in Peril." *Newsweek,* special issue on "How Kids Grow: Health, Psychology & Values." (Summer):18–21.

Cowley, Geoffrey. 1992a. "A Quit-Now Drive That Worked." *Newsweek* (April 6):54.

Cowley, Geoffrey. 1992b. "Poison at Home and at Work." *Newsweek* (June 29):55.

Crooks, Louise. 1991. "Women and Pensions." *Vital Speeches of the Day* 57 (February 15):283–285.

Crooks, Robert, and Karla Baur. 1987. *Our Sexuality.* 3d ed. Menlo Park, Calif.: Benjamin Cummings.

Crystal, Stephen, and Dennis Shea. 1990. "Cumulative Advantage, Cumulative Disadvantage, and Inequality among Elderly People." *The Gerontologist* 30 (August):437–443.

Cumming, Elaine, and Willing E. Henry. 1961. *Growing Old: The Process of Disengagement.* New York: Basic Books.

Cummings, Judith. 1987. "Hispanic Workers Gaining a Big Share of New Jobs." *New York Times* (April 2):11.

Curran, Daniel J., and Clair M. Renzetti. 1987. *Social Problems: Society in Crisis.* Boston: Allyn and Bacon.

Currie, Elliott. 1985. *Confronting Crime: An American Challenge.* New York: Pantheon.

Currie, Elliott, and Jerome H. Skolnick. 1984. *America's Problems: Social Issues and Public Policy.* Boston: Little, Brown.

Currie, Elliott, and Jerome H. Skolnick. 1988. *America's Problems.* 2d ed. Glenview, Ill.: Scott, Foresman.

Curtain, Sharon R. 1972. *Nobody Ever Died of Old Age.* Boston: Atlantic Monthly Press.

Cuskey, Walter R., and William Krasner. 1973. "The Needle and the Boot: Heroin Maintenance." *Society* 10 (May/June):49.

Cutler, Blayne. 1989. "Up the Down Staircase." *American Demographics* 11 (April):32–41.

Dallek, Geraldine. 1990. "Hospital Care for Profit." In *Readings on Social Problems,* William Feigelman (ed.). Fort Worth: Holt, Rinehart and Winston, pp. 19–26.

David, Deborah S., and Robert Brannon. 1980. "The Male Sex Role." In *Family in Transition,* 3d ed., Arlene S. Skolnick and Jerome H. Skolnick (eds.). Boston: Little, Brown.

Davidson, Nicholas. 1990. "Life without Father: America's Greatest Social Catastrophe." *Policy Review,* no. 51 (Winter):40–44.

Davis, Cary, Carl Haub, and JoAnne Willete. 1983. "U.S. Hispanics Changing the Face of America." *Population Bulletin* 38 (June):entire issue.

Davis, Ged R. 1990. "Energy for Planet Earth." *Scientific American* 263 (September):55–62.

Day, Janet. 1990. "Parents Debating Diaper Dilemma." *Rocky Mountain News* (May 16):32.

Days, Samuel H., Jr. 1982. "Reinventing the World." *The Progressive* 46 (April):13–14.

de Beauvoir, Simone. 1970. *The Second Sex.* Translated by H.M. Parshley. New York: Bantam Books.

de Beauvoir, Simone. 1973. *The Coming of Age.* New York: Warner Paperback Library, pp. 57–131.

Deckard, Barbara Sinclair. 1983. *The Women's Movement.* 3d ed. New York: Harper & Row.

Deets, Horace B. 1989. "Health Care for a Caring America." *Vital Speeches of the Day* 55 (August 1):636–637.

D'Emilio, John. 1983. *Sexual Politics, Sexual Communities: The Making of a Homosexual Minority in the United States 1940–1970.* Chicago: University of Chicago Press.

D'Emilio, John. 1990. "The Campus Environment for Gay and Lesbian Life." *Academe* 76 (January/February): 16–19.

Dennis, Richard J. 1990. "The Economics of Legalizing Drugs." *Atlantic Monthly* 266 (November):126–132.

Denver Post. 1982a (October 22):11A.

Denver Post. 1990. "Long-Term Care Cost Soars." (January 23):A3.

Denver Post Wire Services. 1992. "Poverty Rolls Soar over 35 Million." *Denver Post* (September 4):lA.

DeParle, Jason. 1992. "Why Marginal Changes Don't Rescue the Welfare State." *New York Times* (March 1):E3.

Deutsch, Albert. 1949. *The Mentally Ill in America.* 2d ed. New York: Columbia University Press.

Diamond, Stuart. 1985. "U.S. Toxic Mishaps in Chemicals Put at 6,928 in 5 Years." *New York Times* (October 3):1, 13.

Diamond, Stuart. 1986. "Chernobyl Rouses Bad Memories, New Fears." *New York Times* (May 4):E3.

Di Baggio, Thomas. 1976. "The Unholy Alliance." *Penthouse* (May):74–91.

Dibble, Ursula, and Murray S. Straus. 1980. "Some Social Structure Determinants of Inconsistency between Attitudes and Behavior: The Case of Family Violence." *Journal of Marriage and the Family* 42 (February):71–80.

Di Leonardo, Micaela. 1992. "Boyz on the Hood." *The Nation* (August 17/24):178–186.

Dohrenwend, Bruce P., and Barbara S. Dohrenwend. 1969. *Social Status and Psychological Disorder.* New York: Wiley.

Domhoff, G. William. 1978. *The Powers That Be: Processes of Ruling Class Domination in America.* New York: Random House.

Domhoff, G. William. 1990. *The Power Elite and the State: How Policy Is Made in America.* Hawthorn, N.Y.: Aldine de Gruyter.

Donaldson, Kenneth. 1976. *Insanity Inside Out.* New York: Crown.

Dorning, Mike. 1992. "Upgrading Infrastructure Linked to Rebuilding U.S. Productivity." *Chicago Tribune* (September 27):1C, 4C.

Dorris, Michael A. 1981. "The Grass Still Grows, the Rivers Still Flow: Contemporary Native Americans." *Daedalus* 110 (Spring):43–69.

Doyle, Jack, and Paul T. Schindler. 1974. "The Incoherent Society." Paper presented at the American Sociological Association, Montreal, August 25–29.

Draguns, Juris G., and Leslie Phillips. 1971. *Psychiatric Classification and Diagnosis: An Overview and Critique.* New York: General Learning Press.

Dreier, Peter. 1992. "Bush to Cities: Drop Dead." *The Progressive* 56 (July):20–23.

Drucker, Peter F. 1972. "School around the Bend." *Psychology Today* 6 (June):49.

Duncan, Greg J. 1984. *Years of Poverty, Years of Plenty: The Changing Economic Fortunes of American Workers and Families.* Ann Arbor: Institute for Social Research.

Duncan, Greg J. 1987. "On the Slippery Slope." *American Demographics* 9 (May):30–35.

Dunn, Marcia. 1989. "White Men Dominate Transplant Operations." *Fort Collins Coloradoan* (May 30):A6.

Dunn, William. 1987. "1-Parent Families Total 8.9 M." *USA Today* (December 17):3A.

duRivage, Virginia L. 1992. "Flexibility Trap: The Proliferation of Marginal Jobs." *The American Prospect,* No. 9 (Spring):84–93.

Durkheim, Emile. 1958. *The Rules of Sociological Method.* Translated by S. A. Solovay and J. H. Mueller. Glencoe, Ill.: Free Press.

Durkheim, Emile. 1960. *The Division of Labor in Society.* Translated by George Simpson. Glencoe, Ill.: Free Press.

Durning, Alan B. 1990. "Ending Poverty." In *State of the World 1990.* Lester R. Brown et al. (ed.). New York: W. W. Norton, pp. 135–153.

Durning, Alan B. 1991. "The Health of the Planet." In *World Military and Social Expenditures 1991* by Ruth Leger Sivard. Washington, D.C.: World Priorities, pp. 28–35.

Durrett, M. A., S. O'Bryant, and J. W. Pennebacker. 1975. "Child-Rearing Reports of White, Black and Mexican-American Families." *Developmental Psychology* 11:871.

Duster, Troy. 1970. *The Legislation of Morality: Law, Drugs, and Moral Judgment.* New York: Free Press.

Dychtwald, Ken, and Joe Flower. 1990. "Meeting the Challenges of an Aging Nation." *Utne Reader,* No. 37 (January/February):82–86.

Dyer, Everett D. 1979. *The American Family: Variety and Change.* New York: McGraw-Hill.

The Economist. 1992a. "America's Cities: Doomed to Burn?" (May 9):21–22, 24.

The Economist. 1992a. "Pull Together?" (May 9):25, 28.

The Economist. 1992b. "Bad Apples?" 324 (July 18):29.

Edsall, Thomas Byrne, with Mary D. Edsall. 1991. "Race." *Atlantic Monthly* (May):53–86.

Edwards, Richard C., Michael Reich, and Thomas E. Weisskopf. 1978. "Sexism." In *The Capitalist System,* 2d ed., R. C. Edwards, M. Reich, and T. E. Weisskopf (eds.). Englewood Cliffs, N.J.: Prentice-Hall, pp. 331–341.

Ehrenreich, Barbara. 1991. "Welfare: A White Secret." *Time* (December 16):84.

Ehrenreich, Barbara, and Karin Stallard. 1982. "The Nouveau Poor." *Ms.* (August):217–224.

Ehrlich, Paul R., and Anne H. Ehrlich. 1972. *Population/Resources/Environment: Issues in Human Ecology.* 2nd ed. San Francisco: Freeman.

Ehrlich, Paul R., and Anne H. Ehrlich. 1988. "Population, Plenty, and Poverty." *National Geographic* 174 (December):914–945.

Ehrlich, Paul R., and Anne H. Ehrlich. 1990. *The Population Explosion.* New York: Simon & Schuster Touchstone.

Eisenstein, Zillah. 1979a. "Developing a Theory of Capitalist Patriarchy and Socialist Feminism." In *Capitalist Patriarchy and the Case for Socialist Feminism,* Zillah R. Eisenstein (ed.). New York: Monthly Review Press, pp. 5–40.

Eisenstein, Zillah. 1979b. *Capitalist Patriarchy and the Case for Socialist Feminism.* New York: Monthly Review Press.

Eitzen, D. Stanley. 1984. "Teaching Social Problems: Implications of the Objectivist-Subjectivist Debate." *Society for the Study of Social Problems Newsletter* 16 (Fall):10–12.

Eitzen, D. Stanley, and Maxine Baca Zinn, eds. 1989. *The Reshaping of America.* Englewood Cliffs, N.J.: Prentice-Hall.

Eitzen, D. Stanley, and Maxine Baca Zinn. 1990. *In Conflict and Order: Understanding Society.* 5th ed. Boston: Allyn and Bacon.

Eitzen, D. Stanley, and George H. Sage. 1993. *Sociology of North American Sport.* 5th ed. Dubuque, Ia.: Wm. C. Brown.

Elias, Marilyn. 1987. "Safe Sex and the Heterosexual." *USA Today* (November 3):D1–2.

Elmer-Dewitt, Philip. 1991a. "Love Canals in the Making." *Time* (May 20):51.

Elmer-Dewitt, Philip. 1991b. "Machines from the Lunatic Fringe." *Time* (November 11):74–75.

Elmer-Dewitt, Phillip. 1992. "Rich vs. Poor." *Time* (June 1):42–58.

Elson, John. 1990. "Dumping on the Poor." *Time,* August 13):46–47.

Elson, John. 1991. "Drink until You Drop." *Time* (December 16):64–65.

English, Carry W. 1984. "From High Unemployment to a Labor Shortage." *U.S. News & World Report* (September 17):56.

Environmental Action. 1989. "Reforming the Auto." 21 (July–August):17–26.

Epstein, Cynthia Fuchs. 1970. *Woman's Place.* Berkeley: University of California Press.

Erikson, Kai T. 1962. "Notes on the Sociology of Deviance," *Social Problems* 9 (Spring).

Erikson, Kai T. 1966. *Wayward Puritans: A Study in the Sociology of Deviance.* New York: Wiley.

Esters, Stephanie, and Jean Seligmann. 1990. "A Call for More Donors." *Newsweek* (September 10):53.

Estes, Ralph. 1992. "Enterprise Zones: Urban Hope or Trickle-Down Hokum?" *In These Times* (September 16–29):16.

Estrada, Leobardo F., et al. 1981. "Chicanos in the United States: A History of Exploitation and Resistance." *Daedalus* 110 (Spring):103–131.

Etzioni, Amitai. 1974. "Grass, Greed, and the Slow Gain of Social Progress." *Human Behavior* 2 (February): 4–5.

Etzioni, Amitai. 1987. "Corporations on the Government Gravy Train." *Business and Society Review,* no. 62 (Summer):4–10.

Eyesenck, Hans J. 1970. "The Effects of Psychotherapy." In *Social Psychology through Symbolic Interaction,* Gregory P. Stone and Harvey A. Farberman (eds.). Waltham, Mass.: Ginn-Blaisdell, pp. 718–770.

Faltermayer, Edmund. 1992. "Let's *Really* Cure the Health System." *Fortune* (March 23):46–58.

Faludi, Susan. 1991. *Backlash: The Undeclared War against Women.* New York: Crown.

Farnsworth, Clyde H. 1992. "Canadians Defend Care System Against Criticism." *New York Times* (February 17): C8.

Feagin, Joe R., and Clairece Booher Feagin. 1990. *Social Problems: A Critical Power-Conflict Perspective.* 3d ed. Englewood Cliffs, N.J.: Prentice-Hall.

Feagin, Joe R., and Robert Parker. 1990. *Building American Cities: The Urban Real Estate Game.* 2nd ed. Englewood Cliffs, N.J.: Prentice-Hall.

Ferree, Myra Marx. 1991. "Feminism and Family Research." In *Contemporary Families: Looking Forward, Looking Back,* Alan Booth (ed.). Minneapolis: National Council on Family Relations, pp. 103–121.

Findlay, Steven. 1986. "Cancer Risk Higher for Poor." *USA Today* (October 7):D1.

Finkel, Norma J. 1976. *Mental Illness and Health: Its Legacy, Tensions, and Changes.* New York: Macmillan.

Finkelstein, Michael O. 1987. "A Shared Fate." *The Nation* (May 9):599.

Finn, Chester E., Jr. 1989. "A Seismic Shock for Education." *New York Times* (September 3):E13.

Fischer, Claude. 1976. *The Urban Experience.* New York: Harcourt Brace Jovanovich.

Fischman, Joshua. 1986. "A Journey of Hearts and Minds." *Psychology Today* (July):42–47.

Fishman, Pamela M. 1978. "Interaction: The Work Women Do." *Social Problems* 25 (April):397–406.

Fiske, Edward B. 1987. "Integration Lacks at Public Schools." *New York Times* (July 26):1, 15.

Flavin, Christopher. 1990. "Detroit: America's Best Source of Oil." *New York Times* (August 26):F13.

Forbes. 1990a. "Forbes 500s." (April 30):entire issue.

Forbes. 1990b. "The 100 Largest U.S. Multinationals." (July 23):362.

Forbes. 1992a. "Made in America." 150 (July 20):161.

Forbes. 1992b. "U.S. Corporations with the Biggest Foreign Revenues." 150 (July 20):298–300.

Ford, Clellan, and Frank Beach. 1951. *Patterns of Sexual Behavior.* New York: Harper & Row.

Fordham Institute for Innovation in Social Policy. 1991. *1991 Index of Social Health/The Social Healty of America's Cities.* Tarrytown, N.Y.: Fordham University Graduate Center.

Fort, Joel, and Christopher T. Cory. 1975. *American Drugstore: A (Alcohol) to V (Valium).* Boston: Little, Brown.

Fortune. 1991. "The Fortune 500." (April 22):280–286.

Fost, Dan. 1991. "American Indians in the Nineties." *American Demographics* 13 (December):26–34.

Foucault, Michael. 1973. *Madness and Civilization: A History of Insanity in the Age of Reason.* New York: Random House/Vintage.

Frankel, Bruce. 1991. "Public Hospital System Is Suffering: Feds Aren't Shouldering the Burden." *USA Today* (December 18):1–2.

Franklin, Ben A. 1987. "Violations Cited in Utah Mine Fire That Killed 29." *New York Times* (March 25):24.

Freeman, Jo. 1979. "The Women's Liberation Movement: Its Origins, Organizations, Activities, and Ideas." In *Women: A Feminist Perspective,* 2d ed., Jo Freeman (ed.). Palo Alto, Calif.: Mayfield, pp. 557–574.

Freiberg, Peter. 1987a. "The March on Washington." *Advocate* (November 10):11–22.

Freiberg, Peter. 1987b. "New Report on Hate Crimes." *Advocate* (November 25):10–20.

Freudenheim, Milt. 1992. "Health Costs up 12.1% Last Year, a Study Says." *New York Times* (January 28):C2.

Frey, William H. 1990. "Metropolitan America: Beyond the Transition." *Population Bulletin* 45 (July).

Frey, William H. 1991. "Are Two Americas Emerging?" *Population Today* 19 (October):6–8.

Friedman, Milton. 1978. *The Economics of Freedom.* Cleveland: Standard Oil Company.

Friend, Tim. 1991. "Hypertension Linked to Discrimination." *USA Today* (February 6):A1.

Fuentes, Annette, and Barbara Ehrenreich. 1983. *Women in the Global Factory.* Boston: South End Press.

Futurist. 1987. "The Economics of Garbage." 21 (November/December):42.

Gallup, George, Jr. 1990. *The Gallup Poll: Public Opinion 1989.* Wilmington, Del.: Scholarly Resources.

The Gallup Report. 1987. "Homosexuality." 258 (March):12–18.

The Gallup Report. 1989a. "Poverty." 287 (August):4.

The Gallup Report. 1989b. "Homosexuality." 289 (October):11–15.

Gannett News Service. 1992. "Huge Gap in Funds for Children Seen from State to State." (March 6).

Gans, Herbert J. 1971. "The Uses of Power: The Poor Pay All." *Social Policy* 2 (July–August):20–24.

Gardner, Robert W., Bryant Robey, and Peter C. Smith. 1985. "Asian Americans: Growth, Change, and Diversity." *Population Bulletin* 40 (October):entire issue.

Garreau, Joel. 1991. *Edge City: Life on the New Frontier.* New York: Doubleday.

Geiger, H. Jack. 1990. "Generation of Poison and Lies." *New York Times* (August 5):E19.

Gelles, Richard J. 1976. "Demythologizing Child Abuse." *Family Coordinator* 25 (April).

Gelles, Richard J. 1977. "No Place to Go: The Social Dynamics of Marital Violence." In *Battered Women,* Maria Roy (ed.). New York: Van Nostrand.

Gelles, Richard J. 1979a. "The Myth of Battered Husbands." *Ms.* 8 (October):65–66, 71–74.

Gelles, Richard J. 1979b. "Violence at Home." *Rocky Mountain News* (December 11):62.

Gelles, Richard J., and Murray A. Straus. 1979a. "Determinants of Violence in the Family." In *Contemporary Theories about the Family,* Vol. 1,

Wesley R. Burr et al. (ed.). New York: Free Press, pp. 549–581.

Gelles, Richard J., and Murray A. Straus. 1979b. "Domestic Violence and Sexual Abuse of Children." In *Contemporary Families: Looking Forward, Looking Back,* Alan Booth (ed.). Minneapolis: National Council on Family Relations, pp. 327–340.

Gelles, Richard J., and Murray A. Straus. 1988. *Intimate Violence.* New York: Simon & Schuster.

Gelman, David. 1992. "Born or Bred?" *Newsweek* (February 24):46–53.

Gerth, Hans, and C. Wright Mills. 1953. *Character and Social Structure: The Psychology of Social Institutions.* New York: Harcourt, Brace, and World.

Giele, Janet Z. 1988. "Gender and Sex Roles." In *Handbook of Sociology,* Neil J. Smelser (ed.). Newbury Park, Calif.: Sage, pp. 291–323.

Gilder, George. 1981. *Wealth and Poverty.* New York: Basic Books.

Gilderbloom, John I. 1991. "Housing in America: It's Time for a New Strategy." *USA Today* (magazine) 120 (November):30–32.

Gilderbloom, John I., and Richard Appelbaum. 1988. *Rethinking Rental Housing.* Philadelphia: Temple University Press.

Gillie, Oliver. 1977. "Did Sir Cyril Burt Fake His Research on Heritability of Intelligence?" *Phi Delta Kappan* 58 (February):469–471.

Gilman, Richard. 1971. "Where Did It All Go Wrong?" *Life* (August 13):40–55.

Gillmour, Dan, and Steven K. Doig. 1992. "Segregation Forever?" *American Demographics* 14 (January): 48–51.

Giovannoni, Jeanne M. 1971. "Parental Mistreatment: Perpetrators as Victims." *Journal of Marriage and the Family* 33 (November):649–657.

Giovannoni, Jeanne M., and Rosina M. Becerra. 1979. *Defining Child Abuse.* New York: Free Press.

Glenn, Evelyn Nakano, and Roslyn L. Feldberg. 1984. "Clerical Work: The Female Occupation." In *Women: A Feminist Perspective,* 2d ed., Jo Freeman (ed.). Palo Alto, Calif.: Mayfield, pp. 316–336.

Glick, Paul C. 1975. "Some Recent Changes in American Families." *Current Population Reports,* Series P–23, No. 52. Washington, D.C.: Government Printing Office.

Goetting, Ann. 1983. "Divorce Outcome Research: Issues and Perspectives." In *Family in Transition,* 4th ed., Arlene S. Skolnick and Jerome H. Skolnick (eds.). Boston: Little, Brown, pp. 367–387.

Goffman, Erving. 1959. *The Presentation of Self in Everyday Life.* Garden City, N.Y.: Doubleday.

Goffman, Erving. 1961. *Asylums: Essays on the Social Situation of Mental Patients and Other Inmates.* Garden City, N.Y.: Doubleday/Anchor.

Goffman, Erving. 1963. *Stigma: Notes on the Management of Spoiled Identity.* Englewood Cliffs, N.J.: Prentice-Hall.

Goffman, Erving. 1979. *Gender Advertisements.* New York: Harper & Row/Colophon.

Goldfarb, Bruce. 1990. "Eye Problems More Likely among Blacks." *USA Today* (February 7):1.

Goldman, Ari L. 1986. "As Call Comes, More Women Answer." *New York Times* (October 10):E6.

Goldman, Benjamin A. 1992. "Polluting the Poor." *The Nation* (October 5):348–349.

Goldman, Daniel. 1978. "Who's Mentally Ill?" *Psychology Today* 11 (January):34–41.

Goldman, Daniel. 1990. "Us vs. Them: Profiling the New, Violent Hate." *International Herald Tribune* (May 30):1.

Goldsmith, William W., and Edward J. Blakely. 1992. *Separate Societies: Poverty and Inequality in U.S. Cities.* Philadelphia: Temple University Press.

Goode, Erica E. 1992. "Sick, or Just Quirky?" *U.S. News & World Report* (February 10):49–50.

Goode, Erich. 1989. *Drugs in American Society.* 3d ed. New York: Knopf.

Goode, William J. 1971. "Force and Violence in the Family." *Journal of Marriage and the Family* 33 (November):624–636.

Goode, William J. 1973. *The Drug Phenomenon: Social Aspects of Drug Taking.* Indianapolis: Bobbs-Merrill.

Goode, William J. 1976. "Family Disorganization." In *Contemporary Social Problems,* 4th ed., Robert K. Merton and Robert Nisbet (eds.). New York: Harcourt Brace Jovanovich.

Goodman, Ellen. 1990. "More Women Being Seen, but Still Not Being Heard." *Rocky Mountain News* (October 1):37.

Gordon, David M., Richard C. Edwards, and Michael Reich. 1982. *Segmented Work, Divided Workers.* Cambridge, Eng.: Cambridge University Press.

Gordon, Diana R. 1990. *The Justice Juggernaut: Fighting Street Crime, Controlling Citizens.* New Brunswick, N.J.: Rutgers University Press.

Gordon, Suzanne. 1983. "The New Corporate Feminism." *The Nation* (February 5):129, 143–147.

Gore, Al, Jr. 1990. "To Skeptics on Global Warming. . . ." *New York Times* (April 22):E27.

Gore, Al, Jr. 1992. *Earth in the Balance: Ecology and the Human Spirit.* New York: Houghton Mifflin.

Gorman, Christine. 1991a. "Are Gay Men Born That Way?" *Time* (September 9):60–61.

Gorman, Christine. 1991b. "Why Do Blacks Die Young?" *Time* (September 16):50–52.

Gornick, Vivian. 1976. "For the Rest of Our Days, Things Can Only Get Worse." *Village Voice* (May 24).

Gould, Meredith. 1979. "Statutory Oppressions: An Overview of Legalized Homophobia." In *Gay Men: The Sociology of Male Homosexuality,* Martin P. Levine (ed.). New York: Harper & Row, pp. 51–67.

Gove, Walter R. 1970. "Societal Reaction as an Explanation of Mental Illness: An Evaluation." *American Sociological Review* 35 (October):873–884.

Graham, James M. 1972. "Amphetamine Politics on Capital Hill." *Transaction* 9 (January):14.

Green, Mark J. 1990. "Luring Kids to Light Up." *Business and Society Review* 73 (Spring):22–26.

Green, Mark J. 1972. "The High Cost of Monopoly." *Progressive* 36 (March):15–19.

Green, Mark J. 1984. "When Money Talks, Is It Democracy?" *The Nation* (September 15):200–205.

Green, Marshall. 1981. "Urban Overcrowding Threatens Stability in LDCs." *Intercom* 9 (February):5.

Greenwald, John. 1991. "Time to Choose." *Time* (April 29):54–61.

Greider, William. 1992. *Who Will Tell The People: The Betrayal of American Democracy.* New York: Simon & Schuster.

Griffith, Jeanne E., Mary J. Frase, and John H. Ralph. 1989. "American Education: The Challenge of Change." *Population Bulletin* 44 (December):entire issue.

Grochot, J. C., Sr. 1992. "Wealth-Fare Cheaters." *In These Times* (January 15–21):24.

Grzywinski, Ronald. 1991. "The New Old-Fashioned Banking." *Harvard Business Review* (May/June):87–88.

Gutman, Herbert. 1976. *The Black Family in Slavery and Freedom: 1750–1925.* New York: Pantheon Books.

Gwynne, S. C. 1988. "Are You Better Off?" *Time* (October 10):28–32.

Hacker, Andrew. 1986. "Women at Work." *New York Review of Books* 33 (August 14):26–32.

Hagan, Frank E. 1990. *Introduction to Criminology.* 2d ed. Chicago: Nelson-Hall.

Hagedorn, John M., with Perry Macon. 1988. *People and Folks: Gangs, Crime and the Underclass in a Rustbelt City.* Chicago: Lake View Press.

Hall, Edwin L., and Albert A. Simkus. 1975. "Inequality in the Types of Sentences Received by Native Americans and Whites." *Criminology* 13 (August):199–222.

Hanrahan, Patricia, and Katharine Rankin. 1990. "How Lawyers Can Help Provide Housing for the Neediest." *Human Rights* 17 (Summer):37–39.

Harper's Magazine. 1992. "Harper's Index." 284 (April):13.

Harrington, Michael. 1963. *The Other America: Poverty in the United States.* Baltimore: Penguin Books.

Harrington, Michael. 1965. *The Accidental Century.* Baltimore: Penguin Books.

Harrington, Michael. 1968. "The Urgent Case for Social Investment." *Saturday Review* (November 23).

Harrington, Michael. 1976. *The Twilight of Capitalism.* New York: Simon & Schuster.

Harrington, Michael. 1979. "Social Retreat and Economic Stagnation." *Dissent* 26 (Spring):131–134.

Harrington, Michael. 1984. *The New American Poverty.* New York: Holt, Rinehart and Winston.

Harrington, Michael. 1987b. "New Poverty." *USA Today* (October 7):11A.

Harris, Diane. 1987. "We'll All Pay." *Money* 16 (November):109–134.

Harrison, Bennett. 1990. "The Wrong Signals." *Technology Review,* (January):65.

Harrison, Bennett, and Barry Bluestone. 1983. "An Interview with Bennett Harrison and Barry Bluestone." *Working Papers* 10 (January/February):42–51.

Harrison, Bennett, Chris Tilly, and Barry Bluestone. 1986. "Wage Inequality Takes a Great U-Turn." *Challenge* 29 (March–April):26–32.

Harry, Joseph. 1983. "Gay Male and Lesbian Relationships." In *Contemporary Families and Alternative Lifestyles,* Eleanor D. Macklin and Roger H. Rubin (eds.). Beverly Hills, Calif.: Sage, pp. 216–234.

Harsh, Joseph C. 1984. "U.S. Military Strength." *Christian Science Monitor* (October 23):18.

Hartjen, Clayton A. 1977. *Possible Trouble: An Analysis of Social Problems.* New York: Praeger.

Hartjen, Clayton A. 1978. *Crime and Criminalization.* 2d ed. New York: Praeger.

Hartmann, Heidi I. 1976. "Capitalism, Patriarchy, and Job Segregation by Sex." *Signs* 1 (Spring):137–169.

Hartmann, Heidi I. 1983. "Changes in Women's Economic and Family Roles in Post World War II United States." Paper presented at the Conference on Women and Structural Transformation, New Brunswick, N.J., November 18–19.

Hasson, Judi. 1992. "Firms Give Both Ways to Assure Their Access." *USA Today* (June 11):11A.

Haub, Carl. 1992. "New UN Projections Show Uncertainty of Future World." *Population Today* 20 (February):6–7.

Hausknecht, Murray. 1987. "The Secret Life of Capitalism." *Dissent* 34 (Winter):63–65.

Hawley, Willis D. 1981. "Increasing the Effectiveness of School Desegregation: Lessons from the Research." In *Race and Schooling in the City,* Adam Yarmolinsky. Lance Liebman, and Corinne S. Schelling, (eds.). Cambridge, Mass.: Harvard University Press, pp. 145–162.

Hayakawa, S. I. 1949. *Language in Thought and Action.* New York: Harcourt, Brace & World.

Hayes, Cherly D., John L. Palmer, and Martha J. Zaslow (eds.). 1990. *Who Cares for America's Children? Child Care Policy for the 1990s.* Washington, D.C.: National Academy Press.

Hayes-Bautista, David E., Warner O. Schinek, and Jorge Chapa. 1984. "Young Latinas in an Aging American Society." *Social Policy* 15 (Summer):49–52.

Hayghe, Howard V. 1990. "Family Members in the Work Force." *Monthly Labor Review* 113 (March):14–19.

Heard, Jacquelyn, and Robert Davis. 1992. "Daley Lashes Out at Kimbrough." *Chicago Tribune* (September 24):1, 24.

Heilbroner, Robert L. 1974. *An Inquiry into the Human Prospect.* New York: Norton.

Heiman, Diane, and Phyllis Bookspan. 1992. "Word on the Street: Bias There, Too." *Rocky Mountain News* (July 28):30.

Hendricks, Jon, and C. Davis Hendricks. 1977. *Aging in Mass Society: Myths and Realities.* Cambridge, Mass.: Winthrop.

Henry, Jules. 1963. *Culture against Man.* New York: Random House/Vintage.

Henry, Tamara. 1988. "Working Women's TV Roles." *Philadelphia Inquirer* (December 14):7E.

Henry, William A. III. 1990. "Beyond the Melting Pot." *Time* (April 9):28–35.

Henslin, James M. 1976a. "The Drugged Society." In *Down to Earth Sociology: Introductory Readings,* 2d ed., James M. Henslin (ed.). New York: Free Press, pp. 365–378.

Henslin, James M. 1976b. "Growing Old in the Land of the Young." In *Social Problems in American Society,* 2d ed., James M. Henslin and Larry T. Reynolds, (eds.). Boston: Holbrook Press.

Henslin, James M. 1990. "Dreams and Realities: Reflections on War." In *Social Problems Today,* James M. Henslin (ed.). Englewood Cliffs, N.J.: Prentice-Hall, pp. 377–381.

Henslin, James M., and Larry T. Reynolds, eds. 1976. *Social Problems in American Society.* 2d ed. Boston: Holbrook Press.

Herrnstein, Richard. 1971. "I.Q." *Atlantic* 228 (September):43–64.

Herrnstein, Richard J. 1973. *I.Q. in the Meritocracy.* Boston: Little, Brown.

Hess, Beth B., Elizabeth W. Markson, and Peter J. Stein. 1988. *Sociology.* 3d ed. New York: Macmillan.

Higham, Charles. 1983. *Trading with the Enemy.* New York: Dell.

Hightower, Jim. 1987. "Where Greed, Unofficially Blessed by Reagan, Has Led." *New York Times* (June 21):25.

Hills, Howard. 1977. "Society's Outcasts." *Center Magazine* 10 (July–August):2–14.

Hills, Stuart. 1980. *Demystifying Social Deviance.* New York: McGraw-Hill.

Hilton, Bruce. 1990. "Bigotry against Women Extends Even to Those in Coma." *Rocky Mountain News* (November 15):52, 55.

Hilts, Philip J. 1991. "Black Teenagers Smoke Less Than Whites, Federal Study Says." *New York Times* (September 15):14.

Himmelstein, Jerome L. 1978. "Drug Politics Theory: Analysis and Critique." *Journal of Drug Issues* 8 (Winter):37–52.

Hirsch, Arnold R. 1983. *Making the Second Ghetto: Race and Housing in Chicago 1940–1960.* Cambridge, Eng.: Cambridge University Press.

Hoch, Charles, and Robert A. Slayton. 1989. *New Homeless and Old: Community and the Skid Row Hotel.* Philadelphia: Temple University Press.

Hochschild, Arlie Russell. 1973. "A Review of Sex Role Research." *American Journal of Sociology* 78 (January):1011–1029.

Holden, Karen C., and Pamela J. Smock. 1991. "The Economic Costs of Marital Dissolution: Why Do Women Bear a Disproportionate Cost." *Annual Review of Sociology,* 17:51–78.

Hole, Judith, and Ellen Levine. 1979. "The First Feminists." In *Women: A Feminist Perspective,* Jo Freeman (ed.). Palo Alto, Calif.: Mayfield.

Holusha, John. 1991. "The Nation's Polluters—Who Emits What, and Where." *New York Times* (October 13):F10.

Horn, Miriam. 1987. "The Burgeoning Educational Underclass." *U.S. News & World Report* (May 18):66–67.

Horn, Patricia. 1991. "Fringe Benenfits for Gay Spouses." *Dollars & Sense,* No. 172 (December):10–11, 22.

Horwitz, Allan V. 1984. "The Economy and Social Pathology." *Annual Review of Sociology.* Vol. 10. New York: Annual Reviews.

Hughes, Dana, Kay Johnson, Sara Rosenbaum, and Joseph Liu. 1989. *The Health of America's Children.* Washington, D.C.: Children's Defense Fund.

Hugick, Larry. 1991. "American Unhappiness with Health Care Contrasts with Canadian Contentment." *The Gallup Poll Monthly,* No. 311 (August):2–3.

Hugick, Larry, and Jennifer Leonard. 1991. "Despite Increasing Hostility, One in Four Americans Still Smokes." *The Gallup Poll Monthly,* No. 315 (December):2–9.

Humphreys, Laud. 1972. *Out of the Closets: The Sociology of Homosexual Liberation.* Englewood Cliffs, N.J.: Prentice-Hall.

Hunter, Nan D. 1991. "Sexual Dissent and the Family." *The Nation* (October 7):406–411.

Huntington, Samuel P. 1965. "The Marasmus of the ICC." In *Bureaucratic Power in National Politics,* Francis Rourke (ed.). Boston: Little, Brown, pp. 73–86.

Hutchins, Robert M. 1976. "Is Democracy Possible?" *Center Magazine* 9 (January–February):2–6.

Hymowitz, Carol, and Timothy D. Schellhardt. 1986. "The Glass Ceiling." *Wall Street Journal* (March 24):1, 4.

Inciardi, James A. 1986. *The War on Drugs: Heroin, Cocaine, Crime, and Public Policy.* Palo Alto, Calif.: Mayfield.

ISR Newsletter. 1982. "Why Do Women Earn Less?" Ann Arbor: University of Michigan, Institute for Social Research, Spring/Summer.

Jackson, Kenneth T. 1985. *Crabgrass Frontier: The Suburbanization of the United States.* New York: Oxford University Press.

Jacobs, Jerry. 1980. "Corporate Subsidies from the Fifty States." *Business and Society Review* 33 (Spring):47–50.

Jacobson, Joan. 1992. "City Has Lost $25 Million in Bad Development Loans." *Baltimore Sun* (August 2):1A, 12A–13A.

Jacobson, Sherry. 1992. "Many Hospitals Spurn Indigent." *The Coloradoan* (Fort Collins) (June 22):A3.

Jasinowski, Jerry J. 1990. "Quality Control for Health Care." *New York Times* (March 11):F13.

Jaynes, Gerald David, and Robin M. Williams, Jr. 1989. *A Common Destiny: Blacks and American Society.* Washington, D.C.: National Academy Press.

Jencks, Christopher, et al. 1972. *Inequality: A Reassessment of the Effect of Family and Schooling in America.* New York: Basic Books.

Jencks, Christopher, et al. 1979. *Who Gets Ahead? The Determinants of Economic Success in America.* New York: Basic Books.

Jensen, Arthur R. 1969. "How Much Can We Boost IQ and Scholastic Achievement? *Harvard Educational Review* 39 (Winter):1–123.

Jensen, Arthur R. 1980. *Bias in Mental Testing.* New York: Free Press.

Johnson, Julie. 1989. "One in 8 Physicians Involved in Medicare Is an Investor in Labs." *New York Times* (April 29):1.

Johnstone, Diana. 1991. "Under the Big Lie." *In These Times* (February 6–12):13.

Joint Economic Committee. 1986. *The Concentration of Wealth in the United States.* Washington, D.C.: Government Printing Office.

Jones, Barry. 1991. *Sleepers Awake! Technology and the Future of Work.* 2nd ed. Melbourne: Oxford University Press.

Jones, Jacqueline. 1992. *The Dispossessed: America's Underclasses from the Civil War to the Present.* New York: Basic Books.

Jones, Rachel L., and Lisa Capitanini. 1991. "Asthma Deaths in Chicago Double; Two-Thirds of Victims are Black." *The Chicago Reporter* 21 (January):1, 6–9.

Journal of the American Medical Association. 1991. "Alcohol and Other Drug Use among High School Students—United States 1990." Vol. 266 (December 18):3266–3267.

Kagan, Jerome. 1973. "What Is Intelligence?" *Social Policy* 4 (July–August):88–94.

Kagan, Jerome. 1978. "The Parental Love Trap." *Psychology Today* 12 (August):54–61, 91.

Kamerman, Sheila B., and Alfred J. Kahn. 1988. "What Europe Does for Single-Parent Families." *The Public Interest* 93 (Fall):70–86.

Kaminer, Wendy. 1992. "Crashing the Locker Room." *The Atlantic Monthly* 270 (July):59–70.

Kammeyer, Kenneth C. W., George Ritzer, and Norman R. Yetman. 1990. *Sociology: Experiencing Changing Societies.* 4th ed. Boston: Allyn and Bacon.

Kanamine, Linda. 1992. "Report: Toxic Emissions Down, but They Still Pose a Health Risk." *USA Today* (October 1):13A.

Kanamine, Linda, and Jack Kelly. 1991. "1990: World's Warmest Year." *USA Today* (January 4):1–2.

Kanter, Rosabeth Moss. 1977. *Men and Women of the Corporation.* New York: Basic Books.

Kaplan, Mark S. 1990. "AIDS: Individualizing a Social Problem." *Society* 27 (January/February):4–7.

Kart, Cary S. 1981. *The Realities of Aging.* Boston: Allyn and Bacon.

Kasarda, John D. 1983. "Caught in the Web of Change." *Society* 21 (November/December):41–47.

Kasarda, John D. 1985. "Urban Change and Minority Opportunities." In *The New Urban Reality,* Paul E. Peterson (ed.). Washington, D.C.: The Brookings Institution, pp. 33–67.

Kasinitz, Philip. 1984. "Gentrification and Homelessness." *The Urban and Social Change Review* 17 (Winter):9–14.

Katz, Michael B. 1968. *The Irony of Early School Reform: Educational Innovation in Mid-Nineteenth Century Massachusetts.* Cambridge, Mass.: Harvard University Press.

Kaufman, Debra Renee. 1984. "Professional Women: How Real Are the Recent Gains?" In *Women: A Feminist Perspective,* 3d ed., Jo Freeman (ed.). Palo Alto, Calif.: Mayfield, pp. 353–369.

Keegan, Patricia. 1989. "Playing Favorites." *New York Times Magazine,* (August 6):A26.

Keen, Sam. 1991. *Fire in the Belly: On Being a Man.* New York: Bantam Books.

Kelly, Dennis. 1992a. "Minorities Make Gains on Campuses." *USA Today* (January 20):D1.

Kelly, Dennis. 1992b. "Black, Hispanic Kids Lack Computer Access." *USA Today* (July 7):D1.

Kemper, Vicki. 1991. "Operation Urban Storm." *Common Cause Magazine* (July/August):10, 12–16, 39–40.

Kemper, Vicki, and Viveca Novak. 1992. "What's Blocking Health Care Reform?" *Common Cause Magazine* 18 (January/February):8–13, 25.

Kempton, Murray. 1979. "Arithmetic of Inequality." *The Progressive* 43 (November):8–9.

Kerr, Peter. 1991. "Mental Hospital Chains Accused of Much Cheating on Insurance." *New York Times* (November 24):1, 20.

Key, V. O., Jr. 1949. *Southern Politics.* New York: Random House.

Keyserling, Leon H. 1960. "Programs: Present and Future." In *Dialogue on Poverty,* Paul Jacobs et al. (eds.). Indianapolis: Bobbs-Merrill.

Kilborn, Peter T. 1992. "Sad Distinction for the Sioux: Homeland Is No. 1 in Poverty." *New York Times* (September 20):1, 14.

Kinsey, Alfred S., et al. 1948. *Sexual Behavior in the Human Male.* Philadelphia: Saunders.

Kinsey, Alfred S., et al. 1953. *Sexual Behavior in the Human Female.* Philadelphia: Saunders.

Kirkland, Richard I., Jr. 1992. "What We Can Do Now." *Fortune* (June 1):41–48.

Kittrie, Nicholas. 1973. *The Right to Be Different: Deviance and Enforced Therapy.* Baltimore: Penguin Books.

Kleinman, Paula Holzman, Irving F. Lukoff, and Barbara Lynn Kail. 1977. "The Magic Fix: A Critical Assessment of Methadone Maintenance Treatment." *Social Problems* 25 (December):208–214.

Kluckhohn, Florence, and Fred L. Strodtbeck. 1961. *Variations in Value Orientation.* New York: Harper & Row.

Knowles, Louis L., and Kenneth Prewitt, eds. 1965. *Institutional Racism in America.* Englewood Cliffs, N.J.: Prentice-Hall.

Kosberg, Jordan I. 1976. "Differences in Proprietary Institutions Caring for Affluent and Nonaffluent Elderly." In *Aging in America,* Cary S. Hart and Barbara B. Manard (eds.). Port Washington, N.Y.: Alfred.

Kozol, Jonathan. 1985. *Illiterate America.* Garden City, N.Y.: Anchor Press/Doubleday.

Kozol, Jonathan. 1988. *Rachel and Her Children: Homeless Families in America.* New York: Crown.

Kozol, Jonathan. 1991. *Savage Inequalities: Children in America's Schools.* New York: Crown.

Kramer, Heinrich, and James Springer. 1942. *Malleus Maleficarum.* Translated by Montague Summers. New York: Dover.

Kriesberg, Louis. 1979. *Social Inequality.* Englewood Cliffs, N.J.: Prentice-Hall.

Kunnes, Richard. 1972. *The American Heroin Empire: Power, Profits, and Politics.* New York: Dodd, Mead.

Kurz, Demie. 1989. "Social Science Perspectives on Wife Abuse: Current Debates and Future Directions." *Gender and Society* 34 (December):489–505.

Kutscher, Ronald E., and Valerie A. Personick. 1986. "Deindustrialization and the Shift to Services." *Monthly Labor Review* (June):3–13.

Kuttner, Bob. 1984. "Jobs." In *Alternatives: Proposals for America from the Democratic Left,* Irving Howe (ed.). New York: Pantheon Books, pp. 19–40.

Kuttner, Robert. 1986. "Unions, Economic Power and the State." *Dissent* 33 (Winter):33–44.

Labell, Linda S. 1979. "Wife Abuse: A Sociological Study of Battered Women and Their Mates." *Victimology* 4, No. 20.

Lacayo, Richard. 1991. "Death on the Shop Floor." *Time* (September 16):28–29.

Lacayo, Richard. 1992. "Abortion: The Future Is Already Here." *Time* (May 4):27–30.

Ladner, Joyce A. 1971. *Tomorrow's Tomorrow.* New York: Doubleday.

Laing, R. D. 1967. *The Politics of Experience.* New York: Pantheon.

Lakoff, Robin. 1975. *Language and Woman's Place.* New York: Harper & Row/Colophon.

Lamar, Jacob V., Jr. 1986. "Crack." *Time* (June 2):16–18.

Lamm, Richard. 1989a. "America's Health Hinges on Finding Health-Care Cure." *Rocky Mountain News* (October 8):65.

Lamm, Richard. 1989b. "U.S. Must Cure Health-Care Ills." *Rocky Mountain News* (July 23):59.

Lamm, Richard D. 1990. "Again, Age Beats Youth." *New York Times* (December 2):2E.

Langer, Elinor. 1990. "The American Neo-Nazi Movement Today." *The Nation* (July 16–23):82–107.

Langlois, Judith H., and A. Chris Downs. 1980. "Mothers, Fathers, and Peers as Socialization Agents of Sex-Typed Play Behaviors in Young Children." *Child Development* 57:1237–1247.

Langone, John. 1989. "A Stinking Mess." *Time* (January 2):44–47.

Lappe, Frances Moore, and Joseph Collins. 1979. *Food First: The Myth of Scarcity.* New York: Ballantine Books.

Lappe, Frances Moore, and Joseph Collins. 1986. *World Hunger: Twelve Myths.* New York: Grove Press.

Lasch, Christopher. 1977. *Haven in a Heartless World: The Family Besieged.* New York: Basic Books.

Laslett, Barbara. 1977. "The Family as a Private and Public Institution: An Historical Perspective." In *The Family: Functions, Conflicts, and Symbols,* Peter Stein, Judith Richman, and Natalie Hannon (eds.). Reading, Mass.: Addison-Wesley, pp. 44–59.

Leary, Warren E. 1992. "10% of Spending on Health Found Lost through Fraud." *New York Times* (May 8):A8.

Lee, Felicia R. 1991. "Poor Record Seen in Immunizations." *New York Times* (October 16):B12.

Leigh, Wilhelmina. 1992. *A Health Assessment of Black Americans.* Washington, D.C.: Joint Center for Political and Economic Studies.

Leinberger, Christopher B. 1992. "Business Flees to the Urban Fringe." *The Nation* (July 6):10–14.

Lekachman, Robert. 1979. "The Spector of Full Employment." In *Crisis in American Institutions,* 4th ed., Jerome H. Skolnick and Elliott Currie (eds.). Boston: Little, Brown, pp. 50–58.

Lekachman, Robert. 1987. "The Craze for 'Privatization.' " *Dissent* 34 (Summer):302–307.

Lemann, Nicholas. 1986. "The Origins of the Underclass." Parts 1 and 2. *Atlantic Monthly* (June):31–55; (July):54–68.

Lemert, Edwin M. 1967. *Human Deviance, Social Problems and Social Control.* Englewood Cliffs, N.J.: Prentice-Hall.

Lemonick, Michael D. 1989. "Feeling the Heat." *Time* (January 2):36–39.

Lennard, Henry L., Leon J. Epstein, Arnold Bernstein, and Donald C. Ransom. 1971. *Mystification and Drug Misuse.* New York: Harper & Row.

Leo, John. 1984. "Polling for Mental Health." *Time* (October 15):80.

Leonard, Arthur S. 1990. "Gay/Lesbian Rights: Report from the Legal Front." *The Nation* (July 2):12–15.

Leung, Yin Ling. 1987. "The Model Minority Myth: Asian Americans Confront Growing Backlash." *Minority Trends Letter* 1/2 (Winter):5–7.

LeVay, Simon. 1991. "A Difference in Hypothalamic Structure Between Heterosexual and Homosexual Men." *Science* 253:1034–1037.

Lever, Janet. 1976. "Sex Differences in the Games Children Play." *Social Problems* 23 (April):478–487.

Levine, Art. 1988. "AIDS and the Innocents." *U.S. News & World Report* (February 1):49–51.

Levine, Martin P. 1979. "Employment Discrimination against Gay Men." *International Review of Modern Sociology* 9 (July–December):151–163.

Levine, Martin P., and Robin Leonard. 1984. "Discrimination against Lesbians in the Work Force." *Signs* 9:700–710.

Levitan, Sar A., and Richard S. Belous. 1981. *What's Happening to the American Family?* Baltimore: Johns Hopkins University Press.

Levitan, Sar A., Richard S. Belous, and Frank Gallo. 1988. *What's Happening to the American Family?* Rev. ed. Baltimore: Johns Hopkins University Press.

Levitan, Sar A., and Frank Gallo. 1990. "Work and Family: The Impact of Legislation." *Monthly Labor Review* 113 (March):34–40.

Levitan, Sar A., and Clifford M. Johnson. 1982. *Second Thoughts on Work.* Kalamazoo, Mich.: W. E. Upjohn Institute for Employment Research.

Lewin, E., and T. A. Lyons. 1982. "Everything in Its Place: The Coexistence of Lesbianism and Motherhood." In *Homosexuality: Social, Psychological, and Biological Issues,* W. Paul, J. D. Weinrich, J. C. Gonsiovek, and M. E. Hotvedt (eds.). Beverly Hills, Calif.: Sage.

Lewin, Tamar. 1988. "Day Care Becomes a Growing Burden." *New York Times* (June 5):11.

Lewis, David L. 1976. "Color It Black: The Failure of Drug Abuse Policy." *Social Policy* 6 (March–April):26–32.

Lewis, Michael. 1972. "There's No Unisex in the Nursery." *Psychology Today* 5 (May):54–57.

Lewis, Paul. 1987. "World Hunger Found Still Growing." *New York Times* (June 28):3.

Lewotin, Richard C., Steven Rose, and Leon J. Kamin. 1984. *Not in Genes: Biology, Ideology, and Human Nature.* New York: Pantheon Books.

Liazos, Alexander. 1972. "The Poverty of the Sociology of Deviance: Nuts, Sluts, and Preverts." *Social Problems* 20 (Summer):103–120.

Liazos, Alexander. 1982. *People First: An Introduction to Social Problems.* Boston: Allyn and Bacon.

Liebow, Elliot. 1967. *Tally's Corner.* Boston: Little, Brown.

Linden, Eugene. 1989. "The Death of Birth." *Time* (January 2):32–35.

Lindsay, Sue. 1983. "Hard Times Mark Children with Abuse." *Rocky Mountain News* (January 9):7.

Lindsey, Linda L. 1990. *Gender Roles: A Sociological Perspective.* Englewood Cliffs, N.J.: Prentice-Hall.

Lipman-Blumen, Jean. 1984. *Gender Roles and Power.* Englewood Cliffs, N.J.: Prentice-Hall.

Lobsenz, Norman M. 1976. "Sex and the Senior Citizen." In *Aging in America,* Cary S. Hart and Barbara B. Manard (eds.). Port Washington, N.Y.: Alfred, pp. 200–212.

Lockheed, Marlaine. 1985. "Sex Equity in the Classroom Organization and Climate." In *Handbook for Achieving Sex Equity through Education,* Susan S. Klein (ed.). Baltimore: Johns Hopkins University Press, pp. 189–217.

Long, Gary T., and Faye E. Sulton. 1987. "Contributions from Social Psychology." In *Male and Female Homosexuality: Psychological Approaches,* Louis Diamant (ed.). Washington, D.C.: Hemisphere Publications, pp. 221–237.

Lord, Walter. 1955. *A Night to Remember.* New York: Henry Holt.

Lott, Juanita Tamayo, and Judy C. Felt. 1991. "Studying the Pan Asian Community." *Population Today* 19 (April 1):6–8.

Louie, Elaine. 1989. "Unequal Contest." *New York Times* (August 6):A28.

Lubeck, Sall, and Patricia Garrett. 1988. "Child Care 2000: Policy Options for the Future." *Social Policy* 18 (Spring):31–37.

Luhman, Reid, and Stuart Gilman. 1980. *Race and Ethnic Relations.* Belmont, Calif.: Wadsworth.

McAdoo, John. 1988. "Changing Perspectives on the Role of the Black Father." In *Fatherhood Today, Men's Changing Role in the Family,* P. Bronstein and C. P. Cowan (eds.). New York: John Wiley, pp. 79–92.

MacAndrew, Craig, and Robert Edgerton. 1969. *Drunken Comportment: A Social Explanation.* Chicago: Aldine.

McAneny, Leslie. 1992. "Number of Drinkers on the Rise Again." *The Gallup Poll Monthly,* No. 317 (February):43–47.

McBean, Bill. 1992. "No Car Often Means No Job at New Airport." *Denver Post* (October 4):1C, 5C.

McCaghy, Charles H. 1976. *Deviant Behavior: Crime, Conflict, and Interest Groups.* New York: Macmillan.

McCaghy, Charles H., and Stephen A. Cernkovich. 1987. *Crime in American Society.* 2d ed. New York: Macmillan.

McCord, Colin, and Harold P. Freeman. 1990. "Excess Mortality in Harlem." *The New England Journal of Medicine* 322:173–177.

McFalls, Joseph A., Jr. 1991. "Population: A Lively Introduction." *Population Bulletin* 46 (October):entire issue.

McGhee, Paul E., and Terry Frueh. 1980. "Television Viewing and the Learning of Sex-Role Stereotypes." *Sex Roles* 6:179–188.

Mach, Henry Jay. 1987. "Shrink, Shrank, Shrunk: The Stormy Relationship between Gays and the Mental Health `Experts.' " *Advocate* (October 13):43–49.

Machung, Anne. 1984. "Word Processing: Forward for Business, Backward for Women." In *My Troubles Are Going to Have Trouble with Me,* Karen Brodkin Sacks and Dorothy Remy (ed.). New Brunswick, N.J.: Rutgers University Press, pp. 124–139.

McIntosh, Pegg. 1992. "White Privilege and Male Privilege." In *Race, Class, and Gender,* Margaret L. Andersen and Patricia Hill Collins (eds.). Belmont, Calif.: Wadsworth, pp. 70–81.

McLanahan, Sara, and Karen Booth. 1991. "Mother-Only Families." In *Contemporary Families: Looking Forward, Looking Back,* Alan Booth (ed.). Minneapolis: National Council on Family Relations, pp. 405–428.

Macmurray, Val D. 1979. "The Effect and Nature of Alcohol Abuse in Cases of Child Neglect." *Victimology* 4 (1):29–45.

McNish, Jacquie. 1991. "New York Baby Deaths Rival Third World." *Rocky Mountain News* (June 25):4, 23.

McWilliams, Carey. 1949. *North from Mexico.* Philadelphia: Lippincott.

Maharidge, Dale. 1992. "And the Rural Poor Get Poorer." *The Nation* (January 6–13):10–12.

Maher, Walter B. 1989. "Reform Medicare: The Rest Will Follow." *New York Times* (July 9):B13.

Mann, Eric. 1990. "L.A.'s Smogbusters." *The Nation* (September 17):257, 268–274.

Marger, Martin N. 1987. *Elites and Masses: An Introduction to Political Sociology.* 2d ed. Belmont, Calif.: Wadsworth.

Mariani, John, 1980. "Husbands without Wives: The Impact of Divorce on Men." *Family Weekly* (March 9):4, 7.

Markoff, John. 1991. "Denser, Faster, Cheaper: The Microchip in the 21st Century." *New York Times* (December 29):5F.

Martin, Teresa Castro, and Larry L. Bumpass. 1989. "Recent Trends in Marital Disruption." *Demography* 26:37–51.

Marx, Karl. 1956. *Karl Marx: Selected Writings in Sociology and Social Philosophy.* Translated by T. B. Bottomore. New York: McGraw-Hill.

Maslow, Abraham H. 1954. *Motivation and Personality.* New York: Harper & Row.

Massey, Douglas, and Nancy Denton. 1989. "Hypersegregation in U.S. Metropolitan Areas: Black and Hispanic Segregation along Five Dimensions." *Demography* 26 (3):373–389.

Mattera, Philip. 1983. "Home Computer Sweatshops." *The Nation* (April 2):390–392.

Mattox, William R., Jr. 1991. "The Parent Trap: So Many Bills, So Little Time." *Policy Review,* No. 51 (Winter):6–13.

Mauer, Marc. 1991. *Americans behind Bars: A Comparison of International Rates of Incarceration.* Washington, D.C.: The Sentencing Project.

Mayfield, Mark. 1992. "Hate Groups Increase—As Do Their Crimes." *USA Today* (February 20):A3.

Mechanic, David. 1962. "Some Factors in Identifying and Defining Mental Illness." *Mental Hygiene* 46 (January).

Meddis, Sam Vincent. 1991. "Black Imprisonment Highest in USA." *USA Today* (January 7):2.

Meisler, Stanley. 1990. "Rich Get Wealthier While Poor Take Cut." *Denver Post* (July 24):C1–2.

Merton, Robert K. 1957. *Social Theory and Social Structure.* 2d ed. Glencoe, Ill.: Free Press.

Meyer, Thomas J. 1986. "1 in 3 College Students Tries Cocaine." *Chronicle of Higher Education* (July 16):1, 30.

The Michigan Daily. 1987. "Why Women Faculty Are So Few." (March 13):6–7, 12.

Miles, Jack. 1992. "Blacks vs. Browns." *The Atlantic Monthly* 270 (October):41–68.

Miller, David. 1991. "A Vision of Market Socialism." *Dissent* 38 (Summer):406–414.

Miller, Mark. 1987. "Drug Use: Down, but Not in Ghetto." *Newsweek* (November 23):33.

Mills, C. Wright. 1956. *The Power Elite.* New York: Oxford University Press.

Mills, C. Wright. 1962. *Power, Politics, and People: The Collected Essays of C. Wright Mills.* Irving Louis Horowitz (ed.). New York: Ballantine Books, pp. 395–402.

Minority Trendsletter. 1987. "AIDS and Minorities." (Winter):17.

Mintz, Morton. 1991a. "Tobacco Roads: Delivering Death to the Third World." *The Progressive* 55 (May):24–29.

Mintz, Morton. 1991b. "A Reporter Looks Back in Anger." *The Progressive* 55 (December):29–32.

Moberg, David. 1992. "Decline and Inequality After the Great U-Turn." *In These Times* (May 27–June 9):7, 22.

Mokhiber, Russell. 1987. "Corporate Crime and Violence." *Multinational Monitor* 8 (April):4.

Mokhiber, Russell. 1988. *Corporate Crime and Violence: Big Business Power and the Abuse of the Public Trust.* San Francisco: Sierra Club Books.

Mokhiber, Russell. 1989. "The 10 Worst Corporations of 1989." *Multinational Monitor* 11 (December):10–17.

Mokhiber, Russell. 1991. "Corporate Crime & Violence in Review: The 10 Worst Corporations of 1991." *Multinational Monitor* 12 (December):9–17.

Moore, Joan W. 1976. *Mexican Americans.* Englewood Cliffs, N.J.: Prentice-Hall.

Moore, Joan W. 1978. *Homeboys: Gangs, Drugs, and Prison in the Barrios of Los Angeles.* Philadelphia: Temple University Press.

Moore, Kristin A., and Isabell V. Sawhill. 1984. "Implications of Women's Employment for Home and Family Life." In *Work and Family,* Patricia Voydanoff (ed.). Palo Alto, Calif.: Mayfield, pp. 153–171.

Morgan, Patricia A. 1978. "The Legislation of Drug Law: Economic Crisis and Social Control." *Journal of Drug Issues* 8 (Winter):53–62.

Morganthau, Tom. 1987. "Hard Choices, Less Money." *Newsweek* (November 16):60–63.

Morris, David. 1989. "Tolerance, Respect Work for Dutch." *Des Moines Register* (October 12):3A.

Morris, Julie. 1987. "Methodist Ministers Plan Battle." *USA Today,* (December 14).

Moynihan, Daniel P. 1988. "Our Poorest Citizens— Children." *Focus* 11 (Spring):5–6.

Mullins, Marcy E. 1992. "How Minority Groups Are Faring." *USA Today* (January 20):A11.

Multinational Monitor. 1989a. "An Energy Policy with a Future." 10 (January–February):5–6.

Multinational Monitor. 1989b. "Stopping Toxic Trade." 10 (July–August):6.

Multinational Monitor. 1990. "Criminal Business." 11 (June):6.

Multinational Monitor. 1991. "Fight for the Living." 12 (April):5.

Multinational Monitor. 1992a. "America's Killing Ground." 13 (September):5.

Multinational Monitor. 1992b. "Selling Pollution." 13 (June):5.

Munoz, Eric. 1991. "Minority Americans Are Being Shortchanged." *USA Today* (magazine). (November):28–29.

Murdoch, William M. 1980. *The Poverty of Nations: The Political Economy of Hunger and Population.* Baltimore: Johns Hopkins University Press.

Murdoch, William M. 1981. "Hungry Millions in World That Could Feed All." *Los Angeles Times* (October 18):pt. 1, p. 3.

Murdock, George P., and Caterina Provost. 1973. "Factors in the Division of Labor by Sex: A Cross-Cultural Analysis." *Ethnology* 12 (April):207.

Murray, Charles. 1984. *Losing Ground.* New York: Basic Books.

Muwakkil, Salim. 1987. "AIDS Hits Hard at Blacks and Hispanics." *In These Times* (August 19):6.

Muwakkil, Salim. 1989. "Drugs as a Life (Style) and Death Issue." *In These Times* (October 3):7.

Mydans, Seth. 1989. "Book Ban in California School Strikes Down Familiar Target." *New York Times* (September 3):1, 11.

Mydans, Seth. 1992. "An Invisible Presence Grows in the Barrios of Los Angeles." *New York Times* (May 24):D1.

Myrdal, Gunnar. 1944. *An American Dilemma.* New York: Pantheon Books.

Nadelmann, Ethan A. 1989. "Drug Prohibition in the United States: Costs, Consequences, and Alternatives." *Science* 245 (September):939–947.

Nader, Ralph. 1970, 1977. Speeches at Colorado State University in May 1970 and November 1977.

Nash, Nathaniel C. 1992. "Squalid Slums Grow as People Flood Latin America's Cities." *New York Times* (October 11):1, 10.

The Nation. 1982. "The Death Lobby." (September 11):196–197.

The Nation. 1986. "Tax Cut for the Rich." (August 30):1.

National Association of Working Women. 1986. *Computer Monitoring and Other Dirty Tricks.* Cleveland: National Association of Working Women, 9 to 5.

National Center for Education Statistics. 1980. Cited in "Bilingual Hispanics Do Better in School." *Phi Delta Kappan* 62 (December):235.

National Center for Health Statistics. 1990a. *Health, United States, 1989* (pamphlet). Hyattsville, Md.: Public Health Service.

National Center for Health Statistics. 1990b. *Health, United States, 1989.* Hyattsville, Md.: Public Health Service.

National Committee on Pay Equity. 1987. *Pay Equity: An Issue of Race, Ethnicity and Sex.* Washington, D.C.: National Committee on Pay Equity.

National Geographic. 1988. "Two Ways to Cope" (174):942–943.

National Institute on Drug Abuse. 1989. *National Household Survey on Drug Abuse: Population Estimates 1988.* Rockville, Md.: National Institute of Drug Abuse.

National Urban Coalition. 1978. *Displacement: City Neighborhoods in Transition.* Washington, D.C.: National Urban Coalition.

Navarro, Vincente. 1991. "Class and Race: Life and Death Situations." *Monthly Review* 43 (September):1–13.

Nazario, Sonia L. 1991. "Views of Women Are as Varied as the Women." *Wall Street Journal* (October 18):B4.

Neaman, Judith S. 1975. *Suggestion of the Devil: The Origins of Madness.* Garden City, N.Y.: Doubleday/Anchor.

Nettler, Gwynn. 1976. *Social Concerns.* New York: McGraw-Hill.

Neugarten, Bernice L. 1980. "Grow Old Along with Me! The Best Is Yet to Be." In *Growing Old in America,* Beth Hess (ed.). New Brunswick, N.J.: Transaction Books, pp. 180–197.

Newcomer, Kris. 1990. "Coors Will Pay $650,000 for Polluting Creek." *Rocky Mountain News* (October 24):6.

Newman, Katherine S. 1988. *Falling from Grace: The Experience of Downward Mobility in the American Middle Class.* New York: Free Press.

Newsweek. 1988. "AIDS and the Real Electorate." (February 1):7.

Newsweek. 1990a. "How to Teach Our Kids." Special issue (Fall/Winter): entire issue.

Newsweek. 1990b. "Troubled Waters." (April 16):66–80.

Newton, Jan. 1973. "The Political Economy of Women's Oppression." In *Women on the Move: A Feminist Perspective,* Jean Ramage Lepaluoto (ed.). Eugene: University of Oregon Press.

New York Times. 1987a. "Homosexuals Held Unsuited to Adopt." (December 6):13.

New York Times. 1988. "Despite a 5-Year Upturn, 9.7 Million Jobs Are Lost." (December 13):A12.

New York Times. 1992. "Hispanic Residents Face Health Gap." (May 5):A15.

Nichols, Bill. 1990. "Study: Crime Hits Blacks Hardest." *USA Today* (April 23):1.

Nielsen, Joyce, McCarl. 1990. *Sex and Gender in Society.* Prospect Heights, Ill.: Waveland Press.

Nossiter, Bernard D. 1986. "The Red Shame of New York City." *The Nation* (April 19):546–548.

Novak, Viveca. 1991. "Why Workers Can't Win." *Common Cause Magazine* 17 (July/August):28–32.

Nussbaum, Bruce. 1988. "Needed: Human Capital." *Business Week* (September 19):100–103.

Oakes, Jeannie. 1985. *Keeping Track: How Schools Structure Inequality.* New Haven: Yale University Press.

Oakes, Jeannie, and Martin Lipton. 1992. "Detracking Schools: Early Lessons from the Field." *Phi Delta Kappan* 73 (February):448–454.

O'Connell, Martin, and David E. Bloom. 1987. *Juggling Jobs and Babies: America's Child Care Challenge.* Washington, D.C.: Population Reference Bureau.

O'Hare, William P. 1985. "Poverty in America: Trends and New Patterns." *Population Bulletin* 40 (June):entire issue.

O'Hare, William P. 1986. "The Eight Myths of Poverty." *American Demographics* 8 (May):22–25.

O'Hare, William P. 1987. "America's Welfare Population: Who Gets What?" *Population Trends and Public Policy,* No. 13 (September):entire issue.

O'Hare, William P. 1990. "A New Look at Asian Americans." *American Demographics* (October):26–31.

O'Hare, William P., and Brenda Curry-White. 1992. "Is There a Rural Underclass?" *Population Today* 20 (March):6–8.

O'Hare, William P., and Judy C. Felt. 1991. "Asian Americans: America's Fastest Growing Minority Group." *Population Bulletin,* No. 19 (February):entire issue.

O'Hare, William P., and Margaret L. Usdansky. 1992. "What the 1990 Census Tells Us about Segregation in 25 Large Metros." *Population Today* 20 (September):6–7, 10.

O'Kelly, Charlotte. 1980. *Women and Men in Society.* New York: Van Nostrand.

Omi, Michael, and Howard Winant. 1986. "By the Rivers of Babylon: Race in the United States, Part One." *Socialist Review* 71 (September–October):31–66.

O'Reilly, Brian. 1992. "The Job Drought." *Fortune* 126 (August 24):62–74.

Oski, Frank. 1989. "How to Raise Money for the Class of 2000." *The Nation* (February 20):217, 221.

Ostling, Richard N. 1988. "Gays vs. the Vatican." *Time* (December 5):60.

Oxford Analytica. 1986. *America in Perspective: The Social, Economic, Political, Fiscal, and Psychological Trends That Will Shape American Society for the Next Ten Years and Beyond.* Boston: Houghton Mifflin.

Painter, Kim. 1992b. "NIH Offers 'Promise' to Women." *USA Today* (September 22):A1.

Painton, Priscilla. 1992. "After Willie Horton Are Gays Next?" *Time* (August 3):42.

Palen, John. 1975. *The Urban World.* New York: McGraw-Hill.

Parenti, Michael. 1978. *Power and the Powerless.* 2d ed. New York: St. Martin's Press.

Parenti, Michael. 1980. *Democracy for the Few.* 3d ed. New York: St. Martin's Press.

Parenti, Michael. 1983. *Democracy for the Few.* 4th ed. New York: St. Martin's Press.

Parenti, Michael. 1988. *Democracy for the Few.* 5th ed. New York: St. Martin's Press.

Parlee, Mary Brown. 1979. "Conversational Politics." *Psychology Today* 12 (May):48–56.

Passell, Peter. 1990. "More Oil from More Places Could Loosen Gulf's Grip." *New York Times* (September 2): E3.

Paton, Bruce. 1992. "Physician-Hospital Pacts Deserve Stricter Scrutiny." *Denver Post* (July 26):I1, I5).

Patton, Cindy. 1985. Sex and Germs: The Politics of AIDS. Boston: South End Press.

Pay Equity: An Issue of Race, Ethnicity, and Sex. 1987. Washington, D.C.: National Committee on Pay Equity, February.

Pear, Robert. 1988. "In AIDS Research, Money Is Just the Start." *New York Times* (January 10):E36.

Pear, Robert. 1992. "Ranks of U.S. Poor Reach 36.7 Million, the Most Since '64." *New York Times* (September 4):A1, A10.

Pear, Robert, and Erik Eckholm. 1991. "When Healers Are Entrepreneurs: A Debate over Costs and Ethics." *New York Times* (June 2):1, 17.

Pearce, Diana. 1978. "The Feminization of Poverty: Women, Work, and Welfare." *Urban and Social Change Review* 11:28–36.

Pearl, Arthur. 1977. "Public Policy or Crime: Which Is Worse?" *Social Policy* 7 (January–February):47–54.

Pelton, Leroy H. 1981. "Child Abuse and Neglect: The Myth of Classlessness." In *The Social Context of Child Abuse and Neglect,* Leroy H. Pilton (ed.). New York: Human Sciences Press, pp. 23–28.

Pepinsky, Harold E., and Paul Jesilow. 1985. *Myths That Cause Crime.* 2d ed. Cabin John, Md.: Seven Locks Press.

Peplau, Letitia Ann. 1981. "What Homosexuals Want." *Psychology Today* 15 (March):28–38.

Persell, Caroline Hodges. 1987. *Understanding Society.* 2d ed. New York: Harper & Row.

Peters, Peter J. 1992. *Intolerance of, Discrimination against, and the Death Penalty for Homosexuals as Prescribed in the Bible.* LaPorte, Colo.: Scriptures for America.

Peterson, Iver. 1991. "Why Older People Are Richer Than Other Americans." *New York Times* (November 3):E3.

Peterson, Linda, and Elaine Enarson. 1974. "Blaming the Victim in the Sociology of Women: On the Misuse of the Concept of Socialization." Paper presented at the Pacific Sociological Association, San Jose, California, March.

Philippus, M. J. 1989. "Hispanics Fail Tests Because Tests Fail Them." *Rocky Mountain News* (June 15):59.

Phillips, Kathryn. 1987. "Making a Killing from AIDS Drugs." *In These Times* (November 11–17):6, 10.

Phillips, Kevin. 1990. *The Politics of Rich and Poor.* New York: Random House.

Phillips, Leslie A. 1986. "Leaving the House." *USA Today* (June 30):4B.

Pike, Otis. 1982. "The Cancer of Congressmen and Campaign Funds." *Denver Post* (August 31):B2.

Pinsky, Mark A. 1987. "VDT Hazard: Is High-Tech Work High Risk?" *In These Times* (November 18–24):12–13, 22.

Piore, Michael J. 1975. "Notes for a Theory of Labor Market Stratification." In *Labor Market Segmentation,* Richard L. Edwards et al. (eds.). Lexington, Mass.: Heath, pp. 125–150.

Piven, Frances Fox, and Richard A. Cloward. 1971. *Regulating the Poor.* New York: Random House.

Pleck, Joseph H. 1981. "Prisoners of Manliness." *Psychology Today* 15 (September):68–83.

Pollin, Robert, and Alexander Cockburn. 1991. "The World, The Free Market, and the Left." *The Nation* (February 25):224–236.

Pomeroy, W. 1965. "Why We Tolerate Lesbians." *Sexology* (May):652–654.

Popenoe, David. 1989. "The Family Transformed." *Family Affairs* 2 (Summer–Fall):1–3.

Population Reference Bureau. 1986. "Anti-Asian Violence Pattern Probed." *Population Today* 14 (July–August):9–11.

Population Reference Bureau. 1989. *America in the 21st Century: Human Resource Development.* Washington, D.C.: Population Reference Bureau.

Population Reference Bureau. 1990. *1990 World Population Data Sheet.* Washington, D.C.: Population Reference Bureau.

Population Today. 1990. "Population Update." 18 (December):6.

Porterfield, Andrew, and David Weir. 1987. "The Export of U.S. Toxic Wastes." *The Nation* (October 3):325, 341–343.

Portes, Alejandro. 1992. "Immigration and the Reshaping of America." *The Baltimore Sun* (May 13).

Postel, Sandra. 1991. "Restoring Degraded Land." *The World Watch Reader,* Lester R. Brown (ed.). New York: W. W. Norton, pp. 25–42.

Postel, Sandra. 1992. "Denial in the Decisive Decade." *State of the World 1992,* Lester R. Brown et al. (eds.). New York: W. W. Norton, pp. 3–8.

Press, Aric. 1983. "Divorce American Style." *Newsweek* (January 10):42–48.

Preston, Samuel H. 1984. "Children and the Elderly: Divergent Paths for America's Dependents." *Demography* 21 (November):435–457.

Price, Sharon J., and Patrick C. McKenry. 1988. *Divorce.* Beverly Hills, CA: Sage.

The Progressive. 1980. "Out of the Bottle." 44 (August):8.

Puckett, Sam B. 1988. "When a Worker Gets AIDS." *Psychology Today* (January):26–27.

Purnick, Joyce. 1983. "State Cites City for Sex Bias at Trade Schools." *New York Times* (August 13):25, 28.

Purvis, Andrew. 1990. "Research for Men Only." *Time* (March 5):59–60.

Quadagno, D. M., R. Briscoe, and J. S. Quadagno. 1977. "Effect of Perinatal Gonadal Hormones on Selected Nonsexual Behavior Patterns." *Psychological Bulletin* 84:62–80.

Quadland, Michael C., and William D. Shattls. 1987. "AIDS, Sexuality, and Sexual Control." *Journal of Homosexuality* 14 (1/2):277–298.

Quindlen, Anna. 1990. "Latchkey Summer." *New York Times* (July 8):E17.

Quindlen, Anna. 1992. "49 to 1." *New York Times* (May 31):E19.

Quinney, Richard. 1970. *The Social Reality of Crime.* Boston: Little, Brown.

Quinney, Richard. 1979. *Criminology.* 2d ed. Boston: Little, Brown.

Quint, Michael. 1992. "Aa Bank Shows It Can Profit and Follow a Social Agenda." *New York Times* (May 24).

Rachlin, Jill. 1989. "The Label That Sticks." *U.S. News & World Report* (July 3):51–52.

Ramirez, Blandina. 1992. "Minority Students Make Some Gains." *USA Today* (January 20):All.

Ramos, Suzanne. 1979. "When Parents Steal Their Own Children." *New York Times* (November 15):C1.

Rapp, Rayna. 1982. "Family and Class in Contemporary America." In *Rethinking the Family: Some Feminist Questions,* Barrie Thorne and Marilyn Yalom (eds.). New York: Longman, pp. 168–187.

Raymond, Chris. 1990. "Researchers Say Debate over Drug War and Legislation Is Tied to American Cultural and Religious Values." *Chronicle of Higher Education* (March 7):A6–A11.

Reasons, Charles. 1974. "The Politics of Drugs: An Inquiry in the Sociology of Social Problems." *Sociological Quarterly* 15 (Summer):381–404.

Reeves, Richard. 1988. "The Developing New Politics of a Rapidly Aging America." *Denver Post* (December 18):3H.

Register-Guard (Eugene, Ore.). 1990. "Medical Dilemma: Costs of High-Tech Procedures." (April 29):5A.

Reich, Michael. 1978. "Military Spending and Production of Profit." In *The Capitalist System,* 2d ed., Richard E. Edwards, Michael Reich, and Thomas E. Weisskopf (eds.). Englewood Cliffs, N.J.: Prentice-Hall, pp. 409–417.

Reich, Robert B. 1989. "The Future of Work." *Harper's Magazine* 278 (April):26, 28, 30–31.

Reiman, Jeffrey H. 1990. *The Rich Get Richer and the Poor Get Prison: Ideology, Class, and Criminal Justice.* 3d ed. New York: Macmillan.

Renzetti, Claire M., and Daniel J. Curran. 1989. *Women, Men, and Society.* Boston: Allyn and Bacon.

Renzetti, Claire M., and Daniel J. Curran. 1992. *Women, Men, and Society,* 2nd ed. Boston: Allyn and Bacon.

Reskin, Barbara F., and Heidi I. Hartmann, eds. 1986. *Women's Work, Men's Work: Sex Segregation on the Job.* Washington, D.C.: National Academy Press.

Rich, Adrienne. 1983. "Compulsory Heterosexuality and Lesbian Existence." In *Powers of Desire: The Politics of Sexuality,* Ann Snitow, Christine Stansell, and Sharon Thompson (eds.). New York: Monthly Review Press, pp. 177–205.

Richardson, Laurel Walum. 1981. *The Dynamics of Sex and Gender.* 2d ed. Boston: Houghton Mifflin.

Riche, Martha Farnsworth. 1991. "We're All Minorities Now." *American Demographics* 13 (October):26–31.

Richmond-Abbott, Marie. 1983. *Masculine and Feminine: Sex Roles over the Life Cycle.* Reading, Mass.: Addison-Wesley.

Richmond-Abbott, Marie. 1992. *Masculine and Feminine: Sex Roles over the Life Cycle.* 2nd ed. New York: McGraw-Hill.

Ricks, Thomas E. 1987. "Coming Down: Signs Indicate That America's Cocaine Habit Is Easing." *Wall Street Journal* (July 20):sec. 2, p. 1.

Ries, Paula, and Anne J. Stone (eds.). 1992. *The American Woman, 1992–93.* New York: W. W. Norton.

Riley, Matilda White, and Joan Waring. 1976. "Age and Aging." In *Contemporary Social Problems.* 4th ed., Robert K. Merton and Robert Nisbet (ed.). New York: Harcourt Brace Jovanovich, pp. 357–410.

Ritzer, George. 1993. *The McDonaldization of Society: An Investigation into the Changing Character of Contemporary Social Life.* Newbury Park, Calif.: Pine Forge Press.

Rivlin, Leanne G. 1986. "A New Look at the Homeless." *Social Policy* 16 (Spring):3–10.

Rix, Sara E., ed. 1990. *The American Woman 1990–91.* New York: W. W. Norton.

Robinson, David, Jr. 1986. "Sodomy and the Supreme Court." *Commentary* 82 (October):57–61.

Rocky Mountain News. 1992. "Vatican: There Is No 'Right' to Be Gay." (July 24):3.

Roebuck, J., and S. C. Weeber. 1978. *Political Crime in the United States: Analyzing Crimes by and against Government.* New York: Praeger.

Rogers, Susan Carol. 1978. "Women's Place: A Critical Review of Anthropological Theory." *Comparative Studies in Society and History* 20 (1):123–162.

Rom, Mark. 1992. "Reversing America's Welfare Magnets." *USA Today* 120 (periodical) (March):16–18.

Ropers, Richard H. 1991. *Persistent Poverty.* New York: Insight Books.

Rosaldo, Michelle Zimbalist. 1974. "Women, Culture, and Society: A Theoretical Overview." In *Woman, Culture, and Society,* Michelle Zimbalist Rosaldo and Louise Lamphere (eds.). Stanford: Stanford University Press, pp. 17–42.

Rosaldo, Michelle Zimbalist. 1980. "The Use and Abuse of Anthropology." *Signs* 5 (Spring):389–417.

Rose, Stephen J. 1986. *The American Profile Poster.* New York: Pantheon Books.

Rosenhan, D. L. 1973. "On Being Sane in Insane Places." *Science* 179 (January):250–258.

Rosenthal, Robert, and Lenore Jacobson. 1968. *Pygmalion in the Classroom: Teacher Expectations and Pupils' Intellectual Development.* New York: Holt, Rinehart and Winston.

Ross, Ellen, and Rayna Rapp. 1983. "Sex and Society: A Research Note from Social History and Anthropology." In *Power of Desire: The Politics of Sexuality,* Ann Snitow, Christine Stansell, and Sharon Thompson (eds.).New York: Monthly Review Press, pp. 51–73.

Rothman, David J. 1971. *The Discovery of the Asylum: Social Order and Disorder in the New Republic.* Boston: Little, Brown.

Rubin, Isadore. 1976. "The 'Sexless Older Years': A Socially Harmful Stereotype." In *Growing Old in America,* Beth B. Hess (ed.). New Brunswick, N.J.: Transaction Books, pp. 435–448.

Rukeyser, Louis, and John Cooney. 1991. *Louis Rukeyser's Business Almanac.* Rev. ed. New York: Simon & Schuster.

Ryan, Barbara Haddad. 1980. "Common Cause: Special Interests Won on Nov. 4." *Rocky Mountain News* (November 16):4.

Ryan, William. 1970. "Is Banfield Serious?" *Social Policy* 1 (November–December):74–76.

Ryan, William. 1972. "Postscript: A Call to Action." *Social Policy* 3 (May–June).

Ryan, William. 1976. *Blaming the Victim.* Rev. ed. New York: Random House (Vintage).

Sacks, Karen. 1974. "Engels Revisited: Women, the Organization of Production, and Private Property." In *Woman, Culture, and Society,* Michelle Zimbalist Rosaldo and Louise Lamphere (eds.). Stanford: Stanford University Press, pp. 207–222.

Saker, Ann. 1992. "Medium-Sized Cities Cut Smog; Clean Cars, Cool Weather Cited." *Denver Post* (October 20):5A.

Salholz, Eloise. 1990. "The Future of Gay America." *Newsweek* (March 12):20–25.

Salvatore, Nick. 1992. "The Decline of Labor." *Dissent* 39 (Winter):86–92.

Samuelson, Robert J. 1984. "We're Not a National Laundromat." *Newsweek* (July 9):61.

Samuelson, Robert J. 1988. "Child Care Revisited." *Newsweek* (August 8):53.

Sancton, Thomas A. 1989. "What on Earth Are We Doing?" *Time* (January 2):24–30.

Sandefur, Gary. 1989. "American Indian Reservations: The First Underclass Areas?" *Focus* 12 (Spring):37–41.

Sandefur, Gary D. 1990. "Census Volume on the American Indian." *Social Science Research Council Items* 44 (June/September):37–40.

Santrack, John W. 1972. "Relation of Type and Onset of Father Absence to Cognitive Development." *Child Development* 43:455–469.

Sapiro, Virginia. 1986. *Women in American Society.* Palo Alto, Calif.: Mayfield.

Saturday Review. 1970. "Welfare: Time for Reform." (May 23):19.

Scarpitti, Frank R., and Margaret L. Andersen. 1992. *Social Problems.* 2nd ed. New York: HarperCollins.

Schafer, Walter E., Carol Olexa, and Kenneth Polk. 1972. "Programmed for Social Class." In *Schools and Delinquency,* Kenneth Polk and Walter E. Schafer (eds). Englewood Cliffs, N.J.: Prentice-Hall.

Scheff, Thomas J. 1966a. *Labeling Madness: Being Mentally Ill: A Sociological Theory.* Chicago: Aldine.

Scheff, Thomas J. 1966b. *Mentally Ill.* Chicago: Aldine.

Scheff, Thomas J. 1968. "The Role of the Mentally Ill and the Dynamics of Mental Disorder: A Research Framework." In *The Mental Patient: Studies in the Sociology of Deviance,* Stephan P. Spitzer and Norman K. Denzin (ed.). New York: McGraw-Hill.

Scheff, Thomas J. 1974. "The Labeling Theory of Mental Illness." *American Sociological Review* 39 (June):444–452.

Scheff, Thomas J. 1975. "On Reason and Sanity: Some Political Implications of Psychiatric Thought." In *Labeling Madness,* Thomas J. Scheff (ed.). Englewood Cliffs, N.J.: Prentice-Hall, pp. 12–20.

Schinto, Jeanne. 1977. "The Breathless Cotton Workers." *Progressive* 41 (August):27–29.

Schlesinger, Mark. 1987. "Paying the Price: Medical Care, Minorities, and the Newly Competitive Health Care System." *Milbank Quarterly* 65 (Supplement 2):270–296.

Schmoke, Kurt L. 1992. "Forward." In Sam Staley, *Drug Policy and the Decline of American Cities,* Sam Staley (ed.) New Brunswick, N.J.: Transaction Publishers, pp. xiii–xvi.

Schneider, David M., and Raymond T. Smith. 1973. *Class Differences and Sex Roles in American Family and Kinship Structure.* Englewood Cliffs, N.J.: Prentice-Hall.

Schneider, Keith. 1990. "Pesticide Makers Fight Export Curb." *New York Times* (August 26):17.

Schneider, William. 1987. "Homosexuals: Is AIDS Changing Attitudes?" *Public Opinion* 10 (July–August):6–7, 59.

Schorr, Lisbeth B., with Daniel Schorr. 1988. *Within Our Reach: Breaking the Cycle of Disadvantage.* New York: Doubleday Anchor Press.

Schur, Edwin M. 1965. *Crimes without Victims.* Englewood Cliffs, N.J.: Prentice-Hall.

Schur, Edwin. 1971. *Labeling Deviant Behavior: Its Sociological Implications.* New York: Harper & Row.

Schur, Edwin. 1973. *Radical Nonintervention: Rethinking the Delinquency Problem.* Englewood Cliffs, N.J.: Prentice-Hall.

Schwartz, Joe, and Thomas Exter. 1989. "All Our Children." *American Demographics* 11 (May):34–37.

Scrimshaw, Nevin S. 1991. "The Consequences of Hidden Hunger." *Vital Speeches of the Day* 58 (December 15):138–144.

See, Katherine O'Sullivan, and William J. Wilson. 1988. "Race and Ethnicity." In *Handbook of Sociology,* Neil J. Smelser (ed.). Newbury Park, Calif.: Sage, pp. 223–242.

Serbin, Lisa, and K. Daniel O'Leary. 1975. "How Nursery Schools Teach Girls to Shut Up." *Psychology Today* 9 (December):56–58, 102–103.

Shabecoff, Philip. 1987. "With No Room at the Dump, U.S. Faces a Garbage Crisis." *New York Times* (June 29):11.

Shanker, Albert. 1990a. "The Family Medical Leave Act." *New York Times* (June 24):E7.

Shanker, Albert. 1990b. "The French System of Child Care: A Welcome for Every Child." *New York Times* (November 11):E7.

Shanker, Albert. 1991. "Dumbing Down America." *New York Times* (January 27):E7.

Shanker, Albert. 1992a. "Children in Crisis." *New York Times* (February 16):E9.

Shanker, Albert. 1992b. "Improving Our Schools." *New York Times* (May 17):E7.

Shanker, Albert. 1992c. "How Far Have We Come?" *New York Times* (August 16):E9.

Shannon, Thomas R., Nancy Kleniewski, and William M. Cross. 1991. *Urban Problems in Sociological Perspective.* 2nd ed. Prospect Heights, Ill.: Waveland Press.

Shapiro, Andrew L. 1992. *We're Number One: Where America Stands—and Falls—in the World Order.* New York: Vintage.

Shapiro, Judith. 1981. "Anthropology and the Study of Gender." In *A Feminist Perspective in the Academy,* Elizabeth Langland and Walter Gove (eds.). Chicago: University of Chicago Press, pp. 110–129.

Shapiro, Robert J. 1987 "A Frightening New Numbers Game." *U.S. News & World Report* (September 28):32–33.

Shinoda, Tomohito. 1990. "Letter to the Editor." *Harvard Business Review* 68 (November–December):187, 190.

Shortridge, Kathleen. 1989. "Poverty Is a Woman's Problem." *Women: A Feminist Perspective.* 2nd ed. Mountain View, Calif.: Mayfield, pp. 485–492.

Shreve, Anita. 1984. "The Working Mother as Role Model." *New York Times Magazine* (September 9):43.

Sidel, Ruth. 1986. *Women and Children Last: The Plight of Poor Women in Affluent America.* New York: Viking Press.

Sidel, Ruth. 1991. "Separate and Unequal." *The Nation.* (November 18):620–622.

Silberman, Charles E. 1970. *Crisis in the Classroom.* New York: Random House.

Silberner, Joanne. 1990. "Health: Another Gender Gap." *U.S. News & World Report* (September 24):54–55.

Silverstein, Charles. 1981. *Man to Man: Gay Couples in America.* New York: Morrow.

Silvestri, George, and John Lukasiewicz. 1989. "Projections of Occupational Employment, 1988–2000." *Monthly Labor Review* 112 (November):42–65.

Simon, David R., and D. Stanley Eitzen. 1990. *Elite Deviance.* 3d ed. Boston: Allyn and Bacon.

Simon, David R., and D. Stanley Eitzen. 1993. *Elite Deviance.* 4th ed. Boston: Allyn and Bacon.

Simons, Geoffery. 1985. *Silicon Shock: The Menace of the Computer.* Oxford: Basil Blackwell.

Simpson, Peggy. 1985. "The Fight for Pay Equity." In *Crisis in American Institutions,* 4th ed., Jerome H. Skolnick and Elliott Currie (eds.). Boston: Little, Brown, pp. 208–216.

Sivard, Ruth Leger. 1989. *World Military and Social Expenditures 1989.* Washington, D.C.: World Priorities.

Sivard, Ruth Leger. 1991. *World Military and Social Expenditures 1991.* Washington, D.C.: World Priorities.

Sklar, Holly. 1992. "Reaffirmative Action." *Zeta Magazine* 5 (May/June):9–15.

Skolnick, Arlene. 1983. *The Intimate Environment.* 3d ed. Boston: Little, Brown.

Skolnick, Arlene. 1991. *Embattled Paradise: The American Family in an Age of Uncertainty.* New York: Basic Books.

Skolnick, Jerome. 1966. *The Politics of Protest.* New York: Ballantine Books.

Skolnick, Jerome, and Elliott Currie. 1973. "Introduction: Approaches to Social Problems." In *Crisis in American Institutions,* 2d ed., Jerome Skolnick and Elliott Currie (eds.). Boston: Little, Brown, pp. 1–17.

Slobodin, Alan M. 1990. "Never Mind 'Causes'; Get after the Criminals." *USA Today* (August 8):10A.

Smith, Dave. 1983. "Black Babies Death Rate Twice Whites." *Los Angeles Times* (July 7):2D.

Smith, Gayle. 1991. "The Hunger." *Mother Jones* 16 (September–October):36–37, 41, 61–62.

Snell, Bradford. 1974. "GM and the Nazis." *Ramparts* (June):14–16.

Snider, Dixie E., John J. Seggerson, and Mary D. Hutton. 1991. "Tuberculosis and Migrant Farm Workers." *Journal of the American Medical Association* 265 (April 3):1732.

Snider, Mike, Michelle Healy, and Leslie Miller. 1992. "Women Likely to Get Less Pain Medication." *USA Today* (July 27):D6.

Snipp, C. Matthew. 1989. *American Indians: The First of This Land.* New York: Russell Sage.

Snipp, C. Matthew. 1992. "Sociological Perspectives on American Indians." *Annual Review of Sociology* 18:351–371.

Snow, David A., Susan G. Baker, Leon Anderson, and Michael Martin. 1986. "The Myth of Pervasive Mental Illness among the Homeless." *Social Problems* 33 (June):407–423.

Sociologists for Women in Society. 1986. *Facts about Pay Equity.* April.

Soldo, Beth J., and Emily Agree. 1988. "America's Elderly." *Population Bulletin* 43 (September):8.

South Shore Bank. 1992. *Development Deposits* (pamphlet). Chicago: South Shore Bank.

Sowell, Thomas. 1978. "Debate: Equal Opportunity or the Numbers Game?" *American Educator* (Fall).

Sowell, Thomas. 1981. *Ethnic America: A History.* New York: Basic Books.

Spector, Malcolm, and John I. Kitsuse, 1987. *Constructing Social Problems.* Hawthorne, N.Y.: Aldine de Gruyter.

Sperling, Dan. 1990. "Bill Would Boost Female Health Care." *USA Today* (July 27):D1.

Spitzer, Steven. 1975. "Toward a Marxian Theory of Deviance." *Social Problems* 22 (5):638–651.

Spring, Joel H. 1972. *Education and the Rise of the Corporate State.* Boston: Beacon Press.

Squitieri, Tom. 1990. "Health Chief: Show 'Ethics,' Put End to Ads." *USA Today* (February 2):1.

Srole, Leo, et al. 1962. *Mental Health in the Metropolis: The Midtown Manhattan Study.* New York: McGraw-Hill.

Stack, Carol B. 1990. "Different Voices, Different Visions: Gender, Culture, and Moral Reasoning." In *Uncertain Terms: Negotiating Gender in American Culture,* Faye Ginsburg and Anna Lowenhaupt Tsing (eds.). Boston: Beacon, pp. 19–27.

Staley, Sam. 1992. *Drug Policy and the Decline of American Cities.* New Brunswick, N.J.: Transaction Publishers.

Stallard, Karin, Barbara Ehrenreich, and Holly Sklar. 1983. *Poverty in the American Dream: Women and Children First.* Boston: South End Press.

Steif, William. 1979. "U.S. Government, Slowly Aiding Battered Wives." *Rocky Mountain News* (October 27):76.

Stein, Peter J., Judith Richman, and Natalie Hannon. 1977. *The Family: Functions, Conflicts, and Symbols.* Reading, Mass.: Addison-Wesley.

Steinberg, David. n.d. "Racism in America: Definition and Analysis." In *People against Racism.* Detroit.

Steiner, Claude. 1974. "Radical Psychiatry." In *Is America Possible?* Henry Etzkowitz (ed.). St. Paul, Minn.: West, pp. 191–195.

Steinmetz, Suzanne K. 1977. "Wifebeating, Husband-beating—A Comparison of the Use of Violence between Spouses to Resolve Marital Conflicts." In *Battered Women: A Psychological Study of Domestic Violence,* Maria Roy (ed.). New York: Van Nostrand.

Steinmetz, Suzanne K. 1977–1978. "The Battered Husband Syndrome." *Victimology* 2 (3–4):449–509.

Steinmetz, Suzanne K. 1978. "Battered Parents." *Society* 15 (July/August):54–55.

Stengel, Richard. 1987. "The Changing Face of AIDS." *Time* (August 17):12–14.

Sterling, Eric E. 1991. "What Should We Do about Drugs?" *Vital Speeches of the Day* 57 (August 1):626–632.

Stern, Philip M. 1988. *The Best Congress Money Can Buy.* New York: Pantheon.

Stevens, William K. 1989. "Racial Differences Found in Kind of Medical Care Americans Get." *New York Times* (January 13):1, C18.

Stewart, Sally Ann. 1989. "Heart Disease Decreases as Income Goes Up." *USA Today* (February 21):D1.

Stewart, Thomas A. 1991. "Gay in Corporate America." *Fortune* (December 16):42–56.

Stone, Lawrence. 1985. "Sex in the West: The Strange History of Human Sexuality." *New Republic* (July 8):25–37.

Stone, Marvin. 1978. "Political Spending Running Wild." *U.S. News & World Report* (October 23):112.

Straus, Murray A. 1974a. "Leveling, Civility, and Violence in the Family." *Journal of Marriage and the Family* 36:13–27.

Straus, Murray A. 1974b. "Sexual Inequality, Cultural Norms, and Wife Beating." *Journal of Marriage and the Family* 36 (February):13–30.

Straus, Murray A. 1977. "A Sociological Perspective on the Prevention and Treatment of Wifebeating." In *Battered Women,* Maria Roy (ed.). New York: Van Nostrand.

Straus, Murray A., and Richard J. Gelles. 1985. "Societal Change and Change in Family Violence from 1975 to 1985 as Revealed by Two National Surveys." Paper presented at the American Society of Criminology, San Diego, November. Published by the Family Violence Research Program, University of New Hampshire, Durham.

Straus, Murray A., and Suzanne K. Steinmetz. 1980. *Behind Closed Doors: Violence in the American Family.* New York: Anchor Books.

Stuart, Richard B. 1970. *Trick or Treatment: How and When Psychotherapy Fails.* Champaign, Ill.: Research Press.

Sullivan, Mercer L. 1989. *"Getting Paid": Youth Crime and Work in the Inner City.* Ithaca, N.Y.: Cornell University Press.

Swanson, Stevenson. 1992. "For Poor, Pollution Just One More Hazard." *Chicago Tribune* (June 29):1, 8.

Swartz, Joel. 1975. "Silent Killers at Work." *Crime and Social Justice* (Spring/Summer):15–20.

Swartz, Steve. 1989. "Why Mike Milken Stands to Qualify for Guinness Book." *Wall Street Journal* (March 31): 1, 4.

Swedish Institute. 1988. "General Facts on Sweden." *Fact Sheets on Sweden* (5 December):2. Stockholm: The Swedish Institute.

Swinton, David. 1987. "Economic Status of Blacks 1986." In *The Status of Black America 1987,* Janet Dewart (ed.). New York: National Urban League, Inc, pp. 49–73.

Sykes, Gresham M., and Francis T. Cullen. 1992. *Criminology.* 2nd ed. Orlando, Fla.: Harcourt Brace Jovanovich.

Szasz, Thomas S. 1970. *The Manufacture of Madness.* New York: Delta Books.

Szasz, Thomas S. 1972. "The Ethics of Addiction." *Harper's* (April):74–79.

Szasz, Thomas S. 1974a. *The Myth of Mental Illness.* Rev. ed. New York: Harper & Row.

Szasz, Thomas S. 1974b. *The Second Sin.* Garden City, N.Y.: Doubleday/Anchor.

Szasz, Thomas S. 1975. *Ceremonial Chemistry: The Ritual Persecution of Drugs, Addicts, and Pushers.* Garden City, N.Y.: Doubleday/Anchor.

Takaki, Ronald. 1990. "The Harmful Myth of Asian Superiority." *New York Times* (June 16):15.

Tannen, Deborah. 1990. *You Just Don't Understand: Women and Men in Conversation.* New York: Ballantine Books.

Tatge, Mark. 1986. "Study: For-Profit Hospitals Cost More." *Denver Post* (January 9):E1–2.

Taylor, Robert Joseph, Linda M. Chatters, M. Belinda Tucker, and Edith Lewis. 1991. "Developments in Research on Black Families." In *Contemporary Families: Looking Forward, Looking Back,* Alan Booth (ed.). Minneapolis: National Council on Family Relations, pp. 275–296.

Taylor, Ronald A. 1987a. "Another Day Older and Deeper in Trash." *U.S. News & World Report* (May 11):20–21.

Taylor, Ronald A. 1987b. "Why Fewer Blacks Are Graduating." *U.S. News & World Report* (June 8):75–76.

Taylor, William L. 1978. "Debate: Equal Opportunity or the Numbers Game?" *American Educator* (Fall).

Temkin, Barry. 1992. "City Schools Budget Cuts Will Leave Deep Scars on a Lot of Young Lives." *Chicago Tribune* (September 27):section 3:24.

Terkel, Studs. 1975. *Working: People Talk about What They Do All Day and How They Feel about What They Do.* New York: Avon Books.

Thorne, Barrie. 1982. "Feminist Rethinking of the Family: An Overview." In *Rethinking the Family: Some Feminist Questions,* Barrie Thorne and Marilyn Yalom (eds.). New York: Longman, pp. 1–24.

Thorne, Barrie. 1992. "Feminism and the Family: Two Decades of Thought." In *Rethinking the Family,* 2nd ed. Barrie Thorne and Marilyn Yalom (eds.). Boston: Northeastern University Press.

Thorne, Barrie with Marilyn Yalom. 1992. *Rethinking the Family,* 2nd ed. Boston: Northeastern University Press.

Thornton, Arland, and Deborah Freedman. 1983. "The Changing American Family." *Population Bulletin* 38 (October):entire issue.

Tifft, Susan. 1989. "The Big Shift in School Finance." *Time* (October 16):48.

Tilly, Chris. 1986. "U-Turn on Equality: The Puzzle of Middle-Class Decline." *Dollars & Sense,* No. 116 (May):11–13.

Tilly, Chris. 1990. "The World Is Their Ashtray." *Dollars & Sense,* No. 160 (October):12–15, 18.

Tilly, Louise A. 1982. "Women's Employment—Past, Present, and Future." *University Record* (University of Michigan) (July).

Time. 1979a. "Forewarnings of Fatal Flaws." (June 25):58–61.

Timmer, Doug A. 1991. "Drug War: The State in the Inner-City." Paper presented to the joint meeting of the Law and Society Association and the Research Committee on the Sociology of Law of the International Sociological Association, University of Amsterdam, the Netherlands (June).

Timmer, Doug A., and D. Stanley Eitzen. 1992. "The Root Causes of Urban Homelessness in the United States." *Humanity and Society* 16 (2):159–175.

Timmer, Doug A., D. Stanley Eitzen, and Kathryn D. Talley. Forthcoming. *Paths to Homelessness: Extreme Poverty and the Urban Housing Crisis.* Boulder, Colo.: Westview Press.

Tivnan, Edward. 1987. "Homosexuals and the Churches." *New York Times Magazine* (October 11):84–91.

Tobias, Sheila. 1989. "Tracked to Fail." *Psychology Today* 23 (September):54–60.

Toch, Thomas. 1991. "The Great College Tumble." *U.S. News & World Report* (June 3):50.

Toffler, Alvin. 1990. *Powershift.* New York: Bantam.

Tolchin, Martin. 1989. "Richest Got Richer and Poorest Poorer from 1979 to 1987." *New York Times* (March 23):1, 12.

Toufexis, Anastasia. 1989. "Too Many Mouths." *Time* (January 2):48–50.

Toufexis, Anastasia. 1990a. "A Call for Radical Surgery." *Time* (May 7):50.

Toufexis, Anastasia. 1990b. "From the Asylum to Anarchy." *Time* (October 22):58–59.

Trafford, Abigail. 1982. "New Health Hazard: Being Out of Work." *U.S. News & World Report* (June 14):81–82.

Turner, Jonathan H. 1977. *Social Problems in America.* New York: Harper & Row.

Turque, Bill. 1992. "Gays under Fire." *Newsweek* (September 14):35–40.

Uhlenberg, Peter. 1992. "Population, Aging and Social Policy." *Annual Review of Sociology* 18:449–474.

United Nations. n.d. *Daily World in U.N. Action Pact for World Development.* New York: United Nations Information Division.

Urban Institute. 1990. "Comparable Worth Policies That Work: The Minnesota Case." *Policy and Research Report* (Summer):10–12.

USA Today. 1989a. "Ethnic, Racial Divisions Still Deeply Rooted." (August 30):1–2.

USA Today. 1989b. "Media Coverage of Women 'Poor.' " (April 11):2B.

USA Today. 1989c. "Pay Equity Lobby Helps Raise Wages." (October 20):1.

USA Today. 1990a. "Debate: Taxpayers, Officials Betray Our Children." (May 1):8A.

USA Today. 1990b. "Nursing Homes Must Clean up Their Act." (May 30):10A.

USA Today. 1990c. "We Must Get after Violent Crime Causes." (August 8):10A.

USA Today. 1991a. "Give Shareholders Say in Chief Executives Pay." (December 18):12a.

USA Today. 1991b. "More Kids at Risk from Alcohol than Drugs." (November 5):A15.

USA Today. 1992a. "Plight of Cities Worsen." (May 5): 13A.

USA Today. 1992b. "Traffic Deadlock Nearing." (July 14):2A.

USA Today. 1992c. "Cancer-Causing Chemical Releases." (October 1):13A.

USA Today. 1992d. "Unemployment." *USA Today* (July 7):2B.

U.S. Bureau of the Census. 1990. "The Hispanic Population in the United States." *Current Population Reports,* Series P–20, No. 444. Washington, D.C.: Government Printing Office.

U.S. Bureau of the Census. 1991a. "Population Profile of the United States 1991." *Current Population Reports,* Series P–23, No. 173 (July). Washington, D.C.: Government Printing Office.

U.S. Bureau of the Census. 1991b. *Statistical Abstract of the United States 1991.* Washington, D.C.: Government Printing Office.

U.S. Bureau of the Census. 1991c. "The Black Population in the United States: March 1990 and 1989." *Current Population Reports,* Series P–20, No. 448 (August). Washington, D.C. Government Printing Office.

U.S. Bureau of the Census. 1991d. "Money Income of Households, Families and Persons in the United States." *Current Population Reports,* Series P–60, No. 174. Washington, D.C.: Government Printing Office.

Usdansky, Margaret L. 1991. "USA at Home: Streets Still Isolate Races." *USA Today* (November 11):1A–2A.

Usdansky, Margaret L. 1992a. "Middle Class 'Pulling Apart' to Rich, Poor." *USA Today* (February 20):A1.

Usdansky, Margaret L. 1992b. "Income Inequality Gap Widens for Minorities." *USA Today* (July 24):A3.

Usdansky, Margaret L. 1992c. "Immigrant Tide Surges in 80s" *USA Today* (May 22):1A.

U.S. Department of Health and Human Services. 1991. "Research on the Prevention of Alcohol-Related Problems Among Ethnic Minorities." (June). Washington, D.C.: Government Printing Office.

U.S. Department of Health and Human Services. 1992. "Smoking and Health in the Americas." Washington, D.C.: Government Printing Office.

U.S. Department of Justice. 1988. *Report to the Nation on Crime and Justice.* 2d ed. Washington, D.C.: U.S. Department of Justice.

U.S. Department of Justice. 1989. *Sourcebook of Criminal Justice Statistics—1988.* Washington, D.C.: Government Printing Office.

U.S. Department of Justice. 1992a. *Correctional Populations in the United States, 1990.* Washington, D.C.: Government Printing Office.

U.S. Department of Justice. 1992b. *Prisons and Prisoners in the United States.* Washington, D.C.: U.S. Department of Justice.

U.S. Department of Justice. 1992c. *Uniform Crime Reports 1991.* Washington, D.C.: Government Printing Office.

U.S. Department of Labor. 1965. *The Negro Family: The Case for National Action.* Washington, D.C.: Government Printing Office.

U.S. Department of Labor. 1988. "Facts on U.S. Working Women." Women's Bureau Fact Sheet, No. 88 (January). Washington, D.C.: Government Printing Office.

U.S. Department of Labor. 1990. "Earnings Differences between Women and Men, Facts on Working Women." Washington, D.C.: U.S. Department of Labor, Women's Bureau.

U.S. News & World Report. 1987. "The Burgeoning Educational Underclass." (May 18):66–67.

U.S. News & World Report. 1992. "Hispanics' Tale of Two Cities." (May 25):40–41.

U.S. Senate Committee on Governmental Affairs. 1978. *Interlocking Directorates among the Major United States Corporations.* Washington, D.C.: Government Printing Office.

Valdivieso, Rafael, and Cary Davis. 1988. *U.S. Hispanics: Changing Issues for the 1990s.* Population Reference Bureau 17 (December):entire issue.

Verbrugge, Lois M. 1985. "Gender and Health: An Update on Hypotheses and Evidence." *Journal of Health and Social Behavior* 26 (September):156–182.

Vilbig, Peter. 1992. "Treatment Delay Could Mean Death." *Rocky Mountain News* (May 19):4, 28.

Wald, Matthew L. 1990. "America Is Still Demanding a Full Tank." *New York Times,* (August 2):E3.

Waldman, Steven. 1990. "The Stingy Politics of Head Start." *Newsweek,* Special Issue on Education (Fall–Winter):78–79.

Waldrop, Judith. 1990. "Up and Down the Income Scale." *American Demographics,* (July):24–30.

Waldrop, Judith, and Thomas Exter. 1991. "The Legacy of the 1980s." *American Demographics* (March):32–38.

Walker, Lenore E. 1979. *The Battered Woman.* New York: Harper & Row.

Walker, Michael. 1989. "Beware of Bargains." *Reason* 21 (November):40–41.

Walley, Dean. n.d. *What Boys Can Be.* Kansas City: Hallmark.

Walley, Dean. n.d. *What Girls Can Be.* Kansas City: Hallmark.

Wall Street Journal. 1992. "Breast Cancer Takes Bigger Toll among Poor." (June 19):B1.

Walmer, Tracy. 1990. "For USA's Third World, Illness a Way of Life." *USA Today* (November 14):A9.

Walmer, Tracy. 1991. "Costs, Lack of Health Care Hurt Rural Poor Most." *USA Today* (March 13):A8.

Walter, Dave. 1987. "The Supreme Shift." *Advocate* (August 14):10–11, 20.

Warren, William J. 1988. "Tutoring Becomes a Tool to Provide an Edge." *New York Times* (July 20):24.

Wartzman, Rick. 1992. "Segment of Full-Time Workers Earning Very Low Wages Surged in Past Decade." *Wall Street Journal* (May 12):A2.

Weitzman, Lenore J. 1984. "Sex-Role Socialization: A Focus on Women." In *Women: A Feminist Perspective,* 3d ed., Jo Freeman (ed.). Palo Alto, Calif.: Mayfield, pp. 157–237.

Weitzman, Lenore J. 1985. *The Divorce Revolution: The Unexpected Social and Economic Consequences for Women and Children in America.* New York: Free Press.

Weitzman, Lenore J., Deborah Eifler, Elizabeth Hokada, and Catherine Ross. 1972. "Sex-Role Socialization in Picture Books for Preschool Children." *American Journal of Sociology* 77 (May):1125–1150.

Wellman, David T. 1977. *Portraits of White Racism.* Cambridge, Eng.: Cambridge University Press.

Werlin, Robert J. 1972. "Marxist Political Analysis." *Sociological Inquiry,* No. 3–4.

Wertheimer, Fred. 1986. "A Boost for Campaign Finance Reform." *Common Cause Magazine* 12 (January–February):60.

West, Candace, and Don Zimmerman. 1987. "Doing Gender." *Gender and Society,* 1, 125–151.

Wetzel, James R. 1990. "American Families: 75 Years of Change." *Monthly Labor Review* 113 (March):4–13.

Wheeler, David L. 1992. "Studies Tying Homosexuality to Genes Draw Criticism from Researchers." *Chronicle of Higher Education* (February 5):A1–A2, A9.

White, Jason M. 1991. *Drug Dependence.* Englewood Cliffs, N.J.: Prentice-Hall.

Whitman, David. 1988. "America's Hidden Poor." *U.S. News & World Report,* (January 11):18–24.

Whitman, David. 1990. "The Rise of the 'Hyper-Poor.' " *U.S. News & World Report,* (October 15):40–41.

Wicker, Tom. 1987. "How We Got Here." *New York Times* (November 16):19.

Wickham, DeWayne. 1989. "Violence Shows Race Relations Still Sit on Powderkeg." *Fort Collins Coloradoan* (September 2):A10.

Wilkerson, Isabel. 1987. "Infant Mortality: Frightful Odds in Inner City." *New York Times* (June 26):1, 14.

Wilkins, Roger. 1981. "Sowell Brother?" *Nation* (October 10):333.

Wilkins, Roger. 1992. "Don't Blame the Great Society." *The Progressive* 56 (July):16–18.

Will, George. 1991. "A Plan to Pull Poor Up and Out." *Rocky Mountain News* (March 24):115.

Williams, Daniel, and Marc Breslow. 1992. "Can the Cities Be Saved?" *Dollars & Sense,* 180 (October).

Williams, David R. 1990. "Socioeconomic Differentials in Health: A Review and Redirection." *Social Psychology Quarterly* 53 (June):81–99.

Williams, Gertrude. 1980. "Toward the Eradication of Child Abuse and Neglect at Home." In *Traumatic Abuse and the Neglect of Children at Home,* Gertrude Williams and John Money (eds.) Baltimore: Johns Hopkins University Press, pp. 588–605.

Williams, J. Allen, JoEtta A. Vernon, Martha C. Williams, and Karen Malecha. 1987. "Sex Role Socialization in Picture Books: An Update." *Social Science Quarterly* 68 (March):148–156.

Williams, Juan. 1987. "Racism Revisited." *Utne Reader,* (May/June):54–61.

Wilson, Edward O. 1975. *Sociobiology: The New Synthesis.* Cambridge, Mass.: Harvard University Press.

Wilson, James Q. 1990. "Against the Legalization of Drugs." *Commentary* 89 (February):21–28.

Wilson, James Q., and Richard J. Herrnstein. 1985. *Crime and Human Nature.* New York: Simon & Schuster.

Wilson, Ted. 1989. "What Shall We Call Each Other?" *Equity Coalition,* (Fall):7.

Wilson, William J. 1987. *The Truly Disadvantaged: The Inner City, the Underclass, and Public Policy.* Chicago. University of Chicago Press.

Wines, Michael. 1988. "Mental Institutions May Be as Empty as They'll Ever Be." *New York Times,* (September 4):6E.

Wing, J. K. 1967. "Institutionalism in Mental Hospitals." In *Mental Illness and Social Processes,* Thomas J. Scheff (ed.). New York: Harper & Row, pp. 219–238.

Winslow, Ron. 1990. "Physicians Offered Incentives at Clinics Prescribed Far More Lab Tests, X-Rays." *Wall Street Journal* (April 12):B4.

Wise, Arthur E., and Tamar Gendler. 1989. "Rich Schools, Poor Schools: The Persistence of Unequal Education." *College Board Review,* 151 (Spring):12–17, 36–37.

Wise, Tim. 1989. "Radical Surgery." *Dollars & Sense,* 150 (October):6–9.

Woller, Barbara. 1991. "Women Earn Less Than Men Despite Equal Pay Legislation." *Lansing State Journal* (November 8):4B.

Wysocki, Bernard Jr. 1991. "American Firms Send Office Work Abroad to Use Cheaper Labor." *Wall Street Journal* (August 14):A1, A6.

Yancey, Matt. 1987. "Chrysler Fined $1.5M by U.S." *Boston Globe* (July 7):1, 10.

Yeager, Matthew G. 1975. "The Political Economy of Illicit Drugs." *Contemporary Drug Problems* 4 (Summer):141–178.

Yetman, Norman R. 1991. "Introduction." In *Majority and Minority: The Dynamaics of Race and Ethnicity in American Life,* Norman R. Yetman (ed.). Boston: Allyn and Bacon, pp. 1–29.

Zarsky, Lyuba, and Samuel Bowles, eds. 1986. *Economic Report of the People.* Boston: South End Press.

Zeitlin, Maurice, Kenneth G. Lutterman, and James W. Russell. 1977. "Death in Vietnam: Class, Poverty, and the Risks of War." In *American Society, Inc.,* 2d ed., Maurice Zeitlin (ed.). Chicago: Rand McNally, pp. 143–155.

Zipser, Andy. 1989. "Cooking the Books: How Pressure to Raise Sales Led MiniScribe to Falsifying Numbers." *Wall Street Journal,* (September 11):1, 8.

Name Index

Ackland, Len, 95
Acuna, Rudolfo, 198
Adams, Terry K., 129
Agel, Jerome, 535
Agree, Emily, 276–278, 297
Ahlburg, Dennis A., 216, 330
Ahmad, Eqbal, 77
Albee, George W., 531
Albelda, Randy, 165
Aldous, Joan, 339
Alford, Dolores M., 291
Alley, Janet M., 292
Altman, Lawrence K., 146, 405, 411
Andersen, Margaret L., 232–233, 246,
    380, 403, 519
Anderson, David, 554–555
Anderson, Jack, 401
Anderson, Walt, 537–538
Angier, Natalie, 308, 409
Anslinger, Harry J., 567
Anthony, Susan B., 248
Aponte, Robert, 216
Appelbaum, Richard, 132
Arendell, Terry, 351
Aschauer, David, 140
Atchley, Robert, 302–303
Atkins, Elizabeth, 405
Atkins, Gary L., 316
Atwater, Carol, 357
August, Allison, 412

Baca Zinn, Maxine, 131, 135, 194, 208,
    308, 334–335, 339, 345, 349, 355,
    377, 448
Baker, Eugene C., 198
Baldus, David, 502
Balswick, James, 265
Bane, Mary Jo, 229, 345
Banfield, Edward C., 173
Barbara, John, 573
Barlett, Donald L., 35, 453
Barnes, William, 151
Baron, Harold M., 443
Barrera, Mario, 198–199
Barringer, Felicity, 220, 409
Baskir, Laurence M., 48
Bass, Paul, 551
Baur, Karla, 306, 311–313
Bayles, Fred, 421
Beck, Jim, 195
Beck, Melinda, 289
Becker, Howard S., 5–6, 305, 492,
    558–559
Begley, Sharon, 91
Begtson, Vern L., 283
Bell, Alan P., 308–310
Bell, Inge Powell, 264, 273–274
Belsky, Jay, 342
Bengston, Vern L., 276, 290–292
Benjamin, Susan, 394
Bennett, Amanda, 461–462
Benokratis, Nicole, 210–211
Bentsten, Lloyd, 158
Bernstein, Aaron, 461–462, 466

Bickel, Janet, 409
Birdwhistell, Ray L., 330
Birnbaum, Norman, 440
Bishop, Katherine, 316
Blackmun, Harry, 503
Blauner, Robert, 213, 433
Blieszner, Rosemary, 292
Block, Fred, 189
Bluestone, Barry, 460
Blumberg, Paul M., 335
Blumberg, Rae Lesser, 235
Blume, Judy, 368
Blumstein, Philip, 309
Bock, Gordon, 436
Bograd, Michele, 353
Bonacich, Edna, 441
Bond, Burnie, 470
Bonnie, Richard J., 565
Bookspan, Phyllis, 238
Booth, Karen, 343
Borkin, Joseph, 45
Bosco, Doug, 39
Bourke, Jaron, 46
Bowles, Samuel, 214, 369–371, 373, 391
Boxer, Barbara, 250
Boyd, Robert S., 461
Bradley, Bill, 129
Brannon, Robert, 236
Brecher, Edward M., 562, 571
Breines, Wini, 352, 358
Brennan, William, 503
Brenner, M. Harvey, 169
Breslow, Marc, 152
Brimelow, Peter, 200
Briscoe, R., 233
Brody, Jane E., 353
Brooks-Gunn, Jeanne, 239
Brown, E. Richard, 398
Brown, Lester R., 57, 60, 82–83
Brownworth, Victoria A., 323
Bruce, Gerry, 568
Bruce, Lenny, 555
Bryan, William Jennings, 569
Buder, Leonard, 488
Bukovinsky, Janet, 353
Bullard, Robert D., 142
Bumpass, Larry, 348, 351
Burnham, Linda, 163
Burns, Haywood, 493
Burr, Chandler, 308
Burt, Cyril, 171
Burton, Linda, 276, 290–292
Bush, George, 38, 68, 128, 135, 141,
    157–158, 180, 222, 227, 339, 389,
    405, 489–490
Butler, Matilda, 246
Butterfield, Fox, 201
Bybee, Rodger, W., 356

Calvin, John, 521
Camus, Albert, 433
Capitanini, Lisa, 145
Caplan, Nathan, 13–15
Carmichael, Stokeley, 209–210, 476

Carnoy, Martin, 369
Carpenter, Betsy, 99–100
Carter, Jimmy, 389
Carter, Michael J., 259
Carter, Susan Boslego, 259
Castenada, Carlos, 537
Castro, Janice, 413
Cernovich, Stephen A., 546
Chafetz, Janet Saltzman, 235
Chambliss, William, 492
Chatters, Linda M., 350
Cherlin, Andrew, 344
Chiang Kai-shek, 49
Choate, Pat, 52–53
Choldin, Harvey, 119–120
Christensen, Kathleen, 336, 339
Chung Hee Park, 49
Cimons, Marlene, 407
Clarke, Leroy D., 574
Clay, Phillip, 134, 139
Cleveland, Grover, 43
Clinton, Bill, 152, 157, 227, 250, 260, 316,
    339, 456
Cloward, Richard A., 44–45, 187, 189, 229
Cobb, Jean, 39
Cockburn, Alexander, 29
Cockerham, William C., 542
Cohen, Linc, 143
Cohn, Anne, 357
Cohn, Bob, 321
Cole, Stephen, 533
Coleman, James S., 373
Coleman, James William, 379
Coles, Robert, 536
Collins, Joseph, 60–62, 81–82
Collins, Patricia Hill, 232
Columbus, Christopher, 205
Comfort, Alexander, 281
Commoner, Barry, 91, 110
Cook, James, 204–205, 463
Coolidge, Calvin, 45
Cooney, John, 37
Cornell, George, 248
Cory, Christopher T., 546, 548–550
Cosby, Bill, 195
Cousteau, Jacques, 93
Cowden, Richard, 158
Cowley, Geoffrey, 550, 553
Cressey, Donald R., 379
Crooks, Louise, 278, 282
Crooks, Robert, 306, 311–313
Cross, William M., 120, 140, 142
Cruzan, Nancy, 412
Crystal, Stephen, 278
Cullen, Frances T., 480–483
Curran, Daniel J., 238–241, 243, 287
Currie, Elliott, 7–8, 16, 148, 167–168, 216,
    340, 342, 466, 482
Curry-White, Brenda, 165
Curtain, Sharon, 279
Cuskey, Walter R., 573

Dallek, Geraldine, 398, 415
Darwin, Charles, 15

608

Subject Index

Photo Credits

Chapter 1: p. 2: Rick Reinhard/Impact Visuals; p. 6: Northwind Picture Archives; p. 7: Dan Ford Conolly/Picture Group; p. 11: John Coletti/Stock Boston; p. 13: Eugene Richards/Magnum; p. 15: Lyrl Ahern. Chapter 2: p. 22: Bob Daemmrich/Stock Boston; p. 24: Lyrl Ahern; p. 25: Lyrl Ahern; p. 26: Jacques Chenet/Woodfin Camp & Associates; p. 28: Rob Crandall/Picture Group; p. 30: Lyrl Ahern; p. 34: Lester Sloan and Jose Fernandez/Woodfin Camp & Associates; p. 37: Tomas Muscionico/Contact Press Images; p. 47: AP/Wide World Photos. Chapter 3: p. 44: Betty Press/Picture Group; p. 61: AP/wideworld photos; p. 66: Jehangir Gazdar/Woodfin Camp Associates; p. 71: Jeff Speed/JB Pictures p. 76: Paul Chesley/Photographers Aspen. Chapter 4: p. 84: Courtesy of NASA; p. 89: Cindy Reiman/Impact visuals; p. 94: Carl Ganter/Contact Press Images; p. 97: Stephanie Maze/Woodfin Camp Associates p. 109: Cindy Reiman/Impact Visuals. Chapter 5: p. 118: Miro Vintoniv/Stock Boston; p. 121: Catherine Karnow/Woodfin Camp Associates; p. 125: Brad Bower/Picture Group; p. 133: Cindy Reiman/Impact Visuals; p. 139: Jacques Chenet/Woodfin Camp & Associates. Chapter 6: p. 160: Gabe Kirchheimer/Impact Visuals; p. 164: Lester Sloan/Woodfin Camp & Associates; p. 168: Catherine Karnow/Woodfin Camp & Associates; p. 175: Mike Clemmer/Picture Group; p. 180: Robert Fox/Impact Visuals. Chapter 7: p. 190: Robert Fox/Impact Visuals; p. 201: Paul Fusco/Magnum; p. 206: Nicolas DeVore III/Photographers Aspen' p. 221: Will McIntyre/Photo Researchers; p. 222: AP/Wide World Photos. Chapter 8: p. 230: Mark Ludak/Impact Visuals; p. 237: Valerie Bloomberg; p. 241: Stephen Marks; p. 250: Mark Ludak/Impact Visuals; p. 260: Gary Hershorn Reuters/Bettman Archive. p. 270: John Ficara/Woodfin Camp Associates; p. 277: Jeff Greenberg/Photo Researchers Inc.; p. 287: Kevin Horan/Picture Group; p. 292:

Paul Fusco/Magnum. Chapter 9: p. 270: John Ficara/Woodfin Camp Associates; p. 277: Jeff Greenberg/Photo Researchers Inc.; p. 287: Kevin Horan/Picture Group; p. 292: Paul Fusco/Magnum. Chapter 10: p. 304: Robert Fox/Impact Visuals; p. 313: Tom McKitterick/Impact Visuals; p. 316: Michael Blackburn/Picture Group; p. 322: Timoty Eagan/Woodfin Camp & Associates. Chapter 11: p. 328: Susan Van Etten/Picture Cube; p. 331: Andy Levin/Photo Researchers, Inc.; p. 348: Robert V. Eckert/Stock Boston; p. 354: Donna Ferrato/Black Star. Chapter 12: p. 364: Phil Schermeister/Photographers Aspen; p. 367: Lawrence Migdale/Photo Researchers, Inc.; p. 375: Brian Smith; p. 381: Rob Crandall/Picture Group; p. 386:j Andrew Lichenstein/Impact Visuals. Chapter 13: p. 396: Matthew Borkoski/Stock Boston; p. 399: Reed Saxon/ AP wide world Photos p. 410: Sepp Seitz/Woodfin Camp Associates; p. 416: Gary Wagner/Picture Group; p. 423: Alon Reininger/Contact Press Images. Chapter 14: p. 430: Jim West/Impact Visuals; p. 432: Gerd Ludwig/Woodfin Camp Associates; p. 436: Andy Levin/Photo Researchers, Inc.; p. 442: Lawrence Migdale/Photo Researchers, Inc.; p. 459: Michael Abramson/Woodfin Camp Associates; Chapter 15: p. 474: Larry Downing/Woodfin Camp Associates; p. 477: Lyrl Ahern; p. 480: Danford Connoly/Picture Group; p. 491: AP/Wide World Photos; p. 501: Steve Starr/Picture Group. Chapter 16: p. 510: Courtesy of Alex Wilhite/Very Special Arts; p. 515: Deanne Fitzmaurice/The San Francisco Chronicle; p. 518: Eugene Richards/Magnum; p. 526: Lyrl Ahern; p. 535: Bettman Archive. Chapter 17: p. 544: Chuck Nacke/Picture Group; p. 557: Rick Smolan/Woodfin Camp Associates; p. 560: Sylvain Legrand/Photo Researchers, Inc; p. 565: Andrew Lichtenstein/Impact Visuals.